Exploring Careers for the 21st Century

Second Edition

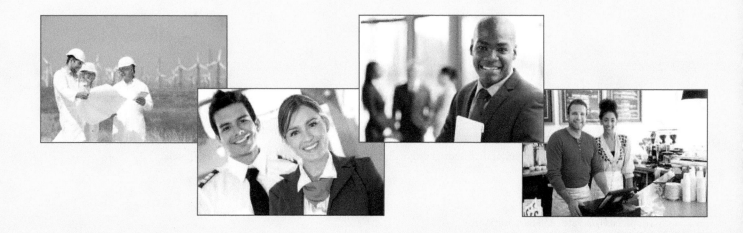

Steve Mariotti

Neelam Patel Chowdhary

Suzanne Weixel

PEARSON

ISBN 10: 1-269-65230-3
ISBN 13: 978-1-269-65230-8

Contents

Contents

13 ▪ Managing a Job Search 219

14 ▪ Getting Started in Your Career 241

15 ▪ Being Productive in Your Career 265

Part V Financial Management

About the Authors

Steve Mariotti

Steve Mariotti, founder of the Network for Teaching Entrepreneurship (NFTE), is an expert in education for at-risk youth. He has been helping young people develop marketable skills by learning about entrepreneurship for more than 25 years.

Mr. Mariotti received an M.B.A. from the University of Michigan, Ann Arbor, and has studied at Harvard University, Stanford University, and Brooklyn College. His professional career began as a Treasury Analyst for Ford Venezuela, Mexico, Caribbean, Argentina, Peru, Chile, South Africa and the Export Division (1976–1979). He introduced financial systems that saved the company over $5 million per annum via interest-expense reduction and improved cash management. After leaving Ford, Mr. Mariotti founded—and for the next three years operated—Mason Import/Export Services in New York, eventually acting as sales representative and purchasing agent for 32 overseas firms.

In 1982, Mr. Mariotti made a momentous career change and became a Special Education/Business Teacher in the New York City school system, choosing to teach in such at-risk neighborhoods as Bedford-Stuyvesant in Brooklyn and the "Fort Apache" section of the South Bronx. It was at Jane Addams Vocational High School in the Bronx that Mr. Mariotti had the idea to bring entrepreneurial education to low-income youth. This inspiration led to the founding of the National Foundation for Teaching Entrepreneurship (NFTE) in 1987, and 501(c)(3) non-profit status was granted by the IRS the following year.

Mr. Mariotti and NFTE have received numerous awards, including the 2004 Ernst & Young National Entrepreneur of the Year Award; the Golden Lamp Award from the Association of Education Publishers (2002); and the National Federation of Independent Businesses—Best Business Teacher, 1988, as well as major media exposure that includes pieces in *The New York Times* and other prominent publications, and profiles on ABC News and CNN. Mariotti has co-authored some two dozen books and manuals that have sold close to one million copies. To learn more about NFTE, visit the Web site at www.nfte.com.

Neelam Patel Chowdhary

Neelam Patel Chowdhary joined NFTE in 2006. She has over 15 years of experience in the field of education, professional development, and curriculum design.

Prior to coming to NFTE, Mrs. Chowdhary taught in public schools within the Los Angeles Unified School District and the New York City Board of Education. In addition, Mrs. Chowdhary has been an instructor and supervisor for Education students in the Master's programs at Mercy College and at Teachers College, Columbia University. Mrs. Chowdhary has a B.A. from the University of Southern

California (Los Angeles, CA), a M.S. in Educational Leadership from Pepperdine University (Malibu, CA), and Doctorate Degree from Teachers College, Columbia University in Curriculum Studies (New York, NY). She is a 2003 National Board Certified Teacher and an editor of *Entrepreneurship: Owning Your Future*, 11th Edition, by Mr. Mariotti.

Mrs. Chowdhary is currently the Executive Director of Global Learning Programs at Asia Society.

Suzanne Weixel

Suzanne Weixel has been writing career and technical education textbooks for so long that she has lost count of the number of books she has had published.

Ms. Weixel also currently serves as the Director of Research for Emergent Learning, LLC. In that role, she particularly enjoys talking with CTE educators to learn directly from them how to develop curriculum materials that suit their needs.

Ms. Weixel graduated from Dartmouth College in 1981 with a degree in art history. She and her husband currently live in Marlborough, MA, where they enjoy cooking (and eating), biking, and watching sports. They have two grown sons who make them very proud.

Letter to the Students

Dear Student,

This book has been designed to help you explore careers, learn about financial literacy, and discover the role that entrepreneurship can have in your life. We hope that what you learn here will help you achieve financial independence and personal satisfaction. Knowing your role in your family, community, and future will be of great value in any employment you may have.

Learning the principles of careers and entrepreneurship will teach you about more than just business and money, however. In this book, you will learn how to plan for your future, develop an academic plan, communicate with others, analyze mathematical and financial information, and write a business plan. These are skills that apply to your personal, as well as your professional, life. Even if you don't become a lifelong entrepreneur, learning how to start and operate a small business will give you an understanding of the business world, which will make it much easier for you to get jobs and create a fulfilling career for yourself.

The characteristics of the successful member of the community—a positive mental attitude, the ability to recognize opportunities where others only see problems, and openness to creative solutions—are all qualities worth developing. They will help you perform better in any situation life throws at you.

Owning your future is the key to your happiness. You can do so much good for your family, friends, and community by being aware of the opportunities and resources that are around you. Thinking about your future career is a way to do that—make your dreams come true and help support the dreams of those that you care about.

I know that you will learn a lot from this course that will help you make the best decisions for yourself. Good luck!

Sincerely yours,

Steve Mariotti

Founder, NFTE

Introduction

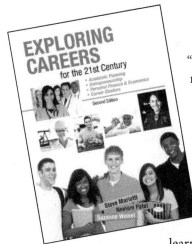

"What will I be when I grow up?" is an age-old question that, for most students, has no easy answer. *Exploring Careers for the 21st Century, Second Edition,* is a broad exploration of career opportunities and the rewards of different career pathways. It provides the essential tools that students need to set and achieve career and academic goals and make positive decisions that will affect their futures.

Exploring Careers for the 21st Century, Second Edition, highlights the most promising careers and prepares students to connect academic achievement to real-world success. Students learn to identify their career interests, aptitudes, and learning styles. They discover that they can gain critical experience and develop job-related skills, including math, technology, teamwork, leadership, and effective communications. This book also helps students recognize and manage their resources and develop a career portfolio while practicing the principles of personal finance, economics, and entrepreneurship.

Exploring Careers for the 21st Century, Second Edition, is a clear and concise text, designed to engage students by focusing on topics that are relevant to their lives today. It uses contemporary, real-world examples to encourage students to apply their skills in practical situations and to meet responsibilities by providing them with challenging learning experiences that require practical application of academic skills.

Content Overview

Exploring Careers for the 21st Century, Second Edition, is organized into five parts.

In **Part I, Careers and You**, students are encouraged to identify how their skills and interests can help them succeed in the world of work. They learn about the different roles and responsibilities they have in the five critical areas of living: home, school, peers, community, and careers. In addition, they are introduced to the career clusters and pathways and to the risks and rewards of entrepreneurship.

Part II, Career Preparation, emphasizes the importance of using processes for decision making, goal setting, and problem solving. The relationship between academic planning, goal setting, and future success takes center stage; students are encouraged to develop an academic plan, and to take advantage of opportunities to develop their skills and interests through high school and beyond. Students have the opportunity to practice effective communication, management, leadership, and teamwork, and learn how math and technology are used in real-world situations.

Part III, Career Development, takes students through the process of identifying career opportunities, planning for a career, and conducting a career search. Students learn to perform a career self-assessment so they can match their interests and abilities with career opportunities. Students are given the opportunity to create career search documents and practice interviewing for a job. Key concepts include making lifestyle choices, balancing work and family life, and making use of lifelong learning opportunities.

In **Part IV, Entrepreneurship**, students are introduced to the role entrepreneurship plays in the economy, as well as the basic types of businesses and the types of business ownership. Students learn how to recognize, interpret, and take advantage of trends in business opportunities, how to develop a business plan, how to raise money, and how to use basic business management skills, such as marketing, organization, and sales to create and grow a successful business.

In **Part V, Financial Management**, students study personal and business finance and consumer responsibility. They are introduced to the concept of money, and how to differentiate between needs and wants. They are encouraged to set financial goals and manage a budget to achieve those goals. In addition, they identify the benefits and drawbacks of different types of payment methods. They learn about bank accounts and the difference between saving and investing. Responsible use of credit is emphasized, along with how to keep personal and financial information safe. They are introduced to the role they play in the global economy, and the importance of making wise consumer decisions. Finally, they learn basic skills for business financial management.

A set of comprehensive appendices complete the text.

A **Business Management Issues** provides an introduction to some of the more complex business issues, including how to reduce risk by using insurance. It covers important legal issues that entrepreneurs and business managers should understand, such as contracts, government regulations, and how to protect intellectual property.

B **Sample Business Plan** illustrates the components of a business plan that students can use as a model for developing a business plan of their own.

C **The NFTE Story** profiles the Network for Teaching Entrepreneurship, Inc., whose mission has expanded into an international movement for teaching entrepreneurship, academic skills, and technology skills to young people worldwide.

D **Joining a Student Organization** explains the importance of joining Career and Technical Student Organizations (CTSO) and lists the major CTSOs.

E **Language Arts Review** provides a review of essential grammar and punctuation skills, including how to identify subjects and verbs, sentence structure, and the use of punctuation.

F **Basic Math Review** provides a review of essential mathematics lessons, including place value, addition, subtraction, multiplication, and division, as well as working with decimals, fractions, and percents.

G **Glossary** provides an alphabetical list of terms found throughout the text.

21st Century Learning

As the future leaders of our families, communities, government, and workforce, it is imperative that today's students develop the skills they need to succeed in work and life. The Partnership for the 21st Century, an advocacy organization focused on infusing 21st Century Skills into education, has created the Framework for 21st Century Learning, which describes the skills, knowledge, and expertise students must master to succeed in work and life (www.p21.org).

Among other things, the Framework for 21st Century Learning identifies the following:

- *Core subjects.* English, reading or language arts, world languages, arts, mathematics, economics, science, geography, history, government, and civics.

- *21st Century interdisciplinary themes.* Global awareness; financial, economic, business, and entrepreneurial literacy; civic literacy; health literacy.

- *Learning and innovation skills.* Creativity and innovation; critical thinking and problem solving; communication and collaboration.

- *Information, media and technology skills.* Information literacy; media literacy; information, communications and technology literacy.

- *Life and career skills.* Flexibility and adaptability; initiative and self-direction; social and cross-cultural skills; productivity and accountability; leadership and responsibility.

Preview of the Textbook

Parts

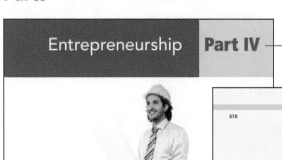

There are five **parts** in the book. Each part focuses on a group of important career-related concepts.

Parts are organized into **chapters**. There are between three and six chapters in each part.

Chapters and Skills

Each chapter has between two and seven objectives that identify the key **skills** explained in the chapter.

Each chapter begins with an introduction, called **Getting Started**, that highlights the concepts covered.

The introduction includes a **"bellringer"** activity designed to focus the class on the current concept while encouraging discussion and collaboration.

Working within a Chapter

Margin features enhance and support the text, and prompt the students to apply critical thinking and 21st Century Skills to the covered concepts.

Main headings correspond to the objectives listed at the beginning of each chapter.

Each objective has at least two sections, which are identified by a **subheading**.

After important figures, an open-ended **figure question** asks the students to consider relevant issues related to the figure and text.

Vocabulary terms are in bold and are defined in the text and in the glossary at the end of the book.

Career Facts, **Tips**, and **Trends** throughout the chapter provide useful information to help the students put the concepts into real-world context.

Features and Activities

Integrated throughout *Exploring Careers for the 21st Century* are opportunities for the student to use critical 21st Century Skills to solve problems, make decisions, and develop and present information individually and cooperatively with their classmates.

Career Profile is a career exploration activity. It highlights a career within one of the 16 career clusters, and prompts the student to use available resources to investigate the skills, qualities, education, and abilities that might be necessary to succeed in that career.

Tech Connect is a technology awareness feature that introduces a technology concept relating to the current topic. The student is asked to research the concept and use available technology to illustrate and present the information they discover to their teacher or classmates.

Money Madness is a financial literacy activity that invites the student to use their problem solving, goal setting, and decision-making skills along with math to solve a problem involving money.

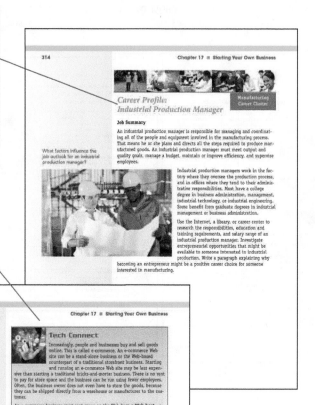

Global Awareness feature illustrates how the current topic relates to the world outside of students' own community. Each feature includes a critical-thinking prompt or activity that encourages students to investigate the topic to learn more.

Career Counsel is a 21st Century Learning activity. It presents a story or scenario about a real-world career situation that has no conclusion. Students are asked to use 21st Century Skills such as decision making, critical thinking, and problem solving to think of an ending and discuss, write, or perform it for their peers.

Starting Your Own Business ■ Chapter 17   321

North American Industry Classifications

The North American Industry Classification System (NAICS—pronounced NAKES) assigns a numerical code to every industry in North America based on its primary business function. The system was developed cooperatively by the United States, Canada, and Mexico. NAICS codes are useful for classifying different types of business and for analyzing trends such as which industries are growing economically and which are shrinking. For example, the Bureau of Labor Statistics uses the system to track employment, earnings, and growth.

NAICS classifies all economic activity in North America into twenty industry sectors; five are goods-producing sectors such as apparel manufacturing and food manufacturing, and fifteen are services-producing sectors, such as home health care services, financial services, and child daycare services.

Why do you think it is important for different countries to work together to develop systems such as NAICS? How can it help entrepreneurs?

Sources of Business Opportunities

Staying aware of things going on around you can help you recognize potential business opportunities and identify trends. Five basic sources of opportunity include problems that need to be solved, change, new discoveries, improvements to existing products or services, and the development of unique knowledge.

■ Problems are often the source of opportunity. You might have a problem you want to solve, or you might see that others have a problem. Problem solving has led to the invention of new products ranging from the light bulb to the cell phone and to services ranging from pizza delivery to online check-in for air travel.

■ Changes occur in every area of life. Laws and regulations change, social customs evolve, even the weather changes. Change often presents new opportunities. For example, a growing interest in protecting the environment has led to opportunities for "green" businesses.

■ New discoveries include the creation of a totally new product or service. The discovery of new materials such as Teflon® led to new products such as non-stick cookware.

■ Improvements to existing products and services lead to new opportunities as well. Consider hybrid cars, low-energy light bulbs, and even potting soil that includes fertilizer. These are all examples of how improving existing products can lead to opportunity.

■ Unique knowledge is when a person has an ability that no-one else has, and can turn it into an opportunity.

Watch the Trends!

You have an idea for starting a business helping senior citizens prepare their homes for the winter. How can paying attention to trends help or hurt the success of your startup?

◆ You ignore the impact of technological developments in building materials that provide year-round weather protection.

◆ You fail to notice the growing trend of seniors moving to assisted-living communities.

◆ You do not take into account that there are other, similar businesses already established in the area.

◆ You change your plan to offer renovations using energy-saving building materials for year-round protection.

◆ You contact assisted-living communities to offer your service.

◆ You consider investing in an existing company.

Can you think of other ways you could adapt your idea based on current trends in business opportunities?

...cts business in at least two different industries is called a ...industry corporation. Because revenue comes from differ-...nerate may be better positioned to withstand problems ...stry, but not another. One risk of this type of organization ...take resources from one area of the business to subsidize ...rea vulnerable. Another risk is that available resources ...all areas, so that no area can succeed. Examples of a con-...company that operates a ...edit financing business or a ...hat manufactures mobile ...l Web site.

Why might it make sense for farmers to form cooperatives?

Cooperative

A **cooperative** is a business owned, controlled, and operated for the mutual benefit of its members. The members may be people who use the company's services, buy its goods, or work for it. For example, farmers form cooperatives to sell crops and buy farming equipment. Cooperatives often share their earnings with the membership as dividends.

21st Century Learning

CAREER COUNSEL

Tamara and William met in a digital photography class. They discussed plans to start a part-time business converting printed pictures into digital format, so people can store and view them on a computer, digital picture frame, or handheld device. William already had a digital scanner and computer set up at his house. They each invested $100.00 to use for purchasing storage devices, other supplies, and advertising. They practiced, and decided they could convert 40 pictures an hour. If they charged 75 cents per picture, they could make a profit.

Soon, they had a long list of customers and a stack of pictures waiting to be converted. They worked together six hours a week, but Tamara was on the school basketball team, so William worked alone an additional three to four hours. The first time the partners met to divide the profits, they each took back their $100.00 investment, and there was still $550.00 left to share. Tamara assumed they would split it equally, but William thought he should get more. After all, it was his scanner and computer, his home, and he was putting in more hours.

What challenges are facing William and Tamara? How can they solve their conflict? Use 21st Century Skills such as problem solving, decision making, critical thinking, and effective communication to help them resolve their conflict. Write an ending to the story and share it with your class.

 business ■ Chapter 17   319

Margin Features

Margin features within each chapter are designed to stand out visually on the page. They support and reinforce the chapter content.

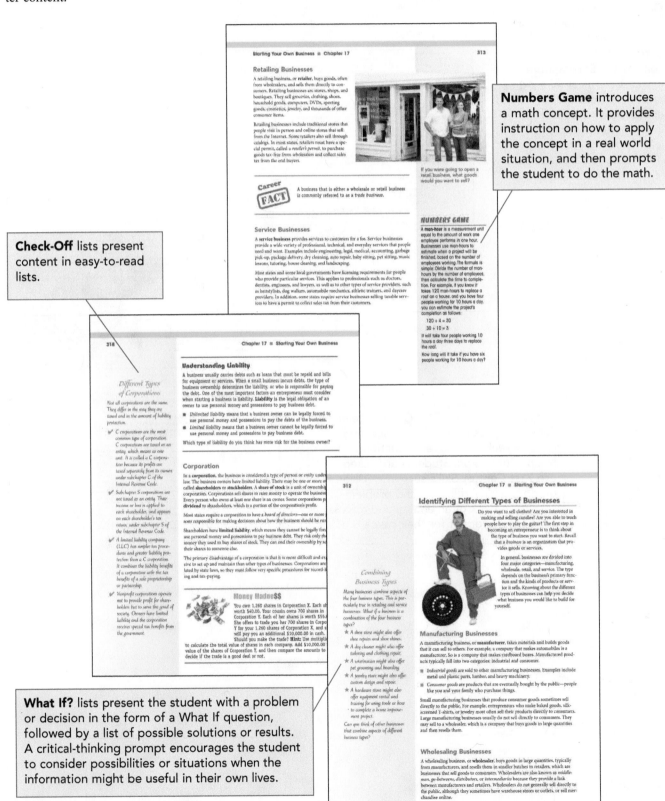

Numbers Game introduces a math concept. It provides instruction on how to apply the concept in a real world situation, and then prompts the student to do the math.

Check-Off lists present content in easy-to-read lists.

What If? lists present the student with a problem or decision in the form of a What If question, followed by a list of possible solutions or results. A critical-thinking prompt encourages the student to consider possibilities or situations when the information might be useful in their own lives.

No Excuses is a list of possible pitfalls or problems relating to the topic, marked with thumbs-down icons, followed by a list of positive actions, marked with thumbs-up icons. A critical-thinking prompt encourages students to consider how you might act in a similar situation.

Myth/Truth presents a common misconception and the facts behind the truth.

Starting Your Own Business ■ Chapter 17   321

North American Industry Classifications

The North American Industry Classification System (NAICS—pronounced NAKES) assigns a numerical code to every industry in North America based on its primary business function. The system was developed cooperatively by the United States, Canada, and Mexico. NAICS codes are useful for classifying different types of business and for analyzing trends such as which industries are growing economically and which are shrinking. For example, the Bureau of Labor Statistics uses the system to track employment, earnings, and growth.

NAICS classifies all economic activity in North America into twenty industry sectors: five are goods-producing sectors such as apparel manufacturing and food manufacturing, and fifteen are services-producing sectors, such as home health care services, financial services, and child daycare services.

Why do you think it is important for different countries to work together to develop systems such as NAICS? How can it help entrepreneurs?

Sources of Business Opportunities

Staying aware of things going on around you can help you recognize potential business opportunities and identify trends. Five basic sources of opportunity include problems that need to be solved, change, new discoveries, improvements to existing products or services, and the development of unique knowledge.

■ Problems are often the source of opportunity. You might have a problem you want to solve, or you might see that others have a problem. Problem solving has led to the invention of new products ranging from the light bulb to the cell phone and to services ranging from pizza delivery to online check-in for air travel.

■ Changes occur in every area of life. Laws and regulations change, social customs evolve, even the weather changes. Change often presents new opportunities. For example, a growing interest in protecting the environment has led to opportunities for "green" businesses.

■ New discoveries include the creation of a totally new product or service. The discovery of new materials such as Teflon® led to new products such as non-stick cookware.

■ Improvements to existing products and services lead to new opportunities as well. Consider hybrid cars, low-energy light bulbs, and [...] includes fertilizer. These are all examples of how impro[...] can lead to opportunity.

■ Unique knowledge is when a person has an ability that [...] can turn it into an opportunity.

Watch the Trends!

You have an idea for starting a business helping senior citizens prepare their homes for the winter. How can paying attention to trends help or hurt the success of your startup?

👎 You ignore the impact of technological developments in building materials that provide year-round weather protection.

👎 You fail to notice the growing trend of seniors moving to assisted-living communities.

👎 You do not take into account that there are other, similar businesses already established in the area.

👍 You change your plan to offer renovations using energy-saving building materials for year-round protection.

👍 You contact assisted-living communities to offer your service.

👍 You consider investing in an existing company.

Can you think of other ways you could adapt your idea based on current trends in business opportunities?

Starting Your Own Business ■ Chapter 17   317

TIPS

Career Tips

All businesses should be set up legally by a lawyer in order to make sure that the rights of owners, partners, investors, and customers are protected.

Sole Proprietorship

A **sole proprietorship** is a business that is owned by a single individual. The owner collects all profit from the business and has unlimited liability for its debt. Most small businesses operate as sole proprietorships.

A sole proprietorship is the simplest and least expensive option for business ownership. Business income and costs are reported on the owner's personal income tax return, which means less paperwork and easier tax accounting. The sole proprietor is also the sole decision maker, with complete control over the management of the business.

However, he or she is also responsible for raising the money for setting up, operating, and expanding the business. Also, with unlimited liability for any business debts, the owner's personal money and possessions are at risk if there is not enough money in the business to pay debts.

Partnership

In a **partnership**, at least two individuals share the management, profit, and liability for the business. There are two basic types.

■ In a *general partnership*, all partners have unlimited liability.

■ In a *limited partnership*, one general partner has limited liability. The other partners are investors only and have no say in how to run the company on a day-to-day basis.

A general partnership is much like a sole proprietorship. The primary advantage is that a general partnership has at least two people contributing to its success, rather than just one. Of course, the unlimited liability is shared by all owners, as well, so all are at risk of losing personal money and possessions to pay business debts. Other disadvantages include the possibility of conflict between the owners about how the business should be run, the fact that profits are shared among all owners, and that each partner is equally responsible for the business-related actions of all the others.

Myth It takes a lot of money to start a business.

Truth Most new businesses are started with less than $10,000.00. Most entrepreneurs are able to raise the money from investors—including family and friends—and from loans. They may even be able to obtain government grants.

What are some benefits and drawbacks of organizing a business as a partnership?

End-of-Chapter Activities

At the end of every chapter is a series of questions and activities.

Career-Ready Practices is a group activity designed to encourage teamwork and to support career-ready practices. It provides the opportunity for students to work collaboratively on projects ranging from research presentations to debates and competitive games.

Case Study presents a real-life career-related scenario, followed by a series of open-ended questions designed to provide students with the opportunity to use 21st Century Skills.

Web Extra provides suggestions for using the Internet to locate additional information about the chapter topics.

Answer It! is a set of ten questions designed to assess reading comprehension.

Career Portfolio provides students with the opportunity to develop a collection of documents and other items that they can use to illustrate their accomplishments, skills, and abilities to potential employers.

Business Plan Project is designed to guide students through the steps of developing an actual business plan. The business plan is developed throughout the book.

Write Now is a language arts activity that encourages students to use language to answer questions, research and present information, or respond to critical-thinking prompts.

Companion Web Site (www.pearsoncustom.com/us/exploringcareers)

The *Exploring Careers for the 21st Century* companion Web site includes additional material—including chapter outlines, quizzes, and additional activities—to support the textbook. Teachers can register from this site to access support material, such as the teacher's wraparound edition, test bank, PowerPoint slides, and answer keys.

Acknowledgments

First, I would like to thank my writing partners, Neelam Patel Chowdhary and Suzanne Weixel, for the excellent thought and writing on this book. I must also thank Rupa Mohan, for her leadership and insights are deeply appreciated.

A very special thanks to the MetLife Foundation for supporting NFTE to make this project a reality. Their kindness and generous donation have made this book possible. We look forward to working with the MetLife Foundation for many years to come.

Special thanks to the team at Emergent Learning for helping us put together this amazing project. Also, thank you to Gary Bauer, Vernon Anthony, Robin Balizewski, Leigh Ann Sims, and the entire team at Prentice Hall for their professionalism and support.

Special thanks to Amy Rosen, who NFTE is thrilled to have as our president and CEO. She is sure to take NFTE to a new level of success.

I would like to recognize the efforts and contributions of members of NFTE's National Board of Directors: Albert Abney, Patricia Alper, Bill Daugherty, Phillip A. Falcone, Michael L. Fetters, Lawrence N. Field, Donald Friedman, Thomas Hartocollis, Landon Hilliard, Sanford Krieger, James Lyle, Consuelo Mack, Alan Patricof, Marsha Ralls, Donna Redel, Amy Rosen, Mary Myers Kauppila, Robert Refkin, Arthur J. Samberg, Diana Davis Spence, Peter B. Walker, and Tucker York; and I would like to acknowledge the inspired guidance provided by our National Executive Committee: Bart Breighner, Steven Breninkmeijer, Kathryn Davis, Lewis M. Eisenberg, Theodore J. Forstmann, Sir Paul Judge, Elizabeth B. Koch, Abby Moffat, Jeffrey S. Raikes, Kenneth I. Starr, and the Hon. John C. Whitehead. I am deeply grateful as well to the many philanthropists who have supported our work, including Raymond Chambers, Charles G. and David H. Koch, Chris Podoll of the William Zimmerman Foundation, The Shelby Cullom Davis Foundation, the Microsoft Corporation, The Nasdaq Educational Foundation, and the Legatum Institute.

I would like to express my thanks to the following reviewers for their insightful feedback, support, and help throughout developing the book:

Anthony Salcedo, Carole L. Christensen, Connie C. Woody, Cynthia R. Tyler, Marilyn Robinson, Rebecca Booth, Rupa Mohan, and Steven Trust.

Thanks to Dave Anderson, Nathaniel Brown, Michael Frew, and Nathalie Jean for their contributions to the book.

Finally, I want to thank my mother, Nancy, a wonderful special education instructor who showed me that one great teacher can affect eternity. Any errors are mine alone.

—Steve Mariotti

Careers and You

Part I

In This Part . . .

1 Your Personal Strengths

Skills in This Chapter . . .

- **Analyzing Career Requirements and Rewards**
- **Recognizing Your Values**
- **Identifying Your Strengths and Interests**
- **Recognizing Character Qualities**
- **Analyzing Employability Skills**

GETTING STARTED

Has anyone ever asked you what you want to be when you grow up? Did you answer firefighter or doctor? Did you answer artist or president of the United States? These are all good careers. However, they are not the right careers for everyone. If you choose a career that interests you and that makes use of your skills and abilities, you are more likely to be happy and satisfied with your work.

Why do people work? Ask ten people that question, and you are likely to get ten different answers! Yes, people work to make money. They also work to feel pride and satisfaction, to stay busy, and because it

can be fun. The average person spends between 40 and 50 hours a week at work. If that work is enjoyable and rewarding, that person is going to be happier in all areas of life.

➤ In two groups, take a few minutes to select and write down a career without the other group knowing what you have picked. Take turns asking the other group "Yes" or "No" questions about their career, until you can guess what it is. As a class, discuss the skills and abilities you might need for the careers each group picked, and what it would be like to work in those careers.

Analyzing Career Requirements and Rewards

A **career** is a chosen field of work in which you try to advance over time by gaining responsibility and earning more money. A **job** is any activity that you do in exchange for money or other payment. A job does not necessarily lead to advancement. **Occupation** is a word that means career or job.

Every career comes with its own **requirements**—things you must do or have—and **rewards**—things you receive in return. The specific requirements and rewards of the career you choose have a major impact on the kind of life you will lead.

- A doctor spends years in school and in training. It is expensive and leaves little time for extra activities. But, doctors help people and save lives, which can be very rewarding.

- A restaurant owner invests his own money in the business. He works long hours and must interact with temperamental chefs, kitchen staff, and customers. However, he is his own boss and can take pride in starting and running his own exciting business.

Understanding the requirements and rewards can help you choose a career that you will enjoy for many years.

Career Requirements

Career requirements are the responsibilities that you must perform in order to succeed in the career. A **responsibility** is something people expect you to do, or something you must accomplish. As a student, your teachers expect you to come to class and do your homework. As an employee—worker—your supervisor expects certain things from you, too.

You Want Me to Do What?

When you consider a career, it is important to think about whether or not you are willing to meet its requirements. If you do not live up to your responsibilities at work, you will soon be looking for a new job. What are some ways you show that you can or cannot meet responsibilities?

👎 Showing up late and leaving early

👎 Letting co-workers do your job

👎 Skipping meetings

👍 Cooperating with co-workers

👍 Always trying your best

👍 Making sure you have the training you need to complete your work

How can researching the requirements of a job help you avoid problems at work?

The requirements of a career determine things such as the type of training and education you will need. Career requirements might also determine where you will live, how you will spend your time, and who you will be working with.

■ If you choose to become an electrician, you will need education and training different from that of someone who chooses to become a chef.

■ A kindergarten teacher spends most of the day with 5-year-olds.

■ A lawyer must read and prepare legal documents.

■ A software programmer is alone in front of a computer for hours at a time.

What are the requirements and rewards of a career as a firefighter?

 Career FACT The word *career* first appeared in the middle 1500s. Its original meaning was "road" or "race course."

Career Rewards

What are some of the rewards of being a health care professional?

Recall that the average person spends between 40 to 50 hours per week at work. Most people work because they require money to buy things they need, such as food, clothes, and shelter. Some people choose their careers based on how much money they can earn on the job. The money that you receive in exchange for work performed is called **wages** or a **salary**.

Money is a good reason to choose a career, but it is not the only reason. People who are happy with their careers usually do something they enjoy. Even if the job does not pay very well, people might choose a career because it gives them satisfaction, fits their values, uses their skills and abilities, and gives them a role in the community.

■ A woman who starts a small jewelry business may enjoy being her own boss and setting her own hours.

■ A social worker who helps homeless people may believe she is making the world a better place.

■ An artist may feel he is making the world more beautiful by creating paintings or sculptures.

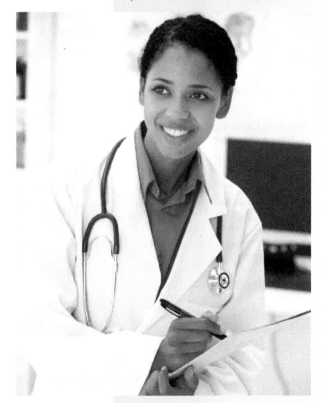

Identifying Work Values

Identifying your work values can help you choose a career that you will enjoy. Some common work values include:

✔ Creativity: Having a job that allows you to express yourself or use your imagination

✔ Physical activity: Having a job that allows you to move around and be active

✔ Independence: Being your own boss, an entrepreneur

✔ Good salary: Being paid well for your work

✔ Job security: Having a steady, long-term job

✔ Work environment: Being able to work in a space where you are comfortable, such as outside, or in an office

✔ Leadership opportunities: Directing or managing the work of others

✔ Prestige: Having a job that commands the respect and admiration of others

✔ Challenge: Having the opportunity to perform difficult or important tasks

✔ Work safety: Being able to work in a predictable job, or in a job where there is no risk

✔ Variety: Having the opportunity to do different things

✔ Working with people: Being able to work closely with others

✔ Thinking: Having a job that requires you to use your brain and intellectual abilities

Recognizing Your Values

Values are the thoughts, ideas, and actions that are important to you. You use them to gauge or evaluate the people and things in your life. Knowing what you value is key to choosing an occupation that is right for you.

You develop values by figuring out what is important to you. When you are young, your values might reflect the values of the people in your life. For example, you might value the same things your parents and friends value.

As you grow and learn more about the world around you, you can develop your own values. Your parents might value job security more than you do, or your friends might not value protecting the environment as much as you do.

Types of Values

Something has **instrumental value** if it is important for acquiring something else. For example, money has instrumental value because you use it to buy other things. A car has instrumental value because you use it to drive to school or work. Clothes and an education also have instrumental value.

Something has **intrinsic value** if it is important in and of itself. Things with intrinsic value may be hard to explain. They might include emotions or feelings. For example, happiness, love, respect, justice, and beauty have intrinsic value. If you do something because it makes you feel good about yourself and not because someone is going to give you credit for it, then it has intrinsic value.

As soon as you are old enough to tell right from wrong, you develop **moral values**. Moral values help us judge behavior based on what we think is good compared to what we think is wrong. Moral values usually include positive character traits such as honesty, respect, justice, and responsibility.

Work-related values refer to how you like to work and the results that you produce. Your work-related values can help you make career decisions.

■ If you value adventure, you might consider a career in tourism or recreation management.

■ If you value job security—knowing you will have your job for a long time—you might consider a career in government.

■ If you value time with your family, then you may not want a job that requires you to travel a lot.

Changing Values

Of course, values can change. When you are young, you might value the opportunity to travel and meet new people. You might consider a career as a flight attendant.

As you get older, you might value job security and a steady salary. You might consider a career in hotel management.

Not everyone values the same things. Your mother might value a flexible work schedule so she can spend more time at home. Your cousin might value expensive things, so he works a lot of hours to earn more money. It is important to be able to respect other people's values even if you don't agree with them.

What types of careers might suit someone who values working outdoors?

Money Madne$$

You have been offered two jobs for the summer. They are both in food service, which is a field that interests you, and they have similar responsibilities. You have decided to choose the one that offers the best wages.

The first position is as a bus person at a restaurant. A bus person supports the wait staff by setting up and clearing tables, and performing tasks such as filling water glasses. It pays $6.15 per hour, and you are expected to work 30 hours a week for 8 weeks. The second position is as a caterer's assistant. A caterer's assistant also sets up and clears, and may also help prepare and transport food. It pays $1,500.00 for the summer. Which position should you accept?

NUMBERS GAME

Employees earning an hourly rate are paid for the number of hours they work. You can calculate the number of hours you work by measuring the **elapsed time**, which is the amount of time that has passed from one time to another. You find the amount of elapsed time by subtracting the earlier time from the later time.

For example, if you start working at 3:00 and finish at 5:00, how long did you work? 5:00 – 3:00 = 2:00, so you worked 2 hours.

If you start working at 3:30 and finish at 6:00, how long did you work?

Myth Once you develop a value, it stays with you for life.

Truth Values change over time. Things that are important to you when you are young might become less important as you grow older.

Are Your Standards Flexible?

We use values to set standards. Setting a high standard shows that you value something a lot; a lower standard shows that you don't value it so much. **Standards** are really just guidelines for whether or not something meets expectations. We use standards to measure performance on everything from how many miles per gallon a car gets, to how well students do in a class.

You probably know when someone is judging you to see if you meet his or her standards: a teacher gives you a test or a parent comments on your table manners. You might not realize that you set standards, too, and you use them to measure whether people and things meet your expectations. At work, an employer expects you to meet certain standards such as dressing appropriately and respecting your co-workers. You also expect your employer to meet your standards.

Why might someone who values the environment be unhappy working in a factory that creates pollution?

- If you value the environment, you will probably be happier working for an employer that supports environmentally-friendly practices, such as recycling.
- If you value making money, you might prefer an employer that rewards hard work with high pay.

Sometimes, having different values can cause conflicts—disagreements. One way to avoid conflict is to have **flexible standards**—standards that you can adapt to different situations. For example, you might lower your standard for high pay if your employer provides rewards such as more vacation time. Having flexible standards shows you are **tolerant** or willing to consider the opinions of others.

Tech Connect

Technology has made the option of working at home a reality for many employees.

- E-mail, instant messaging, and voice over Internet protocol (VOIP) make it easy to communicate.

- Applications and documents stored on Internet servers let workers collaborate on projects no matter where their desks are. Likewise, employees can sync multiple devices, allowing them to access the same information from any location on whichever device they choose.

- Video conferences make it possible to meet face to face—even when you are miles apart.

What qualities and values might a person have who enjoys working at home? What might be some benefits and drawbacks? What technology do you think would be most useful? Use a word processing program to write an essay that answers these questions.

Understanding Ethics

Your values and standards are also influenced by your **ethics**. Ethics are a set of beliefs about what is right and what is wrong.

■ Some ethics are established by society. They determine how people are supposed to behave, usually in terms of human rights, responsibilities, and justice. They may be based on customs or on law.

■ Some ethics are established by groups of people, such as the members of certain professions. For example, doctors and lawyers must abide by strict ethical standards, or they can lose their licenses to practice.

■ Some ethics are personal and usually measure **virtues**—or positive character traits—such as honesty, compassion, and loyalty.

People don't always agree on what is ethical. One employee may think it is ethical to make personal phone calls while at work, while another employee may think it is unethical.

Even when there are laws defining what is ethical, some people still don't agree. For example, one person might think it is ethical to take paper or staples from an office, even though it is illegal.

Identifying Your Strengths and Interests

If you are like most people, you will spend half your life or more working. So, choosing a career that will bring you satisfaction makes good sense. How can you know what will bring satisfaction? One way is to choose a career that gives you a chance to use and develop your strengths and interests.

Being able to identify your strengths and interests will help you choose a career that is right for you. It will also help you set realistic educational and career goals.

What Are Strengths?

Your **strengths** are your positive qualities and skills. Your personal qualities are the characteristics and traits that make you unique. A **skill** is an ability or talent—something you do well.

■ You might have a talent for growing flowers.

■ You might understand how machines work.

■ You might speak multiple languages.

Interests and Careers

You don't have to be an expert in something to have an interest in it. An interest might be a favorite activity or something you just like to do. For example, you might not be a star basketball player, but you can still seek a career that satisfies your interest in basketball and also uses your other skills and abilities. What if you are interested in basketball but know you do not have the talent to be a professional player?

★ *If you have an ability for communications, you might consider a career as a sports journalist.*

★ *If you have an ability for food and nutrition, you might consider a career as a sports dietitian.*

★ *If you have an ability for marketing, you might consider a career in public relations, sales, or marketing for a sports team.*

What interests and abilities do you have that you think might relate to a career?

Sometimes it is hard to recognize your own strengths. You must be very honest about what you do well, and what you do not do very well. Sometimes other people can help. You can ask family members and friends who you trust, or a teacher or counselor at school, to help you identify your strengths.

Strengths also include **accomplishments**, which are things you have achieved at home, in school, or in the community. Accomplishments might include specific skills, such as knowing how to create a chart using a spreadsheet program or how to change a flat tire on a car. Accomplishments might also include achievements such as being the treasurer of a club or scoring a goal in a soccer game.

Discovering Your Interests

Often, people have strengths that relate to their interests. **Interests** are subjects or activities that attract your attention and that you enjoy doing or learning about. You can have interests in the different areas of your life.

■ At home, you might have interests in cooking, gardening, sewing, or design.

■ At school, you might have interests related to your class subjects, music, theater, athletics, and clubs.

■ With peers, you might share interests in movies, music, and sports.

■ In your community, you might have interests in volunteer activities, politics, and public service.

Many of your interests are probably related to activities such as sports, arts, and entertainment. These interests may be useful in your career, or they may be things you do outside of work for fun.

For example, if you are interested in music, you might consider a career such as a music teacher, a disc jockey, an agent for a musician, an owner of a club that hosts performers, or a radio host. You might consider performing with a band for fun.

What interests do you have that might be useful in a career?

Multilingual Employees

Are you multilingual? Multilingual means that you can communicate in more than one language. It is an ability that is an advantage to anyone looking for a career.

Many businesses have offices in countries all around the world. Even those that have offices in only one country have customers who speak different languages. Employers are eager to hire qualified candidates who can speak multiple languages. If you understand different cultures and are interested in living internationally, that is an advantage as well.

What languages do you think are spoken by the most people around the world? Use the Internet or the library to find the answer. Make a poster showing how you might use multiple languages to succeed in a career.

Recognizing Character Qualities

Your **character** is the personal qualities or traits that make you unique. You show your character qualities by the way you act and the things you say. Most people have both positive and not-so-positive character traits.

These character traits combine to make you the type of person you are. You might be kind, helpful, or considerate. You might be stubborn, sad, or mean.

Your character traits influence the way other people see you and the way you see yourself. They can contribute to your self-esteem and your well-being. You are not stuck with the same character traits for your whole life. You might change some traits, and you might gain new ones.

Myth If a person has one bad quality, he is bad through and through.

Truth Most people have both positive and negative character qualities. To be a good person, you might want to try to have more positive qualities than negative ones.

Personal Qualities and Your Career

Everyone has positive and negative personal qualities. When you start looking for a career, it helps to understand the situations that bring out both types of qualities.

■ Are you happy working alone, or would you get lonely and sad?

■ Do you enjoy talking on the phone, or would you prefer to meet with people face to face?

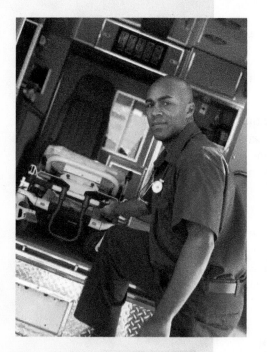

What character qualities do you think are important for a paramedic?

- Are you relaxed sitting at a desk for a long time, or would you rather be outdoors and active?
- Do you enjoy the excitement of having to meet a deadline, or does it cause you to feel stress?

You will spend a lot of time and energy at work. The best work environment will bring out your positive personal qualities.

Developing Your Character

You develop character qualities over time as you come to understand what is important to you. You can also work to develop character qualities. For example, you can decide you want to be more **compassionate**—caring about the suffering of others.

- Can you show compassion by walking dogs at an animal shelter?
- Can you show compassion by stocking shelves at the food pantry?
- Can you show compassion by speaking up when someone is mean to another person?

Another way to develop character qualities is to find someone who has the character you admire and then try to **emulate**—or copy in a respectful manner—his or her behavior.

Sometimes, your character traits show up only in certain situations. You might be shy in class but outgoing when you are with your family and friends. You might be lazy when you have homework to do but enthusiastic when you play soccer.

Recognizing Your Character

Sometimes it is hard to recognize your own character qualities. You might be embarrassed to think about your positive traits. People might think you are bragging or conceited.

You might be unwilling to think about your negative traits. You might not want to admit you can sometimes be mean or stubborn.

The more you understand about yourself, the easier it is to identify all of your traits. You can accept both the good and the bad, and understand how you might try to improve.

One way to tell a positive character trait from a negative character trait is to ask yourself whether you would like that trait in someone else. For example, do you like it when someone else is rude? Do you like it when someone else is bossy? If not, you might not want to show those character traits yourself, either.

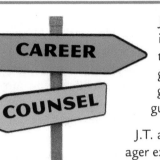

J.T. is looking for a summer job. His friend Alex is a lifeguard and works at the town pool. He tells J.T. that lifeguarding is fun. The pay is good, he gets to be outside all day, the other guards are nice, and the girls all think the life-guard is cool.

J.T. applies for the job. The town's recreation man-ager explains that the town will pay for the lifeguard training and certification as long as J.T. works all sum-mer. If he quits, he will have to repay the cost of the training.

The training is harder than J.T expected. He does not enjoy learning first aid and CPR. The job is not much fun, either. Little kids are constantly asking for bandages. J.T. has to clean the bathrooms at the end of the day. After one week, J.T. is regretting his decision to become a lifeguard. He is thinking about quitting.

What problems are facing J.T.? Can he find solutions? Did he make the best decisions while looking for a summer job? What could he have done different-ly? Use your 21st Century Skills such as decision making, problem solving, and critical thinking to help J.T. Write an ending to the story. Read it to the class, or form a small group and present it as a skit.

Benefits of Character Qualities

Positive character qualities—or virtues—make you feel good about yourself and contribute to your well-being.

- People recognize that your character is positive, and they respect you for it.
- Positive character qualities also make you feel proud of yourself and confident in your abilities.
- When people think your character is negative, they don't trust or respect you.

Positive character qualities contribute to your well-being. Some common positive traits include enthusiasm, thoughtfulness, compassion, trustworthiness, tolerance, and kindness.

Negative character qualities interfere with your well-being. Some common nega-tive traits include laziness, indifference, dishonesty, intolerance, meanness, and stubbornness.

Character Qualities of an Entrepreneur

An entrepreneur is a person who organizes and runs his or her own business. Being your own boss has advantages, such as independence, flexibility, and the pride and excite-ment that come with ownership. It also has disadvantages, such as no regular salary, an unpredictable work schedule, and the risk of losing everything if the business fails.

What are some of the character qualities you think would be useful for someone who wants to be an entrepreneur? Make a list of at least five qualities and write a brief expla-nation of how each quality would help an entrepreneur succeed.

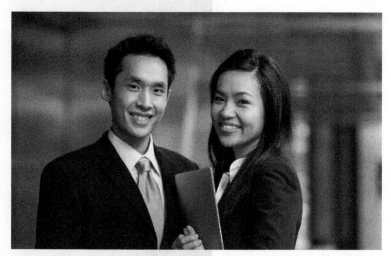

Why do you think an employer would prefer an employee with a positive attitude?

Appearance and Attitude

Do people judge your attitude based on your appearance? It might be a bias or a prejudice, but it happens all the time. Can you convey an attitude by the way you look or dress?

👎 Scowling and slouching

👎 Wearing clothing that doesn't fit

👎 Wearing heavy dark make-up and black nail polish

👍 Smiling

👍 Wearing neat, well-fitting outfits

👍 Making eye contact

Do you think people should judge you by the way you look and dress? How can you convey a positive attitude no matter what you look like?

A Positive Attitude

Attitude is the way you think, feel, or behave, particularly when you are with other people. If you have a **positive attitude**, you are happy, you think life is good, and you have confidence in yourself and the people around you. If you have a **negative attitude**, you are unhappy, you think life is unfair, and you have little confidence in yourself and others. When you have a positive attitude, people want to be around you.

Attitude changes depending on your situation. You might have a positive attitude about school and a negative attitude about your family. You might have a positive attitude about language arts class and a negative attitude about social studies.

Most employers want to hire people who have a positive attitude. You can develop a positive attitude by developing positive character traits. You can pay attention to the good things in your life and learn how to change the bad things, or let them go, so they don't bother you or make you sad.

Career Trend

According to the Bureau of Labor Statistics, occupations related to healthcare are projected to add the most new jobs between now and 2022. Total employment in that sector is projected to increase 10.8 percent, or by 15.6 million. The healthcare occupation that will have the highest number of new jobs is that of personal care aide. The projected number of new personal care aide jobs between 2012 and 2022 is 581,000.

Analyzing Employability Skills

You might graduate from college with a bachelor's degree in design, but if clients think you are unfriendly, or if they question your confidence, they are unlikely to hire you. Attitude and confidence are part of employability. **Employability** means having and using your life skills and abilities to be hired and stay hired. It is more than just meeting the qualifications for a position. It also means knowing how to:

- Present your positive qualities to an employer
- Communicate effectively with employers, co-workers, and customers
- Meet your responsibilities at work

Having employability skills will give you an advantage when you are ready to apply and interview for a position, no matter what career you choose.

Employability Characteristics

Some of the same personal qualities that make you successful in other areas of your life help make you employable. Positive qualities such as honesty, tolerance, patience, and responsibility show a potential employer that you are someone who will not only get the work done, but be good to have around the workplace. You can develop other positive qualities to improve your employability.

- A positive attitude shows that you enjoy your work. You do not complain or criticize others.

- Being cooperative shows that you respect your employer, co-workers, and customers. You meet your responsibilities, value other team members, and help others when it is necessary.

- Accepting and using **criticism**—advice about how to make positive changes in your actions or behavior—show that you want to improve and are willing to learn.

- Flexibility shows that you can accept change and adapt to new situations.

- Leadership shows that you are capable of making decisions and solving problems. It shows that others respect you and want to work with you.

Employers want to see that you are generally happy and easy to work with. Developing positive personal qualities and showing these qualities to an employer improves your chances of finding and keeping a job.

Myth Once I choose a career, I am stuck with it.

Truth Most people change careers at least three times in their lives, and many change more than that. Skills that you develop in one job can be used in a different line of work. Attending school or training programs at night or on the job may lead you in a different direction. Your goals are likely to change over time. You can change careers, too.

What Skills Are Transferable?

Here is a list of some transferable skills.

✔ *Negotiating*

✔ *Problem solving*

✔ *Management*

✔ *Leadership*

✔ *Accepting responsibility*

✔ *Honesty*

✔ *Decision making*

✔ *Cooperating*

✔ *Respect*

✔ *Creativity*

✔ *Independence*

✔ *Communications*

Can you think of skills you have that you can transfer to many different situations?

How can joining a career and technical student organization help you build employability skills?

Transferable Skills

A skill is the ability to do a task well. Skills can generally be placed into two groups: hard skills and **transferable skills**.

Hard skills relate to specific jobs or tasks. For example, operating a cash register is a hard skill. Baking a cake is a hard skill. Sewing a seam is a hard skill. Employers often look for people with hard skills to fill specific jobs. For example, an auto repair shop looks to hire people who are skilled at repairing automobiles. A florist looks to hire people skilled at arranging flowers.

Transferable skills can be used on almost any job. They are called transferable skills because you can transfer them from one situation or career to another. Being able to communicate effectively with other people is a transferable skill. So is being able to manage time and other resources. Employers are always looking for employees who have transferable skills.

How Can I Build Employability Skills?

You develop character qualities over time as you come to understand what is important to you. You can also work to develop character qualities by taking active steps. For example, you can make an effort to be more cooperative in school, or more flexible with your family. You can also emulate—copy—someone who shows qualities that you admire.

You can build employability skills that will appeal to an employer by practicing them in all areas of your life.

- At home, you can practice conflict resolution. Look for ways to fight less with your siblings and to communicate more effectively with your parents.

- At school, you can set academic goals and work with a teacher or counselor to create a plan for achieving them.

- With your peers, you can practice leadership by standing up against bullies or becoming active in a club or career technical student organization such as Family, Career and Community Leaders of America (FCCLA), or Health Occupations Students of America (HOSA).

- In your community, you can practice problem solving by looking for ways to support public resources. You might look for ways to reduce trash or to improve safety.

Career Profile: Employment and Placement Manager

Business Management & Administration Career Cluster

Job Summary

An employment and placement manager is a professional who advises other people on the process of choosing a career. Other job titles for the same position are career counselor, vocational counselor, and employment counselor.

Employment and placement managers meet with clients who are looking for jobs and help them assess their interests, skills, and abilities in order to identify suitable jobs. They may also work to help people develop job search skills as well as to locate and apply for jobs. Some employment and placement managers help clients cope with career-related issues such as job loss or stress.

Employment and placement managers may work in schools, for private companies, or for government agencies. Managers should be trustworthy and honest and enjoy helping others. Education requirements vary, but in most states, counselors must earn a master's degree in order to receive a license or become certified.

Use the Internet, a library, or career center to research the responsibilities, education and training requirements, and salary range of an employment and placement manager in your state. Write a job description for the position.

What might be the qualities and interests of a person who would be successful as an employment and placement manager?

Case Study

Casey is preparing to attend a job fair to find part-time work. He is not sure what type of job he wants. His mother suggests he consider a position as a bank teller, because banking careers are generally secure and pay well. His father—a landscape architect—thinks Casey might want to be a landscape assistant.

Casey has a list of the companies that will be at the fair. There are more than 50! He is not sure if he will be able to visit every booth, and he is worried he might miss the one that has the best opportunity for him.

■ What can Casey do to narrow the list of companies he should visit at the job fair?
■ What else can Casey do to prepare for the job fair?
■ Do you think Casey's parents are being helpful with their suggestions?

Career Portfolio

A **portfolio** is a collection of information and documents. A career portfolio can help you stay focused and organized as you explore career options and develop a career plan. A career portfolio includes information and documents that show the progress you make in school and in your career plan. It helps you stay on track to achieve your educational and career goals. You can also take it to job interviews and job fairs, so you have the information you need to fill out applications and the documents you want to show to potential employers.

As a class, discuss the types of information and documents you might include in a career portfolio. For example, you might include a list of skills, interests, and abilities; a personal academic plan; a resume; and a sample cover letter. You might also include examples of achievement, such as a brochure you designed, artwork, or writing samples, as well as report cards or other assessments.

On your own, set up a career portfolio. It might be a paper folder or an electronic folder on your computer. For the first document, make a list of the documents and information you plan to include in the portfolio. As you collect the items, you can cross them off the list.

Web Extra

Many job Web sites include sections specifically for teens, such as groovejob.com and myfirstpaycheck.com.

Use the Internet to identify the sites that you think might be the most useful for your peers. Make a directory of the sites, including the Web site address and a brief description. Post the directory on your school Web site or in your school career center or library.

Answer It!

1. What is a career?
2. What is a job?
3. List three things that might be determined by career requirements.
4. List four reasons people might choose a career.
5. What are values?
6. What are interests?
7. Define character.
8. List five positive character qualities.
9. List five negative character qualities.
10. What are transferable skills? Give at least one example.

Career-Ready Practices

Participating in school clubs and organizations can provide valuable opportunities to gain career-related experience. As a class or in small groups, brainstorm ways you can inform students and families about the different clubs and organizations at your school. For example, you might publish a booklet, design a Web site, or organize an Activity Fair. Make sure you consider the importance of using reliable and thorough research strategies to brainstorm ideas and gather information.

Working together, select one idea that will let you educate students and families about the clubs and organizations available at school. Make a plan for completing the project, and then put the plan into action. Keep in mind that career-ready individuals work productively in teams to evaluate the methods for sharing and presenting information to others. They find ways to encourage all team members to participate and contribute to the team's goals.

When the project is complete, evaluate your success. Did you achieve your goal? Did you create a useful product? Did the students and families find it useful and informative? Did you run into any obstacles? If so, how did you overcome them? Did you have to make any trade-offs? Write a report explaining what you learned, whether you were successful or not, and what you would do differently if you were going to start the project all over again.

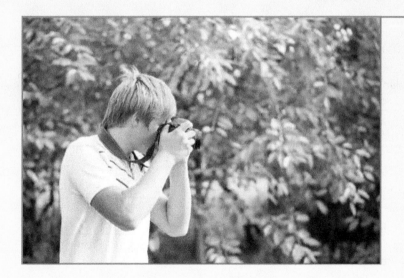

Write Now

Sometimes it is difficult to identify your own interests, skills, and abilities. Working in pairs, spend 15 minutes talking to your partner about the things you like to do. Discuss the things you think you are good at, your favorite subjects in school, and the clubs or organizations you have joined. Take notes so you will remember what your partner tells you.

When you have finished talking, look over your notes and select a career that you think suits your partner's interests, skills, and abilities. Write a letter of recommendation to a potential employer on behalf of your partner, explaining why you think this would be the right career match.

Business Plan Project

A business plan is a map that an entrepreneur draws to organize his or her goals for building a business. In addition to listing the goals, the business plan identifies the actions the entrepreneur will take to achieve those goals, and the challenges he or she is likely to face in the process. In addition to creating a map for the entrepreneur, the business plan also shows potential investors (the people who loan entrepreneurs money to start the business) that the entrepreneur has thought through the process and is prepared for the challenges that lie ahead.

Creating a business plan might seem like a large and overwhelming task. As with any long-term goal, breaking it into smaller, more manageable goals can help make it easier. In each chapter of this book, the **Business Plan Project** activity will give you the opportunity to create a piece of a business plan for your own business. By the end, you will have a complete, thorough map for taking that business from an idea to profitability. Appendix B includes a sample business plan that you can use as a guide as you build your business plan project.

In your career portfolio, create a section titled **Business Plan Project**. On page 1, enter the chart below. You can draw the chart, or use a software tool such as the Table feature in Word or a spreadsheet program such as Excel. Enter the text in both columns. You will use the information in this chart to organize your thoughts and develop your plan. Don't worry if it doesn't make sense yet. By the end of this book it will.

On page 2 of your **Business Plan Project**, draw a 2-column chart. In small groups or own your own, brainstorm a list of activities you do well and like to do, such as hobbies, part-time work, sports, classes, and after-school clubs. Record the list in the left column of the chart. In the right column, record the types of skills and characteristics required for each activity and whether or not these skills and characteristics will help you be an entrepreneur. Compare this list of skills and characteristics to the five qualities/characteristics you completed on page 13.

Your Business Idea	Describe your business idea. What is the name of your business? Explain how your idea will satisfy a customer need.
Business Ownership	What type of business are you starting? What type of business ownership?
Economics of One Unit	What are your costs to make the product? What is your selling price? Calculate Your Economics of One Unit.
Goals	What are your business goals? What are your personal/educational goals?
Opportunity Recognition	Conduct a SWOT (Strengths, Weaknesses, Opportunities, and Threats) analysis on your business idea. What qualifications/skills do you have to run this business?
Competition	List two primary competitors. What is your company's competition advantage?
Marketing & Market Research	Describe the Four P's for your business (Product, Place, Price, and Promotion). Complete a marketing plan chart. Who is your target market? List five questions you could include in a market research survey.
Fixed Expenses	List your average fixed expenses for a month. Why does your company need these expenses?
Projected Income Statement	How many units will you sell in one month? Complete the income statement for the month. Use the income statement & fixed expenses to calculate: • Break Even Units for the month
Financing Strategy	Make a list of all the items you will need to start the business. Use the Start up and Income Statement to calculate: • Return on Investment for the month • Return on Sales for the month

Skills in This Chapter . . .

- **Identifying Roles and Responsibilities**
- **Analyzing Well-Being**
- **Recognizing Influences**
- **Identifying Resources**

GETTING STARTED

How well do you know yourself? You know the facts: your birthday, your address, what grade you are in. But do you know what makes you happy? Do you know why you choose one flavor of ice cream over another, or why you would rather play soccer than basketball—or basketball instead of volleyball? These are hard questions to answer. Thinking about them might even make you uncomfortable. But understanding yourself is an important step in understanding the world around you, how you fit in, and why you might find one career more satisfying than another.

➤ Make a list of the things that are important to you, such as people, pets, sports, places, and even things. Pick the one that you think best defines you, write it on a slip of paper, and then give it to your teacher. As a class, read the slips of paper and try to figure out who wrote each one.

Identifying Roles and Responsibilities

An actor might play one **role** in a movie and a different role on television. In real life, you play different roles, too. That doesn't mean you pretend to be someone you are not—it just means you act differently depending on who you are with and what you are doing.

A role is the way you behave in a specific situation. As a student, you are expected to behave a certain way in school, but that's not the same way a coach expects you to behave as an athlete in practice, or an employer expects you to behave on the job.

A **responsibility** is something people expect you to do, or something you must accomplish. Responsibilities help define the way people interact and communicate with each other in different circumstances. When you live up to your responsibilities, you are successful in your role.

Different Roles = Different Responsibilities

You have roles in five main areas of your life: at home, at work, in school, with people your own age, or **peers**, and in your community. You also have a role as an individual—a **unique** (or one-of-a-kind) person.

You relate to people in each area in different ways. For example, you probably use different words when you talk to your friends than you do when you talk to your parents or teachers. You might dress differently, too. At home, you might wear sweats, at school you might want to express your style, and at work you might wear a uniform.

Responsibilities are different in each role, too.

- As an employee, you are responsible for showing up on time.
- As a family member, you are responsible for making your bed.
- As a friend, you are responsible for being a good listener.
- As a student, you are responsible for completing your assignments.
- As a neighbor, you are responsible for picking up trash in front of your house.

Working Americans spend an average of 8.8 hours a day at work or on work-related activities. High school students spend an average of 7.5 hours a day attending class and doing homework.

Assigned Roles vs. Acquired Roles

Many of our roles happen because of who we are. Take the role of family member, for example. We don't choose to be a brother or sister or son or daughter. These roles are assigned to us.

Some roles we choose for ourselves.

■ You might want to be a musician, so you learn to play an instrument and audition for a band.

■ You might want to be a member of the student government, so you campaign for office.

■ You might want to work in a restaurant, so you apply for a job.

■ You might want to contribute to your community, so you volunteer at a senior center.

Not everyone chooses the same roles. We choose certain roles because they are important to us. The roles we choose are the ones that make us unique—different from other people.

A person who starts a small business is said to "wear many hats." That means he or she has to play many different roles at work. For example, you might start a company to sell hand-printed T-shirts because you are skilled at designing the artwork. But you must also manage the other aspects of the business if you want to succeed, including advertising and sales, filling orders, purchasing supplies, and handling customer complaints.

Who Am I Now?

Your roles vary depending on the five main areas of your life:

✔ *Family:*
- *Son or daughter*
- *Brother or sister*
- *Niece or nephew*
- *Grandchild*

✔ *Work:*
- *Employee*
- *Co-worker*
- *Manager*
- *Owner*

✔ *Peers:*
- *Friend*
- *Rival*
- *Teammate*

✔ *School:*
- *Student*
- *Classmate*

✔ *Community:*
- *Neighbor*
- *Volunteer*

Think about a small business you might like to operate. What different roles would you play in the business? What responsibilities might you have in each role?

Roles and Responsibilities Change

Roles change depending on your **stage of life**, or how old you are. Right now, you might not have a paying job; in a few years, you might work part-time after school or in the summer. One day, you will start a career and work full time.

Like roles, responsibilities change over time or in different situations.

■ Now, you might be responsible for watching your little brother in the afternoon. Someday, you might be a paid babysitter for your neighbor's children, care for your own children, or run a daycare center.

■ Now, you might be responsible for making your own lunch. Someday, you might be responsible for preparing dinner for your whole family, managing a kitchen as a head chef, or owning your own restaurant.

Just because the role and responsibility are the same for you as for someone else doesn't mean you will both behave the same way. Everyone in your math class is responsible for doing the homework, but one person might do it every morning on the bus, while you meet with a classmate to do it after school.

The way we meet our responsibilities is unique, because we are unique. When you understand your roles and responsibilities, you understand more about yourself and why you behave the way you do in a certain situation.

Fulfilling Your Responsibilities

You might think responsibilities are a burden. After all, why should you care what other people expect from you? But people treat you with more respect if you fulfill your responsibilities.

Why do you think an employer would prefer to hire someone who fulfills his or her responsibilities?

■ They trust you.

■ They take you seriously.

■ They enjoy being with you.

If you do not fulfill your responsibilities, people stop expecting very much from you. They think you are immature.

■ People feel you let them down.

■ They see you as a slacker.

■ They find someone else who will meet their expectations.

Rules and Responsibilities

Living up to your responsibilities means playing by the rules. A **rule** is a written or unwritten statement about how something is supposed to be done. Rules are meant to protect people and to help people live together in communities. When you follow the rules, you show people that you are responsible.

There are rules in every area of your life—home, at work, in school, in the community, and even when you are with your peers.

- At home, you may have to be in bed at a certain time. You may not be able to watch television or use your phone until your homework is complete.
- At work, you may have to arrive at a specific time, or wear your hair a certain way.
- In school, you may have to sit in assigned seats. You may have to raise your hand to speak in class.
- In your community, you may have to turn off your phone in a movie. You may have to wait for the signal to cross a street.

When you break the rules, you show that you are not responsible. There may be consequences for breaking the rules.

- If you arrive late for work, your supervisor may fire you.
- If you use your phone during a movie, the usher may ask you to leave.

Different Rules for Different People

If you think that there are different rules for different people, you are right—there are. Many rules are meant to protect people, such as rules for wearing a seatbelt or a motorcycle helmet. Some rules vary depending on factors such as your age or your occupation.

- Health care workers are not allowed to discuss their client's health with others.
- Politicians are not allowed to keep secrets from the public.

If you think a rule is unreasonable, try to find out why the rule is in place. Once you understand the reason for the rule, you might understand why it is important not to break it.

You may be able to change some rules. For example, if you show your employer you are responsible and can be trusted to complete your assigned tasks, he or she might be more flexible about the time you are expected to start working.

NUMBERS GAME

You can use a circle—or pie—chart to show the relationship of parts to a whole. The entire circle represents the whole—or 100%. Each part represents a portion—or percentage—of the whole.

For example, you can use a circle chart to show the relationship among the times you spend in the different roles in your life.

The entire circle represents 24 hours, or one day. Sections of the circle represent the number of hours you spend in each role.

Say you spend 7 hours a day as a student in school, 2 hours as a teammate in practice, 1 hour a day as a friend, and 14 hours as a family member. First, calculate the percentage of time spent in each role relative to one day. (*Hint:* Divide the number of hours in each role by the total number of hours in a day. Round the answer to the nearest whole number.)

- 29%—student
- 8%—teammate
- 5%—friend
- 58%—family member

Next, draw the sections to represent each role. Your circle chart would look like this:

What would the chart look like if you spent 3 hours at work, no time as a teammate, and 13 hours at home? What about a chart representing the roles you play?

Analyzing Well-Being

Well-being is the feeling and understanding that everything is going right in your life. It is when you have a positive outlook about yourself and the people and things around you. You are happy, healthy, confident, and satisfied. Often, well-being has a lot to do with how well you meet your responsibilities.

Having a career that brings you satisfaction is important for your well-being. When you enjoy your work, you are more likely to be happy and have a positive attitude. If you do not enjoy your work, you are more likely to feel angry, sad, and frustrated. Recognizing the things that contribute to your well-being can help you choose a satisfying career path.

Well-Being: Six Ways

Six areas of your life contribute to your well-being, and when all six work together successfully, you experience an overall feeling of well-being, or **wellness**.

- **Emotional well-being** depends on your ability to deal with problems and stress.
- **Physical well-being** depends on your health.
- **Social well-being** depends on how you get along with other people.
- **Personal well-being** depends on how satisfied and confident you are with yourself.
- **Intellectual well-being** depends on your ability to think and learn new things.
- **Environmental well-being** depends on your comfort and satisfaction with the environment in which you live and work.

Wellness is not an accident. It happens when you make healthy choices about the way you live your life. When you make wellness part of your **lifestyle**—the way you think and behave every day—you take control of your health and well-being. You accept responsibility for your health and happiness instead of letting other people determine what is best for you.

Whose Well-Being Is More Important?

Sometimes, looking out for your own well-being could actually interfere with the well-being of others. While some people, such as your parents, might be willing to put your well-being first, you cannot expect that from everyone. What if you want to take a long lunch in order to attend an exercise class?

★ *Your co-workers must cover for you, and they may miss their own lunch time.*

★ *Your customers must wait until you are back at work.*

★ *Your supervisor may turn to someone else for assistance.*

★ *You may lose pay, which affects your family.*

Is your action fair to everyone else? What could you do so that your well-being does not interfere with the well-being of others?

Promote Your Own Well-Being

You are responsible for your own well-being. It is not up to other people to make sure you are happy and confident. To promote your own well-being, you can be aware of what makes you happy and satisfied, and then take the action you need to make it happen. You can take action in one particular area, such as attending a class to learn a new skill, or you can make general changes that will promote overall wellness and well-being, such as getting more exercise or eating a healthy diet.

- To promote emotional well-being, you can start writing your thoughts, fears, worries, and concerns in a journal.
- To promote physical well-being, you can make sure you get enough sleep.
- To promote social well-being, you can join a club or student organization.
- To promote personal well-being, you can be honest with yourself and the people around you.

Roadblocks to Well-Being

A **roadblock** is something that gets in the way and interferes with your progress. Lots of things get in the way of well-being. You might feel tired or sick. You might be frustrated with a co-worker who has trouble understanding a new responsibility, or angry because a customer complains.

Problems in one area of well-being can affect the other areas. If you're tired, you might have less patience with a co-worker. If you're angry at your supervisor, you might be rude to a customer.

It is important to recognize roadblocks that are interfering with your well-being so you can take action. For example, you might make time to help your co-worker learn a new skill.

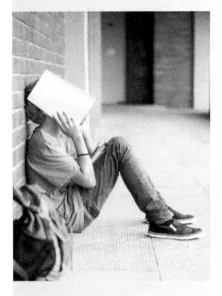

Why do you think problems in one area of well-being affect you in other areas?

CAREER

COUNSEL

Malik recently started working after school as a cashier at the grocery store. He earns a good hourly wage and is gaining work experience. Most of his friends do not have jobs. They spend their afternoons hanging around and playing video games.

One day, Malik's friends show up at the grocery store. They follow him around while he stocks the shelves. They make a lot of noise, knock things over, and move items from one shelf to another, where they don't belong. Malik asks them to cut it out, but they just laugh. Finally, Malik's supervisor asks them to leave. The next day, Malik's friends come back.

What challenges are facing Malik? Use 21st Century Skills such as problem solving, decision making, and critical thinking to help Malik recognize the obstacles in front of him, and to make and implement a plan of action. Write an ending to the story and read it to the class, or form small groups and present it as a skit.

Promoting Your Well-Being

Wanting something that will promote your well-being shows that you are responsible. Interfering with the well-being of others in order to get what you want is not. What are some of the positive and negative ways you might promote your own well-being?

👎 Taking credit for someone else's achievement

👎 Stealing someone else's belongings

👎 Putting someone down to make you look better

👍 Recognizing roadblocks to well-being and finding ways to overcome them

👍 Being aware of the way your actions and words affect others

Can you think of responsible ways to promote your own well-being?

Recognizing Influences

An **influence** is something that affects the way you think and act. You are influenced by pretty much everything in your life.

When you are young, your biggest influence is your family. That's who you spend the most time with and who teaches you about life. As you grow older, you are influenced by a wider range of people and information, including friends, teachers, current events, advertising, and celebrities.

Recognizing the things that influence you can help you understand yourself better.

When you know where influence comes from, you can make up your own mind about whether the influence would be positive—a good influence—or negative—a bad influence. This knowledge can help you make decisions about which career will be right for you.

Understanding Influence

There are major influences in all areas of your life. You are influenced by your family and friends, by your culture and community. You may be influenced by things you read or see on television. You may be influenced by the behavior of athletes and celebrities you don't even know. A lot of influence happens without your even knowing it.

■ For example, just living in a certain neighborhood can influence you and your opinions of others. In a friendly neighborhood, you might feel safe and spend a lot of time outside, but in a less friendly neighborhood, you might be wary and stay indoors.

■ The media—television, radio, magazines, and the Internet—can influence you. For example, you see pictures of attractive, happy people in an ad for a particular store, and you want to shop in that store so you can be pretty and happy, too.

Good Influence or Bad Influence?

Sometimes it's pretty easy to tell whether an influence is positive or negative.

■ If something influences you in a way that promotes your well-being, it's a good bet the influence is positive.

■ If something influences you to break the law, or risk your life or health—or someone else's life or health—it's a good bet the influence is bad.

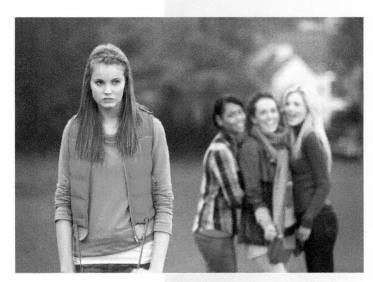

Sometimes it's not so easy to tell a good influence from a bad influence. A friend might want you to join a club or organization—usually that's a positive influence. But it's still a good idea to check out the club first and make sure it is right for you.

Some influences might create roadblocks to your success. For example, the behavior of the people around you can be a roadblock. You might see your co-workers making personal telephone calls or playing games online and be influenced to do the same.

Can you think of a situation when someone asked you to do something you knew was not good for your health or wellness? What did you do? How did you feel?

Identifying Resources

Resources are things you can use to get something else. We need resources to help us achieve our goals, which are the plans we make to obtain something. For example, if you set a career goal to become a kindergarten teacher, you might use resources such as high school classes in child development, volunteer opportunities at a day care center, and your ability to communicate with small children to achieve your goal.

What Influences You?

Your thoughts, beliefs, and actions are influenced by the people and things in your life. Major influences include:

✔ *Family*
✔ *Friends*
✔ *Culture*
✔ *Community*
✔ *Current events*
✔ *Media*

Sharing Resources

Lots of resources can be used by more than one person at a time. A family shares a home. In school, a whole class shares one teacher. A whole community shares the public library. Everyone shares the national parks. What if people don't manage shared resources very well?

★ Some resources might run out, such as coal and other fossil fuels.

★ Some resources might become unusable, such as parks overrun by criminals or destroyed by vandals.

★ Access to resources might cause conflicts, such as fighting over land or water rights.

★ Access to resources might be restricted to a few, such as beaches owned by the wealthy.

How might you be affected by mismanagement of shared resources?

Types of Resources

You can categorize resources into seven main groups.

■ **Human resources** are the resources people provide that things cannot. Human resources include knowledge, talent, physical and intellectual abilities, time, energy, and even personal character.

■ **Nonhuman** or **capital resources** include things such as money and cars.

■ **Technological resources** have a great impact on your life. They include everything from computers to automated teller machines to medical equipment.

■ **Community resources** are services that the government provides, such as public parks, public schools, libraries, and police and fire departments. Some businesses contribute to community resources as well. For example, a company might sponsor a softball team.

■ **Natural resources** are things that exist in nature and are available for everyone. Natural resources include air, water, wildlife, minerals, and plants.

■ **Renewable resources** are natural resources that can be recreated in unlimited quantities, such as air and sunlight.

■ **Nonrenewable resources** are natural resources that are available in limited quantities and may one day be used up. Coal is a nonrenewable resource.

Available Resources

Some resources are available to everyone, such as air and water. Other resources may be available only to some people, such as artistic ability or talent. Some resources depend on your current role and your stage of life. For example, you might not have money if you're too young to have a job. You might have more physical strength and energy than a senior citizen.

You can develop your resources in order to make sure you have them available when you need them.

■ You can eat well and exercise to develop your health.

■ You can work and save money to develop financial security.

■ You can practice to develop a skill or talent.

Whose Resources Are They?

Experts estimate that there are about 7 billion people living in about 195 countries on the planet Earth. Most people manage and use the resources available in their own communities. But who is responsible for managing the resources we all share?

One issue that affects the resources we all share is global warming. Scientists explain global warming as a gradual increase in the temperature of the Earth's atmosphere. Representatives from around the world have worked together to set rules and regulations to manage global warming, but they are not always successful.

Why is it important for people to work together to manage global resources? Can you think of reasons why it may be difficult to succeed? Individually or with a partner, research an issue affecting global resources. Write a letter to a politician explaining how the issue affects your community. Suggest ways to manage the resource for the benefit of all.

Managing Resources

Sometimes it's hard not to worry if you don't have as many resources as someone else, or if you have different resources. You might think someone who knows the president of a company will be hired for the job you want. Or you might worry that someone who has enough money to pay for a private college will have an advantage if you can only afford a public university.

Why is it important to manage the resources you have available?

You can make the most out of the resources you have by managing them. That means making sure you use your resources at the right time and for the right purpose.

For example, you and your parents may have been saving for your college education. You could spend your entire college fund on four years at a private college, or you could use it for four years at a public school and have enough left for graduate school as well. How will you manage your college fund resources?

To make that decision, you consider your values, standards, and ethics. You recognize the things that are influencing you. For example, are your friends going to public or private universities? Do you value the **prestige**—positive recognition and admiration—that comes with a degree from a private school? Finally, you ask yourself which option gives you the best opportunity to achieve your goals.

Making the Most of What You Have

Not everyone has access to the same resources. What if you want to play guitar in a band but cannot afford lessons?

■ You could get a job and earn the money you need.

■ You could offer to do chores for the guitar teacher in exchange for lessons.

■ You could borrow a guitar lesson book from the library and teach yourself.

Can you think of creative ways you could manage your resources?

Myth Money is the most important resource.

Truth Money is important if you want to buy something. Other resources are important for achieving different goals. If you want to run a race, you need your health more than you need money. If you want to make a new friend, you need a sense of humor more than you need money.

Money Madne$$

Money is a resource we use to acquire things. For most people, money is a limited resource—we do not have an unending supply. That means we have to make decisions about how we use money. If you have $10.00 in your pocket, and you spend $6.75 to rent a video game, how much will you have left over to buy something to eat? What if you have $22.50 and rent two video games? (Hint: Multiply $6.75 times 2 to find out the cost of renting two video games.)

Tech Connect

Time is a valuable resource. An electronic day planner can help you manage your time effectively. It's a calendar you can use to enter appointments, activities, notes, and other information. Most let you view days, weeks, or even a month at a time so you can see what's coming in the days ahead and stay prepared and organized. Day planners are available for computers and cell phones.

Can you think of other technologies that can help you manage your resources? Research one and use a presentation graphics program to create a presentation about it.

Career Profile: Environmental Scientist

Science, Technology, Engineering & Mathematics Career Cluster

Job Summary

Environmental scientists study ways to use science to protect the environment. They work to identify and fix problems with the air, water, and soil to make sure that the environment is safe.

Some environmental scientists work in laboratories, conducting experiments. Some work in offices, advising politicians and business owners. Some work outside—or in the field—collecting samples.

Environmental scientists study all fields of science, including biology and chemistry. They must know how to use math and computers. Some also study business, law, or engineering. They must have at least a college degree, and most need a master's or a doctoral degree.

Use the Internet, a library, or career center to research the responsibilities, education and training requirements, and salary range of an environmental scientist. Prepare a presentation about the career.

What skills and interests do you think might lead someone to pursue a career as an environmental scientist?

Career Trend

According to jobmonkey.com, jobs in the environmental science industry are expected to grow in the next decade. Find out more at jobmonkey.com/greenjobs/environmental-science.html.

Case Study

Melissa has an interest in finance and does well in math class. She applies for an after-school job as a bank teller. The bank manager, Karen Johnson, calls Melissa and asks her to come in for an interview.

Melissa's friend Jenna suggests that Melissa try appearing very grown up at the interview. Melissa borrows clothes from her older sister, including shoes with high heels, and calls the bank manager by her first name throughout the meeting. Melissa does not get the job.

- Did Melissa behave appropriately at the interview?
- What influenced Melissa's behavior?
- What could Melissa have done differently?
- Do you think Melissa understands the roles she plays in the different areas of her life?

Career Portfolio

Resources are things you use to accomplish something else. Career resources are the things you will use to identify, get, and succeed in the career of your choice.

Make a table with three columns. In the left column, list career resources you think would be helpful. The list might include a career counselor or teacher, books about careers, computers and the Internet, and your parents. In the middle column, indicate whether you have the resource available to you or not. In the right column, if you have the resource, describe how you will use it. If you do not have the resource, describe how you might get it, or how you will make do without it.

Add the document to your career portfolio.

Web Extra

Use the Internet to locate information about community resources in your area. Are there state parks? National parks? How about libraries or museums? What types of career opportunities are available in these resources? Select one, and write a job description for it.

Answer It!

1. What are the five main areas of your life that define your roles and responsibilities?
2. What is the purpose of rules?
3. What are the six areas of well-being?
4. Define the term roadblock.
5. Define the term influence.
6. What are six major influence factors?
7. Define the term resources.
8. List the seven main groups of resources.
9. List four examples of human resources.
10. How can you make the most of the resources you have available?

Career-Ready Practices

The purpose of advertising is to influence people to buy a certain product, use a certain service, or even think a certain way. In a small group, select an advertisement from a magazine, the Internet, or television and look at it closely to figure out how it influences people. Answer the following questions:

■ What is being advertised?

■ Who is doing the advertising?

■ What methods does the ad use to influence you?

■ Is the ad effective?

Then, pick a product, service, or idea and create your own advertisement. It might be a poster, video, presentation, or even a song. Use your communication skills, both written and verbal, to present your idea. Make sure you consider the audience you want to target with your advertisement. Career-ready individuals understand that knowing your audience is critical to communicating clearly and effectively. Work together as a team to complete the project, using cooperation, compromise, and teamwork to achieve your goal.

Write Now

Think about your roles and responsibilities. What roles do you play in your family, with your peers, at school, at work, and in your community? Is one role more important to you?

Write a personal essay describing the role you think is most important and why. Be sure to contrast it to some of your other roles that you think are less important.

Business Plan Project

It is important to know what resources you have available for building a business and how you can use them. Working on your own, make a list of the financial resources you have available, such as money in a savings account, income from a part time job, and even money you might be able to borrow from a friend or family member. Record the list in your **Business Plan Project**. Next, make a list of human resources you have available, such as your skills, talents, and abilities, and the skills, talents, and abilities of people who might help you, such as friends or family members. (*Hint: Take a look at the 2-column chart you created in Chapter 1.*) Finally, make a list of the technological resources you have available, such as a computer, tablet, or smartphone.

With a partner, brainstorm different businesses you could start with your resources and record them in your **Business Plan Project**. Help your partner brainstorm businesses he or she could start with his or her resources.

3 | Why We Work

Skills in This Chapter . . .

- **Examining Lifestyle Goals and Factors**
- **Recognizing Needs vs. Wants**
- **Measuring the Value of Work**
- **Examining Career Trends**

GETTING STARTED

People work to achieve the things they want and need in life, from shelter and clothing to respect and pride. Do you daydream about things you want in life when you are an adult, such as the type of home you will live in, the car you will drive, or the number of children you will have? If you start planning now, you can identify a career path that will help make those daydreams become reality.

➤ Draw a picture of yourself twenty years in the future. What will you be doing? Where will you be? Who will you be with? What can you do now to make that vision of yourself come true?

Examining Lifestyle Goals and Factors

Does a clinical laboratory technician earn enough money to afford a vacation home? How many hours a week does an agricultural inspector spend on the job? Is a hotel clerk expected to work nights and weekends? Does a sales representative travel a lot?

The career you choose helps determine the lifestyle you will achieve, and your lifestyle might impact the career you choose. Recall that your lifestyle is the way you think and behave every day. Your lifestyle is the way you reflect personal values, standards, and attitudes in your life.

■ If you value expensive items such as designer clothes, you might choose a career because it pays a high salary.

■ If you value time with your family, you might choose a career with a flexible schedule, even if it pays less than other jobs.

You can consider lifestyle factors such as location, salary, education, time, and environment when you choose a career. You can also set goals for the way you want to live your life and the things you want to have in life as part of your career plan.

What Are Lifestyle Factors?

The things about your job that affect the way you live your life are **lifestyle factors**. There are five basic lifestyle factors you might want to consider when you are making decisions about the career that will be right for you.

1. *Location.* Where do you want to live? Do you want to be near your family? Do you want to live in the mountains or near the ocean? Do you prefer a city, the country, or the suburbs?

2. *Salary.* How much money do you think you must earn to pay for your needs and wants? Are you willing to work for less money to achieve other goals, such as more free time or less work-related stress?

3. *Education.* How many years are you willing to spend in school? Would you be happy taking classes at night while you work during the day? Would you be willing to earn less money while you train on the job?

4. *Time.* How many hours a week do you want to spend at work? Would you work at night or on weekends? Would you mind being **on-call**, which means being available at any time to cope with emergencies? Do you want to work part-time, even if it means earning less money?

5. *Environment.* What type of space do you want to be in? Do you like sitting at a desk? Do you want to be outdoors? What type of people do you want to work with? Do you need windows in your office? Do you like to dress in a suit or do you prefer casual clothes?

About 80% of the U.S. population lives in urban areas (cities) while about 20% lives in rural areas (the countryside).

Setting Lifestyle Goals

Lifestyle goals are the things you want in life such as a family, where you want to live, how much money you have, and how much free time you have for friends, sports, and other activities that you enjoy.

- You might want to live in the mountains and spend as much time as possible out of doors. You might consider a career in recreation.

- You might want to have children and be available in the afternoons when they get home from school. You might consider a career in part-time sales.

- You might want to have enough money to travel, even if it means working many hours between trips. You might consider a career such as corporate lawyer or surgeon.

Selecting a career path that gives you the opportunity to achieve your lifestyle goals will make you a happier, more satisfied person.

Making Trade-Offs

When you make decisions about your lifestyle and career plans, you may have to make trade-offs. A **trade-off** is a compromise, or giving up one thing in order to get something else.

Why do you think a career that matches your lifestyle goals will be more enjoyable and satisfying?

You might want to be a social worker helping young adults in New York City. You might also want to live in a house with a backyard. Houses in New York City are very expensive, and social workers typically do not earn very high salaries. What trade-off could you make?

- You could choose to rent an apartment in the city, and put off the goal of living in a house with a backyard.

- Or, you could choose to live in a less expensive community outside the city. You would have a long commute to work, but you would be able to afford a house with a backyard.

Focusing on the things that are most important to you and setting priorities can help you make the best decisions. You can use the decision-making process described in Chapter 6 to consider all possible options and the consequences of each option. Then, choose the option that helps you achieve your career goals and your lifestyle goals.

Are Your Lifestyle Goals Realistic?

Like career-related goals, lifestyle goals should be realistic. While you might choose to aim high, it is important that you believe your goals are attainable, which means that you have the skills and resources to achieve them. Are the following goals realistic and attainable, or not?

- 👎 Work 10 hours a week and earn a $1,000,000.00 annual salary

- 👎 Live in a mansion and be named the NBA's most valuable player for three years in a row

- 👍 Study hard to become a doctor and open your own medical practice

- 👍 Enlist in the United States Air Force, learn to fly jet planes, and then travel the world as a commercial pilot

- 👍 Attend cosmetology school and get a job as a stylist at a salon in a city

Knowing you can achieve your lifestyle goals will help you work hard and stay on track. What lifestyle goals do you have that might influence your career plans?

How Long Is Your Work Week?

A **work week** is the number of hours you work per week. How do you think the length of a work week affects your lifestyle? How might it affect the employer's business, as well as the economy?

In the United States, the number of hours an employee works is set by the employer and agreed to by the employee. Typically, a full-time employee works 8 hours a day, 5 days a week, which equals a 40-hour work week.

In France, most employees work a 35-hour work week. In South Korea, they work 44 hours per week.

Make a chart comparing the typical work-week hours in three or four countries around the world. Use the Internet or the library to find the information.

Recognizing Needs vs. Wants

When you say that you absolutely, positively need a new video game, you're wrong. You might *want* a new video game. But you don't *need* it.

- A **need** is a something you can't live without.

- A **want** is something you desire.

Humans *need* certain basic items in order to survive. We *want* things to improve our quality of life, or to achieve a certain lifestyle. Our wants and needs and how we achieve them influence the career decisions that we make.

Why Do Needs and Wants Matter?

Wanting or needing something can be a powerful **motivator**, which means it can encourage you to set goals and make decisions. Recall that a goal is a plan to obtain something. Goals help you focus on what is really important to you and what you are willing to work for. When you know what you need and what you want, you can use goals to get those things.

For example, wanting a red convertible can motivate you to set a goal.

- You study hard in school so you become qualified for a career.

- The career brings you personal satisfaction as well as a good salary.

- You earn enough to pay for your needs and save to buy the car you want.

Do You Want It or Need It?

There are two categories of human needs: physical needs and psychological needs. Physical needs are basic items you need to survive, such as food, water, shelter, and clothing. Psychological needs are things that affect the way you think and feel, such as safety, security, love, acceptance, and respect.

Wants are things that are not necessary for survival. They are things that you think will make you happy and contribute to your well-being—and they might. But you can make do without them.

There are some things most people want, such as entertainment and dessert. Some wants are very personal and help define us as individuals.

People want different things in life. What do you want that's different from what your friends want?

They are influenced by our values, standards, and goals. For example, you might value creativity and independence and want a career as a musician. Your friend might value job security and adventure and want a career in the military.

Money Madne$$

You work eight hours a week at the public library shelving books. You earn $7.50 an hour. Your Spanish teacher is organizing a class trip to Mexico during spring break. It costs $589.00. How many weeks must you work to earn enough to pay for the trip? Do you think a trip to Mexico with your Spanish class is a good thing to spend your money on? Why or why not?

Measuring the Value of Work

Value is a measure of the quality or importance of something. So, how do you measure the importance of work? Start by defining the word *work*. Work has different meanings in the different areas of your life.

In terms of a career, work refers to the way you spend your time in order to earn an income.

- At home, it might mean the chores you do around the house.
- At school, it might mean homework, tests, or class projects.
- With your peers, it might mean the effort you put into friendships.
- In your community, it might mean the time you spend volunteering.

In this book, of course, the focus is on careers and the work you do to earn an income. Recognizing the value of work in a career will help you choose a career that is right for you.

The Economic Value of Work

Economics is the study of the way people use resources to achieve their needs and wants. If you have a job now, you probably know the economic value of work. You work, and you are paid for it. When you receive a paycheck, you can use the money to buy things you want and need. You can contribute to your family's finances. You can save for the future.

The economic value of work is greater than just putting cash in your pocket. When you work, you contribute to the success of the economy. The **economy** is activity related to the production and distribution of goods and services.

- *Goods* are things you can see, touch, buy, and sell. Clothing, food, cell phones, and televisions are goods.
- *Services* are work that one person does for other people, in exchange for payment. Doctors, hairstylists, bus drivers, and lawyers are people who provide services.

Work produces the goods and services that people need and want. People who work are able to buy the goods and services. The stronger the economy, the more jobs there are, and the more people work.

Employers measure the value of work in terms of **productivity**—the amount of work an employee accomplishes. When workers are productive, the employer is successful.

The community measures the value of work in terms of taxes. When you earn an income, you pay taxes that support your local community, your state, and the federal government.

Benefits of Feeling Good About Work

A positive work environment contributes to your overall wellness. What if you successfully complete a complicated project?

★ *Your employer appreciates your efforts.*

★ *Your customers respect your knowledge.*

★ *Your co-workers enjoy working with you.*

★ *Your family recognizes that you can achieve goals outside the home.*

When you feel good about yourself, you put more effort into your work. How might feeling good about yourself help you achieve your career goals?

Tech Connect

One way employers measure productivity is by keeping track of how many hours each employee works. Some ask employees to fill out a **time sheet**, or table with cells for entering the time in, time out, and total hours at work.

Some use time clocks to record employee hours. A **time clock** is a machine that automatically records the time you *clock-in*—arrive—and the time you *clock-out*—leave. With older, mechanical time clocks, you actually insert a card in the machine and the current time prints on the card.

Newer time clocks are computerized. The current time is recorded when you swipe your ID card or punch in a code. **Biometric time clocks** use a fingerprint or handprint to record when an employee comes and goes.

Why do you think employers want to track their employees' hours? Can you think of any advantages to using a biometric time clock? Use a spreadsheet program to make a sample time sheet for one employee for one week. If you know how, use a formula to total the number of hours for each day and for the whole week.

The Emotional Value of Work

Some days you might think your job is not worth your paycheck. Your friends might be playing games while you are stocking shelves at the market. Or they are watching videos while you are babysitting.

Recall from Chapter 1 that every job has rewards as well as responsibilities. Luckily, the benefits of work include more than just money. A career can meet emotional needs by providing respect, satisfaction, and pride. You also gain confidence knowing you are developing skills and experience you will be able to use later on in life. When you have a career that meets emotional needs, it helps you feel good about yourself. It contributes to emotional well-being and overall wellness.

The Educational Value of Work

Jobs you have when you are still in school provide the opportunity to gain knowledge that will be valuable as you begin to plan and search for a career. You can discover more about the workplace and about the types of jobs you enjoy.

- As a data entry clerk, you might realize that you have a knack for computer programming.
- As a landscaping assistant, you might realize that you get satisfaction from working outdoors.

*Value of Work
As an Entrepreneur*

Entrepreneurs—people who start their own businesses—must work many hours to build a successful business. Sometimes it takes a long time before they earn a profit. How do you think being an entrepreneur might impact your lifestyle? How might you measure the value of work as an entrepreneur?

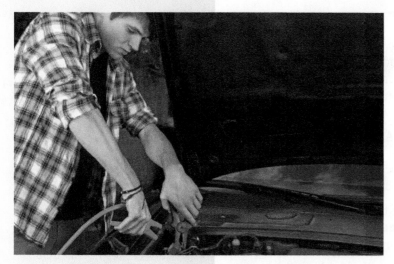

Can you think of skills you have developed while working or in school that will help you succeed in a future career?

Myth There is one perfect job for everyone.

Truth Trying to find one perfect job limits your opportunities. Many occupations can satisfy your career goals, and most people will have several jobs and careers throughout life.

Throughout your life, work is valuable because it provides an opportunity to learn new skills and information.

■ A waiter learns how to take orders and serve food.

■ A childcare assistant learns how to clean up after snack time and monitor children in a play area.

■ An office assistant learns how to answer phones, manage inventory, and use the office computer system.

■ A sale representative learns about new products and services.

Every job you have—for wages and as a volunteer—provides an opportunity to develop skills that will help you succeed in the present and in the future. Useful skills you can develop on the job include:

■ Showing respect to employers, customers, and co-workers.

■ Dressing appropriately for the workplace.

■ Arriving on time.

■ Making healthy decisions.

■ Solving problems.

■ Setting and achieving goals.

■ Working as part of a team.

Examining Career Trends

Will there be jobs for construction workers when you get out of school? Will California be hiring music teachers? Is the salary for transportation managers increasing or decreasing? One way to learn the answers to these questions is to look at career, or employment, trends. A **trend** is a general move in a certain direction. An employment trend is one way the labor market is changing over time. The **labor market** refers to any situation in which workers compete for jobs and employers compete for workers. Knowing how to identify employment trends can help you choose a career with a positive outlook.

What Are Employment Trends?

Employment trends include things such as the number of jobs and workers in a certain industry. For example, experts see a growing need for healthcare workers and educators, but a shrinking need for assembly-line workers. Other employment trends include where the jobs are. For example, if businesses are opening offices in the Southwest and closing them in the Northeast, there will be more job openings in the Southwest.

Employment trends are influenced by trends in other areas of life. There are four major factors:

- The economy
- Technology
- Lifestyle trends
- Changes in population

Economic Trends

The economy impacts employment in many ways. The **unemployment rate** is the percentage of unemployed people looking for jobs. The economy affects the unemployment rate, and the unemployment rate affects the economy.

- When the economy is strong, there is demand for goods and services. Businesses hire workers, so the unemployment rate is low.
- When the economy is weak, there is less demand for goods and services. Businesses cannot afford to pay wages. The unemployment rate is high.
- When the unemployment rate is low, many people are working and earning income. They have money to spend, which increases the demand for goods and services and boosts the economy.
- When the unemployment rate is high, many people are out of work. They have little money to spend, which decreases the demand for goods and services.

Why do you think high demand for goods and services leads to lower unemployment?

Is This Industry Growing?

You can spot career trends by looking for statistics that show how industries are changing over time. How can you tell if an industry is growing—a positive sign for jobs—or shrinking—a negative sign?

- There are fewer jobs in this field than there were last year.

- The salaries in this industry are the same or lower than they were last year.

- Companies in this industry are closing.

- Companies in this industry have higher profits than they did last year.

- Companies in this industry are hiring more employees than they did last year.

- There are more training programs for jobs in this industry than there were last year.

How can identifying employment trends help you choose a career in a growing industry?

Can you think of current lifestyle trends that might affect careers?

Impact of Technology

Technology has a strong influence on employment. It creates new jobs, replaces old jobs, and changes the way some people perform their existing jobs.

■ The development of new software and apps for mobile devices creates new jobs in areas such as application development, sales, and research and development.

■ The trend toward smaller computers and mobile devices has shifted the manufacturing of systems from desktops to laptops, notebooks, and netbooks.

■ Improvements in robotics have made it possible to use robots in positions that people once held, such as on automobile assembly lines.

■ Electronic recordkeeping in fields such as healthcare has changed the way medical professionals enter patient information, order prescriptions, and access patient records.

■ The trend toward storing information and applications on the Internet instead of on local computers has eliminated the need for some information technology managers at large companies.

■ The trend toward using videoconferencing instead of traveling to meetings impacts travel agents, hotel workers, and people who work in restaurants where travelers might eat.

Changing Lifestyles

Lifestyle trends affect employment. For example, the trend toward **dual-income families**—both parents working to earn a salary—and the trend toward divorce both cause an increase in demand for childcare workers. Other lifestyle trends that affect employment include:

■ The number of children in a family

■ The number of adults in a family

■ Where a family lives

■ How a family chooses to spend and save money

Improved health also impacts employment. When people have an increased lifespan—when they live longer—jobs are affected. People may retire at an older age, so there are fewer jobs for younger workers. There is more demand for housing, care, and activities for senior citizens, and therefore more jobs in those areas. The government must pay more Social Security, which can reduce resources for other groups.

Career Profile: Flight Attendant

**Hospitality &
Tourism
Career Cluster**

Job Summary

A flight attendant is a member of the cabin crew employed by an airline to ensure the safety and comfort of airplane passengers. Airlines are required by law to provide at least one flight attendant for every 50 passenger seats.

Flight attendants spend a lot of time away from home. They usually have to work some nights, weekends, and holidays. Their most important responsibility is to help passengers in case of an emergency. They communicate directly with many different people, and they must be friendly and patient but also assertive in order to command respect.

Use the Internet, a library, or career center to research the responsibilities, education and training requirements, and salary range of a flight attendant. Make a chart or table comparing the benefits and drawbacks of the position.

What lifestyle goals might influence a person's desire to become a flight attendant?

Flexible Lifestyles

A trend to a more flexible lifestyle is impacting employment. People in your grandparents' generation may have chosen a career early in life and then stayed in that business until retirement. **Retirement** is when someone leaves a job or career after many years and does not return to a paid job.

For some of these people, the biggest reward was **job security**—knowing that they would always have a job and receive a paycheck. They knew they would receive a pension when they retired. A **pension** is a regular payment given to a retired person by a former employer.

Career Trend

Some trends toward flexibility are the result of employers looking for ways to save money or increase productivity. Instead of hiring permanent full-time employees, companies may want to hire temporary workers. That means some industries are trending toward a just-in-time workforce, which is made up of part-time, temporary, and consulting positions.

Population Shifts

Where people live, the number of people in a community, and lifespan—how long people live—affect the number of jobs, the types of jobs, and the level of pay. What if people leave rural areas to live in cities? In the rural areas:

★ *There are fewer people available to work in agricultural careers. Farmers might have to pay high wages to hire farm hands.*

★ *Businesses in rural towns might not have enough customers.*

★ *The towns will not collect enough taxes to support community programs and services.*

★ *In the cities, there will be more competition for existing jobs. Employers might be able to pay lower salaries.*

★ *New businesses will open in the cities to provide goods and services for the many residents.*

★ *City services such as trash collection and schools may be overwhelmed by demand.*

Why do you think employers might have to pay higher wages when there are fewer job applicants and lower wages when there are more job applicants?

Today, workers are more flexible, or willing to make changes. People want careers that let them spend time with their families or doing leisure activities that they enjoy. They may want to work from a home office, have flexible hours, or even **job-share**, which means share the responsibilities for one job with another person. They change companies, locations, and even careers in order to find the job they like the best.

■ A television news reporter might move to a station in a different city because the salary is higher, or because the station is watched by more viewers.

■ A teacher may switch to selling real estate.

■ A factory worker may retrain to become a nurse.

Entrepreneurship

Entrepreneurship is a trend resulting from a number of factors. A desire for independence, the possibility of great rewards, and even the lack of more traditional opportunities all encourage people to start their own businesses. Therefore, the number of entrepreneurs in the United States is rising, as people look for options that let them be their own boss and set their own working conditions.

Nontraditional Occupations

A **nontraditional occupation** is any job that a man or woman does that is usually done by someone of the other gender. For example, nurse is an occupation usually done by women, so it is nontraditional for men. Construction worker is an occupation usually done by men, so it is nontraditional for women. Some other nontraditional careers include:

Men	Women
■ Receptionist	■ Auto mechanic
■ Librarian	■ Detective
■ Hair stylist	■ Security guard
■ Childcare worker	■ Farmer
■ Elementary school teacher	■ Pilot

Try not to rule out a nontraditional career because you associate it with one gender or another; it might be a good match for your skills and abilities.

Career Tips

The Bureau of Labor Statistics (BLS) tracks the number of jobs in different careers and uses the data to develop the *Occupational Outlook Handbook*. You can use the OOH to identify careers with a positive outlook.

Diversity in the Workforce

Population is the number of people in a country or area. Facts about a population are called **demographics**. These facts include information such as age, sex, cultural background, and race. Trends in demographics impact trends in employment. For example, new businesses often open where there are a lot of people.

Increased cultural diversity in the population leads to increased cultural diversity in the workplace. For example, between 2000 and 2010, both the Hispanic/Latino and Asian populations in the United States grew by more than 40 percent. The change is reflected in the diversity of the workforce.

Annual Average of Employment by Race and Ethnicity

	2003	2008	2011
Black or African American	10%	11%	12%
Hispanic or Latino	12%	14%	15%
Asian	Less than 1%	4.8%	5%

Source: Bureau of Labor Statistics, www.bls.gov/cps/cpsrace2011.

What might be some of the benefits and challenges of a diverse workforce?

CAREER COUNSEL

Ari is 15. His father works as a financial analyst for a large company. His mother is a bank teller. Ari has one sister and two brothers. They live in a two-bedroom apartment in Pittsburgh, Pennsylvania.

One day Ari's parents say they have good news. The family is moving to Charlotte, North Carolina. The company has offered Ari's dad a promotion, with more responsibilities and a much larger salary. The family will be able to buy a house, and Ari's mom will be able to work part-time so she can be home more.

Ari's sister and brothers are excited, but Ari is angry. He does not think it is good news at all.

What are the benefits of making the move? What are the drawbacks? Use your 21st Century Skills such as problem solving, decision making, and critical thinking to help Ari and his family successfully meet the challenges to come. Write an ending to the story and read it to the class, or form small groups and present it as a skit.

Case Study

In clothing lab at school, Matthew discovers he has a talent for clothing construction. He understands the way the patterns work, and he has a good eye for selecting fabric and colors. Other students like his designs. One girl asked if she could buy a pillow he made.

Matthew tells his parents about it. He says he is thinking about buying a sewing machine. He thinks he can develop his skills and make some money selling his work. He thinks he might want to study textile and fashion design in college. His parents do not think it is a good idea. They tell him to look for a different hobby.

■ Why do you think Matthew's parents don't want him to continue sewing?

■ Do you agree that he should look for a different hobby?

■ What can Matthew do to convince his parents that sewing is right for him?

Web Extra

The Bureau of Labor Statistics publishes information and statistics about employment trends on its Web site: bls.gov.

Use the Web site to research current trends affecting the careers that interest you. Make a list of at least three important trends, and share it with your class.

Answer It!

1. List the five basic lifestyle factors.
2. What is a trade-off?
3. List four physical needs.
4. Why can wanting or needing something be a powerful motivator?
5. List four psychological needs.

6. List four examples of goods.
7. List four examples of people who provide services.
8. List three ways people measure the value of work.
9. What is the labor market?
10. List four types of demographic facts.

Career-Ready Practices - - - - - - - -

As a class, brainstorm different ways to measure the economic, emotional, and educational value of work. Divide into teams of four or five and select a career you all find interesting. Write and present a skit that demonstrates the different ways you can measure the value of work in your selected career.

Make sure you consider the impact your career has on the economy, the community, and the environment. Career-ready individuals are aware of how their roles and responsibilities on the job can have an effect—positive or negative—on other people, organizations, and the environment.

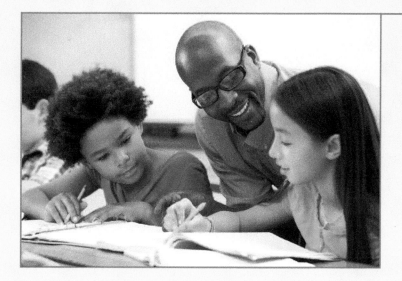

Write Now

Can you picture yourself in a nontraditional occupation? Many employers actively recruit males for traditionally female careers and females for traditionally male careers. Spend some time researching different types of nontraditional occupations, so you can understand the benefits or drawbacks they might provide.

Write a want ad for a nontraditional occupation that you think might appeal to the underrepresented gender—men for a traditionally female career or women for a traditionally male career. Share your ad with the class.

Career Portfolio

Do you have lifestyle goals that might influence the career path you choose? How are those goals affected by the five lifestyle factors? Make a list of the lifestyle factors, including an explanation of how each factor might impact your choice of career. Add the list to your career portfolio.

Business Plan Project

Working individually or in pairs, develop a list of the economic, emotional, and educational value of being an entrepreneur. On your own, write a paragraph no more than five sentences long explaining why these values make you personally want to be an entrepreneur. Enter the paragraph in your **Business Plan Project**.

4 Exploring the Career Clusters

Skills in This Chapter . . .

- **Analyzing the Career Clusters**
- **Exploring Other Resources for Identifying Careers**

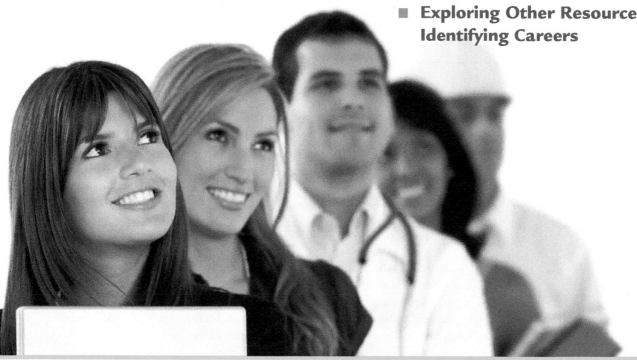

GETTING STARTED

There are an overwhelming number of available career opportunities. How can you possibly identify the ones that might be of interest to you? The 16 career clusters—developed by the National Association of State Directors of Career Technical Education Consortium (NASDCTEc)—are a good place to start. They can help you identify types of careers and specific jobs and help you pick out the ones that you might find interesting. They also show you the educational and skill requirements you might need and the path you might take to achieve the career of your dreams.

➤ Think of some of the activities that interest you. For example, do you like to write stories or climb trees? Do you like solving math problems or fixing broken toys or machines? Write a list of five things you like to do. As a class or in small groups, discuss possible career pathways that might match those interests and activities.

Analyzing the Career Clusters

The U.S. NASDCTEc (National Association of State Directors of Career Technical Education Consortium) identifies 16 career clusters by classifying specific jobs and industries into similar categories. You can use the information on career clusters to learn about careers while you are in school or any time you are doing career research.

Within each of the 16 career clusters are related job, industry, and occupation types known as **pathways**. For example, the Architecture & Construction cluster has three pathways: Construction, Design/Pre-Construction, and Maintenance/Operations. The pathways are the building blocks of the 16 career clusters. Each pathway offers a variety of careers you might choose. There are also relationships between occupations in different clusters. For example, an information technology manager (Information Technology cluster) may work in almost any industry, including health care (Health Science cluster), legal services (Law, Public Safety, Corrections & Security cluster), and airline reservation systems (Hospitality & Tourism cluster).

The clusters and their pathways help job seekers and individuals interested in specific careers to identify professions that best suit their interests and abilities. Through the clusters and pathways, you can learn about the education and skills you will need to be effective in a specific job and career. They provide you with clear-cut choices and options as you begin your career exploration.

Tech Connect

Almost every job requires you to use technology in one way or another. For example, a bank teller uses technology to:

■ Electronically process customer transactions

■ Ensure the security of the bank through computerized code entries

■ Create and generate financial reports

Select a profession that interests you. In your school library or on the Internet, research the types of technology someone in that profession might use. Then, use a presentation software program to create a presentation about it, and share your presentation with the class.

Agriculture, Food & Natural Resources

The Agriculture, Food & Natural Resources career cluster is for people interested in the production, processing, marketing, distribution, financing, and development of agricultural commodities—economic goods—and resources. Their interests in the field might include food, fuel, fiber, wood products, natural resources, horticulture, and other plant and animal products and resources. People in this field select jobs as diverse as farmer, food scientist, and meat inspector.

Pathways

Agribusiness Systems

Animal Systems

Environmental Service Systems

Food Products and Processing Systems

Natural Resources Systems

Plant Systems

Power, Structural and Technical Systems

Sample Occupations

Agricultural Communications Specialist

Animal Scientist

Greenhouse Manager

Embryo Technologist

Feed Sales Representative

Fish and Game Warden

Food Scientist

Livestock Buyer

Microbiologist

Tree Trimmer and Pruner

A fish and game warden are responsible for enforcing laws relating to the hunting, fishing, and trapping of wild animals. What skills and interests do you think might be necessary to become a fish and game warden?

Working Abroad

Of course you are not limited to working only in the United States to pursue a career. You might want to move to Germany, China, Nigeria, Australia, Panama, or Martinique to work.

Before you move to another country to work, there are things you should know and questions you should ask: Will you need a work permit? Are there language barriers? What will be the cost of living there? Who will be there for you if you get homesick or ill?

Select a country that interests you. Use your school library or the Internet to look for information about the rules and policies that govern foreign workers. Focus on finding answers to the questions on work permits and cost of living in an area. Share your findings with your classmates.

Architecture & Construction

People in the Architecture & Construction career cluster design, plan, manage, build, and maintain the built environment. Take a look around you. The houses across the street, the roads that cars drive on, and the parks that you walk through every day were created or maintained by the people performing jobs in this cluster and its pathways.

Pathways

Construction

Design/Pre-Construction

Maintenance/Operations

A construction worker builds houses and buildings. What skills and interests do you think might be necessary to become a construction worker?

Sample Occupations

Architect

Architectural and Civil Drafter

Carpenter

Civil Engineer

Civil Engineering Technician

Code Official

Computer Aided Drafter (CAD)

Concrete Finisher

Construction Worker

Cost Estimator

Drywall and Ceiling Tile Installer

Pipelayer

Entrepreneurial Opportunities

Many careers in the Architecture & Construction cluster are well-suited for someone interested in being an entrepreneur. An architect might work for a large firm for a while then start her own business when she feels that she has gained enough experience to succeed on her own. A drywall installer might prefer working independently instead of for a contractor. What are some of the benefits and drawbacks to working as an entrepreneur in the Architecture & Construction industry?

Arts, Audio/Video Technology & Communications

Have you ever wanted to design, produce, exhibit, perform, write, and publish anything by making music or creating multimedia visual content? Do you love the performing arts? You could be dreaming of becoming an actress on the stage or television. Or perhaps you would rather be a world-renowned painter. Then again, your interests might direct you to journalism as the next star anchor of the evening news or as a respected blogger. You might want to be a public-relations specialist working behind the scenes to guide the careers of the rich and famous. If so, this cluster is for you.

Journalists report the news in newspapers and on television and radio stations. What skills and interests do you think might be necessary to become a journalist?

Pathways

Audio and Video Technology and Film

Journalism and Broadcasting

Performing Arts

Printing Technology

Telecommunications

Visual Arts

Sample Occupations

Animation Technician

Broadcast Technician

Cinematographer

Editor

Graphics and Printing Equipment Operator

Journalist

Publisher

Reporter

Special Effects Technician

Video Graphics Engineer

Video Systems Technician

Business Management & Administration

Every business hires individuals to manage its operations. Businesses need office managers and accountants to ensure that the calls are answered and that the books are in order. These businesses can range in size from small convenience stores to large hospitals. They all need employees who ensure that operations run smoothly within the organization. The employees who choose careers in the Business Management & Administration cluster play this role.

Pathways

Administrative Support

Business Information Management

General Management

Human Resources Management

Operations Management

A payroll manager ensures that all employees in a company receive accurate paychecks on time. What skills and interests do you think might be necessary to become a payroll manager?

Sample Occupations

Accountant

Accounting Manager

Accounts Payable Manager

Assistant Credit Manager

Billing Manager

Business and Development Manager

Chief Executive Officer

Compensation and Benefits Manager

Credit and Collections Manager

Entrepreneur

General Manager

Payroll Manager

Risk Manager

Career Trend

Accountants and auditors perform similar functions by tracking how companies spend their money. In 2010, there were more than 1.2 million accountants and auditors in the United States. According to the U.S. Bureau of Labor Statistics (www.bls.gov), employment of accountants and auditors is expected to grow 16 percent between 2010 and 2020.

Education & Training

Much thought and care go into planning, managing, and providing education as well as training and related learning-support services. People employed in this field educate children and adults. Workers in this cluster need patience and good customer service skills to be effective in their jobs.

Pathways

Administration and Administrative Support

Professional Support Services

Teaching/Training

A corporate trainer provides short, specialized courses to employees of large and small firms. What skills and interests does a corporate trainer need?

Sample Occupations

College President, Dean, Department Chair, Program Coordinator

Corporate Trainer

Curriculum Specialist

Education Researcher, Test Measurement Specialist/Assessment Specialist

Elementary and Secondary Superintendent, Principal, Administrator

Museum Coordinator

Post-Secondary Administrator

Supervisor and Instructional Coordinator

Teacher

Career Tips

Teaching is a key profession in the Education & Training cluster. If you are considering a teaching career, keep in mind that you must be certified to instruct in public schools.

There are different levels of teaching certification. Some teachers are licensed to teach through grade three. Others are licensed only for the middle and high school levels or for specialized subjects.

Check with your state or local government to find out the certification requirements in your community..

Finance

Finance is often linked to banking, but the industry has many facets because there are so many different types of financial institutions. Employees in this field provide services for financial and investment planning, banking, insurance products, business/financial management, and more. This field is directly connected to the stock market, which monitors the economic stability of the world's financial markets.

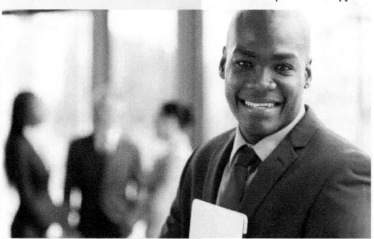

An insurance agent sells insurance to people who need it. What skills and interests do you think might be necessary to become an insurance agent?

Pathways

Banking Services

Business Finance

Insurance

Securities and Investments

Sample Occupations

Brokerage Representative

Development Officer

Insurance Agent

Investment Advisor

Personal Financial Advisor

Sales Agent, Securities and Commodities

Securities/Investments Analyst

Stock Broker

Tax Preparation Specialist

NUMBERS GAME

You are considering opening your own business but need $5,000.00 to start it. You have decided to borrow from your local bank. The bank charges 10% interest, so you will have to repay the loan plus the additional 10%. How much will you have to pay back?

First, calculate the 10% interest rate on your $5,000.00 loan:

1. Change the percentage to a decimal by replacing the percent sign with a decimal point and moving the decimal point two spaces to the left.

2. Multiply the decimal by the number. For example, to find 10% of $5,000.00:
   10% = .10
   5,000 × .10 = 500

So when you add the interest to the amount borrowed, how much will you repay the bank? What if the interest rate is 13%?

Government & Public Administration

Local, state, and federal governments need employees to perform functions that include **governance**—or making decisions about how government will act—national security, foreign service, planning, revenue flows and taxation, regulation, and management and administration. For example, the Secretary of State is the chief diplomat for the United States. As chief diplomat, the Secretary of State represents the United States at important meetings on the world stage. People employed in this field typically develop strong communication, problem-solving skills, and critical-thinking skills.

Ambassadors represent their governments in foreign countries. What skills and interests do you think might be necessary to become an ambassador?

Pathways

Foreign Service

Governance

National Security

Planning

Public Management and Administration

Regulation

Revenue and Taxation

Sample Occupations

Abassador

Airborne Warning/Control Specialist

Assessor

Congressional Aide

Diplomatic Courier

Equal Opportunity Representative

Legislative Aide

National Security Advisor

President

Senator

Special Forces Officer

Tax Attorney

Vice President

Doctors consult with their patients about their ailments and recommend treatments they need to recover from illnesses. What skills and interests do you think might be necessary to become a doctor?

Health Science

Health Science cluster employees plan, manage, and deliver therapeutic services, diagnostic services, health informatics, support services, and biotechnology research and development to individuals throughout the United States. They work in cities, suburbs, rural areas, and other communities to provide crucial services to a diverse client base. Individuals employed in these fields take on legal responsibilities, must have strong ethics, and often use their technical skills.

Pathways

Biotechnology Research and Development

Diagnostic Services

Health Informatics

Support Services

Therapeutic Services

Sample Occupations

Acupuncturist

Anesthesia Technologist/Technician

Anesthesiologist/Assistant

Art/Music/Dance Therapist

Athletic Trainer

Audiologist

Certified Nursing Assistant

Chiropractic Assistant

Chiropractor

Dental Assistant/Hygienist

Dental Lab Technician

Dietitian/Nutritionist

Doctor

Nurse

Career Profile: Nurse

Health Science Career Cluster

Job Summary

One of the occupations within the Health Science cluster that appeals to a lot of individuals is nursing. Individuals interested in nursing typically have a passion for helping sick or injured people recuperate. They also participate in giving the preventive care that keep people healthy so they do not end up in hospitals at all.

Registered nurses (RNs) have direct interactions with patients. They take care of the sick and injured, give medicine, treat wounds, and often provide emotional support to patients and their families. Not all nurses are involved in providing direct care. Nurses also work in research or as administrators who manage clinics, nursing homes, or hospitals.

Use the Internet, a library, or career center to research the responsibilities, education and training requirements, and salary range of a nurse. Write a job description for the position.

Career Trend

The job outlook for the nursing field is very good. Employment of RNs is expected to grow 26 percent from 2010 to 2020. In 2010, the median pay for RNs was $64,690 per year.

Reasons for Choosing a Career

Sometimes people choose their careers for the wrong reasons. Someone interested in the creative arts might choose finance because he thinks he will earn more money. Someone interested in science might avoid the Health Science cluster because she thinks all health science jobs require direct contact with patients. How do you plan to choose a career?

👎 Choose a career because your parents say it is right for you

👎 Enter a field because it is popular and "hot"

👎 Select a job based only on the salary

👍 Match your career to your interests

👍 Do career research to find a career that appeals to you

👍 Dedicate yourself to getting the proper training for the career that most interests you

How might choosing a career for the wrong reasons lead to frustration and unhappiness?

Hotel managers are responsible for making sure guests are happy and satisfied. What skills and interests do you think might be necessary to become a hotel manager?

Hospitality & Tourism

Hospitality and tourism careers comprise the world's largest industry. Its workers manage, market, and operate restaurants and other food services, lodging, attractions, recreation events, and travel-related services. They are very busy people who cater to the needs of individuals that visit your town, city, state, and other countries of the world as tourists. If you enjoy a vacation, a large part of the reason why is the services these employees perform.

Pathways

Lodging

Recreation, Amusements and Attractions

Restaurants and Food/Beverage Services

Travel and Tourism

Sample Occupations

Bell Captain

Catering and Banquet Manager

Chef

Concierge

Convention Planner

Gaming and Casino Manager

Hotel Manager

Kitchen Manager

Restaurant Owner

Service Manager

Tour Guide

Travel Agent

Making Travel Fun

There are millions of people employed in the tourism and hospitality industries worldwide. What if there were no tourism and hospitality employees? Who would:

★ Call a cab to take vacationers to the beach?

★ Direct visitors from out of town to the best local restaurants?

★ Clean a traveler's hotel room?

★ Deliver room service to a hungry guest?

★ Serve meals in a resort dining room?

★ Sell souvenirs to remind people of the fun they had on vacation?

What problems might arise if you arrived at a hotel for a vacation and there were no hospitality workers?

Human Services

Human services careers prepare individuals for employment in pathways that relate to families and human needs. They work in daycare centers, drive the elderly and disabled to their appointments, provide massages in spas, and counsel those in need of emotional support. Their clients include students having problems in school, brides needing beautiful hairstyles for a wedding, congregants looking for guidance from their clergy, and homeless families trying to find housing. Working in this field can be very rewarding if you like to interact with people. The work that you do will help children and adults, but you must have a lot of compassion and patience to be effective in this field.

Social workers help people focus on improving their lives. What skills and interests do you think might be necessary to become a social worker?

Pathways

Consumer Services

Counseling and Mental Health Services

Early Childhood Development and Services

Family and Community Services

Personal Care Services

Sample Occupations

Barber

Clergy

Embalmer

Guidance Counselor

Hairdresser/Cosmetologist

Manicurist and Pedicurist

Nanny

Social Worker

Getting the Right Training for Jobs at School!

Just because you think a career cluster sounds interesting doesn't mean you have the skills or education you will need to land a job in that field. Use your time in school to make sure you are qualified for it.

✔ Stay on track to develop basic skills such as reading, writing, math, and languages.

✔ Work with a career counselor to select elective courses that match your interests and abilities.

✔ Spend time researching the career clusters and pathways.

✔ Build technology skills to help you with your job search.

You can use this approach to explore careers throughout your life until you find a good fit for you, your interests, and personality type.

Career Tips

If you need extra help in figuring out the right career for you, visit the Web site of the U.S. Bureau of Labor Statistics at www.bls.gov. It produces reports that outline the fastest growing industries, their salary range, and educational requirements.

Computer technicians work to build or repair computer systems. What skills and interests do you think might be necessary to become a computer technician?

Myth Education beyond high school is unnecessary.

Truth Today, the careers that offer the best growth opportunities and pay the most require at least a two- or four-year degree. If you are considering a career path that will require a lot of education, begin to view graduating from high school as the start of your education. Embrace the idea of learning as a lifetime effort. Part of that lifelong process will include constantly training and updating your skills.

Information Technology

Individuals employed in this cluster build the bridges between people and technology. They design, develop, support, and manage hardware, software, multimedia, and systems integration services that allow you to have access to the Internet, operate your remote control device, and use your mobile devices. Most people in this field have a strong mathematical and scientific academic foundation and are willing to learn information technology applications and systems. Its employees are constantly working on cutting-edge technology aimed at making life easier for everyone.

Pathways

Information Support and Services

Network Systems

Programming and Software Development

Web and Digital Communications

Sample Occupations

Analyst

Computer Programmer

Computer Security Specialist

Computer Technician

Database Developer

Modeler

Network Designer

Network Developer

Web Administrator

Law, Public Safety, Corrections & Security

Individuals who plan, manage, and provide legal, public safety, protective services, and homeland security, including professional and technical support services, play important roles in your community. They are police officers, lawyers, security guards, and firefighters, and they deliver the services that make you feel safer in times of crisis.

Pathways

Correction Services
Emergency and Fire Management Services
Law Enforcement Services
Legal Services
Security and Protective Services

Sample Occupations

Arbitrator, Mediator and Conciliator
Correctional Officer and Jailer
Detective and Investigator
Dispatcher
Firefighter
Immigration and Custom Inspector
Judge
Lawyer
Paramedic
Police Officer

Police officers keep you safe, respond to emergencies, and issue citations to people who break the law. What skills and interests do you think might be necessary to become a police officer?

21st Century Learning

Sam has been having problems receiving and making calls on his cell phone. Finding solutions to the problem has been challenging yet interesting. The process has him curious about the clusters and pathways connected to the cell phone industry, such as Marketing, Manufacturing, and Transportation, Distribution & Logistics.

He is doing research to contact and meet with a career counselor at school to discuss the skills he will need to become employable in those clusters within cell phone companies. What are some of the ideas that the counselor might suggest to Sam? Do you think Sam will need to consult with professionals in those fields? What new information might the conversation with his counselor reveal? How would you advise Sam to use 21st Century Skills such as decision making, problem solving, and goal setting to learn more about the cell phone industry as a career path? Write a letter advising Sam, or form small groups and present your advice as a skit.

Factory workers assemble a wide variety of products. What skills and interests do you think might be necessary to become a factory worker?

Manufacturing

Products ranging from plastic bottles to cars are built in factories and developed in manufacturing plants all over the world through specific processes. Those employed in the Manufacturing cluster perform the steps that go into intermediate or final products and related professional and technical support activities such as production planning and control, maintenance, and manufacturing/ process engineering. They are in a field for individuals who love to use their hands to make things that are important to daily living such as cars, cabinets, or books.

Pathways

Health, Safety and Environmental Assurance

Logistics and Inventory Control

Maintenance, Installation and Repair

Manufacturing Production Process Development

Production

Quality Assurance

Sample Occupations

Assembler

Automated Manufacturing Technician

Bookbinder

Calibration Technician

Electrical Installer and Repairer

Electromechanical Equipment Assembler

Logistical Engineer

Machinist

Energy Career Cluster

To meet the growing demand for skilled workers in the energy industry, a number of states have developed an Energy career cluster to identify energy-related occupations that are critical to their economic development.

Energy jobs fall within four of the 16 Career Clusters identified by NASDCTEc:

✔ *Agriculture, Food & Natural Resources*

✔ *Architecture & Construction*

✔ *Science, Technology, Engineering & Mathematics*

✔ *Manufacturing*

Investigate your state's career clusters to determine if an Energy cluster has been adopted.

Marketing

Marketing professionals plan, manage, and perform activities to reach organizational objectives. Their work can range from handing out flyers to publicizing an event or working in an office to researching consumers' spending habits. They work for small or large firms or independently as contractors in a number of roles where they develop their leadership and teamwork abilities as well as their analytical skills.

Pathways

Marketing Communications

Marketing Management

Marketing Research

Merchandising

Professional Sales

Sample Occupations

Account Executive

Creative Director

Key Account Manager

Market Research Analyst

Merchandise Displayer and Window Trimmer

Real Estate Agent

Sales Representative

Store Manager

Telemarketer

Wholesale and Retail Buyer

Store managers oversee the day-to-day operations of the stores, shops, and retail outlets in which you buy things. What skills and interests do you think might be necessary to become a store manager?

Money Madne$$

Esther is studying communications in college and is exploring careers in the Marketing career cluster. In the meantime, she is looking for a summer job. She is offered a position as a sales associate at a shoe store. It pays $10.25 per hour, for 25 hours per week. She will be able to work for 8 weeks until school starts again. She is also offered an internship at a public relations agency. The internship is full time, and it pays $2,500.00 for the entire summer. Which position do you recommend Esther accept? What factors should she consider? **Hint:** Use multiplication to calculate the amount Esther would earn.

Science, Technology, Engineering & Mathematics

Can you see yourself planning, managing, and providing scientific research as a career? Are you interested in laboratory and testing services or in research and development? If so, are you also willing to earn the certification or advanced education necessary to work in this career cluster? If your answer is a "yes" to any of these questions, then take a closer look at these pathways and occupations.

Pathways

Engineering and Technology

Science and Math

Academic institutions, government laboratories, and private industry hire physicists to study matter or energy within the universe. What skills and interests do you think might be necessary to become a physicist?

Sample Occupations

Anthropologist

Biologist

Geneticist

Mathematician

Nuclear Chemist

Paleontologist

Physicist

Statistician

Technical Writer

Transportation, Distribution & Logistics

How does food get to your supermarket shelves or fuel to your local gas station? A lot of planning goes into the transportation and shipping of products around the globe. Many people work behind the scenes to coordinate, manage, and move these goods to their final destinations by arranging for their transportation by road, pipeline, air, rail, and water. They also oversee the related professional and technical support services that are a part of the process. Beyond planning for the transportation of goods, there is another related sector in this field: urban planning. Planners decide where houses, parks, and stores should be built so that neighborhoods are organized in a way that is convenient for everyone living in them. Here are the pathways and some of the occupations that make up this cluster.

Urban planners oversee how land is used by and in communities. What skills and interests do you think might be necessary to become an urban planner?

Pathways

Facility and Mobile Equipment Maintenance

Health, Safety and Environmental Management

Logistics Planning and Management Services

Sales and Services

Transportation Operations

Transportation Systems/Infrastructure Planning, Management and Regulation

Warehousing and Distribution Center Operations

Sample Occupations

Air Traffic Controller

Driver

Industrial and Packaging Engineer

Logistician

Storage and Distribution Manager

Surveying and Mapping Technician

Traffic Manager

Traffic, Shipping, and Receiving Clerk

Urban and Regional Planner

Warehouse Manager

Exploring Other Resources for Identifying Careers

In addition to the career clusters, you have many resources to help you identify the types of careers that are available. Recall that a resource is something you use to get or achieve something else. Some resources that will help you identify careers are available at school, and some you will find in your community. These and other resources will be discussed throughout this book.

You can use career search resources to learn about the types of jobs that are available and to locate jobs that match your interests, skills, and abilities.

Resources at School

Some of the best resources for learning about career opportunities are available at school. Your guidance and career counselors have books, computer programs, videos, and lists of useful Web sites that provide information about types of careers. Your teachers can help you identify your strengths and abilities and match them with career requirements.

School clubs and organizations may also have information about types of careers. A business club might invite a representative from the community to speak about his or her occupation. An organization such as Family, Career and Community Leaders of America (FCCLA) or Health Occupations Students of America (HOSA) has career-related projects and activities.

The Bureau of Labor Statistics

The U.S. Bureau of Labor Statistics (BLS) is a government agency responsible for tracking information about jobs and workers. Its Web site has a section specifically for students (www.bls.gov/audience/students.htm). It includes information on more than 60 occupations, including descriptions of responsibilities, education requirements, salary ranges, and job outlook. A **job outlook** includes statistics and trends about whether the job is in an industry that is growing or shrinking.

The BLS also publishes the *Occupational Outlook Handbook* (OOH) in printed and online editions. The OOH describes more than 200 occupations, including responsibilities, working conditions, education requirements, salary ranges, and job outlook.

Identifying Careers through Job-Related Activities

Even if you do not hold a full- or part-time job, the tasks you do and activities in which you are involved on a daily basis can help you identify the career clusters that best match your interests, skills, aptitudes, and values. For example:

✔ *Helping a younger sibling with his homework might lead you to a career in the Education & Training career cluster.*

✔ *Volunteering at a local park or zoo might mean you are cut out for a career in the Agriculture, Food & Natural Resources career cluster.*

✔ *Taking photos for your school newspaper could prepare you for a career in the Arts, Audio/Video Technology & Communications career cluster.*

Think about the job-related activities you perform at home, in school, and in the community. How can they help you identify the career cluster(s) best suited to you?

The *Occupational Outlook Handbook* is massive. There may be a printed copy of the OOH in your local library or career center. You can start by looking through the table of contents to get an idea of how careers are organized. You may find it easier to use the online version at www.bls.gov/ooh. Online, you can search for specific careers, use the alphabetical listing to locate a career that interests you, or browse through the career clusters. As you look through the OOH, you might want to take notes on the information you find, and record the source—including the page number in the printed copy or the Web page address online.

Resources in Your Community

One of the best ways to learn about different careers is from someone who is employed. For example, you can job-shadow someone who has a job you find interesting. Job shadowing means to follow someone around at work for a day or part of a day. By job shadowing, you can see exactly what the responsibilities, tasks, and rewards are for a particular job.

Informational interviews are also a good way to explore careers. An informational interview gives you the opportunity to sit down with someone who is employed in a career or industry that interests you. You can ask specific questions about the job responsibilities, see the work environment, and maybe even meet other people in the industry.

Talking directly to someone in the job can teach you a lot more than you can learn from a book or online. For example, a roofer can tell you what it feels like to work on top of a house, 30 feet above the ground. Your career counselor may be able to help you arrange an informational interview.

Why do you think you should only request an informational interview when you are serious about a career?

Steps for Managing an Informational Interview

Follow these steps to plan, schedule, and conduct an informational interview:

✔ Find a person who has the job you are interested in.

✔ Call and make an appointment.

✔ Write down the questions you want to ask before the interview.

✔ Arrive on time for the interview.

✔ Write down the answers to your questions.

✔ Thank the person when you leave, and follow up by sending a written thank you note.

Career Trend

More informational interviews are being held over the telephone or by e-mail than in the past. People are busy and always on the go. Sometimes it is easier to make time for an interview using technology.

Career Tips

Do not ask for a job during an informational interview. If you ask for a job, the person you are interviewing might feel that you misled him or her about the purpose of the interview.

Case Study

Michael works as a full-time firefighter for his local municipality, making $35,000.00 a year. He has seen many of his colleagues laid off recently as a result of a downturn in the economy. In his firehouse of ten firefighters and two part-time clerical staff, half of the firefighters and one of the clerks lost their jobs.

He has been thinking about a career change because he wants more job and financial security. Many close friends have advised him not to change careers at this time, but to consider it in the future.

For now, Michael has decided to remain in his current position, but he will continue looking into other opportunities. He also decides to take classes in areas of interest as he waits to make a final decision about his future.

- What decisions did Michael face?
- Do you agree with his choices? Why or why not?
- How can the information on career clusters and their pathways be helpful to Michael?
- What other steps can Michael take now, while he waits for the right time to make a career change?

Web Extra

Many Web sites provide information on career clusters. One site is careertech.org.

Do you have effective research skills? Test them by using the Internet to locate resources that help you determine job and career opportunities related to your state's career clusters. Include a brief description of the information available through each resource.

Create a directory of all of the sites that you find. Post it on your school Web site, make it available in your school library, or add it to the school blog.

Answer It!

1. How many career clusters are defined by the National Association of State Directors of Career Technical Education Consortium?

2. List the pathways in the Architecture & Construction cluster.

3. What is the title of the chief diplomat for the United States?

4. List five sample occupations in the Hospitality & Tourism cluster.

5. What career cluster has a pathway for computer programmers?

6. In which cluster are firefighters and police officers employed?

7. What career cluster includes a pathway for urban planners?

8. List two resources available at school to help you identify career opportunities.

9. What government agency is responsible for tracking information about jobs and workers?

10. List five things you can learn about an occupation from the Occupational Outlook Handbook.

Career-Ready Practices - - - - - - - -

Divide into teams of four or five. Each team will select a career cluster and pathway. Use the Internet or other resources to research companies that work in your cluster and pathway. If possible, visit the Web sites of these companies and locate the employment opportunities section where job openings are listed. As a team, note the skills and educational requirements for available positions. Discuss your findings as a class. How can you and your classmates prepare yourselves for the requirements of the positions that most interests you?

Career-ready individuals recognize that nearly all career paths require ongoing education and experience. They understand the time, effort, and experience that will be required to pursue the pathways that interest them. In addition, they seek counselors, mentors, and other experts to help them plan and meet their career and personal goals.

Write Now

To attract new employees, companies post want ads on online job listings or in electronic or printed publications and newspapers announcing their vacancies. Now that you know about and understand the career clusters and their pathways, create ads for the occupations in the three career clusters that most interest you. Look at examples of want ads online or in your local newspaper. Use them as models of how your ads should look. Show your ads to the class and discuss them.

Career Portfolio

Matching your interests and abilities to a career is an important step in finding job satisfaction. After reviewing the 16 career clusters, make a list of the four that you find most interesting. Write a description of each, and include the reasons they appeal to you. You may list the clusters in a word processing document, or write them on a piece of paper. Include the title *Career Clusters that Interest Me* at the top of the page. Add the document to your career portfolio.

Business Plan Project

Problem-solving is an important part of being an entrepreneur. All careers and businesses face problems and challenges every day. Review the career clusters covered in this chapter, and then pick one that interests you. Brainstorm the challenges that people working in that career cluster might face on a daily basis and record the list in your **Business Plan Project**. For example, the reservation system might crash at a hotel, or a drought might affect a farmer's crops. When you have compiled your list, think like an entrepreneur and brainstorm ways to solve each problem with a business solution. Record your solutions in your **Business Plan Project**.

5 Think Like an Entrepreneur

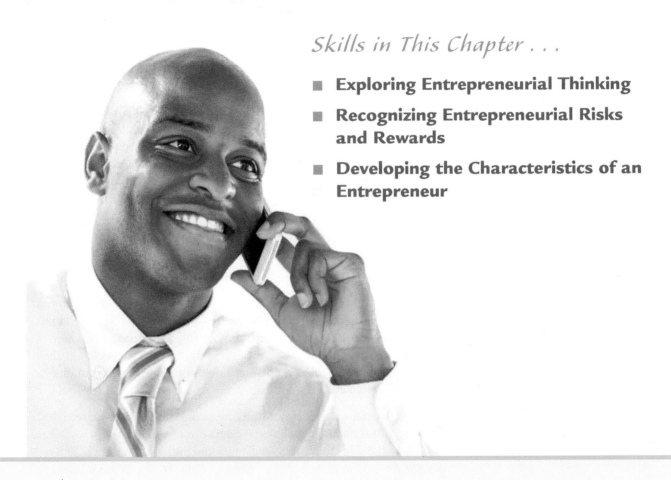

Skills in This Chapter . . .

- **Exploring Entrepreneurial Thinking**
- **Recognizing Entrepreneurial Risks and Rewards**
- **Developing the Characteristics of an Entrepreneur**

GETTING STARTED

Have you ever thought about starting your own business? Do you have ideas about what kind of business it would be? An entrepreneur is someone who creates and runs a business. If you have a business idea and can imagine a way to make it come true, you could be an entrepreneur. Even if you don't want to be an entrepreneur, thinking like one can help you develop a vision, or plan, of what you want your future to be.

➤ Make a list of the character qualities you think make someone a good boss. Put a star next to the ones that you think you possess. Would you be a good boss? Do you think it would be easier to work for yourself or for someone else?

Exploring Entrepreneurial Thinking

Most people earn a living by working in a **business**. A business is an organization that provides goods or services, usually to make money. A person who works in a business owned by someone else is an **employee** of that business. On the other hand, someone who creates and runs his or her own business is called an *entrepreneur*.

Owning a business isn't for everyone. But that's okay because both employees and entrepreneurs are needed in the world of work. Whether or not you become an entrepreneur, understanding entrepreneurial thinking can help you in any career you choose.

What Is Entrepreneurial Thinking?

Entrepreneurial thinking is the process of starting a new business. It may mean thinking of, creating, and developing a brand-new product or service. For example, you might develop a new type of fuel for powering automobiles, or a new method of fitness training. It may also mean creating a new business to sell an existing product or service, such as opening a new restaurant or selling online jewelry that you design and create yourself.

Entrepreneurial thinking is not easy. More new businesses fail than succeed. Just having a good idea is not enough. Entrepreneurs must be motivated to work hard. They must have the skills to identify challenges and find solutions, including raising money and other resources. They must also be able to determine whether a risk has a better chance of bringing rewards or causing failure.

Career Trend

Many businesses today encourage **intrapreneurship**, which means acting like an entrepreneur while working as an employee. They give employees opportunities to be creative, try out new ideas, and sometimes even to develop a new business within the existing one.

Do You Think Like an Entrepreneur?

Thinking like an entrepreneur can help you succeed in school as well as in your career.

- 👎 Arrive late for class
- 👎 Never participate in class discussions
- 👎 Turn in incomplete assignments
- 👍 Come to class prepared
- 👍 Listen to your teachers
- 👍 Respect your classmates
- 👍 See projects through to completion
- 👍 Contribute new ideas in class

Can you think of other ways you can use entrepreneurial skills and qualities to succeed in school?

Thinking Like an Entrepreneur

Thinking like an entrepreneur and being aware of how to make a business run more successfully can help you do well at school, home, and in your community, as well as at work for someone else. Successful entrepreneurs know how to come up with an idea and then set up a plan to make it a reality. They set goals, manage their time effectively, and are 100 percent committed to their plan.

When you think like an entrepreneur, you show that you are creative, independent, and responsible. In school, you participate, pay attention, and show respect. As an employee, you treat someone else's business as if it were your own. Here are three ways to think like an entrepreneur even when you are not running your own business.

Why might an employer like to hire and promote an employee who thinks like an entrepreneur?

- *Observe.* Keep on the lookout for chances to learn new skills and accept new responsibilities. At work, staying aware of what goes on around you can help you identify new ideas for business growth, such as new products or services that customers may need or want.

- *Listen.* Pay attention to what others have to say. Your classmates may have a different view of things. Challenges that other employees are facing may give you ideas for making business improvements.

- *Think.* Instead of complaining about a problem, analyze it. Then, suggest possible solutions.

Career FACT

According to a survey by the U.S. Census Bureau, about 37% of business owners are over 55 years old; 30% are between 45 and 54; 21% are between 35 and 44; 11% are between 25 and 34; and 2% are under 25.

Recognizing Entrepreneurial Risks and Rewards

Being an entrepreneur has benefits and drawbacks. It involves risk—but not being risky. *Risk* refers to the chance of danger or loss. In terms of business, it usually refers to the risk of losing money. Being *risky* means acting in a way that puts you or your belongings at risk. In business, being risky usually refers to taking unnecessary chances with your money.

As business owners, entrepreneurs are in control of the money made by their business. They also have the final say in all business decisions. As a result, entrepreneurs are ultimately responsible for the success or failure of their businesses. It is a lot of responsibility, but it can also bring a lot of rewards.

You might think of many reasons to start your own business. Before doing so, however, it's a good idea to consider the pros and cons of being an entrepreneur. The key is evaluating whether the potential rewards are worth more to you than the drawbacks and risks you will take.

International Entrepreneurial Thinking

Entrepreneurs can benefit from international trade. They can sell goods or services that people in other countries need, or buy goods made somewhere else to sell in the United States.

However, there are many risks associated with international trade. For example, governments might place restrictions called **trade barriers** on international trade. Exchange rates—the value of the currency used in one country compared to the value of currency in a different country—change daily and can affect the cost of items sold across borders. Also, cultural differences can impact business decisions.

Using the Internet or your library, research the benefits and drawbacks an entrepreneur might encounter when trying to start an international business. Select one and report on it to your class.

What Are the Rewards?

Of course, entrepreneurs want to make money. A successful business lets you earn enough so that you fulfill your needs and wants without depending on others. If the business grows, entrepreneurs can create even greater wealth by selling it for more money than they used to start it. They may even be able to use the money from the sale to start another business.

In addition to the financial rewards, entrepreneurs can benefit in other ways.

- Entrepreneurs achieve pride and personal satisfaction from starting and growing a business. Not only do you have freedom and independence, you also display your skills and abilities for your family and friends to see. Entrepreneurs also feel excitement and joy from taking a chance and trying something new.

- As an entrepreneur, you get to make your own rules. Depending on your business, you can decide what type of schedule you work, where you work, and how and when you get paid. You also have the final word on which products or services the business provides and how they are provided. For example, when you have a creative idea, you have the power to put that idea into action.

- Being an entrepreneur opens up opportunities that help make your community and the world a better place in which to live. Entrepreneurs often start a business because they see a need in the community. They might start small, but if the business succeeds, they are soon creating jobs, paying taxes, and giving back by donating time and money to worthy causes.

Do you think the benefits of being your own boss would outweigh the drawbacks? Why or why not?

Facts About Entrepreneurs

Following are some facts about business owners taken from a survey conducted by the U.S. Census Bureau.

- ✔ Of the business owners who were surveyed, 68% had some college education when they started the business.

- ✔ More than 34% of the business owners used money of their own, or from their families, to start or buy the business.

- ✔ Slightly more than 50% of the business owners worked more than 40 hours per week.

- ✔ About 30% of the businesses were home-based.

Tech Connect

Entrepreneurs are always looking for ways to use the newest trends and technologies to start or grow a business. You probably think of a social networking Web site as a place to communicate with your friends. Entrepreneurs see it as a business opportunity.

For example, can a fashion designer trying to start a new business draw in customers by tweeting? If a restaurant owner offers discount coupons on a social networking site, will people tell their friends?

Use the Internet to research one way an entrepreneur has tried to use social networking or another type of technology to develop a business. Then, use a word processing program to write a report about what you discover.

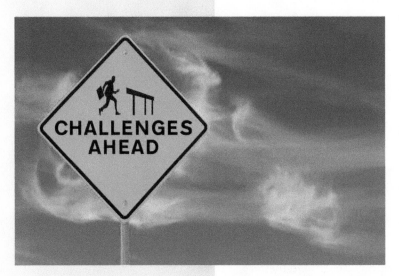

How does the saying, "Nothing ventured, nothing gained" relate to entrepreneurs?

Myth Most entrepreneurs take wild and uncalculated risks when they start their businesses.

Truth Entrepreneurs know that taking high risks is a gamble. They are not afraid of risk, but they know how to assess a situation and take on challenges when they feel confident they have the skills for success.

What Are the Risks?

When an entrepreneur starts a new business, risk is involved. **Risk** is the chance of losing something. An entrepreneur invests money, time, and energy in his or her business in the hope of receiving greater rewards, or benefits. Being fully responsible means the success or failure of your business rests on you. Even if you make all the right decisions, the business might fail. In that case, you may walk away with nothing—or worse, **debt**, which is money you owe to others. The failure can affect your family and friends, too. They may lose money they invested in the business, and they may suffer from stress.

Other risks include unexpected problems, unreliable income, and time away from family and friends.

■ Unexpected problems are challenges for which you are unprepared. They can be discouraging and frustrating and can cause **stress**, which is a physical reaction to a difficult or demanding situation. Facing these challenges can get scary and lonely, especially if you don't have the emotional support of family and friends.

■ Unreliable income is when the amount of money you pay yourself changes month to month. The amount of money you can pay yourself may go up or down, depending on how well your business is performing. Many new businesses don't make much money in the beginning, so you may not always be able to pay yourself. During rough times, you may even have to put more money into the business to pay your business bills, leaving less money to pay your personal expenses..

■ It's not unusual for entrepreneurs to work a lot of extra hours to make their businesses successful. This is especially true during the initial start-up process. These long hours can decrease the time you have available for your friends and family. Until you can afford to hire other people to help, you may have to perform many types of tasks. This will require discipline and a willingness to do whatever needs to be done.

Developing the Characteristics of an Entrepreneur

Recall that your *character* is the personal qualities or traits that make you unique. Most entrepreneurs share some similar characteristics that make them suited to starting a business. For example, they tend to be creative, hard working, and willing to take risks.

Entrepreneurs also have certain skills that help them succeed. A *skill* is an ability that you learn through training and practice. For example, they understand how to create and manage a business, and they are able to keep tasks and information organized.

No one is born with all the characteristics and skills needed to be a successful entrepreneur. But if you keep a positive attitude and believe in yourself, you can develop many of them. They can help you succeed as an entrepreneur, and also in other areas of your life.

Qualities of an Entrepreneur

Do you have the qualities of an entrepreneur? Can you develop them?

- *Entrepreneurs have courage.* They are willing to take risks in spite of possible losses. They tend to be creative. They invent new ways of doing things, and they see possibilities where others see only problems.

- *Entrepreneurs are curious.* They are eager to learn, and they know how to ask questions and find answers. They are determined. They refuse to quit even when they are faced with many obstacles.

- *Entrepreneurs are disciplined.* They stay focused, and they are able to follow a schedule to meet deadlines. They are enthusiastic. They are passionate about their goals and see problems as opportunities. Entrepreneurs are flexible. They can adapt to new situations and are not afraid to make changes.

- *Entrepreneurs have empathy.* People who have **empathy** are sensitive to the thoughts and feelings of other people. They have patience and recognize that most goals cannot be achieved in a short time.

- *Entrepreneurs are honest.* They are committed to being truthful and sincere with others. They are responsible. They do their best to live up to others' expectations. They are accountable for their decisions and actions, and they do not blame others for their own mistakes.

Which personality traits do you have that might help you be a successful entrepreneur? Which do you need to develop?

Entrepreneurial Skills

The skills you use to be a successful entrepreneur are the basic skills you need for success in all areas of your life. You can work in school, at home, and in your community to develop these skills through practice, and with the help of adults. You learn about many of these skills in this book. Some of the basic skills entrepreneurs need include the following.

■ *Business skills:* Understanding how to create and manage a business

■ *Communication skills:* The ability to listen well, write well, and speak well

■ *Computer skills:* The ability to use technological tools effectively

■ *Decision-making and problem-solving skills:* Knowing how to apply logic, information, and past experiences to new decisions and problems

■ *Mathematical skills:* Using math to create budgets, keep accurate records, and analyze financial statements

■ *Organizational skills:* The knack of keeping tasks and information in order; the ability to plan well and manage your time

■ *Relationship skills:* The ability to persuade and motivate people; knowing how to be a leader and to work as part of a team

Building on Experience

Make a list of activities or tasks you've done in the past, such as hobbies, part-time jobs, volunteerism, clubs, sports, science fairs, school activities, and classes. Then create another list that identifies the kind of personal characteristics and skills you need to perform those activities. Based on the two lists, write an essay that describes how your past experiences could help you as an entrepreneur.

Money Madne$$

Every year the Fourth of July parade passes in front of your house. You and a friend decide this year you will set up a stand to sell bottles of water. You decide to purchase 250 bottles. The bottles come 25 in a case, and each case costs $10.99. How much money will you need to purchase the bottles of water? **Hint:** Calculate the number of cases you need, and then multiply that number by $10.99.

If you sell each bottle for $1.50 and sell all 250 bottles, how much profit will you make? **Hint:** Your profit is the amount of money you earn less the amount of money you spend.

Keys to Success

Don't be discouraged from becoming an entrepreneur just because you don't yet have all the traits and skills you will need. You can increase your entrepreneurial potential by focusing on six specific areas. Even if you never become an entrepreneur, paying attention to these areas will help you be more successful in life.

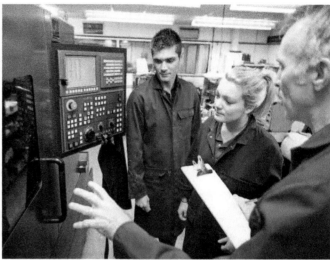

■ *Business knowledge.* Make a habit of reading magazine and newspaper articles on business topics. Use the Internet to research business subjects. Watch films or television programs about successful entrepreneurs. This can help you learn more about business. If you know someone who owns a business, discuss the business with that individual.

■ *Financial skills.* Strengthen your math skills by taking a course in accounting, personal finance, or investing. If you find that math is a difficult subject, ask a teacher to spend a little extra time with you before or after school. Team up with a friend who is good at math. Play math games or do math homework together.

How can developing relationships with experienced workers help you develop entrepreneurial skills?

■ *Career exploration.* It is not too early to begin thinking about your career. You can identify your strengths and weaknesses and work to develop the qualities you think you will need. You can also develop your interests, build a career portfolio, and talk to people who have jobs you think are interesting.

■ *Community awareness.* Look for opportunities to become involved in your community.

■ *Education.* Learning is important, no matter what career you choose. Take advantage of opportunities to learn new things, ask lots of questions, and work hard to do your best. Obtaining an educational certificate, diploma, or degree not only benefits you personally, it can also help open doors to more career opportunities.

■ *Relationships.* Spend time with people who believe in you and inspire you. Being around positive people will help you stay positive and accomplish more. Find opportunities to develop leadership skills and to gain experience working as a member of a team.

Career FACT

According to the Small Business Administration (SBA), an agency of the U.S. government that provides aid and advice to small businesses, a small business is defined by the number of employees or its average annual receipts, depending on the type of industry. The primary size standard is 500 or fewer employees for most manufacturing and mining industries, and $7 million or less in annual receipts for most non-manufacturing industries.

Career Profile: Electrician

> Architecture &
> Construction
> Career Cluster

Job Summary

An electrician is someone who installs the wires that carry electricity through houses, offices, factories, and other buildings. Some electricians build or repair machines that run on electricity.

Why is problem solving an important skill for an electrician?

Electricians must have a lot of specialized, technical knowledge. For example, they must understand the dangers of electricity and how to follow rules and regulations controlling wiring. They must read blueprints to see where to put wires, electrical equipment, and outlets for plugs. Some electricians create blueprints to show others how the wiring should be installed.

To become an electrician, people take classes about electricity, often starting in high school. It also helps to take classes in math and science. Once they receive a high-school diploma, they work as assistants or apprentices to get on-the-job training, while taking additional classes toward certification. It takes many years to become skilled enough to be certified or licensed and longer to become a Master Electrician.

Electricians may work for construction companies, or they may work in factories. Many start out working for someone else, and then begin operating their own, independent businesses.

Use the Internet, a library, or career center to research the responsibilities, education and training requirements, and salary range of an electrician. Write a letter of recommendation for someone who might want to become an electrician.

CAREER COUNSEL

Camille is quiet and shy. She is a talented artist and particularly enjoys decorating fabrics with original designs. She often makes T-shirts, scarves, and other items to give to her friends and family as gifts.

Camille's friend Anna thinks Camille's art is good enough to sell. Anna has always wanted her own business. She studied marketing in school and has worked as a sales clerk for five years. She has researched ways to start a small business. Anna offers to handle the business side of things, so Camille can concentrate on designing and creating the products. Anna thinks that together they could be very successful. Camille is hesitant. She does not think enough people would buy her products to make it worthwhile.

What are the challenges facing Anna and Camille? What are the potential rewards? Use your 21st Century Skills such as problem solving, decision making, and critical thinking to help Anna and Camille come to an agreement about what to do next. Write an ending to the story and read it to the class, or form small groups and present it as a skit.

21st Century Learning

Can an artist be an entrepreneur? What type of skills might he or she need to develop to grow a successful business?

Case Study

When Jackson was 12 years old, his state passed a recycling law. As part of the law, consumers received 10 cents apiece for returning certain types of glass bottles and aluminum cans. Jackson started collecting returnable bottles and cans and bringing them back to stores to receive the refund. He saved the money he earned in a bank account.

When Jackson turned 17, he used the money that he had saved as a down payment on a pickup truck. He used the truck to start a business picking up unwanted items from neighbors and friends. He was amazed at the items people didn't want—furniture, clothing, books, and even appliances. He sold most of it to stores or recycling facilities, donated some to charity, and disposed of the rest.

Jackson used some of the money he earned to pay for college tuition and saved the rest. When he graduated, the bank gave him a small business loan so he could open his own store selling used goods.

■ Do you think Jackson is an entrepreneur? Why or why not?

■ What entrepreneurial characteristics does Jackson display?

■ What entrepreneurial skills has Jackson developed and demonstrated?

Web Extra

You can find a lot of useful information about entrepreneurial thinking and small businesses at sba.gov, the Web site for the U.S. Small Business Administration. Start on the home page, and explore the links to learn more about how to plan, start, and manage your own business.

Answer It!

1. What is the difference between an employee and an entrepreneur?

2. List three ways an employee can think like an entrepreneur.

3. What is the difference between risk and being risky?

4. List four benefits of entrepreneurial thinking.

5. What are three things an entrepreneur invests in his or her business?

6. List four risks of entrepreneurial thinking.

7. List five characteristics of an entrepreneur.

8. What is empathy?

9. List seven entrepreneurial skills.

10. List three ways an entrepreneur uses mathematical skills.

Career-Ready Practices

Career-ready individuals recognize the time, effort, and experience needed to pursue their career goals, even if that goal is owning their own business. They recognize the value of building skills and gaining experience that are aligned with their personal and career goals.

As a class, review the 16 career clusters. Then, divide into teams of three or four and select one of the career clusters. Make a list of entrepreneurial opportunities within your selected career cluster. Pick one, research it, and make a presentation about it to your class.

Be sure to discuss the seven entrepreneurial skills and how they would be of use in your business.

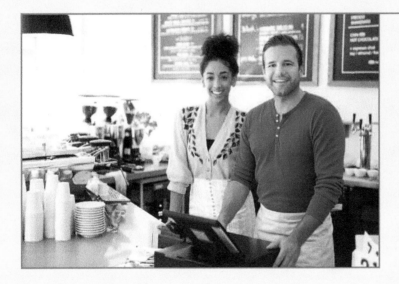

Write Now

Interview an entrepreneur or small business owner in your community. Ask the person about the challenges, risks, and rewards of being an entrepreneur. Ask which personal characteristics or skills have contributed most to business success. Then ask what the owner would do differently if starting the business today. Use the information from your interview to write a newspaper article about the person.

Career Portfolio

Entrepreneurial characteristics and skills can help you succeed in school and as an employee. Make a list of entrepreneurial characteristics and skills. Describe how you exhibit each item or how you can develop it. Include an explanation of how each characteristic or skill can help you succeed. Add the list to your career portfolio.

Business Plan Project

People are born with some skills and qualities, but many skills and qualities are developed over a lifetime. Thinking like an entrepreneur comes from developing the skills and qualities that can help you succeed.

- **Qualities of an Entrepreneur:** Courageous, Creative, Curious, Determined, Disciplined, Empathetic, Enthusiastic, Passionate, Flexible, Honest, Patient, Responsible

- **Skills of an Entrepreneur:** Business, Communication, Computer, Decision-Making, Mathematical, Organizational, Relationship

In your **Business Plan Project**, create a 4-column chart. From left to right, label the columns: **Skills I Have**, **Skills I Need to Develop**, **Qualities I Have**, and **Qualities I Need to Develop**. Fill in the rows under each heading, thinking about the skills and qualities necessary for becoming an entrepreneur. Review the items in columns 2 and 4 and pick the two items you think are most important. Write 3–4 sentences explaining how you will develop these two skills and/or qualities.

Career Preparation

Part II

In This Part . . .

6 Skills for Success

GETTING STARTED

What does success mean to you? Are you successful if you get a B on a math test? Do you feel successful if you beat your personal best at sports, even if your team loses?

Success is the completion of anything intended or finishing what you planned to do. In other words, **success** is when you set a goal for yourself and then achieve that goal. Because we all set different goals, success means different things to different people. But no matter how you measure success, there are basic skills that can help you get there. When you recognize how to set goals, make decisions, and solve problems, you can apply these skills to all areas of your life.

➤ Look through magazines and cut out pictures of at least three people you think are successful. As a class, discuss why you picked the pictures. How can you tell the person is successful? What do your selections say about how you measure success?

Making Decisions

Any time you make up your mind about something, or choose one option over another, you are making a **decision**. Some decisions are simple—what time will I leave for school? Some are more difficult—what will I do after high school? The results—or **consequences**—of your decisions affect you in big and small ways.

■ If the consequences of a decision are positive and contribute to your well-being, it means you made a healthy—or good—choice.

■ If the consequences are negative and interfere with your well-being, that means you made an unhealthy—or poor—choice.

Decisions give you power and control over your life. When you make a decision, you are showing yourself and others that you are independent and responsible.

Every Decision Is Unique

Clearly, not everyone will make the same decision in the same situation. That's because we each use our own character qualities, values, and available resources when we make a choice.

You and a friend might both decide to join your community's recycling action committee, but you might have different reasons for doing so. You might be disgusted by the trash you see along the road, but your friend might want to meet new people. A third friend might opt not to join the committee at all.

Six Steps to a Decision

You can take some of the uncertainty and doubt out of decision making by turning it into a process. A **process** is a series of steps that leads to a conclusion.

1. *Identify the decision to be made.* Make sure you recognize and understand the choice. Define the decision as a goal—what do I want to achieve with this choice?

2. *Consider all possible options.* You usually have lots of options for each decision. Try to think of as many as you can, and write them down. Don't just consider the obvious choice; some of the best options might seem pretty bizarre at first. Consider your available resources and what you are trying to achieve.

Influences

Things that influence your decisions:

✔ Values

✔ Goals

✔ Standards

✔ Ethics

✔ Roles

✔ Stage in life

✔ Other people

✔ Resources

✔ Experience

✔ Knowledge

3. *Identify the consequences of each option.* Each option will have consequences—some positive and some negative; some long-term and some short-term. Recognizing all the consequences will help you predict the outcome of your decision.

4. *Select the best option.* Once you consider the options and identify the consequences, you have the information you need to make your decision.

5. *Make and implement a plan of action.* Making the decision is not the end of the process. You must take steps to make it happen. Until you do, the decision is just an idea or thought in your head.

6. *Evaluate the decision, process, and outcome.* After you have acted on your decision, you can look back and evaluate it, based on your values and standards. Did you achieve the goal you defined in step 1? Did you miss any possible options? Did you correctly identify the consequences? Did you make use of your resources? Was the outcome what you hoped for?

Can Your Decisions Be Hurtful?

How can you be sure your decisions won't interfere with the well-being of yourself and others? When you are evaluating your options while making a decision, consider these questions.

- Is it hurtful to me?
- Is it hurtful to someone else?

If the answer to the questions above is "Yes," you might want to look for other alternatives. If the answer to the following questions is "Yes," you are on the right track.

- Is it fair?
- Is it honest?
- Is it legal?
- Is it practical?

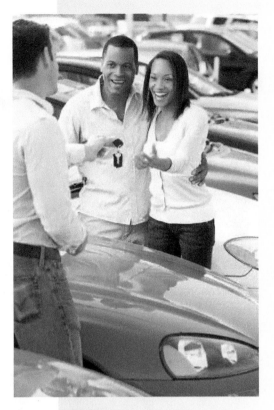

Some decisions are easy to make, and others are more difficult. What is one of the more difficult decisions that you've had to make? What were the consequences of your decision?

Myth All healthy choices lead to positive consequences.

Truth Sometimes even the best decisions lead to negative consequences. Life is unpredictable. When that happens, we have to try to learn from the experience and make the best possible choices going forward.

How can you reduce the stress you feel when you must make a choice?

Overwhelmed by Options

Decision making can be stressful. Even simple choices can seem overwhelming at times. For example, should you wear a suit coat when you apply for a job or is a clean, pressed shirt appropriate? Once you make a decision, you might *second-guess* yourself, which means doubting your own choice. You wore the clean, pressed shirt, but you continue to wonder whether the suit coat might have been better.

- If you are **indecisive**—unable to make a decision—you might think about what will happen if you choose one option over another and never make a decision at all.

- If you are **impulsive**—inclined to act without thinking—you might make a snap decision without considering the consequences.

Predicting Consequences

Do you need a crystal ball to predict the long-term consequences of a decision? What if you decide to volunteer to read to children at the local kindergarten?

★ *Short-term consequence: You have fun with the young children.*

★ *Long-term consequence: You consider a career in early childhood education.*

★ *Consequence that affects others: One of the kindergarteners loves the story you read and is inspired to work hard to learn to read herself.*

Can you think of other long-term consequences that might come from a simple decision?

Career Tips

When you are faced with a decision that affects your career, discuss it with someone who understands your career plan. A career counselor, a teacher, or your supervisor at work will be able to help you assess your options.

More About Consequences

Consequences of our choices can be short-term or long-term. What you eat for breakfast might affect your energy level for a few hours. Whether you go to college can affect your whole life.

Most decisions actually have both long-term and short-term consequences. Long-term, what you eat for breakfast might affect your health and wellness. Short-term, it might affect how you do on a test.

Sometimes, consequences have both positive and negative results. Take the breakfast decision: On the up side, a doughnut tastes good and gives you a sugar boost of energy. On the down side, a doughnut raises your cholesterol level, which might lead to a heart condition. The good news is that you can learn how to make healthy decisions that turn out positive more often than they turn out negative.

Did I Make the Best Choice?

How can your values, standards, and ethics help you make healthy choices? We all make mistakes. Despite our best intentions, we make poor choices. Most of the time, it doesn't matter too much. If you cut your hair too short, it will grow. You can choose a different style next time or even go to a different shop for the cut.

Sometimes, though, we must live with the consequences of our actions for a long time—maybe even our whole lives. It's part of the deal—if you are independent and responsible enough to make the decision, you're stuck with the results. If you choose to cut class or hang out with friends instead of studying, you might not qualify for the college of your choice. But even when we make a poor choice with long-term consequences, we can learn from our mistakes and try to make better choices going forward.

If you make a decision that has negative consequences, what can you do next time to make a better choice?

NUMBERS GAME

You can use **probability**—the chance that something will happen—to measure how likely it is that a particular outcome will occur. The **formula**—rule or method of doing something—for probability is the number of times the particular outcome occurs divided by the total number of possible outcomes. In fractional form, it looks like this:

$$\text{Probability} = \frac{\text{Number of particular outcomes}}{\text{Total number of possible outcomes}}$$

As an example, consider that you are a clerk at a pet store. You have a box of dog collars. There are five blue collars, three red collars, and one black collar. A customer asks for a red collar. What is the probability that you pick a red collar from the box your first time?

Hint: Divide 3 (the number of red collars) by 9 (the total number of collars).

What is the probability that you pick a blue collar your first time? **Hint:** Divide 5 by 9.

Myth All poor choices lead to negative consequences.

Truth As luck would have it, sometimes things work out OK even when you make really poor decisions. Just breathe a sigh of relief, recognize that you were fortunate that nothing negative happened, and once again, make the best possible choices going forward.

Solving Problems

A **problem** is a difficulty or challenge that you must resolve before you can make progress. In other words, any barrier or obstacle between you and a goal is a problem.

Problems pop up all the time. Mostly, we come up with a solution without thinking too hard. Say you want to meet friends for dinner after work, but you promised your supervisor you would complete a report. You have a problem: The unfinished report is an obstacle between you and dinner with friends. Solving the problem is easy: You finish the report or reschedule the dinner.

Some problems sneak up on us over time, sometimes hidden or obscured by something else. You might want to do well at work, but you fall asleep in staff meetings. Is the problem that the meeting is boring, that the conference room is too warm, or is it that you are staying up late at night playing video games? Recognizing the real problem is the first step in solving it.

Owning the Problem

One difficulty with solving problems is figuring out whose problem it really is. Generally, the person who is blocked from a goal is the one who owns the problem.

If your co-worker leaves his copy of a report at home and wants to borrow yours, is it your problem or his? What if you loan him the report and he loses it? Is it his problem or yours? Who should take responsibility for solving it?

If you own the problem, you are responsible for solving it. If someone else owns the problem, you may be able to help solve it, but ultimately it is not your responsibility. Taking responsibility for your own problems, and working to find solutions, shows that you are independent and capable.

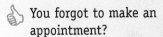
Why do you think employers value employees who are able to solve problems in the workplace?

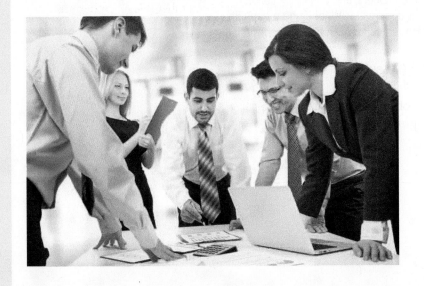

Six Steps to a Solution

When problems are harder to identify, or harder to solve, you can use the problem-solving process to figure out the best solution.

1. *Identify the problem.* This is your chance to be honest, acknowledge the problem, and determine what goal it is blocking.

2. *Consider all possible solutions.* There may be one obvious solution or there may be many possible solutions. Write down as many as you can think of. You will need to consider your values, standards, and resources, too. Some solutions might be harder to make happen or take longer than others. Some might cost money, and some might be free. Some might solve only part of the problem.

3. *Identify the consequences of each solution.* As for decisions, each solution will have consequences, and it is important to recognize how the consequences will affect you and others. Again, write them down.

4. *Select the best solution.* The best solution offers the best possible opportunity for you to continue your progress toward your goal.

5. *Make and implement a plan of action.* Recognizing and selecting a solution are only part of the process. You must take the necessary steps to make the solution real.

6. *Evaluate the solution, process, and outcome.* Did your solution work? Did you achieve your goal? Would you do anything differently if you had the same problem again?

Asking for and Giving Help

You do not have to make every decision or solve every problem on your own. You have many people around to help, including family, friends, and teachers. You might think asking for help is a sign of weakness, but it's really a sign of strength. Recognizing that you need help shows that you are responsible. It proves that you understand your limitations. Face it—you don't know all the answers. Asking for help shows that you want to learn from the experience of others.

However, when someone comes to *you* for help, remember it is his or her problem to solve, not yours. With that in mind, you should listen carefully and critically, and then share your thoughts and opinions. Try not to make the decision or solve the problem yourself—it's not your responsibility. If you don't think you are qualified to help, say so, and then suggest someone who might be. You can probably help a friend decide what to wear on a date, but a parent, teacher, or counselor might be better equipped to offer advice on how to prepare for a job interview.

Career Profile:
Computer Support Specialist

Information Technology Career Cluster

Job Summary

Why is problem solving an important skill for a computer support technician?

When someone has computer trouble, he or she asks a computer support specialist for help. A computer support specialist works to identify the problem and then tries to fix it.

In addition to knowledge about computer systems, computer support specialists must be able to communicate effectively with the people who come to them for help. They often work over the phone or by using e-mail to help people solve the problem themselves. Some do the actual repair work. Many computer support specialists also set up computer systems, and then train people on how to use them.

To become a computer support specialist, people take classes about building, installing, repairing, and using computer systems. They also study math and develop problem-solving skills. Most employers look for computer support specialists who have a college degree and experience working with computers.

Use the Internet, a library, or career center to research the responsibilities, education and training requirements, and salary range of computer support technicians. Write a want advertisement for a computer support specialist job opening.

Money Madne$$

You are responsible for purchasing supplies for a meeting. There will be 50 people at the meeting. You need pens, pads of paper, and folders for each attendee. Pens come 25 in a box. Each box costs $3.25. The paper costs $1.25 per pad. Folders cost $2.10 per box of 50. There is a 6% sales tax in your state. How much money do you need to purchase all of the supplies?

Setting Goals

Recall that a **goal** is something you are trying to achieve. Goals help direct your actions and guide your decision-making because they give you something to work toward. They help give your life meaning, because you know that there is a purpose in what you do. When you achieve a goal, you can be proud and express satisfaction.

If all you do is think about a goal, it's just a dream. You make goals real by deciding what you want to achieve and then planning how to get there. A successful entrepreneur, for example, has a vision of what he or she expects to accomplish. To achieve that vision, it is important to set realistic and attainable goals. Goals help an entrepreneur plan, develop, and grow a business. They let the entrepreneur identify the challenges ahead, so he or she is prepared when problems arise. While you should set goals that are within reach, there is nothing wrong with challenging yourself to push harder.

Goals are not written in stone. As you progress through different stages of your life, you will learn more about yourself, your values, and your standards. Your resources will change. You can change your goals at any time and develop new goals. Most people do.

Five Steps to a Goal

You can use the following process to help identify, assess, and set goals.

1. *Identify the goal.* Write down the goal using as much detail as you can. This helps you understand and recognize the goal. Be positive, not negative: "I will attend the FCCLA meeting" rather than "I won't skip the FCCLA meeting."

2. *Assess the goal.* Determine if it is something you really want and if it is realistic and attainable. It might be a fad or something that sounds good or even something someone else wants for you.

3. *Make an action plan for achieving the goal.* What resources will you need? If you cannot come up with a plan that works, it may mean the goal is not realistic or attainable. If so, you may need to go back to step 1.

4. *Write down your action plan.* Be as specific as possible.

5. *Reevaluate your goals.* Every once in a while, make sure they are still important to you and, if so, that you are on track to achieve them.

Goals in All Areas of Your Life

You can set goals for all your roles in life that help you prepare for and achieve a satisfying career. What if you are interested in a career in health sciences?

★ At home: Investigate the items necessary for a home first aid kit and enlist your family's help in preparing one.

★ At school: Enroll in classes and extracurricular activities that will help you develop the skills you need to pursue an education in health science.

★ With friends: Help your friends recognize the importance of safety precautions such as wearing bike helmets and buckling seat belts.

★ In your community: Volunteer at a hospital or medical center.

★ At work: Consider part-time or volunteer opportunities that will contribute to your knowledge about the health sciences industry.

Can you think of other ways to integrate your career goals into many areas of your life? Make a list and discuss it in class.

Make a Plan

Just because a goal is short-term doesn't mean you can achieve it without a plan. What if you have a short-term goal to meet friends at the mall?

★ *Where will you meet?*

★ *What time will you meet?*

★ *How will you get there?*

★ *What time should you leave?*

Considering all of the factors helps you make decisions and form a realistic plan. The more specific the plan, the easier it will be to achieve your goal. How can you make a plan for long-term goals?

Short-Term Goals

When you want to achieve something quickly, you set **short-term goals**. You can accomplish short-term goals in the near future—maybe even today. For example, finishing your homework on time is a short-term goal. It is usually easy to define short-term goals because they are specific and not very complicated. If you keep a to-do list, it is full of short-term goals—meet friends at the mall, call your grandmother, make your bed.

Long-Term Goals

A **long-term goal** is something you want to achieve in the more distant future—maybe a year from now or maybe even more distant than that. Graduating from college is a long-term goal. So is buying a car.

Defining long-term goals may be more difficult than defining short-term goals. You might know you want to get married some day, but you don't know when or to whom. You might know you want to travel, but you don't know where or how.

What Are Milestones?

What can you do now to make long-term goals a reality?

Sometimes it's harder to stay focused on a long-term goal—it seems far away. Breaking the long-term goal down into a series of short-term goals—or **milestones**—makes it easier to stay on track.

Becoming a nurse might be a long-term goal. To achieve that goal, you can set a series of realistic and attainable milestones, such as:

■ Volunteering at a hospital or senior care center

■ Working part-time in a clinic

■ Graduating from high school

■ Attending college

Thinking Critically

Critical thinking is the ability to be honest, rational, and open-minded. It can help you evaluate your options in many situations. You can use it when you are making decisions, setting goals, and solving problems. When you think critically, you try not to let emotions get in the way of choosing the best course of action.

- Being honest means acknowledging selfish feelings and preexisting opinions.

- Being rational means relying on reason and thought instead of on emotion or impulse.

- Being open-minded means being willing to evaluate all possible options—even those that are unpopular.

Thinking critically doesn't mean you should ignore emotions or any of the other influence factors. It just means you should consider all possibilities before rushing to judgment.

Critical Thinking in Action

When you think critically, you consider all possible options and other points of view. You look objectively at information. **Objective** means fairly, without emotion or prejudice. Then, you use your values, standards, and ethics to interpret the information subjectively. **Subjective** means affected by existing opinions, feelings, and beliefs.

Looking at things both objectively and subjectively can help you make choices that are right for you. For example, you can look at a candidate for class president objectively and see that she is smart, hard-working, and honest. Subjectively, you can disagree with everything she stands for and vote for someone else.

You can think critically about a lot of things, not just decisions and problems. You don't have to believe everything you hear or read. You can question a news report, look more deeply into the meaning of a magazine article, or investigate the truth behind a rumor.

Myth You can't trust your gut and think critically at the same time.

Truth Trusting your gut is not the same as being impulsive. Sometimes your gut—or that little voice inside your head—is really your values, standards, and ethics pointing you in the right direction. If you use the decision-making process and your gut is pointing out the best choice, go with it.

Are Emotions Always a Problem?

Emotions can affect critical thinking. That's not necessarily bad, but it's not necessarily good, either. Skipping class because you are angry about a low grade might seem like a good choice at the time, but the consequence might be more low grades.

If you think critically, you acknowledge that you are angry and are honest about why. Then, you can let the anger go and assess your options with a clear head. Maybe it would be better to go to class and ask the teacher what you can do to improve. The consequences might be better grades, an improved relationship with the teacher, and—best of all—no more anger.

How can thinking critically help employees make decisions or solve problems in the workplace?

21st Century Learning

CAREER

COUNSEL

Alyssa is friendly and nice and likes being around people. In school, she enjoys classes in business math and technology. She is thinking about studying finance in college. She applies for a summer job as a bank teller. The branch manager hires someone else, but tells Alyssa she is a strong candidate, and he will call her if another position becomes available.

Alyssa accepts a job as a data records assistant at a hospital. She is assigned to work on a project to convert paper files to electronic files. She spends her days alone at a computer.

After two weeks, the bank branch manager calls. A teller position has become available, and he offers the job to Alyssa.

What should Alyssa do? Use your 21st Century Skills such as decision making, problem solving, goal setting, and critical thinking to help Alyssa examine her situation and move forward. Write an ending to the story. Read it to the class, or form a small group and present it as a skit.

Using Management Skills

You are already a manager. A **manager** is someone who makes decisions, solves problems, and uses resources to achieve specific goals. A manager thinks critically and communicates effectively.

Being a manager means that you are in control and responsible. You are willing to take the blame when something goes wrong, and you are willing to share the credit when something goes right.

What a Manager Does

A good manager uses a three-step process to make thoughts and ideas become reality. He or she knows how to use goal setting, decision making, and critical thinking to find a way to get things done. You can use these steps to solve problems the way a manager does.

■ First, you figure out what needs to be done. You set a goal. You consider your resources. You assess problems that might be in the way. And then you develop an action plan.

■ Next, you put the plan into action. You monitor the plan to make sure it is going the way you expect. You might even need to make changes along the way.

■ Finally, you look back to assess and evaluate. Did the plan work the way you expected? Did you achieve your goal?

What Makes a Manager Effective?

A manager is effective when he or she achieves a goal. An effective manager knows how to recognize and use available resources, including:

■ Time   ■ Energy

■ Technology   ■ People

An effective manager knows how to make healthy choices in all areas of life. For example, an effective manager knows how to:

■ Communicate with family members

■ Think critically about friends and peers

■ Set goals for school and career

■ Solve problems in the community

Cross-Cultural Management

Management culture—a companywide attitude toward workplace values and standards—is often influenced by the culture of the country where the business is located. For example, in some countries, it is not important to be on time for meetings. In other countries, businesses close for an hour or more in the middle of the day.

In today's global economy, it is important for managers working internationally to understand and respect differences in cultural management. Managers who do not may have trouble earning the respect of their international employees.

Use the Internet or the library to research management culture around the globe, then make a chart comparing at least three countries. What cultural differences do you think would pose the biggest challenge to international managers?

What Does the Title "Manager" Mean?

At work, some people have the job title "Manager." Usually, a manager supervises other employees to make sure all responsibilities are met. For example, at a bank, the branch manager supervises the bank tellers and others who work at the branch. At a supermarket, the bakery manager supervises the bakers and others who work in the bakery department.

Managers generally earn more money because they have more experience and more responsibility in the workplace. You become a manager at work by showing you are responsible, independent, and capable of making decisions and solving problems. You increase your chances of becoming a manager by taking classes in school to learn how to manage effectively. You can also attend graduate school after college to earn a Masters in Business Administration—MBA—degree.

Becoming a Leader

A **leader** is a type of manager. A leader is someone who unites people to work toward common goals. If you are a leader, it means others trust you and trust your judgment. In the world of work, leaders supervise other employees and manage projects.

Although you might have heard that someone is a "born leader," that's not usually the case. Becoming a leader takes time and patience. Leaders have to prove that they can make healthy decisions, set goals, and solve problems. They have to know how to use their resources to help others achieve their goals. Leaders usually start out as good employees. They are promoted into management positions as they develop and display leadership qualities. For example, a teacher may continue his or her education, assume leadership roles, and become a principal or superintendant.

Leaders are successful in their different roles and meet their responsibilities. For example, in school, you might participate in clubs and organizations. At work, you might accept responsibility for new projects. In the community, you might attend meetings and help organize events. At home, you might show your siblings how to cooperate with each other.

What Makes a Leader?

Leaders exhibit positive qualities that other people respect, such as self-confidence. They use skills such as goal setting and critical thinking to make healthy decisions for the benefit of the group. If you are an effective leader you:

What skills and resources can you use to be an effective leader?

■ Respect others

■ Know how to compromise

■ Know how to communicate

As a leader, you understand your own strengths and weaknesses. You also know how to accept responsibility when something goes wrong and how to give credit to others when something goes right. Finally, a strong leader is willing to take a stand, even if it's unpopular.

Tech Connect

In most businesses, managers are responsible for keeping projects on time, on track, and on budget. Even small projects may become overwhelming at times. To make the job easier, many use project management software tools for collecting data, tracking tasks, and enabling everyone involved to communicate effectively.

Project management software programs vary in terms of complexity. Most include such features as scheduling, assigning tasks, file storage, file sharing, to-do lists, time tracking, and security.

Use the Internet or magazines or visit a local computer/electronics store to research project management software. Imagine you are a department manager for a small business. Select a product and prepare a list that outlines its features and capabilities that you will share with your employees. Present the list to your class.

Case Study

Jamal has been taking karate classes after school since the age of 11. Now he is a sophomore in high school. He has earned a first-degree black belt and works at the dojo (karate school) to earn money to pay for his lessons.

Jamal's friend has asked him to join the wrestling team at school. The practices are fun, and Jamal is good at wrestling. The coach thinks he can start on the varsity team if he works hard. The problem is, practices are at the same time that Jamal usually works at the dojo.

■ What decision does Jamal have to make?

■ Are there any problems he has to solve?

■ What resources can Jamal use to make his decision?

■ What do you think Jamal should do? Why?

Web Extra

acrn.ovae.org/links.htm is the Web site for America's Career Resource Network, a group of state and federal organizations that provide information, resources, and training about career and education planning. Use the link for Students to explore the topics and resources and to access the site's Career Decision-Making Tool.

Answer It!

1. Explain the difference between a healthy choice and an unhealthy choice.

2. List the six steps in the decision-making process.

3. List at least three things that influence your decisions.

4. How can you tell who owns a problem?

5. List the five steps in the goal-setting process.

6. What is the difference between short-term goals and long-term goals?

7. List three qualities of critical thinking.

8. What is the difference between being objective and being subjective?

9. What is a manager?

10. List at least three qualities of a leader.

Career-Ready Practices

Career-ready individuals recognize that problems arise in the workplace. They understand the first step in solving a problem is to identify its cause. Then, they consider options for solving the problem. Once they determine the best solution, they follow through to ensure it is solved.

In teams of four or five, brainstorm a list of different types of businesses. Pick one business, and, on a separate piece of paper, write down one problem or challenge that employees of that business might run into. Do not identify the type of business. Exchange problems with another team. Work as a team to identify the type of business and brainstorm solutions to the problem. Discuss your results with your class.

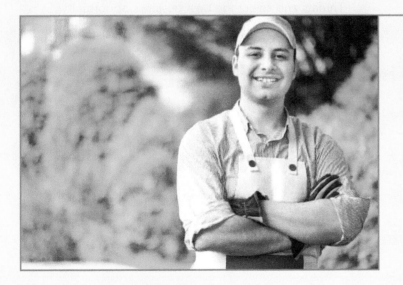

Write Now

What do think you are going to do after high school? Do you have a goal? Are there obstacles between you and that goal? Imagine yourself ten years from now. Write an autobiography—essay about your life—explaining the goals you set, decisions you made, and problems or challenges you overcame during those ten years to become your future self.

Career Portfolio

Setting goals is an important part of the education and career planning process. Make a list of long-term and short-term goals for yourself. Select one, and use the five-step goal-setting process to develop the goal and make an action plan for achieving the goal. Include a timeframe and assess the plan to make sure it is reasonable and attainable. Add both the list of goals and the action plan to your career portfolio.

Business Plan Project

To select the best idea for a new business, entrepreneurs conduct SWOT analyses. SWOT stands for **S**trengths, **W**eaknesses, **O**pportunities, and **T**hreats. To complete a SWOT analysis, you identify the **S**trengths and **W**eaknesses of yourself and your team, and the **O**pportunities and **T**hreats that come from outside the business. For example, existing competition might be a threat. If the strengths and opportunities outweigh the weaknesses and threats, then it's a good business opportunity.

From the list of businesses you developed in the **Business Plan Project** for Chapter 2, pick two business ideas and complete a SWOT analysis for each. You might draw a table with five columns and three rows to organize the SWOT. For the column headings, enter Idea, Strengths, Weaknesses, Opportunities, and Threats. Enter each idea in a separate row, and fill in the SWOT information. (*Hint: Refer to the lists you developed in earlier chapters, such as your resources, qualities, and skills.*) When the table is complete, compare the Strengths, Weaknesses, Opportunities, and Threats and select the best business opportunity.

Skills in This Chapter . . .

- **Recognizing the Value of School**

- **Analyzing Your Learning Style**

- **Developing an Academic Plan**

- **Developing Career-Related Skills in School**

- **Planning for Postsecondary Education**

- **Identifying Career-Related Opportunities for Students**

GETTING STARTED

Can you name one thing you can do to increase the amount of money you will earn in your lifetime? How about graduating from high school? Even better, graduating from college!

High school graduation might seem very far away. The thought of studying for so many years, of taking—and passing—so many classes, might feel like a heavy burden. But the benefits of success are worth the effort. Graduates are more likely to be hired than nongraduates. They earn more money, are healthier, and live better lifestyles. Completing your education is one of the best things you can do for yourself and your career. Academic planning can help you reach that goal.

➤ Fold a piece of paper in half. On one side, make a list of jobs you think you could get without a high school diploma. On the other side, list jobs you think you could not get without a high school diploma. As a class, discuss which jobs offer better benefits and rewards.

Recognizing the Value of School

Finishing school is an investment in your future. Studies show that people who stay in school have higher self-esteem, better physical health, and a more positive attitude. They are more likely to have a job, and they earn more money.

School is an opportunity. When you stay in school, you can learn new things, meet new people, and try new activities. You can practice skills you will need when you graduate, such as getting along with others, speaking up for yourself, and being on time for appointments.

Why School Matters

School also provides an opportunity to prepare for a career. Core subjects such as reading, writing, and math are vital for the career-search process. Science, social studies, music, art, technology, family and consumer sciences, and sports all help you gain knowledge and build skills you will need to succeed at work, such as teamwork, leadership, and problem solving. School clubs and organizations also help you build skills for future success.

Why Dropping Out Is Not Cool

You might think dropping out of school to get a job is a good idea. Maybe you need money. Maybe you are tired of going to class. Maybe you think you are ready to live like a grownup. However, when you are not in school, you will be expected to pay your own rent, pay for your own transportation, and pay for your own food. If a company does hire you, it will likely pay you about 35 percent less than if you had graduated.

A **dropout**—someone who leaves school without receiving a diploma—is more likely to be poor, receive assistance from the government, and be a single parent. Dropouts are more likely to commit crimes and go to jail, to suffer from depression, and to have substance abuse problems.

According to the U.S. Census Bureau, the average dropout can expect to earn an annual income of $20,241. A high school graduate, on the other hand, can expect to make about $30,500 a year, and those with a bachelor's degree can expect to make more than $50,000 a year.

How Education Affects Employment

Education teaches you skills and information you need to get and keep a job. Think about this: Most companies will not hire an employee who has not graduated from high school. Some will not hire an employee who has not graduated from college. If a company does hire dropouts, it usually pays them less than it pays graduates.

Employers assume that graduates have certain characteristics that dropouts don't have. If a graduate and a dropout apply for the same job, the employer thinks that the graduate:

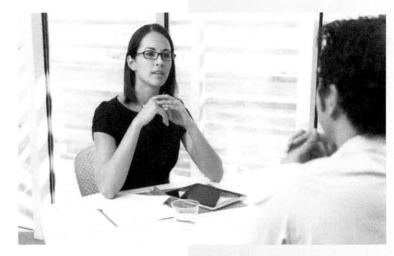

- Knows how to read and write
- Understands basic math
- Can communicate with others
- Knows how to solve problems
- Has a good work ethic
- Has a positive attitude
- Is self-disciplined
- Is motivated to succeed

If you were an employer, what characteristics would you look for in someone you were going to hire? Would you rather hire a graduate or a dropout?

Meeting Career Goals

Developing strong academic skills can help you in any career you choose. What skills can you acquire and strengthen in school in order to achieve your career goals?

Money Madne$$

Research shows that high school dropouts in the United States earn a lot less than high school graduates. In fact, they earn 35% less. What exactly does that mean? It means that if a high school graduate working as a chef earns $27,000.00 a year, a high school dropout would only earn $17,550.00.

How much more does the graduate earn?

To find the **difference**, or how much more the graduate earns than the dropout, subtract the dropout's salary from the graduate's salary.

What if the graduate earns $32,000.00 a year? To find the dropout's salary, you multiply the grad's salary by 35%, and then subtract the answer from 32,000.00. If you have a calculator, press 32000 * 35%. Then, subtract the result from 32000 to get the amount of the dropout's salary.

If you don't have a calculator, convert the percentage to a decimal so you can multiply it by the graduate's salary. To convert to a decimal, divide the percent by 100: 35 ÷ 100 = 0.35.

👍 Prioritize assignments and manage your time to complete them.

👍 Listen carefully and follow instructions.

👍 Enroll in courses related to the career you want to pursue.

👎 Cram for a test the night before it's scheduled.

👎 Socialize and talk a lot during class.

👎 Enroll in easy classes so you can get a good grade and improve your GPA.

What other academic skills can help you meet your career goals?

Analyzing Your Learning Style

A **learning style** is a way of taking in information so that you remember it and can use it in a practical way. Researchers have identified three major learning styles—visual, auditory, and tactile—although every person learns in his or her own unique way. Some do better when they can see information and examples; some do better when they hear it. Some people learn by doing—which means they need practical experience with tasks.

No single learning style is better than any of the others. Each has its own strengths and weaknesses. Recognizing your own learning style can help you succeed in school, as well as in other areas of life. Your teachers, parents, and guidance counselors can help you identify your learning style and find methods of learning that work best for you.

Visual Learners

Visual learners take in information best when they see it. They tend to have excellent imaginations. They think in pictures and remember things best if they see them. They are usually good spellers and may have art skills.

- Visual learners may need to hear spoken instructions more than once before they understand them.
- Visual aids such as charts, illustrations, maps, notes, and videos help visual learners absorb information.
- Visual learners often benefit from marking or highlighting written information.
- Visual learners might find it helpful to sit in the front of a class so they can see the teacher's facial expressions clearly.

Auditory Learners

Auditory learners take in information best when they hear it. They listen well and like to talk about what they learn. They follow spoken instructions better than written instructions. They are usually good at giving speeches and presentations.

- Auditory learners remember information when they hear it in a lecture or on a recording.
- **Reciting**—speaking—information out loud helps auditory learners remember it.
- Auditory learners benefit from a spoken explanation of visual material, such as charts, diagrams, and maps.
- Auditory learners might find it helpful to use rhymes, raps, or musical jingles to remember information.
- Dictating—speaking ideas aloud while another person writes them down—is a good way for auditory learners to organize their thoughts.

Studying Works!

Choosing the correct study methods for your own learning style is important, but some study methods work for everyone. How can you use studying to improve your chances of academic success?

👎 Study while watching television

👎 Cram in all your studying right before a test

👎 Stay up all night to study

👍 Study a little bit every day

👍 Organize a study group

👍 Ask your teacher for study tips

What other study methods do you think might improve your chances of academic success?

Tactile Learners

Tactile learners learn best by touching things. They tend to express themselves physically. For example, they might move their hands or gesture when they speak, and they might like to walk around when they are listening. They usually are not effective listeners and lose interest in lectures or speeches. Tactile learners often learn best by practicing what they learn and relating information to real-life situations.

■ Tactile learners may find it helpful to take frequent breaks and move around while studying.

■ They may benefit from studying while standing up or eating while studying.

■ Acting out scenarios can help tactile learners remember information.

■ Tactile learners remember information better if they take notes while listening.

■ Tracing written words with their fingers can help them remember the text.

Study Strategies for Success in School

People who do well in school usually work very hard. They know how to use study **strategies**—careful plans and methods—that improve their ability to remember new things. Once you identify your learning style, you can select study strategies that work for you.

■ *General strategies.* Sit near the front of the class so you pay attention; take notes; set a daily study goal, such as completing your homework.

■ *Strategies for memory.* Study your notes soon after class; make flash cards with a key idea on one side and a definition or explanation on the other side.

■ *Strategies for listening and note-taking.* Listen for clues that the speaker is giving a key point; underline or star the main points; use abbreviations for commonly used words.

■ *Strategies for planning and organization.* Keep a calendar, schedule, or to-do list; write assignments and due dates in an assignment notebook and on a calendar; prioritize your responsibilities and tasks; break a large project into smaller steps, and set a deadline for each step.

■ *Strategies for tests.* Ask your teacher what the test will cover and what type of questions it will include; don't wait until the night before to study—study a little bit each evening in the days leading up to the test; read test directions carefully; check your answers; skip questions you are unsure of and go back to them after you have completed the others.

What study strategies do you find most useful?

Tech Connect

Schools take advantage of technology in many ways, including to communicate with parents and the community and to cut costs. However, the main reason for using technology in school is to teach.

Some technologies such as interactive white boards, digital text books, online videos, and collaborative Web sites can make learning more engaging. Some make teaching more effective. For example, specialized technologies such as voice recognition software help students with disabilities succeed.

Do you think you need technology to learn? Do you think technology makes school more effective? Interview someone in your school community about technology in the classroom. Then, write an article about it to print in your school newspaper or post on your school Web site.

Developing an Academic Plan

What to Put in an Academic Plan

Some things that you might put in your personal academic plan include:

✔ Goals beyond high school

✔ Assessment of your skills, knowledge, and experience

✔ Assessment of factors that will contribute to your success

✔ Assessment of factors that might interfere with your success

✔ Graduation requirements

✔ Plan for achieving graduation

✔ Plan for achieving goals beyond high school

Recall that part of the goal-setting process is to make a plan for achieving the goal. A **personal academic plan** is a document that you use to set goals for the things you want to accomplish while you are in school. Some schools call it a *personal education plan*, a *personal career plan*, or even a *personal life plan*. It serves as a map that you can follow and helps you achieve your educational, career, and lifestyle goals.

Goal-setting skills can help you manage the academic planning process from start to finish. It can help you stay focused on the educational objectives that you need to achieve your career and lifetime goals.

The Purpose of the Plan

A personal academic plan can help you make sure you graduate from high school, take advantage of opportunities to develop your skills and abilities while you are in school, and help prepare you for life after graduation.

At a very basic level, a personal academic plan will help you keep track of your progress toward achieving your school's graduation requirements. An academic plan can help you assess your achievement at each grade level. You can use the information to prepare for and select appropriate courses for the next year.

At a higher level, a personal academic plan can help you identify areas of opportunity in school and out. It can:

- Help you identify your academic strengths and weaknesses

- Help you find ways to overcome challenges, obstacles, and problems

- Assist you with developing strategies to improve your success in all areas

- Encourage you to participate in **co-curricular** activities such as athletic teams, clubs, and career student organizations

- Inspire you to become involved in your community

- Help you identify the skills you need to meet the requirements for certification in the career of your choice

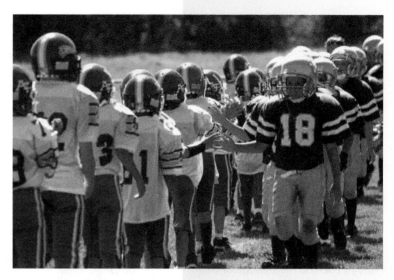

Why is it important to include co-curricular activities as part of your academic plan?

How Do I Create an Academic Plan?

Your teachers and school counselor can help you develop an academic plan. Some schools have forms you can use; if not, you can organize your plan in a way that maps your academic achievement and future plans. You may also be able to find an academic plan form online.

Most personal academic plans include goals in four basic areas.

- Career-related planning, skills, and experiences
- Academic preparation and planning
- School and community involvement
- Plans and goals for after high school

When you create your academic plan, make it realistic and attainable. You want to feel confident that you can put the plan into action and achieve your goals. Keep in mind that your plan may change over time. Your goals might change, or your available resources might change.

Setting Long-Term and Short-Term Academic Goals

Start your academic plan by writing a statement that describes your long-term ultimate goal. The goal should be specific and should include career, education, and lifestyle goals. For example, you might write: *I will be an occupational physical therapist in California by the time I am 30 years old.* Or, *I will be a commanding officer in the Navy by the time I am 30 years old.* Or, *I will own and operate an Italian restaurant in Chicago by the time I am 30 years old.*

Meeting High School Graduation Requirements

Before you create an academic plan, make sure you understand your high school's graduation requirements.

Each state defines the minimum course requirements a student must complete in order to graduate. Individual school districts may adopt additional requirements beyond those defined by the state.

Explore your school's graduation requirements. Make a list of the requirements or print an existing one and create a schedule or plan for how you will meet them.

Add short-term goals that define how you will gain the skills, knowledge, and experience that you need to achieve your ultimate goal. Include a timeline for achieving each one. For example, for the first long-term goal listed on the previous page, you might set the following short-term goals:

■ Get an A in health class this semester

■ Enroll in advanced science classes next semester

■ Volunteer at a physical rehabilitation center this summer

■ By the end of the school year, research colleges and universities in California that offer physical therapy degrees

Developing Career-Related Skills in School

How will you find a job if you cannot read the job description? How will you prepare a cover letter if you cannot write a paragraph? How will you compare salaries if you cannot do basic math?

Luckily, you have the opportunity in school to develop the basic skills you need to succeed in a career, by taking core courses such as math, language arts, social studies, and science. You also have the opportunity to explore courses that relate to your interests and abilities, such as music, art, carpentry, textiles, nutrition, and other electives.

Building Math Skills

Basic math skills such as addition, subtraction, multiplication, and division are vital for success in careers ranging from nursing to inventory control. Most schools require students to pass a basic math test in order to graduate.

■ If you are a nurse's aide, you count a pulse for ten seconds, and then multiply the number by six to find a patient's heart rate.

■ If you are installing drywall, you measure the square footage of a room to determine how much building material to buy.

You might benefit from a business math class if you are interested in a career in business. Business math covers topics such as accounting, tax management, reading and creating charts and graphs, and personal finance.

You will need advanced math skills for a career in technology, business, engineering, or science. Advanced math includes subjects such as advanced algebra, calculus, and trigonometry.

NUMBERS GAME

An **average** is the sum of two or more quantities divided by the number of quantities. A **grade point average** (GPA) is the average of all grades that you receive. Colleges and universities use GPA as one measure of an applicant's qualifications for admission. You can use your grade point average to assess your overall academic achievement.

To calculate your GPA, you must convert letter grades to their numeric equivalent, and then find the average.

A+ = 4.0	A = 4.0	A– = 3.7
B+ = 3.3	B = 3.0	B– = 2.7
C+ = 2.3	C = 2.0	C– = 1.7
D+ = 1.3	D = 1.0	D– = 0.7
F= 0.0		

For example, to find your GPA if you received an A–, a B+, a B, and a C+:

1. Convert the grades:

   A– = 3.7

   B+ = 3.3

   B = 3.0

   C+ = 2.3

2. Add the values of the grades:

   3.7 + 3.3 + 3.0 + 2.3 = 12.3

3. Divide the sum of all grades by the number of grades:

   12.3 ÷ 4 = 3.075

What would your GPA be if you received a B+, B–, C+, and a C– for the first semester, and then a B+, B, B–, and a C for the second semester?

Developing Communication Skills

Almost every employer wants workers who can read, write, and speak effectively. Communications skills are the tools you need to share information with others.

- ■ You might need to write an order for supplies.
- ■ You might need to explain the features of a product to a customer.

In school, language arts classes help you develop communications skills. You learn to organize written information, understand the things you read, and speak out loud in front of an audience.

Clubs and organizations also help you build communications skills. You can join the debate team to learn how to argue politely and effectively. You can write for the school newspaper or Web site. You can perform with the drama club.

Choosing Electives

Most of the classes you take in school are required. But, as you move into higher grades, you will have more opportunity to take **electives**—classes you choose because you are interested in the subject. When you take an elective, you can discover how your interests might lead to a career. Electives often align with the career clusters. For example, you might take a Foods and Nutrition elective and discover that you would be interested in a career as a dietitian. Or, you might take a drafting elective and learn that you have a talent for architecture.

Electives allow you to explore new subjects outside the standard core courses. The number and type of electives vary from school to school. Your school counselor can help you select courses that match your career and academic goals.

Choosing Advanced Courses

If you have ability in a subject, you might choose to take advanced-level courses. Advanced-level courses challenge you to work harder and learn more about a subject. Teachers or counselors may recommend you for advanced courses, or you could ask to enroll.

Some advanced courses have the added benefit of letting you earn college credit while you are still in high school. Advanced Placement (AP) and International Baccalaureate (IB) courses are offered at most high schools. At the end of the course, you have the opportunity to take an exam; if you do well, most colleges give you course credit for it.

In some states, dual credit courses let you earn high school and college credit. Some colleges have *articulation agreements* with local high schools that enable students to earn credit for certain courses. For example, you might receive college credit for taking a Culinary Arts course or an Introduction to Agriculture course.

Access to Electives

Not all schools have the resources to offer a wide range of electives. What if your school doesn't offer electives in areas that interest you?

★ Take a class outside of school.

★ Explore virtual or online learning options.

★ Read books on the subject.

★ Find a work-based opportunity to learn more about the subject.

What electives does your school district offer? Which do you find most interesting?

How can electives help you learn more about your skills and interests?

Learning Beyond High School

After you receive your high school diploma—the document that certifies that you successfully completed your high school course of study, you may enroll in college to continue your education or earn a professional degree. A degree is awarded by an institute such as a college or university when you complete the requirements of an academic or vocational program. Many careers require a minimum of an **associate's degree**—two years after high school—and many require a **bachelor's degree**—four years post high school (see the table on page 122). Professions such as doctor, lawyer, and teacher require additional education. But even if you don't go directly to college, you have opportunities to continue your education and develop career-related skills.

- You may enlist in the military.

- You may enroll in a technical or vocational program to earn a professional certificate for a career such as master electrician or certified nurse's aide (CNA).

- You may become an **apprentice**—someone who works with a professional to learn a skill or trade.

- You may find an on-the-job training program.

Can you think of ways to continue achieving your career goals even if you do not go directly from high school to college?

Military Service

When American students turn 18, they have the option of enlisting in the military. Other countries *require* citizens to serve in the military. Austria, Brazil, Denmark, Finland, Israel, Mexico, Norway, Russia, South Korea, Sweden, Switzerland, and Turkey are all countries that have mandatory military service requirements for citizens when they turn 18 years old. The U.S. Armed Forces are all-volunteer. That means citizens serve voluntarily, not because they have to.

Do you know anyone in the military? Do you know why they volunteered? Use the Internet or the library to learn more about the differences between mandatory—required—and voluntary military service. Which do you think is better? Write an essay explaining your point of view.

Planning for Postsecondary Education

Is a high school diploma enough education to land you the career of your choice? If not, you will want to start thinking about **postsecondary education** or school after high school. For most people, postsecondary education means college, but it can also include military training and apprenticeships.

Planning for postsecondary education involves:

■ Selecting a school or program

■ Making sure you have the necessary qualifications

■ Applying for admission

■ Obtaining financial aid

Myth I need to decide on my career before I can choose a college.

Truth Most students start college without knowing what they will do after graduation. Having career goals might help you select a college, but it is not necessary.

Researching Colleges

You can find information about different postsecondary opportunities online, in your school guidance center, and at the library. As you research the programs, ask yourself the following questions:

■ Does it offer a degree in my field of interest?

■ Where is it? Will I live at home or on campus? Is it in a city or a small town?

■ How many students are there? Will I be more comfortable in a small school or a large school?

■ How much does it cost? What is the annual **tuition**—cost of education? How much is **room and board**—the cost of meals and a dorm room? What is the cost of books? Are there lab fees or other additional fees?

■ Am I qualified for admission? Does my grade point average meet the school standards? Did I score high enough on the ACT or Scholastic Aptitude Test (SAT)—the standardized college entrance exams? Do I have the right co-curricular activities?

Career Tips

You can prepare for a future career by researching the skills you will need to receive a license or certification. Then, you can select a program that best meets your needs. Look for the information on industry association Web sites, or contact the government agency that awards certification.

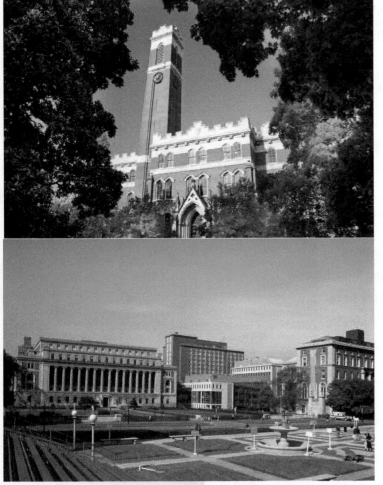

What type of college interests you?

Which College Is Right for Me?

There are more than 3,500 colleges in the United States. They range from technical colleges that award certification for a specific job or career, to universities that grant bachelors' and graduate degrees. Use the chart at the bottom of this page to compare postsecondary programs.

Applying to College

A college application form asks for information about yourself and your family. It has space for listing your co-curricular activities and for a personal essay that tells the college about you, your goals, and your abilities. In addition to the application form, you will also need:

- An official **transcript**, which is a record of the courses you took in high school and the grades you earned
- An official score report, which gives the results of the standard college entrance exams, such as the Scholastic Aptitude Test (SAT) or American College Test (ACT)
- Recommendations, which are forms that you ask one teacher and one counselor to fill out, describing your qualities as a student and a person
- Financial aid forms, which provide information about your ability to pay

	Technical College/ Vocational School	Community College/ Junior College	Four-Year College	University
Focus of program	Specialized training for particular occupation	Two-year degree in career area or academic course credit that transfers to a four-year college	Four-year degree; general academic courses plus focus on major	Four-year degree plus graduate programs
Length of program	Nine months to two years	Two years	Four years or more	Four years or more

Paying for College

Postsecondary education is expensive. Tuition alone may range from a few thousand dollars for a year at a community college to more than $50,000.00 at a private university. Add room and board, books, and other fees, and the amount seems overwhelming. While a few people might have enough money saved in a bank account, most must try to find other resources to pay.

- First, it is never too late to start saving, and no amount is too small. You can use a standard savings account or a special college savings account. College savings accounts usually have restrictions on how the funds can be used and may also have tax benefits.

- Most schools offer financial aid to qualified students. **Financial aid** is money to help you pay for education. It may be in the form of **grants**, which you do not have to repay, or **loans**, which you do have to repay along with interest. It may also include a **work-study program**, which is the opportunity to work while you are in school so you can earn money to help pay your costs.

- Schools and other organizations offer scholarships to qualified students. **Scholarships** are grants, so you do not have to repay them. Often, they are merit-based, which means you must meet specific academic or other criteria.

- You can take out a loan from a bank. Most education loans are supported by the government; others are funded by financial institutions such as banks.

Career Tips

Talk to your parents as soon as possible about the cost of college and how you and your family will pay for it. The conversation will make it easier for you to develop your academic plan.

Myth I will only be accepted to college if I earn all A grades.

Truth Colleges look at the complete student, not just the grades. Admission is also influenced by factors such as letters of recommendation and participation in co-curricular activities. As for grades, showing improvement and taking advanced courses that challenge you to work hard help make a positive impression.

Things to Do on a College Visit

You can take virtual college tours online, but the best way to get a sense of whether you would be happy at a college is to visit. On a college visit, you can:

✔ Tour the campus

✔ Talk to students

✔ Stay overnight in a dorm

✔ Eat meals in a dining hall

✔ Sit in on a class

✔ Talk to a professor

✔ Attend an information session

Career Profile: College Admissions Officer

Education & Training Career Cluster

What personal characteristics do you think would benefit a college admissions officer?

Job Summary

A college admissions officer is an education administrator responsible for making decisions about whether or not to admit an applicant. He or she spends a lot of time reading applications and discussing them with other admissions officers.

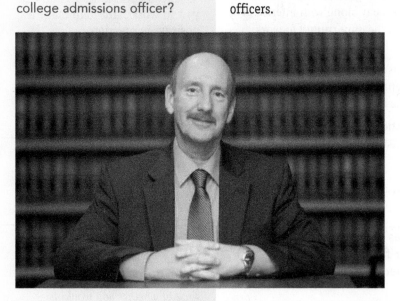

A college admissions officer represents the college on and off campus by leading information sessions or presentations for potential students and their families. Other duties may involve traveling to high schools to promote the college and conducting one-on-one interviews with applicants.

Admissions officers usually have a bachelor's degree and may obtain advanced degrees in college student affairs, counseling, or higher education administration. They benefit from courses in computers and statistics. Experience with computer systems is helpful because much of the application process is completed electronically.

Use the Internet, a library, or career center to research the responsibilities, education and training requirements, and salary range of a college admissions officer, or another education administrator position that interests you. Write a sample job description for the position.

Identifying Career-Related Opportunities for Students

Employers like to hire people who have experience. But most teens don't have much work experience. Some states have laws restricting the number of hours a teen can work, and many companies won't even hire people under 16.

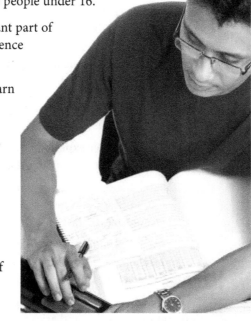

Gaining job experience is an important part of developing an academic plan. Experience serves two main purposes.

■ It gives you the opportunity to learn about a career first-hand. While you are working, you can find out if you enjoy the environment, feel comfortable with the responsibilities, and see a future for yourself in the industry.

■ It gives you the opportunity to build a work history that you can include on job and school applications. A **work history** is a list of jobs you have held from the past through the present, showing your experience as an employee.

You can explore career-related opportunities with the help of your parents, teachers, or school counselor. They can show you how to identify opportunities that relate to your skills, interests, and abilities, and how to apply for positions.

What Is an Internship?

An **internship** is a temporary job, usually for students. Internships may or may not pay a salary, but they provide other useful benefits. You have the opportunity to work in a field that interests you and to build skills. You meet people who might act as **references**—people who will provide a recommendation for you when you apply for jobs or school in the future.

■ An internship might be part-time after school. For example, you might intern at a law office two afternoons a week.

■ Many internships are in the summer. You might intern full-time at a television station during summer vacation.

■ Some internships are for a specific project or time period. You might intern at a company to develop a Web site or to digitize records. When the project is complete, the internship ends.

Usually you apply for an internship using a process similar to applying for a job. Your school counselor can help you find internship opportunities.

Volunteer!

Have you ever considered volunteering? Many volunteers are looking for ways to help others and contribute to their communities. But volunteering is also an opportunity to gain career-related experience, meet people who work in a field that interests you, and do something you can put on job and college applications.

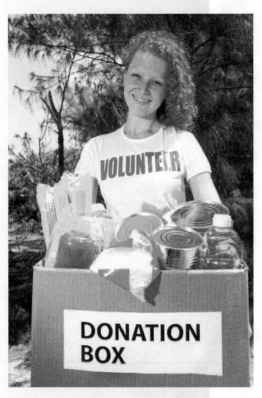

Have you ever volunteered? What job-related experience did you gain?

Volunteers are unpaid workers. Many volunteer positions are in service organizations, such as homeless shelters, health clinics, animal shelters, and food pantries. These organizations are usually short on money to pay workers, so they depend on volunteers to perform a full range of responsibilities. They need people to do everything from answering telephones to maintaining mailing lists to communicating directly with clients.

- If you are interested in the arts, you might volunteer as a **docent**—guide—at a museum.
- For health career experience, you might volunteer as a receptionist in a hospital, clinic, or nursing home.
- If you are considering a career in communications, you might volunteer as a production assistant at a public access cable station, public television station, or public radio station.
- If you are thinking about a career in recreation, many nature centers and state parks hire volunteers to run gift shops, clean, maintain trails, lead tours, and answer visitors' questions.

The opportunities for volunteering are nearly endless. Select an organization that interests you and ask what positions are available. The organization may even offer training.

Other Ways to Gain Experience

In addition to part-time jobs, internships, and volunteering, there are other ways you can gain valuable career-related experience.

- Mentoring programs pair experienced workers with students or less-experienced employees. The mentor acts as an advisor, providing advice, job contacts, and tutoring.
- Apprenticeships allow a worker to learn a trade by working with someone who has already mastered that trade. An apprenticeship combines on-the-job training and classroom education. Some trades require a worker to complete an apprenticeship in order to qualify for certification.
- Job shadowing allows you to follow an experienced worker through his or her work day to see the specific responsibilities and tasks required on the job.

■ School clubs and organizations offer opportunities to gain management and leadership skills.

■ Entrepreneurial thinking can help you create your own job and gain valuable experience. Are you patient, responsible, and good with kids? You can babysit. Do you love animals and exercise? You can walk dogs. Do you know how to play the guitar? You can teach others. If you have a skill or ability that other people will pay for, you can gain work experience by being an entrepreneur.

21st Century Learning

Julio's favorite subject in school is biology. He loves watching medical shows on television. He thinks he is quick to react and solve problems. He thinks he might be interested in a career in health care—specifically as an emergency medical technician. He knows he will need money for an education, so he starts looking for his first job.

His mother works as a dispatcher for the local emergency service center. She says they need temporary office help to catch up on filing. If Julio is interested, she can set up an interview with the office manager.

Julio thinks office work is boring. He would like to find a part-time job that relates directly to emergency medical care. He visits the hospital to see what part-time openings they have, but they tell him they don't hire anyone under 17. He contacts a medical clinic, but they say he needs training and experience.

What problems are facing Julio? Use your 21st Century Skills such as decision making, problem solving, goal setting, and critical thinking to help Julio decide what to do next. Write an ending to the story. Read it to the class, or form a small group and present it as a skit.

Case Study

Sophia moved to a new city three months ago and started at a new school. She thinks the work is much harder than at her old school, and she is having trouble keeping up. Sophia's teachers think she is not trying very hard. One told her that if she didn't improve, she would have to repeat the grade.

She misses her old school and her old friends. She has made only one good friend in her new neighborhood—Selena—but Selena goes to a different school. Sophia will be 16 in three months. She is thinking about getting a job and quitting school.

■ Do you think Sophia is right about getting a job and quitting school?

■ What problems does she have to deal with?

■ What can she do to solve the problems?

Web Extra

There are many Web sites that offer academic planning advice to students. One useful site is www.mycollegecalendar.org. Starting as a freshman—ninth grade—you can select your grade level for customized assistance with the college search and application process. Or you can use the links to research more general information, including preparing for standardized tests and identifying college majors.

Answer It!

1. **List at least three benefits of staying in school.**
2. List the three major learning styles.
3. **List three types of visual aids that might help visual learners.**
4. What is one study method that might help auditory learners remember information?
5. **What type of learner tends to gesture when speaking?**

6. What is a personal academic plan?
7. **What is the basic purpose of an academic plan?**
8. How can you build communications skills in school?
9. **List four items you need to apply to college.**
10. What are the two main purposes of gaining job experience?

Career-Ready Practices

Maya is interested in a career in recreation management. She was offered a volunteer position at a professional golf tournament at a golf course in her area. She would work as an assistant to the Volunteer Coordinator. The position would be part-time for three months, and then full-time for the week of the tournament. It does not pay any wages. In fact, Maya would have to pay $50.00 to buy a uniform! She has asked you to help her decide whether she should accept the position or not.

Working in teams of three or four, use the decision-making process to help Maya decide what to do. Analyze the situation, look for all possible options, and consider the consequences of each option. Make sure you consider the benefits of acquiring career-related skills. Career-ready individuals use volunteer opportunities to gain knowledge and experience. Likewise, they can strengthen their academic skills by applying them to real-world, workplace situations. Write a report or prepare a presentation that explains your advice to Maya. Be specific about the reasons for your decision.

Write Now

Most community service organizations welcome volunteers of all ages. Contact organizations in your community and ask them if they have positions for volunteers from your school. Create a directory of volunteer opportunities. Categorize the positions according to career cluster or pathway, and include a brief description. Make the directory available in your classroom, library, or career center, or post it on the school Web site.

Career Portfolio

Your career portfolio should include a personal academic plan. Working with your teacher, a counselor, or a family member, develop a personal academic plan that starts now and takes you through to high school graduation. If your school has a form for the plan, use it. Otherwise, use the Internet to locate a form that you might be able to use or adapt for your needs. Be sure to include your academic and career goals and an assessment of your skills, interests, and abilities. You can include your school report card or transcript, as well as a list of your co-curricular and community activities. Add the plan to your career portfolio.

Business Plan Project

Once you select an idea for your business, you can start defining the specific goals you will need to achieve to make the business successful. In your **Business Plan Project**, enter these five questions and your answers. Refer to the business plan in Appendix B to make sure you are on track.

1. What is the name of your business?

2. What is the purpose of your business? For example, what will you provide or sell.

3. How will your business satisfy customer needs?

4. What are your personal and educational goals?

5. What are your business goals?

8 Communicating with Others

Skills in This Chapter . . .

- **Using Written Communication**

- **Using Verbal Communication**

- **Developing Listening Skills**

- **Identifying Nonverbal Communication**

- **Recognizing Obstacles to Communication**

GETTING STARTED

Human beings are born with a desire to communicate. Over millions of years, we have developed many ways to communicate, from gestures and body language to pictures to verbal and written language. Communication is not only important in your daily life. It is also the key to career success. It prevents misunderstandings. It gives you a way to share ideas. It even makes it easier for you to appreciate and respect other's opinions.

At its most basic, communication is an exchange between a sender and a receiver. The sender transmits the message with a specific intent. The receiver interprets the message and responds. Being able to identify types of communication will help you master the art of communicating.

➤ Using a piece of paper, create a mind-map of the different forms of communication. At the center of your paper write the word "Communication" in a bubble. Branching from that word, make bubbles for as many different types of communication you can think of. Share your mind-map with the class and discuss how many types of communication the class identified.

NUMBERS GAME

Often, authors who write books are paid a royalty, which is an amount based on how many books are sold. That means that a percentage of the amount you pay for a book goes to the author, while the rest goes to the publisher.

The word *percent* means by the hundred. Each percent represents one part of 100; 100 percent equals the whole or all of something—no matter how much is in the whole.

To find the percentage of a number:

1. Change the percentage to a decimal by replacing the percent sign with a decimal point and moving the decimal point two spaces to the left.

2. Multiply the decimal by the number.

For example, to find 10% of 150:
    10% = .10
    150 × .10 = 15

If you are an author earning a 7% royalty, and a book costs $15.50, how much of that money will you earn, and how much will go to the publisher?

Using Written Communication

Many historians believe that the printing press, invented and built by Johannes Gutenberg in 1440, was the single most important invention of all time. Most agree that its invention marks the transition from the Middle Ages to the **Renaissance**, a period of artistic and intellectual revival in Europe. Why is that? The printing press made it easier and cheaper to create printed communications such as books and newspapers, and this in turn allowed for information to spread more easily. When people began to read books for themselves, they began to think for themselves.

Before the printing press, creating written communications was a time-consuming and costly business. Books were usually written by hand. Paper was scarce and expensive. Written communications were therefore rare. These days, you are surrounded by written communications, from the textbook in front of you to the notes in your notebook to the information written on your class whiteboard. Everyone now has the ability to use written communications to transfer ideas. This ability will be **integral**—necessary or essential—to almost any career you might enter.

Reading

Why do you think it is important to learn how to read? If you did not know how to read, you would have to learn all of your ideas from people speaking to you. Reading allows you to learn on your own. You can learn ideas that were developed and written down in the past, even centuries ago.

Reading will be essential for your career. Whether you want to be a doctor, car mechanic, astrophysicist, or firefighter, you will need to read every day you are on the job.

There are different ways to read, depending on what you are reading. You can read *passively* or *critically*.

- **Passive reading** is the kind of reading you do for entertainment, such as when you read a magazine or a comic book. In this kind of reading, you are just taking in information or following the plot.

- When you read critically, you take time to really think about what is written and why. **Critical reading** happens when you are actively engaging the subject as you read.

The difference between passive and critical reading is like the difference between listening to your friend talk and having a debate with her. When you read critically, you are having a debate with the text. Here are the steps to critical reading:

■ Determine the best reading strategy for the text. This means that you need to figure out whether to skim the text, read closely for detail, or read for meaning or critical analysis.

■ As you read, stop and think about what is being said and try to put it in your own words or rephrase it from your own point of view.

■ Take notes while you're reading to make sure you are understanding and remembering the main points.

Money Madne$$

You find two jobs that you think you would be qualified for. One pays an annual salary of $57,000.00, with no bonus. The other pays $45,000.00, but if you meet all goals set by your employer, you can earn a bonus equal to 15% of your annual salary. Which job would you rather have? What factors other than pay might influence your decision?

Writing

Like peanut butter and jelly, reading and writing go together. In fact, you cannot do critical reading without also writing. But not all writing is the kind you do in English or Creative Writing class. Jotting down notes and scribbling a message to a friend also count as writing.

Writing is something you get better at with practice. You can think of words as being like tools. Writers who are just learning to write use simple words to communicate their ideas, just as beginning builders start with basic tools to put together small projects. The more words you learn and the more you learn how to put them together, the bigger the projects you can build.

Just like learning any skill, learning to write is an ongoing process. You should always expect to get better, and accept **constructive criticism**—suggestions from others on how to improve your writing—and consider how it can make you a better writer.

What are the benefits and drawbacks of having a career as a writer?

What If You Couldn't Read?

In this country, most—but not all—people learn to read as children. What if you were an adult and you couldn't read?

★ You could not get a driving license, because you would not be able to read the written part of the license test.

★ You could pick out items at the grocery store, but you would not be able to read the nutritional information and you might have trouble comparing pricing.

★ You would have to depend on other people to tell you what was written in instructional manuals and brochures.

★ The Internet, the largest source of information on the planet, would be relatively useless to you, since it is mostly text-based.

Can you think of any more reasons why knowing how to read is important in modern life?

How Do You React to Constructive Criticism?

Even the best writers in the world have editors. And this means that writers accept and use constructive criticism in developing their writing. How do you respond to constructive criticism?

- 👎 You ignore it, because you think your way is best.

- 👎 You get angry and assume that the constructive criticism is meant to hurt you personally.

- 👎 You accept it all without thinking hard about whether it is right or not.

- 👍 You take each suggestion as a part of the writing process, not a personal attack.

- 👍 You consider each criticism one by one and put yourself in the shoes of your editor.

- 👍 You accept the criticisms that make the most sense to you, revise your writing, and resubmit to your editor, with explanations of which criticisms you agreed with, which you did not, and why.

What do you think are other ways that constructive criticism can be taken? List three reasons why it is important for any piece of writing.

Like reading, writing well will be essential in almost any career you choose. Even before you begin work at a job, you will usually have to write three important documents:

- Applying to most jobs requires submitting a resume. You write a resume to explain your skills, tell where you went to school, share information about your other talents, and give the names of references—people who can verify your experience.

- When you submit a resume, you usually also submit a cover letter. A **cover letter** is a short one-page summary of who you are, why you are applying for the job, and why you are the best person for it.

- After you have had an interview, you should submit a follow-up letter to emphasize your continued interest in the job and review why you would be the best candidate for the job.

While you are employed, you may have regular writing tasks such as preparing letters to clients, creating written reports for customers, or writing memos to your co-workers. You might also have to write a letter of resignation, if you have decided to change from one job or career to another. This is a letter that expresses your reasons for leaving and your appreciation for your former employer.

Career Trend

In an increasingly digital age, distributing written information has never been easier. This means that there are more opportunities for careers in writing. Blogging and self-publishing are two great examples of this.

Using Verbal Communication

You were born with the ability to learn how to speak and understand others. This ability to use and understand language is something that all human beings have, and it is something that makes us unique among all other animals on the planet.

Of course, just because you know how to talk does not mean you know how to speak *well*. Even if you were the smartest person in the world, it would be very hard for you to get the career you want if others did not understand you.

Mastering the art of verbal communication is a very important part of getting the career you want, because you will have to use this skill to convince an employer to hire you. You will also have to use verbal communication every day on your job, no matter what it is.

Using the Communication Process

You can communicate effectively by using a six-step process:

1. *Be clear.* The receiver is more likely to get your message if you deliver it in a way he or she can understand. Speak slowly. Consider who you are talking to. You probably use different language when you talk to a teacher than when you talk to a friend. You might even use a completely different type of communication. For example, you probably talk to your teacher face to face, but you might text your friend.

2. *Be personal.* Use the other person's name so there's no doubt who you are talking to. Use an "I" statement—a statement that starts with the word "I"—to frame the statement in terms of you and your goals. An "I" statement indicates that you are taking responsibility for your thoughts and feelings. It helps the receiver understand your point of view and respond to you.

3. *Be positive.* Phrase your message in positive terms. Say what you want, not what you don't want. For example, say, "I want to leave at 3:30," instead of saying, "I don't want to leave at 4:00."

4. *Get to the point.* Follow the "I" statement with an explanation of the message you are sending. Explain how or why you feel a certain way, or how or why you think a certain thing. For example, say, "I want to leave at 3:30. I think that will give us enough time to get there without having to rush."

5. *Listen to the response.* Pay attention and use active listening techniques to make sure you hear the response.

6. *Think before you respond.* Make sure you understand the message. Repeat it, if necessary, and ask questions for clarification. Use critical thinking to make sure you are not letting emotions and preconceived ideas get in the way.

Different Types of Verbal Communication

The way you speak can determine the outcome of a conversation. Which of these examples of verbal communication is more likely to have a positive conclusion? Why?

As you already know, the ways you speak to your friends, your parents, your teachers, or your siblings differ greatly. For instance, you might get in trouble with your teachers if you spoke with them as if they were your friends. On the other hand, speaking to your friends as if they were your teachers wouldn't be any fun.

Just as you use different types of verbal communication when speaking to your friends and your parents, you use different types of verbal communication when speaking to people with whom you relate on the job, such as your boss, your co-workers, your customers, and your **subordinates**—the people you supervise.

■ Your boss has a higher rank in the company than you do and has control over your job. When communicating with a boss, you usually use a formal style of verbal communication. You show **deference**—courteous regard or respect—by using her title and refraining from jokes or casual remarks you might use with a friend. You must also recognize that your boss has the final say on most matters, and so you must know when to agree with her decisions, even if you disagree with them personally.

■ Your co-workers, or **colleagues**, have the same rank in the company that you do. This does not mean that you should joke around with them as you do with your friends. It also does not mean you should use the same style of verbal communication you would use with your boss. You can speak to them more casually.

■ Your customers are the source of your business. When communicating with customers, remember the old saying, "the customer is always right." This means that in order to be successful, you must respect your customers and speak with them positively.

■ If you supervise others in the company, you communicate with them using the respect that is due to any worker. You can also use an assertive or positive style of verbal communication, so that they know exactly what is expected of them.

Not only is what you say important, but so is how you say it. In addition to the different ways you can verbally communicate with others in the workplace, you can use different tones to make your meaning clear. These include:

■ Assertive speech, which includes action verbs such as "should," "does," and "will."

■ Aggressive speech, which you should avoid in the workplace, since it can lead to arguments or hurt feelings. An example of aggressive speech would be, "You better help me now!"

■ Passive speech, which is usually best to use when you also want to show respect or deference. Examples of passive speech include words such as "can," "might," and "could."

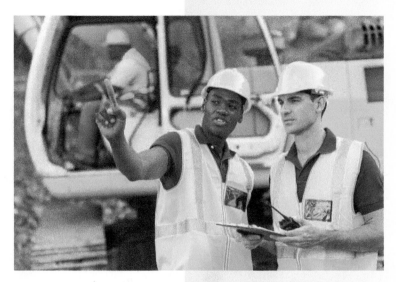

What do you think it takes to be an effective communicator?

21st Century Learning

CAREER COUNSEL

Laura has an after-school job at a local coffee shop. The job allows her to earn some extra money and interact with different people. Her co-workers are all very nice and there are even a few regular customers whom she sees every day. She really enjoys having the extra spending money and not having to ask her parents for an allowance.

But Laura is not happy. She feels her boss does not respect her. His tone of voice is usually harsh and aggressive. He makes sarcastic remarks about her work. And he has asked her to work more hours, even though Laura is in school and has many other responsibilities besides work. Even though Laura likes everything about her job except her boss, she is thinking about quitting.

What problems are facing Laura? What can she do to fix them? Use your 21st Century Skills such as identifying different types of communication, problem solving, and critical thinking to help Laura. Write an ending to the story. Read it to the class, or form a small group and present it as a skit.

How Verbal Communication Helps You Think

There is a difference between speaking out loud and thinking to ourselves. How might speaking without thinking cause problems or conflict?

Myth All debates must be personal and must involve two passionate advocates who oppose each other.

Truth Debating can be a productive way to solve a difficult problem, as long as both sides keep in mind that they are actually on the same team!

Often, the best way to think something through is to talk about it with someone else. Why is that? The answer is that one mind is only so powerful, but two minds can think of twice as much. In other words, when you take a difficult problem and talk about it with someone else, you are doubling the brainpower devoted to solving it. And sometimes, having to explain something to someone else helps you understand it yourself.

Talking or debating about something is a great way to learn. But this strategy can be an even better way to problem solve in the workplace.

■ Talking critically about a difficult problem is not so different from thinking critically about a difficult problem. One benefit of talking over a problem with someone is that you get a different perspective from the other person.

■ Using verbal communication to problem-solve allows you to take sides and debate the problem. You may even take the position of being **the devil's advocate**. This is a label used to describe taking a position you do not necessarily agree with, but pretending you do for the sake of argument. Playing, or having someone play, the devil's advocate can be a powerful way to work through a difficult problem.

■ Using verbal communication to help you think and problem-solve only works if you strike a balance between caring too much or too little about the topic under debate. You must be actively engaged in order to move the debate along. But you must not get too passionate about your side. After all, you are both striving towards the same goal, which is to solve your problem!

Steps to Becoming a Great Speaker

Great speakers are rare and easy to recognize. Many of our U.S. presidents were great speakers. Why is that? Because being able to communicate is one of the most important skills needed in a career in politics. The best among the political communicators often become president.

You don't have to be the president to be an expert at using verbal communication. Here are a few steps on the way to becoming a great speaker.

■ It is said that great speakers "know their audience." But do you know what this actually means? It means you must know what your audience wants to hear. It also means that you must be considerate of the person (or persons) you are speaking to. What the president says to the American people—and how he says it—is usually different in tone and content from what he might say to a foreign leader.

■ You must know what you are talking about. This seems obvious, but it actually takes a lot of work. Being a great speaker means that before you speak, you take the time to really consider what you say, what it means, and how it will be received. This means thinking before you speak.

■ Never stop learning! The greatest speakers would all admit that they are always learning. You might sometimes think that you have learned all you need to know on a certain topic. But if you keep an open mind, you might find that you learn something new every day. The ability to keep an open mind and continually learn new things can make you not only a better speaker, but a better person as well.

Why is being a great speaker an important skill for a career in politics?

Career Profile: Politician

Government & Public Administration Career Cluster

Job Summary

Whether they are local, regional, statewide, or national, politicians are representatives of some group of people. What can you expect of a career in politics? Since democracy involves citizens voting for their representatives, you can expect to talk with a lot of people. This means you must communicate well, not only in speaking but in writing.

A career in politics can be very rewarding. Politicians speak and act on behalf of all those who they represent. Politicians are usually well respected. Keep in mind, however, that the job is always hard work!

Use the Internet, a library, or career center to research the responsibilities, education and training requirements, and salary range for a career in politics. Then, imagine you are running for a political position. Use a word processor to write a campaign speech announcing that you are running and why.

Communication in and out of the Workplace

Being an effective verbal communicator is essential to being good at your job. Here are some characteristics of a good communicator.

✔ You avoid passive communication when speaking.

✔ You do not automatically treat your co-workers as your friends. You speak with them with the degree of respect and formality that is common in a workplace.

✔ You speak to your superiors with deference.

✔ Your tone of voice is appropriate for your audience. This means that you do not use aggressive speech when assertive speech is best.

Developing Listening Skills

Consider the question, "If a tree falls in the woods and no one is there to hear it, does it make a sound?" Do you think the answer is yes or no? In fact, the answer depends on how you define "sound." But the question raises an important point. In verbal communication, half of the process is speaking. The other half is hearing, or listening. It may surprise you to learn that there is a difference between hearing and listening.

The Difference Between Hearing and Listening

How can listening be different from hearing? Sound is all around us, all the time, so we often cannot help hearing sounds. It may even seem unavoidable to hear certain people speak. But there is an important difference between merely hearing and actively listening. That difference is up to you. It depends on how much you are thinking about what you are hearing. If you are really thinking, considering, and engaged with the words you hear, then you are actively listening. If, on the other hand, the words you hear go into your head and you soon forget them, then you are merely hearing.

A good way to consider the difference is to think of hearing as *passive* and listening as *active*. In other words, "hearing" is something that happens to you. You cannot avoid hearing, unless you plug or cover your ears. On the other hand, listening is something you actually do. It involves thinking about what you are hearing.

Active listening is an important part of effective communication. When you are an active listener, you pay attention to the speaker and make sure you hear and understand the message. Active listening is also a sign of respect. It shows you are willing to communicate and that you care about the speaker and the message. When you listen actively, the other person is more likely to listen when you speak, too.

Which group of students is listening, and which is hearing?

Listening on the Job

How is listening relevant to your career? No matter if you are a boss, a subordinate, or a co-worker, you will need to listen at some point. The better you are at it, the more successful you will be. Here are a few reasons why:

■ Good listeners often pick up **subtle**—unmentioned or implied—cues in conversation. This means that a person's tone of voice or his word choice tell you more about what he thinks than what he says. In your career, you might have a great advantage if you can pick up these clues.

■ Good listeners are often more trusted than bad listeners. If you listen carefully to what people tell you, you deliver the message that they are important to you. They are more likely to trust you and like you.

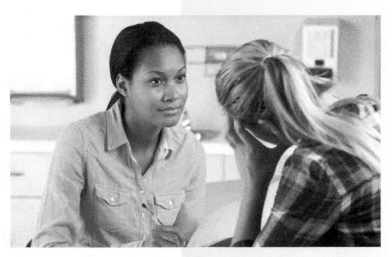

Can you think of a career in which your primary responsibility is listening?

■ Being a good listener will make you a better worker. When you listen carefully to instructions, for example, you are more likely to be able to carry out your tasks without having to be reminded what to do. You are able to act to resolve problems that people tell you about so that your workplace is a more positive environment.

Active Listening Skills

Practice your active listening skills by working in groups of three.

■ One person will be the active listener

■ One person will discuss a topic of interest (such as a planned vacation, a new job, or an upcoming college visit)

■ The third person will observe to see if the active listener is using active listening skills

Take turns playing each role. Develop a list of the active skills your group members applied and which ones they didn't.

Share your list with the rest of the class. As a group, discuss how active listening can make you a more powerful communicator.

Skills for Active Listening

Use these skills to be an active listener:

✔ Show interest using eye contact and positive nonverbal messages.

✔ Let the other person finish speaking before you respond.

✔ Ignore distractions such as cell phones and other people.

✔ Set your preconceived opinions and emotions aside.

✔ Repeat the message that you hear out loud to make sure you received it correctly.

Identifying Nonverbal Communication

Besides reading, writing, and speaking, what other types of communication are there? Two other important ways of communicating are sign language and body language.

Did you know that sign language is just as powerful as spoken language? You can communicate everything you would with speech using sign language, without saying a word. Using sign language requires that all parties in the conversation know how to understand the various signs. This problem is often solved using sign language interpreters who sign as someone is speaking to deliver spoken messages to those who cannot hear them.

Body language is a different type of nonverbal communication that everyone uses every day, sometimes without knowing it. Did you ever notice that if you didn't do your homework somehow your teacher knows it and calls on you anyway? Your body language may be giving you away. Body language can be either positive or negative. It can show you are confident and prepared, or that you are unsure or afraid.

Finally, one other way to communicate without speaking or writing is to use **visual aids**—pictures, graphs, charts, or anything without words that conveys your ideas. Visual aids can often deliver a clearer or more easily understood message than written or verbal communication.

Cross-Cultural Communications

Nonverbal communications can be tricky when you are communicating with people from different cultures. Personal space, touching, and gestures frequently mean different things depending on where in the world you live.

For instance, in the United States we beckon one another by crooking our index finger. In Asian cultures, that gesture is used to call dogs and other animals and is considered insulting if used to a person.

Do you know of any other types of communication that mean different things to different people? Can you find examples on the Internet? Make a poster that shows an example and display it in your classroom.

Positive Body Language

Have you ever come away from a conversation feeling good about how you communicated with the other person? Chances are that most of your good feeling was caused by what she said. But equally important is how she said it. Along with verbal cues such as a pleasant tone of voice, you may have picked up other important cues from that person's body language. Did he or she smile during the conversation or look you in the eye without staring intently? These are both aspects of positive body language. Here are some other ways you can communicate using positive body language.

- *Watch your posture.* Stand up and sit straight without bending backward, and keep your shoulders square with the person to whom you are speaking. If sitting, you may lean slightly forward to show that you are interested in what the other person has to say.

- *Open arms communicate an open mind.* Standing or sitting with your arms at your sides or in front of you indicates that you are open and receptive to your conversation partner's ideas.

- *Active hand gestures indicate active debate.* This means that you move your hands to show and demonstrate ideas. Why is this important? Because it shows that you are actively engaged in the conversation, not just passively hearing and responding.

- *Maintain adequate eye contact.* This does not mean you must lock eyes with the person you are speaking with at all times. It does mean that you must at least meet his eyes when he looks at you.

In your career, you will probably encounter situations where positive body language will serve you well. Calming an upset customer and reassuring a nervous co-worker are two situations when positive body language can help you succeed.

How can you use body language to make a positive impression when you are communicating?

Negative Body Language

Just as positive body language can affect your interactions with others, so too can negative body language. Negative body language can portray you as hostile, combative, and unwilling. Here are some examples of negative body language.

- *Avoid unnecessary movements.* Don't repeatedly tap your fingers or a foot, scratch, put your head down on your desk, or look out the window. These actions give the impression you are impatient or uninterested.

- *Avoid closed or folded arms.* When you close your arms across your chest, you signal that your mind is closed to new ideas.

■ *Don't stare intently.* While you should make eye contact with the person to whom you are speaking, you should not stare a long time. A prolonged stare may seem threatening to another person.

■ *Don't signal that you've stopped paying attention.* Failing to maintain some eye contact and letting your eyes wander are telltale signs that you are no longer paying attention.

Being aware of and avoiding negative body language will make you a far more effective communicator.

Career Tips

Practice being a positive body language communicator. Stand in front of a mirror and act as if you are speaking with another person. Look at how you stand, where your arms fall, and what your body language says. Mastering of your body language can be your secret weapon in getting the career you want!

Using Visual Aids

Can you think of a time when pictures are more effective than words?

Have you ever heard the expression, "A picture is worth a thousand words"? Do you know what that means? Not only pictures, but any **graphical representation**—or way of conveying information without words—can be a great way of communicating ideas without saying them directly. And there are times when this is the best way to communicate. For instance, visual aids can sometimes make us see ideas that would be difficult to explain otherwise. Graphs and charts are excellent examples of this.

Graphical representations can also make us feel emotions in ways words sometimes cannot. For instance, reading a description of the first moon landing might make you think the achievement was interesting and worthwhile, but actually seeing a picture of it can make you well up with national pride.

In your career, you might sometimes find that using visual aids will be the most effective way to communicate. This includes putting a picture or graph in your presentation, making a chart instead of describing a trend in your data set, or drawing a picture to explain what you are talking about. Visual aids are often helpful in communicating ideas that you have so far been unsuccessful at communicating with words.

The possibilities for using visual aids are endless. Can you think of other examples of when using a visual aid is the best way to communicate?

Recognizing Obstacles to Communication

Because human beings are unique individuals, not everyone communicates in the same way. Differences in culture, values, and personal characteristics can affect communication, making it difficult for even the best communicators to get their message across.

The best approach for solving this problem is to learn to recognize obstacles to communication. You can then try to avoid or overcome them by changing the way you communicate. Being sensitive to communication obstacles, and being able to avoid problems caused by miscommunication, will make you a great candidate in any career field.

Tech Connect

Modern technology is helping people overcome obstacles to communication more than ever before. People with disabilities often have special challenges to overcome. Using technology such as voice-recognition software, which converts spoken words to digital text, many disabled individuals can communicate with ease.

Use the Internet to find out more about the ways modern technology helps us overcome obstacles to communication. Then, use your computer to prepare a list of three examples, including links to the research you have done.

Communication Skills for the Entrepreneur

While large companies have human resources departments to manage the process of hiring new employees, entrepreneurs often must handle advertising, interviewing, and hiring on their own. What communication skills do you think an entrepreneur might need to successfully identify and hire a suitable employee? What communication skills do you think an entrepreneur might look for in an employee? Create a poster with a T-chart that shows communication skills that are important for the entrepreneur and the employee. Discuss how these are different and similar.

Recognizing Communication Barriers

Have you ever felt there was a barrier between you and the person you are speaking with? How could you overcome this problem?

In the workplace as in school, people are all different. A good word for this is **diversity**, which means an environment that includes variety, such as people of different ages, cultural backgrounds, and race. Diversity is generally a good thing. Diversity allows for different ideas and opinions. You can learn from people who are different from you, because they can bring different perspectives to your attention.

However, diversity can also bring special challenges to communication. When people have ideas and opinions different from yours, it can sometimes be difficult for you to communicate with them. The trick is to figure this out before your miscommunication becomes a problem.

Here are some common differences in communication that can become obstacles to effective communication. We call these differences **communication barriers**, because they can sometimes be like a wall between you and the person you are trying to communicate with.

▪ *Language barriers.* When two people who have different native tongues try to communicate in a single language, problems may arise if one person does not understand the language well enough.

▪ *Cultural barriers.* People of different cultures may have differing expectations or express themselves in different ways. Many cultures avoid direct eye contact as a sign of respect, for example, whereas direct eye contact is considered a sign of active listening in the United States.

▪ *Gender barriers.* Women and men communicate in different ways. For example, men may communicate by means of short statements and facts, while women often prefer more detail and the "big picture." This means that there can sometimes be problems when men and women do not recognize their different communication styles.

▪ *Value/belief barriers.* You do not have to be from a different culture to have a different set of values or beliefs. Even though the United States is a single culture, it is also a diverse country. This means that barriers can arise when people do not have the same ideas about morality, religion, and other life issues. Differences of opinion are perfectly fine, but sometimes these differences cause problems in communication.

Remember that in all cases of communication barriers, it is not about who is right and who is wrong. Rather, it is about recognizing and accepting diversity for what it is. You will confront some or all of these barriers. If you can recognize them, then you can take steps to resolve or avoid them.

Overcoming Miscommunication

Once you recognize that there is a communication barrier, you can try to overcome it. One method is to change the tone of voice you are using. For instance, a gender barrier might arise from too aggressive a tone of voice in a conversation between you and someone of the opposite gender. Changing your tone of voice to be more neutral or passive can overcome the barrier.

Another way to overcome a communication barrier is to change your body language. As you learned already, negative body language can turn a conversation sour. But it can also create a communication barrier. For instance, language barriers can be made even worse by negative body language. On the other hand, positive body language can often help you get your point across, even when there is a language barrier.

Finally, value/belief barriers present problems for communication, because they often arise from issues that people usually feel very passionate about. In cases where you recognize a value/belief barrier, the best way to overcome it is to stop the conversation, take a step back, and re-evaluate. Even when two people have opposing beliefs, there may be some common ground on which they can agree. A good way to overcome a value/belief barrier is to figure out what this common ground is and restart the conversation from there.

Do you go to school with people whose families are from different cultural backgrounds? Are there certain aspects of communicating that might seem inappropriate to one culture, but not another?

Case Study

Peter works for a large international clothing chain. He is in charge of offices all over the world. This means that he must go to meetings with people from different countries who speak different languages, have different cultural expectations, and have different values and beliefs.

One of the more difficult annual meetings Peter must attend takes place in a country that is very different from the United States. At this meeting, Peter must give a presentation that explains the sales for the year and discusses where the company is heading in the future.

Peter does not believe he is a good speaker. Although he always prepares a draft of his presentation, he never asks anyone to review it because he doesn't want any more criticism. In years past, he has simply stood at the front of the meeting and spoken, with his hands in his pockets. These meetings have not gone well. This year, Peter is dreading having to present at the meeting.

■ What are the reasons that Peter's past presentations have not gone well? Prepare a list with at least five reasons that you could give to Peter.

■ What advice can you give Peter on getting help with his speech in advance?

■ How can Peter make his presentation more interesting?

■ What are some of the ways Peter can avoid communication barriers that arise from the meeting that takes place in a culture so different from Peter's?

■ How can Peter best get the difficult sales information across?

Web Extra

The Internet is the world's biggest forum for communication. Social network sites such as Facebook.com, Twitter.com, and Pinterest.com are places where people from all over the world communicate with one another. And the best part is, this communication comes in all forms: written, verbal, visual, etc. With a parent, teacher, or librarian, go to one of these social network sites. Find one example of positive and one example of negative communication. These examples can be in any of the communication forms. Then, make a short report on your findings and why they were positive and negative.

Answer It!

1. Why is good communication key to your success in finding a career?

2. Why is Gutenberg's printing press considered by many to be the most important invention of all time?

3. What are two different ways to read?

4. Why do we say that reading and writing go hand-in-hand?

5. List three types of documents you will write while you search for a job.

6. Why is it a good idea to speak with deference to your boss?

7. Why can talking about a difficult problem with another person sometimes help solve the problem better than just thinking about it alone?

8. What is the difference between hearing and listening?

9. When is it a good idea to use a visual aid to communicate?

10. How can different cultures create a problem for communicating?

Career-Ready Practices ----------

Imagine that your school is planning on changing the school hours to start much later in the morning and go until later in the afternoon/evening. Divide into groups of eight to ten people to debate this issue.

There will likely be some in your group who are for this and some who are against it. Split into two sides along these lines. Make the groups even. Then, the group that was for your school changing the hours will argue that the hours should not change. The group that was against the change will argue in favor of it. Make sure you pay attention to your tone and presentation skills as you share your opinions. Career-ready individuals are skilled at interacting with others and articulating ideas. They speak clearly and with purpose.

Use this debate to make a list of pros and cons. Which side won? As a class, compare the outcomes for each group.

Write Now

You are applying for a job as a teacher in a school like yours. You consider yourself to be well qualified for the job. Write a four-paragraph cover letter that expresses your interest in becoming a teacher. In the first paragraph, introduce yourself and express your desire to apply for a job. Be specific about the job you are applying for, including what subject you want to teach. In the second paragraph, list your qualifications and explain why they make you the best candidate for the job. In the third paragraph, include some specifics about the school, the subject, and your teaching style. In the fourth paragraph, summarize your interest, your qualifications, and the reasons why you should be hired. Try to summarize your work without repeating anything.

Submit your cover letter to your teacher, and she will act as your potential employer and let you know if you got the job.

Career Portfolio

Developing strong communication skills will help you find, get, and keep a job. Do you have strong communication skills? Are there some you could work to improve? Make a table listing different communication skills, and rank your strength in each on a scale of 1 to 10—with 1 being weak and 10 being strong. Make a written plan for improving the communication skills you consider to be the weakest, and for practicing those you consider strong. Add the table and the plan to your career portfolio.

It is also a good idea to add documents that illustrate your successful communication skills. For example, you might include a list of skill competencies you have achieved; licenses or certificates you have obtained; any awards or scholarships you have received; projects you have completed as a volunteer or member of a career and technical student organization; and an evaluation from a teacher. Prepare a multimedia presentation of your portfolio to deliver to the class, a teacher, a career counselor, or an employer to demonstrate your effective communication skills.

Business Plan Project

Being able to communicate your business ideas is an important entrepreneurial skill. You will need to convey your message to different types of people, such as potential investors, customers, and employees. In your **Business Plan Project**, write a script that describes your business to a friend. Then, write a second script that describes your business to a potential client. Read both scripts out loud to a partner and listen to your partner's scripts. Try to identify which script is for the friend and which is for the client. Discuss the differences and similarities between the two.

9 Building Relationships

Skills in This Chapter . . .

- **Relating to Others**
- **Building Team Relationships**
- **Managing Conflict**

GETTING STARTED

People are naturally social. We live in groups, socialize in groups, and work in groups. Like success in school, career success has a lot to do with your ability to get along with the people around you. When we have healthy relationships with other people, we are happier than when we have unhealthy relationships. We can use skills such as decision making, problem solving, and—most of all—communicating to build healthy relationships with all the people in our lives.

➤ Write down one person in each area of your life—family, school, peers, community, and work if you have a job. Next to the name, write whether you think the relationship you have with that person is healthy or unhealthy, and list at least one reason why. As a class, discuss the reasons you think a relationship is healthy or unhealthy.

Relating to Others

Whenever you interact with someone else, you are **relating**. Relating includes the way you communicate and behave when you are together. You might be friendly, you might be mean, or you might be competitive.

A **relationship** is a connection or association between two or more people. It describes the way you relate. You have personal relationships with people such as family and friends, but you also have relationships with others—a stranger who bumps into you and apologizes or the mail carrier who delivers your mail.

Developing a healthy relationship with someone contributes to your well-being. It is satisfying and makes you feel good. When a relationship is unsatisfying, it can interfere with your well-being. Recognizing factors that contribute to healthy relationships can help you succeed in all areas of your life.

Relating to People at Work

Relationships you build at work—like relationships you build at school or at home—can have a major impact on your overall well-being.

- You have relationships with your co-workers and your supervisor. As a team, you work together to achieve common goals. For example, you might work as a flight attendant. The other members of the flight crew are on your team. You work together to make sure that you depart on time and arrive safely.

- You may also have relationships with customers or clients. You work to provide them with goods or services that satisfy their needs. The passengers are your customers. You work to provide them with information about the flight, drinks or snacks, and other things to make them comfortable.

You may have relationships with other people in your work environment, such as the baggage handlers and cleaning crew. Knowing how to get along and avoid or solve conflicts is an important part of your career success. You can start building these skills today by how you build relationships with other students and teachers in your school or how you relate to family members.

Building Relationships in Your Own Business

Entrepreneurs are more involved in the day-to-day operations of their business than owners and managers are at a large company. Entrepreneurs interact with their employees on a regular basis and must be able to build relationships with everyone. Often, the success of the start-up business depends on the entrepreneur's ability to communicate, resolve conflict, and work together with his or her employees. How do you think building relationships is different at a small start-up company than at a large corporation?

Career Tips

Being nice is a good way to start developing positive relationships with people in all areas of your life. For example, if you offer to help a co-worker or classmate, others will recognize you as supportive. If you compliment or praise someone's work or effort, they will recognize you as appreciative.

Qualities of a Healthy Relationship

A relationship is healthy and functional if both parties give and receive what they need. A healthy personal relationship has these important characteristics:

- Respect
- Trust
- Honesty
- Responsibility
- Open communication

Relationships that are full of conflict or are not satisfying are unhealthy, or **dysfunctional**—they are not working correctly. One way to tell if a relationship is unhealthy is that you are unhappy. You might not feel respect or trust for the other person, or you might fight a lot.

What can you do if you have an unhealthy relationship with your employer?

A Two-Way Street

All relationships are a two-way street. That means both people involved share the responsibility of keeping the relationship healthy.

When you have a relationship with someone, you exchange resources. That means you give and take. For example, you might exchange respect and support with co-workers. You might give advice to customers in exchange for money. You might give labor—your work—to your employer in exchange for salary and benefits.

When the exchange is equal—you give as much as you receive—both people are satisfied. When the exchange is unequal—you are either giving or receiving more than the other person—it may lead to problems.

- If you don't have time to help your co-worker with a project, but you expect her to help you, you are receiving more from the relationship than you are giving.

- If your employer asks you to work late but does not pay you for the additional hours, you are giving more to the relationship than you are receiving.

Communicate, Communicate, Communicate!

Effective communication is the foundation for a healthy relationship. When you communicate openly and honestly, you understand each other. You avoid misunderstandings.

- When you listen and respond to someone, you show respect.
- When you share your thoughts and opinions, you show trust.
- When you honor a confidence—listen to someone's private thoughts without telling anyone else—you show that you are trustworthy.
- When you are willing to discuss differences, you show openness.

Using communication to build a healthy relationship helps you enjoy being with other people, as well as be more productive at work. You are more likely to be comfortable and happy when you are with people who you respect and trust, and who respect and trust you.

NUMBERS GAME

How are decisions made in teams? Sometimes, the leader makes decisions, taking the suggestions and ideas of the team members into consideration. Another method of team decision making is majority rule, which means the decision is made based on what most people want. A **majority** is a greater number or part. For example, if there are eight people on a team, and five prefer the color pink while three prefer the color yellow, the group preferring pink is the majority. The opposite of majority is **minority**—the lesser number or part. In this example, the group preferring the color yellow is the minority.

- If a team consists of ten people, how many need to agree to make a majority?
- What if the team consists of eleven?

Of course, when there is an even number of people in a group, there might be a tie. How might you make a decision if there is a tie?

Expecting Too Much

Expecting too much means you are taking more than you are giving. You are too needy—you need more resources than you give in order to feel satisfied with the relationship. What are the consequences of expecting too much from a relationship, compared with expecting equality?

- 👎 You expect others to listen to you complain all the time.
- 👎 You expect others to provide constant reassurance about your appearance, personality, and abilities.
- 👎 You expect others to put up with you even when you are dishonest, irresponsible, or disrespectful.
- 👎 You expect others to share your values and standards.
- 👍 You expect to exchange resources equally and to give as much as you receive.

How can a positive attitude and high self-esteem help you build healthy relationships at work?

Building Team Relationships

A **team** is a group of two or more people who work together to achieve a common goal. When you are part of a team, you have access to all the knowledge, experience, and abilities of your teammates. Together you can have more ideas, achieve more goals, and solve more problems. A healthy relationship as a team member contributes to your well-being. Your teammates respect you and value your contribution to their success.

A successful team relationship depends on all team members working together. They rely on each other. They trust one another. If one team member does not do his or her share, the entire team suffers.

Career Trend

More and more companies today organize their employees into teams made up of people from different departments. For example, a team might include representatives from research, development, design, marketing, and finance. The goal is to bring different thoughts and ideas together from the start to produce higher quality products and services.

Challenges of Teamwork

The challenges of a team relationship come from having different people working together. Even if everyone agrees on a common goal, they may not agree on how to achieve that goal. Your friends might agree to celebrate the end of the school year together, but:

■ Some of you might want to go to the lake.

■ Some might want to play Frisbee in the park.

■ Some might want to have a picnic.

To be successful, a team needs all members to agree about how to achieve your goal. To achieve agreement, teams must be able to communicate and negotiate, which means to give and take until you find a solution that satisfies everyone. They must also be ready to resolve conflicts in an open and honest way. You might also have to make personal sacrifices for the success of the team.

What If You Hate Your Team?

You might not want to be part of a team. Maybe you were placed on a team that you did not choose. Maybe you think you are the only one on the team who is making an effort. How might your behavior influence the team's success?

👎 Refuse to cooperate.

👎 Do not participate in team discussions.

👎 Do what you think is best, even if the rest of the team has a different plan.

👎 Yell at your teammates until they do what you want.

👍 Listen respectfully, keep a positive attitude, and present your opinions in a clear and concise way.

Sometimes being an effective member of a team does not depend on the actual outcome of the project. Sometimes it depends on how well you get along with your teammates and whether you give your teammates a chance to succeed.

What Makes a Team Successful?

What can you do to encourage team members to cooperate?

Teams are influenced by different things, including the personal qualities of the team members, the resources available, and the purpose or goals of the team.

When you first join a team, you and your fellow team members might feel nervous and uncomfortable. You might not know each other very well. You might wonder what to expect.

At first, you might misunderstand each other or misinterpret communications. One teammate might say she can't come to a meeting, and you might think she means she doesn't want to be part of the team. Another teammate might have lots of plans and ideas, and the rest of you might think he is trying to take over and be the boss.

As you get to know each other, and learn how to communicate, you might feel a sense of belonging. You might develop common bonds. You will be able to work together to achieve your goal.

21st Century Learning

Jesse is 13. He signed up as a volunteer for his town's community clean-up day. When he arrives, he is assigned to work with three other people picking up trash in a neighborhood park. The group is diverse. There are two high school girls who Jesse thinks are Asian and an African American man about the same age as Jesse's dad.

At the park, Jesse puts on his gloves, grabs a trash bag, and looks around for a good place to get started. The girls take out their cell phones and text their friends. The man yells at the girls to get to work. Then, he turns his attention to Jesse. He points out trash and orders Jesse to pick it up. Jesse feels like he is the only one doing any real work. He begins to regret his decision to volunteer.

How can Jesse make the best of the situation? Use 21st Century Skills such as problem solving, critical thinking, communications, and decision making to help Jesse identify the challenges he is facing and to find solutions. Write an ending to the story and read it to the class, or form small groups and present it as a skit.

Developing As a Leader

Even when all members of a team have an equal role in decision making and problem solving, it is important to have a leader. Recall that a *leader* is a type of manager who knows how to use available resources to help others achieve their goals.

Leaders exhibit positive qualities that other people respect, such as self-confidence. They use skills such as goal setting and critical thinking to make healthy decisions for the benefit of the team. If you are the leader, you take on the responsibility for:

■ Organizing the team's activities

■ Encouraging everyone to share ideas and give opinions

■ Motivating all team members to work toward established goals

Being the leader does not mean you are always right. The leader's opinion does not count more than the opinions of the other team members. An effective leader keeps the team on track and focused on achieving its goals.

What personal qualities does a leader display?

Career Profile: Video Director

Arts, A/V Technology & Communications Career Cluster

Job Summary

A video director is responsible for directing the work of the cast and crew during the production of a video. Directors interpret scripts, select the cast, and manage rehearsals. If necessary, they approve the sets, costumes, choreography, and music.

A few directors succeed in the motion picture industry, but many work for businesses creating training and marketing videos. Many are self-employed, which means they must work hard to promote themselves to get new jobs.

Video directors must prove they have skill and talent. They must also manage a diverse team of people, including actors, producers, and writers, and keep track of the budget. Most attend college to study theater arts, while taking advantage of opportunities to direct videos while in school. They may start their careers as an assistant director.

Use the Internet, a library, or career center to research the responsibilities, education and training requirements, and salary range of a video director. Write a video script for a biography of a successful video director. If possible, turn the script into an actual video, or perform it with a team of classmates.

What leadership qualities might help a video director succeed?

What About Team Members?

While a strong leader is important to the success of a team, team members must also be committed to the group's success. An effective team member helps teammates if they need help, does not blame teammates for problems or mistakes, and offers ideas and suggestions instead of criticism.

You are a good team member if you are:

- Open minded
- Cooperative
- Trustworthy
- Willing to compromise
- Friendly

Recognizing Peer Pressure

Peer pressure is when your peers such as friends, classmates, or co-workers influence you to do something. They might actively try to convince you to do something you haven't done before or to stop doing something you are doing. For example, a co-worker who is a vegetarian might try to convince you to stop eating meat.

Or, you might decide to do something or stop doing something because of what you think your peers might think. For example, you might start drinking soda instead of juice because everyone else drinks soda. No one actually told you to drink soda, but you think you will fit in better and they will like you more if you do.

- Peer pressure can be positive if it contributes to your well-being and does not interfere with your values, standards, and beliefs. For example, a friend might love mountain biking, so you try mountain biking and find out you love it, too.
- Peer pressure can be negative. It might interfere with your well-being or go against your values. For example, you might know taking more than one hour for lunch is wrong, but your co-workers convince you to do it anyway.

Recognizing peer pressure can help you make healthy choices and achieve your career goals. You can decide for yourself whether it is positive or negative and whether you want it to influence you.

Qualities of an Effective Team

An effective team cooperates to achieve a specific goal. Members of an effective team:

✔ *Listen to each other*

✔ *Respect each others' opinions*

✔ *Recognize each others' skills and abilities*

✔ *Share the work load*

✔ *Share responsibility*

Money Madne$$

You like a turkey sandwich on whole-wheat bread with lettuce for lunch. At the supermarket, the sliced turkey costs $5.75 per pound. A head of lettuce costs $1.25. A loaf of whole-wheat bread costs $3.15. You can use the items to make more than enough sandwiches for a whole week.

Your co-workers eat in the cafeteria. They buy freshly made sandwiches for $4.25.

How much does it cost you to bring a sandwich for lunch five days a week? How much does it cost to buy a sandwich for five days? Which option do you think you should choose? Is cost the only thing to consider? Write a paragraph explaining your decision to your co-workers.

Building Ethical Relationships

Recall that *ethics* are a set of beliefs about what is right and what is wrong. When you build ethical relationships, you treat others with respect and honesty and they trust you in return. Your ethics help you set standards for relationships in all areas of your life.

You don't leave your ethics behind when you enter a workplace. As a co-worker, employee, or supervisor, you have a responsibility to behave ethically. For example, you should not lie, steal, or make fun of other people. Employers are always looking for ethical employees.

Work ethics are beliefs and behaviors about what is right and wrong in a work environment. The business where you work may have a set of corporate or business ethics. Business ethics set standards for how the company relates to others, including customers, employees, competitors, and even the government. For example, the company might believe that it has a responsibility to protect the environment, so it takes steps to conserve natural resources by turning off lights, keeping the air conditioning low, and buying recycled paper products.

How can your ethics help you develop strong relationships in a work environment?

Not everyone has the same set of ethics. For example, you might think it is wrong to gossip about others, but your co-workers do it all the time. You cannot control someone else's ethics. All you can do is make sure you relate to others in a way that is true to your own ethics.

However, if someone behaves illegally, or against your company's code of ethics, you have a responsibility to your employer to report it to your supervisor or to the human resources department.

Tech Connect

In general, technology improves worker productivity and makes it easier for companies to succeed. It also brings new ethical problems and decisions.

For example, technology has made it easier for people to steal intellectual property, such as written words or recorded music. It has made it easier for thieves to steal credit card and bank account information. It has even made it easier to edit photographs so people cannot be certain if the picture they are looking at is real.

Use the Internet or your library to research some of the ways developments in technology have impacted ethical behavior in the workplace. Select one and write a newspaper article about it. Use a desktop publishing or word processing program to make a newsletter that includes articles written by your classmates.

Is the Conflict Your Fault?

Your co-workers are angry at you. They have been "forgetting" to tell you about meetings. They do not listen to your suggestions or ideas. What do you do to affect their attitude towards you?

👎 Make excuses to cover up your mistakes.

👎 Blame your co-workers for your errors.

👎 Take credit for others' work.

👍 Find ways to cooperate and compromise.

👍 Show appreciation for their efforts.

👍 Take responsibility for your work.

How can unhealthy relationships with your co-workers interfere with your career success?

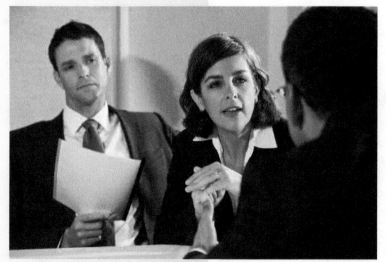

How can you use respect and honesty to manage conflict at work?

Managing Conflict

Conflict is a disagreement between two or more people who have different ideas. Conflict occurs in all relationships at one time or another. It can cause stress and interfere with your well-being if it is not resolved.

■ When a relationship is healthy, people talk about what is causing the conflict and work together to find a solution.

■ When a relationship is not healthy, conflict can go unresolved. Unresolved conflict interferes with well-being and can cause stress, depression, anger, and resentment.

Managing conflict does not always mean eliminating the conflict completely. It means you are able to recognize what is causing the conflict and that you can cope with it in an honest and respectful way.

Types of Conflict

There are different types of conflict. The way you respond to conflict depends on what it is and how it affects your well-being.

Some conflict is minor and short-lived—such as disagreeing with a co-worker about who should clean up the lunchroom. You can usually resolve minor conflicts easily by talking about them and coming to a compromise or agreement.

Some conflict is serious or ongoing—such as refusing to promote a product your company sells or disagreeing with the way your supervisor treats co-workers. Serious conflicts often come from conflicting values and could be difficult—or even impossible—to resolve. You may not want to compromise your ethics or values. Sometimes, you can agree to disagree. Other times, you may have to end the relationship.

Causes of Conflict

Any disagreement can cause conflict. Sometimes understanding what causes the disagreement can help you resolve the conflict more quickly. When you recognize the cause of the conflict, you can take steps to find a solution.

- Differences in values and standards cause conflict. Your supervisor might schedule you to work on Sunday, but it is important to you to spend Sundays with your family.

- Ineffective communication and misunderstandings can cause conflict. If your supervisor doesn't tell you she will be late for work, you might schedule a meeting for her. Then you are angry when you must change the schedule.

- Conflict may be caused by personal qualities such as stubbornness or conceit. Your co-worker might refuse to turn down the music volume when you are trying to talk to a customer on the phone.

How can an apology show you understand that the other person is hurt or angry?

Resolving Conflict

At the root of all conflict there is a problem that blocks you from achieving a goal. You can use the problem-solving process to find a solution. You will be more successful in resolving or minimizing the conflict if you work with the other person or people who are involved in the conflict. Together you can identify the disagreement or problem. You can then **negotiate**, or discuss options that will lead to an agreement that satisfies everyone. Finally, you can compromise and select and implement—put in action—the best solution.

When you work together to resolve conflict, keep these tips in mind:

- Show respect and understanding for the other person.
- Remain calm and objective.
- Take responsibility for your own actions and feelings, without blaming anyone else.
- Remember to use the six key factors of effective communication, including sending a clear, concise message; listening carefully; and using "I" statements to focus on your point of view.
- Insults hurt and cause new conflicts. You can attack the conflict without attacking the other person.

The hardest thing of all might be to apologize. Even if you don't think you caused the conflict or did anything wrong, you can apologize for making the other person feel bad.

Sometimes you might not be able to get the other person to cooperate. He or she might not want to resolve the conflict or might refuse to admit there is a conflict. Then, you will have to decide whether you need to take action on your own or just walk away.

Anger Management

Conflict can make you mad. When you are angry, you might not be reasonable or realistic about the conflict. You might say or do something you will regret later. What if you are too angry to talk to the other person?

★ Take a deep breath.

★ Count to ten.

★ Exercise.

★ Identify your role in the conflict.

★ Brainstorm solutions.

★ Consider what you could say to start resolving the conflict.

★ Ask someone you trust for advice.

Once you calm down, you will be better able to think critically about what is causing the conflict and how to resolve it. Can you think of other ways to control your anger and resolve the conflict?

Team Conflicts

Conflicts in a team can interfere with the team's ability to achieve its goals. Because there are many people involved, the type of conflict can vary.

- Sometimes, the conflict might have nothing to do with the team. One member might have a personal conflict that is getting in his way. For example, your co-worker might not be able to concentrate on a project because he has a family problem.

- There may be conflict between two team members. You and your co-worker may not agree about whether you should contact a customer using e-mail or the telephone.

- There may be conflict between one team member and everyone else in the team. Your supervisor might want the team to meet in the morning, but the rest of you want to meet in the afternoon.

To be successful, the whole team should work together to resolve the conflict. Each team member can contribute to identifying the problem and brainstorming solutions.

Asserting Yourself

One positive way to cope with conflict is to be assertive. Being **assertive** means that you stand up for yourself. You express your feelings and thoughts with confidence, in a strong, honest, and direct way. When you are assertive, you show others that you have the right to be treated with respect.

One negative way to cope with conflict is to be aggressive. Being **aggressive** means that you force your opinions on others. You express your feelings and thoughts in a hostile, or angry, way. When you are aggressive, you show others that you have no respect for their thoughts or feelings.

Resolving Team Conflicts

Follow these important steps for resolving conflicts as a team.

✔ *Give all team members a chance to express their views.*

✔ *Be respectful of all team members.*

✔ *Deal with one problem at a time.*

✔ *Focus on your common goals.*

✔ *Find ways for all team members to be involved in the solution.*

✔ *Encourage all team members to take responsibility for their actions—positive and negative.*

✔ *Avoid blame.*

Finding Common Bonds

In order to succeed in your career, it is important to build relationships with all of your co-workers. In most work environments, you will have the opportunity to work with people from different cultures and backgrounds. One way to develop a relationship with people who seem different is to find common bonds. When you look for common bonds, you focus on the things that make you like someone else. You do not spend time worrying about what makes you different.

For example, you might work with someone who was born in Brazil. You might have different traditions or eat different food, but you might both enjoy playing soccer. You might both have brothers or sisters. You might both play the guitar. Discovering common bonds helps you understand the other person so you can work together successfully as a team.

Select a country and use the Internet to research its cultural traditions. Make a three-column chart comparing your cultural traditions with the cultural traditions of your selected country and identifying areas with common bonds.

Unresolved Conflict

When you let conflict go unresolved, it can slowly eat away at a relationship. You might not want to speak up about what is bothering you. You might think it is silly. You might worry the other person will be hurt or angry. When you don't speak up, you can start to **resent** the other person, or blame him for your unhappiness.

Do you expect the other person to know what you are thinking or feeling? You might be annoyed because your co-worker did not respond to your text message. You might be hurt because you think she is ignoring you. It is possible she did not receive the message, or that she accidentally hit delete instead of send. Unless you speak up, you will not be able to resolve the conflict and move forward toward your common goals.

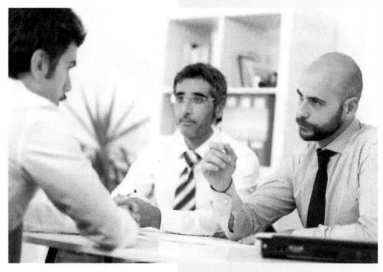

How can unresolved conflict interfere with your success at work?

Odors in the Office

The co-worker who sits at the next desk wears very strong cologne. It gives you a headache and makes it difficult for you to concentrate on your work. What steps can you take to successfully solve the problem?

👎 Take lots of ibuprofen to make your headache feel better.

👎 Sit at your desk and complain about it in a loud voice, hoping he will overhear you.

👎 Leave an anonymous note about it on his desk.

👎 Buy him a brand of cologne that you like.

👍 Ask to speak with him privately, explain the situation, and see if you can work together to find a solution.

👍 Ask your supervisor to speak with him about changing his behavior.

👍 If he will not change his behavior, request a different desk.

Does wearing strong cologne show respect for your co-workers? What other personal behaviors might interfere with a co-worker's ability to do her job?

Myth Only bad employees cause conflict.

Truth While negative attitudes and inflexible opinions can cause conflict, there are lots of other causes, too. Very good employees can cause or contribute to conflict if they don't understand how to use effective communications, team-work, leadership, and problem solving to manage and solve conflict when it occurs.

Case Study

Kali babysits for her neighbor's two children every Friday night. She arrives at 6:00 p.m., gives the children dinner, cleans up, plays with them until bedtime, and then puts them to bed. She spends the rest of the time watching television and chatting with her friends. The parents come home at 10:00, pay Kali $25.00, and walk her home. Kali likes her neighbors and the kids, and enjoys babysitting. She is happy earning $25.00 each week.

One Friday when she arrives, her neighbors tell her that their niece and nephew are sleeping over. Kali prepares dinner for all four kids and cleans up after them all. They have a hard time deciding what to do before bed and argue a lot. It takes a long time to get them all settled and asleep. Kali barely has time to do anything before the parents arrive home. They pay her $25.00, thank her, and walk her home. Kali feels used and resentful. She tells her neighbors that she cannot babysit anymore.

- What do you think caused Kali to feel hurt?
- Do you think Kali is right to quit the babysitting job?
- How could Kali have acted differently?

Web Extra

There are many Web sites that publish team-building advice and activities for teens, as well as for professionals. Use the Internet to identify some reputable sites you think might be useful for yourself and your classmates. Make a directory of the sites to leave in your classroom or school guidance office.

Answer It!

1. List at least three groups of people you might have relationships with at work.
2. List at least five characteristics of a healthy relationship.
3. What is the foundation for a healthy relationship?
4. List at least three responsibilities of a team leader.
5. List at least five qualities of a good team member.
6. Explain the difference between positive and negative peer pressure.
7. Define conflict.
8. List at least three reasons for conflict in the workplace.
9. Explain the difference between assertive and aggressive behavior.
10. What is one risk of letting conflict go unresolved?

Career-Ready Practices ----------

Form groups of five to eight. Take five minutes to write a list of things that everyone in the group has in common. For example, everyone is in the same grade or everyone lives in the same town. Next, using a different piece of paper, take five minutes to write at least two things that are unique about each person in the group. For example, one person might be the only one who plays the violin or one person might be the only one who has an older brother. Keep in mind that recognizing unique abilities or characteristics of each group member can help build strong team relationships. Career-ready individuals do not allow differences among team members to create barriers. Instead, they focus on positive interaction with others and encourage all team members to contribute in a productive manner. Share your lists with the other groups in the class.

Write Now

Are the relationships you have with your family different from the relationships you have with friends? Are the relationships you have with teachers different from the relationships you have with neighbors? Select two relationships that are important in your life, and then write an essay comparing and contrasting them.

Career Portfolio

Employers want to hire ethical employees who they can trust to represent the company in a fair and responsible way. Make a list of the personal and work ethics that are important to you, and explain why these ethics would make you a valuable employee. Add the list to your career portfolio.

Business Plan Project

There is a saying in business: "The customer is always right." This means that it is important to make a customer happy if you want your business to succeed. A happy customer will return, and will tell others good things about the business. But customers are not the only people an entrepreneur must treat well. There are employees, investors, suppliers, and many other people who interact with a business who must be treated fairly, honestly, and with respect. In your **Business Plan Project**, develop a code of ethics, or a list of rules, to govern how you will behave towards everyone who interacts with your business. Think of positive statements that will guide the way you treat others. Once you complete your list, write a paragraph explaining why these rules are important to you personally and to your business.

10 Basic Math Skills

Skills in This Chapter . . .

- **Adding, Subtracting, Multiplying, and Dividing**

- **Working with Percentages, Fractions, and Decimals**

- **Working with Ratios and Proportions**

- **Analyzing Data and Probability**

- **Analyzing Charts**

GETTING STARTED

Every year since you started school, you have taken math. You count. You add. You subtract. You memorize your multiplication tables. Why?

Math is essential. You use math every day in many situations. You calculate how much time you have to get to class. You count your change at lunch. You dole out portions of a snack to friends. Math not only helps you in your daily life, it also helps you succeed in other classes in school. You use math in core courses such as social studies and science. You use it in electives for tasks such as measuring ingredients for a recipe or constructing sets for drama.

And, of course, developing basic math skills will help you succeed in whatever career you choose. For example, in business you use math to create budgets and analyze financial statements. In health care occupations, you use it to measure medicine. In construction trades, you use it to calculate how much material you need and what it will cost.

➤ Make a list of everyday tasks for which you use math. Then, write down how you would accomplish each task if you couldn't add, subtract, multiply, or divide.

Adding, Subtracting, Multiplying, and Dividing

The basic mathematical operations are addition, subtraction, multiplication, and division. You use them to manipulate numbers to find answers to common questions. For example, if you want to know how much money you earned selling clocks today, you would add together all of the sales receipts for clocks. If you want to know how much each share of company stock is worth, you would divide the total value of the company by the number of shares of stock.

Knowing how to add, subtract, multiply, and divide is a necessary skill for everyday life, as well as for any career you choose. You can develop these skills in math class at school and by practicing them at home, at work, and in your community.

What Good Is Addition?

Addition is the totaling of two or more numbers. Each number you are adding is called an **addend**. The result is called the **sum**, or **total**. For example, two computers in the reception area + three computers in accounting = a total of five computers in the office.

At work, you use addition for tasks such as calculating income, preparing expense reports, totaling sales, and ordering **inventory**—goods you have available to sell. If you work in health care, you might use addition to total the amount of fluids administered to a patient during the day or to count medication in a pharmacy. If you work in construction, you might add the total linear feet of lumber you need. If you work in transportation, you might add the number of miles you drove.

When Do I Subtract?

Subtraction is the opposite of addition. Subtracting numbers means taking one number away from another number. The result is called the **difference**. For example, if you have six sweaters in stock and sell four of them, you have two sweaters left in the store.

At work, you need subtraction for tasks such as tracking inventory, checking payroll deductions and withholdings, monitoring debit and checking account balances, and calculating net profits. If you are a police officer or a nurse, you might use subtraction to calculate how many hours you have left on your shift. If you are a hotel manager, you might use subtraction to determine how many rooms are vacant.

Memorize Those Multiplication Tables!

Multiplication is a quick method of adding numbers. It lets you repeat an addition problem in one step. For example, if a customer wants to buy four sweaters for $12.50 each, you could add $12.50 + $12.50 + $12.50 + $12.50 = $50.00, or you could multiply $12.50 × 4 to find the answer of $50.00. The numbers you multiply—in this case $12.50 and 4—are called **factors**. The answer is the **product**.

Some tasks for which you use multiplication at work include calculating hourly pay, finding the total cost of multiple items, and managing inventory. If you are a lawyer, you might use multiplication to calculate your billable hours. If you are a scientist, you might use multiplication to forecast the growth of cells.

How would you use math if you worked as an air traffic controller?

Do I Need Division?

Division is the opposite of multiplication. It is the process of separating a whole into parts. For example, if you have four employees and want to schedule them each for an equal number of hours, you divide the total number of hours in the week by four: 40 hours ÷ 4 = 10 hours each. The whole—in this case 40 hours—is called the **dividend**. The number you divide the dividend by—in this case, the four employees—is called the **divisor**. The result is the **quotient**.

You use division at work for tasks such as sharing profits, deciding how to spend your budget, deciding how to use floor space in a store or warehouse, and calculating per unit costs. A teacher might use division to organize a class into groups.

Career Trend

Many companies are screening job applicants for basic math skills before hiring. They administer tests to verify that candidates can add, subtract, multiply, and divide. The trend is occurring in many industries, but it is particularly common for jobs that require employees to handle money, such as cashiers, bank tellers, and waitstaff at a restuarant.

International Measurements

In the United States, we use a measurement system called the U.S. customary system, which is sometimes called the conventional or traditional measurement system. Most other countries use the International System of measurement, or the metric system.

The metric system is a decimal system, which means it is based on multiples of ten. Meters, grams, and liters are the basic units of measurement. Prefixes—letters added to the beginning of a word—indicate the size of the units. For example, a kilometer is 1,000 meters. A kilogram is 1,000 grams, and a kiloliter is 1,000 liters.

The customary system is not based on any one unit. Distance is measured in inches, feet, yards, and miles. Weight is measured in ounces, pounds, and tons. Volume is measured in cups, pints, quarts, and gallons.

Why do you think it is important for employees in the United States to understand the metric system? Use measurement tools in your classroom to measure distance, weight, and volume of common items with both systems. Make a chart showing the comparison.

What's Geometry?

Geometry *is math that deals with the size, position, and shape of 2- and 3-dimensional objects. Some occupations that require the use of geometry include:*

✔ *Carpenter*

✔ *Astronomer*

✔ *Interior designer*

✔ *Surveyor*

✔ *Structural engineer*

✔ *House painter*

✔ *Robotic engineer*

Working with Percentages, Fractions, and Decimals

Percentages, fractions, and decimals are different ways to represent the same thing: a number less than a whole. The main difference is the context in which you use each one. For example, ¼, .25, and 25% all represent the same value, but you use them in different situations:

■ 25% to represent a sales discount

■ ¼ teaspoon to represent an amount of an ingredient in a recipe

■ .25 to represent part of a dollar

You will benefit in any career by knowing how to work with percentages, fractions, and decimals in different situations. The first step is to understand the difference between them and when to use one or another.

What's a Fraction?

A **fraction** is a *ratio*—or comparison—of two whole numbers, or one whole number divided by another whole number. You write a fraction in a way similar to writing a division problem. A dividend, called the **numerator**, is written above a line, called the **fraction bar**. A divisor, called the **denominator**, is written below the fraction bar.

For example, if you have three-quarters of an hour to travel to a meeting, you can write the fraction like this: ¾. The number 3 is the numerator, or dividend. It represents the number of quarter-hours you have. The number 4 is the denominator, or divisor. It represents the total number of quarter-hours in a whole hour.

A mix of whole numbers and fractions is called a mixed fraction. For example, 1¼ is a mixed fraction.

At work, you most often use fractions to measure quantities. For example, a chef uses fractions to measure ingredients and a tailor uses fractions to measure fabric or thread. You might also use fractions to explain statistics. For instance, a market research analyst might notice that half—½—of a group prefers one product over another. A third use of fractions is to refer to time. For example, you might schedule an appointment for a quarter—¼—of an hour.

What's a Decimal?

A **decimal** is a different way of writing a fraction. You write a decimal using a decimal point, or dot. Numbers to the left of the decimal point are whole numbers. Numbers to the right of the decimal point are less than one. Each place in a decimal represents a multiple of ten. The first place to the right of a decimal is tenths. The second place is hundredths. The third place is thousandths. For example, .25 means there are two tenths and five hundredths. The number 2.25 means there are two wholes, two tenths, and five hundredths. One of the most common uses for decimals is to write dollar values. The numbers to the left of the decimal point represent whole dollars, and the numbers to the right represent the cents.

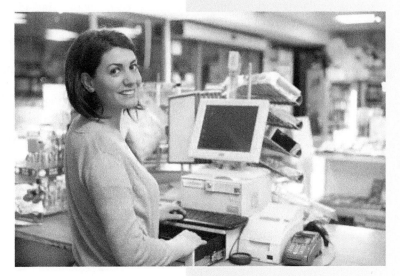

Could you make change if you did not know how to work with decimals?

Many occupations use decimals. In health care, decimals indicate body temperature—98.6 is normal. Mileage is measured using decimals. Often, people convert fractions to decimals so they can work with the numbers more easily. For example, it is easier to add .25 + .33 than it is to add ¼ + ⅓.

Money Madne$$

Counting change is an important skill for many workers as well as for consumers. Bank tellers count change for customers cashing checks or withdrawing money from an account. Cashiers count change when a customer pays more than an item costs and receives the difference back. Consumers count change to make sure they receive the correct amount.

You and a friend are going to the movies. The tickets cost $10.75 each. You buy both tickets online. At the theater, your friend gives you a $20.00 bill to pay for his ticket. How much change do you give him? What if the tickets cost $11.50 each?

Myth There is only one way to solve a math problem.

Truth As for any problem, there are always multiple options for coming up with a solution to a math problem. The method that works best for you might depend on your own learning style. For example, if you are a visual learner, you might illustrate the problem in order to see it clearly. If you are a tactile learner, you might use manipulatives—or objects that you can handle or count.

What's a Percent?

A **percentage** is also part of whole. Specifically, 1 percent is one part out of 100. That means that 100 percent equals the whole, or all, of something—no matter how much is in the whole.

You can quickly calculate a percentage by dividing the amount you have by the total amount, and then multiplying the quotient by 100. For example, if there are 500 sweaters in the stockroom, and 45 are blue, you can calculate the percent of blue sweaters by dividing 45—the number of blue sweaters—by 500—the total number of sweaters. Then you multiply the quotient—.09—by 100. The answer is 9%. If 55 are red, the percent of red sweaters is $55 \div 500 = .11 \times 100 = 11\%$.

To calculate the amount of a percent, multiply the total number by the percent. For example, if you know 6% of the 500 sweaters are brown, multiply $500 \times 6\%$ to learn that you have 30 brown sweaters. You can convert the percent to a decimal first, to make the multiplication easier: Replace the percent sign with a decimal point and move the decimal point two spaces to the left. So, $500 \times .06 = 30$.

How do you use percents at work? To determine market share; to track inventory; to calculate interest; or to compare sales of different products, sales to different customers, sales by region, sales by store, or sales by salesperson. A salesperson uses percentages to calculate commission. A farmer might use percentages to decide how many acres to use for a specific crop.

Career Tips

Studying math is an excellent way to prepare for many careers. It provides a foundation for all areas of science and engineering as well as social sciences such as anthropology, sociology, and psychology. Lawyers, business professionals, and health care workers all require a solid background in math and statistics.

Tech Connect

A spreadsheet is a grid of columns and rows used for storing numerical or financial data. Once, spreadsheets were written on paper; now, almost all spreadsheets are created using computer programs such as Microsoft Office Excel. Spreadsheet programs are used in any job that works with numbers—which is pretty much every job. For example, you can use one to set up a budget, create charts, track data, forecast sales, analyze statistics, and record the results of scientific experiments.

Spreadsheet programs have made workers more productive by automating tasks they used to do by hand. For example, they have features that let you set up equations or formulas so your computer can automatically perform calculations. The formulas might be simple, such as totaling a column of numbers, or complex, such as generating a chart based on data in multiple columns or rows. Workers can use the same spreadsheet in different situations by changing the values but keeping the formulas in place.

How much time do you think a spreadsheet saves? Write a column of ten numbers, with at least three digits in each number. Exchange your paper with a partner and see how long it takes to add the column without using a calculator or computer. Change three of the numbers. How long does it take to recalculate the sum? Using a computer, enter the numbers in a spreadsheet program such as Excel. Use the SUM formula to find the total. Change three numbers and recalculate the sum. Which method is faster? Which is more likely to result in an error?

Working with Ratios and Proportions

Have you heard the term *scale* used for changing the size of something? For example, you might scale a digital photograph to make it bigger or smaller. You might scale a recipe to make more or less. When you scale, you use ratios and proportions. A ratio lets you compare two values—even when the units are different. For example, you can compare the number of apples in a display case to the number of oranges. Then, you can use proportions to adjust the values an equal amount.

Ratios are useful in industries where you combine different components to create a product or when you want to compare two different units. For example, a chef who combines ingredients uses ratios to make sure the dish tastes good. An entrepreneur uses ratios to track the amount of profit compared to the amount of loss.

Proportions come in handy for people who adjust the sizes of things: That same chef might want to feed four people using a recipe written for two—so he increases the amount of ingredients while keeping the proportions the same. An architect builds a scale model of a house by keeping the measurements in proportion.

Can I Use a Calculator?

A calculator can make coming up with the right answer to a math problem easier—as long as you know what operations to use! What are some of the benefits and drawbacks of relying on a calculator?

- You might not have the calculator with you.
- You might not know how to set up the equation to get the right answer.
- You might be able to perform the calculation faster in your head.
- You will get the correct answer to basic math problems.
- You can perform more complex problems faster.

Can you think of other benefits and drawbacks of using a calculator?

What's a Ratio?

A ratio compares two numbers. For example, if there are three employees in the sales department and one manager, the ratio of employees to managers is 3 to 1. You often write a ratio using a colon to separate the two numbers, like this: 3:1. You can also write the ratio as a fraction, like this: ³⁄₁.

Ratios are often used to measure rate. The basic difference between rate and ratio is that the two things either have the same unit—a ratio—or a different unit—a rate. For instance, when a person runs 7 miles per hour, it indicates a rate of 7:1, which is commonly written as 7 miles/hour. The different units are miles and hours.

Ratios help workers perform a variety of tasks. An artist might combine a ratio of red to blue paint to create a desired shade of violet. If the ratio of red to blue changes, the shade of violet changes, too. A baker might use 2 parts sugar to 1 part flour, which is a ratio of 2:1. If he changes the ratio—say he uses 1 part sugar to 2 parts flour—1:2— the dough will not come out correctly.

Ratios are also useful in other careers. A grocer might notice that she sells four dozen McIntosh apples for every one dozen of Delicious apples, a ratio of 4:1. She can use that information to decide how many apples of each type to buy in the future.

What might happen if the concrete is not mixed using the proper ratios of ingredients?

Financial Ratios for the Entrepreneur

One of the most effective ways for an entrepreneur to analyze financial information is to use financial ratios. Some of the most useful financial ratios include:

- **Operating ratio**, which shows the percentage of each dollar of sales needed to cover expenses.
- **Return on sales (ROS)** ratio, which is calculated by dividing net profit by sales.
- The **quick ratio**, which is a comparison of cash to debt.
- **Current ratio**, which is current assets divided by current liabilities.

Pick one of these financial ratios and research how it can help an entrepreneur understand his or her financial situation.

What's a Proportion?

A **proportion** is when you have two ratios that equal each other. For example, one class might have 1 teacher for every 15 students (a ratio of 1:15), and another class might have 2 teachers for every 30 students (2:30, which is the same as 1:15). The ratios are equal.

You use proportions to maintain equality between two things, even when the number of things changes. For example, a window washer might use 1 cup of ammonia for every 2 gallons of water—a 1:2 ratio. If he wants to use 4 gallons of water, how much ammonia should he use? Since he doubled the amount of water, to maintain the ratio he must double the amount of ammonia—2 cups of ammonia for 4 gallons of water—still a 1:2 ratio.

Anyone who uses ratios in a career is also likely to use proportions. For example, if a baker wants to increase the number of rolls she gets from a recipe, she can increase the amount of dough. To make sure the dough comes out right, she must keep the ingredients in proportion to each other. If she uses 1:2 parts sugar to flour in the smaller amount, she must use 1:2 parts sugar to flour in the greater amount.

Proportions are also used to measure equality in other areas. A school might want to keep the ratio of teachers to students in proportion—or the same. A city planner might want to keep the ratio of residential homes to businesses in proportion.

NUMBERS GAME

Measuring with a ruler or tape measure is an important skill for many careers, such as tailor, carpenter, or architect. An inch ruler or tape measure is divided into inches, and each inch can be divided into 16 parts. Marks on the ruler indicate the parts: the shortest lines mark ¹⁄₁₆, the next shortest mark ¹⁄₈, then ¼ and ½. Each inch line is marked with a number (refer to the illustration).

1/16 inch mark | 1/2 inch mark
1/4 inch mark
1/8 inch mark

To measure, you line up an inch mark at the edge or point where you want to start measuring, use the lines to count off the length, and mark the spot where you want to stop measuring. For example, to measure ³⁄₈ from the edge of fabric, you line up the edge with the inch mark, count three ¹⁄₈ inch marks, and draw a line to mark the spot. To measure ⁵⁄₈ from the edge, you line up the edge, count five ¹⁄₈ inch marks, and mark the spot.

Using a blank piece of paper and a ruler, tape measure, or the illustration, measure ¼ inch from the left edge of the page, and draw a line to mark the spot. Then, measure the distance from the ¼ mark you made to the right edge of the page. Write the measurement next to the line marking the ¼ spot.

Measure ⁵⁄₈ from the right edge, mark the spot, then measure the distance from the mark to the left edge of the page. Write the measurement next to the ⁵⁄₈ mark.

Measure 1¹⁄₈ from the top edge, mark the spot, then measure the distance from the mark to the bottom edge. Write the measurement next to the 1¹⁄₈ mark.

Analyzing Data and Probability

Statistics, or **data analysis,** is a type of math used to collect, organize, and analyze **data**—information. Statistics are bits of numerical information. They are used to make sense of things that have happened in the past, to help make decisions, and to predict—or forecast—what might happen in the future, based on what has happened before. The chance that something might happen is called **probability**.

Data and statistics help to prove facts, illustrate goals, and forecast possibilities. Almost all careers use statistics and probability. Meteorologists collect statistics about weather and use the information for forecasting. Geologists collect statistics about mineral deposits and use the information to predict the probability of locating oil. Market researchers collect statistics about people's buying habits and use the information to predict the probability of a product's success. Insurance actuaries collect statistics about risk factors and use the information to predict the probability of illness, accidents, or death.

Data Analysis

To collect data, you ask questions or conduct a survey. For example, you can conduct a survey of your classmates to find out whether they prefer cats or dogs or how many siblings they have or if they like the taste of mushrooms. You can also collect data from history. For example, a retail chain might collect sales data from the past three years for each of its stores.

Once you collect the data, you analyze it and turn it into statistics. For example, a dietitian might ask, "How many servings of vegetables did you eat each day this week?" You might answer two on Monday, three on Tuesday, none on Wednesday, one on Thursday, two on Friday, three on Saturday, and three on Sunday.

From the information, the dietitian can calculate many things: the average number of servings you ate each day, the total number of servings you ate this week, the least number of servings you ate, the most number of servings you ate, and so on. If he has asked other people the same question, he can combine all of your answers and start to look for patterns. For example, he might be able to identify whether people eat more servings on Fridays than on Wednesdays. He can use the information to make decisions such as how to get people to eat more vegetables on Wednesdays.

You might use data analysis at work in marketing, pharmaceutical research, or retail sales. A politician might use it to decide whether to run for office, a banker might use it to decide where to invest funds, and an entrepreneur might use it to convince investors to back his start-up. Schools use statistics to decide how many teachers to hire, and colleges use statistics to help determine which applicants to admit.

Common Statistics

Some common statistics include:

✔ *Median: The middle value in a set*

✔ *Average or mean: A typical value calculated by adding all values and dividing the total by the number of values*

✔ *Mode: The number that occurs most often in a set*

✔ *Range: The difference between the lowest and highest values in the set*

✔ *Frequency: The number of times an event occurs*

International Currency

Currency is the unit of money used in a country. For example, the dollar is the currency in the United States. The euro is the currency in the European Union. When you travel to a different country, you exchange the currency you have—dollars—for the currency you need. The **exchange rate** determines how much of the foreign money you can buy for one dollar.

So, if the current dollar exchange rate for euros is 0.731608, it means you can exchange $1.00 for 0.731608 euros.

To find out how much you will get for more than $1.00, you multiply the amount you have in dollars by the exchange rate. To exchange $25.00:

$25.00 × 0.731608 = 18.29 euros.

If the current exchange rate for the Mexican peso is 13.1, how many pesos will you get if you exchange $25.00?

The exchange rate changes constantly and it is different for each currency around the world. You can find the current exchange rates online at sites such as x-rates.com.

What's the Chance of That?

You can use probability—the chance that something will happen—to measure how likely it is that a particular outcome will occur. The formula for probability is the number of times the particular outcome occurs divided by the total number of possible outcomes.

For example, a piano teacher can assess the probability of a particular student being late for class by dividing the number of times the student has been late by the total number of classes the student has had. If she has been late three times out of nine, the probability is 3 ÷ 9, or .33, which is the same as 33%. So, there is a 33% chance the student will be late.

An event that is certain to happen has a probability of 1—or 100%. If your birthday is March 10, and today is March 9, the probability that tomorrow is your birthday is 100%. An event that cannot happen has a probability of 0—or 0%. If your birthday is March 10, and today is April 6, the probability that tomorrow is your birthday is zero.

How often do you consider probability in everyday life?

How is probability used at work? Almost every business uses probability to assess risk. Insurance agencies assess the risk of loss. Manufacturers assess the risk of product failure; farmers use probability to determine whether it will rain; military leaders use probability to determine whether a campaign will succeed or fail; school counselors use probability to determine if a student is at risk of dropping out; and parole boards use probability to determine if an inmate will reoffend if released.

Career Profile: Actuary

**Finance
Career Cluster**

Job Summary

What are the benefits and drawbacks of working as an actuary?

An actuary is a business professional who analyzes the financial consequences of risk. For example, an actuary might analyze data to estimate the probability of an event such as death or illness. Actuaries also determine the potential cost of such an event and help companies set policies to minimize the risk.

Most actuaries work for insurance companies, but some work in other businesses, including the government, hospitals, banks, and investment firms. They must have a strong foundation in mathematics, statistics, and general business and should know how to use computer programs such as spreadsheets and databases. Actuaries must have a bachelor's degree and are required to pass a series of exams in order to become certified.

Use the Internet, a library, or career center to research the responsibilities, education and training requirements, and salary range of an actuary. Write a **cover letter** to a potential employer applying for a position as an actuary. (A cover letter is a letter explaining your interest and qualifications for a job that you send along with a resume.)

21st Century Learning

Olivia wants to be a pediatric nurse. She knows she needs strong math skills to be accepted into a training program. She works hard in math class. She sits in the front row and takes notes. She does all her homework, every day. She studies for tests and quizzes. But she has never received a grade higher than a C.

Olivia's friends think she should consider a career that does not require as much math. Olivia loves children and thinks she would be an excellent pediatric nurse. She volunteers at the hospital and sees how important pediatric nursing is. She cannot think of another career that would be as rewarding. Her mother tells her to keep trying, but Olivia is very discouraged. She doesn't even want to go to math class anymore.

What should Olivia do? Use 21st Century Skills such as problem solving, critical thinking, communications, and decision making to help Olivia identify the challenges she is facing and to find solutions. Write an ending to the story and read it to the class, or form small groups and present it as a skit.

Analyzing Charts

A **chart**—also called a **graph**—is a picture that displays data. You use charts to compare data, identify patterns, or show trends over time. For example, an entrepreneur might use a pie chart to compare amounts provided by different investors.

A doctor might use a line chart to show changes in a patient's temperature over time.

Most people respond better to visual information than to numbers. Charts help people understand data quickly because they can see what the numbers mean. For that reason, charts are useful in any career where you use data to make a point or to communicate.

Jobs That Use Charts

If you can create and interpret charts, you will be an asset in any career. Health care professionals use charts to track patient progress. Business managers use charts to display financial information. Human resources managers use charts to track employee data such as salary and staffing levels. Zookeepers use charts to schedule feedings, warehouse managers use charts to monitor inventory, and wholesalers use charts to track sales.

Viet is very creative. He has artistic talent for painting, drawing, and design. He plans to study art and design in college, and to pursue a career as a graphic artist.

Although Viet has always done well in math, he does not enjoy math class. He does not think he needs math skills to achieve his career goals. To meet his school's graduation requirements, he enrolls in a low-level math class. He puts in very little effort, preferring to spend his time working on his art. At the end of the year, he has all A's on his report card except for a B– in math.

- Do you think Viet made the right choice by taking a low-level math class?

- What problems might Viet encounter because of his decision?

- Do you agree that Viet does not need math skills to achieve his career goals?

Web Extra

There are many Web sites that provide enrichment math activities for students or let you ask math-related questions. For example, mathforum.org provides information about many math topics, has a question and answer section, and lists activities illustrating many math concepts. Use the Internet to find a math activity you could do at home or in school.

Answer It!

1. List the four basic mathematical operations.
2. What is addition?
3. What is the opposite of addition?
4. What do you call the answer to a multiplication problem?
5. What do you call the answer to a division problem?
6. What part of a fraction is written above the fraction bar?
7. Why do you use proportions?
8. What type of math deals with collecting, organizing, and analyzing data?
9. What is the probability of an event that is certain to happen?
10. What is the probability of an event that can never happen?

Career-Ready Practices

As you have learned, math skills are important for just about any career you choose. Career-ready individuals use the knowledge and skills they have acquired in school to be more productive on the job. They apply what they have learned to solving problems and making decisions.

Form teams of three or four. Select a job in one of the career clusters. Think of a situation in which a person in that job would need to use math. Write a math problem for that situation. Exchange your problem with a problem developed by another team. Work together to come up with the solution.

Write Now

What would you say to a friend who was thinking of skipping math class? Write a letter explaining why skipping math might have a long-term effect on his or her career and life goals.

Career Portfolio

Create a math academic plan for yourself, mapping out the courses you will take from now until graduation and the skills you will develop. Explain how each course will help you achieve your career goals. Add the plan to your career portfolio.

Business Plan Project

Entrepreneurs use charts to illustrate many types of information relating to their business. Among other things, charts can be used to forecast income, show growth over time, or identify the size of a target audience. Consider one aspect of your business you could illustrate using a chart. Then, use a charting tool in a program such as Microsoft Excel and create your chart to add to your **Business Plan Project**. Deliver a short presentation to your class or to a small group showing and explaining your chart.

11 | Technology and Your Career

Skills in This Chapter . . .

- **Recognizing the Impact of Technology**
- **High Technology in Industry**
- **Using Technology in Your Career**

GETTING STARTED

We all use technology, but can you tell which kinds of technology might be useful in your career? What makes a certain technology useful? Does a cell phone make communication easier? Does a computer make you more productive? How do you know which technology to use?

Technology is the use of resources such as scientific knowledge and methods to make our lives easier or better. This includes devices such as smartphones that allow you to send e-mail messages, documents, and pictures via wireless networks and video games that allow players to enjoy the experience of virtual reality, a computer-generated simulation of the world. But there is a key difference between tech-

nologies that make our lives and jobs easier and those that make our lives and jobs more fun. Those that make our jobs easier, and therefore allow us to produce more products, are likely to also be the most important technologies of the 21st Century. They might have an impact on you one day by expanding the range of possible careers available.

➤ Take out a piece of paper and fold it in half. In the top half, write five careers. In the bottom half, list one type of technology that would make you better at each career. As a class, discuss your choices, and consider the various ways technology makes it easier to accomplish everyday tasks in your career.

Recognizing the Impact of Technology

What would you do without your cell phone or the Internet? Technology makes our lives easier, and as soon as a new technology is introduced, it becomes hard to imagine life without it. For instance, before the Wright brothers invented an airplane, most people never even thought about traveling to far off countries. Now, companies have offices around the globe, people travel for business, education, and vacation, and the world is a much smaller place.

Remember: Although technology can be very useful, it cannot do your work for you. The most it can do is make it easier for *you* to do your work. Sometimes this means you can get your work done more quickly. Sometimes this means you can do more work or do your work more efficiently.

Videoconferencing uses technology to make long-distance meetings less expensive and more convenient for businesses. Can you think of other ways technology has changed business in recent years?

How Technology Impacts Career Options

Before the high-tech revolution that began in the 1980s, deciding on a career and finding a job required a lot of manual labor. In the past, finding a career usually meant going to the library to research various industries or spending a lot of time with a career counselor. Job seekers had few options for finding specific jobs other than reading the want ads in the newspaper. After identifying a potential job, the job seeker would usually have had to type a resume on a typewriter—retyping the whole page if he or she misspelled a word. Communications between the applicant and the employer usually required letters sent by the U.S. Postal Service, which took days or longer.

But thanks in large part to technology, finding a career and working at a job today are much different.

■ You can use computer programs to help you determine which careers you might like or might be good at.

■ You can use the Internet to research careers with a specific employer quickly and efficiently, because nearly every company has its own Web site.

■ You can find jobs in your area—or anywhere in the world—using job search Web sites.

■ You can use business social networking sites to get the word out that you are looking for a job, and use online contact lists to network with people who might be able to steer you to a new job.

■ You can fill out application forms online or send your resume by e-mail, saving time and money.

■ If you have a phone, a computer, and Internet service, you can become a **telecommuter** who works from home. This means that some geographically distant career choices could be possible options for you without having to relocate or travel.

High-tech devices such as smart phones and computers and the Internet have expanded the range of possible careers for you, and thanks to them, the U.S. Bureau of Labor Statistics estimates that you will likely have as many as three different careers in your working life.

New Careers Driven by Technology

Not only has technology changed the way you find a career and do your work, it has also launched many new careers. Some that have emerged in the last decade include:

■ App developer, who designs computer programs that can run on mobile devices.

■ Data scientist, who uses statistics and computer programming to analyze huge amounts of data and identify useful information.

■ Social media manager, who uses social networks to identify customers, generate sales, and build awareness.

■ Nursing informatics specialist, who oversees the integration of data, information, and medical knowledge to help patients and their health care providers make decisions.

Technology Trends in the Workplace

You will encounter new trends in the workplace when you start your career. Typically, new technologies are used in the workplace when they save time and money compared with traditional ways of working. Just as word processing programs have replaced typewriters, so new technology trends have begun to replace more time-consuming or inefficient ways of working in many areas of business. Consider some of these cutting-edge technologies and how they speed up our work.

■ **Videoconferencing** enables people to meet "face-to-face" without having to travel any distance at all. By setting up two video cameras and establishing an Internet link, employees at distant offices are able to see and speak to each other without spending time and money on traveling.

■ **Collaborative software** allows more than one person to work on a document at one time. For example, more than one person at a time, working at different computers in different locations, can work on the same word processing document, spreadsheet, or presentation. Collaboration software increases productivity. It also saves time, money, and trees (paper).

Does the Internet Help or Hurt My Career Search?

Technology can be an incredibly useful tool, but it can also slow you down if you are unfocused. It is your responsibility to use technology wisely, to recognize when it becomes a distraction, and to avoid letting it waste your time.

👎 You e-mail a company your resume when the want ad states that the company will not accept e-mailed applications.

👎 You instant message with your friends when you are supposed to be doing career research.

👎 You play Internet games and visit social networking sites instead of industry and company Web sites.

👍 You find salary and employment data for careers you are considering.

👍 You e-mail your resume to potential employers that accept online applications.

👍 You use a job placement Web site to find and research career options.

What are other ways that the Internet can both help and hurt your career search? List two new examples of each.

NUMBERS GAME

Graphs (or charts) let you display numerical information in a visual way that is easy to understand. A graph shows the relationship between different types of data, such as number of items sold each month or trends in sales over a year's time. A graph has a vertical line, the Y-axis, which shows values such as prices, and a horizontal line, the X-axis, which shows categories such as years, months, or departments.

One of the easiest types of graphs to create is a **bar graph**, which is useful for showing comparisons among individual items. In a bar graph, categories appear along the vertical axis and values display on the horizontal axis. This is a good graph to use if your category labels are long or you want to show how items compare over time.

The following bar graph makes it easy to compare the prices of three notebook computers.

Notebook Computer
Cost Comparison

Make a bar graph comparing the costs of the following three printers:

Printer 1: $129.99

Printer 2: $85.49

Printer 3: $149.99

Which printer would you buy? Is cost the only consideration?

■ **Wi-Fi** is a technology that allows you to connect to the Internet without having to be connected to any wires or cords. This means that you can be online in a coffee shop, airport terminal, or even in a public park, so long as there is a Wi-Fi "hotspot," or source. Like a radio, Wi-Fi broadcasts a signal through the air to your computer or other device. Wi-Fi allows your office to be virtually anywhere you are with your computer.

■ Not all repetitive tasks must be done by people anymore, thanks to **automation software**. Skilled programmers can create scripts that use the power of a computer to complete tasks that are repetitive, time-consuming, and boring. For instance, most computers can now perform data backups, software updates, and virus scans automatically. Another example is software that lets a computer calculate large data-sets using only a few bits of user input.

Money Madne$$

Your parents pay the monthly charge for your no-contract prepaid cell phone, but you pay for your data usage. The plan charges you $19.99 per month for unlimited talk and text. Data costs $3 a month extra for 50 megabytes (MB). If you download 22 songs at 3.5MB per song and 18 photos at 5MB per image, how many megabytes will you use? How much will you pay for the data services?

High Technology in Industry

Have you ever seen a printing press or a steam engine? Do you think of them as old or modern? High-tech or low-tech? In their day, these inventions were certainly fine examples of high technology. Yet now, high technology, what you might call "high-tech," is a term for only the most advanced or specialized technological developments. Examples of high-tech products range from tiny microchips inside computers to unmanned robots that roam the surface of mars. High technology is all about "pushing the envelope," or developing technologies that make things that might seem impossible, possible.

Many industries have seen significant growth because of the development of new technologies. Retail has grown thanks to online shopping. Health care has improved thanks to diagnostic systems. Agriculture has become more efficient due to irrigation systems.

Technology has reduced the drudgery and unsafe working conditions of many manufacturing jobs. Instead of a person tightening one bolt on each piece of machinery that goes by or breathing paint fumes for eight hours a day, robots can perform these tasks. But at a cost: there are fewer people employed in manufacturing these days because technological advances have eliminated their jobs.

Technology does more than just help an industry grow, it also affects careers. In some cases, high technologies create jobs or improve conditions for workers. In other cases, high technology can actually take the place of a worker or make it easier for one worker to do the job of several, which can result in fewer jobs in the industry.

Technology in Manufacturing

Have you ever wondered how your parents' car was built? Most likely, it was put together with the help of a **hydraulic arm**, a machine that creates power by pumping water through a confined space. This allows a kind of robot to lift objects much heavier than any person could lift on his or her own. And like a computer, a hydraulic arm is an example of high technology.

The hydraulic arms of a robot are just one example of high technology in manufacturing. **Manufacturing** is the making of things on a large scale using machinery. This means that a factory that produces toys is an example of manufacturing. A plant that produces microchips for computers is also a manufacturer. Usually, the machinery used in manufacturing is a good example of technology. This can be heavy machinery, like the hydraulic arm used in making cars.

This car assembly plant uses advanced technology to produce goods. How can learning about computers help you pursue a career in manufacturing?

High-Tech Careers

Do you know someone who works in one of these high-tech jobs?

✔ Computer chip manufacturers work in completely dust-free environments where they wear special white full-body suits and masks.

✔ In the finance industry, programmers write complex computer *algorithms*—computer programs made especially for problem solving—that help bankers and stockbrokers make important financial decisions.

✔ In the alternative energy industry, technicians climb hundreds of feet in the air to maintain and fix the machinery of giant wind turbines that generate energy for nearby cities or towns.

✔ In the entertainment industry, digital graphic artists use specialized computer programs to create animated features or enhance live-action movies with CGI, or "computer generated images."

✔ In medicine, surgeons use special joysticks to control miniature robotic fingers with special surgical tools to operate on sensitive areas of the body that are out of reach of human hands.

Can you think of other careers that make use of high technology?

It can also be small and highly specialized technology, like the tools used to make computer chips. Technology in manufacturing comes in a large range of sizes and applications:

■ Giant cranes make modern skyscrapers.

■ Robotic hydraulic arms manufacture cars.

■ Computers control automated assembly lines.

■ Just-in-time computerized inventory control means that companies don't have to waste time and money on inventory that just sits around in the warehouse. Instead, these systems order inventory at the exact right time and only for the exact right amount.

■ High-powered lasers etch and cut giant slabs of metal used in oil tankers.

■ Microscopic computer chips are configured using microscopic tools.

Keep this in mind: Even if a computer controls an assembly line, or if a robotic hydraulic arm can put together a car, none of these examples of technology in manufacturing work without skilled people controlling, programming, troubleshooting, and operating them.

Technology in E-Commerce

"Electronic commerce," or **e-commerce**, is the buying and selling of goods or services over the Internet. Some popular examples of e-commerce include: online banking, online retail sales, online travel resources, online ticket auctions, and so on. For instance, it used to be that in order to buy shoes, you needed to go into a store and try them on. Nowadays, you can buy shoes online and return them overnight if they do not fit. Likewise, buying tickets, books, or movies was only possible from inside the stores that sold them. But now, you can buy all of those things from your living room. And banking is never easier than when it is done on the Internet.

Many technological breakthroughs had to happen before widespread e-commerce became possible. Mathematicians invented encryption software to keep our credit card numbers safe. Systems engineers invented computerized inventory systems to keep track of products and orders. Even the hand-held scanner that your local package delivery employee uses is important for e-commerce because it allows businesses to instantly see that you have received your products.

How does e-commerce affect careers? Unfortunately, the convenience of online shopping has caused some small businesses to close. As a result, there may be fewer career opportunities in retail. However, there may be increased opportunities at online retail businesses.

Myth Computers are replacing people in the workplace.

Truth The workplace will always need skilled workers; computers are only as powerful as the people using them.

Careers in Information Technology (IT) Systems

Information technology systems, or **IT**, is a term used to describe computer and telecommunication systems that transmit and store information. Almost every business has an IT department, responsible for managing the data and computer systems that keep the company running. For example, the IT department makes sure that the human resources department has the tools it needs to keep track of employees, benefits, and training. It makes sure that the accounts receivable department can track and record payments.

A career working in an IT department would involve setting up, maintaining, and repairing the computer systems of an organization. Since virtually every large company uses some kind of computer system, there is great demand for skilled IT technicians. IT departments are usually separate from the rest of a company, since their employees are specifically dedicated to maintaining a computer **infrastructure**, which is the computer systems, networking, and other devices. Because many computer systems are similar, the skills you might develop in the IT department of one company are the same skills you would need in another. This means that if you decide on a career in IT, you can potentially work for many different companies. A good word for this is **fungible**, which means being able to trade one item or quality for another, interchangeably—as in, "your skills as an IT technician are fungible."

As an IT technician, you might:

- Resolve a problem with a company's e-mail system.
- Configure a wireless Internet network for thousands of employees.
- Recommend the purchase of certain computer hardware, such as servers, printers, or consoles.
- Do regular maintenance and backup on servers.
- Install programs, or write programs for specific uses.
- Maintain a company Web site.
- Deal with security issues, such as attempts to hack into company files and viruses.
- Train company personnel on IT issues.

IT technicians are usually highly respected, because they have knowledge of complex technologies. Most other members of a company generally do not have this knowledge, so the importance of having skilled IT technicians in any company makes a career in IT desirable.

What are some requirements and rewards of a career as a computer service technician?

Does Everyone Use Technology?

Even if you don't have a cell phone or computer, you use technology if you ride a bus, drive a car, or even write with a ballpoint pen. What if you don't want to use technology?

★ *You would have to forgo using any indoor plumbing or electricity in your home.*

★ *You could only go places that are within walking distance— unless you have a horse.*

★ *You could communicate with people only if you are face to face.*

★ *You could sit and tell stories with friends and family for entertainment.*

Can you think of other ways you could remove technology from your life?

Career Profile: Information Technology Manager

Information Technology Career Cluster

What skills and interests do you think would help someone succeed in a career as an information technology manager?

Job Summary

Working as an IT manager requires knowledge of both technology and business practices. The duties of an IT manager will vary depending on the work environment, company size, experience level, and other factors.

However, you can expect to deal with a wide range of issues. You must have excellent people skills, an understanding of business management, and technical expertise in some aspects of computer infrastructure. All of these skills are equally important. Technical expertise is often gained through previous professional experience, especially working in a related information technology position.

Use the Internet, a library, or career center to research the responsibilities, education and training requirements, and salary range of an information technology manager. Prepare a presentation about the career.

Career Trend

Careers in IT are becoming more desirable as we rely on technology in the workplace more. In economic terms, this means that a career in IT may pay more now than ever before.

Technology in Agriculture

Believe it or not, technology has had a big impact on our food over the past fifty years. Prior to the 1950s, American farms were usually small, family-owned operations that could not output a large number of crops per year. However, important advances in agricultural technologies have enabled large-scale farm practices. Technologies such as modern fertilizers, pesticides, genetically engineered seeds, and farm equipment have shaped what we eat. The food available to us in grocery stores depends on what our farmers produce. And what our farmers produce is affected by the kinds of technologies available to them. Here are some examples of how farm technology has affected the foods you eat:

Technology affects our food supply in many ways. How would a farmer plant and harvest crops without technology?

■ Science has allowed food manufacturers to process corn into a cheap sweetener, known as high-fructose corn syrup, which is used in thousands of different products, from soft drinks to soups.

■ Large-scale harvesting of wheat is possible with modern tractors, which can turn thousands of pounds of wheat into usable crops per day. This has increased the American output of wheat by a huge amount, making America one of the biggest wheat producers in the world. This means that the foods you eat that contain wheat, like bread and cereal, are all very inexpensive.

■ Industrial meat production has increased the amount of beef, pork, and poultry we can produce per day. This makes meat less costly.

Tech Connect

Technology has helped make food supplies around the world safer. Refrigeration keeps food fresher longer. Water purification systems kill harmful germs and insects. **Irradiation** exposes fruit and other food products to a source of radiation that kills bacteria and insects.

Technology has also caused safety problems. Chemicals used in farming to promote growth or kill insects can get into the water supply or into the meat and plants we eat. Bacteria such as salmonella can transfer from farms that produce meat, eggs, and poultry into the water supply and contaminate plants that we eat.

Use the Internet or your library to research technologies that protect or harm the food supply. Pick one, and then create a presentation about it to show your class.

Using Technology in Your Career

Can you think of a job that does not require you to use technology? Phone systems, computers, printers, copy machines, and fax machines are standard equipment in almost every office. Even entry-level positions that require no previous work experience often require some use of technology. Your best bet in preparing for almost any career is to become familiar with technology so that you can become an expert when the time comes.

Technology for the Entrepreneur

For many years, entrepreneurs have started successful businesses—and sometimes kept them running for a long time—from inside their own homes. It has become even easier as technology has improved and come down in cost. Home computers, all-in-one printers that scan, copy, and fax as well as print, software for scheduling and data management, Internet access, and mobile phones allow entrepreneurs to function as if they had an office and staff—even when they are home alone working at the kitchen table. What technologies do you think an entrepreneur might find most useful when starting a business?

Laptops That Make a Difference

One Laptop per Child is a nonprofit organization with a goal of creating educational opportunities for the world's poorest children by giving them laptop computers they can use to access and share information.

To achieve its goal, the organization developed a low-cost, rugged laptop called the XO. It has built-in wireless communications and a screen that can be read even in bright sunlight—so it can be used outdoors. The battery lasts about six hours, or 24 hours for reading only, and features 2,000 recharge cycles, which is about four times more cycles than the typical laptop.

Use the Internet to learn more about One Laptop per Child and the XO. Why does the XO need to be rugged? How can providing children with laptops help solve problems associated with poverty and the lack of education? Can you think of other solutions that might work? Use presentation software to make a short presentation about the topic. Keep a bibliography listing the sources you consult in your research. Then, share your presentation with the class.

Career Tips

You can make your Internet searches more powerful by using what's called **Boolean operators**, special words or quotes that make your searches more specific. For instance, putting quotes around a phrase searches for that phrase exactly, instead of just searching for sites that contain at least one of the words from the phrase.

Transferrable Computer Skills

Do you type? Have you ever used the Internet to search for information? If so, then you already possess several basic, transferable skills that you will need to interact with technology in your career. And the best part is, since technology is everywhere in the world of work, if you have one or more of these basic skills, you can take them wherever you go.

What are basic skills you need when you start almost any career? You need to be able to:

■ Run and use various computer programs and take measures to secure your data.

■ Type on a computer keyboard without making many mistakes.

■ Access the Internet and move from one Web site to another.

■ Use a search engine to do basic Internet research.

■ Log on to work groups and use collaboration technology.

■ Write and send e-mail.

Some of these skills might seem easy to you. Others might sound difficult or new. Either way, these are all skills worth having. The important thing to know is that you might be asked to use these or other basic, transferrable skills at some point in your career. Even if you do not know how to do some of these things, you can learn. Being flexible, open-minded, and willing to learn new skills is the key to success.

21st Century Learning

Jessica is a recent retiree who worked her career in a textile manufacturing plant. She has never used a computer, but since most of her extended family uses social networking sites, she would like to be able to connect with them over the Internet. There are computers at her local library, but she doesn't know how to use them. Her local community center offers classes, but she is embarrassed to admit she needs lessons.

Jessica feels that it's too late to learn and that she will be doomed to computer illiteracy forever.

What steps can Jessica take to become comfortable using a computer? Should she try to learn, or is it too late? How can she overcome her fear and embarrassment? Use your 21st Century Skills such as setting goals, managing resources, and recognizing the impact of technology to help Jessica. Write an ending to the story. Read it to the class, or form a small group and present it as a skit.

Using Communications Devices

Do you text? Can you send e-mail? Do you have a phone that can do either of these things? If yes, you are like millions of Americans who own a smartphone. If not, chances are, you will one day soon.

Cell phones make it possible to communicate with others from almost anywhere in the world. At the same time cell phones were becoming an important means of communication, **personal digital assistants (PDAs)** were developed to help people track their appointments and business contacts. Gradually, cell phones added more features like those of PDAs, and PDAs added wireless communications and calling capability. The combination of features from both types of devices resulted in smartphones.

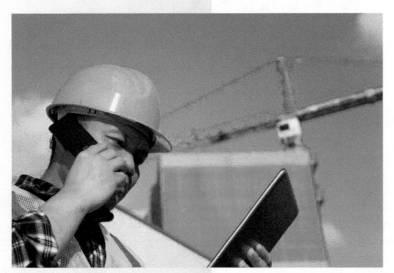

Why is it important for construction workers to have cell phones?

Besides being able to communicate with your parents and friends, what is the value of having one of these devices?

■ Employees with smartphones can be reached by e-mail, the communications medium of choice, at any time of day. In fact, many companies give their employees a smartphone for free. But with this free device comes the understanding that employees are reachable for work even when they are at home. Therefore, they can work longer hours.

■ "Texting," sending small written messages from one cell phone to another, can be an efficient way to communicate. Sending a text instead of placing a call can save both the caller and the recipient time. And in some businesses, getting information from one person to another quickly is essential to making money.

■ Employees can access the Internet to look up information when they are not at their office.

A **smartphone** is a cell phone that is also a miniature computer. What makes a smartphone "smart"? How can it help you in your career?

Using Computer Applications

A **computer application**, or **program**, is a tool you use to perform specific tasks on a computer. Employers look for employees who have experience using computer applications. Some of the most common and useful include:

■ Modern word processors allow you to quickly edit and rearrange your written thoughts. If you are unhappy about a certain paragraph, you can move it somewhere else in the document or delete it entirely. Word processors also automatically check your spelling, so there are fewer mistakes in your work.

■ Presentation software can produce slide shows that are very helpful for presenting certain types of information.

■ Spreadsheets can take tens of millions of pieces of data, usually in the form of numbers, and organize them quickly. This is why many companies use spreadsheet software to contain and manipulate their data.

■ Web browsers are becoming so important to modern computing that some computers are nothing but a Web browser! This means that the files normally on a computer—your documents, photos, music, etc.—are all stored online and accessed through the Internet. This type of computing is called **cloud computing**.

■ A database management program helps you organize and manipulate data.

■ A Web design program helps you create Web pages.

■ A graphic design program lets you create sophisticated graphics or repair or manipulate photographs.

■ A page layout program lets you place type and graphics on pages for publications.

Understanding Mobile Apps Is Important, Too!

An *app* is a computer program designed for use on a mobile device. There are literally millions of apps available for download. They enable you to do many things directly from your smartphone or other mobile device, such as play games, transfer bank funds, or purchase tickets to a concert.

Many companies have found apps to be useful tools for communicating with customers and promoting their products and services. Employees, too, use apps to schedule appointments, track inventory, and manage information.

What type of apps do you think an employee could use in any career?

You can use a spreadsheet to store data, create graphs, and perform calculations. How many careers can you think of where spreadsheet skills might be necessary?

Case Study

Bethany really wanted a new bicycle. But her allowance was too small to pay for it, and her parents did not want to buy it for her. So she decided to try to get a part-time job after school. She felt she had some good job skills, including familiarity with using a computer, phone skills, and typing skills.

Bethany's parents were too busy at work to take her around to any local shops that might be interested in hiring her part-time. She felt unsure walking around by herself. A friend recommended that Bethany use the Internet to find out more information before going to look for a part-time job, but Bethany had never done a job search online before. She had heard of some Web sites where people got jobs, but never used one herself.

■ How can Bethany use technology to help her find work?

■ What Internet sites could help Bethany find part-time, after-school work?

■ What kind of job might Bethany look for?

■ How can Bethany find out how much money she might expect her job to pay her?

Web Extra ▼

Many informational Web sites provide reliable and accurate information for job seekers, including monster.com, careerbuilder.com, and payscale.com.

Use the Internet to locate some sites that you think might be useful for your peers. Using a spreadsheet application, make a directory of the sites. Include the Web site address, a brief description, and whether the site is free or has a fee. Post the directory on your school Web site or in your school career center or library.

Answer It!

1. What is technology?

2. How has technology changed the way your generation might plan for and settle on a career?

3. According to the U.S. Bureau of Labor Statistics, how many careers will a person from your generation probably have in a lifetime?

4. How has videoconferencing affected the way companies conduct meetings?

5. What are the three reasons any business would use any type of technology?

6. Name at least three examples of manufacturing.

7. Why is it that technology will never replace people?

8. What would a career in an IT department involve?

9. Why do many companies give their employees smartphones for free?

10. What reason do companies have for using spreadsheet software?

Career-Ready Practices

Information technology has a significant impact on consumers. Advertising on television and the Internet influences our buying decisions, access to online shopping affects how and where we shop, and access to information helps us compare and evaluate products and stores before we shop. To remain competitive and be successful, businesses have had to adjust to these changing consumer buying habits. For example, many companies now have Web sites—in addition to bricks-and-mortar locations—where consumers can buy products and services.

Career-ready individuals recognize that using and maximizing technology can enhance workplace productivity and give their employer a competitive edge. They equip themselves with basic technology skills and embrace new skills that will help them accomplish their tasks and meet the needs of their customers.

Imagine you work in the IT department of a large corporation. Working in teams of four or five, research the influence technology has on products and services, and how it impacts consumer decision making. Then explore how these changes affect the use of technology in the workplace. Using a presentation program, organize the information into a presentation that you can deliver to the class.

Write Now

Applying for jobs online can be more convenient than doing it in person. You can mail hundreds of resumes and cover letters with the click of a button. This would take far more work when done by hand. But, with this convenience comes a downside. Just as easy as it is to send e-mail to a potential employer, it is also just as easy for a potential employer to ignore you.

Write an essay about the benefits and drawbacks of applying for jobs over the Internet. Include information about why the Internet can make it both easier and harder to get a job. Then, think of ways you can avoid being ignored and how you can make your job application stand out. Talk with people who have experience—your parents, siblings, a teacher, or librarian. Use examples that you find online, if possible. In your essay, provide examples from the Career Portfolio that you are working on.

Career Portfolio

Many computer applications are common in business these days. Mostly, this software is related to everyday productivity. This includes software that helps people write, organize data, and present information. Knowing how to use these types of software is usually essential for even entry-level jobs. Being an expert at one or more of these applications is almost always a good skill. And since the software is used nearly everywhere, knowing how to use it is a transferable skill.

Your Career Portfolio is a place to showcase the basic, transferrable skills that you possess. For instance, have you used word processing software to create letters or reports or spreadsheet software for analyzing numerical information? Make a list for your Career Portfolio. Include any of these pieces of productivity software (or others) that you have used. Briefly describe your familiarity with each as "Basic," "Intermediate," or "Expert." Include samples of your work.

Business Plan Project

Every business uses technology in one form or another. With a partner, brainstorm the type of technologies that you think you will need to make your business succeed. Then, use the Internet to learn more about how those technologies are used. In your **Business Plan Project**, make a list explaining what you learned, and how you might develop the skills you need to implement the technologies as part of your **Business Plan Project**. For example, you could select a class to learn how to design a Web page, read a book about robots, or ask your teacher to organize a videoconference with a class at a different school.

Career Development

Part III

In This Part . . .

Chapter 12 ■ **Career Planning**

Chapter 13 ■ **Managing a Job Search**

Chapter 14 ■ **Getting Started in Your Career**

Chapter 15 ■ **Being Productive in Your Career**

Chapter 16 ■ **Balancing Work, Family, and Friends**

12 Career Planning

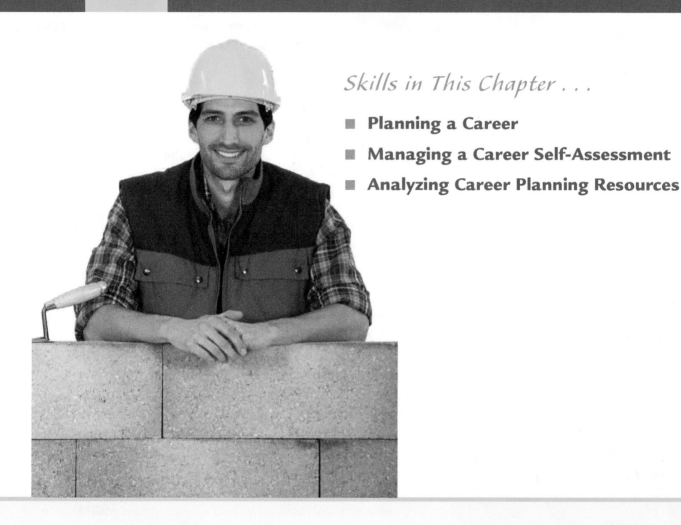

Skills in This Chapter . . .

- **Planning a Career**
- **Managing a Career Self-Assessment**
- **Analyzing Career Planning Resources**

GETTING STARTED

Planning for a career is a job in itself. It takes time, energy, and careful management. So why do it? Putting effort into career planning can help you set realistic and attainable goals for education. It can help you identify your strengths and weaknesses, so you focus your resources on finding a career that you will enjoy. Spending time exploring career opportunities can also be fun and exciting, because you experience new situations and activities. Career planning allows you to gather the information you need to make healthy decisions and take control of your future.

➤ Working in small groups, take three minutes to make a list of the most exciting and interesting careers you can think of. Next to each one, write whether or not it is a career you might realistically be able to attain. Why or why not?

But I Haven't Chosen a Career!

How can you use career-related goals to help identify a career that matches your interests and abilities? What if you are unsure about the career path you will follow?

★ Set goals for academic achievement.

★ Set goals for volunteering.

★ Set goals for researching different types of careers.

★ Set goals for building skills and abilities.

★ Set goals for earning and saving money.

Can you think of career-related goals you can set right now? Make a list and discuss it with the class.

How can planning your career help you take control of your future?

Planning a Career

You might be wondering why you should care about planning your career now. You might be thinking that you have time for that in the future. In truth, the sooner you start thinking about your future options, the easier it will be to make those options attainable.

Planning a career involves assessing your career-related skills and interests and then setting goals. It also involves exploring the career clusters, pathways, and jobs so you recognize the possibilities. Finally, it involves analyzing career resources so you can recognize opportunities that can help you achieve your goals.

Steps for Planning a Career

A career, if it is the right one for you, can be very rewarding. The following steps outline the basic process of planning a career.

1. *Assess your interests, skills, values, and abilities.* What are your talents and interests? What do you value? What rewards do you want from a career?

2. *Research the big picture.* Which job areas are the fastest-growing in your area? What kind of education and training will workers need for these jobs?

3. *Explore career options.* What types of careers are there? What are the requirements for different careers? What are the day-to-day responsibilities?

4. *Create a career plan.* What are your career goals? How will you get the education and training you need to achieve those goals? How long will it take?

5. Get hired. Are you employable? Are there opportunities for you to work right now that might build your skills and provide you with valuable experience?

6. Be successful. Do you have the skills you need to keep up with your work responsibilities? Do you have the personal qualities other people admire and respect? Do you know how to make decisions, set goals, and solve problems?

7. Continue planning. Are you satisfied in your current position? Are there new goals you might want to achieve? How can you continue to grow and develop new skills and experience?

Mapping out a Career Plan

A **career plan** is a map that shows you the way to achieve your career goals. You use it to identify your skills and interests, to find a career or career cluster that suits your skills and interests, and to determine the type of education and training you will need to succeed.

A career plan is similar to an academic plan. In fact, you can't really have one without the other.

■ Your academic plan should include goals for developing career-related skills and abilities.

■ Your career plan should include goals for achieving academic requirements.

As with an academic plan, your career plan should be specific, realistic, and attainable. It should include a long-range career goal as well as a series of short-term milestones that will help you get there. Every once in a while, you should revisit your career plan and make adjustments or corrections. Your goals might change as you develop new interests and abilities, so your career plan will change, too.

What to Include in a Career Plan

There are different ways to develop a career plan. Your teacher or counselor may have a form for you to use. It may be part of your academic plan or a separate document. Most career plans include the following information:

■ A career self-assessment, including a prioritized list of skills, interests, and abilities

■ An analysis of careers or career clusters that match personal skills, interests, and abilities

■ An academic plan aligned with a selected career or career cluster

■ An analysis of the outlook for the selected career or career cluster

■ An assessment of the financial resources required to achieve career goals

Myth Once you make a career plan, you are stuck with it for life.

Truth A career plan is flexible. Most people revise and refine their career plans many times in their lives. Your plan might change because your interests or abilities change, or you might discover new opportunities or resources.

Surveys show that high pay does not necessarily lead to job satisfaction. While it is important to consider salary when choosing a career, it is also important to look for a job that you enjoy.

I Hate This Job!

Problems can come from choosing a career without careful planning. Just because a career is right for someone else doesn't mean it is right for you. Here are some of the reasons a job might work out—or not.

- 👎 You don't have the skills or abilities.

- 👎 You think it is boring.

- 👎 You think it does not pay enough.

- 👍 You spend time looking for a career that matches your interests.

- 👍 You succeed because of your education.

What are some reasons people work in careers they do not enjoy? What steps can you take to find a career you do enjoy?

College Entrance Exams

In the United States, most colleges and universities consider a wide range of factors when assessing applicants, including scores from standardized tests such as the Scholastic Aptitude Test (SAT) and ACT. In other countries, standardized exams may be the only factor that determines whether a student is accepted.

In South Korea, for example, all students interested in attending a university must take a day-long national college entrance exam. That adds up to more than half a million students taking the same test at the same time. The results determine which school each student will be qualified to attend, which directly affects his or her ability to obtain a job.

Brazil also bases university admission solely on a student's score on a national standardized test. Of course, some countries make it much easier to achieve higher education. In Belgium, the only requirement for enrolling in a public university is a high school diploma.

Do you think it is fair to judge a college applicant on standardized test scores alone? Why do you think most American colleges and universities consider factors such as high school grades, teacher recommendations, and a personal essay? Use the Internet or your library to research the college or university entrance requirements in the United States and in another country. Write an essay or create a chart comparing the two systems.

NUMBERS GAME

The ability to add fractions is important in many careers. Chefs use fractions when developing recipes. Carpenters use fractions to measure lumber and other materials. All workers use fractions to measure time and money.

To add fractions that have the same denominator, simply add the numerators, leaving the denominator unchanged. So, $\frac{3}{8} + \frac{3}{8} = \frac{6}{8}$ (which can be simplified to $\frac{3}{4}$).

To add fractions that have different denominators, such as $\frac{3}{8}$ and $\frac{3}{4}$, you must rewrite the fractions using the **least common denominator** (LCD). The LCD is the smallest number that two different denominators can divide into evenly. In other words, it is a multiple of all the denominators.

To find the LCD, write down the multiples of one denominator, and then write down the multiples of the next denominator. (That means multiplying the denominator by one and writing down the product, multiplying it by two and writing down the product, multiplying by three, etc.) Then, circle the numbers that are on both lists, and pick the smallest.

So, the first step is to find the LCD for $\frac{3}{8}$ and $\frac{3}{4}$. List the denominators and circle the ones they have in common:

⑧ ⑯ 24, 32, …   4, ⑧ 12, ⑯ …

Next, rewrite the factions using the LCD, which in this case is 8 (multiply the numerator and the denominator by the same multiple):

$\frac{3}{8} = \frac{3}{8}$ $\frac{3}{4} = \frac{6}{8}$

Finally, add the fractions:

$\frac{3}{8} + \frac{6}{8} = \frac{9}{8}$, which can be written as the mixed number $1\frac{1}{8}$.

You do the math: A tailor has $\frac{3}{4}$ of a yard left on one bolt of fabric, and $\frac{2}{3}$ of a yard left on another bolt. How many total yards does he have?

Managing a Career Self-Assessment

Recall that a self-assessment process helps you identify the things you enjoy and do well. When you focus the self-assessment process on career-related skills, interests, values, and abilities, it is called a **career self-assessment**. A career self-assessment can help you choose a career path that will bring you satisfaction.

A career self-assessment can be hard, but rewarding. At this point, how do you identify your career-related abilities? How do you apply your values to a work environment? To perform a career self-assessment, you use a process to examine your strengths and weaknesses honestly and objectively.

Developing a Career Self-Assessment Worksheet

There are many ways to assess your career interests, skills, and abilities. One way is to use a six-step process to help you complete an objective career self-assessment. The result will be a worksheet that you can use to set academic and career goals. You can develop the worksheet on your own, but it may be easier if you work with an adult such as a teacher or counselor. The adult can help you be objective and honest about your skills, interests, and abilities.

1. List your two favorite school subjects. Usually—but not always—these are the subjects you do well in. They might be core subjects, such as science or social studies, or they may be electives, such as technology education or art.

2. List at least four specific skills you have acquired in your favorite subjects. For example, if you chose Spanish, your skills might include reading or speaking Spanish or understanding Spanish culture, or even cooking Spanish food. If you chose science, your skills might include understanding chemical properties, using a microscope, or valuing peer review.

3. List at least four achievements in your favorite subjects. Your achievements are the things you have earned based on your performance. They might include good grades, awards, acknowledgments, or even an assignment you are proud of. For example, for language arts, you might list a poem you wrote for class. For music, you might list a solo in the fall concert.

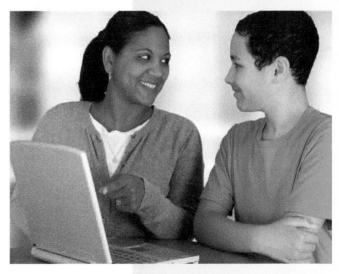

4. List at least four abilities—the things you do well or your talents. You can list specific abilities, such as playing guitar or repairing machines. You can also list qualities that help you succeed in many areas, such as being a good listener or having good time management skills. (Refer to the table on the following page for categories of abilities.)

5. List at least two interests. Again, you can list specific interests, such as working with animals or photography, or you can list interest areas. (Refer to the table on page 208 for descriptions of six common interest areas.)

6. List at least four work values.

Career Tips

There are many ways to conduct a career-self-assessment. Your teacher or counselor might use a different process or have a form for you to complete. You can try different methods to find one you are comfortable using.

21st Century Learning

Maria is a junior in high school. She plays on the school basketball team. She is a member of the school's chapter of Future Business Leaders of America. She does very well in school and takes advanced-level classes in math, science, and language arts.

Maria works part-time helping her father with his landscape business. Her father wants her to join the business after graduation, and he plans to give her the business when he is ready to retire. Maria enjoys landscaping because it is active, outdoor work, but she is not sure if it is the right career for her. She wonders if she will get bored or miss out on other opportunities if she joins her dad's business right after high school.

What can Maria do now to start planning for her career? What resources can she use to determine whether landscaping is right for her or if she should consider other career opportunities? Use 21st Century Skills such as problem solving, critical thinking, communications, and decision making to help Maria assess her options. Write an ending to the story and read it to the class, or form small groups and present it as a skit.

Identifying Your Abilities

Use the chart below to find the ability (or abilities) that describe you best and the corresponding careers.

Ability	Description	Related Careers
Artistic	If you have artistic ability you are creative and understand artistic ideas.	Fashion designer, graphic designer, interior decorator, or photographer
Clerical	If you have clerical ability you pay attention to detail and do precise, accurate work.	Administrative assistant, bookkeeper, medical, public safety dispatcher, or records technician
Interpersonal	People with this ability relate well to others. They are good communicators, friendly, polite, and adapt well to different situations. Most careers require strong interpersonal ability.	Customer service representative, flight attendant, home health aide, retail salesperson, or social worker
Language	If you have language ability you are an excellent reader, writer, and speaker. You know how to ask questions and listen to answers.	Editor, social worker, speech therapist, or translator
Leadership	People who have leadership ability are able to get others to work together toward a common goal. They also manage resources effectively.	Athletic coach, chef, educational administrator, firefighter, or lawyer
Manual	If you have manual ability you are skilled using your hands, fingers, and eyes, and are good at operating equipment and following directions. This area also includes athletic ability.	Animal caretaker, athlete, auto mechanic, carpenter, or conservation worker
Mathematical/ Numerical	If you have mathematical/numerical ability you are good at solving problems and using math skills.	Financial analyst, network administrator, pharmacist, or software engineer
Musical/ Dramatic	People who have musical ability have a keen ear for sound. People who have dramatic ability are skilled at acting.	Actor, director, music or drama educator, musician, or producer
Organizational	People with organizational ability are good at planning and managing tasks and maintaining records.	Air traffic controller, computer systems analyst, nurse, or travel agent
Persuasive	If you have persuasive ability you can influence others by sharing your own views and opinions.	Advertising executive, lawyer, psychiatrist, or retail salesperson
Scientific	If you have scientific ability you are good at research, logic, and critical thinking.	Agricultural inspector, chemical engineer, dental assistant, dietitian, or physical therapist
Social	People with social ability use logical thinking and effective communication to help others.	Home health aide, recreational worker, school counselor, or social worker
Visual	People with visual—or spatial—ability can see differences in size and shape and understand how objects fit together or come apart.	Architect, carpenter, dentist, graphic designer, landscaper, or mechanical engineer
Technical/ Mechanical	If you have technical/mechanical ability you understand how to set up and operate machines.	Airline pilot, auto mechanic, electrician, or master mechanic

Identifying Your Interests

Use the chart below to find your interest areas and the corresponding careers.

Interest Area	Description	Related Careers
The Arts	If you enjoy music, painting, writing, entertaining others, and are creative and independent, you may be interested in the arts.	Actor, artist, editor, fashion designer, musician, photographer, or reporter
Business	If you enjoy coming up with new ideas, managing projects and other people, and selling things, you may be interested in business.	Bank manager, business executive, entrepreneur, lawyer, or salesperson
Crafts	If you enjoy working with tools and building things, you may be interested in crafts.	Architect, auto mechanic, cook, electrician, fashion designer, or graphic artist
Office Operations	If you enjoy working with words and numbers and if you like being organized and accurate, you may be interested in office operations.	Accountant, administrative assistant, bank teller, computer operator, medical records, tax preparer, or technician
Scientific	If you enjoy math and science, study a lot, work independently, and are curious and creative, you may have scientific interests.	Architect, biologist, computer scientist, economist, mechanical engineer, medical lab technician, pharmacist, physician, or veterinarian
Social	If you enjoy helping others, get along well with other people, have a lot of patience, and enjoy communicating, you may have social interests.	Clinical psychologist, counselor, nurse, police officer, recreation worker, school administrator, social worker, or teacher

What abilities might be useful for a career as a social worker? What interests might a social worker and a teacher have in common?

Completing Your Career Self-Assessment Worksheet

Once you have filled in your career self-assessment worksheet, you can look through the information to find connections that might point to a possible career path. For example, your favorite subject might be history, your abilities might include patience with senior citizens, and you might have an interest in social services. Can you see any connection between them?

For the final step to complete the worksheet, list your top two preferred career clusters—the clusters that best match your skills, interests, and abilities.

Using Your Career Self-Assessment Worksheet

Every career self-assessment worksheet will be unique, because you are unique. You might share interests with a friend, but you might have different abilities or work values. What career path might you consider if your self-assessment profile includes the following?

- Subject: Technology
- Skill: Computer programming
- Achievement: Award for Web page design
- Ability: Artistic
- Interest: Business
- Work value: Independence

You might look at the Information Technology career cluster and the Web and Digital Communications pathway, or you might consider the Business Management & Administration career cluster and the Business Information Management pathway. Can you think of other career opportunities that might appeal to someone with the profile above?

Self-Assessment, a Valuable Tool for Entrepreneur

Entrepreneurs might conduct a self-assessment for reasons other than identifying career opportunities. An entrepreneur can use an honest self-assessment to identify his or her strengths and weaknesses. Then, he or she can use the information to hire employees who are stronger where the entrepreneur may be weak. An entrepreneur might also use a self-assessment to determine if he or she is starting the business at the right time, for the right reasons. In such a situation, the self-assessment might include questions such as, "Is this the right time in my life for this opportunity?" "Am I committed to this venture?" and "Is there another way to achieve my career goals?" How might an entrepreneur and his or her investors benefit from this type of self-assessment?

Analyzing Career Planning Resources

Part of career planning is identifying career opportunities that meet your needs and fit your skills, interests, and abilities. In addition to the resources discussed in Chapter 4, such as the Occupational Outlook Handbook and informational interviews, you can also use **job search resources**—tools designed to help you find **job leads.**

You can use a variety of resources to identify career opportunities. You will probably need to use more than one of the following resources.

- Networking uses people you know to help you find opportunities.
- Online resources let you access information and job listings on the Internet.
- Want ads are a traditional source for job listings.
- Career counselors help you identify jobs that match your skills, interests, and abilities.
- Employment agencies work to match employers with employees.
- Job fairs provide an opportunity to introduce yourself to many different employers.

What Is Networking?

Networking in career planning means sharing information about yourself and your career goals with personal contacts—people you know already or new people you meet in any area of your life. Hopefully, one of the contacts works for a company that is hiring or knows someone at a company that is hiring. The contact recommends you for the position. Employers like to hire people who come with a recommendation from someone they know and trust.

Here's how it works:

1. You see a cousin at a family party and tell him that you are trying to find a job as a paralegal—someone who works in a law office assisting lawyers with legal paperwork.

2. Your cousin is bowling with friends and mentions that you are looking for a position as a paralegal.

3. One of the bowling buddies tells his mother, who is a lawyer, about you.

4. The law firm where she works is looking for a paralegal. She invites you to apply for the job.

Some studies show that nearly 80 percent of all job openings are never advertised.

How Do I Network?

The first step in networking is to tell everyone you know that you are planning your career. Be specific about your career goals. Tell your family, friends, classmates, and teachers. If you volunteer, tell the people at the volunteer organization. If you are a member of a club or organization, tell the other members.

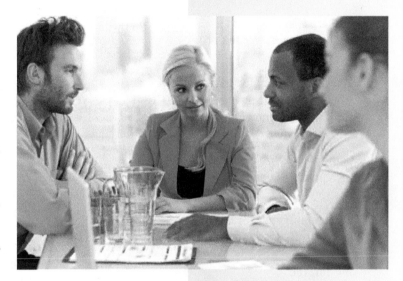

Once you make a contact, it is important to stay in touch through regular calls or e-mails. The first time you call or e-mail a contact, explain who you are and why you are reaching out. Do not ask for a job. Instead, ask for:

■ Information about occupations and companies, such as what trends are affecting a certain industry

■ Introductions to people who might become part of your network

■ Job leads

How can meeting new people help you find career opportunities?

Remember to give the contact your phone number and e-mail address so he or she can reach you. Always be polite, speak clearly, and say thank you.

Money Madne$$

You currently work at the information booth in a local state park. You earn $10.75 an hour. Recently, you met a woman who works as a wilderness first responder—someone who helps people injured while participating in a wilderness activity such as hiking or skiing. The job sounds like something you might be interested in. She suggests you take a wilderness first aid course, which is the first step toward certification. The course costs $175.00. How many hours must you work to save enough money to pay for the course?

Job Search. Career Research. What's the Difference?

You completed a career self-assessment worksheet. You picked two careers that match your interests, skills, and abilities. Why haven't you found a job?

👎 You are spending only a couple of hours a week on your job search.

👎 You are applying for positions that require more skill and training than you currently have.

👎 You do not have personal recommendations for the positions.

👎 You are applying for the same job that hundreds of other candidates are applying for, too.

👍 You are continuing to spend time building a network of contacts.

👍 You keep your job search materials organized to make it easy to apply to any new job opening.

👍 You use all available job search resources to increase your chances of finding a job.

Remember, career research helps you identify types of careers that match your skills, interests, and abilities. A job search identifies specific job openings and opportunities for employment. How can you use your career research to help you in your job search?

Organizing Your Contacts

Set up a networking file to keep track of each contact. That way, you will have a record of each communication to help you stay organized and focused. Set up the file using index cards or a computer program. In the file, include:

■ The name, occupation, mailing address, phone number, and e-mail address of each contact.

■ A reminder of how you know the contact. Is it a personal friend? Did you meet through someone else? Did you meet through a club or organization?

■ The date and time of each phone call, message, or other type of communication with the contact

■ Notes about each conversation or exchange with the contact.

Using Online Resources

The Internet is a great tool for finding a career. You can even use it to make contacts for networking. Some of the more effective online resources include:

■ *Company Web sites.* You can learn a lot about a company from its Web site, including what they do, the backgrounds of the people who work there, and who to contact in each department. Most sites also have a page listing job openings, with information on how to apply. Even if there are no openings that interest you, you can contact the human resources department to try to set up an informational interview.

■ *Government sites.* Like corporations, government agencies list information and job openings. There are also government Web sites that provide job listings.

■ *Industry sites.* Many industries and industry associations have Web sites that list job opportunities. For example, if you are interested in a career as a social worker, you could look for positions on socialworkjobbank.com.

■ *Online job agencies.* Companies such as Monster.com or CareerBuilder.com list job openings and let you upload your resume for employers to look at. You can search these sites for jobs in a field or career that interests you. Some of these sites charge fees.

■ *Social networking sites.* You can use social networking sites such as Facebook or LinkedIn to meet contacts and learn about jobs. There are groups for people in certain careers or who work for specific companies. Employers join these sites, as well. They look for potential employees based on the personal profile you create. That's an important reason for posting only information that would be appropriate for a potential employer to see!

Using a Career Center or Agency

A career center is an excellent place to start planning your career. Your school might have a career center that you can use free of charge. Career centers have job listings, research resources, and counselors who will help you identify jobs that match your skills and interests. They can also introduce you to former students who are now employed—giving you more opportunities for networking.

Employment offices are similar to career centers. Some are sponsored by the state or local government. They provide job search resources and assistance free of charge.

Private employment agencies charge a fee to match employees with employers. Sometimes you pay the fee, and sometimes the employer pays the fee. Sometimes you pay even if you don't find a job. They all have different policies, so be sure to ask before you sign a contract.

Does your school have a career center? What resources does it have that you might use?

Career Profile: Human Resources Manager

Business Management & Administration Career Cluster

Job Summary

Human resources managers supervise the staff in a human resources department—or a personnel department. They oversee all personnel-related activities. For example, people who work in human resources review job applications, advise employees on work- and career-related issues, administer compensation and benefits policies, manage training for new and current employees, represent the company at career fairs and other events, and manage employee records.

The role of a human resources manager often depends on the size of the organization. If the company is small, he or she may be responsible for all aspects of human resources work. In a larger company, he or she may specialize in one human resources activity, such as employment and placement, compensation and benefits, training and development, or labor relations.

Use the Internet, a library, or career center to research the responsibilities, education and training requirements, and salary range of a human resources manager in your state. Write a job description or want ad for the position.

Government Job Search Resources

Some Web sites that link to government job search resources include:

✔ *usajobs.gov*

✔ *governmentjobs.com*

✔ *www.jobsfed.com*

✔ *www.studentjobs.gov*

Temporary employment agencies are hired by a company to fill temporary jobs. For example, a company might need temporary data entry help to complete a large project or help to fill in for a worker on vacation or on a leave of absence. Temporary jobs can lead to a permanent position. They are also a good way to build skills, gain experience, and meet people in the industry.

Career Fairs

An event such as a career or job fair is a great opportunity to meet representatives from many different companies. Companies set up booths where you can talk to representatives to learn more about the business, types of careers, and even available positions. Some companies use career fairs to collect resumes and set up interviews; some conduct interviews on the spot.

What might be some benefits and drawbacks of attending a job fair that focuses on a specific industry?

Although many career fairs are general, which means there are companies from many different industries, there is a growing trend toward career fairs that focus on a specific industry. For example, at a high technology career fair, you can meet representatives from companies in the high technology industry. At a health sciences career fair, you can meet representatives from companies in the health sciences industry. Attending a focused career fair may be useful if you know the industry or cluster that interests you, but you may miss the opportunity to learn about other industries or types of jobs.

When you attend a career fair, assume you are being evaluated as a potential employee. You may be interested in collecting information for career planning, but the company representatives are looking for people to hire. Dress appropriately, be confident and outgoing, and be prepared to ask and answer questions.

What About Want Advertisements?

Another resource that can help you identify career opportunities are help wanted ads. **Help wanted ads**—which are sometimes called classified ads—are job listings for specific positions. They are printed in newspapers and magazines and posted online at newspaper and magazine Web sites. You can use the help wanted ads to find a specific job, but also to learn about career outlooks in your area. For example, you can identify companies that are hiring, industries that appear to have many openings—or very few—and salary ranges for listed jobs.

Usually, there are many ads listed alphabetically. They may be organized into general categories, such as Medical, Professional, and Education. For example, if you are looking for a teaching position, you would look at the listings under Education.

Help wanted ad listings usually include a job title and a very brief description of the responsibilities and experience required. Sometimes they include information about wages and hours. There may be a phone number or e-mail address to call for more information or to apply, or a mailing address where you can send a resume.

What can you learn about career opportunities from a help wanted ad?

Tech Connect

Printed newspapers once graced the front porch of nearly every home in America. Now, easy access to the Internet and 24-hour news cycles on television have helped to push newspapers online. While printed editions are still available, you can access and read articles and features in papers around the world using the Internet.

The online editions make it easy to read want ads in any area of the country—and in other countries, too. When you are ready to apply for jobs, you can use search tools to identify the ones that meet your criteria. You might also be able to upload your resume and apply for available positions.

Does your local newspaper have an online edition? If so, can you access its help wanted ads online? Use the Internet or your library to find out. Then, use a word processing program or a desktop publishing program to create a flyer advertising the benefits of using online newspaper help wanted ads to identify career opportunities.

Help Wanted Shorthand

Help wanted ads must convey a lot of information in a small amount of space. Here are some common want ad abbreviations.

✔ Appt	Appointment
✔ Avail	Available
✔ Eves	Evenings
✔ Exp	Experience
✔ F/T	Full-time
✔ H.S. Grad	High school graduate
✔ Hr	Hour
✔ Immed	Immediately
✔ M-F	Monday through Friday
✔ Nec	Necessary
✔ P/T	Part-time
✔ Perm	Permanent
✔ Pref	Preferred
✔ Refs	References
✔ Resp	Responsible
✔ Wkdays	Weekdays
✔ Wkends	Weekends

Case Study

Marcus is a shy, quiet young man who does well in math and science. In fact, he won the school science fair and has the highest average in advanced algebra. He does not play any sports, but he sings in the school choir, is a member of the drama club, and plays on the school chess team.

Marcus filled out a career self-assessment profile in school. He selected language arts and music as his best subjects. Among his skills he listed "strong communications" and "excellent singer." He included musical/dramatic, language, and social for his abilities. His achievements included second place in the school spelling bee and chorus in the school musical. He listed his interests as social and the arts. He selected entertainment and music as his preferred career groups. His work values included independence, creativity, and working with people.

■ Do you think Marcus was honest and accurate in his self-assessment?

■ Do you think Marcus selected career groups that match his values, interests, and abilities?

■ If you were Marcus's career counselor, what would you recommend he consider?

Web Extra

Bls.gov/k12/ is an official U.S. government Web site that provides links to careers that relate to your interests and presents fun facts about the economy and jobs. Use the Student Resources link to explore the careers that are related to your interests. Use the information you find to develop a list of potential careers, and create a table for each that identifies the average salary, education requirements, work experience requirements, and the job outlook.

Answer It!

1. What is the first step in the basic process of planning a career?

2. What is the purpose of a career plan?

3. Why is it important to revisit your career plan every once in a while?

4. List five things to include in a career plan.

5. Why might it be easier to work with an adult when you develop a career-assessment worksheet?

6. What is the final step to complete your career self-assessment worksheet?

7. List at least five resources for identifying career opportunities.

8. What is one reason networking is an excellent way to find career opportunities?

9. Why is it important to keep track of your networking contacts?

10. Why is it important to dress appropriately when you attend a job fair?

Career-Ready Practices

As you have learned, networking is a valuable career-planning tool that allows you to share information about yourself and your career goals with personal contacts. Career-ready individuals understand that in order to build a network of quality contacts—people who are eager to help you meet your career goals—they must demonstrate employability characteristics and skills such as leadership, flexibility, cooperation, and a positive attitude. They exhibit integrity and use a variety of means to positively influence others. They are honest and ethical in the roles they have in all areas of their lives.

Write a short paper that explains to a potential contact why he would want to include you in his network of personal contacts. Summarize your employability characteristics and skills and provide examples of how you have had a positive impact on others.

Write Now

Use the six-step process to create a career self-assessment worksheet for yourself. Be honest and accurate. Work with a partner, teacher, or counselor, if necessary. Analyze the worksheet and look for connections that point to a possible career path.

Complete the worksheet by listing two career clusters that interest you, based on the career assessment worksheet. Select a pathway in each cluster, and research the job outlook for each. Write a paragraph explaining how you might explore the opportunities in each pathway.

Career Portfolio

Your career portfolio should include your career plan. Working with your teacher, a counselor, or a family member, develop a career plan that starts now. The plan may be part of the academic plan you developed in Chapter 7, or it may be a separate document. If your school has a form for the plan, use it. Otherwise, develop the plan on a sheet of paper. Be sure to state a realistic and attainable long-term career goal that matches your skills, interests, and abilities. Also include short-term education and career goals that map out the steps you will take to achieve your ultimate career goal. Add the plan to your career portfolio along with your career self-assessment.

Business Plan Project

There are entrepreneurs in every type of career. No matter what career goals you choose or how you build your career plan, you can look for opportunities to create a business. On your own, consider the business you have selected for your business plan. Write a career plan for yourself that will lead you to achieve the goal of starting your selected business. Add this to your **Business Plan Project**. Then, in pairs or small groups review the career clusters and brainstorm entrepreneurial opportunities that are available in each one.

13 | Managing a Job Search

Skills in This Chapter . . .

- **Creating Job Search Materials**
- **Preparing a Resume**
- **Applying for a Job**
- **Interviewing for a Job**
- **Evaluating a Job Offer**

GETTING STARTED

Searching for a job is hard work. You will need all of your 21st Century process skills. For example:

- Communications skills to write job search materials, describe your strengths, and convey your interests nonverbally
- Decision-making skills to identify job opportunities and to accept or turn down a job offer
- Problem-solving skills to negotiate employment needs and improve your search materials or interviewing technique

A successful job search depends on being organized and thorough, as well as knowing how to use all available resources—in other words, on being an effective manager.

➤ As a class, brainstorm resources you think would be helpful for managing a job search. Be creative. For example, in addition to a computer with Internet access, you might think of a relative with a business that needs employees or a new outfit to wear on an interview. After you compile the list, discuss how you could effectively use each resource in a job search.

Creating Job Search Materials

Employers often consider tens or even hundreds of candidates for every job opening. Sometimes they shuffle through stacks of letters or field multiple phone calls. How can you make a positive impression and show you are serious and qualified for the job?

You can prepare professional, accurate job search materials, including a resume, cover letter, and list of references.

■ Your resume may be your most important job-search document. It is a written summary of your work-related skills, experience, and education.

■ A cover letter is sent along with your resume. It introduces you to a potential employer and highlights the qualities that make you suitable for the position you want.

■ A list of references includes the names and contact information of people who know you and your qualifications, and who are willing to speak about you to potential employers.

Why Do I Need a Cover Letter?

When you include a cover letter with your resume, you make a better impression on the employer than if you send the resume alone. Including a cover letter shows that you have taken the time to match your qualifications with a specific job.

A cover letter should be short and to the point. Direct it to the person who is responsible for hiring. If you do not know the person's name, title, and address, call the company and ask.

You can customize the cover letter to the job opening you are applying for. Use it to tell the employer why you are interested in that job and why you are qualified to do the work.

Career Tips

Even when you send a resume electronically, it is important to send a cover letter. For example, you can write the cover letter in an e-mail message and include the resume as an attachment.

When you write a cover letter, ask yourself these questions:

- Have I identified the job title for the job I want?
- Have I stated where I learned about the position?
- Have I listed the skills I have that qualify me for the position?
- Have I thanked the reader for his or her time and consideration?
- Have I corrected all spelling and grammatical errors?

Listing References

A **reference** is someone who knows you well and is willing to speak to employers about your qualifications. A good reference knows your positive work qualities and values, understands your abilities and interests, and can describe how you behave in a work environment. People such as relatives and friends should not be used as references because they may not be objective about you and your strengths and weaknesses.

Create a reference list to include in your career portfolio, and make sure you have it available to give to employers when they ask. Put your name and contact information at the top, and use the heading "References."

Select at least three people, and ask them for permission to use them as a reference. On the list, include each person's full name, occupation, mailing address, e-mail address, and daytime telephone number, including area code.

October 3, 2015

Ms. Helen White
MNO company
4671 Highland Avenue
Palatine, IL 60067

Dear Ms. White,

I am writing in response to the job posting for a human resources assistant that I saw on your Web site. I am enclosing my resume for your review.

For the past two years, I have worked as an account assistant at Employ Action, LLC., an employment agency. In that time, I have learned a great deal about employment options and opportunities. I am a hard worker who is looking for new challenges.

I would welcome the opportunity to speak with you personally about the human resources assistant position. You can contact me by phone or e-mail using the information below.

Thank you for your time and consideration,

Sincerely,

Thomas Leslie

Thomas Leslie
2323 McCloud Street
Palatine, IL 60067
555-555-5555
thomasleslie@mail.net

What message do you think spelling errors in a cover letter sends about your qualifications as an employee?

A good reference can speak objectively about your strengths and weaknesses. Can you think of three people you can include on your reference list?

Choosing a Reference

People who make good references include:

✔ Former or current employers

✔ Coaches or club advisors

✔ Teachers

People who do not make good references include:

✔ Your parents

✔ Any relative

✔ Friends

Do I Need a Portfolio?

Everyone looking for work should keep a career portfolio for storing documents such as a resume, cover letter, personal data sheet, and list of references. You can use a career portfolio as a resource when you are applying for jobs or going to an interview. For example, if you have your reference list with you when you are filling out a job application, you do not have to worry about remembering names and contact information.

If you are looking for a position in a creative career, such as photography, graphic design, or journalism, a portfolio that includes samples of current work is an important part of your job search materials. It lets you show potential employers your abilities and achievements.

■ For a job as a reporter, you would want to have a portfolio of published writing samples—clips from newspapers, magazines, newsletters, or printouts from a Web site. If you do not have published samples, you can include samples from your school work.

■ For a graphic designer, you would want to have a portfolio of materials you have designed, such as logos, business cards, or stationery.

It is a good idea to have the original sample in the portfolio, if possible, and to have copies available to give to potential employers. Artists sometimes create slides of their artwork to include in a portfolio.

Money Madne$$

Can you save money and time by submitting your resume and cover letter electronically? How much does it cost to send a first-class letter using the U.S. Postal Service? How many resumes are you going to send out?

Say it costs 52 cents for each resume, and you plan to send out 20 resumes. How much will it cost? What if you send out 55 resumes? Write a paragraph explaining why the cost of mailing a resume and cover letter is worth it, or not.

Recent research indicates that the average length of a job search is now more than seven months! In a down economy with a high unemployment rate, it can take longer than that. Knowing that it can take a long time to find a job helps keep you from becoming discouraged, or giving up.

Managing Your Job Search Materials

Keeping your job search materials organized in a folder or binder will help you follow up every possibility. When you are actively looking for work at many companies, it is easy to forget who you spoke to and even what you spoke about. An employer might not look favorably on someone who repeats the same conversation or cannot remember who referred her in the first place.

- Keep a to-do list of tasks you want to accomplish each day, such as people you want to contact, resumes you have to send out, and thank-you notes to write. Cross off each item you complete, and add new items as they come up.

- Contact some people in your network every day. Make brief phone calls, or send brief e-mail messages to let them know you are looking for work, and to ask for assistance finding job opportunities.

- Follow up on all leads. Keep a record of the people you contact, including phone numbers, e-mail addresses, and mailing addresses. Include the dates and times, the method of communication, and the result. Did they invite you in for an interview? Did they refer you to someone else?

Why is it important to keep your job search materials organized?

- Set up folders for storing documents that relate to your job search. Use the folders to keep track of information you send to each contact or potential employer and the response you get back. The folder might include copies of the cover letter and samples of your work that you sent. It might also include notes you took during a phone call or interview, a brochure about the company, and a printout of an e-mail message you received.

Typo!

Even the best candidate might not get an interview if there's a spelling error in the cover letter or resume. What can you do to avoid that problem?

Career Tips

Some experts recommend that you begin an active job search six to nine months before the date you hope to start working.

If you treat your job search like a job itself, you know you are actively working to achieve your career goals. How much time would you spend working each day if you had the job you want? Try to spend that time working on your job search.

You might not be earning an income, but you can meet your responsibilities by developing your employability skills, creating and improving job search materials, and exploring resources that might lead to job prospects—the possibility of employment.

👎 Assume your word processor's spell check feature will catch all errors.

👎 Hit the Send button without previewing the documents.

👎 Proofread your documents when you are tired.

👍 Use a spelling checker, but also proofread it yourself.

👍 Ask two other people to proofread your documents.

👍 Preview all documents before sending them electronically.

What could you do if you discover a typo after you have already sent your resume to a potential employer?

Is It Too Good to Be True?

Do not fall for employment scams, such as a job ad that promises income of thousands of dollars a week and requires no experience or education. If a job description sounds too good to be true, it probably is. Be wary of any job that:

✔ *Asks you to pay for something up front*

✔ *Asks for a scan of your passport or other personal information*

✔ *Offers a part-time, work-from-home job that earns a large salary*

✔ *Includes money transfers or money transactions in the job description*

✔ *Comes from an agency representing a cruise ship*

Jane is looking for a summer job. She is considering a career in hospitality, so she would like to work in a hotel. Glenna is also looking for a summer job. She is considering a career in law, so she would like to work in a law office.

Jane goes online and starts looking through want ads. She sends out her resume to a few hotels in the area, but she does not hear back from any. She goes to the library and looks through the want ads in newspapers and magazines. She sends out more resumes and still gets no response. She is beginning to think she will never find a job.

Glenna also looks online and in newspapers and magazines. She makes an appointment with a career counselor at school, who helps her compile a list of law offices in the community. The counselor gives Glenna the name and phone number of a lawyer she knows. Glenna makes time one afternoon to personally drop off her resume at a few of the local law offices. She calls the lawyer and asks if she can come in for an informational interview. She feels that her chances of finding a job she wants are pretty good.

What is different about the way the two girls are approaching their job searches? Which girl do you think has a better chance of finding a summer job? Use 21st Century Skills to answer these questions. Write an ending to the story. Read it to the class, or form a small group and present it as a skit.

Tech Connect

Most word processing programs such as Microsoft Office Word come with resume templates or let you download resume templates from a Web site. A template is a form, or sample document, that provides text and formatting to help you create standard documents. A resume template helps you quickly create a professional-looking resume.

When you use a resume template, you create the document, then replace the sample text with text customized for your own experience. The template prompts you to insert specific information, such as your name and address, and indicates where you should type your work and education experience. The template also includes formatting, such as lists, bullets, and fonts. Some have graphics, such as lines or shapes, or prompt you to insert your own graphics.

The benefits of using a resume template are obvious—a template saves time and makes it easy to produce a neat, complete resume. There are drawbacks, too. For example, other people might use the same template.

Explore the resume templates available with your word processing program at home or at school. Select a template and use it to create your resume.

Preparing a Resume

A **resume** is a document that provides a snapshot image of your qualifications. It summarizes you, your skills, and your abilities. It is a statement of who you are, what you have done in your life, and what you hope to do next. Your resume may be the first communication between you and a potential employer. You will make a positive impression if your resume is:

- Neatly printed on white paper
- True and accurate
- Free of any typographical, grammatical, or spelling errors
- Direct and to the point

You want your resume to describe you in a way that makes the employer want to meet you. A well-written resume will help you to get an interview.

How Should I Format My Resume?

There are many ways to organize or format a resume. Most word processing programs come with resume **templates**—sample documents. You can also find sample resume designs in books and on the Internet.

Choose a format that highlights your experience and skills so they stand out to someone who might just glance at the resume quickly. You may also want to consider these tips:

- Make it easy to read. Leave space between lines so it is not crowded or overloaded.
- Use one, easy-to-read font, and apply different font styles and sizes for emphasis.
- Bullets are effective for making lines of text stand out.
- Use proper spelling, punctuation, and grammar.
- Keep it to one page, if possible; two pages at the most. (If you use two pages, be sure to put your name in the header or footer on page 2, in case it becomes separated from page 1.)

Sometimes you will mail your resume in an envelope with a cover letter. Sometimes you will send it electronically by e-mail. Make sure it looks professional when it is printed, as well as when you view it on a computer.

What Do I Include on My Resume?

A typical resume has four main sections:

■ *Contact information.* Include your full name, address, telephone number, and e-mail address at the top of the page. This gives the employer all the information necessary to get in touch with you.

■ *Objective.* An objective describes your career goal. It should be short and clear. You can have a general, long-term goal as your objective, or you can customize your resume for a specific position by using a short-term goal. For example, a general objective might be, "To work in fashion sales." A customized objective might be, "To work as a part-time sales associate in a fashion clothing store."

■ *Education.* If you have little work experience, it is important to highlight your education. List the name, city, and state of every school where you earned a degree, starting with high school (or the last school you attended). Include the years you attended the school, the degree you earned, and any special courses or certificates that relate to your career. You might want to include your grade point average, as well.

■ *Work experience.* Include all full-time and part-time jobs, internships, apprenticeships, and volunteer experience, starting with the most recent experience first. Include employment dates, job titles, company names, city, and state. Briefly describe your main responsibility, and list your duties and accomplishments. Be specific. If you have work experience, you might want to put this section before Education.

Clyde Duggan
2556 Granger Avenue
Palatine, IL 60067
(555) 555-5555
clydeduggan@mail.net

Objective	To work as a part-time sales associate in a fashion clothing store.
Education	Currently enrolled in Wickham High School; expect to graduate in June 2013.

Work Experience

9/10–present	Fashion consultant, HH Shelter for Women and Children, Palatine, IL • Select and coordinate outfits for women preparing for job interviews.
5/09	Fashion show organizer, Wickham High School, Palatine, IL • Proposed, planned, and managed fashion show of student designs to raise funds for the HH Shelter for Women and Children.
Skills	• Sewing • Clothing coordination and fit • Basic math skills • Fluent in Spanish

Extracurricular Activities

Family, Career and Community Leaders of America (FCCLA); member since 2008; chapter treasurer 2010–present

Why do you think it is important to include co-curricular activities on your resume?

You may also include a Skills section for listing jobs skills such as your ability to use computers or speak a foreign language. You might also want to include a Personal Information section that lists co-curricular activities, awards, and honors. You can include all clubs and organizations of which you are a member, and things you do in your school or community. Remember to update your resume on a regular basis, so employers will see the most current and accurate information.

Use Action Words!

Action words are verbs that describe your actions in a way that makes them stand out to the reader. When you use action words to describe your responsibilities and skills in a cover letter or on your resume, it will bring your actions to life.

■ Instead of *Made lunch,* try *Cooked healthy lunches for 50 people.*

■ Instead of *Filed papers,* try *Organized customer files alphabetically.*

■ Instead of *Took pictures,* try *Photographed school events and functions for use on Web site and in newspaper.*

■ Instead of *Know CPR,* try *Certified by the American Red Cross in cardiopulmonary resuscitation (CPR).*

Applying for a Job

When you find a job you think you want, you apply for it. Applying means that you present yourself as a **candidate**—possible employee—for the position. A successful job application leads to an invitation for a job interview.

Applying usually starts with sending in your resume and a cover letter. Sometimes you can improve your chances of landing an interview by applying in person.

- In a small company, that means speaking directly with the owner or manager. For example, if you are applying for a position in a local restaurant, you would speak with the manager.

- In a large company, applying in person might mean going to the human resources department. Employees in the human resources department often meet job applicants first to decide whether they meet the qualifications for the position.

Be sure to bring a few copies of your resume and reference list to hand out when you apply in person. Also, ask for business cards from the people you meet so you know how to contact them.

Tips for Applying

When you apply for a job, your short-term goal is to get invited for an interview. There are a few things you can do to improve your chances and to make your application stand out from the crowd.

- Use a professional e-mail address. A cutesy address such as suzieq, lonewolf, daredevil, or wildgirl828 is not likely to impress a potential employer.

- Even when you are asked to fill out a standard job application form, submit a resume as well.

- Be polite and professional to everyone you meet. Whether you apply in person or are speaking on the phone, be courteous and respectful to everyone.

- When you submit a resume online, ask whether you must use a specific format. Some companies want resumes in plain text format, others accept files created using a word processing program.

- Customize your resume for a specific job. You can customize the objective, or rearrange your experience and skills to highlight the information you think is most appropriate for the position.

Other Action Words to Consider

Use a thesaurus—reference book of definitions and synonyms—to find action words to replace common verbs, such as *go*, *have*, or *get*. Some attention-getting action words for resumes include:

- ✔ Created
- ✔ Operated
- ✔ Supervised
- ✔ Prepared
- ✔ Built
- ✔ Produced
- ✔ Published
- ✔ Planned
- ✔ Coached
- ✔ Improved

Filling out a Job Application

What resources might help make filling out a job application easier?

A **job application** is a standard form you will fill out when you apply for a job. You might fill it out in person when you visit a potential employer, or you might fill it out online. It requires a lot of the same information that you put on your resume, such as your contact information, as well as details about your education and work experience. (It may ask for your Social Security number, but you can withhold such information until after you receive a job offer.)

Filling out an application form may seem simple, but a lot of people make mistakes or forget important information. A messy or incomplete job application will not make a positive impression on the employer.

- Read the form before you start filling it out.
- Follow all instructions.
- Be truthful and accurate.
- Write neatly.
- Enter N/A for not applicable if there is a question that does not apply to you.
- Check your spelling and grammar.
- If you make a mistake, ask for a new form and start again.

Practice Makes Perfect!

When you apply for a job, many employers expect you to complete the application on the spot. Providing accurate information and writing legibly can mean the difference between your application making the cut or ending up in the reject pile.

That's why you will find it useful to fill out a practice application before you actually start applying for jobs. Your school's career center or counseling office may have sample applications on file. You can also find practice applications online. Some Web sites that provide applications are jobsearch.about.com and careerchoices.com/lounge/files/jobapplication.pdf.

With your instructor's permission, download and complete a sample job application. Then exchange it with a classmate and make suggestions on how it could be improved.

Use a Personal Information Card

You might find it helpful to bring a personal information card with you when you apply for a job. A **personal information card** is an index card—or other piece of paper—on which you write or print the information you might need to fill out a job application accurately. You may even be able to store the information in your cell phone or other handheld device.

To create a personal information card, simply write the information you will need, including:

- The names, addresses, and contact information of your current and previous employers, including dates and the amount you were paid
- The names and addresses of schools where you earned a diploma or degree, including dates
- The names, addresses, and contact information of your references

Career Tips

You can use the documents you have in your career portfolio to help fill out a job application. Your resume includes facts you will need about your previous employers. Your reference list includes the names and contact information of your references.

Interviewing for a Job

What happens when an employer reads your cover letter and resume and thinks you have the qualifications that she is looking for? She invites you for a job interview. A **job interview** is a formal meeting between a job seeker and a potential employer—the interviewer. The job interview helps you and the interviewer make important decisions regarding the position at stake.

■ The interviewer decides if the job seeker is the best person for the position.

■ You decide if the position is one you really want.

Both you and the interviewer can use the job interview to get to know each other. You learn information that you cannot learn from a cover letter or resume. For example, the interviewer learns whether or not you make eye contact. You learn if people at the company are friendly. A job interview is successful if you convince the interviewer to offer you the job. It is also successful if you learn that the position would not be right for you.

Preparing for a Job Interview

A test is always easier if you are prepared. A job interview is like a test—if you pass, you are offered the job. Use these four steps to prepare for a job interview.

1. Research the company or organization where you are going for the interview. Talk to someone who works there. Visit the company's Web site.

2. Make a list of questions an interviewer might ask you. Common questions include, "Tell me about yourself," "Why do you want to work here?" "Do you have the skills to get the work done?" and "Why should I hire you?"

3. Prepare answers to the questions. Be specific. Emphasize your strengths, skills, and abilities. Explain how you solved a problem, made an important decision, or showed responsibility. Mention your goals, and briefly explain how you plan to achieve them.

4. Make a list of five to ten questions you can ask the interviewer. Ask about the company, the work environment, and the position. Common questions include, "What kinds of projects or tasks will I be responsible for?" "Is there opportunity for advancement?" "What are the hours?" "What is the salary range?" and "When will you make a hiring decision?"

How can practicing for an interview help you perform better in an actual interview?

Practicing for a Job Interview

A job interview is stressful. You are trying to make a good impression. You want to look and sound your best. You want the interviewer to like you and to respect you. Practicing for the interview by rehearsing your behavior and answers to questions helps give you confidence.

Working with a partner is probably the best way to practice. You can take turns being the interviewer and the job seeker. If you are alone, practice in front of a mirror. If possible, record your practice so you can watch yourself.

Making the Most of the Job Interview

Many interviews are 10–15 minutes long. How can you best use that time to get a job offer?

- Arrive ten minutes early.
- Introduce yourself to the receptionist, and explain who you are there to meet.
- Be polite and respectful to everyone you meet.
- Shake hands with your interviewer when you arrive and before you leave.
- Listen carefully, using positive body language. For example, smile and lean forward slightly when the interviewer is talking.
- Use proper English when you speak; no slang.
- Avoid chewing gum.
- Turn off your cell phone. If you forget and it rings or vibrates, apologize and ignore it or turn it off without checking to see who called.
- At the end of the interview, shake hands again, and thank the interviewer. Ask for a business card, so you have the interviewer's contact information.

Tips for Practicing for a Job Interview

Practicing your interview will help you feel comfortable and prepared. Use the time to rehearse your words and actions for the actual interview. Here are some tips for practicing.

✔ *Be truthful.*

✔ *Pronounce your words in a strong, clear voice.*

✔ *Keep your answers brief and to the point.*

✔ *Use positive nonverbal communication, such as eye contact, relaxed arms, and good posture.*

✔ *Dress as you would for an actual interview.*

✔ *Avoid fidgeting or playing with your hair.*

✔ *Ask someone to critique your interviewing skills and use his or her comments to improve your technique.*

Career FACT

Studies show that interviewers judge job seekers first by appearance, next by behavior, and third by what they say. So, having a neat appearance, positive attitude, and showing confidence all help you make a good first impression

Telephone Interviews

Many companies use telephone interviews to *screen*—make a first decision about—potential employees. They might be interested in you based on your cover letter and resume, but want to see how you present yourself during a conversation before they invite you for a face-to-face interview.

■ Some employers will call or e-mail to schedule a telephone interview. Then, you can prepare for the call the same way you would prepare for a face-to-face interview.

■ Some employers will call out of the blue. This lets them learn how well you handle stress and if you are able to communicate effectively without preparation.

You can prepare for surprise calls by practicing with a friend or relative. You can also make sure you are always prepared to talk about a company you apply to, the position, and yourself.

Why do you think some companies screen applicants by phone before meeting them?

Write a Thank-You Note

The interview is over. Now what? Start by writing a thank-you note. A thank-you note reminds the interviewer that you are serious about wanting the job.

You use a thank-you note to restate your interest in the job and your qualifications and to thank the interviewer for spending time with you. Refer to something specific that you discussed during the interview. Address the note to the person who interviewed you—that's why you asked for the business card! Send the note within 24 hours of the interview.

Follow Up

During the interview, you asked how long it would be before the interviewer made a decision. If you do not hear from the interviewer within that timeframe, you can call or send an e-mail. Ask if he or she has made a decision, and say again that you are interested in the position.

Sometimes, one interview leads to another. The first interviewer might like you for the job, but not be authorized to make hiring decisions. Or, he or she wants to see how other employees react to you. Being called back for a second interview is a good thing. It means you passed the first test.

Looking Your Best for an Interview

Some tips for presenting a professional appearance:

✔ *Wash, dry, and comb your hair.*

✔ *Trim and clean your fingernails.*

✔ *Use deodorant.*

✔ *Brush your teeth.*

✔ *Avoid products such as perfume or body spray that have a strong odor.*

✔ *Wear small, neat jewelry.*

✔ *Wear clean, neat clothes that are appropriate for the work environment.*

✔ *Avoid bright or contrasting colors that might distract the employer.*

✔ *Avoid revealing too much skin.*

✔ *Arrive early enough so you have time to visit the restroom to check your appearance and freshen up.*

When You are the Interviewer

Entrepreneurs might not have to interview for a job—after all, that's one of the benefits of being your own boss. But they may find themselves on the other side of the table, interviewing job applicants. Once an entrepreneur makes the decision to hire, he or she is the one who must write the job description, determine the compensation, and advertise the position. The entrepreneur must evaluate applicants based on the cover letter and resume and invite the most promising candidates in for an interview. How would you go about hiring employees if you were an entrepreneur? What questions would you ask in an interview? What challenges might you encounter, and how would you deal with them?

Myth   All interviewers ask the same questions.

Truth   Most interviewers ask questions that relate to the job opening, the company, and the individual candidate. A good interviewer will know how to ask questions that encourage you to describe your own strengths and weaknesses.

What If You Get the Job?

If you are offered the job, you have reason to celebrate. But, before you accept the offer, make sure you have all the information you need to make the best decision. You should not have to accept or reject the offer immediately. If possible, ask to talk to someone in the human resources department who can explain the company policies to you. For example, you might want to ask:

■ What is the salary?

■ What benefits—health insurance, vacation time—come with the position?

■ When does the job start?

■ What are the hours?

■ When does the company need to know your decision?

When you have all the information you need, use the decision-making process to decide whether to accept the position or not.

■ If you accept the offer, thank the employer and ask when and where you should report to work. You may have to sign a formal letter of acceptance, or write a letter of intent, which states that you are accepting the position.

■ If you reject the offer, you should still write a letter of intent, thanking the employer and stating that you are not accepting the position.

What If You Do Not Get the Job?

If you do not get a job offer, it is alright to be disappointed. It will be very helpful if the interviewer can explain why you were not selected for the job. When you are feeling calm:

■ Call the interviewer and politely ask what you could have done differently to get the job.

■ Listen carefully and take notes. The information will help you succeed at your next interview.

What can you learn from a job rejection that might help you get an offer in the future?

■ Say thank you at the end.

■ Ask the interviewer to keep you in mind for other opportunities.

Some interviewers will not want to talk to you. Do not be discouraged. Remind yourself that the interviewer thought highly enough of you to invite you for an interview. Sooner or later, you will find the right position, and you will get the job.

Career Profile: Image Consultant

Human Services Career Cluster

Job Summary

An image consultant is someone who advises clients on factors that contribute to making a positive first impression. That includes personal appearance, fashion, and style as well as effective verbal and nonverbal communication and etiquette.

Clients may be either individuals or corporations looking to change or enhance their image. For example, image consultants might run training sessions to teach corporate employees how to dress for business meetings or casual Fridays or how to provide customer service.

Image consultants are usually self-employed. They often study human ecology, psychology, and sociology in college, as well as public speaking and general business management. They also benefit from training and certification programs offered by professional organizations.

Use the Internet, a library, or career center to research the responsibilities, education and training requirements, and salary range of an image consultant. Create an advertisement for an image consultant, including information about the services the consultant provides and how clients will benefit from them.

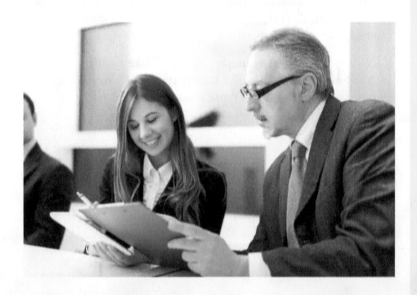

I Thought It Went Well, But ...

You showed up on time. Your hair was neat. Your tie was clean. But you didn't get the job. You asked the interviewer why. She said you came across as uninterested. What actions might affect an interviewer's opinion of you?

👎 You don't shake hands.

👎 Your cell phone buzzes during the interview.

👎 You are chewing gum.

👎 You don't make eye contact.

👎 You ask no questions.

👍 You are knowledgeable about the company.

👍 You ask lots of questions.

👍 You smile and lean forward to listen when the interviewer talks.

👍 You follow up immediately with a thank-you note.

How can you use the information an interviewer gives you about your behavior during an interview to improve your chances of getting a job offer in the future?

What type of skills do you think would help someone succeed as an image consultant?

Evaluating a Job Offer

When you receive the job offer you have been working for, it's time to think about your employment needs. Employment needs range from **compensation**—wages and benefits—to recognition; from training to accommodations for disabilities.

Employers provide compensation to employees in exchange for work. You may be satisfied with the first offer from the employer. It may meet your requirements. However, if you believe that the company could pay more, or offer different benefits or accommodations, knowing how to negotiate for the things you need will help you make sure the exchange is fair.

How Much Does It Pay?

Usually, the most important consideration when evaluating a job offer is the **monetary compensation**, or how much the job pays. Monetary compensation comes in different forms. There is **base pay** which is the hourly wage or annual salary that you earn. Some employees are paid a commission instead of base pay, or in addition to base pay. A **commission** is a payment based on a percentage of sales. Some employees earn a **bonus**, which is a lump sum paid in addition to base pay, usually once a year. Some employees receive tips, or *gratuities*, in addition to base pay. Tips are paid by customers, not the employer.

When you evaluate the salary and other monetary compensation, it helps to be prepared. Do some research on how much comparable jobs pay in the area. The Bureau of Labor Statistics publishes salary information on its Web site (www.bls.gov). You can also find information about salary ranges in classified want ads and other job postings.

It also helps to know how much you need. Make a budget to identify expenses such as food, rent, utilities, and transportation. Then, you know how much income you require to meet those needs.

Can I Count on a Bonus?

Unless a bonus is guaranteed in writing, it is never a sure thing. What if your employer says you may receive an annual bonus?

★ *A bonus might be based on your personal performance, such as meeting certain sales goals.*

★ *You might receive a bonus if the company achieves goals, such as a certain profit level, or landing a major contract.*

★ *Some bonuses are standard and are a set percentage of your annual base pay.*

★ *You might receive a bonus for signing a contract or if you refer someone who is hired by your employer.*

Do you think it is better to receive a higher salary or to receive an annual bonus?

What Are Benefits?

Benefits are things other than wages that have value. Most companies offer some type of benefits, although smaller companies may not. Some benefits, such as unemployment insurance, are required by law. Some types of benefits include:

- Health insurance
- Life insurance
- Long-term care and disability insurance
- Vacation time
- Holiday time
- Sick time
- Tuition assistance for work-related classes
- Retirement plan
- Stock options

Some companies offer benefits in the form of a **subsidy**, which is a cash payment toward a specific work-related need. For example, a company might offer a child- or elder-care subsidy to use to pay a caregiver or a transportation subsidy to use for travel or parking expenses.

Career Trend

There is a trend toward flexible—or cafeteria style—benefits. With flexible benefits, an employee can choose the benefits that are appropriate. For example, a single adult might choose an education benefit instead of a child-care benefit.

Analyzing Insurance

An important benefit to consider when you evaluate a job offer is the insurance plan that the employer provides. **Insurance** is an investment that protects you financially against everyday risks. It protects you from the costs of an unexpected emergency. Insurance is available to cover almost anything, including your health, car, home, belongings, and even life. If you suffer an accident or loss in any of the covered areas, you can collect money to pay for the loss or to repair the damage.

Employers often offer some types of insurance to employees. Large employers may be able to pay a portion of the premiums or to negotiate lower, group rates.

Job Offer Factors to Consider

Before deciding whether to accept a job offer, consider these factors.

✔ Responsibilities. Will you enjoy the work?

✔ Employer. Do you respect your supervisor?

✔ Compensation. Does the salary meet your needs?

✔ Benefits. Are the benefits standard for the industry?

✔ Co-workers. Will you get along with the other employees?

✔ Hours. Will you be able to balance the time commitment with other responsibilities?

✔ Location. Is the position in a convenient location?

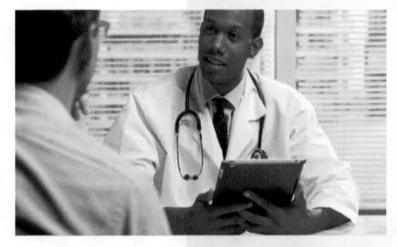

Why is medical insurance an important part of a job offer?

Insurance Terminology

Understanding insurance starts with understanding the terminology.

✔ *Insurance policy.* The contract issued by the insurance company.

✔ *Insurance agent.* Someone who sells insurance.

✔ *Premium.* The amount of money paid by the policy holder.

✔ *Claim.* A request for payment to cover a loss.

✔ *Beneficiary.* The person who collects the money if there is a claim.

✔ *Deductible.* A set amount the beneficiary must pay toward a claim before the insurance company pays any money.

Usually, the employer pays a percentage of the cost of the insurance, and the employee pays the rest. When you evaluate benefits, you must carefully read the information about the insurance policies so you understand your portion of the costs, as well as the actual benefits you will receive.

Medical insurance is probably the most important, and every policy is different. For example, your employer might offer a plan that pays a set percentage of the bill—say 80%—leaving you responsible for the rest. Or, you might make a co-payment of $25.00 every time you see a doctor, but the insurance pays the rest. Most medical policies are very specific about what is covered and what is not covered. They also vary in terms of the doctors you can use. For example, a fee-for-service policy lets you choose any doctor, while a preferred-provider policy has a list of doctors from which you can choose.

Other types of insurance often offered by employers include life insurance, which pays money to your family if you die, long-term care insurance, which pays for care if you are unable to care for yourself, and disability insurance, which pays money if you are disabled and cannot work. Both sums are usually a percentage of your annual salary.

How to Negotiate Your Compensation

Do not automatically turn down an offer if the salary and benefits are lower than you expected. You may be able to **negotiate**—discuss options until you reach a compromise—with the employer. Negotiating is a bit like problem solving. The employer makes you an offer. You point out the things about the offer that you think are problems. You work together to find solutions that make you both happy.

For example, you might think the salary is too low. Your employer might not be able to offer you more money, but maybe he can offer a benefit that has value to you, such as free parking or a flexible schedule. Or, he may be able to offer you a raise if you meet expectations for three months.

When you negotiate, always be polite and positive. State your goals clearly so your employer knows what you are trying to achieve. Be prepared to compromise. Remember, you want the job.

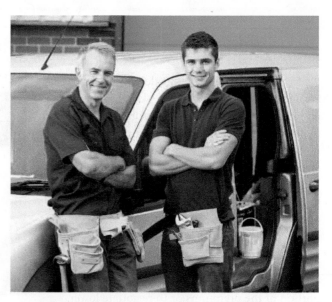

How can you use the problem-solving process to negotiate employment needs?

Do You Need Accommodations?

An **accommodation** makes it possible for a disabled employee to perform his or her job responsibilities in a safe and accessible work environment. If you have a disability that might get in the way of your performing a task the same way a nondisabled person would, you may need to negotiate for accommodations when you receive a job offer. For example, if you use a wheelchair to move around, you might not be able to access a storage room that is down a flight of stairs.

By law, employers who are aware of an employee's disability must make accommodations, if the accommodations do not impose an extreme hardship on the business. Tell your employer if you need an accommodation to do your job. Not all disabilities are visible—your employer may not know that you have one.

Examples of common accommodations include:

- Making nonwork areas such as cafeterias and lounges accessible by installing wheelchair ramps or elevators
- Modifying work schedules
- Replacing or modifying equipment
- Changing exams, training materials, or policies to accommodate factors such as reading disabilities
- Providing sign-language interpreters or assistive equipment for the hearing impaired

---

Who Made Your Sneakers?

Laws protect workers in the United States. Workers in other countries might not be as fortunate.

Many of the pieces of clothing sold in the United States are made in Southeast Asia. In countries such as Thailand and Cambodia, workers have very few rights and very few opportunities. Sweatshops—unsafe factories—are common. Children as young as seven years of age may work, and wages for everyone may be very low.

Do you own clothes made in Southeast Asia? How do your own buying habits impact sweatshops in Southeast Asia? How do the sweatshops impact the economy of the United States? Use the Internet or the library to learn more about working conditions in other parts of the world. Write an essay on the topic, "Should We Care About Workers in Other Countries?"

NUMBERS GAME

Some salespeople are paid a commission in addition to or in place of a salary. A **commission** is a payment calculated as a percentage of total sales. Earning a commission encourages sales people to sell more, because the more they sell, the more they earn.

Expensive items such as cars, boats, recreational vehicles, houses, and furniture are commonly sold on commission.

If you are a real estate agent earning a 7% commission, how much would you earn by selling a house for $195,000.00?

Multiply $195,000.00 by 7%:

$195,000.00 × .07 = $13,650.00

What if you sell a house for $242,900.00?

What if you sell cars and earn 8% on your total monthly sales. In one month, you sell one car for $13,955.00, one for $15,495.00, and one for $14,455.00. How much commission will you earn for that month?

Case Study

Claude is hoping to land an internship at a company where he can use his skills in computer programming. He researches companies in his community and identifies five that hire student interns. He picks the one that is closest to his home and calls the human resources department. The assistant tells him to send in a resume and cover letter, along with a school transcript.

Claude wants his application to stand out from those of the other students who apply. He inserts his class photo at the top of his resume. He prints his cover letter on neon yellow paper.

Two weeks after sending in his information, Claude receives a letter telling him that he will not get the internship.

■ What do you think Claude did well in his job search?

■ What do you think Claude could do to improve his job search?

■ What do you think Claude should do next?

Web Extra

There are Web sites for teens that provide useful information about managing a job search. For example, gotajob.com has a section on resume-writing tips and links to sample cover letters.

Use the Internet to identify the sites that you think might be the most useful for your peers. Make a directory of the sites, including the Web site address, a brief description, and whether the site is free or has a fee. Post the directory on your school Web site or in your school career center or library.

Answer It!

1. What is the purpose of a cover letter?
2. Why don't relatives and friends make good references?
3. What are four things you can do to keep your job search materials organized?
4. What is the most important job search document?
5. What are the four main sections of a resume?

6. List four types of information you are likely to need to complete a job application.
7. List four steps for preparing for a job interview.
8. List at least four things you can do to make a good impression at a job interview.
9. List at least six types of benefits.
10. What is the purpose of an accommodation in the workplace?

Career-Ready Practices

As you have learned, managing a job search can be a complex and time-consuming undertaking. But it all begins with basic research. Career-ready individuals realize that using valid and reliable research strategies will help them focus their job search. It also provides them with valuable information that can help them prepare for interviews and make decisions about prospective employers.

With a partner, write a job description for a specific job at a specific company. Prepare for an interview by researching the company, its competitors, and the industry in general. Based on your research, prepare a list of questions and answers. Take turns acting as the interviewer and the job seeker. If possible, videotape the practice. Analyze the interview carefully. Was your research helpful in answering questions? Can you identify ways to improve your interviewing skills?

Write Now

The government protects the rights of children as workers. The Fair Labor Standards Act (FLSA) sets the rules for workers under the age of 18. Use the Internet or your library to research the laws that set policies for youth workers in your state. Write an advertisement, flyer, or brochure explaining the laws and providing the address, URL, and phone number for the government agency where people can go for more information.

Career Portfolio

The most important documents in your career portfolio may be your resume and list of references. Sample cover letters and thank-you letters are also useful. If you have not already done so, prepare these documents for your portfolio.

■ Develop a resume. Be complete and accurate. Include an objective specific to the job for which you plan to apply. Use action words to describe your experience and skills. Use formatting that is professional and easy to read.

■ Write a cover letter to submit with your resume. Customize it for a specific job that interests you. Keep it brief and to the point.

■ Develop a list of references. Try to include at least three people who are willing to speak on your behalf. Ask them for permission to include them on the list.

■ Write a sample thank-you letter that you could send after an interview. Use the letter to remind the interviewer about your particular skills and qualifications.

Ask a classmate, teacher, or advisor to review the materials and offer comments and suggestions. Use the comments and suggestions to improve the documents, and then add them to your career portfolio. Periodically, look over the documents and revise them in order to keep them up-to-date.

Business Plan Project

Entrepreneurs need to sell their business ideas to potential customers and investors. Sometimes they only have a minute or two to pitch the benefits of their business. If they don't capture the interest of the audience in that short time, they may never have another chance. In your **Business Plan Project**, write a 30–60 second pitch you could present to a potential customer. (Alternatively, write a TweetPitch—a pitch that is not more than 140 characters long.) Describe your product or service and what makes it interesting and unique. Deliver your pitch to a small group or to the class, and listen to their feedback. Use the feedback to improve your pitch.

14 Getting Started in Your Career

Skills in This Chapter . . .

- **Beginning a New Job**
- **Building Work Relationships**
- **Benefiting from a Performance Review**
- **Requesting Additional Education and Training**
- **Obtaining a Raise or Promotion**
- **Making a Career Change**

GETTING STARTED

Starting a new job can be stressful, like starting a new school year. Will you show up on time? Will you make new friends? Will the work be difficult? Like adjusting to a new year or a new school, you will have to meet new responsibilities. Most important, starting a new job requires a positive attitude. Remember that your employer hired you over a lot of other candidates. He or she is confident that you have the skills to be a successful employee; you should be confident, too. To make the first days less stressful, it helps to be prepared by knowing what to expect.

➤ Imagine you are an employer. Make a list of five reasons you would promote someone on the job. Then make a list of five reasons you would fire someone. Share your lists with other members of the class. What did you have in common? What does this tell you about being successful at work?

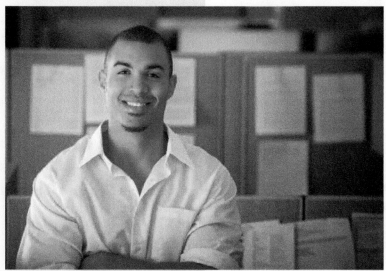

What can you expect on your first day of work? Is it normal to be nervous?

Beginning a New Job

Like all new ventures, being successful at work requires you to put your best foot forward. The first day—even the first week or month—is full of new information and new experiences. It can be stressful, and sometimes even overwhelming.

Many people worry about whether they will get along with their co-workers. They are not sure how they will handle their job duties. They are afraid of making a mistake. These feelings are natural. However, there are things you can do to make a new job less stressful.

■ *Understand exactly what you are supposed to do.* If you are confused about what is expected of you, talk to your manager.

■ *Make a commitment to do your best.* Everyone has a "learning curve," and it may take you a while to learn how to do certain tasks. If you are determined and work hard, your employer will recognize the effort and help you to do your work to the best of your ability.

■ *Get to know your co-workers.* They can answer questions, show you how to do your work more efficiently, and, most important, they can make you feel more comfortable on the job.

You can expect quite a few experiences during your first day and first week at work: forms and rules and tours, to name a few. However, one thing you can always be certain of is that you will learn something new.

Filling out Forms

Your first day will probably include time for filling out forms. One of the first forms you will fill out is a **W-4**—the Employee's Withholding Allowance Certificate. It is a form employees fill out to provide information the employer needs in order to calculate how much money to withhold from wages to pay taxes. You can follow the instructions on the form to fill it out correctly, or ask someone in human resources to help you.

Other forms you may need to fill out include the following:

■ State tax withholding form.

■ Employment Eligibility Verification form, which proves you are a U.S. resident or are authorized to work in the United States.

- Authorization to deposit your paycheck directly into your bank account.
- An application for an identification card.
- Benefits selection forms. For example, you may have to make decisions about the type of health insurance plan you want.

Most employers expect you to bring proof of residency (that you are a United States citizen) and all necessary documents with you on the first day—if not before. If your employer does not tell you what to bring, call and ask, so you have the right documents ready. Be prepared to bring the following:

- Your birth certificate or passport, or resident card
- Your Social Security card (If you don't have a Social Security card, you can apply for one by visiting your local Social Security office.)
- A work permit, which is required before anyone under the age of 18 is allowed to work in most jobs, or employment certificate, if necessary

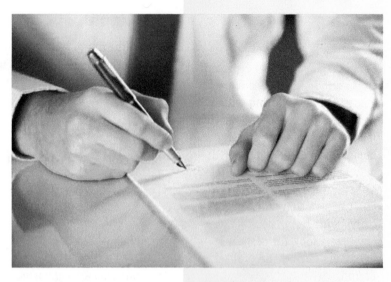

You will spend part of your first day filling out forms. What should you do if you have questions?

Making the Most of Orientation

When you start a new job, you will likely have an orientation your first day. It may be led by someone from human resources or by the manager of your department, or it may be an online or video presentation. Orientation will answer most of your questions and provide the information you need to get started.

At orientation, you are likely to receive an employee handbook. An **employee handbook** describes company policies and procedures, such as how to request vacation time, and the different benefits that are available.

In addition to the orientation, many companies provide new-employee training on the first day, or within the first few days. Some training may be for all new employees. For example, you may receive training about safety procedures, or about harassment policies.

Some training may be specific to your job. For example, if you are a cashier, you may receive training on how to use the cash register. If you are a salesperson, you might learn about the different products available. If you are a cook, you may start learning how to prepare food. Make sure you pay attention during training, and ask questions.

Why should new employees take the time to read their employee handbook?

Making It Through Probation

Some employees have a probation period, which is a set amount of time during which you prove you are right for the job. Probation varies in length depending on the company. It may be a matter of a few weeks or several months. Because they don't expect you to know everything right from the start, employers look for certain behaviors during the probation period.

👎 Taking time off or calling in sick

👎 Showing up late or leaving early

👎 Not following the dress code

👎 Failing at basic tasks that you said you were qualified for

👍 Making an effort to get along with co-workers

👍 Asking questions when appropriate

👍 Taking initiative to learn new things

👍 Following the rules and regulations

Can you think of other behavior an employer might look for during the probation period?

Making a Good Impression

Recall the importance of making a positive first impression in a job interview? It doesn't stop there. You need to approach your first few days of work the same way you approached the interview that landed you the job. That means staying positive and enthusiastic.

Keep in mind that the person who *hired* you isn't always the person who will be *managing* you. In fact, most of the people you will be working with will probably be meeting you for the first time on your first day. You need to make a good first impression on everybody from day one: your supervisor, your co-workers, and your customers. Some tips to keep in mind:

■ *Come to work a little early the first few days.* This will not only help you get adjusted to your surroundings, it will also show that you are eager to do a good job.

■ *Dress the part.* Read about the dress code (if there is one) in your handbook. If it's not specific, pay close attention to what your co-workers are wearing and dress similarly. It is better to overdress than to underdress.

■ *Be proactive.* Take the initiative to meet your co-workers and learn new job tasks.

■ *Keep any negative opinions to yourself.* While other employees may not always seem happy to be at work, avoid passing judgment yourself.

Should you make an effort to introduce yourself to your co-workers or wait until they approach you?

Building Work Relationships

Like any other relationship, the relationships you build at work can affect your on-the-job success, job satisfaction, and overall well-being. Building positive working relationships helps you in the following areas.

■ Makes you more productive. Working well with others helps avoid conflict, which usually leads to work being done faster and better.

■ Gives you additional opportunities to learn. Your co-workers can be excellent resources for helping you improve your skills.

■ Makes work more enjoyable. While work isn't meant to be all fun and games, it can be less stressful and more agreeable if you like the people you work with.

On the other hand, negative working relationships can lead to conflicts, which can decrease productivity, increase stress, and even be the cause of dismissal.

Perhaps the most important thing you can do during your first week of work is to get to know your fellow workers. Be sure to introduce yourself (without being intrusive), keep an open mind, and don't be afraid to ask questions. You might even consider asking co-workers if they'd like to have lunch (or they might ask you). Take advantage of opportunities to help out as well. Co-workers will remember the offer even if they don't take you up on it.

Employers are looking for team players. How much easier is it to complete group projects when you get along with your group members?

NUMBERS GAME

At your job, you may have to choose how much you want to deposit in a retirement plan, such as a 401(k). Many companies offer a matching contribution for retirement plans. They often state the contribution as a ratio, such as 2:1 or 1:1.

A **ratio** is a proportional relationship between two numbers or quantities. For example, if there is one teacher in your class and 24 students, the ratio of teachers to students is 1 to 24, which is written as 1:24.

A 2:1 ratio means that for every $2.00 you contribute, the company will contribute $1.00. A 1:1 ratio means that for every $1.00 you contribute, the company will contribute $1.00.

If you contribute $100.00 a week into your 401(k), and your employer makes a 2:1 matching contribution, how much is deposited into your account each week?

Your contribution:

$100.00

Employer contribution:

$100.00 ÷ 2 = $50.00

Total contribution:

$100.00 + $50.00 = $150.00

How much is contributed each month if your employer makes a 3:1 contribution and you put in $525 a month? How much is deposited each week if you contribute $126.00 at the same 3:1 rate?

Career Trend

You already know that you will hold several different jobs over the course of your career. Did you know that some people choose not to hold a job longer than a few years? These job jumpers aren't interested in moving up the corporate ladder. More often than not, they simply get bored with the work they are doing and want to try something new. Job jumping has become much more expected in today's working world.

Types of Work Relationships

Imagine you are hired as a server at a family restaurant. What work relationships will you build? Naturally you will build relationships with the other servers, the hosts and hostesses, the cooks, and the bussers who clear and set the tables. You will also build a relationship with your manager, and maybe even the restaurant owner. But what about customers? There may be some repeat customers who ask for you specifically because you provide excellent service. You may even have working relationships with people you only see occasionally, such as delivery people or maintenance staff.

Regardless of the person—customer or co-worker, manager or peer—it's important to have a positive attitude. Consider the following tips, no matter whom you are working with:

■ Be enthusiastic.

■ Don't make excuses.

■ Pitch in.

■ Adapt to changes quickly.

■ Try not to complain.

■ Smile!

Also remember that work relationships are just that—*work* relationships. While you may be friends with your co-workers and see them outside of the work setting, while you are on the clock, you should try to keep any personal problems to yourself.

Would you act differently around your co-workers than you would around your supervisor? Would you treat some customers differently than others?

Teamwork and Leadership

People who can work successfully as part of a team—whether as a leader or a team member—are valued in the work environment, just as they are valued in school, the community, and at home.

As a team member, you should do the following:

■ Use active listening to make sure you understand the needs and opinions of others.

■ Show cooperation in order to achieve your team's common goals.

■ Compromise when necessary—be sure all parties come away with something positive.

■ Complete your tasks and responsibilities on time, and to the best of your ability.

As a leader, you can do the following:

■ Help build cooperation among team members.

■ Show *initiative*, which means you take charge to accomplish a task that needs to be done.

■ Make healthy choices at work.

■ Respect the diverse opinions of others while still getting your point across.

■ Be assertive, but not aggressive. Don't force other people to follow your lead—encourage and persuade them to.

Remember: No two team members will always agree on everything or be equally skilled at all tasks. Good team members recognize that each person on the team has different ideas and skills. They use these differences to achieve their common goals.

Career Tips

It is important to treat your co-workers with respect. If you are honest and respectful toward others, they are likely to be honest and respectful toward you.

Who Would You Pick?

Unless you are the boss, you don't get to pick your co-workers, but you still have to interact with them on a daily basis. But suppose you could pick them? What if you got to choose a group of five people that you would work with at a new job?

★ Would they be close friends or just acquaintances?

★ Would they do what you told them?

★ Would you want them to be smarter, faster, or better workers than you?

★ Would you pick people on the basis of their skills or their personality?

★ Would you hire strangers if you thought they were qualified?

Think about your answers to these questions. Then think about the people who make hiring decisions. Do you think they would make the same choices?

Benefiting from a Performance Review

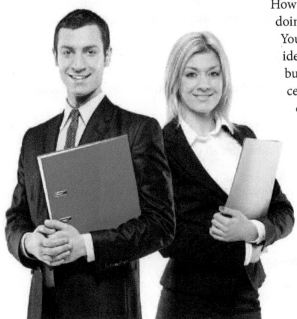

How do you know when you are doing well in a certain class? You probably have a general idea as the term progresses, but you can't be absolutely certain until your report card comes in. The same is true of the working world. When you are an employee, you receive a job review or **performance review**—a report that rates how well you do your job.

A performance review evaluates you in different areas, depending on your job. For example, if you are a carpenter, it might evaluate you on your ability to use tools or follow safety procedures. If you are a salesperson, your review will likely be based on your sales history, quotas (sales goals) reached, and customer feedback. Regardless of the job, some common areas for evaluation include the following:

- Job performance
- Attendance
- Attitude and behavior
- Ability to communicate with customers
- Relationships with co-workers
- Relationship with manager

A performance review is a resource that helps you understand how your supervisor views your ability to manage your work-related tasks. You can use the information to improve and advance in your career.

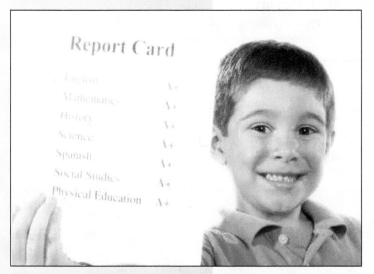

What if you received an actual report card every three months at work? How do you think you would do? What kinds of grades would you earn? How is a performance review rating similar to a report card?

Knowing What to Expect

While you are being graded in a way, performance reviews aren't like final exams that you can cram for. However, knowing what you can expect—and when you can expect it—can help you ensure that your work is up to par and that your review will be a good one.

Most companies schedule performance reviews on a regular basis. Your supervisor or a representative from human resources should tell you the schedule, or you might find it in your employee handbook.

Many companies use an assessment form, similar to a report card. Your supervisor will rate your performance in different areas. If you are not sure how performance is rated, ask your supervisor to explain the performance standards ahead of time, so you know what is expected of you.

Some performance reviews will involve your supervisor watching you work—completing specific job tasks while the supervisor observes and takes notes. Other reviews will be more like meetings where you and the supervisor discuss your work more generally.

While your performance review will likely be based on your work as a whole and over a certain period of time, it doesn't hurt to put forth extra effort on the day you are being reviewed—and even a few days before.

If you had to rate yourself as a student, what aspects of your performance would you include? How would you do?

Career Trend

Some companies use peer reviews, in which your co-workers rate your performance, or self-reviews, in which you rate your own performance. This can be harder than you think. Some people are harder on themselves than an employer would ever be.

Money Madne$$

Your performance review is coming up and you want to make sure you've met your annual sales quota. You are required to sell $200,000.00 in digital widgamadigits each year. It's December 30, and so far you've only sold $188,000.00. Widgamadigits cost $100.00 each, though the price is reduced to $75.00 for customers who buy quantities of 100 or more. You are in the process of closing a sale of 18 widgamadigits for one customer and are hoping for one more big sale to put you over the top. How many widgamadigits would you have to sell to one customer to meet your quota?

What the Performance Review Means

As part of your review, you will probably sit down with your supervisor to discuss your scores. Though every review is different, reviews generally evaluate employees in terms of their ability to meet expectations.

- You might receive a score of Meets Standards if you consistently complete your responsibilities on time.

- You might receive a score of Exceeds Standards if you often help others complete their own work.

- You might receive a score of Needs Improvement if you are frequently late for work.

What does it mean if you receive a score of "Needs Improvement" on a performance review? Does your supervisor hate you? Will you lose your job? Don't panic. The information in your performance review is intended to help you succeed at work. Use the time in the meeting to discuss with your supervisor ways you can make the most of your strengths at work, as well as how you can improve in the areas where you may be underperforming.

Use these tips to make the most of your performance review.

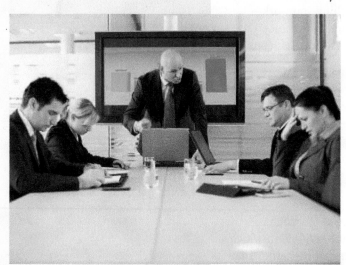

- Listen attentively to everything your supervisor says.

- Take note of areas in which your supervisor expects you to improve.

- Be prepared to talk about yourself and your role at work.

- Accept criticism calmly; it is meant to help you improve.

Why is it difficult for people to accept criticism? What can you do to make sure you don't take any criticism too personally?

- Ask questions so you fully understand what is expected of you.

Your performance review is also a good time to discuss the goals you have achieved and to set new goals for the coming year. You can discuss things that are on your mind, such as requesting training or asking about opportunities for new responsibilities.

Requesting a Review

Sometimes, a supervisor does not schedule a performance review. He or she may be busy, or might not enjoy the process. While this may sound like a good thing—like the teacher who forgets to give a quiz—it's not. Passing up a performance review means passing up a chance to improve, to show off your successes, and to ask for more responsibility and possibly more money.

If, for some reason, your supervisor neglects to schedule a review, you will have to speak up. Be polite but assertive. Remind your supervisor that it is time for the review, and that you would welcome information that will help you succeed at your job.

Requesting Additional Education and Training

To keep up with changes in the workplace, you may need to develop new skills. Some careers, such as those in health care, require that you update your certification on a regular basis. For other careers, it is up to you to make sure you stay up to date on changes and advancements.

- A computer technician must keep up with changes in technology.

- A tax accountant is responsible for knowing about changes to tax policy and regulations.

- A travel agent may want to keep up with world events so she can recommend safe vacation spots.

Ask your teacher if he or she has to undergo additional education and training on a regular basis and he or she will likely tell you about conferences, teacher training, and in-service days. Regardless of the profession, you almost always have opportunities for improving your skills and learning more about your job. Seek out additional education and training, and make sure you are prepared for changes and advancement opportunities that come your way.

Career Tips

When a manufacturing plant replaces old equipment with new, updated equipment, it's called retooling. Nowadays, more and more workers are *retooling* as well—replacing old skills with new ones. Community colleges, for example, are experiencing record enrollment from students headed back to school for more training. This not only makes workers better at their jobs, it often leads to better jobs.

Do You Make the Grade?

Here are four reasons employees might not meet performance standards, and actions for improvement.

✔ Not enough training. If you do not know the proper procedure, it is difficult to perform up to expectations. Ask for training so that you can improve.

✔ Distractions. Problems in the workplace can interfere with performance. For example, you might be bothered by noise, conflict with co-workers or customers, poor lighting, or equipment that does not work. Politely discuss the problems with your supervisor.

✔ Lack of motivation or encouragement. You may be bored or tired, or you may feel as if your work is not valued by your supervisor or co-workers. It is hard to be positive if you are not motivated. Discuss your feelings with your supervisor to see what steps you can take to improve conditions.

✔ Failure to follow rules. If there are company policies or rules that you haven't complied with, then you should either start complying or look for a different job. If there are policies you don't agree with, you can discuss the matter with your supervisor, provided you have a good reason. Be sure to listen openly to feedback.

What kinds of workers would you expect to stay most up-to-date with their knowledge and skills? Why?

How Can You Develop New Skills?

There are many ways to develop new skills. Co-workers and supervisors often provide on-the-job training simply by showing you how to improve the way you do your regular tasks, or teaching you new skills. For example, a co-worker might train you on a new computer application, teach you how to install a piece of drywall, or simply show you how to make a conference call.

Your company might also offer other opportunities for education and training.

- Specialized courses, such as a seminar about customer service for sales representatives, or a session on how to use Web-based storage for data management employees.

- **Professional development**—training in your chosen career. Teachers, lawyers, and nurses, for example, are usually required to participate in professional development to learn about new trends in their fields or to prepare for certification exams.

- Tuition reimbursement programs. If you take a class, your company may pay the tuition costs. You can take classes at a local college on nights or weekends to earn a degree or certification, or simply to learn material that might help you advance.

Developing new skills prepares you for new responsibilities and helps you achieve career, academic, and life goals. Even if your employer does not offer these opportunities, you can take steps to continue your education and training on your own by taking classes or reading books. This kind of education makes you a more valuable worker and helps you grow as a person.

Volunteering Overseas

One of the best ways to learn new skills and to further your professional development is to volunteer. You have hundreds of options for volunteering in this country, and hundreds more opportunities abroad. Underdeveloped countries especially have a tremendous need for educated, committed volunteers. You could teach English, help build a school, or help run an orphanage.

The benefits of volunteer service overseas are numerous. You'll have a chance to learn a new language, experience a different culture, travel to new places, and develop key career and leadership skills. Volunteering abroad can enhance long-term career prospects whether you want to work for a corporation, a nonprofit organization, or a government agency.

In addition, several organizations, such as the Peace Corps, offer educational benefits, such as college credit or student loan deferment, for service. The Peace Corps can even open doors to graduate school.

Use the Internet to research your options for volunteering in another country. You might start with peacecorps.gov or globalservicecorps.org. Learn what the requirements are and what specific opportunities are available. Pick one program that you would like to teach your class about and develop a three-minute presentation, including photos and contact information, to give to your class.

Finding a Mentor

One of the best ways to develop your skills is to find a mentor. A **mentor** is someone knowledge-able and experienced in your field who is willing to teach you, advise you, and help you reach your goals. While all mentors are teachers of sorts, not all teachers are mentors. A mentor is someone who is willing to give you extra individual attention, to guide you along your career path, and to pass along what he or she has already learned.

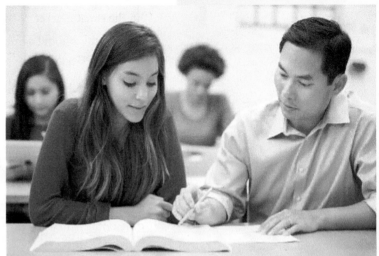

Finding a mentor at work can be as easy as asking someone you know and respect at work to train you or help you learn new skills. Consider these other tips when finding and choosing a mentor.

- *Know what you want.* Are you looking for someone to teach you specific skills, to help you make important career decisions, or to just be a sounding board for when you have problems? Know what you'd like your mentor to do for you and be clear about this up front.

- *Explore your network.* Your mentor doesn't have to be your supervisor or another member of your work team or department, though that is often the case. He or she may be a teacher or a counselor, a coach, or even a family member.

- *Show your gratitude.* Most mentors will help you because they honestly want to see you succeed. However, it doesn't hurt to thank them for their efforts and to help them out if ever the occasion arises.

Have you ever had someone "take you under their wing" and help you to improve? Have you ever considered being a mentor to somebody else?

Becoming a Lifelong Learner

Lifelong learning means continually acquiring new knowledge and skills through-out the course of your life. While this might sound like a given, it actually goes against traditional thinking that education ends the moment one graduates from high school or college. The truth is you never stop learning. It's just that nowadays people are making a more concentrated effort to *keep* learning, and not just because their careers demand it.

Education and training are not limited to learning new skills for the workplace. You should consider educational opportunities to enrich your life at home, with friends, and in your community. Studies have shown that people who continue to take an active role in their learning lead happier, even healthier lives. To become a lifelong learner, consider the following.

- Take a class to learn a new hobby, such as Web design or woodworking.

- Join an exercise program, such as karate, golf, or fitness.

- Enroll in a community college to improve your personal finance skills or learn more about computers.

■ Join a book club to develop your reading skills and expand your social group.

■ Attend a seminar at your bank about starting your own business or investing in the stock market.

■ Teach others about something you are good at or knowledgeable about, such as art, sports, or music.

Regardless of what you study, remember that the goal of lifelong learning is not simply to advance your career, but to cultivate your interests and gain new experiences.

Lifelong learning doesn't mean you always have to improve your job skills. What would you learn how to do if you had the time?

Tech Connect

Can you imagine graduating from college without ever leaving your home? Welcome to the world of online education. Many colleges offer strictly online courses that you access over the Internet. The instructor posts video lectures, notes, and assignments on a Web site. You log in and participate as if you were on campus. Sites often have tools that allow students to communicate in real time so they can study together, or work on group assignments. Some of these courses are even free. Though they are generally for no credit, they provide a new way to learn about something that interests you.

Some companies provide online training, too. You might be able to complete a course in ethics online, or use a simulation training program to learn how to use new equipment.

Use the Internet to research the online courses offered by colleges in your area. Do they lead to a degree? What requirements must you meet to enroll? Make a presentation about the benefits and drawbacks of taking a course online. Try to find at least one class that you think you would be interested in taking online.

Obtaining a Raise or Promotion

In school, you are rewarded for all of your studying and hard work with good grades. You may be rewarded for your performance in a sport or club with a ribbon or a trophy. In the working world, your rewards come in the form of raises and promotions.

A **raise** is an increase in pay. A **promotion** is an advance in your career that includes a new job title and additional responsibilities. Both are ways that a company recognizes your achievements.

Earning a raise and/or promotion is an important part of career success and satisfaction. It is proof that your employer appreciates your contributions. In addition to the financial rewards, promotions bring with them new challenges. They also may open up even more rewarding career opportunities down the road.

The Importance of Advancement

Promotions often come with an increase in pay, but they also come with added responsibilities. You may be asked to take on additional or more challenging work tasks. You may be asked to work different hours, to travel more, or to supervise others. You might also experience more pressure to perform. You might even question if it is worth the raise.

It's important to remember that advancing in your career is about much more than a pay increase. The money is nice, but a promotion offers other benefits.

■ Promotions sometimes include added **perks**—which is compensation in addition to wages or salary—and benefits, such as a nicer office, better parking, more vacation time, or better health insurance.

■ Advancing in your career provides a boost to your self-esteem.

■ Being recognized and rewarded brings career satisfaction.

■ Achieving certain goals allows you to set new goals for the future.

■ Earning a promotion makes you look more attractive to other employers, which could lead to even better job offers.

Not to mention that new challenges can be exciting. Staying in the same position and doing the same work every day can become tedious. By moving up, you learn new skills and push yourself to grow as a person.

Myth Companies are required to give employees a raise every year.

Truth Companies understand that the cost of living goes up every year. While most companies try to reward their employees with annual raises, they are not required to do so. Raises are often based on merit. That is, they have to be earned. There are times when employers can't afford to give raises even to the people who deserve them. In the working world, nothing is a given.

Do you want to be recognized for the work you do? Are the benefits worth the hard work required?

Career Profile: Veterinarian

Health Science Career Cluster

Job Summary

Veterinarians take care of pets and other animals. They treat injuries and illnesses, perform surgery, administer vaccinations, prescribe medicines, and inform animal owners of the proper way to care for their pets. Some are involved in research and work with laboratory animals. Others work for farms, ranches, or zoos. More than half of all veterinarians treat small animals—cats, dogs, birds, and rabbits, with the occasional snake thrown in for good measure.

Becoming a veterinarian is no easy feat, however, requiring much the same educational requirements as a physician. A doctorate of veterinary medicine usually takes four years; that's above and beyond other postsecondary requirements, such as a bachelor's degree. Veterinarians also must be licensed—which requires them to pass an 8-hour examination! Once you become a veterinarian, don't expect an easy job. Unlike human patients, most animal patients have few reservations about biting, clawing, kicking, and hissing.

Use the Internet, a library, or career center to research the responsibilities, education and training requirements, and salary range of a veterinarian. Prepare a presentation about the career.

What skills do you think a veterinarian would need?

How Can You Earn a Raise or a Promotion?

So, how do you achieve a raise or promotion? The best way is to work hard, excel at your job, and show your supervisor that you have the skills, interests, and abilities to take on more responsibility.

How long does it take to earn a raise? The answer depends on your job and on company policies. There are two basic types of raises:

■ An *annual raise* is awarded to all employees on a regular basis—usually once a year. It may be based on seniority—how long you have worked for the company—or on how successful the company has been. You will be notified of the increase a few weeks in advance. It is usually a percentage of your current pay.

■ A *merit raise* is based on your performance. If you are exceeding expectations, or if you are promoted to a new job or assume new responsibilities, you might earn a merit raise. A merit raise can be awarded at any time.

What does it take to earn a promotion? First, you must prove to your supervisor that you are ready for more responsibility. Then, there must be an opportunity.

■ You might earn a promotion if someone with more seniority leaves. For example, your supervisor might retire, or a co-worker with more responsibility might take a job in a different department.

- Another way to earn a promotion is if the company grows. Companies that do well might expand into new areas of businesses. They will need employees to take on the new tasks and responsibilities.

- A third way to earn a promotion is to create a new job for yourself. You might see an opportunity for something new in your department. For example, if you work in a restaurant, you might suggest to your manager that you could expand business by offering home delivery. Your manager might put you in charge of the new home delivery service.

Making a Career Change

You've already learned that the average worker changes jobs many times over his or her working career. But how do you know when it is time for a change?

That depends on whether it is a decision you make for yourself, or one that your employer makes for you.

- You might feel that you have reached your potential, and that there is no more room for advancement at your current place of work.

- Your family might move to a different city, making the commute to your current job impossible.

- You might just want to try something new.

- New family or personal responsibilities may require you to take a job with different hours, different pay, or different benefits.

Or, it could be because of one of the following reasons.

- Your employer might not be satisfied with your performance.

- Your job might be eliminated.

- Your company might go out of business or move operations to another country.

Changing jobs is stressful, just like changing schools or starting a new grade, and there is often much more at stake. It means leaving a familiar situation. It means beginning your job search all over again. It may even mean going back to school or learning new skills.

A job change is also an opportunity to think critically about your career and to set new career goals. Looking at a job change as an opportunity instead of a loss can lead to greater career satisfaction and positive well-being.

Is leaving a job ever an easy decision to make? Think of one or two examples.

Going Above and Beyond

Imagine you have been with the same company a few years. Your reviews have been good. You earn an annual raise every year. But you can't seem to earn a promotion. What can you do to get recognized?

- 👎 Start acting as if you were promoted anyway and boss your co-workers around.

- 👎 Be disrespectful to your supervisor.

- 👎 Pass up opportunities for developing new skills.

- 👍 Join a professional organization.

- 👍 Propose new projects or suggest ways to improve productivity.

- 👍 Meet with your supervisor to discuss opportunities in your department, or in other departments.

How could you advance in your career if there are no opportunities for a promotion available?

How to Say Goodbye

Even when you are the one who makes the decision to leave, changing jobs can be confusing and depressing. There are some things you can do to make the process easier for yourself and your employer.

- Giving plenty of notice. **Giving notice** means telling your employer you are leaving. You should be clear about the date you plan to stop working. Most companies ask you to give notice two weeks before your last day. That gives them time to look for your replacement. You may also need to write a **letter of resignation**—a brief, formal, and positive letter that states that you are leaving the job, the date your employment will end, and thanks your employer for the opportunity to have worked there.

- Creating a job folder for your replacement. The folder should contain lists of the responsibilities, procedures, and resources needed for the job. It will help your replacement settle in and become productive.

- Meeting with a human resources representative to discuss your benefits, including what to do with your 401(k) or other retirement account. This may be part of your **exit interview**—a meeting with your supervisor or human resources representative to discuss why you are leaving.

Leaving on good terms is important. You want to maintain positive relationships with your supervisor and co-workers. You may want them as references for future jobs or as contacts for networking, or you may want to work for the company again someday.

Jobs That Lead to Business Start-Ups

Every business is owned by someone. Technically, that means *any* job can lead to an opportunity to be your own boss. However, some jobs have higher proportions of self-employed workers than others. Often this has to do with the kind of work being performed—whether it can be done by an individual or a group, for example, or whether it can be done from home or by telecommuting.

Below are some of the jobs with high percentages of self-employed workers.

- Personal financial advisors
- Chiropractors
- Interior designers
- Creative writers
- Property managers
- Construction managers
- Veterinarians
- Graphic designers
- Lawyers
- Podiatrists
- Real estate agents

Pick one of these jobs and research it. In particular, try to discover why these jobs are more attractive to people interested in self-employment. Write a brief (two- to three-paragraph) report on the job you've choosen and present it to the class.

Josh has always wanted to move to California. He has lived in a small town all of his life and is thinking about heading to downtown Los Angeles or San Francisco. He's worried about getting a job there, however. He knows that the cost of living in those cities is high. He has a bachelor's degree in English and has some work experience building Web sites. He also has four years of experience as a waiter and another two years working as a junior copywriter for a local advertising agency.

Use your 21st Century Skills such as problem solving, critical thinking, and decision making to help Josh decide what his options are. What kinds of jobs are plentiful in those cities? What kind of work do you think he could do? How much would he have to earn in order to afford a place to live? Write two endings to Josh's story: an ending in which Josh is successful and an ending in which he isn't. Share your stories with your class.

Career Tips

Just because you have a job doesn't mean you must stop looking for another. Even if you are satisfied with your current position, you might find one that has a similar work environment and responsibilities that offers better pay or benefits. Just don't surf the job boards or want ads while you are at work.

Coping with a Layoff

At some point, through no fault of your own, you may lose your job. You might be working hard and doing everything right and still find yourself let go or laid off. A **layoff** is a job loss caused when a company has no work for certain employees for a period of time. Some layoffs are short—you might work at a factory that receives no orders for new products for six months, but when new orders come in, you are called back to work. Some layoffs are permanent. The factory might shut down and never reopen.

Losing your job can make you angry or depressed. It seems unfair. You lose your income. You lose your daily routine. You may even lose friends. To better cope with a job loss, consider the following.

■ Make sure you understand the reason for your termination. Try to get it in writing.

■ Ask for letters of recommendation. Most likely these will come from supervisors, though you might ask co-workers for recommendations as well.

21st Century Learning

In Good Times and Bad

Layoffs are more likely to happen when the economy is slow, such as during a recession. To make up for lost profits, companies will look to cut costs by trimming personnel or outsourcing work. There are some jobs and industries, however, that are more naturally resistant to tough economic times. Consider the following careers that tend to have more staying power:

✔ Nurses
✔ Teachers
✔ Firefighter
✔ Government Employees
✔ Veterinarians
✔ Accountants
✔ Pharmacists
✔ Database Administrators
✔ Engineers
✔ Police Officers

Have you ever asked anyone for a letter of recommendation? Why do you think employers request them?

- Analyze the terms of your **severance package**—the compensation you receive because you are being terminated. It may include wages, training, career counseling, and temporary continuation of medical insurance.

- File for unemployment benefits as soon as you are eligible. Unemployment benefits include money and free career counseling services that are available to unemployed workers while they are looking for new jobs.

- Check into your health insurance options. If you were insured through a company policy you will need to get your own health insurance.

- Reevaluate your budget. The loss of income may require you to make changes to your spending until you can find a new job.

- Ask for help. Make sure you have a support network in place to help you deal with the stress of losing your job and finding a new one. This same network may be able to help you to find work as well.

- Stay positive. Feelings of anger or sadness are natural, but they can lead to hopelessness or depression. By staying positive you will be more likely to seek out new opportunities and will find work faster.

You've probably heard the phrase, "a blessing in disguise." Many times, a job loss is exactly that. While it is stressful and life-altering, it can also provide the incentive for you to move on to something more rewarding.

Though the name may suggest otherwise, if you are laid off, COBRA can be a good thing. COBRA provides former employees and their families the right to temporary continuation of their health coverage at group rates. COBRA helps make sure that individuals don't have to go without health insurance while they are looking for a new job.

Finding a New Job

The best time to look for a new job is while you still have the old one. If you make the decision to resign, or if you know a layoff is coming, you can update your resume and start your job search before you are unemployed.

The process for finding a new job is basically the same as for finding a first job. Assess your skills, abilities, and interests; research job opportunities; and send out your resume. However, there are a few advantages to finding a second (or third or fourth) job.

- *You have experience.* Make sure your resume highlights your most recent job description. Give specific examples of your successes.

- *You have developed contacts in the industry.* Get in touch with people you met through work, including customers and clients, members of professional organizations, and even your competition. Let them know you are looking for work.

- *You know more about yourself.* You know if the kind of work you have been doing is right for you. You know what it takes to succeed in that industry. You know if you are ready to try something new.

You should be careful about where and when you look for work, however. Surfing job boards for new opportunities from the workstation of your current job could get you laid off faster. If you are thinking about making a career change, it is best to keep that information to yourself—at least while you are at work. Once a new opportunity arises, however, you should discuss it with your current employer. The possibility of your leaving might persuade him or her to make a counter offer—perhaps giving you enough reason to stay.

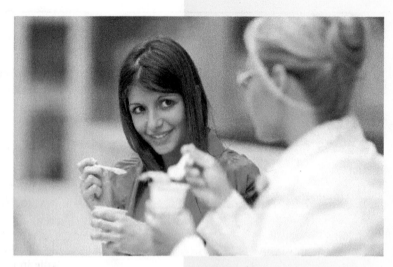

Taking Time Off

Every day, thousands of people put their careers on hold. Often it's time needed to raise a family or care for relatives. Others take time off to travel, go back to school, or start their own business. Sometimes people just need time away to reevaluate their career choices. At some point, however, many of those same people will want to reenter the workforce. Going back to work after substantial time off isn't always easy. Workers trying to find jobs after taking time off can feel under-skilled and overwhelmed. It can sometimes be even more difficult to reenter the workforce than it was to enter it in the first place. Returning to work after taking time off brings with it several considerations.

■ Should you go back to your previous career or at least work in that same industry?

■ Do you still have contacts you can count on for job leads and references?

■ Do you still have the education and skills required, or will you need to go back to school?

■ Have your career values and priorities changed? For example, do you need work that pays more, has more time off, or is less stressful?

■ Has the job market changed? Are there new jobs available that you'd consider?

You also will need to consider the time off from an employer's perspective. While it may seem unfair, most employers see a gap in employment history and assume that it means a worker with out-of-date skills and training. For that reason, you'll want to think about how you will approach your time off on your resume or in an interview.

Use a functional type resume that emphasizes your key skills rather than your work history. Use your cover letter as an opportunity to explain the time off and emphasize any non-work related activity you've done to improve your knowledge and skills and keep up with the industry.

In the interview, focus on why you want to return to work rather than why you left in the first place. Emphasize what you hope to accomplish for the future.

Remember that no matter what you did in your time off—whether it involved traveling the world, raising a family, or volunteering for a good cause—it helped you grow as a person and probably improved important skills that you can transfer to your job.

Why is it important to keep in contact with co-workers, clients, and other people you work with even after leaving a job?

A Closed Door or an Open One?

Being unemployed may be an opportunity to expand your knowledge and skills. What if the restaurant you are working for closes permanently?

★ *You might decide to open your own sandwich shop.*

★ *You might retrain in an industry that is growing, such as health care.*

★ *You might move to a part of the country that has low unemployment.*

★ *You might take a temporary job while you decide what to do next.*

★ *You might take time to travel.*

★ *You might join a not-for-profit organization such as the Peace Corps.*

What skills and resources can you use to turn a job loss into an opportunity for advancement?

Case Study

Leah has been working as an assistant in a medical office for three months. At her first performance review, her supervisor praised her for having a perfect attendance record. However, Leah received a score of Needs Improvement for organization, because she often filed patient records incorrectly.

Leah did not like the Needs Improvement score. She interrupted her supervisor to say that she thought it was one of the other assistants who made the errors. She said that filing was too easy, anyway, and that she needed something more challenging to do.

Leah's supervisor replied that if Leah was not happy with her role in the office, maybe the job was not right for her. Leah was stunned. Was she being fired?

■ Do you think Leah handled herself appropriately at her performance review?

■ What could she have done differently?

■ What decisions does Leah have to make now?

■ How should she respond to her supervisor?

Web Extra

Each state has its own system for handling unemployment benefits. Use the Internet to research the procedure for your state. You might start at doleta.gov, the site for the U.S. Department of Labor's employment and training administration.

Summarize the information in a report, and include links to important information for your state. Publish the summary on your school Web site, or make it available in your career center or library.

Answer It!

1. List two things you can do to make a new job less stressful.

2. Name three kinds of forms you might be expected to fill out on your first day at work.

3. What does an employee handbook do?

4. Name some strategies for making a good impression during your first few days at work.

5. List three characteristics of being a good leader.

6. List the six areas that are commonly evaluated on a performance review.

7. What should you do to get the most out of a performance review?

8. What is a tuition-reimbursement program?

9. What is the difference between an annual raise and a merit raise?

10. Why might it be easier to find a second job than a first one?

Career-Ready Practices

Career-ready individuals seek new methods, practices, and ideas from a variety of sources that they can apply to their own workplace. A professional organization is one such resource.

Joining a professional organization provides you with opportunities to learn more about your industry, strengthen your job skills, and expand your network of personal contacts. To an employer, it shows that you are motivated to look beyond the workplace to find new and innovative ideas that can help you and your organization be more productive.

One way that a professional organization helps its members is by distributing information about the industry through Web sites, newsletters, or magazines.

Working in teams of three or four, select an industry and create a two-page publication for its professional organization. Try not to be too general in your choice (choose nursing instead of medicine or marketing instead of business). Use the Internet to research current trends, policies, or events affecting the industry. Give the publication a suitable name, and write three or four articles that the members would find useful. Include pictures if appropriate.

When your project is complete, print it to share with the class, or publish it on your class Web site.

Write Now

Can you think of reasons why someone might become dissatisfied with a job that he or she used to enjoy? Is it because of changing values? Changing goals? Could changes in other areas of life affect his or her job satisfaction?

If you were a career counselor, how would you advise someone who is dissatisfied with work? Write a report describing the person. Include information about the job and the person's career history, such as how long he or she has had the job, what responsibilities there are, and the quality of his or her relationships with co-workers.

Describe the reasons the person is dissatisfied. Explain how you would recommend he or she approach the problem and find solutions.

Career Portfolio

A performance review makes an ideal piece for a career portfolio—provided it is a good one, of course. Such reviews showcase specific skills and exhibit your performance on the job in ways that general recommendations or a resume can't. Plus, several performance reviews together can show a history of improvement and personal growth, providing a kind of timeline of your work experience.

Some employers may be reluctant to provide you with a copy of your review for your own records. If that is the case, consider asking your supervisor to type up a summary of the review that you can include in your portfolio in lieu of the actual review.

In addition to the performance review, this chapter discussed several other kinds of experiences and documents that you might want to include in your portfolio. Can you think of any?

Business Plan Project

There are many people in your life that could help you achieve your goals. Review the skills and qualities you would like to develop. In your **Business Plan Project**, make a list of adults you know or would like to know from whom you could learn the skills and qualities you need to achieve your goals. Contact at least one person on your list and discuss what you would like to learn, and how that person could help. Record his or her response in your **Business Plan Project**.

15 | Being Productive in Your Career

Skills in This Chapter . . .

- **Being a Successful Employee**
- **Applying Time-Management Techniques in the Workplace**
- **Managing Workplace Conflict**
- **Recognizing Your Rights and Responsibilities**

GETTING STARTED

What does it take to succeed? Think about your classes, hobbies, or co-curricular activities. Think about what it takes to get an A on a test, to finish a project, or to cross the finish line first. Like success in school, career success has a lot to do with your ability to adapt to changes, to work well with others, to think clearly and critically, and to manage your resources effectively to continue to learn and grow. Most important, career success requires you to take responsibility for your actions.

➤ Think of a class or an activity (such as a sport or hobby) in which you do well. Make a list of five personal traits you have that help you to succeed in that class or activity. Now think of different work situations or scenarios in which that personal characteristic would come in handy, one scenario for each trait. Pick one of those scenarios and write a paragraph describing how your personal characteristics would help you to excel.

Being a Successful Employee

The qualities that make you successful in other areas of your life make you successful at work, too. The determination required to run a race or work through a complex math problem would come in handy when you need to work extra hours to complete a marketing project or finish your delivery route. The critical thinking skills you use to perform a science experiment would be valuable when you are diagnosing a patient or preparing a legal brief. The communication skills you use to keep two friends from arguing would also be helpful when you are dealing with an angry customer insisting on a refund.

Think about someone you know who is good at his or her job. Why do you think he is good at what he does? Is he smarter than others who do similar jobs? Does he have more resources? Or does he simply work harder than the rest?

What does it take to be the best at something? Do you want to be the best at your job, or do you want to do "just good enough" to get a paycheck?

Successful employees exhibit the traits that employers need most. According to the National Association of Colleges and Employers, employers look for job candidates who are honest and motivated, who have a good work ethic, and who have strong communication and teamwork skills. Think of just about any job on the market: Who doesn't want a motivated and honest worker who knows how to get along with others and be part of a team? It doesn't really matter *what* you are doing: The skills and qualities that make for a successful employee apply across the board.

Employee of the Month
awarded to

_____

Sarah Chen

for outstanding work ethic

Dept. Manager   May 19, 2015
GRANTED BY   ON THE DAY OF

Being Professional

Have you ever heard someone say that a worker exhibits *professionalism*? Maybe a repair worker calls back two days after fixing your furnace to make sure your house is still warm. Maybe an emergency dispatcher calmly talks a frantic mother through the steps necessary to stop her child's bleeding while waiting for the ambulance. Maybe a busy waiter takes the time to help you select a meal and feel comfortable.

Professionalism is the ability to show respect to everyone around you while you perform your responsibilities as best as you can. It includes a basic set of personal qualities that make an employee successful—no matter what job or career he or she has. The personal qualities that combine to create professionalism include the following:

■ Integrity

■ Courtesy

- Honesty
- Dependability
- Responsibility

When you show professionalism, you earn the trust and respect of your supervisor, co-workers, and customers. You contribute to your own well-being, because you can feel good about the way you treat others and the way you meet your work responsibilities. Generally, when you feel good about the work you do, it means you are doing good work.

Career FACT

In today's workplaces, people change jobs often, and companies have trouble hanging on to qualified workers. That's why employers value *loyalty* almost as much as hard work, honesty, and dependability. Many employers still reward loyalty with raises, promotions, bonuses, and other incentives.

Is "being a professional" the same as "showing professionalism"? Can anyone show professionalism, regardless of the kind of work he or she does?

Being a Problem Solver

While many of the characteristics that make you successful at school will help you to succeed at work, you will still run into problems and obstacles that you have not encountered before. Businesses and organizations want workers who can take the initiative and solve problems as they arise. In fact, the ability to solve problems is consistently ranked by employers as one of the most important skills.

Recall that a problem is a difficulty you must resolve before you can make progress. You are likely to encounter a wide variety of problems depending on your work role.

- Should you give a customer a discount in order to make the sale?
- Should you buy cheaper materials in order to finish a job under budget?
- What do you do if your computer crashes in the middle of a multimedia presentation?
- Do you know the right person to speak to about ordering supplies?
- What should you do if a co-worker wants to gossip about your supervisor?

Meeting Your Employer's Expectations

Every employer will have different expectations, just as every job will come with a different set of duties. There are some expectations that almost every employer can agree on.

✔ *Work hard for a full day.*
✔ *Follow the rules.*
✔ *Be honest.*
✔ *Get along with others.*
✔ *Respect people's differences.*
✔ *Show up every day on time.*
✔ *Meet deadlines.*
✔ *Stay positive.*
✔ *Avoid mistakes.*
✔ *Accept responsibility.*

Can you think of other expectations that employers have? Have you ever had trouble meeting any of these expectations at work or at school?

Someone You Can Count On

Regardless of the job, employers need their workers to be reliable. If an employer can't count on you to show up and do your work to the best of your ability, he or she will find someone else who will.

👎 Showing up late day after day

👎 Taking too many sick or personal days

👎 Taking longer than allowed breaks and lunches

👎 Missing deadlines

👍 Completing work accurately and on time

👍 Calling ahead if you are going to be late

👍 Scheduling days off well in advance

👍 Working overtime if required

👍 Helping out co-workers when they need it

Are you reliable? Can your friends and family members count on you? Is there anything you could do to be more dependable?

Because the kinds of problems you'll face will vary, it's important to have a process for resolving them. You can use your problem-solving skills at work the same way you use them in other areas of your life.

■ Identify the problem.

■ Consider all possible solutions.

■ Identify the consequences of each solution.

■ Select the best solution.

■ Make and implement a plan of action.

Taking responsibility for your problems and working to find solutions shows you are independent and capable. That, in turn, can lead to increased responsibility and more recognition.

Can you think of a single job in which workers *aren't* expected to solve problems?

Being Ethical at Work

Recall that *ethics* are a set of beliefs about what is right and what is wrong. **Work ethics** are beliefs and behaviors about what is right and wrong in a work environment. When you behave ethically at work, others will trust and respect you.

Most work ethics are similar to principles from other areas of life that you apply to your workplace.

■ Always try to do your best.

■ Respect the authority of your supervisor.

■ Respect your co-workers.

■ Respect company property.

Not everyone behaves ethically at work. When you are in a situation where others are acting in a way that you know is unethical, you will have to use your decision-making skills to choose how to respond.

■ You might see someone taking office supplies home for personal use, which is stealing.

■ You might hear co-workers insulting a customer or manager, which is disrespectful.

■ Someone might leave early and ask you to lie about it to your supervisor, which is dishonest.

Of course, ethics extends beyond the actions and behaviors of individual workers. It applies to companies and organizations as a whole.

■ You might work for a company that dumps chemical waste into a nearby river.

■ You might work for an employer who neglects safety procedures in order to cut costs.

■ You might work for an organization that doesn't report all of the taxes it owes.

It's important to remember that being ethical means standing up for what you believe, even if that goes against the actions and beliefs of others—even your employer.

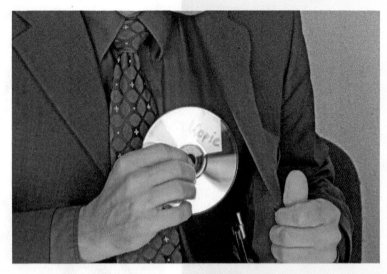

What would you do if you caught someone stealing at work?

NUMBERS GAME

Imagine you work at a factory. At a recent meeting, your supervisor happily noted that work-related injuries were down 20% from the previous month. During the current month there had only been 16 injuries. In the month prior, there were 20.

A percentage *increase* represents how much *more* of something there is compared to a previous number or amount. A percentage *decrease* represents how much *less* of something there is.

In the example above, there were four fewer injuries in the current month compared to the previous month. To find the percentage *decrease*, first find the *difference* of the two numbers. Then divide that answer by the *higher* number. Finally, multiply that number by 100.

$20 - 16 = 4$

$4 \div 20 = .20$

$.20 \times 100 = 20\%$

To find the percentage *increase*, divide the difference of the two numbers by the *lower* number. Then multiply the answer by 100.

Now imagine it is a month later and your supervisor sadly reports that the number of injuries rose from 16 to 24. What is the percentage increase?

Applying Time-Management Techniques in the Workplace

You arrive at your work as a marketing assistant at 8:50 a.m. You look at your to-do list. It has ten tasks on it. You get started on task one. The phone rings. Your supervisor asks you to reschedule an appointment. Then, a co-worker needs help preparing a mailing that has to go out today. Your sister calls. She's in the area and wants to meet for lunch. After lunch, a customer calls to inquire about a new product. Then, your supervisor wants you to sit in on a meeting. You look at your watch and it is 5:05. You look at your to-do list. The day is over, and you are only halfway through item one.

Time management is a critical skill for succeeding at work. Employers want you to make the most of your time—to them, time is money. To achieve your career goals, you will have to manage your time effectively and *set priorities*—decide which tasks must be completed first.

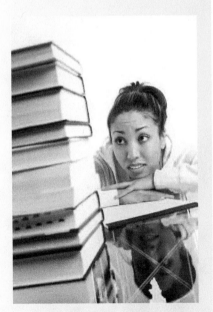

Should you work on the project worth half your grade due next week or finish your math homework due tomorrow? What time management skills do you use to succeed at school?

Tech Connect

Sometimes it seems everyone needs a personal assistant . . . or at least a digital version of one. A personal digital assistant (PDA) is a handheld computer, sometimes called a palmtop computer. Most PDAs are smartphones: mobile phones capable of browsing the Web, creating and storing documents, and acting as portable multimedia players. This technology allows users to stay connected to almost everyone from almost anywhere.

But how smart is a smartphone? While the applications available can certainly make you a more productive worker, they can also be a distraction. While your smartphone may alert you to your upcoming meeting, it also tempts you to play games instead of paying attention to the latest sales figures. Technology is only as valuable as the person using it.

Imagine you are the manager of information technology at a small business. Department managers are all issued company smartphones. You are responsible for developing a list of applications that each manager should download to his or her phone. Research business-oriented applications that would help a department manager work more productively. Create a table that describes each application and why you would recommend it. Share your findings with the class.

Employers expect you to respect your time at work. That means showing up on time, taking breaks at scheduled times, meeting deadlines, and taking care of personal business on your own time. Making the most of your time demonstrates to your supervisor that you take your responsibilities seriously.

Career Tips

School, practice, clubs, meets, homework . . . not to mention your social life—knowing how to manage your time is a skill you should start developing immediately. Think about how busy you are now. Now imagine balancing your career with the rest of your adult life.

Tools for Managing Time at Work

You can use many of the same time-management tools you use at home and at school to manage your time at work. Schedules and goal-setting can keep you focused on the tasks at hand. Computer programs can help you organize and meet your responsibilities. Set realistic and attainable goals using daily, weekly, and monthly schedules.

- Different schedules can help you identify tasks that must be accomplished within a specific timeframe. For example, you may have to call a customer today, but you may have to submit a report sometime this week. You may have to request vacation time before the first of next month, and you may have to attend a safety training session before Wednesday.

- Make use of the calendar program on your computer or handheld device. With programs such as Microsoft Office Outlook or Google Calendar, you can enter schedules, phone calls, and appointments. Use the tasks list feature to record and prioritize the things you need to accomplish. Set the program to display a message or make a sound to remind you of deadlines.

Myth　Americans work too hard.

Truth　It is all relative. Compared to other countries, Americans do work longer hours than average. According to the Organization for Economic Cooperation and Development, U.S. workers work an average of 1,790 hours per year. That puts them 10th in the rankings. At the top: the Mexicans, who work 2,226 hours per year, on average.

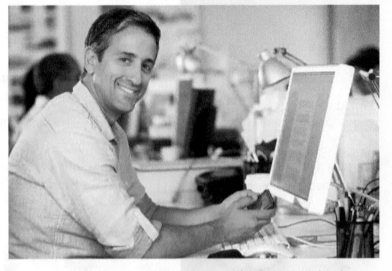

Have advances in technology made it easier or harder for people to manage their time?

Did I Wake You?

The earth is divided into 24 different **time zones**—geographic regions that use the same standard time. When you cross from one time zone into another, the time is different.

When you work in an office that does business with people living in different time zones, it is important to know the **local time**—time in the time zone where the other people are located.

For example, if you work in Miami, Florida, you are in the U.S. Eastern Time Zone. The local time for a client in London, England, is five hours later, in the Western European Time Zone. When it is 9:00 a.m. in Miami, it is 2:00 p.m. in London. While that time difference is certainly manageable, think about a business call from Miami to Japan, which is *13* hours later.

Can you think of jobs that might have problems resulting from differing time zones? Write about a work problem caused by time zones. Be specific about the job, the problem, and the time zones. Describe how you would solve the problem.

Tips for Managing Time at Work

The most important way to manage your time at work is to *prioritize*.

- Identify the tasks that must be done immediately and finish them first.
- Identify tasks that have multiple steps and plan when steps will be completed.
- Use your goal-setting skills to help you decide how to break larger projects into smaller chunks.

Something as simple as a daily to-do list may be all you need to keep your work priorities in order. However, it doesn't hurt to check in with your supervisor from time to time and make sure that what you are working on is the top priority.

Would your friends be happy if you said you'd meet them at 4:00 but you didn't show up until 4:45? Employers and co-workers expect you to honor and respect time in the workplace, too.

Following are some other tips for managing your time.

- *Give no for an answer.* Some people may ask for too much of your time. They may expect you to take on more responsibility than you can handle. It is okay to say no. Be polite and respectful, but explain that your schedule is full.

- *Ask for help.* If you are having trouble completing tasks that are part of your assigned responsibilities, you will need to find a way to get them done. Ask your supervisor, a co-worker, or someone in human resources to help you learn how to organize your time, or find ways to be more efficient so you can get more work done.

■ *Notify your supervisor if you are late.* Most people try to be **punctual**—on time. They don't intend to be late for work or meetings. But things come up to delay them. Your morning bus is late because of traffic or you receive an unexpected phone call just as you are heading for a conference. When possible, call to notify your employer that you will be late, or request the time off for unplanned absences.

Career Profile: Occupational Therapist

Health Science Career Cluster

Job Summary

Occupational therapists help patients to develop, recover, or maintain their daily living and work skills. Often they work with individuals who suffer from a mental, physical, developmental, or emotional disability. The goal of all therapists is to help their clients lead independent, productive, and satisfying lives.

Occupational therapists help clients perform daily activities, engage in rehabilitative exercise, and improve their mental functioning. They work in rehabilitation centers, schools, hospitals, and other healthcare settings, though many of them also work out of patients' homes. Being an occupational therapist requires a college degree and a license. Employment of occupational therapists is expected to grow much faster than most other occupations, especially for those treating the elderly.

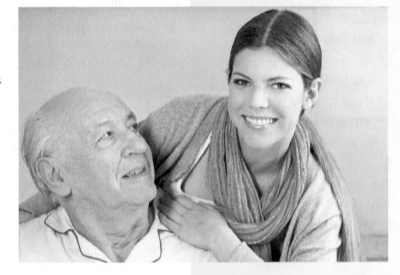

Use the Internet, a library, or career center to research the responsibilities, education and training requirements, and salary range of an occupational therapist. Prepare a presentation about the career.

Occupational therapists do more than just help people get back to work—they help people of all ages improve their quality of life. What kinds of skills are necessary for this type of work?

Communications

Review

Knowing how to use communication skills to manage workplace conflict will make you a valuable member of your work team. Remember some of these important steps for effective communication.

✔ *Be clear. Use words and body language that the other person can understand.*

✔ *Be personal. Address the other person by his or her name or title. Use "I" statements to show that you take responsibility for your role in the conflict.*

✔ *Be positive. State your message in positive terms directed at how to achieve your common goal.*

✔ *Get to the point. Explain why you feel or think this way.*

✔ *Use active listening to be sure you hear the response.*

✔ *Think before you respond. Use critical thinking instead of emotions.*

The ability to communicate effectively is a transferable skill that you will use no matter what direction your career takes.

Managing Workplace Conflict

No matter how well you get along with your friends or how much you love your family, you are bound to disagree with them every now and then. It is no different at work. If anything, the pressure to succeed can make workplace conflicts even more intense.

Recall that conflict is a disagreement between two or more people who have different ideas. Conflict at work can interfere with your career goals. It can make you angry and cause you to resent the other people at work. If it is left unresolved, conflict can make it difficult or even impossible to successfully meet your responsibilities.

Some workplace conflicts are small, such as a disagreement about who gets to use the printer first or who put a file in the wrong drawer. Others are more significant, such as a disagreement over who will be the manager of a new project or who will get a promotion.

As in other areas of your life, managing workplace conflict does not always mean eliminating the conflict completely. It means that you are able to recognize what is causing the conflict and that you can cope with it in an honest and respectful way.

Valuing Differences

You will encounter people with different backgrounds and experiences in your workplace. You are also likely to encounter people from different cultures. Sometimes, these differences can cause conflict.

■ You might think the food a co-worker eats in the lunchroom smells bad, even though it is common in his or her native country.

■ You might be frustrated trying to understand an order placed by a customer who speaks English as a second language.

■ You might become impatient waiting for a disabled co-worker to complete a task you know you could do faster.

Understanding the differences between your co-workers makes it easier to communicate, which, in turn, helps you to find common bonds. Though you may have different cultures, beliefs, backgrounds, or skills, you are all working toward the same goals: to get your work done and help your organization succeed. At work, focusing on the common goals you and your co-workers share will help you see past the differences to resolve conflicts.

Breaking Down Workplace Barriers

Workplace barriers are anything that keeps you from doing your job to the best of your ability. Such barriers often *cause* conflict, but they may be caused *by* conflict, too.

- You might not understand your responsibilities.

- You might not feel that you have received adequate training.

- You might think a team member is not pulling his or her weight on the job.

- You might find your supervisor is not helpful or supportive.

Effective communication is one of the best ways to avoid barriers at work. Be respectful and polite. Show that you value the opinions of others, and present your point of view in a clear and positive way.

You can also knock down a lot of barriers by maintaining a positive attitude. A negative attitude can quickly cause conflict and result in the loss of support from the rest of your team.

Peer Pressure at Work

You are probably aware of the power of peer pressure among your friends at school. Co-workers, customers, and supervisors can influence your thoughts and actions as well. Is peer pressure at work positive or negative?

- Co-workers convince you to leave work early to go to the movies.

- Your supervisor asks you to tell an angry customer that he is out when you know he is in the office.

- A vendor says she will pay you cash on the side if you buy office supplies from her.

- Co-workers encourage you to exercise during lunch.

- Your supervisor invites you to join a professional organization that can help your career.

- Team members convince you to work overtime to finish a project ahead of schedule.

How can recognizing peer pressure at work help you make healthy decisions and achieve your career goals?

How does respecting cultural and social differences help you avoid conflict at work?

Can't We All Get Along?

You respect the opinions of all of your co-workers, make an effort to get to know them, and hope that you get along with them all. But sometimes there is simply a personality clash. What if you just don't like someone you work with?

★ You could avoid working with that individual whenever possible.

★ You could have a talk with the co-worker and find ways to cooperate and compromise.

★ You could discuss any problems you are having with your supervisor.

★ You could ask for a different schedule or a transfer to a different department.

What are the consequences of each of these actions? How can unhealthy relationships with your co-workers interfere with your career success?

Recognizing Your Rights and Responsibilities

What would you do if an employer did not pay you for two months? What if an employer expected you to use a dirty bathroom, or work in a building without smoke detectors? What would you do if an employer promoted someone less qualified instead of you simply because that person was the opposite gender?

As a worker in the United States, you have rights that are protected by law. Federal and state agencies are responsible for making sure your employer treats you fairly and obeys the law. Your employer is responsible for the following:

- Paying you on time
- Providing you with safe working conditions
- Allowing you to leave to care for your family
- Preventing discrimination against you

Understanding your rights as a worker will help you make decisions about where to work and what type of career to choose Moreover, it can help you to decide if an employer *is* treating you fairly and what steps you can take if the answer is no.

Overcoming Discrimination and Harassment

Have you ever felt that you were treated differently from others because of a quality or characteristic that you cannot control? Maybe girls did not want you walking home with them because you are a boy. Maybe a teacher did not choose you to narrate a class presentation because you have an accent. Perhaps you weren't picked to be part of a club because you are in a wheelchair. If you thought the treatment was unfair, you were right. In fact, it was discrimination. **Discrimination** is unfair treatment of a person or group based on age, gender, race, religion, or disability. Discrimination is usually because of **prejudice**, or negative opinions that are not based on fact.

Sometimes employers or co-workers harass others. **Harassment** is unwanted, repeated behavior or communication that bothers, annoys, frightens, or stresses another person. Like discrimination, harassment at work is against the law.

Learning how to cope with and overcome discrimination and harassment can help you achieve success at work. The workplace will be a more productive environment if all employees are happy and comfortable. You can encourage a more productive environment by developing qualities such as tolerance, cooperation, respect, and understanding.

Employers are required to keep your work environment safe, but what can you do to stay safe on the job?

You have the right to be treated fairly in the workplace, and to be safe from harassment. The **Civil Rights Act of 1964** states that employers may not use race, skin color, religion, sex, or national origin as a reason to promote, not promote, hire, or fire an employee. Similarly, the **Equal Pay Act of 1963** prohibits employers from paying workers less simply because of their gender.

Newer laws such as the **Americans with Disabilities Act (ADA)** make it illegal to discriminate based on age or physical disability. States also have anti-discrimination laws, some of which are stronger than the federal laws.

The **Family and Medical Leave Act (FMLA)** provides certain employees with up to 12 weeks of unpaid, job-protected leave per year. The leave must be used for family or medical reasons, such as the birth of a new baby or to care for an ailing parent. The law also requires that the employee's health benefits continue during the leave.

If you believe you are facing discrimination or harassment at work you should do the following.

- Keep a careful written record of every incident. That means writing down what people say or do, including the date, time, and names of all the other people who were there. If you receive written threats or offensive documents such as letters, texts, or e-mails, save them and print them.

- Get a copy of your company's policy on discrimination and harassment. It may be online or in the employee handbook.

- Follow the procedure in the company policy for reporting illegal behavior. If there is no procedure, meet with someone in human resources to report it.

- If the company is not responsive, you can report directly to the **Equal Employment Opportunity Commission (EEOC),** the federal agency responsible for investigating charges of discrimination against employers.

Dealing with discrimination or harassment at work can cause stress and unhappiness. How would this affect an employee's attitude toward work?

Privacy in the Workplace

Would you be angry if you found out your supervisor was reading e-mails from your friends that you received at work? Maybe, but your supervisor did not break the law. Employers have the right to check on their employees to make sure they are being honest and productive. They may:

✔ *Read e-mail messages and personal computer files stored at work*

✔ *Listen to telephone conversations that take place at work*

✔ *Monitor Internet usage, including tracking the sites an employee visits while at work*

✔ *Video employees using hidden cameras, if they suspect them of illegal or unethical behavior*

You can avoid any problems by assuming that your employer is able to read or hear everything that passes through your computer and telephone at work.

CAREER

COUNSEL

Eduardo works at a restaurant, handling take-out orders over the phone. He works hard. He takes extra shifts when his manager needs him. He covers for co-workers who want time off. He likes the work environment. He gets along well with his co-workers and managers.

When a waiter quits, her job becomes available. Eduardo applies. He has the necessary qualifications. He is familiar with the restaurant, the menu, and the procedures. Someone who had never worked in the restaurant is offered the job.

Eduardo is one of the few Latino people who work at the restaurant. He thinks he did not get the job because of his cultural background. Do you agree with Eduardo? Are there other reasons he might not have been hired?

Use your 21st Century Skills such as decision making, goal setting, and problem solving to help Eduardo decide what to do next. Write an ending to the story. Read it to the class, or form a small group and present it as a skit.

Understanding Unions and Trade Organizations

A trade or labor union is an organization of people who do similar work. Trade unions exist for many kinds of workers. The purpose of **trade unions** is to improve wages and working conditions for workers. While every union is different, all unions share some characteristics.

- Unions hold elections to choose representatives.
- Representatives negotiate for workers' contracts.
- They speak up for workers' rights, such as safe working conditions.

Becoming a member of a trade union means that you will have to pay union **dues**—fees for belonging to that union. The dues are used to support the trade union and the work it does. Many teachers belong to unions. Ask your teacher what teachers' unions do and what teachers must do to belong.

Some businesses are "union shops." If you work in a union shop, you *must* join the trade union soon after you start working. In states that have right-to-work laws, workers generally do not have to belong to trade unions.

Why do you think an organization of many workers may be better able to negotiate than one worker alone?

In 2013, a little more than 11% of all wage and salary workers belonged to unions.

Understanding Professional Organizations

Like trade and labor unions, a **professional organization** is an association of people who are all employed in the same field or industry. Usually, the goals of a professional organization include providing education and training and acting as a source of information about the industry. It is similar to a student organization, such as Future Business Leaders of America.

Being a member of a professional organization can help you stay up-to-date on issues affecting the industry, as well as establish contacts with potential customers, suppliers, and employers. There are professional organizations for just about every career you can imagine—sometimes more than one. Benefits of joining a professional organization include:

■ *Opportunities to meet people in the industry.* You can increase the number of contacts you have for networking and make friends who share similar interests. This can be especially valuable for getting advice on job and advancement opportunities in your area of interest.

■ *Access to the most current news and trends affecting the industry.* Professional organizations publish Web sites and newsletters to make sure members have the latest information.

■ *Access to training.* Organizations hold meetings, sponsor speakers and seminars, and offer classes for members.

Joining a professional organization helps you expand your career opportunities and improve your career-related skills. It also shows your employer that you are serious about your career.

Most Dangerous Careers

According to the Bureau of Labor Statistics, the following are some of the most dangerous jobs in America:

✔ *Fishers*

✔ *Loggers*

✔ *Pilots and flight engineers*

✔ *Iron and steel workers*

✔ *Roofers*

Why do you think people choose to work in these dangerous jobs? Are the benefits worth the risks?

Staying Safe at Work

Is the work you do safe? Do only the most dangerous jobs—such as roofer or fisher—require safety procedures? Consider the following situations.

- You are the co-pilot on a jet liner, and the pilot has been flying for 42 hours straight and is noticeably fatigued.

- You work at an autobody repair shop, and your co-worker is trying to use an acetylene torch to weld two pieces of metal together.

- You work for a manufacturing facility testing toxic chemicals, and your supervisor insists that you don't need a respirator because you will only be exposed for a couple of minutes.

- Your company is moving to a new office building, and the owner is looking to cut costs by not installing an emergency sprinkler system.

Part of your rights as a worker is the right to safe working conditions. There are numerous laws and regulations in place to ensure that organizations provide a safe working environment. In addition, most businesses have specific rules and procedures for maintaining workplace safety, whether it's how to correctly operate a machine or how to safely evacuate a burning building.

Is the work we do now more or less dangerous than the work our parents, grandparents, or great-grandparents did? What factors have made work safer?

Money Madne$$

You work for a construction company and are injured on the job when the scaffolding collapses and you break your leg. Your employer provides you with disability insurance equivalent to full-time pay for the period that you will be unable to work. Assuming that it will take six weeks until you can return to work and that you normally work a 40-hour week at $18.50 per hour, how much will the company compensate you for by the end?

In 1970, the federal government passed a law called the **Occupational Safety and Health Act**. This law requires all employers to provide a safe and healthful workplace. Workers must be provided with safe equipment, protective clothing when needed, and education about safety practices. The **Occupational Safety and Health Administration (OSHA)** was formed to inspect companies and enforce safety laws. Even so, more than 4,000 Americans die from on-the-job accidents every year.

As a worker under the Occupational Safety and Health Act, you have the following rights and responsibilities.

- *Right to know.* You have the right to know about hazards in your workplace, as well as the right to training to learn how to identify workplace hazards and what to do if there is an incident.

- *Right to refuse unsafe work.* If you have reasonable grounds to believe the work you do or the piece of equipment you use is unsafe, you can stop work immediately. You cannot be laid off, suspended, or penalized for refusing unsafe work if you follow the proper procedures.

- *Responsibility to follow safety rules.* It is your employer's responsibility to teach you the safety rules; it is your responsibility to follow the rules.

- *Responsibility to ask for training.* If you feel that you need more training than your employer provides, it is your responsibility to ask for it.

- *Responsibility to speak up.* It is your responsibility to report incidents and unsafe work practices as well as unsafe conditions.

Part of your responsibility as a worker is to make sure that you keep your work environment safe for yourself and for others. You have to take some responsibility for your own safety. If you are a new worker, enroll in any safety classes offered by the company. If you work around chemicals, poisons, or dangerous machinery, ask how they can be handled safely. If a company offers you hard hats or other safety equipment, use them. Read your manuals and handbook, and don't take shortcuts if it means endangering your safety or the safety of customers or co-workers. Remember—failure to follow safety guidelines is cause for dismissal.

What do you do to make sure you stay safe at work, at school, or when exercising or playing sports?

Putting Others at Risk

You have the right to a safe workplace, but you also have responsibilities to do your part to keep yourself, co-workers, and clients safe. How might your actions affect the safety of others?

- You fail to report a worn-out electrical cord.

- You do not request training on a new piece of equipment.

- You do not report that a new co-worker does not know how to use the equipment.

- You participate in your company's safety committee.

- You request safety inspections.

- You keep your safety training current.

What careers do you think have the riskiest work environments? Does risky work appeal to you?

Career Tips

Those interested in a career in a growing industry should consider workplace safety. Some occupations within this area include safety training specialists, environmental health specialists, emergency management specialists, health safety technicians, and safety inspectors.

Case Study

Lucy and Amanda work at an afterschool recreation program for elementary school kids in their town. The program uses the gym at the middle school. The girls give the kids snacks and help them do their homework. Then they play games using the middle school gym equipment. At the end of the day, Lucy and Amanda are responsible for making sure all the equipment is locked up in the storage room.

One day, Amanda takes a soccer ball home with her instead of locking it in the closet. Lucy notices but doesn't say anything. She hopes Amanda will bring it back the next day. Lucy never sees the soccer ball again.

■ What do you think of Amanda's actions?

■ Can you identify a problem or challenge facing Lucy?

■ What do you think Lucy should do next? How should she respond to her supervisor?

Web Extra

The nonprofit organization Workplace Fairness provides workers with information about many issues, including employee rights. Use its Web site—workplacefairness.org—to learn about issues facing workers today.

Pick an issue that you find interesting, and write a summary explaining how it affects workers, why you think it is important, and how workers can deal with it.

Answer It!

1. Name three characteristics of professionalism.

2. List five ways you can meet any employer's expectations.

3. What is the key to managing your time at work?

4. What communication skills can help you to manage workplace conflict?

5. What responsibilities do employers have to their workers?

6. True or false: Employers have the right to record employees' phone conversations and read their work e-mails.

7. What federal law protects individuals from workplace discrimination?

8. What steps should you take if you are facing harassment or discrimination at work?

9. What do trade unions do?

10. What are you entitled to under the Occupational Safety and Health Act?

Career-Ready Practices

Students have the right to be free of harassment and discrimination in school, just like employees in the workplace. As a class, discuss the ways harassment and discrimination occur in school and brainstorm ideas for how to eliminate it.

Career-ready individuals look for ways to contribute to the betterment of their families, schools, community, and workplace. They are responsible and eager to participate in activities that serve the greater good. In groups of three or four, brainstorm ideas for an anti-harassment and discrimination theme and slogan. As a group, create a poster that educates people about harassment or discrimination using the theme and slogan you select. Display the posters in your classroom or on a bulletin board in a common area of the school. Notify your local media about the display. They may want to publish examples of the posters in print or online.

Write Now

Do you think there are similarities between your home environment, school environment, and the environment you might encounter at work? Are there differences? Are your roles the same or different? Do you need similar skills to succeed in each environment? Are the kinds of relationships you develop the same?

Write an essay comparing and contrasting the environments of your home and school with the environment you might find at work. Be sure to include what impact the differences might have on your behavior.

Career Portfolio

When most people think of references or letters of recommendation, they immediately look to their supervisor—and for good reason. Your supervisor is generally in the best position to evaluate your overall performance. However, you shouldn't overlook the opinions of your co-workers and peers, either. Sometimes they are in an even better position to discuss some of the skills and personal attributes most valued in the workplace—the ability to communicate effectively, to work as part of a team, and to manage conflicts, to name a few. Because supervisors aren't always around to watch your every move, it is sometimes just as valuable to get the opinions and feedback of the people you work with most closely.

Consider asking one of your co-workers or fellow students—someone whose opinion you value—to write a letter of recommendation for you to put into your portfolio. Stress that you would like him or her to comment on what it is like to be your co-worker. As a gesture of gratitude, offer to write him or her a recommendation in return.

Business Plan Project

Entrepreneurs are pulled in lots of different directions. Every day they must spend hours on the tasks necessary to keep the business running and growing. But there are only 24 hours in a day and 168 hours in a week. An entrepreneur cannot succeed without strong time-management skills. In your **Business Plan Project**, make a table listing the tasks you would need to perform for your new business and the amount of time per week you would spend on each. Add a row for activities outside of your business, such as eating and sleeping and spending time with family and friends. Total the number of hours. Is it more than 168? If so, how can you balance your commitments? Adjust the hours in your table until the total is as close to 168 without going over.

16 | Living a Healthy and Balanced Life

Skills in This Chapter . . .

- **Analyzing Lifestyle Choices**
- **Recognizing the Importance of Lifelong Learning**
- **Living in Your Community**
- **Staying Healthy**

GETTING STARTED

How much time do you want to spend at work or at home? Do you need time to volunteer? When will you see your friends? Do you want to raise a family someday? When do you hope to retire? Though it may seem too early to even think about some of these questions, it is important to start learning how to balance your work with the rest of your life. Balancing work, family, and friends means making the right choices for your education, career, and lifestyle. It means staying active and involved and making time for what's important to you. Finding a balance between all of the demands and desires in your life will lead to happiness and better health.

➤ Imagine you have five hours to do whatever you please. No work. No studying. No bedroom to clean or laundry to put away. What would you do? Would you spend time with friends, with your family, or by yourself? What activities would make you happiest? What activities would enhance your self esteem? Make a detailed schedule of how you would spend that five hours and then share it with one other person in the class. What does your schedule say about your priorities and your ability to balance your responsibilities?

Analyzing Lifestyle Choices

Recall that your *lifestyle* is the way you reflect personal values, standards, and attitudes in your life. It represents all of the choices you make—in the relationships you have, the activities you pursue, and the beliefs you hold. You may have heard that someone leads a carefree lifestyle, a dangerous lifestyle, or an expensive lifestyle. In fact, your lifestyle can seldom be encompassed in just one word, and it changes as you change and grow.

The choices you make—in your career, your relationships, your education, and how you spend your free time—will help dictate your lifestyle and vice versa. The goal is to choose a lifestyle that works for you, one that helps you to meet your goals, fulfill your needs, and find happiness.

Recall that wellness is when all of the areas of your life are working together to make you healthy, happy, and confident. Wellness is not an accident. It happens when you make healthy choices about the way you live your life. In order to stay healthy and happy you will need to learn how to balance all the parts of your life.

Balancing Roles

Part of achieving your lifestyle goals includes balancing the roles you play in all five areas of your life—family, work, school, peers, and community.

- When you spend all of your time on schoolwork, you have no time to volunteer in your community.

- When you spend all of your time at your job, you have no time left to spend with your family.

Of course, achieving balance doesn't mean spending the same amount of time in each role. You might feel balanced spending 45% of your time at school; 35% with your family; 15% at work; and 5% volunteering. Your friend might feel balanced spending 45% at school; 25% with family; 20% at work; and 10% volunteering.

■ Staying balanced also means being flexible. When the demands increase in one role, you may have to adjust the balance temporarily.

■ If you have to study for midterm exams, you may not be able to take an extra shift at work.

■ If your parents expect you to visit your grandmother, you may not be able to hang out with your friends.

Your overall wellness depends on your ability to meet your responsibilities in all of your roles.

Balancing Relationships

Your overall wellness also depends on your ability to balance your relationships. That means knowing how to make space for people and responsibilities without giving up the things that are important to you.

When you achieve balanced relationships, you are more likely to feel confident and happy. You are able to spend time with the people who are important to you, while still meeting your responsibilities in other areas. When you are unable to achieve balance, you may become tired, stressed, and unsatisfied. You may underperform in all areas and have trouble achieving your goals.

Tech Connect

Balancing work, family, and friends can be difficult. Often there isn't enough time in the day to talk to everyone you care about. You might have trouble staying in touch with people who live in a different community, city, state, or even a different country.

Thankfully, the Internet provides many ways for people to meet and socialize online.

■ Social networking sites let you post information and pictures about yourself and your friends. You can join groups, exchange messages, and stay in touch.

■ Chat rooms let you discuss topics with people who have similar interests.

■ Text messaging keeps you in constant contact with friends and family.

■ RSS feeds (a form of Web publishing that is easily updated and downloaded) let you broadcast your thoughts and actions, as well as follow the thoughts and actions of others.

Pick one means of socializing online and research it. Ask your parents if you can set up an account, if required. As you explore what the technology has to offer, consider these questions: How could you use this technology to balance your work, family, and friends? How could you use it to maintain your relationships? When does social networking become a problem? Write a brief report of your findings and present it to the class.

Signs of an Unhealthy Relationship

*Relationships that are full of conflict or are not satisfying are unhealthy, or **dysfunctional**—not working correctly. Ways to tell if a relationship is unhealthy include:*

✔ *You are unhappy in the relationship.*

✔ *You feel you cannot be yourself with that person.*

✔ *You are afraid the other person will end the relationship.*

✔ *You are afraid the other person will hurt you—physically or emotionally.*

✔ *You do not trust the other person.*

✔ *You are dishonest.*

✔ *You cannot or will not talk about your feelings.*

✔ *You do not respect the other person.*

Is the solution to a dysfunctional relationship always to end it? Are there positive ways to "fix" unhealthy relationships?

Have you ever struggled to balance your schoolwork with your social life? Do friends ever make meeting your responsibilities harder?

Think of all of the relationships you have. Parents, siblings, close friends, casual friends, extended family, teachers, teammates—these are all people who demand varying amounts of your time and attention. You have a relationship with anyone you interact with, in all five areas of your life—home, school, peers, work, and community.

Relationships are important in every role of your life and at every stage of your life. They help you share and exchange resources and achieve common goals. Often, relationships motivate us to make the choices we do. Think of the parent who works two jobs to support his or her family, or the friends who apply to the same college so that they can be together.

Money Madne$$

Recently, your friend spent a Sunday afternoon helping you study for a social studies test when she could have been at the movies. You decide to show your appreciation by baking her chocolate chip brownies. You are not sure if you should buy a box of brownie mix or bake the brownies from scratch.

You already have butter, sugar, flour, and salt. You would need to buy the chocolate ($4.85), eggs ($2.25), vanilla extract ($4.25), and chocolate chips ($3.75). The mix would cost $3.49. Which would cost less? Is cost the only factor? Which option would you choose, and why?

Events That Can Change Career Plans

Plan for the possible and be prepared for the unexpected! Flexibility, problem solving, and good decision-making skills will help you cope with events that might disrupt your career plans, including:

✔ *Marriage*

✔ *Parenthood*

✔ *Divorce*

✔ *Sickness or disability*

✔ *Layoffs*

✔ *Relocation to a new city*

Can you think of other events that might alter your career plans?

Career Choices and a Balanced Lifestyle

In Chapter 3, you considered how your choice of lifestyle might impact your career options. It's important to keep those same considerations in mind as you think about your personal well-being and the need for balance. Consider the following careers and the lifestyles and demands that go with them.

■ An attorney works 80 hours a week. She earns enough money to host her extended family for one month each summer at her vacation beach home.

- A chef works nights and weekends, but he is available during the day to volunteer at his child's school.

- A truck driver is frequently out of town, but he calls home every night to talk to his family before bed.

Your career impacts the way you perform your responsibilities in other areas of your life. The choices you make in your career affect your relationships with your family, friends, and community. Using your values and standards to make choices will help you keep the areas of your life in balance.

- Do you pursue a high-paying career because it enables you to provide your family with the things they need and want, and so you can make cash contributions to charities?

- Do you work in human services because you enjoy helping others and think it sets an important example for your family?

- Do you go into medicine not necessarily because you want to help people, but because you like the challenge of the profession and the prestige that comes with being a doctor?

- Do you follow in your parents' footsteps because you think it would make them proud and you hope one day to inherit the family business?

Your values and standards are likely to change over time. You may benefit from reconsidering your choices on a regular basis to make sure they still support your values.

Do you think these people all value the same things in their work? Why or why not?

Career Tips

Finding time for leisure activities may seem difficult. Use goal-setting strategies to incorporate them into your daily schedule and time-management strategies to make sure you stick to your goals.

Balancing Work and Leisure

One hundred years ago, it was common for people in the United States to work 6 days a week, 12 hours each day. They had very little time for **recreation** or **leisure**—fun—activities outside of work. Now, most people value leisure activities and vacation as a necessary part of balancing work with the other areas of their lives.

Leisure activities contribute to your well-being in many ways.

■ They improve your emotional well-being by helping you cope with stress.

■ They improve your social well-being by giving you time with family and friends.

■ Some forms improve your physical well-being by providing exercise.

■ They improve your personal well-being by helping you develop new skills and interests.

Leisure activities can range from reading a book, to playing sports, to taking a hike. The activities that are most satisfying match your interests and values. You might want to volunteer for the Special Olympics, go birdwatching, or attend a concert. Leisure is an opportunity to relax and enjoy yourself, and to take time off from your work responsibilities. Often this allows you to go back to work refreshed and rejuvenated—or energized.

How can having fun outside of work help you to be a better worker?

Myth Balancing work and family is only a women's issue.

Truth Once, traditional roles meant men were responsible for earning money and women were responsible for taking care of the home and family. Now, the responsibilities are more evenly shared, and both men and women are concerned with balancing work and family.

Vacation Around the World

On average, Americans receive 13 days of vacation per year. This amount varies dramatically from one occupation to the next, of course, and with how long you work for a company. Those starting out with a company are likely to have only one or two weeks of paid vacation per year, but after ten years of service, that may increase to three or four weeks.

But how does that compare to other countries? Not so well, according to the World Tourism Organization. Workers in Italy and France enjoy more than 35 days of paid time off per year. Those in Canada, Japan, Korea, and the United Kingdom are entitled to 25 days or more per year. And in Austria, workers are legally entitled to a minimum of 22 vacation days plus 13 public holidays. If you had more than a month of vacation time a year, how would you spend it?

Thinking About the Future

When you become an adult, your roles and responsibilities will change. Some common grownup responsibilities include:

- Voting
- Furthering your education at a college or trade school
- Serving in the military
- Holding a full-time job
- Getting married
- Having children
- Making large purchases such as a home or car
- Making financial investments

The more roles and responsibilities you take on, the more difficult it may be to balance them.

One of the most common lifestyle-changing events is marriage. About 75 percent of the population in the United States will get married. **Marriage** is an institution that grants a couple a unique set of legal, social, and religious rights and responsibilities. Adding the role of spouse often requires a rebalancing of goals and priorities. When people marry, they agree to *share* their lives socially, financially, and spiritually. The relationship between spouses can lead to a change in career plans.

- You might follow your spouse to a different part of the country to pursue a job opportunity.
- You might have to quit your job to take care of your spouse if he or she should become ill.
- You might take a job that requires less travel so that you can have more time to spend together.

Like marriage, the decision to have children is an important one that will shape the rest of your life in significant ways. Whether or not you are raising children could determine things such as:

- *The job you have.* Caring for your children is your first priority, so you might not be able to take a job that involves a lot of travel or long hours.

NUMBERS GAME

How many hours, on average, do you spend a week on homework? How many hours do you spend playing video games? How many hours do you spend chatting with your friends on the phone or online?

An **average** is the sum of two or more quantities divided by the number of quantities. For example, you can calculate the average number of hours you sleep in a week by adding the hours slept each day and dividing by 7.

For example, say you got 7 hours of sleep on Monday, Tuesday, Thursday, and Saturday, 8 hours on Wednesday and Sunday, and 5 hours on Friday (sleepover). How much sleep did you get daily, on average?

1. First, add up the hours:
   $7 + 7 + 7 + 7 + 8 + 8 + 5 = 49$

2. Next, divide the sum by the number of days in the week:
   $49 \div 7 = 7$ hours of sleep per day, on average.

Now imagine that your parents are worried about the amount of time you spend in front of the television. You figure you watch about 1½ hours of television (counting movies and video games) Monday through Friday, about 2 hours on Saturday, and 1 hour on Sunday. About how many hours do you spend in front of the television on average per day?

Do you think you might want to get married someday? How might that decision change your career plans?

Does having children always mean putting careers on hold?

- *Your vacation plans.* Rather than a romantic getaway, you might opt for a vacation at a family amusement park.

- *Your home environment.* A home with small children is often noisy and chaotic, with toys everywhere.

When you have children, your time, money, energy, and relationships are not just your own; you must use them in a responsible way for the benefit of your children. That's why it's important not to enter into parenthood lightly—to make sure that you want to have children, and to have them only when you are emotionally, physically, and financially prepared to take good care of them. That way you can keep your career and family life in balance.

Career Profile: Computer Software Engineer

Information Technology Career Cluster

Job Summary

If you enjoy playing video games in your free time, you might consider pursuing a career as a computer software engineer. These workers research and design computer programs, creating applications to meet specific user needs. They might design software to help run a factory, to keep track of hospital patient files, or to create 3-D designs. They could create software for guiding missiles or saving an arcade princess. While they often have strong programming skills, software engineers are more concerned with creating and designing new applications rather than writing the actual code that makes those applications run. As such, their jobs require a balance of artistic vision, imagination, and technical skills.

Because computers are used in nearly every facet of life, the need for software engineers is great, and average earnings are relatively high. In fact, the profession is expected to grow much faster than average compared to other occupations over the next ten years. While there are a few examples of computer whiz kids who make their fortunes right out of high school, most computer software engineers have a bachelor's degree or higher.

Use the Internet, a library, or career center to research the responsibilities, education and training requirements, and salary range of a computer software engineer. Prepare a presentation about the career.

Recognizing the Importance of Lifelong Learning

Lifelong learning is more than just developing new work skills and maintaining old ones. It means being aware of changes that occur around you and adapting your roles and responsibilities as necessary. Setting goals for lifelong learning can help you achieve your career goals and find career satisfaction. It can also help you balance your responsibilities. Consider these common ways of being a lifelong learner.

■ *Continuing your education* will contribute to your self-esteem and improve your qualifications for achieving career success. It may also help you adapt to changing roles in your family. For example, you may shift from a dependent (someone your parents take care of) to a provider (someone who takes care of others).

■ *Developing hobbies and interests* will help you maintain your role as a friend. You will meet new peers and find new ways to enjoy time with old friends.

■ *Participating in your community* can help you to learn about social and cultural issues that are important to you and those around you, making you a more informed citizen and an active, contributing member of society.

Most important, being a lifelong learner means always being open to new experiences and seeing them as opportunities for personal and professional growth. As your roles and responsibilities grow, you must grow with them in order to stay balanced.

Studies have shown that people with four-year college degrees earn, on the average, over a million dollars more in their lifetime than people without one. Continuing your education can lead to all kinds of rewards.

No More School?

People living in the United States are lucky to have free education provided for every child. Not all children across the world are so fortunate. Imagine that all schools in the United States were suddenly shut down and students and their families were now responsible for educating themselves. What if you had to take full responsibility for your own education?

★ *Would you watch more educational programming on television?*

★ *Would you read more newspapers or watch the news more often?*

★ *Would you spend more time at the library or visit more museums?*

★ *Would you try to learn another language or try to study in another country?*

★ *Would you read more books?*

★ *Would you form a group of people interested in learning about a certain subject and find ways to explore it?*

Think about all of the ways you might educate yourself. Can you use these methods to learn about subjects not taught in school?

Staying Informed

Part of being a lifelong learner is staying in touch with the world around you. That means being aware of what is happening at home and at work, in your neighborhood and in your community, in your city or town, in your state, in the country in which you live, and in the world at large. By taking the time each day to read news online or watch it on television, you can keep up with current events and stay informed. By doing so, you will be prepared to identify trends that might affect your career, family, or community.

Some of the ways that you can stay informed and even get involved include:

■ Reading newspapers, news magazines, and Web sites that publish international and national news stories, so you will know what the key issues are.

■ Sharing with your friends and family what you have learned about the issues, to raise their awareness and to discuss the issues with others.

■ Keeping up on legislation that will affect you and your community.

■ Volunteering for organizations that support your goals, values, and beliefs.

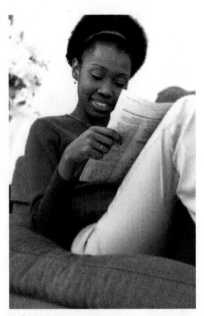

Why is it important to stay informed about what is going on in the world? How can this help you become a well-rounded person?

Rights Around the World

Citizens of the United States have specific rights defined by the Constitution, such as:

■ Freedom to speak about controversial issues

■ Ability to vote in elections, for a voice in government

■ Freedom to travel within the country and outside it

■ Freedom to assemble in groups without government interference

Do other countries afford their citizens the same or similar rights?

Pick one country that you would like to learn more about. Use the Internet or library resources to research the basic rights of that country's citizens. How do they compare to the rights of U.S. citizens? Are there laws or rights that you don't agree with? Are there laws or rights that you think all countries should adopt?

Learning Outside of School

We go to school in order to learn (for the most part). But just as much learning happens outside of school. Think about how much you learn simply by reading books, surfing the Web, traveling to new places, or just talking to your friends. Part of being a lifelong learner is recognizing the many opportunities for learning and growth that exist outside of a traditional school environment.

Of course, there are more formal learning opportunities that exist outside of school as well. Your workplace may offer workshops and training courses, and you may also take advantage of volunteer opportunities. You may take on an **apprenticeship**—a paid training program in a given trade—or an **internship**—an often unpaid, short-term job designed to provide valuable work experience. If you treat your life as an ongoing learning experience, you will soon find educational opportunities everywhere.

Take a moment and think of three or four things you learned yesterday. Did you learn them *all* at school?

21st Century Learning

Hasan looks forward to Sundays. He and his family have always spent Sundays at his grandmother's house. His aunts, uncles, and cousins often come, too. There may be 20 relatives there—eating dinner, playing games, and having a good time.

Hasan is considering a career as a personal trainer. He has a part-time job at a fitness club. He collects towels from the locker room, wipes down equipment, and keeps the floors clean and dry. He usually works on Tuesdays and Thursdays from 3:30 until 6:00, and on Saturdays from 6:00 a.m. until noon.

An instructor offers Hasan the opportunity to help out with a weekly class. She needs someone to demonstrate proper form and to show people the right way to use the equipment. Hasan is very excited, until she explains that the class is on Sundays.

Hasan is faced with a decision that impacts his roles at work and at home. Using your 21st Century Skills such as decision making, goal setting, and problem solving write an ending to the story. Read it to the class, or form a small group and present it as a skit.

Living in Your Community

A community is a group of people who have a common goal. The people might be physically near each other, living in the same neighborhood, or they might be spread out all over the world, connected to each other through the Internet. The people might be very similar to one another, or might have very little in common other than the one interest that draws them together.

Most communities are held together by a shared sense of purpose. That purpose can either be to explore or protect a personal interest (such as a club based around a certain hobby), or to work for a larger cause that the members believe in (such as world peace). A community can have a personal scope or a local, regional, national, or global one.

Examples of communities include:

- Residential neighborhoods
- Small towns
- Religious groups
- Charitable organizations
- Political action groups
- Volunteers for a cause
- Internet message boards and chat rooms
- Girl Scout and Boy Scout troops
- Music, dance, or art-based groups
- Friends who share common interests
- Schools

Recognizing the communities that you are a part of (or that you would like to become a part of) and the roles you play in them is an important step in achieving balance and wellness. Moreover, being involved in your community can lead to increased career opportunities, higher self-esteem, and greater personal growth.

Being a Responsible Citizen

As a citizen of your local community, your state, and the United States, you have certain rights and responsibilities. The service that you owe to such communities is sometimes called **civic responsibility**.

Some civic responsibilities are dictated by law, such as paying taxes, obeying traffic regulations, or serving on a jury. Others, like voting, are not required but are still part of being a good citizen. You can do many things to go the extra mile as a citizen, actively working to make your world a better place. These can include volunteering for worthy causes, serving in local leadership positions such as those on a school or zoning board, picking up litter along the road, or donating money or food to local food banks.

Serving your community is not just a nice thing to do; it can also positively impact your own life. Anything you can do to make your community more safe and pleasant will also make your own life more safe and pleasant within that community.

Volunteering

Volunteering—doing work without pay—is a great way to contribute to the communities you care about and to gain valuable work experience. You have probably done a lot of volunteer activities in your life so far, perhaps without realizing it. For example, when a teacher asked for someone to run an errand or hand out supplies, have you ever raised your hand? That's volunteering for your classroom community.

Volunteering is part of being a good citizen. When everyone pitches in to help, tasks get done more quickly and easily, freeing up the entire group to focus on what's important.

Volunteering also gives you a chance to express your values—in other words, to show what is important to you. For example, if you are passionate about improving the quality of life for children, you might volunteer at an afterschool reading program; if your primary interest is the environment, you might volunteer for a conservation group that plants trees.

What volunteer opportunities are available in your community? How much time do you think students your age should spend volunteering?

What Volunteers Do

Nonprofit organizations use volunteers for almost every aspect of their operations, so there is sure to be something that matches your interests and abilities. For example, volunteers can:

✔ *Staff information booths at fairs and trade shows*

✔ *Tutor children in reading, math, and other subjects*

✔ *Help elderly or disabled people with daily activities*

✔ *Do physical labor such as cleaning, yard work, or even building houses*

✔ *Create flyers, brochures, and other printed materials*

✔ *Provide childcare*

✔ *Collect and distribute donations of food, clothing, or money*

✔ *Give presentations and speeches that promote the group*

✔ *Entertain groups of people with music, dance, acting, or other creative arts*

✔ *Pick up trash or gather materials for recycling*

✔ *Help take care of animals at shelters*

Pick a nonprofit organization that interests you and research what volunteers in that organization do. Share this information with your class and consider taking part in that organization's mission in your free time.

Taking Care of the Environment

As it turns out, you are actually part of a community of some 7.1 billion members and counting. The planet we live on represents its own community and requires responsible actions in order to preserve it. The environment is the natural world—the soil, the water, the air, and the plant and animal life. Volunteering for organizations that promote a healthy environment can pay off in creating a world for yourself—and others—where plants and animals flourish, resources are used responsibly, and the air, land, and seas are free of pollutants.

Some common environmental concerns facing our global community include:

- Global warming awareness and prevention
- Planting trees to re-grow forests that have been cut down
- Setting limits on how much pollution companies can release into the air and water
- Protecting the habitats of endangered species
- Working with auto makers to reduce air pollution from vehicles, and supporting the development of alternative fuels
- Cleaning up landfills, dumps, roadsides, and other areas and preventing harmful substances from entering water supplies
- Promoting the use of recycling programs and recycled paper and plastics

There are many simple things you can do to help preserve the environment in your community and beyond, and most of them don't require a great deal of time or money. Here are some ideas.

- Get literature from local conservation groups to learn what environmental programs are active in your area and how you can participate.
- Volunteer after school and on weekends for organizations that do local environmental cleanup activities such as picking up trash along a river or road.
- If your school or religious institution does not recycle, do research to find out what the costs and benefits would be, and present that information to decision-makers in the organization.
- Encourage family and friends who drive automobiles to consider fuel-efficient models such as gas/electric hybrids.
- Conserve electricity at home by shutting off lights and turning off appliances.
- Go green by bringing your own reusable bags when you shop.

By taking care of the environment, you are not only helping to ensure your own personal wellness, but the health and wellness of billions of others.

Who is responsible for taking care of the Earth? Can the actions of one person really make a difference?

Tech Connect

Almost all organizations have a Web site that publishes contact information, a mission statement, and a schedule of activities and events. Some sites also list requests for volunteer help and application forms for getting started with them. You may need some training or skills development, such as first aid, CPR, child care, or computer training, in order to participate in some programs.

Here are a few sites of popular nonprofit organizations that encourage community involvement.

- American Red Cross: redcross.org
- Habitat for Humanity International: habitat.org
- Heifer International: heifer.org
- Greenpeace: greenpeace.org/usa
- The Nature Conservancy: nature.org
- The Humane Society: humanesociety.org

Pick an organization from the list above or one of your own choosing and research the volunteer opportunities it has available, the skills or training required, and the time commitment involved. Present your findings to the class.

Staying Healthy

Think about a time when you didn't feel well. What did you do? Did you spend as much time with your friends? Did you go to work or struggle to finish school work? Did you feel like doing much of *anything*?

In order to keep all parts of your life in balance, you need to stay balanced yourself. That means looking out for your own health and well-being. When you are healthy, you have more energy to meet your responsibilities and achieve your goals. Good health leads to high self-esteem and a positive attitude.

Staying healthy means keeping both your body and mind in top working order. It means staying in touch with your feelings and understanding how the choices you make affect how you feel. Your personal health is made up of three parts, all interconnected.

- *Physical health.* Being physically fit makes you alert and energetic. You can focus when you are at school or work and have lots of energy for enjoying your friends and other activities.

■ *Emotional health.* Being emotionally healthy makes you confident and enthusiastic. It helps you make the most of your relationships and find satisfaction in your activities.

■ *Mental health.* Being mentally healthy means you can think clearly and critically, set realistic goals, and make healthy choices.

We all have different ways of staying healthy. However, there are a few things everyone can do in order to stay physically, emotionally, and mentally fit.

■ Get enough sleep.

■ Eat right.

■ Get regular exercise.

■ Maintain high self-esteem.

■ Engage in hobbies and leisure activities.

■ Have supportive friends and family members.

■ Keep a positive attitude.

The most important thing is to be aware of what works for you. What makes you feel strong, energetic, and motivated? Once you know the answer, you can make the right choices to ensure your well-being.

Balancing Act

You may think being an entrepreneur or business owner means less stress and more time for fun. You might dream about working in your pajamas or taking time off whenever you please, answerable to no one.

But the truth is that entrepreneurs experience just as much, if not more, stress than their non-self-employed peers. The stress of meeting deadlines, finding new clients, keeping a steady cash flow, balancing the needs of the company with your own personal needs and the needs of your family are all important factors that add up. And the fact that you are the owner of the company means that all decisions and responsibilities ultimately rest with you. In fact, studies have shown that regular employees generally have less job stress and work fewer hours per week than entrepreneurs.

Though most entrepreneurs would probably argue that the added stress and pressure are worth it, it is still important to think about how being self-employed will shift your roles and responsibilities, forcing you to rebalance your work, family, and social lives.

Interview an entrepreneur, asking about how he or she balances work with his or her personal life. What does he do to stay healthy? How does she combat stress? Most important, how did his or her life change as a result of becoming an entrepreneur? Report your findings to the class or ask the person you interviewed to come speak to your class about his or her business and experience as an entrepreneur.

Stress Management

Stress is the way your body reacts to a difficult or demanding situation. You might feel stress in both good situations and in bad. For example:

■ You might feel stress at a birthday party because you have to talk to lots of people and make sure everyone is having a good time.

■ You might feel stress when you start a new job or meet new people.

■ You might feel stress when your teacher gives a pop-quiz.

■ You might feel stress the first time you get behind the wheel of a car.

Any event or situation that is unfamiliar or demanding can be a **stressor**—a cause of stress. Stress can come from serious, life-changing events, such as a death in the family, divorce, a lost job, or a move to a new town. It can also come from small, everyday events, such as missing your ride or losing your lunch money. Some of the most common stressors come from within, from low self-esteem, for example, or from an overwhelming pressure to succeed.

Stress can have positive or negative results. Think about a competition. You might try harder when you are in a real game than when you are in practice. It might bring out the best in you. Your friend might hate competition. It might give him a stomach ache.

Some stress is normal, but too much stress can cause problems and interfere with your overall wellness. It is unrealistic to think you can remove stress from your life, but you can use problem-solving skills to manage it. The key is to identify the source of the stress and then try to deal with *that* problem directly.

However, sometimes you cannot solve the problem causing the stress. You cannot stop your co-workers from fighting. You cannot cure a relative's cancer. **Coping skills** help you deal with or overcome problems and difficulties that you might not be able to solve. Here are some coping skills you can use to relieve stress and make yourself feel better.

■ Relax. Sit or lie down in a quiet place. Breathe deeply.

■ Do something you enjoy with people you like.

■ Stretch your muscles to relieve tension, or be physically active.

■ **Prioritize** your responsibilities.

■ Accept what you cannot change.

■ Try to stay positive.

■ Express your feelings. Write down your thoughts in a journal or blog or talk to someone you trust.

■ Talk with someone you trust or respect as a professional.

■ Take steps to avoid situations that you know will cause you stress.

Not everyone handles stress the same way. What do you do when you get stressed?

Signs of Stress

When you experience stress, your body responds as if you are in danger—your heart beats faster, you breathe faster, and you might have a burst of energy. Following are some other signs of stress.

✔ *Sadness or depression*

✔ *Mood swings*

✔ *Anger*

✔ *Headaches*

✔ *Upset stomach*

✔ *Trouble sleeping*

✔ *Loss of appetite*

Since stress is a common occurrence, how do you know when it becomes dangerous? How much stress is too much?

Career Trend

Employers are recognizing the impact of stress on their employees. Stressed employees work less, get sick more often, have strained working relationships, and make more mistakes. For this reason, many employers take steps to help their workers relieve stress, such as having a gym available for employees to exercise or providing free back massages once a week.

Nutrition

What did you eat for breakfast this morning? Was it the well-balanced meal you always see pictured on cereal advertisements, complete with fresh fruit, orange juice, and lowfat yogurt? Or was it a toasted pastry and a quick gulp of milk? Maybe it was just a granola bar on the bus.

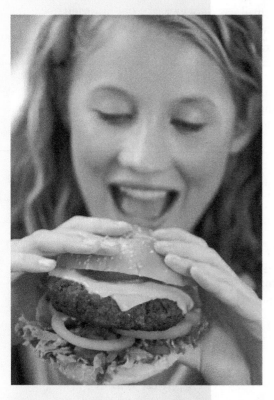

Do your friends have any influence on what foods you eat? How do you decide what is best for you?

Every day, you make choices that affect your physical, mental, and emotional well-being simply by eating the foods you do. Each choice has consequences. Some are positive, such as the health benefits of choosing an apple instead of a bag of potato chips. Some are negative, such as purposely starving oneself in order to maintain an unhealthy body image. It is important to think about your food choices and their impact. Doing so can help you make healthy decisions about what—and how much—to eat.

To make healthy choices, you need to know what your body needs. **Diet** is the food you eat. **Nutrition** is a science that studies the way the food you eat nourishes your body. When you eat a healthy diet and have good nutrition, your body is getting what it needs to work at its best level. Different foods contribute different **nutrients**—the parts of food that your body requires. Recognizing that food is a resource you can use to stay healthy and happy can help you choose the best foods and food combinations and maintain a healthy diet.

So what is a healthy diet? A healthy diet is one that gives your body balanced nutrition. Like a car, if you give your body the right fuel, it will run great and last a long time. If you give it the wrong fuel, it might break down. To achieve a healthy diet, you should eat a balanced variety of foods from different food groups.

Other basic guidelines include:

- Eating a variety of fruits and vegetables, including dark green vegetables, yellow vegetables, and beans
- Eating foods that are rich in calcium, such as low-fat milk, cheese, and yogurt
- Eating whole grains
- Eating lean meats, fish, poultry, and nuts
- Limiting the amount of fats, salts, and sugars that you eat
- Drinking plenty of water

ChooseMyPlate.gov

The United States Department of Agriculture (USDA) developed MyPlate to provide the information you need to choose a healthy diet. Check it out at choosemyplate.gov.

Force of Habit

You can tell a lot about a person from his or her eating habits. Postive habits contribute to health and wellness. Negative habits do not.

- 👎 Eating fast food every day for breakfast or lunch
- 👎 Regularly skipping meals
- 👎 Snacking heavily in front of the television
- 👎 Eating foods high in sugar or fat
- 👎 Eating because you are stressed
- 👍 Eating moderate portions
- 👍 Having regular meals with your family
- 👍 Taking part in food preparation
- 👍 Keeping fruits, vegetables, and nuts handy for snacks
- 👍 Taking your time while eating

Recognizing your own eating habits can help you understand why and how you make the choices you do. How might you adjust your eating habits to stay healthy?

A healthy diet also balances the amount of food you take in with your physical activity. Think of *food* as energy that comes into your body, and *activity* as energy that goes out. For that reason, people with very active lifestyles, such as athletes, generally need to eat more. A healthy goal is to have the same amount of energy in as energy out. That way you can maintain a healthy weight and obtain all the nutrients your body needs to function properly.

Physical Activity

Physical activity is one of the best things you can do to promote your own wellness. It keeps your heart and other muscles strong, increases your energy level, improves self-esteem, and—best of all—it's fun.

Physical activity is also beneficial because it:

- Increases your mental focus
- Helps prevent diseases, such as heart disease, osteoporosis, and breast cancer
- Improves digestion
- Improves endurance
- Improves circulation and helps reduce blood pressure
- Enhances coordination and balance
- Helps to reduce stress

Energy Expenditure

A calorie *is a unit of food energy. You can use online calculators to look up how many calories you burn doing different activities, such as running, biking, or walking. They take into consideration your age, height, and weight. Here are some standard numbers for common activities. The value is the number of calories burned per minute, for a person who weighs 120 pounds.*

✔ *Sitting still*   1.4

✔ *Walking slowly*   2.2

✔ *Walking briskly*   4.8

✔ *Bicycling*   3.8

✔ *Running slowly*   7.6

✔ *Running moderately*   9.5

✔ *Running fast*   13.2

✔ *Yoga*   2.4

How many calories do you take in during a day? How many do you burn?

Do you exercise with your family? What activities could you do as a family to stay active?

Though most people recognize the benefits of physical activity, they complain they just don't have the time. However, researchers have shown that any physical activity can have positive health benefits. In fact, most health professionals recommend that you get at least two to three hours of moderate exercise a week (less than half an hour per day). Moderate physical activity would include:

■ Walking briskly (3 miles per hour or faster)

■ Water aerobics

■ Bicycling

■ Tennis

■ Ballroom dancing

■ General gardening

Staying physically fit doesn't have to mean spending hours in the gym lifting weights or running for hours on a treadmill. Many of the activities you enjoy contribute to your physical health, whether it's playing a sport, hiking in a park, dancing alone in your room, or just walking to a friend's house. By staying physically fit, you will have the energy and focus required to do your best work and meet your career goals as well.

Career FACT

Some medical professionals believe that obesity is the number one killer in the United States. It is a contributing factor in a number of health conditions from diabetes to heart disease. Even more striking is that the cure for most obese Americans has been around for centuries: a healthy diet and daily exercise. That can be difficult in the modern workplace where many jobs involve sitting at a desk for hours on end. What can you do to stay healthy if your job keeps you chairbound all day?

Avoiding Risky Behaviors

Living a balanced and healthy lifestyle means making positive choices every day. Of course there are times when you will make choices that are not so healthy—staying up late on a school night talking to a friend or eating a whole pint of ice-cream in one sitting. While maybe not the smartest decisions, such choices are ultimately not dangerous.

However, you will likely be confronted with choices that are dangerous. Any activity that puts your health and wellness in danger is a **risky behavior**. When you make a choice to participate in risky behavior—and it is your choice—you take a chance of harming yourself and others.

What would you do if you were invited to a party where you know there will be illegal substances?

Perhaps the most common risky behavior that teens must face today is substance abuse. **Substance abuse** is when you eat, drink, smoke, or otherwise use substances—such as food, drugs, or alcohol—that are bad for your health and wellness. The substances can be legal—such as medicines you can buy at the supermarket. They can also be illegal—such as cocaine, marijuana, ecstasy, or even alcohol and tobacco products if you are underage.

Abused substances usually change the way you think and feel. They confuse your brain so you cannot tell right from wrong. You don't remember what's important to you. Things might seem to move faster or slower. You might feel light-headed. You might lose control over your body.

Most people abuse substances because they like the way those substances make them feel. It's fun and social, and everyone seems to have a good time. Some people abuse substances because of **peer pressure**—when your peers and friends influence you to do something. Some people start because they are curious, or because they believe it helps relieve stress.

Regardless of the reason, it's important to realize that substance abuse is a choice with potentially devastating consequences. You can be fired from a job for substance abuse, and many employers require mandatory drug tests. A documented history of substance abuse can negatively impact your ability to even get a job. Even just showing up for an interview smelling like smoke or alcohol might influence an employer's decision on hiring you. The employer might conclude that someone who drinks or smokes might not make the best, most responsible decisions.

Substance abuse can cause you to hurt yourself or someone else. Over the long term, you can even become addicted to the substance. An **addiction** is a need to continue using the substance even though it has negative consequences. The best way to avoid substance abuse is **abstinence**—which means never using the substance at all.

A Deadly Habit

According to the Centers for Disease Control, smoking is bad for almost every organ in your body.

✔ *It causes cancer in many parts of the body, including the lungs, mouth, bladder, and kidneys.*

✔ *It raises the risk of heart disease and stroke significantly.*

✔ *It can lead to emphysema, bronchitis, and many other lung problems.*

✔ *It can cause infertility or lead to problems during pregnancy and at birth.*

As a result, more and more businesses, not to mention state and local governments, have instituted smoking bans. In fact, 28 states and Washington, D.C. have bans on smoking in enclosed public places.

Case Study

Thomas's friends invited him to a party at the house of another student he doesn't know very well. Thomas's parents trust him to make healthy choices and gave him permission to go. Later, he learned that the parents of the student throwing the party would be out of town that weekend. He also heard someone say that there would be alcohol. Of course he knows that underage drinking is illegal, but he has already told his friends that he would go. He feels like they would be disappointed in him if he backed out now—that they would somehow think less of him.

■ Should Thomas go to the party?

■ Should he tell his parents about the situation?

■ Is it okay for him to go the party as long as he promises not to drink any alcohol?

■ What should he say to his friends if he decides not to go?

Web Extra

You can use the Internet to identify ways to become involved in your community. Most cities and towns have Web sites and social networking communities. Neighbors exchange ideas and discuss issues that concern them. Local organizations look for volunteers. Take the time to explore your community's online resources. When you find an issue or organization that interests you, join the conversation or ask how you can help.

Answer It!

1. Define wellness.
2. List the five major roles you must balance in your life.
3. List three characteristics of a healthy relationship.
4. What common life events can alter career plans?
5. How do leisure activities contribute to your well-being?

6. What are important factors to consider when deciding whether or not to have children?
7. True or false: Taking college courses is the only way to be a lifelong learner.
8. List five examples of communities you might belong to.
9. List five general strategies for staying in good health.
10. What is the difference between diet and nutrition?

Career-Ready Practices

Career-ready individuals understand the relationship between personal health and well-being and their performance on the job. They eat healthy, exercise, engage in mental health activities, and avoid risky behaviors.

But finding and keeping a healthy balance can be difficult when you are working hard to reach your career goals. In teams of three or four, create a three-column table with headings for Physical Health, Emotional Health, and Mental Health. In each column, list as many things you can think of that would contribute to that area of your personal health. Create a presentation and share it with your classmates.

Write Now

Knowing how to express your feelings is an important part of maintaining healthy relationships. Think about someone who means a lot to you. Think about the personal qualities he or she has that you admire and the values that you respect. Write a letter to that person expressing how you feel and why.

Career Portfolio

A record of community service can be a point of distinction for your portfolio, as well as a point of personal pride. Employers look favorably upon candidates with a record of community service and volunteerism, and college admissions boards almost expect to see some record of community involvement in the records of applicants. In addition, many high schools now make community service a graduation requirement.

For young people, community service and volunteer work often act as a substitute for paid work experience. In fact, such service often teaches valuable work skills. You might learn how to measure and cut wood while helping to build houses for Habitat for Humanity, learn how to cook or serve food while working at a soup kitchen, or enhance your leadership skills by volunteering to coach sports for young children.

Because of the increasing emphasis on community service, it's important to include any record of your own service in your portfolio. Include photos documenting your efforts and descriptions of what you did. And don't be afraid to ask the program director for a letter of recommendation.

Business Plan Project

In your **Business Plan Project**, review the table you created in Chapter 15. Identify activities that fall into one of the following three categories of well-being: social health, emotional health, and physical health. Then, write down the following four questions and your answers.

1. Which activities do you spend time on that contribute to your well-being?

2. Do you think you spend enough time on activities that contribute to your well-being?

3. How might you add or modify activities to increase the amount of time you spend on your own well-being?

4. Do you spend any time supporting a cause or organization? If so, what is the cause and why is it important to you? If not, name one you would like find time to support.

Entrepreneurial Thinking

Part IV

In This Part . . .

Chapter 17 ■ Starting Your Own Business

Chapter 18 ■ Planning Your Business

Chapter 19 ■ Managing Your Business

17 Starting Your Own Business

GETTING STARTED

How many businesses are there in your community? Do they sell things, such as shoes, food, or electronics? Do they provide a service, such as a law firm, a doctor's office, or an architectural company? Do they have a lot of employees, or just one or two?

Every business starts out as an idea in someone's mind, but the path each one takes to become reality is different. One of the first decisions an entrepreneur makes is what type of business to start. Then, he or she must decide what type of business ownership to set up. Understanding the options can help you focus on the path you will take to make your business a reality. If you do not plan to start a business, it can help you be a better employee.

➤ Write down the name of a business in your community. As a class, work together to group the businesses into types.

311

Identifying Different Types of Businesses

Do you want to sell clothes? Are you interested in making and selling candles? Can you teach people how to play the guitar? The first step in becoming an entrepreneur is to think about the type of business you want to start. Recall that a *business* is an organization that provides goods or services.

In general, businesses are divided into four major categories—manufacturing, wholesale, retail, and service. The type depends on the business's primary function and the kinds of products or service it sells. Knowing about the different types of businesses can help you decide what business you would like to build for yourself.

Combining Business Types

Many businesses combine aspects of the four business types. This is particularly true in retailing and service businesses. What if a business is a combination of the four business types?

★ A shoe store might also offer shoe repairs and shoe shines.

★ A dry cleaner might also offer tailoring and clothing repair.

★ A veterinarian might also offer pet grooming and boarding.

★ A jewelry store might also offer custom design and repair.

★ A hardware store might also offer equipment rental and training for using tools or how to complete a home improvement project.

Can you think of other businesses that combine aspects of different business types?

Manufacturing Businesses

A manufacturing business, or **manufacturer,** takes materials and builds goods that it can sell to others. For example, a company that makes automobiles is a manufacturer. So is a company that makes cardboard boxes. Manufactured products typically fall into two categories: industrial and consumer.

■ *Industrial goods* are sold to other manufacturing businesses. Examples include metal and plastic parts, lumber, and heavy machinery.

■ *Consumer goods* are products that are eventually bought by the public—people like you and your family who purchase things.

Small manufacturing businesses that produce consumer goods sometimes sell directly to the public. For example, entrepreneurs who make baked goods, silk-screened T-shirts, or jewelry most often sell their products directly to consumers. Large manufacturing businesses usually do not sell directly to consumers. They may sell to a wholesaler, which is a company that buys goods in large quantities and then resells them.

Wholesaling Businesses

A wholesaling business, or **wholesaler,** buys goods in large quantities, typically from manufacturers, and resells them in smaller batches to retailers, which are businesses that sell goods to consumers. Wholesalers are also known as *middlemen, go-betweens, distributors,* or *intermediaries* because they provide a link between manufacturers and retailers. Wholesalers do not generally sell directly to the public, although they sometimes have warehouse stores or outlets, or sell merchandise online.

Retailing Businesses

A retailing business, or **retailer**, buys goods, often from wholesalers, and sells them directly to consumers. Retailing businesses are stores, shops, and boutiques. They sell groceries, clothing, shoes, household goods, computers, DVDs, sporting goods, cosmetics, jewelry, and thousands of other consumer items.

Retailing businesses include traditional stores that people visit in person and online stores that sell from the Internet. Some retailers also sell through catalogs. In most states, retailers must have a special permit, called a *reseller's permit*, to purchase goods tax-free from wholesalers and collect sales tax from the end buyers.

If you were going to open a retail business, what goods would you want to sell?

A business that is either a wholesale or retail business is commonly referred to as a *trade business*.

Service Businesses

A **service business** provides services to customers for a fee. Service businesses provide a wide variety of professional, technical, and everyday services that people need and want. Examples include engineering, legal, medical, accounting, garbage pick-up, package delivery, dry cleaning, auto repair, babysitting, pet sitting, music lessons, tutoring, house cleaning, and landscaping.

Most states and some local governments have licensing requirements for people who provide particular services. This applies to professionals such as doctors, dentists, engineers, and lawyers, as well as to other types of service providers, such as hairstylists, dog walkers, automobile mechanics, athletic trainers, and daycare providers. In addition, some states require service businesses selling taxable services to have a permit to collect sales tax from their customers.

NUMBERS GAME

A **man-hour** is a measurement unit equal to the amount of work one employee performs in one hour. Businesses use man-hours to estimate when a project will be finished, based on the number of employees working. The formula is simple: Divide the number of man-hours by the number of employees, then calculate the time to completion. For example, if you know it takes 120 man-hours to replace a roof on a house, and you have four people working for 10 hours a day, you can estimate the project's completion as follows:

$$120 \div 4 = 30$$

$$30 \div 10 = 3$$

It will take four people working 10 hours a day three days to replace the roof.

How long will it take if you have six people working for 10 hours a day?

Career Profile:
Industrial Production Manager

Manufacturing Career Cluster

Job Summary

An industrial production manager is responsible for managing and coordinating all of the people and equipment involved in the manufacturing process. That means he or she plans and directs all the steps required to produce manufactured goods. An industrial production manager must meet output and quality goals, manage a budget, maintain or improve efficiency, and supervise employees.

What factors influence the job outlook for an industrial production manager?

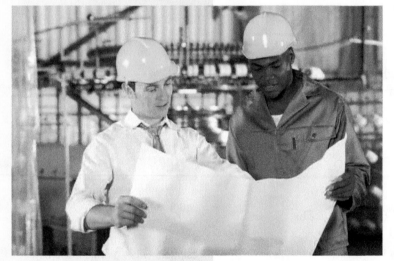

Industrial production managers work in the factory where they oversee the production process, and in offices where they tend to their administrative responsibilities. Most have a college degree in business administration, management, industrial technology, or industrial engineering. Some benefit from graduate degrees in industrial management or business administration.

Use the Internet, a library, or career center to research the responsibilities, education and training requirements, and salary range of an industrial production manager. Investigate entrepreneurial opportunities that might be available to someone interested in industrial production. Write a paragraph explaining why becoming an entrepreneur might be a positive career choice for someone interested in manufacturing.

Special Types of Businesses

Some businesses don't really fall into any of the four basic types. The two most common are farming and mining.

■ *Farming* is a special type of business. Sometimes it is similar to manufacturing. For example, the farm might produce agricultural products that are used to create new products, as when grain is used to make bread. Sometimes it is a combination of manufacturing and retailing. For example, the farm might grow produce—fruits and vegetables—and sell it directly to the consumer at a farm stand.

■ *Mining* is another special type of business. Often referred to as an *extraction business*, mining takes resources from the environment and converts them into a form that can be sold to manufacturers. Examples of extraction businesses are copper mining, oil drilling, and converting sea salt to table salt.

For-Profit or Nonprofit?

Most companies are in business to make a profit. A **profit** is earnings greater than the business's expenses, or the money left over after all the bills are paid. For a for-profit company, the main goal is to make a profit. Many entrepreneurs start businesses that are not initially profitable but work hard to ensure profitability. An entrepreneur whose company makes a profit decides how to use the money. He or she can spend it to improve or grow the business, save it, invest it, donate it to worthy causes, or any combination of these options.

Some companies, called **nonprofit organizations**, are not in business to make a profit. They operate solely to serve the good of society. For example, the American Cancer Society is a nonprofit organization that is in business to raise money for cancer research and education.

Nonprofits earn money through donations, government grants, or the sale of goods and services. Although they operate much like for-profit businesses, by law all earnings must be used to support the organization's social mission. Earnings cannot be used for the financial gain of the people running the nonprofit. Entrepreneurs who start nonprofit organizations do so for reasons other than the chance to build personal wealth and financial independence.

Tech Connect

Increasingly, people and businesses buy and sell goods online. This is called e-commerce. An e-commerce Web site can be a stand-alone business or the Web-based counterpart of a traditional storefront business. Starting and running an e-commerce Web site may be less expensive than starting a traditional bricks-and-mortar business. There is no rent to pay for store space and the business can be run using fewer employees. Often, the business owner does not even have to store the goods, because they can be shipped directly from a warehouse or manufacturer to the customer.

An e-commerce business must rent space on the Web from a **Web host**—a business that stores the Web site information on its server computers. It also needs a commerce server, which is a computer that runs commerce-based applications, such as credit card processing and inventory management, and security programs to protect its customers' financial and personal information. Other expenses include marketing and promotions in order to attract customers to the site.

Identify a business that has a traditional storefront and a Web site. Make a list of at least five criteria you can use to rate the shopping experience at each, such as ease-of-use, convenience, number of products, sales assistance, return policy, and visual appeal. Use a table in a word processing program or a spreadsheet to compare the features of the two.

Identifying Types of Business Ownership

Not only are there different types of businesses, but there are different types of business ownerships as well. Most of the differences are based on liability, taxes, who controls the business, and who shares its profits. There are also legal restrictions and requirements associated with some types of ownership, particularly the corporation.

Each type of business ownership has benefits and drawbacks. As an entrepreneur, you are responsible for selecting the type of business ownership that gives your business the best opportunity for success.

Career Tips

All businesses should be set up legally by a lawyer in order to make sure that the rights of owners, partners, investors, and customers are protected.

Sole Proprietorship

A **sole proprietorship** is a business that is owned by a single individual. The owner collects all profit from the business and has unlimited liability for its debt. Most small businesses operate as sole proprietorships.

A sole proprietorship is the simplest and least expensive option for business ownership. Business income and costs are reported on the owner's personal income tax return, which means less paperwork and easier tax accounting. The sole proprietor is also the sole decision maker, with complete control over the management of the business.

However, he or she is also responsible for raising the money for setting up, operating, and expanding the business. Also, with unlimited liability for any business debts, the owner's personal money and possessions are at risk if there is not enough money in the business to pay debts.

Partnership

In a **partnership**, at least two individuals share the management, profit, and liability for the business. There are two basic types.

- In a *general partnership*, all partners have unlimited liability.

- In a *limited partnership*, one general partner has limited liability. The other partners are investors only and have no say in how to run the company on a day-to-day basis.

A general partnership is much like a sole proprietorship. The primary advantage is that a general partnership has at least two people contributing to its success, rather than just one. Of course, the unlimited liability is shared by all owners, as well, so all are at risk of losing personal money and possessions to pay business debts. Other disadvantages include the possibility of conflict between the owners about how the business should be run, the fact that profits are shared among all owners, and that each partner is equally responsible for the business-related actions of all the others.

Myth It takes a lot of money to start a business.

Truth Most new businesses are started with less than $10,000.00. Most entrepreneurs are able to raise the money from investors—including family and friends—and from loans. They may even be able to obtain government grants.

What are some benefits and drawbacks of organizing a business as a partnership?

Different Types of Corporations

Not all corporations are the same. They differ in the way they are taxed and in the amount of liability protection.

✔ *C corporations are the most common type of corporation. C corporations are taxed as an entity, which means as one unit. It is called a C corporation because its profits are taxed separately from its owners under subchapter C of the Internal Revenue Code.*

✔ *Subchapter S corporations are not taxed as an entity. Their income or loss is applied to each shareholder, and appears on each shareholder's tax return, under subchapter S of the Internal Revenue Code.*

✔ *A limited liability company (LLC) has simpler tax procedures and greater liability protection than a C corporation. It combines the liability benefits of a corporation with the tax benefits of a sole proprietorship or partnership.*

✔ *Nonprofit corporations operate not to provide profit for shareholders but to serve the good of society. Owners have limited liability and the corporation receives special tax benefits from the government.*

Understanding Liability

A business usually carries debts such as loans that must be repaid and bills for equipment or services. When a small business incurs debts, the type of business ownership determines the liability, or who is responsible for paying the debt. One of the most important factors an entrepreneur must consider when starting a business is liability. **Liability** is the legal obligation of an owner to use personal money and possessions to pay business debt.

■ *Unlimited liability* means that a business owner can be legally forced to use personal money and possessions to pay the debts of the business.

■ *Limited liability* means that a business owner cannot be legally forced to use personal money and possessions to pay business debt.

Which type of liability do you think has more risk for the business owner?

Corporation

In a **corporation**, the business is considered a type of person or *entity* under the law. The business owners have limited liability. There may be one or more owners, called **shareholders** or **stockholders**. A **share of stock** is a unit of ownership in a corporation. Corporations sell shares to raise money to operate the business. Every person who owns at least one share is an owner. Some corporations pay a **dividend** to shareholders, which is a portion of the corporation's profit.

Most states require a corporation to have a *board of directors*—one or more persons responsible for making decisions about how the business should be run.

Shareholders have **limited liability**, which means they cannot be legally forced to use personal money and possessions to pay business debt. They risk only the money they used to buy shares of stock. They can end their ownership by selling their shares to someone else.

The primary disadvantage of a corporation is that it is more difficult and expensive to set up and maintain than other types of businesses. Corporations are regulated by state laws, so they must follow very specific procedures for record-keeping and tax-paying.

Money Madne$$

You own 1,260 shares in Corporation X. Each share is worth $40.00. Your cousin owns 700 shares in Corporation Y. Each of her shares is worth $55.00. She offers to trade you her 700 shares in Corporation Y for your 1,260 shares of Corporation X, and she will pay you an additional $10,000.00 in cash. Should you make the trade? **Hint:** Use multiplication to calculate the total value of shares in each company. Add $10,000.00 to the value of the shares of Corporation Y, and then compare the amounts to decide if the trade is a good deal or not.

Conglomerate

A corporation that conducts business in at least two different industries is called a **conglomerate**, or a multi-industry corporation. Because revenue comes from different industries, the conglomerate may be better positioned to withstand problems that might affect one industry, but not another. One risk of this type of organization includes the temptation to take resources from one area of the business to subsidize another, leaving the first area vulnerable. Another risk is that available resources may be spread thin across all areas, so that no area can succeed. Examples of a conglomerate might include a company that operates a department store and a credit financing business or a pharmacy, or a company that manufactures mobile phones and operates a retail Web site.

Why might it make sense for farmers to form cooperatives?

Cooperative

A **cooperative** is a business owned, controlled, and operated for the mutual benefit of its members. The members may be people who use the company's services, buy its goods, or work for it. For example, farmers form cooperatives to sell crops and buy farming equipment. Cooperatives often share their earnings with the membership as dividends.

CAREER COUNSEL

21st Century Learning

Tamara and William met in a digital photography class. They discussed plans to start a part-time business converting printed pictures into digital format, so people can store and view them on a computer, digital picture frame, or handheld device. William already had a digital scanner and computer set up at his house. They each invested $100.00 to use for purchasing storage devices, other supplies, and advertising. They practiced, and decided they could convert 40 pictures an hour. If they charged 75 cents per picture, they could make a profit.

Soon, they had a long list of customers and a stack of pictures waiting to be converted. They worked together six hours a week, but Tamara was on the school basketball team, so William worked alone an additional three to four hours. The first time the partners met to divide the profits, they each took back their $100.00 investment, and there was still $550.00 left to share. Tamara assumed they would split it equally, but William thought he should get more. After all, it was his scanner and computer, his home, and he was putting in more hours.

What challenges are facing William and Tamara? How can they solve their conflict? Use 21st Century Skills such as problem solving, decision making, critical thinking, and effective communication to help them resolve their conflict. Write an ending to the story and share it with your class.

Analyzing Trends in Business Opportunities

In Chapter 3, you read about trends that affect job outlooks and career opportunities. Many of the same factors also affect business opportunities. For example, advances in technology open the door for new types of businesses, such as cell phone applications or social networking sites. They can also close the door on certain businesses, such as video rental stores giving way to movies on-demand and online.

An entrepreneur stands a better chance of success if he or she analyzes the trends in business opportunities before starting a business. Looking at the trends can help an entrepreneur make basic decisions such as where to locate, the type of business to set up, and even how to focus on a certain market.

What trends in lifestyle do you think contributed to the growth of fast-food franchise businesses?

Trends in Business Startups

Over the past fifty years, the business make-up of the United States has changed significantly. In the 1950s, the country's dominant industry, in terms of national income and number of employees, was manufacturing. Wholesale and retail businesses were also important, but service businesses played a relatively minor role in the economy.

During the 1950s and 1960s, America experienced a boom in franchising. A **franchise** is an arrangement in which an established company sells the right for others to use the company's name and operating plan to sell products or services. Franchising became popular in the service and retail industries, particularly among fast-food restaurants.

After 1950, manufacturing began to be less important in the U.S. economy. By 1970, service, wholesale, and retail businesses accounted for the majority of America's economic production. In the first decade of the twenty-first century, most new businesses were in the service and trade businesses.

Career FACT

According to the U.S. Department of Commerce, the service industry in the 1950s and 1960s generated about 60 percent of U.S. output and employment. Today, it accounts for more than 80 percent.

North American Industry Classifications

The North American Industry Classification System (NAICS—pronounced NAKES) assigns a numerical code to every industry in North America based on its primary business function. The system was developed cooperatively by the United States, Canada, and Mexico. NAICS codes are useful for classifying different types of business and for analyzing trends such as which industries are growing economically and which are shrinking. For example, the Bureau of Labor Statistics uses the system to track employment, earnings, and growth.

NAICS classifies all economic activity in North America into twenty industry sectors: five are goods-producing sectors such as apparel manufacturing and food manufacturing, and fifteen are services-producing sectors, such as home health care services, financial services, and child daycare services.

Why do you think it is important for different countries to work together to develop systems such as NAICS? How can it help entrepreneurs?

Sources of Business Opportunities

Staying aware of things going on around you can help you recognize potential business opportunities and identify trends. Five basic sources of opportunity include problems that need to be solved, change, new discoveries, improvements to existing products or services, and the development of unique knowledge.

■ Problems are often the source of opportunity. You might have a problem you want to solve, or you might see that others have a problem. Problem solving has led to the invention of new products ranging from the light bulb to the cell phone and to services ranging from pizza delivery to online check-in for air travel.

■ Changes occur in every area of life. Laws and regulations change, social customs evolve, even the weather changes. Change often presents new opportunities. For example, a growing interest in protecting the environment has led to opportunities for "green" businesses.

■ New discoveries include the creation of a totally new product or service. The discovery of new materials such as Teflon® led to new products such as non-stick cookware.

■ Improvements to existing products and services lead to new opportunities as well. Consider hybrid cars, low-energy light bulbs, and even potting soil that includes fertilizer. These are all examples of how improving existing products can lead to opportunity.

■ Unique knowledge is when a person has an ability that no one else has, and can turn it into an opportunity.

Watch the Trends!

You have an idea for starting a business helping senior citizens prepare their homes for the winter. How can paying attention to trends help or hurt the success of your startup?

👎 You ignore the impact of technological developments in building materials that provide year-round weather protection.

👎 You fail to notice the growing trend of seniors moving to assisted-living communities.

👎 You do not take into account that there are other, similar businesses already established in the area.

👍 You change your plan to offer renovations using energy-saving building materials for year-round protection.

👍 You contact assisted-living communities to offer your service.

👍 You consider investing in an existing company.

Can you think of other ways you could adapt your idea based on current trends in business opportunities?

Case Study

Sasha's parents own and operate a small gas station. A large company opened a bigger station less than a mile away. Sales declined, and Sasha's parents started wondering if they would be able to earn enough profit to stay in business.

Sasha suggested that her parents expand the business to offer services in addition to selling gas. She thought that if they invested in the facilities and equipment for providing services such as oil changes and tire rotation, they would attract more customers, who would also buy gas.

Sasha's parents were worried because they had no experience offering services in addition to pumping gas, but after considering all their options, they decided to give it a try. They applied for a loan at their bank, and made plans to expand the business.

■ Do you think Sasha had a good idea for increasing business at the gas station?

■ What risks and challenges would her parents face?

■ What other ways can you think of to increase business at the gas station?

Web Extra

Both the U.S. Census Bureau (census.gov/eos/www/naics/) and the Bureau of Labor Statistics (bls.gov/bls/NAICS.htm) provide information about NAICS. You can explore the links to locate industry codes and statistics. Select one industry to research, and share one interesting fact about it with your class.

Answer It!

1. List the four major categories of businesses.
2. What are the two typical categories of manufactured products?
3. List two special types of businesses.
4. What is the purpose of a nonprofit organization?
5. Which type of business ownership is the simplest and least expensive?
6. What is the difference between a general partnership and a limited partnership?
7. What do you call the owners of a corporation?
8. What is a cooperative?
9. In what industries did franchising become most popular?
10. List five basic sources of business opportunities.

Career-Ready Practices

Starting a new business takes time, money, hard work, and sacrifice. But most entrepreneurs would never get to that point if they did not have the passion to act on their ideas. Career-ready individuals are constantly thinking of ideas that solve a problem or meet a need in new and different ways. They are creative thinkers and are eager to embrace unconventional and innovative ways to complete a task, fulfill a need, or solve a problem.

In teams of three or four, select a business start-up in your community (one that has been in operation less than three years). Prepare a list of seven to ten questions that you would like to ask the owner. Be sure to find out what inspired him or her to open the business. If possible, record or videotape the interview and share it with your classmates.

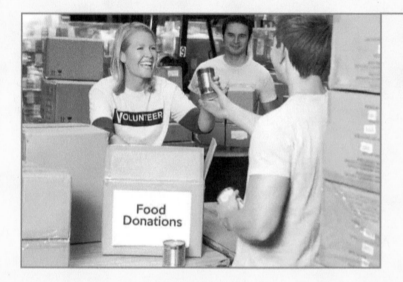

Write Now

Pick a nonprofit organization that interests you. Write a letter that could be sent out to a large mailing list explaining the mission of the organization and requesting a donation. Include an explanation of why the organization needs the money, and how it will be used.

Career Portfolio

Employers will appreciate an employee who understands how business ownerships are structured. Create a table or chart comparing the benefits and drawbacks of the different types of business ownerships discussed in this chapter. After proofreading it and correcting spelling and grammatical errors, print it and add it to your career portfolio as an example of your knowledge and understanding.

Business Plan Project

In your **Business Plan Project**, write a paragraph describing your business and business type. Follow it with another paragraph describing the business ownership structure you will use. Finally, write a third paragraph explaining why the business ownership structure you selected is best for your business. Refer to Appendix B to make sure you are on track.

Skills in This Chapter . . .

- **Developing a Business Plan**

- **Identifying Entrepreneurial Opportunities**

- **Assessing the Market**

- **Developing Plans for Marketing and Promoting Your Business**

GETTING STARTED

Could you bake a cake without a recipe? Maybe, but you would save yourself a lot of time, avoid mistakes, and end up with a better product if you took the time to find a recipe, gather the ingredients, and set up the necessary equipment. Starting a business without a plan is like baking a cake without a recipe. If you start a business without a plan, it might work out in the end, but it is likely to take longer than necessary and lead to costly mistakes along the way.

Planning a business up front takes time, thought, and effort, but the benefits far outweigh the cost. A plan helps you define your goals. It also shows investors that you are responsible and ready to turn your idea into a profitable business.

➤ Have you ever tried to do something important without making a plan first? Did it work out? Were there unexpected challenges? Would you do it differently next time? Write about the experience, or discuss it with your class.

Developing a Business Plan

Creating a business is a complicated process. It makes sense to spend time planning it. Most entrepreneurs develop a business plan as their first step, as a way of describing their business in fine detail. A **business plan** is a statement of your business goals, the reasons you think these goals can be met, and how you are going to achieve them.

A business plan forces you to figure out how to make your business work. A well-written plan helps guide you every step of the way as you develop your business. Sometimes, a business plan can help you focus your thoughts and ideas. It might help you identify different opportunities, or recognize why your original idea might not work out very well. If you start a business without a plan, you are likely to end up overwhelmed by questions you haven't answered.

The Purpose of a Business Plan

A business plan is like a map showing how you will get from your current situation to your successful business. You use it as a guide for yourself, and also to show potential *investors*—the people who will loan you money to start and run your business—that you have thought through the challenges to come and know how to make the business profitable.

To get started developing a business plan, ask yourself the following questions.

- What type of business will I create?
- What type of ownership will it have?

Then focus on financial goals, such as how much it will cost to start and run your business and what your profits will be.

From time to time, you may need to revise your business plan to keep up with the changing nature of your business. For example, if a new technology becomes available that will help you achieve your goals faster, you might revise your plan to include a shorter timeline. On the other side, if a product you require to succeed is not available, you might revise your plan to take longer.

Myth   A business plan must be complete before you start your business.

Truth   A business plan can—and should—evolve and change as you develop your business. No matter how thorough you are up front, you are bound to run into unexpected challenges and situations. Reviewing and updating your business plan on a regular basis can help you stay on track for success.

Types of Business Plans

Business plans have no set format. They vary depending on the type of business and the *audience*—people who will review the plan. However, there are four main types of plans for a start-up business.

- *Quick summary.* This is a brief presentation that lasts between 30 seconds and three minutes. It is used to interest potential investors, customers, or partners. Sometimes, a successful quick summary leads to the opportunity to present a more fully developed plan at a later date.

- *Oral presentation.* This is a short, colorful, and entertaining slide show with spoken narration. It is meant to capture the interest of investors so that they want to read the detailed business plan.

- *Investor's business plan.* This is a detailed business plan that is well-written and arranged so that all the information can be easily understood. It tells potential investors exactly what you are planning.

- *Operational business plan.* This is a plan meant for use within the business only—not for the investors or customers. It describes in great detail how the company will meet its goals.

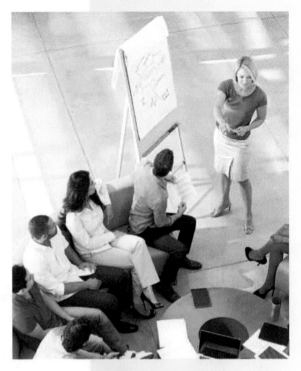

What are some of the ways you could capture the interest of investors when presenting a business plan?

Parts of a Business Plan

Investors typically see many business plans each year. They must decide which one is worth their money. They do not want to spend more than one hour reading a plan, and they will reject an incomplete or poorly written plan.

When you develop a business plan, it is important to include the following seven parts.

- *Business idea.* You describe your product or service, discuss the type of business you will start, and explain the type of business ownership you will use.

- *Opportunity and market analysis.* You describe how and why your product or service will sell. You include the size of the market, its trends and characteristics, and its growth rate. It is important also to include information about your market research, to list your competitors, and to describe why you have an advantage over your competitors. This is the section where you provide your marketing plan, your product and pricing strategies, and your plans for promotion.

- *Financial strategies.* This section shows any available historical financial data, as well as projected figures such as estimated sales and expenses—usually for five years. You should also include the type of loans or other arrangements you want to use to fund the business.

The Three C's of a Business Plan

Every business plan should include information about the three C's: Concept, Customer, and Capital.

- ✔ **Concept.** What is your product or service, and how is it different from similar products or services?

- ✔ **Customer.** Who will buy your product or service, and why?

- ✔ **Capital.** How will you locate the money you need to start your business? What will your costs be, and what kind of profit can you expect?

Why do you think investors want to know the details about the three C's?

- *Organizational structures.* In this part of the business plan, you describe the way the management of the company will be set up. You can provide profiles of managers and information about training and motivating employees.

- *Legal structures.* You describe any legal issues such as contracts or copyrights. You also discuss how your business will be protected by insurance and the effect of taxes on your business, and you address any relevant government regulations that affect the business, as well as the legal ownership structure, such as whether it is a sole propiertorship or a partnership.

- *Business management.* You describe how the business will be managed, focusing on production, distribution, operations, purchasing, and inventory.

- *Plan for growth.* In this section, you describe your plans to grow the business and the challenges you may face.

A business plan that is well thought out and well written may be the most important document an entrepreneur creates. It guides the entrepreneur through every step of developing a business. The entrepreneur uses the business plan to track whether the company is meeting its goals. The business plan becomes a resource for problem solving and decision making. A successful entrepreneur will continue to revise and update the business plan on a regular basis, so it remains relevant as the business grows.

Do I Need an Executive Summary?

What if your investors don't have the time to read the entire business plan? All business plans should include a one- to two-page executive summary that includes the following key points.

★ Mission statement, or explanation of the purpose of the business

★ Business name and location

★ Date the business will begin

★ Owner's name, function, and contact information

★ Opportunity

★ Products or services

★ The economics of one unit, which is a calculation of the profit or loss for each unit of sale the business will make

★ Future plans

Why do you think an executive summary is an important part of any business plan?

Tech Connect

Once, busy investors without a lot of time to spare, might have requested an **elevator pitch**—a business plan presentation that is short enough to be delivered during an elevator ride. Now, entrepreneurs might use a "twitpitch."

A **"twitpitch,"** named for Twitter, the micro-blogging Web site, is a business idea summarized in no more than 140 characters. When an entrepreneur posts a "twitpitch," consultants and venture capitalists can quickly identify the ideas that interest them.

Do you think it's possible to summarize a business plan in 140 characters or less? Think of a business, and try to write a "twitpitch." Use a word processing program that counts characters, so you know when you reach the 140-character limit. Share your "twitpitch" with the class.

Identifying Entrepreneurial Opportunities

Usually you start a business because you see an opportunity. A **business opportunity** is a consumer need or want that can be met by a new business. Not every business idea is a good business opportunity. For example, you might have an idea to open a neighborhood restaurant featuring classic French cooking, but if people in the neighborhood don't like classic French cooking, then your business will not succeed.

A successful entrepreneur knows how to tell the difference between an idea and an opportunity. He or she uses available resources to select an opportunity that shows promise, and then turn it into a business.

Finding Ideas

How does an entrepreneur come up with an idea? Maybe someone has a problem that can be solved with a new product, or is using an existing product that could work better. Maybe someone hears a news story or reads a blog that identifies a need. Often, ideas come from everyday life. Here are some resources you might find in your own community.

- Reading newspapers and magazines can help you identify developing trends in your area, or in a different area. Specialized magazines that focus on something that interests you—such as a hobby—can also help you find opportunities.

- Business and government agencies such as the U.S. Census Bureau, U.S. Department of Labor, and the U.S. Small Business Administration provide statistical data that can help you identify trends. Local organizations such as the Better Business Bureau or Chamber of Commerce provide information on businesses in your local area.

- Trade organizations can provide you with information about a specific industry that interests you, and help you meet and network with people in that industry. Trade organizations are groups that provide training and information for people associated with a particular career or industry. They sponsor meetings and shows and publish newsletters and magazines.

- The Internet lets you explore almost any topic from your own computer. Web sites provide information about industries and companies. Blogs help you learn about consumer problems and opinions.

Can Your Idea Become an Opportunity?

Once you come up with an idea, it is time to explore its potential to be an opportunity. Which of these factors indicate that an idea might make a good business opportunity?

- 👎 You do not have the resources to put the idea into action.

- 👎 Someone else has already made a successful business from the same idea.

- 👎 You cannot provide the product or service at a price that will earn a profit.

- 👍 The idea fills a need or want that's not currently being met.

- 👍 Your community is a great location to make the idea a business.

- 👍 You can provide the product or service at a price that will attract customers.

Can you think of other ways to tell the difference between an idea and an opportunity?

Evaluating an Opportunity

Just because an idea shows promise as an opportunity doesn't mean it is worth pursuing. You can use these three practical methods to determine if an idea is worth the time, effort, and investment that it will take to make it a business.

Why is it important to decide if an idea will make a good opportunity before you start your business?

- *Cost/benefit analysis.* A **cost/benefit analysis** is the process of adding up all the expected benefits of an opportunity and subtracting all the expected costs. If the benefits are greater than the costs, the opportunity may be worthwhile. Costs include money, such as the amount you must spend on supplies and advertising, as well as items such as time and effort. Benefits also include money, such as how much you will earn, and items such as satisfaction and pride. You may have to estimate the costs and benefits at first.

- *Opportunity-cost analysis.* The **opportunity cost** is the value of what you are willing to give up to achieve something else. An opportunity-cost analysis examines the potential benefits that you will give up when you choose one course of action over another. For example, you might choose to accept a position as an unpaid intern in an industry that you find interesting. You give up the wages you might earn in a different job in order to gain experience in the field of your choice.

- *SWOT analysis.* A **SWOT analysis** is a business method used to evaluate four areas: **S**trengths, **W**eaknesses, **O**pportunities, and **T**hreats. Strengths include your skills, knowledge, and resources; weaknesses include the areas where you—or your idea—might be lacking and need improvement. When you assess your opportunities, you look for everything that provides your idea with a business advantage. For example, does your idea fill an unmet need or want, make use of a trend, or surpass the efforts of an existing company? Finally, you analyze the threats, which are obstacles or challenges that might interfere with your success.

Turning an Opportunity into a Business

What action can you take to turn your opportunity into a business? Here are four common ways that entrepreneurs become businessmen and businesswomen.

- *Start a new business.* This is probably the most challenging option. Benefits include the ability to build the business your own way, but there are many drawbacks. You are responsible for making the many decisions and completing the many tasks that are required to set up and run a new business. You will also assume the bulk of the risk. The process may take a long time.

- *Buy a business that already exists.* This option may require a significant amount of money up front, but you will not face the risks and challenges of starting a company from scratch. You will still be responsible for the continued growth and success of the operation.

- *Buy a franchise.* Buying a franchise gives you a legal agreement to sell another company's products or services. Becoming a **franchisee**—someone who buys a franchise—is less risky than starting a new business, or buying an existing business. The **franchisor**—the company that sells the franchise—usually provides training and national advertising. However, you will have less entrepreneurial freedom because you must follow the rules in the legal agreement.

- *Invent something new.* If you invent a new product, design, or process, you can sell or license the invention to someone else, or create a business to use, manufacture, or sell the invention.

Career FACT

Some studies show that most franchise operations have a 90% or better chance of success. Statistics from the Small Business Administration, however, indicate that only about half of all new franchises survive five years or more and roughly a third survive ten years or more, which are the same success rates for independent business startups.

CAREER COUNSEL

21st Century Learning

Evan is not old enough for a driver's license, but he loves cars. One summer, he starts a small automotive detailing business. Detailing involves making the car look clean and new by washing, vacuuming, and buffing every part of it. Evan spends anywhere from two to six hours per car, depending on factors such as the type of car and its condition. He charges $25.00 per hour.

One day Evan receives a call from a man running a classic car show. He wants to hire Evan to detail five classic cars in four days. But he does not want to pay. Instead, he offers to put up signs next to each car at the show with Evan's name and contact information.

What are the benefits and drawbacks of the arrangement for Evan? Use 21st Century Skills such as problem solving, decision making, critical thinking, and effective communication to help Evan decide what to do. Write an ending to the story and share it with your class.

Assessing the Market

A business succeeds if someone buys the goods and services it sells. This group of potential customers is called a **market**. Before an entrepreneur starts a business, he or she does **market research**, which means examining the market to learn as much as possible.

Market research helps entrepreneurs understand customers, the competition, and the current business environment. It helps them identify problems and challenges, so they can avoid costly mistakes. It also provides the information entrepreneurs need to convince others to invest in the business.

Targeting Your Market

You may be tempted to try to **mass market** your product or service, which means sell it to as many customers as possible. Mass marketing is costly and may not be the best approach for a small business. Instead, you can identify a **target market**, which is a group of customers most likely to buy the product or service you are selling.

Market research can help you build a **customer profile**, or description of your ideal customer. When you conduct market research, you collect information about customers to determine who is most likely to buy the product or service you are selling. You can use the information to target customers who best match the profile. Common information you can collect to develop your customer profile includes the following.

- Demographics, such as the age, gender, education, and ethnic background of your customer
- Geography, such as where your customer is located
- Psychology, such as the values, opinions, lifestyle, and politics of your customer
- Buying patterns, such as how often, when, and where your customer shops

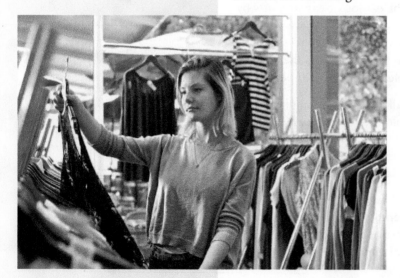

How can a customer profile help you identify your target market?

Career Profile: Market Research Analyst

Marketing Career Cluster

Job Summary

A market research analyst examines market research information to help a company understand the types of products and services people want and how much they are willing to pay. Market research analysts also work to build customer profiles and identify target markets, gather data about competitors, and analyze sales data to predict future sales.

Market research analysts generally work in offices on a regular schedule. They may work alone, or as part of a market research team. They benefit from strong communication skills, because they must be able to explain the data to others. They should pay attention to detail and should have solid problem-solving skills.

Most market research analyst positions require a bachelor's degree in a subject such as business, marketing, or a related area. Some positions may require a master's degree. Studying business, marketing, and consumer research in college is recommended. Courses in mathematics, statistics, computer science, economics, and consumer behavior are recommended.

Use the Internet, a library, or career center to research the responsibilities, education and training requirements, and salary range of a market research analyst. Write an article for a newspaper or Web site describing the position.

Market Research Techniques

Knowing who represents your target market before you open a business can help you avoid costly mistakes. What if you are not sure who your ideal customer is? How can you gather market research information?

★ Conduct interviews or surveys

★ Run a **focus group**, which is a discussion among a small number of people

★ Observe potential customers without talking to them

You can also use **secondary data**, which is existing information collected by someone else. For example, you can use information on the Bureau of Labor Statistics Web site. What might be some benefits and drawbacks of using secondary data?

How can an entrepreneur use market research analysis to improve the chances of success for his or her business?

NUMBERS' GAME

Market share is the percentage of the total sales captured by a product or a business in a particular market. Companies use market share to compare their position in the market to the competition—which company has the greater market share—and also to assess changes in performance from one year to the next—has market share increased or decreased.

The formula for calculating market share is:

(Sales by Business ÷ Total Sales in Market) × 100 = Market Share %

You can calculate market share using the quantity of items sold or revenue earned.

For example, if a company sells 1,000 basketballs in a town where the total sales of basketballs equal 5,000, the company has a 20% market share:

(1,000 ÷ 5,000) × 100 = 20%

If there are 25 dogs in your neighborhood, and you have been hired to walk 10 of them, what is your market share of the dog-walking business in your neighborhood?

Identifying Your Competition

In addition to identifying the target market, a successful entrepreneur investigates the **competition**—the businesses with which you are competing for the dollars your target market spends. Knowing your competition can help you develop a **competitive advantage**—something that makes your business more appealing to your target market than the competitors' businesses.

- **Direct competitors** are businesses that sell a product or service similar to yours. For example, if you open an Italian restaurant, your direct competitors are other Italian restaurants.

- **Indirect competitors** sell different products or services but fill the same need or want. For example, if you open an Italian restaurant, your indirect competitors might be Chinese, French, Brazilian, or American restaurants.

In addition, there may be other options available to your target market. Potential customers may choose to provide the service for themselves rather than paying someone else to do it. For example, some people may cook at home, instead of eating at your restaurant.

Career Tips

A successful entrepreneur will not rely on statistics alone to assess the competition. If possible, he or she will visit the competitor's business to gain firsthand knowledge. For example, a restaurant owner can eat at a competitor's restaurant, or a nail technician can make an appointment at a competitor's nail salon.

Developing Plans for Marketing and Promoting Your Business

Even the best idea will not become a successful business if no one is interested in it. Entrepreneurs—all businesses, in fact—use marketing to communicate the value of their products and services to customers. They use promotion to influence customers to buy.

A **marketing plan** is a detailed guide that identifies your marketing goals and strategies. Part of a successful marketing plan is promotion. Well-thought-out marketing and promotion can be the difference between a product no one has ever heard of and a wildly successful smash hit.

Setting Marketing Goals

Every marketing plan is unique because each business has its own marketing goals. Marketing goals help you define what you want your marketing efforts to accomplish. Your goals should match the overall objectives you outline in your business plan. They should be specific, and they should include a time frame and measurable results. For example, "I want to increase the number of customers who come into my store" is too general. "Within six months, I want to increase the number of customers who come into my store by 25%" includes a specific, measurable goal and a time frame for achieving the goal.

As in other areas of your life, you can set short-term and long-term marketing goals, as well as milestones.

- Short-term goals should define the goals you want to achieve within one year.
- Long-term goals map out the goals you have for ten or even twenty years in the future.
- Milestones help you stay on track to achieve your long-term goals, by breaking them into attainable short-term goals.

Developing Marketing Strategies

Every marketing plan has five main strategy areas: people, product, place, price, and promotion. These strategy areas are sometimes referred to as the "Five P's."

- *People* are your customers. Your marketing plan should include a customer profile. It should also include the ways you plan to appeal to your target market and keep them coming back again and again. People are also your employees. Your plan should include an explanation of who will carry out the marketing plan.

- *Product* is the item or service you offer. Your marketing plan should define the features and benefits of your product, and how it best meets the customer's needs and wants. It should also include information about how you will brand the product. **Branding** is a method of creating a strong, identifiable, and sometimes emotional attachment between your customers and your product. Packaging is also an important part of a product's marketing strategy. Packaging should appeal to your target market, promote the image of your brand, and separate your product from the competition. Packaging may also have to meet industry standards, or protect the product.

Tips for Setting Marketing Goals

Remember to keep the following three considerations in mind when you set marketing goals.

✔ What is your motive? A motive is a reason for doing something. Why do you want to achieve a specific goal? What rewards or benefits do you hope to obtain?

✔ Do some of your goals conflict with other goals? Conflicting goals interfere with your ability to achieve success. For example, you might set one goal of increasing the number of customers who come into your store, and another goal of attracting younger customers. These goals might conflict with each other, lowering your chance of achieving either one.

✔ How much will it cost to achieve your goals? If you do not have the resources you need to achieve a goal, you will not succeed.

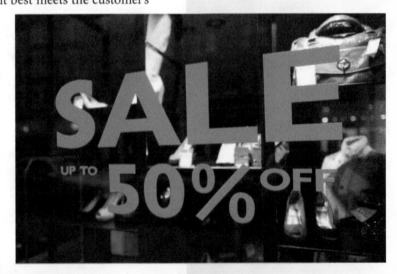

What are some benefits and drawbacks of using discounts to promote your business?

■ *Place* is the way you make the product available to your customer. It includes strategies for distributing the product to customers, the location and hours when the product will be available, and how you will transport and store products.

■ *Price* is how much you will charge customers to buy your product. Although there are many pricing strategies depending on your marketing goals, basic pricing should be based on how much your target market will pay, and how much you must charge to make a profit.

■ *Promotion* is the steps you take to convince customers to buy. It includes strategies for capturing the attention of your target market, holding your customers' interest, and making the product appealing to your customers.

International Distribution

Transportation is used to move a product from one place to another. Ways to transport products include airplanes, trains, ships, and trucks. Some electronic products, such as software, can be transported from a seller's computer to a buyer's computer through the Internet.

In the global marketplace, many factors influence a company's ability to transport goods quickly, efficiently, and at a reasonable cost. For example, a flood in Colombia might wash out the road used to transport coffee beans to a port. Political conflict in the Middle East might cause an increase in the cost of fuel used.

Can you think of other factors a company must consider when selecting transportation methods? Choose a product and research how it is transported from the place where it is manufactured to the place where it is sold. Create a poster showing the route and listing challenges that might arise during transportation.

Basic Promotion Techniques

Promotion is an on-going process. You use it to make sure customers remember your product and think of it first when they are ready to buy. Common promotion techniques include offering rewards such as frequent buyer programs, sponsoring local teams or events, and offering special price discounts.

Methods of promotion have benefits and drawbacks. For example, some cost a lot of money, such as advertising on television, and some are inexpensive, such as sending a press release to a local newspaper or Web site. Your marketing plan should include the promotional methods that best meet your needs.

Most businesses benefit from a **promotional mix**, which is a combination of different methods of promotion. The different methods might be varied, but they all have common goals: to build a favorable awareness of your product and business and to influence people to buy your product. Some common elements of a promotional mix include the following terms:

■ *Advertising*, which is a public, promotional message that your company pays for. Advertising includes printed ads, direct mailings, broadcast ads on radio or television, online advertisements, outdoor advertisements such as billboards or signs, and product placement, which is when you pay a fee to have a product displayed in a noticeable way.

■ *Visual merchandising*, which is when you use artistic displays to attract customers into a store, or to promote products inside a store.

■ *Public relations* (PR), which are activities or events that encourage customers to have a positive attitude about a product or company. PR might include sending a **press release**—a written statement of information about the product or company—to media outlets for publication or broadcast. It might also include sponsoring community events or contests.

■ *Personal selling*, which is direct efforts by sales representatives to convince a particular customer to buy. Personal selling also includes building relationships with customers.

■ *Sales promotion*, which is a short-term activity or incentive that convinces customers to buy. It includes product demonstrations, coupons, and free samples.

Money Madne$$

You have $2,000.00 to start a bicycle repair business. You need $1,250.00 to purchase supplies, and you plan to spend the rest on advertising. The local, weekly newspaper charges $25.00 for a small print advertisement, or $15.00 for a link on its Web site. Your town's cable access station charges $300.00 to produce a basic video commercial and $100.00 each time the commercial airs.

How much money do you have to spend on advertising? How would you allocate the money? Write a paragraph explaining your advertising plan. Show the calculations that you used to make the decision.

Case Study

Sylvie enjoys working with animals. She is thinking of studying to become a veterinarian. A lot of people in her neighborhood have pets. She knows most people don't like to groom their dogs themselves. She thinks she can make money by brushing and washing the dogs in her neighborhood, as well as trimming their nails.

Sylvie visits a local pet store to see how much she will have to spend on equipment. She calls a local pet grooming shop to see how much they charge. She decides she can charge $25.00 for a brush, $45.00 for a brush and wash, and $15.00 for nail trimming. She asks her parents if she can use the patio behind their home; it is fenced in and has a hose and faucet for water. She also asks them to loan her $100.00 to buy the equipment and supplies she will need. Finally, Sylvie uses her computer to design and print advertising flyers. She distributes the flyers to all the homes in her neighborhood where she knows there are dogs.

- How did Sylvie identify a business opportunity?
- What steps did Sylvie take to research her market?
- Do you think Sylvie's business will succeed? Why or why not?

Web Extra

Web sites such as businessplans.org and myownbusiness.org provide information about different types of business plans, as well as how to develop a plan. Use the Internet to explore the different types of plans and to compare the samples. Select one you would like to use.

Answer It!

1. Define business plan.
2. List at least four benefits of a well-written business plan.
3. List four types of business plans.
4. List seven parts of a business plan.
5. List at least four sources that can help you identify business ideas.
6. What is the purpose of market research?
7. What do you call efforts to sell a product or service to as many customers as possible?
8. What is the difference between direct competitors and indirect competitors?
9. What is a marketing plan?
10. List the five "P's" that identify the main strategy areas for a marketing plan.

Career-Ready Practices

Form teams of three or four and randomly select one of the 16 career clusters. Brainstorm a business idea that fits in your selected career cluster. Develop a marketing plan for your business that answers these questions: Who is your target market? What type of advertising will you use to reach your target market? What type of promotions will you use to convince your target market to buy? You will need to conduct thorough research of your selected business and its industry before developing a marketing plan. Career-ready individuals use valid and reliable research strategies. They evaluate the validity of sources from which they gather information. They are selective in how they use information and apply ideas to their workplace situation. Share your business idea and marketing plan with the class.

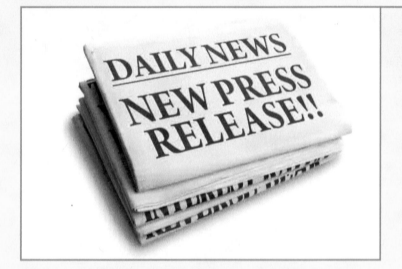

Write Now

A *press release* is a written statement designed to draw attention to a product, service, or event. Look in newspapers or on the Internet for examples of a press release, then write a press release announcing a new product or service.

Career Portfolio

A *business plan* is a written document used by entrepreneurs when they begin the process of starting a business. It defines the business, identifies business goals, and serves as a map for developing the business. It includes specific actions the business will take to achieve its goals. Use a business plan model or template, or refer to the sample business plan in Appendix B, and develop a business plan for a small business you would start if you were an entrepreneur. Add the document to your career portfolio.

Business Plan Project

Developing an understanding of the market and your competitors is a major part of business plan. Identify, research, and record two existing competitors of the business you plan to start. Then, in your **Business Plan Project**, create a table with three columns and seven rows. Label the columns: **Competitive Advantage Area**, **Is it a Competitive Advantage? (Yes or No)**, **Description**. In the rows under the heading Competitive Advantage Area, enter the following: **Quality**, **Price**, **Location**, **Selection**, **Service**, **Reputation**. Consider your business. In the middle column, enter Yes if your business has a competitive advantage in that area, or No if it does not. In the right column, explain why or why not. Circle the row that shows your greatest competitive advantage. Refer to Appendix B to make sure you are on track.

19 | Managing Your Business

Skills in This Chapter . . .

- **Raising Money**
- **Understanding Business Management**
- **Organizing Your Business**
- **Analyzing Successful Selling**
- **Growing Your Business**
- **Creating a Positive Work Environment**

GETTING STARTED

Do you think a manager is someone who tells others what to do? If so, how can an entrepreneur who is the only employee in a start-up business be a manager? Management involves a lot more than just supervising others. It also means making sure all available resources are used in the best way to develop the business, and at the most reasonable cost.

Management keeps a business organized and on track to achieve its goals. An entrepreneur who recognizes the factors that contribute to successful management is prepared to meet challenges, solve problems, and make positive decisions.

➤ Look through magazines and cut out pictures of people you think look like managers. Make a collage of the pictures, adding words that describe and explain what makes each person a manager.

Raising Money

Sometimes entrepreneurs can raise all the money they need to start and operate their business by themselves, using their earnings and savings. Sometimes, an entrepreneur must raise money from other sources to start, operate, and grow the business.

Raising money for a business is called **financing**. If an entrepreneur does not have the money, he or she can consider the following options for financing.

- Debt financing is when you borrow money from a source such as a bank, credit union, relative, or friend.

- Equity financing is when you sell shares of ownership in the business. Buyers might include relatives, friends, investors, or partners.

(Refer to the Big Picture feature on page 345 for more on angel investors.)

The type of financing you choose depends on the business, as well as your own goals. Recognizing the benefits and drawbacks of each type can help you choose the option that is best for you and your business.

How Much Do I Need?

Start-up investment is the one-time sum required to start a business and cover start-up expenses. It may be called seed money or start-up capital. The start-up investment for a new company has two components.

- Start-up expenses such as equipment, space, licensing fees, and advertising

- **Cash reserves**, which is money set aside for emergencies, such as a delivery truck that needs repair, and at least three months of fixed expenses, such as rent and insurance

Bootstrapping

An entrepreneur who starts a business without any outside help is **bootstrapping**. The term comes from the phrase "pulling yourself up by the bootstraps" which means doing something for yourself without help from anyone else.

Many successful entrepreneurs begin their business by using very little or no borrowed money. Instead, they use their own resources. The two most common sources of bootstrap funding are personal savings and credit cards.

- If you have enough money in your savings account to cover your start-up investment, you can be the sole owner of your business. All the profits will belong to you. Of course, if the business fails, you will lose all the money you invested. You also have no savings to use for any other expenses or for emergencies.

- Some entrepreneurs are tempted to charge start-up expenditures to a credit card. However, using credit cards is the same as borrowing money. This is only a good option if you have enough income to pay your credit card account balance in full each month. If not, the interest payments will add up very quickly. You may also reach your **credit limit**, which is the maximum amount you can charge to the card. When you reach your credit limit, you will not be able to use the card for emergencies or other expenses. Finally, keeping high balances on your credit cards affects your credit rating, which affects your ability to obtain loans from other sources.

Debt Financing

One method of obtaining money to fund your start-up investment is to borrow it. When you borrow money, you increase your company's debt, which is why it is called debt financing. There are two main sources of debt financing.

- *Banks and credit unions*, which issue business loans for a set amount of time—called the term—at a specific interest rate. The bank may ask for collateral against the loan. Collateral is property or other assets that you pledge to the bank. If you fail to repay the loan, the bank takes ownership of the collateral. For example, if you own a truck, you might use it as collateral. The bank may also ask for a co-signer for the loan. A co-signer is an individual who agrees to make the loan payments if you cannot.

- *Relatives and friends*, who might loan you the money. This is sometimes called "love money" because people give it to you out of love for you, not necessarily because they have an interest in your business. Borrowing from relatives and friends has both benefits and drawbacks. Benefits include the support from people who care about you and your success. Drawbacks come from the risk of failure. If you are unable to repay the loan, you risk losing a valuable relationship. When you borrow money from family and friends, emotions become involved; it is hard to keep it strictly business. For the arrangement to succeed, it is important that you thoroughly explain the business risks and opportunities. Also, both sides must agree in writing to the terms of the loan, including the schedule for repayment and the interest rate.

How can borrowing or lending money create problems in a relationship?

Career Tips

Banks and other sources of funding are usually more willing to provide financing to people with business experience. If you are just getting started, find a mentor, hire a consultant, or take on a business partner who does have experience.

Equity Financing

Another method of financing a start-up is to sell shares of ownership in your business. This is called equity financing. When you sell **equity**—ownership—you give up some of your company, including profits and possibly some control. There are three main sources of equity financing.

■ Relatives and friends might take a share of the company in exchange for their investment. In this relationship, the funding is not solely based on love. The investors have a greater stake in the success of the business, because they own part of it. They have a right to question your actions and decisions. They may want to play an active role in running the company, or they may be willing to leave the management to you.

■ **Venture capitalists** are companies that invest in businesses. Their goal is to gain large profits. They consider many businesses, but they are more likely to invest in businesses that have moved beyond the initial start-up phase and show great promise of success.

■ **Partners** are people who assume a percentage of the ownership of a business in exchange for equity financing. Partners may be family, friends, acquaintances, or people you do not know at all. It is important, however, that you and your partners share the same basic principles and goals for the business. Partners can bring new ideas and valuable experience, but they may also disagree with the way you want to run the company.

Money Madne$$

You want to start a business selling smoothies on a busy street corner in your neighborhood. You will need a refrigerated cart ($3,250.00); a refrigerator and cabinets for storing supplies in your home ($850.00); a license from the city ($500.00); and starting supplies, such as fruit, yogurt, granola, and nuts ($725.00). You also plan to purchase business cards and make flyers for advertising ($255.00).

How much do you need for a start-up investment? What are your options for obtaining the funding?

Special Sources of Funding

There are many types of government and privately funded sources that provide either debt or equity financing. The following list includes a small sampling.

- *Small Business Investment Companies (SBICs)* are organizations that are partially funded through government loans. They often accept lower interest rates than other sources of debt financing.

- *Specialized Small Business Investment Companies (SSBICs)* are private investment firms chartered by the Small Business Administration. They provide both debt and equity financing to entrepreneurs who have been denied the opportunity to own and operate a business because of social or economic disadvantage.

- *Small Business Innovation Research (SBIR)* and *Small Business Technology Transfer Research (STTR)* are federally funded programs coordinated by the Small Business Administration. They provide grants to technology companies with fewer than 500 employees to fund research on everything from energy independence to transcribing medical records.

- *Business associate financing* is a loan provided by other companies with which you do business. Sometimes customers or suppliers might provide financing in order to help your business succeed. If the business associate provides equity financing, it becomes a co-owner of your business.

- *Barter financing* is the trading of items or services between businesses. It allows both businesses to get what they want without spending any money. For example, if you own a hardware store that sells lawn mowers, you may arrange with a landscape company to care for your property in exchange for a lawn-mower.

Angel Investors

Finding an investor can be a challenge for an entrepreneur. A lucky few establish a relationship with an **angel**, or a wealthy individual or group interested in investing his or her own money in a start-up in exchange for an equity share.

An angel usually has reasons other than profit for investing in a business. For example, an angel investor might be interested in a specific type of business, such as a "green" business that protects the environment; or in a particular type of entrepreneur, such as a member of a minority population; or in a certain community, such as a city that has high unemployment.

Angels differ from venture capitalists in three important ways: Angels typically invest their own money, they are more likely to invest in start-up companies, and they invest smaller amounts—usually between $5,000.00 and $10,000.00.

Many angels look to fund entrepreneurs in their own community, but there is a growing trend toward international angels. International angels recognize the need to support entrepreneurial thinking globally, and focus on investing in businesses that add—and return—value, wherever they are located.

What do you think are the benefits and drawbacks of having an angel investor fund your business?

NUMBERS GAME

Payback is the amount of time, measured in months, that it takes a business to earn enough in profit to cover the start-up investment. To calculate payback, you must know the business's net profit. (Net profit is the gross profit minus expenses and tax. Gross profit is the amount earned from sales, minus the cost of the items being sold.)

The formula for calculating payback is:

Start-up investment ÷ Net profit per month = Payback (in months)

For example, if your start-up investment is $10,000.00, and your net profit per month is $2,000.00, your payback is:

$10,000.00 ÷ $2,000.00 = 5 months

How long is the payback if your start-up investment is $7,500.00 and your net profit per month is $1,200.00?

Tech Connect

Companies that sell products online have a responsibility to protect the personal information of their customers. That means offering a secure Web site that uses **encryption**—code—and authentication standards to protect online transaction information. It also means using tools such as **firewalls**—software that restricts unauthorized access to a site—and anti-virus and anti-spyware programs to keep thieves from accessing personal information stored on servers. A **computer virus** is a software program that spreads from computer to computer destroying data. **Spyware** is a program that lets others access your computer and monitor your keystrokes and other actions.

Implementing the technology to keep a Web site secure is costly and requires a lot of technical expertise. It may be easier and more economical for small businesses to contract with a trusted online security company to make sure their sites are safe and ready for business.

Imagine you own a small business that sells products through its Web site. You have taken measures to ensure that your customers' personal information and transactions are safe and secure. But you want to know what could happen to your business if it fails to secure customer information on its Web site. Use the Internet to research instances where companies have experienced an online breach of security. Select one and use a word processing program to write a short report about how the breach occurred and how the company addressed the issue.

Understanding Business Management

Once an entrepreneur creates a business and gets it running, he or she takes over the business management. **Business management** is the skillful use and coordination of all the business's resources in an organized and efficient way to achieve business goals. Efficiency is important. It means maximizing production, or output, while minimizing expenses.

Experts break down the job of a manager into four interrelated functions:

- Planning
- Organizing
- Directing
- Controlling

Understanding the responsibilities of a manager in each function will help you keep your business running and growing. If you do not have your own business, management skills will prepare you for leadership positions in the future, in your career as well as in other areas of your life.

Planning

Planning is an ongoing process of setting goals and achieving goals. Recall that in Chapter 18 you read about the importance of business planning. A plan is an organized process for achieving a specific goal.

Three types of plans are used frequently in business management.

- A *strategic plan* lays out a broad course of action to achieve a long-term goal, typically three to five years in the future. These plans are usually created by top-level managers with an overall view of what needs to be done and the general way in which those goals will be achieved.

- A *tactical plan* outlines specific milestones for carrying out the strategic plan. Tactical plans typically cover a time period of less than a year and include target dates for accomplishing goals. Tactical plans are usually laid out by midlevel managers.

- An *operational plan* details the everyday activities of a business that will achieve the goals of the tactical plan—and, ultimately, the strategic plan. Operational plans are short-range. They typically cover days or weeks. They are usually drawn up by low-level managers such as supervisors who are very familiar with the actual day-to-day workings of the business and with the capabilities of the employees responsible for accomplishing each goal.

Organizing

Organizing is an ongoing process of arranging and coordinating resources and tasks to achieve specific goals. Organizing creates structure. It puts the people and other resources of a business in the right places and in the right combinations to maximize production and minimize expenses.

One of the most important organizational responsibilities of a manager is to choose and hire the best employees, train them properly, and assign them authority and responsibilities.

Managers must also organize physical resources, as well as the processes, duties, activities, and everyday operations that make a business successful. Physical resources include items such as materials, machinery, supplies, equipment, and inventory.

Is a Manager Always a Leader?

A manager is not necessarily a leader. Which of these actions or behaviors indicates that a manager is also a leader?

- 👎 Employees do as they are told because the manager threatens to fire them.

- 👎 Employees ignore the requests of the manager.

- 👎 Employees go over the manager's head for guidance and leadership.

- 👍 Employees have confidence in the manager.

- 👍 Employees share the manager's vision for the future.

- 👍 Employees work cooperatively as a team to accomplish goals.

Can you think of other actions that indicate a manager is also a leader?

Three Styles of Leadership

Although there are as many leadership styles as there are leaders, the three basic styles are:

✔ Authoritarian, which is practiced when a leader tells employees what needs to be done and how to do it, without seeking their advice. This style works in specific situations, such as with a new employee or when a task needs to be done quickly.

✔ Democratic, which is practiced when a leader seeks input from employees about what tasks need to be done and how to do them, but ultimately makes the final decisions.

✔ Delegating, which is practiced when a leader gives employees complete freedom to decide what tasks need to be done and how to do them. A leader who delegates is able to tackle other, more strategic goals.

Directing

Directing is an ongoing process of leading, influencing, and motivating employees so they will work together to achieve specific goals. It requires strong leadership and interpersonal skills such as communicating clearly, listening, having a positive attitude, and showing respect for others.

The ultimate goal of directing is team building, which is motivating individuals in a group to work together to achieve a shared goal. A group of well-organized people with a solid plan will not be successful without good leadership. They must become a team with a shared goal and have a leader they want to follow.

Controlling

Controlling is an ongoing process of setting performance standards, measuring actual performance, comparing actual performance to the standards, and taking corrective action if actual performance does not meet the performance standards. Standards depend on the business and can include measurements for areas such as production, expenses, customer service, employee actions, equipment, finances, inventory levels, product quality, profits, and sales.

The most difficult component of controlling is usually implementing the appropriate corrective action. Equipment that is not meeting standards may be easy to fix. But if employees are not meeting standards, the company must use training, leadership, and organization to correct the problems.

Making the Most of Available Resources

As mentioned, a manager is responsible for using and coordinating resources to achieve business goals, such as meeting financial targets, or satisfying the needs and wants of customers. A business that establishes priorities for resources and a manager who understands how to make the most of those resources will be in the best position to help the business succeed.

The three most important resources for most businesses are money, people, and technology. Other vital resources include time and materials.

Career Tips

Effective management starts with effective communications. You will be a more successful manager if you take the time to listen and to make sure others understand the message you are sending.

Different businesses might use resources in different ways. A manufacturing company might use a just-in-time strategy to complete an order on time, under budget, and with a minimal number of employees. **Just-in-time** is a method of reducing costs while improving quality and efficiency by limiting the amount of inventory a manufacturer keeps in stock. The business orders new inventory just-in-time to produce an order, instead of keeping unused inventory sitting around in a warehouse.

A business that knows there is increased activity at certain times of the year might make use of temporary employees or consultants. For example, a toy store might hire temporary workers in November and December, while an accounting firm might hire consultants in March and April.

What personal characteristics help a manager become a leader?

CAREER

COUNSEL

21st Century Learning

Meghan makes beautiful pieces of jewelry from beads. She has a lot of patience for beadwork and a talent for designing unique and interesting items. Friends, family, and even strangers often ask her if she can make pieces for them. She recognizes a business opportunity and starts making and selling her designs.

The business takes off, and Meghan has more orders than she can fulfill. Her friends Stacy and Liz make beaded jewelry, too. Meghan asks them to join her growing business, and they agree. Stacy works hard and follows Meghan's instructions. She enjoys talking to customers about what they want and taking orders. She also makes sure items are delivered on time and that payment is received. This gives Meghan more time to design and create the jewelry.

On the other hand, Meghan is finding that Liz is not very good at working independently. She makes a lot of mistakes, asks a lot of questions, and complains about the painstaking work. Meghan must spend a lot of time helping Liz and recreating the pieces that Liz has trouble with. They are beginning to argue a lot, and it is getting more difficult to complete orders on time. Meghan is starting to think about letting Liz go.

What are the problems and challenges facing Meghan? What decisions does she have to make? Use 21st Century Skills such as problem solving, decision making, critical thinking, and effective communication to help Meghan deal with her situation. Write an ending to the story and share it with your class.

Organizing Your Business

When an entrepreneur starts a new business, he or she is likely to be the only employee. As the business succeeds and grows, the entrepreneur hires people to perform specific tasks and to assume responsibility. The system that assigns work, authority, and responsibility within a company is called the **organizational structure**.

An organizational structure is very important. It defines the *chain of command*, which is the path of authority and supervision among employees. A well-organized company clearly identifies the responsibilities of each employee, the relationship between employees, and the relationship between departments within the company.

You can illustrate an organizational structure using an organization chart. The chart shows the chains of command within the business and the working relationships among different groups of people. A good organization chart displays supervisors and their employees, and illustrates the way departments interact.

Traditional Structures

The simplest organizational structure is *line organization*. Line organization is a direct chain of command through levels of personnel. In a school, the principal would be in the top level of a line organization. Teachers are one level below the principal, and students are a level below the teachers.

Who do you think has the most authority in a line organization?

Principal

Teachers

Students

An expanded version of a line organization is the line-and-staff organization, in which staff employees advise, assist, or support the line personnel, but do not have authority over other employees. In a school, maintenance workers fall into the staff category.

Principal

Maintenance

Teachers

Students

Who do you think has authority over staff personnel in a line-and-staff organization?

Sometimes, a business may use a project organization, in which employees from more than one department work as a team on a specific goal. Project organization ends once the project goal is achieved. For example, the owner of the Sea Breeze Restaurant asked the executive chef and the marketing manager to work with a dietitian to develop a line of healthy meals.

Owners/
Finance

Executive
Chef

Sea
Breeze
Project

Outside
Dietitian

Marketing
Manager

What do you think is the relationship between employees in a project organization structure?

Career Trend

Traditional organizational structures do not always fit today's rapidly changing, global economy. Clearly defined roles and responsibilities are giving way to interdepartmental teams and networks that can be put together as the need arises. New communication technology including videoconferencing, collaborative software, and the Internet is playing a role in this evolution.

Setting Up Departments

A small business may not need separate departments to manage everyday tasks and responsibilities. The entrepreneur and a few employees may handle everything from ordering supplies to stocking shelves to meeting with potential investors. As a company grows, however, the number of departments will probably grow, as well.

Some typical business departments include the following:

■ Accounting, to manage the finances

■ Production, to manage the manufacturing

■ Sales, to manage sales

■ Administration, to manage paperwork and legal issues

■ Customer service, to manage relationships between the business and its customers

■ Human resources, to manage staff

■ Research and development, to manage the development of new products and services

■ Advertising, to manage the marketing and promotion of the company

■ Shipping and receiving, to manage inventory

■ Quality control, to manage the quality of goods and services

It is important that a business develop only the departments it needs and can afford. The number and type of departments that a company needs depend on the type of company. For example, a restaurant is not likely to need a research department. A hair salon is not likely to need a production department.

Career Profile: Transportation Manager

Transportation, Distribution & Logistics Career Cluster

Job Summary

Transportation managers work in the transportation and warehousing industry, managing the operations involved in picking up, transporting, and delivering goods between manufacturers and consumers.

These managers are responsible for hiring, supervising, and training the various employees who work in the industry including drivers, warehouse workers, maintenance personnel, sales representatives, and administrative support staff. They also handle logistics, such as scheduling, forecasting, and ordering equipment parts and supplies.

Transportation managers require a college degree in an area such as business, marketing, accounting, industrial relations, or economics. Additional courses or training in logistics is also important. Experience with computer information systems is necessary for handling tasks such as scheduling, ordering, and receiving. Transportation managers should pay attention to details, have strong organization skills, and be able to communicate with a diverse work force. Problem-solving skills are essential.

Use the Internet, a library, or a career center to research the responsibilities, education and training requirements, and salary range of a transportation manager. Write a job description or want advertisement for a transportation managerial position.

What interests do you think might lead someone to a career in transportation and logistics?

Analyzing Successful Selling

The goal of a business is to sell its goods or services. Personal selling is a type of promotion, accomplished by using a sales force. A **sales force** is another term for salespeople, or sales representatives. It is the group of employees responsible for contacting customers and arranging the terms of a sale.

Personal selling has a few advantages over other types of promotion.

■ It helps build personal relationships, because the salespeople meet face-to-face with customers.

■ It allows for customized communication, which means the salespeople can customize their message to each potential customer.

Characteristics of Successful Salespeople

A sales person represents the company to the customer. It is likely that a customer will form an opinion about an entire company based on the attitude and behavior of the sales person. It is very important for sales representatives to be professional, well dressed, knowledgeable, ethical, and polite.

Salespeople have various personalities and styles of selling. However, the following characteristics contribute to selling success.

■ Positive attitude

■ Good listening skills

■ Persistence

■ Willingness to work hard

■ Honesty

■ Dependability

The Selling Process

The selling process refers to the steps involved in personal selling. The selling process is used to identify potential customers and to develop long-term relationships with customers. The process is used for selling both goods and services; however, the order of the steps may vary, depending on the item being sold and the selling situation.

Myth You must talk a lot to make a successful sale.

Truth A successful sales representative listens more than he or she talks. Listening provides the opportunity to hear the prospect's thoughts about the product or service, including positive feelings and objections. The sales representative can then deliver an individual, customized response that addresses the prospect's specific needs.

There are five basic steps in the selling process.

■ *Finding and qualifying sales leads.* A **sales lead** is a person or company that has some characteristics of your target market and might become a potential customer, or **prospect**. Salespeople evaluate, or **qualify**, the lead to determine the likelihood that it will become a prospect. That way, they can avoid wasting time pursuing leads that are unlikely to result in a sale.

■ *Preparing for a sales call.* A sales call is direct contact between the sales person and the customer. It is the sales person's opportunity to present the product to the customer. It may be a phone call, a meeting, or an e-mail exchange. To prepare for a sales call, a sales person first sets up an appointment. He or she then spends time learning about the prospect, learning about the product or service to sell, developing a sales strategy, and writing a presentation outline.

■ *Making the sales call.* Keys to a successful sales call include being on time, using effective communication skills to build trust and respect with the customer, asking questions and taking notes, and responding truthfully to all **customer objections**, which are reasons the customer may be wary or unwilling to buy.

■ *Closing a sale.* Closing a sale means obtaining a commitment, which is an agreement from the customer to buy. Technically, the final closing occurs when the customer accepts delivery of the product or service and payment is received.

■ *Following up.* A successful sales person always follows up a sale by contacting the customer to make sure he or she is satisfied. A happy customer leads to a good relationship and additional sales.

How does preparing for a sales call help you succeed and close a sale?

Closing the Deal

Successful selling involves building a relationship with a potential customer so you can identify and address his or her specific needs. What if a prospect refuses to make a commitment while you are on a sales call?

★ You can spend more time researching the prospect to learn more about how your product addresses his or her needs.

★ You can follow up by phone, e-mail, or another sales call to work on developing your relationship.

★ You can invite an associate to accompany you on a second sales call to see if he or she can develop a bond with the prospect.

★ You can re-qualify the lead to determine if the prospect is really a potential customer, or if you are wasting your time.

Can you think of ways you might build a relationship with a potential customer?

Growing Your Business

When a business succeeds, the owner must eventually decide whether to maintain the original strategy or take the steps necessary to grow the business. Most entrepreneurs choose to grow, because it provides new opportunities for achievement and rewards.

Growth must be carefully planned so that the company maintains its level of quality and success. The original business plan may include steps for growth. If not, the plan should be revised, or completely rewritten to develop a strategy for growth. The plan should set goals for growth and outline the steps necessary to achieve the goals. It should also include an analysis of the benefits and drawbacks that might result from growing the company.

Deciding When to Grow

How do you know if your company is ready to grow? One way is to consider the condition of the business. If the business has a solid base of customers and makes sales that meet or exceed forecasts and contribute to a satisfactory net profit, it is ready to grow.

Another factor to consider is the economic climate in which the business operates. Economies tend to follow cycles of upturns and downturns. An entrepreneur must decide if the economic conditions will support growth. If not, it might be necessary to wait for a better time.

Growing a business is very personal for most entrepreneurs. An owner who decides to grow a business takes on new pressures and demands. Growth will require more time and money and introduce new risks. The decision to grow should include an evaluation of your life goals. It is important that you grow the business because it will bring satisfaction and personal rewards.

Growth Strategies

Businesses can follow many growth strategies in order to expand. The strategies typically focus on new products and possible new markets. There are three broad categories of growth strategies.

- *Intensive growth strategy* focuses on cultivating new products or new markets, and sometimes both. It involves efforts to increase market share, reach new target markets, or develop or enhance products.

- *Integrative growth strategy* emphasizes growing by acquiring or merging with an existing business.

- *Diversification growth strategy* involves expanding the business into new areas by adding new products or services.

Challenges of Growth

There are many challenges to growing a business. If the company is going to succeed, it must maintain its current levels of quality and customer satisfaction. Growth will require changing many of the business processes the smaller company relied on. There are also many practical challenges to growing a business. A business plan for growth should address the following areas.

■ Is there enough physical space for the expansion? For example, is there space for additional employees, or for storing more inventory?

■ Will the business structure accommodate growth? Will you need to add departments, or reorganize management?

■ Can you obtain the materials, equipment, supplies, and other items you will need to support growth? Do your suppliers have the ability to provide more than they have in the past?

■ Do you have the information technology systems in place to support the larger business? Do you have the storage capacity, the Web site capabilities, and the computing power you will need?

■ Do you have the personnel you will need? Are your current employees qualified to handle the expansion or will they need training? Can you locate and hire new employees?

■ Do you have enough money? Can you obtain financing? Is your business prepared for the financial risks and obligations that come with growth?

Why might current employees need training during a business expansion?

To Grow or Not To Grow?

Business growth often poses a dilemma for an entrepreneur. On one hand, it provides new challenges and opportunities. On the other hand, it usually requires the owner to give up some personal control over the business. This may be difficult for an entrepreneur who has been the driving force and creative center of the business. Someone who has been primarily responsible for the creation, development, and success of a business may have a hard time letting go of responsibilities and making the changes necessary to ensure continued success. Entrepreneurs must truthfully examine their personal feelings about giving up some control for the chance to grow. Why do you think some entrepreneurs might choose not to grow their business?

Creating a Positive Work Environment

A positive work environment can contribute to a company's success. Happy, satisfied employees are more likely to be loyal and work hard. Customers are more likely to return. Suppliers will be eager to do business.

As a manager or entrepreneur, you can work to establish a positive work environment using a variety of techniques. For example, you can encourage ethical behavior, demonstrate social responsibility, and treat your employees fairly and with respect.

Business Ethics

As an entrepreneur or manager, you set an example for others. You can take steps to ensure that your company has strong **business ethics**—moral principles applied to business issues and actions. There are several ways to develop an ethical business environment.

- Let people see what the company is doing and why. This is called **transparency**, meaning openness and accountability in business decisions and actions.

- Write and distribute a **code of ethics**, which is a document that describes the business's moral values and sets guidelines for behavior.

- Encourage communication. Employees who feel comfortable communicating with managers and co-workers will be more likely to speak up when they observe a potentially unethical situation.

Practical Reasons for Behaving Ethically

✔ *Customers are more confident when they buy goods and services from an ethical company.*

✔ *Employees are proud to work for a company that has high ethical standards, and where they feel they are treated fairly.*

✔ *Ethical behavior can prevent legal problems, which can cost a company money, customers, and reputation.*

Effective Change

Change is a fact of life. Every business will undergo change at some point. Some companies are constantly changing. Change often makes people nervous and uncomfortable. At work, that can lead to a loss of productivity and conflict between managers and employees, and among co-workers. Managing effective change creates a more positive work environment.

Effective change is change that results in positive gains. To achieve effective change, a manager must encourage trust and respect. Communications must be open and honest, and goals must be realistic and attainable. Change will be most effective when employees understand why change is necessary, how it will affect them, and how they can help make the change happen.

Social Responsibility

Corporate social responsibility—when a business acts in ways that balance profit and growth with the good of society—makes good business sense. Not only does it help those in need, it also creates a positive response in the community, which leads to more business and higher profits. There are three areas where a business can focus its responsibility:

■ Individuals, such as employees, customers, suppliers, and investors

■ The environment

■ The community

There are many ways a business can demonstrate social responsibility. It can sponsor a charity event, donate to community causes, allow employees to take time off to volunteer, or offer customers rebates for participating in programs such as using reusable shopping bags.

Fair Treatment of Employees

A business has a responsibility to treat its employees fairly. A business has a legal obligation to ensure the health and safety of its employees. It has a moral obligation to establish a positive working environment that includes paying a fair wage and offering the opportunity for professional advancement. In addition, employees who know they are valued by the company are more productive and less likely to quit.

An employer can motivate employees in many ways. For example, it can offer a flexible work environment that allows employees to work from home—telecommute—or set their own hours—flextime. This can have a significant positive effect on employee satisfaction and performance. Performance-based rewards such as a bonus, extra time off, or even on-site spa services can also demonstrate the company's commitment to its employees.

Providing access to training and professional development helps employees advance in their career and bring new and improved skills to the workplace. Employees also value prompt and fair performance assessments.

An employer can also respect employee trade unions and guilds. That means recognizing that a union or guild provides important benefits for employees, and negotiating with union leaders in good faith.

Experts calculate that replacing an employee can cost a business up to four times the employee's salary. That includes lost productivity, lost customer loyalty, a drop in company morale, as well as the costs of hiring and training a new employee.

Case Study

Luther loves to read. He has accumulated a lot of books over the years. He often lends them or gives them away to other people. One day, his grandmother says that he ought to open a used book shop. Luther thinks that might be a good idea.

Luther researches the market in his community. There is a neighborhood library and a large chain bookstore, but no used book store. He researches the start-up costs. Renting space is expensive. He decides he would like to start a mobile used book store, using a van that he could drive around to different locations.

Luther will need money to buy a used van and to pay for a license from the city. He has a large inventory of used books but needs cash reserves to buy more if necessary. He also wants to spend money to advertise and promote his new business. He thinks that he will be able to get his business started with about $8,500.00.

Luther does not have enough money of his own. He asks his grandmother. She has $4,000.00 she will loan him. She offers to use her credit card to buy the remaining supplies.

- Do you think Luther's plan to start a mobile used book store will succeed? Why or why not?
- What would you say to Luther's grandmother about her decision to invest in Luther's business?
- What challenges and risks are facing Luther and his grandmother? For example, what additional expenses might he encounter?

Web Extra

You can find helpful information about how to manage and organize a business online. Web sites such as the Free Management Library at managementhelp.org and the Small Business Administration at sba.gov provide articles and links on topics ranging from organizational structure to training and development. Use the Internet to explore different sites, and make a directory of the ones you think would be most useful to an entrepreneur.

Answer It!

1. What are the two components of a start-up investment?
2. Explain the term *bootstrapping*.
3. Explain the difference between debt financing and equity financing.
4. What are three drawbacks of using your credit card to finance your start-up investment?
5. What is business management?
6. What are the four functions of a manager?
7. What is the simplest organizational structure?
8. List at least six characteristics of a successful salesperson.
9. What are the five basic steps in the selling process?
10. List three categories of growth strategies.

Career-Ready Practices

As the owner of a business, you are responsible to your employees, your customers, your suppliers, and your community. You are a leader and a role model to many. You are expected to set an example for others. Career-ready individuals use a variety of means to positively impact the direction and actions of a team or organization. They recognize the short-term and long-term effects that management's actions and attitudes can have on productivity, morale, and organizational culture.

Form teams of three or four. Discuss the ways a business owner can create a positive work environment. Consider the importance of a code of ethics, corporate social responsibility, and the fair treatment of employees. Create a "how-to" presentation for a would-be entrepreneur that provides specific examples of how to create a positive work environment. Share it with your classmates.

Write Now

Write a letter to a friend or relative asking to borrow money for start-up financing. Explain the business and summarize your business plan, including the potential risks and rewards. List the amounts you need for start-up expenses and cash reserves, and specify the total amount you want to borrow. Explain when and how you will repay the loan.

Career Portfolio

Create an organizational chart for a start-up business. You may draw the chart by hand, or use charting software such as Microsoft Office Excel. Add the chart to your career portfolio.

Business Plan Project

As the saying goes, "You're only in business, when you've made your first sale." That's why a successful sales strategy must be part of your marketing plan. One component of a marketing plan is analyzing information you collect from your target market that can help you understand what they want and need. Another component is identifying the 5 P's (Price, Product, People, Place, Promotion) you will use to reach potential customers. In your **Business Plan Project**, brainstorm five questions you could ask your customers to gather information. Then, create a table with four columns. Label the columns: **Method**, **Description**, **Target Market**, and **Amount to Spend**. Fill in the table to show the methods you will use to get the word out about your product or service. For example, one method might be distributing flyers and another might be creating a Facebook page.

Financial Management

Part V

In This Part . . .

Chapter 20 ■ **Personal Money Management**

Chapter 21 ■ **Personal Financial Planning**

Chapter 22 ■ **Basic Economics**

Chapter 23 ■ **Basic Business Financial Management**

Chapter 24 ■ **Basic Business Calculations**

20 Personal Money Management

Skills in This Chapter . . .

- **Why We Use Money**
- **Comparing Financial Needs and Wants**
- **Setting Financial Goals**
- **Managing a Budget**
- **Analyzing Your Paycheck**
- **Choosing a Method of Payment**

GETTING STARTED

There are thousands of different jobs out there, but nearly all of them have one thing in common: a paycheck. What you do with that paycheck is an important part of your ongoing success. Reaching your goals—whether that means owning a house, going to college, or seeing the world—depends a great deal on how well you manage your money. That means creating a personal spending plan and sticking to it. It also means being a smart consumer—understanding where your money comes from and where it goes, and making sure you make the most of the money you earn. Any millionaire will tell you that it's not the size of the paycheck that matters; it's how you use it.

➤ On the front of an index card or a piece of paper, write down one item you own. On the back, write the dollar amount that you think it is worth. Walk around and show your classmates the item you own—without revealing its value. If someone has something you want, see if you can make a trade. When the trading is complete, compare the value of the item you gave with the one you received. Did you get a good deal? As a class, discuss what makes a good deal.

Why We Use Money

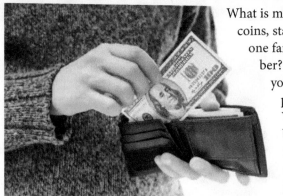

What is money? Is it simply paper or coins, stamped with a picture of someone famous and labeled with a number? What is that dollar bill in your pocket really worth? Is the paper itself worth something? We all know that money can be a powerful thing. It buys us the things that we need and want. But where does its power come from?

Money is anything you exchange for goods or services. In the United States—and most of the world—the money we use is cash. Cash is the money made out of paper—dollar bills—and metal—coins. Money could be made out of anything. Native Americans used shells. Maasai tribes still use cattle. In most countries now, money is made out of paper and metal because these materials are readily available, easy to work with, and convenient for people to carry.

In many countries—including ours—cash money is just one way to pay. We transfer electronic funds between accounts using online banking software or debit cards. We use credit cards to buy something and pay for it later. We write **checks**, which are written orders to a bank to transfer funds from our account to someone else's account. In fact, more and more transactions are done electronically—with no exchange of actual bills or coins involved.

Before money, people **bartered**, or traded, to get things they needed or wanted. If a farmer had a bushel of tomatoes and needed a roll of barbed wire to build a fence, he would trade with someone who had a roll of barbed wire and needed tomatoes. If he couldn't find someone who needed tomatoes and had barbed wire, he wouldn't be able to make the trade. To make the exchange easier, people created money. They assigned a specific value to the money, so everyone knew what they had and what it was worth. The farmer could sell his tomatoes to anyone with money, and then use the money to buy the barbed wire.

What Money Is Worth

The **face value**—or **denomination**—of money is the number printed or stamped on it. If you have a bill in your pocket that has a 5 on it, then its face value is 5 dollars. If you have a coin stamped with 25, then its face value is 25 cents. Face value is determined by the **Federal Reserve**, the government agency responsible for creating and tracking all of the money in the United States. The Federal Reserve decides how many $5.00 bills to print and how many quarters to mint (produce). Obviously, money is worth more to exchange than the paper and metal it is made from. You know what you can get in exchange for the money, because prices are set by people with goods or services to sell.

Money is generally worth more than the paper it is printed on. What is a dollar worth to you?

The real value of money is what it is worth to you. How will *you* spend it? What do you want to get in exchange? The decisions you make about spending your money show what you value.

Different people will spend $5.00 in different ways. Your mother might buy a loaf of bread and a gallon of milk. Your brother might buy a video game. You might download five songs to your smartphone. Your friend might save it, because she wants to buy a sweater that costs $19.99.

The Power to Purchase

We know that money is worth more than the paper or metal it is printed and stamped on. But people who work with money for a living know that money's *power* to buy goods and services changes almost daily. **Purchasing power** is the amount of goods or services that can be purchased with a unit of **currency**, or type of money. For example, in the 1960s, a dollar could buy you five loaves of bread. Nowadays it probably won't even buy you one loaf of bread. Likewise, in the 1950s, it cost two quarters to see a movie. Today the price of admission to the movie theater is more than $10.00.

Purchasing power is tied to the economy and the value of currency. Prices of goods and services rise and fall depending on how well the economy is doing. Historically, prices have risen over time. Thankfully, incomes tend to rise over time as well. For example, the minimum wage in the 1960s was about a dollar an hour. So while our bread may be more expensive than the bread our grandparents bought, we have more dough now to buy it with.

Money Around the World　

In the United States, our currency is the dollar. Other countries have different currencies. For example, Mexico uses the peso and India uses the rupee. Some countries call their currency dollars, but these dollars are not the same as U.S. dollars. For example, Canada, Singapore, Australia, and New Zealand all use dollars.

Each type of currency has a different value, and the values change all the time. Today one U.S. dollar might be worth the same as 48 rupees, but tomorrow it might be worth 50 rupees. European countries formed the European Union (EU) and adopted a standard currency—the Euro—to make it easier for people to travel and trade throughout the region.

Pick another country in the world. Use books or the Internet to learn more about its currency. Be sure to find information about the value of that currency compared to the U.S. dollar. Create a brief presentation about the country's currency and present it to the class.

Do you think your parents or grandparents had an easier or a harder time managing money than you will? Why?

Why Worry About Money?

Some people live "hand-to-mouth," or "paycheck-to-paycheck," which means they spend whatever they earn. These people can have a lot of stress, because they are always worrying about not having enough money. What if you never had to worry about money?

★ You would never have to work.

★ You could buy whatever kind of car you wanted.

★ You could travel the world.

★ You could go to any college or university that accepted you, regardless of cost.

★ You would never have to save for a rainy day.

If you never had to worry about money, would you even need to go to college? Or graduate from high school? What role does money play in how you see your future?

Comparing Financial Needs and Wants

In order to meet your career goals, it helps to understand the difference between your financial needs and wants. Recall that a need is something you can't do without. A want is something you desire but isn't required.

Separating your needs from your wants can be more difficult than it sounds. You may need a car to drive to work, but does that mean you buy a 10-year-old junker, a brand-new fuel-efficient hatchback, or a Ferrari F430 ? Establishing your needs and wants, and learning how to balance the two, is the first step in effectively managing your money.

Establishing Your Needs

Think about what you need to survive. Food, water, and oxygen come to mind. While it's true that these are the absolute basics, your needs actually are much more encompassing. You need a place to live—even if it just means having a roof over your head. You need clothes to keep you warm. Most people need basic utilities such as gas, electricity, and water to cook, clean, and stay warm. While you could go back to the days when you had to dip water from a well, light the house with candles, and cook over an open fire, most people consider a home or apartment with running water, power, and appliances a necessity.

Your **financial needs** and **financial wants** cost money. Your financial needs are the things you must buy in order to survive. Your financial wants are the things you need to maintain a certain **standard of living**. A standard of living measures how comfortable you are based on the things you own.

If you want a standard of living that includes expensive things, such as a big house, fancy car, and designer clothes, then you will spend a lot of money on your wants. If you want a standard of living that includes an apartment, used car, and casual clothes, then you will spend less money on your wants. When you understand the difference between financial needs and wants, you can make responsible choices about what to buy and when to buy it.

Changing Wants and Needs

Financial needs and wants are different depending on your stage of life.

How have your own financial needs and wants changed over time?

- Children and teens can spend the money they have on their wants; their parents pay for their needs. Children want small items such as snacks and toys. Teens might want more expensive items, such as electronic gadgets or special clothes.

- Young adults are responsible for their own needs and wants, though they are not usually responsible for the wants and needs of others.

- Adults are responsible for their own needs and wants, as well as for the needs and wants of their family members. They must use their money to provide for the needs of their spouse, children, and sometimes parents.

As you get older you will not only find that your needs and wants change, but that the financial decisions you make become more and more complicated. This will require you to balance your needs and wants more carefully.

Making Financial Decisions

A **financial decision** is a decision about how to manage your money. A basic financial decision might be what you should buy for lunch. A more complicated financial decision might be how much money to save for college. To make healthy financial decisions, you must consider your financial needs and wants, as well as how much money you have available.

You can use the decision-making process for financial decisions. For example, your bicycle might be broken. How can you decide what to do about it?

1. *Identify the decision to be made.* Do you need a new bicycle? Do you need to have your old bicycle repaired?

2. *Consider all possible options.* You could buy a new bike. You could buy a used bike. You could have your old bike fixed. You could use your brother's bike. You don't need a bike.

3. *Identify the pros and cons of each option.* If you buy a new bike, you will spend a lot of money. You will have less money available for other things. It will cost less to buy a used bike, and less than that to have your old bike fixed. If you have your old bike fixed, it might just break again.

4. *Select the best option.* You decide to have your old bike fixed.

5. *Make and implement a plan of action.* You call a few bike shops to find out what they charge for repairs and how long it will take. You select a shop and take your bike there.

6. *Evaluate the decision, process, and outcome.* Your old bike is working fine now. You are happy that you have a bike. You are happy that you spent some money, but not too much.

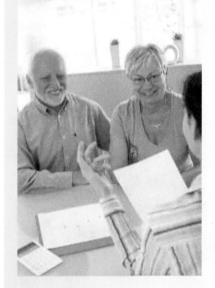

If You Had One Hundred Dollars

People make financial decisions based on how much money they have, what they need, and what they want. What if one hundred dollars was just handed to you?

★ *Would you buy something you need?*

★ *Would you buy something you want?*

★ *Would you save for something more expensive that you might need or want in the future?*

★ *Would you buy something for someone else?*

★ *Would you donate it to charity?*

★ *Would you ask your parent or guardian to invest it?*

How would you spend one hundred dollars?

Not everything you buy will require a thorough six-step decision-making process. Purchasing a bag of chips from the vending matching won't require you to make and implement a detailed plan of action. More-important financial decisions can have long-term consequences, however, expanding or limiting your options for the future. When faced with an important financial decision, consider the following:

■ Do I have enough money to pay for it?

■ Do I need it?

■ Do I need it now?

■ Do I want it?

■ Why do I want it?

■ Are there other things I want more?

■ Is there something less expensive that would be as good?

■ If I buy it, will I have money left over for something else?

Setting Financial Goals

Financial goals are the plans you have for using your money. Financial goals help direct your actions and guide your decision making. They give you something to work toward.

When you set financial goals, you show that you are responsible with money and that you understand the importance of planning for your financial future. There are two main types of financial goals.

■ Spending goals are for buying things you need and want.

■ Saving goals are for saving money for the future.

Setting financial goals helps you focus on how you want to use the money you have available. You can decide what you need and want now, and what you will need and want in the future. Then, you can make and implement an action plan for achieving the goal.

Getting Your Priorities in Order

Your parents or guardians might have told you once that money doesn't grow on trees. You have a certain amount available, and once you use it, it is gone until you earn more. This means that if you pay for one thing, you may not have enough money left to pay for something else.

For example, you might have $4.00 in your pocket. You need $1.50 to pay for the bus home from school. You need $3.50 to buy a snack. What happens if you buy the snack before you pay for the bus? When you set financial priorities, you have guidelines to help you make the best decisions about how to manage your money. Are you going to just buy a cheaper snack to tide you over or are you walking home with a full belly and fifty cents in your pocket? Setting priorities means that you make a decision about which goal is more important, and you make sure you achieve that goal first.

Do you plan to go to college? If so, you might want to think about setting some financial goals now.

Short-Term and Long-Term Financial Goals

You can use both short-term and long-term goals to manage your finances. Recall that short-term goals are for the near future, and long-term goals are for the more distant future. You might set short-term financial goals to make sure you have enough money to go to the movies on Saturday night, or to buy a birthday gift for a friend. You might set long-term financial goals so you can buy a car when you get your driver's license, go to college after high school, or have money in a retirement account.

You might feel overwhelmed by the thought of setting financial goals. You probably don't even have very much money of your own right now. Breaking long-term financial goals into a series of intermediate goals makes it easier.

For example, your goal might be to save $140.00 to buy a new digital music player. That seems like a lot of money all at once, but saving $10.00 each month for a year seems much more realistic.

Why is it so much harder to save money than to spend it? Is there anything you can do to make saving easier?

Avoiding the Impulse

Why do grocery stores keep the candy bars and magazines by the checkout? In general, people buy these things on impulse. Usually impulse purchases are wants (not needs), and often it is a better financial decision to avoid them. Why should you buy something?

👎 Buy something just because someone else has one.

👎 Buy something just because it is on sale.

👎 Buy something just because an advertisement told you to.

👍 Buy something because you need it.

👍 Buy something because you believe it will make you or someone else happy.

👍 Buy something that has value to you.

What is the last thing you bought without thinking? Was it worth it? Do you wish you had made a different decision?

Spending Goals and Saving Goals

When you set financial goals, you will probably think first about what you need or want to buy. These are your spending goals. Most of your spending goals right now are short-term, such as an ice cream on the way home from school or a day at an amusement park. You might have some long-term spending goals, such as expensive clothes or video games. Sometimes in order to meet our spending goals, we have to set saving goals.

It's harder to set saving goals. Saving money is not as much fun as spending. It's also hard to think about what you are going to need and want in the future, and how much those needs and wants might cost. Think about your long-term plans and goals.

- Do you have a vacation to save for?
- Will you need to pay for college?
- Will you want to rent an apartment?
- How much will you spend on a car?

Luckily, you don't always have to be specific about what you are saving for. Your goal might be to buy a car—but you don't have to know exactly which car, or what it will cost. Better yet, you can set a goal to save money without having a specific purpose in mind. Your goal might be to save $5.00 each month, knowing that in the future that money will come in handy. This type of saving goal is open-ended and flexible. It gives you the freedom to know that when you need the money, it will be there.

Managing a Budget

A **budget** is a plan for spending and saving money. It helps you balance your income and expenses so that you can make sure you don't spend more than you have.

When you make a budget, you keep a record of your income, which is the money that comes in to you, and your expenses, which is the money that goes out. The goal is to balance the budget—which means making sure that income is equal to or greater than expenses.

A budget gives you a clear picture of where your money comes from and where it is going. You can use a budget to keep track of the ways you actually use your money, and to set goals and priorities for how you might use your money in the future.

Myth Getting a job with a big salary will make you wealthy for life.

Truth Even movie stars and pro sports players go bankrupt. Wealth is defined by how much money you have accumulated—not how much you earn at work. To be wealthy, you need to save.

Career Tips

The ability to make, analyze, and manage budgets is a valuable skill, and one that is required in many jobs. Of course, accountants, auditors, and business managers have to be budget experts, but almost anyone who is responsible for watching the "bottom line" needs to know something about budgeting. Roofers have to budget for materials and labor costs. Musicians have to budget to cover the cost of equipment and travel. It's an important transferable skill that will come in handy in the future.

What's in a Budget?

Every budget has two main parts: **income** and **expenses**. All the money that comes in to you is income. Income includes the following.

■ Wages and tips you take home from working

■ Gifts you receive for birthdays, holidays, and special occasions

■ An allowance your parents give you on a regular basis

■ Interest that you earn on money in the bank

Expenses are all the ways you use your money. Expenses include the following.

■ Purchases, including needs and wants

■ Savings

■ Charitable donations

You can set up a budget for any length of time, such as a week or a year. Most budgets are set up for a month. A month is convenient because most people pay expenses on a monthly basis, such as rent, phone, and cable bills. They often receive income on a monthly basis, as well.

Do your parents make a budget? Have they ever asked you to give up something because they couldn't afford it?

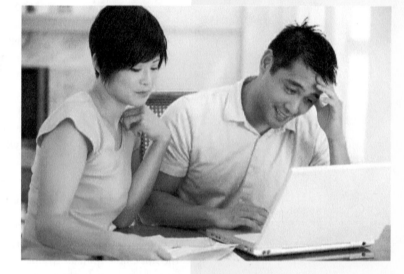

Fixed or Flexible?

In theory, setting up a budget is easy. You list your income in one column and your expenses in another, and then you subtract your expenses from your income.

In practice, setting up a budget is not quite that easy. Some income and expenses are **fixed**, which means you know what they are and have to pay them each month. Others are **flexible** or **variable**, which means they change from month to month.

■ Wages and allowance are fixed income. Gifts and tips are flexible.

■ Rent is a fixed expense. Snacks, clothes, and gasoline are flexible.

You can easily enter your fixed income and expenses in a budget, but what do you do about the flexible items? The answer is to **estimate**. Make your best guess based on past knowledge or facts. If you know you spent $25.00 on snacks each of the past two months, you can estimate that you will spend $25.00 this month, too.

The best way to estimate is to look at records of your past income and expenses. For example, a record of how much money you deposited in the bank after your last birthday will give you a good idea of how much you will receive as birthday gifts this year. Receipts from restaurants will give you a good idea of how much you spent last month eating out.

You can use the estimated amounts when you set up your budget, and then go back and adjust them each month by entering the actual amounts you earned or spent.

Career Trend

Financial records used to only be written in ledgers— notebooks full of debits and credits, numbers and dates. As such they weren't always accessible to everyone in a business all the time. Often only the accountant and the business owner knew how a company was doing. Computers and networking technology make it possible for the most current information to be shared by everyone in an organization. The bottom line: More and more people are responsible for watching their own bottom lines, whether they are accountants or not.

Setting Up a Budget

The best way to set up a budget is to use a table or spreadsheet. That way you can keep your numbers in neat, organized columns and rows. You list categories of income and expenses in one column, actual amounts in the next column, and estimated amounts in the third column.

There are four basic steps for setting up a budget.

1. *List the categories or types of your monthly income.* For example, list wages, allowance, and/or gifts. If you know the amounts, enter them in a column to the right of the category. If you don't know the amount, enter an estimate, or guess, in the third column.

2. *List the categories of your regular expenses.* Include things you spend money on each month, such as transportation to and from school, cell phone service, movies and other entertainment, school supplies, clothing, and food. Don't forget to include a category for saving and one for charity. Also include a "miscellaneous" category that you can use for unexpected or one-time purchases. Again, if you know the actual amounts, go ahead and enter them in the column to the right of the category. If not, enter an estimate.

3. *Balance your budget.* At the end of the month, go back and replace the estimates with the actual amounts that you spent.

4. *Do the math!* Add your total income and your total expenses, then subtract your total expenses from your total income. If the result is zero or more than zero, congratulations! You have a **surplus**, which means you earned more money than you spent. If the result is less than zero, you have a **deficit**, which means you spent more than you earned.

Monthly Budget		
	Actual	**Estimated**
Income		
Wages	$ 150.00	
Allowance	$ 40.00	
Gifts		$ 20.00
Subtotal	**$190.00**	**$ 20.00**
Total Income		**$210.00**
Expenses		
Bus	$ 30.00	
School Supplies		$ 10.00
Food		$ 45.00
Phone	$ 9.99	
Entertainment		$ 25.00
Clothes		$ 25.00
Dues	$ 5.00	
Miscellaneous		$ 50.00
Charity	$ 5.00	
Savings	$ 5.00	
Subtotal	**$ 54.99**	**$155.00**
Total Expenses		**$209.99**

Make Your Budget Work for You

After you set up your budget, you can see exactly how you are spending your money. This might come as a surprise. Did you realize you spent so much money on food and entertainment? Are you shocked by how little you save? To get the most out of your budget, take the time to step back and analyze it. Look at your flexible income and expense categories. Identify areas where you might be able to make changes.

Is it a surplus or a deficit?

What could you do to start spending less and saving more?

- *Reconsider your priorities.* You might see that you spend a lot on clothes, but very little on charity. Maybe you could spend $5.00 a month less on jeans, and donate $5.00 more a month to a good cause.

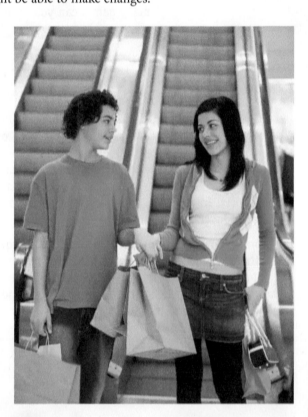

- *Reevaluate your goals.* You might see that you spend a lot of money on the bus. Could you walk to school, or ride your bike? If so, you could save that money. You could then use that savings to meet a long-term financial goal.

Ways to Increase Income

It can be hard for a teen to find income, let alone find a way to earn more. Most states have laws regulating how many hours a teen can work. Many employers don't want to hire anyone younger than 16. What if you want to increase your income?

★ *Could you work more hours?*

★ *Could you ask for a raise?*

★ *Could you find a different job?*

★ *Could you work more than one job?*

★ *Could you ask your parents for a larger allowance?*

One way teens can earn more money is to start their own business. You might be able to mow lawns, babysit, or shovel snow. You might be able to fix computers for your neighbors, or sell jewelry you make yourself. What skills or talents do you have that you could use to start your own business?

Expecting the Unexpected

Remember that miscellaneous category you included in your budget? It's very important. It's the money you use to pay for unexpected expenses, such as when you need to pay your brother back for losing his basketball, or when you go over your allotted cell phone minutes. Unexpected expenses are not covered by the money in one of the regular expense categories. If you leave them out of your budget, you might not be able to pay for them when you need to.

When adults forget to budget for unexpected expenses, they can find themselves in trouble. The car might need a new transmission. A toothache might require oral surgery. If they don't have the money in the budget somewhere, they might be forced to use savings they wanted for something else, or cut back spending in another category, or charge the expense on a credit card to pay for later (with 20% added interest). Sometimes this can lead to even more financial trouble.

Of course, you might decide to use your miscellaneous expense money for something other than an emergency. What could you do with money you budgeted for miscellaneous expenses if you don't use it?

Money Madne$$

Each month you budget $25.00 for your entertainment expenses. This month, you already went to the movies once and rented two video games. Your friends want you to go with them to an arcade where every game is a dollar apiece. If a movie ticket costs $8.50, and the video games cost $2.50 each to rent, how many games can you afford to play at the arcade?

Tech Connect

If you'd like to keep track of your budget on a computer, there are quite a few software options available, such as Quicken®. Such programs not only allow you to track income and expenses. They also help you track investments, make online bank transactions, and create financial reports. In addition, there are several free personal budgeting programs available online.

Of course, if the only income you have is an allowance and you manage less than a hundred dollars a month in expenses, then professional money management software may be more than you need. You might do better to start with a spreadsheet or a blank sheet of paper for now and consider upgrading to a more complex system when your spending habits change.

Staying on Budget

Staying on budget means using your money according to your plan to achieve your financial goals. It doesn't mean you have to earn exactly the amount you entered as income in your budget. It doesn't mean you have to spend exactly the amount you entered as expenses. There's room for flexibility.

For example, you might notice halfway through the month that you already spent the entire amount you budgeted for entertainment. Now, you have choices.

■ Do you stop spending on entertainment?

■ Do you use money you have budgeted for something else to pay for entertainment?

■ If so, which money do you use? Savings? Charity? Food? Miscellaneous?

Of course, if you find that your budget is very different from your actual income and expenses every month, you might want to make some changes. You can evaluate your budget to decide if you need to adjust the amounts. Maybe you were being unrealistic when you set the budget amount for entertainment at $25.00, or maybe you really only need $30.00 a month for food.

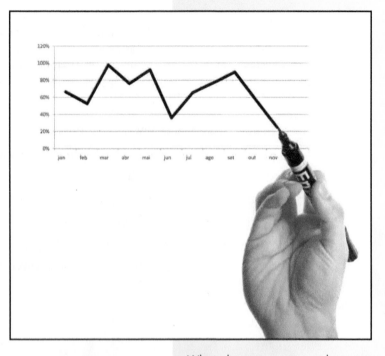

What does a company do when it has a deficit? What kinds of cuts does it make?

Budgeting for the Business Owner

One of the best ways to learn how to use a budget is to start your own business. This can be as simple as setting up a lemonade stand, selling cookies at a sibling's baseball game, or offering to rake leaves around the neighborhood.

Take leaf raking as an example. Suppose you charge $20.00 per yard. That's your income. Now think about your expenses. You will need two rakes ($12.00 each) and bags ($6.00 per box). You will need to make copies of flyers to stuff in neighbors' mailboxes (50 copies at 5 cents each). Also, you hope to enlist the help of your sibling or friend and plan to split your earnings 60/40.

Make a monthly budget that shows your income and expenses. Assuming you can manage to clear two average-size yards per week, how much will *you* make by the end of the first month? What could you do to increase your sales or decrease your expenses?

Running in the Red

If you have a deficit, it means you are spending more money than you are earning every month. In the business world, that's called "running in the red." You might get away with a deficit for a month or two, but eventually you will run out of money. To have enough money to achieve your financial goals, you'll have to eliminate the deficit. That means making tough choices.

Are there expenses you can reduce or eliminate? How much can you save if you did the following:

- Watch free movies instead of going to the theater
- Bring snacks to school instead of buying them
- Shop for clothing, shoes, and accessories at a thrift store instead of buying new
- Drink tap water from a refillable bottle instead of buying bottled water

You might also be able to increase your income. If you have more money to spend, you might be able to cover the expenses the way you have them now, without a deficit.

Career Profile: Financial Planner

**Finance
Career Cluster**

Job Summary

If you think you are good at planning budgets, and you enjoy giving people advice on how to save and spend, you might want to look for a career as a certified financial planner. A financial planner, or personal financial planner, helps people manage their finances by advising them on how to budget, spend, and save.

Certified financial planners must pass a series of certification exams such as those offered by the Certified Financial Planner Board of Standards. Most study financial planning at the college level, as well.

Use the Internet, library, or your school's guidance resources to learn more about a career in financial planning. Write a job description, including the educational requirements, career pathway, and potential salary range.

Analyzing Your Paycheck

Up to now, most of the jobs you have had probably paid you in cash. When you work for a business, however, you receive a **paycheck**. Your paycheck is a written document that tells your employer's bank how much money to give to you. It is your payment for working.

Most paychecks have two parts: the paycheck itself and the **pay stub**. The paycheck is the part you take to the bank to exchange for cash or to transfer funds into your account. The pay stub provides information about your pay, including how much you have earned and how much your employer has deducted from your pay. A **deduction**—which is sometimes called withholding—is an amount that your employer withholds from your earnings to pay for things such as taxes or insurance.

Many employers directly deposit your paycheck in your account instead of giving you a paycheck. Even if you have a direct deposit arrangement, you will receive a pay stub so that you know how much you earned and how much was deducted. It's important to understand the parts of a paycheck so that you know where some of your money goes even before it gets to you.

How You Will Be Paid

You receive a paycheck for every pay period. A pay period is the number of days for which you are being paid. Pay periods are different depending on the employer.

Career Tips

You generally have six months to cash any check you are given. However, you should never wait that long. Whoever paid you, whether it is a paycheck from your employer or a birthday check from a family member, expects you to take that check to the bank. If you hang on to it, you might cause problems with the payer's record keeping. Always cash or deposit your checks in a timely manner.

When Will I Get Paid?

When you are considering a job, one of the things to think about is how often you will get paid. Your employer may pay you:

✔ *Once a week*

✔ *Once every two weeks*

✔ *Once a month*

✔ *Immediately after you complete your work*

✔ *Never—you are a volunteer or intern*

Understanding Your Paycheck

A paycheck looks like a personal check you might write. Most paychecks include the following:

- Your employer's name and address in the upper-left corner
- A check number
- The date of the check
- Your name as the recipient, or payee
- The amount of the check written in numbers and spelled out
- The signature of a person authorized by your employer in the lower-right corner

Your paycheck is just a piece of paper until you deposit it or cash it. You must **endorse**—sign—the back of the check to make it valid. It's a good idea to sign it at the bank, because once you sign it, anyone can cash it or deposit it.

What did you do or what will you do with the money from your first paycheck?

There are two types of endorsements.

- A blank endorsement is when you just sign your name. The check can then be cashed or deposited by anyone, for any purpose.
- A restrictive endorsement is when you sign your name and below it write how the check should be used. For example, you can write "For Deposit Only," if you want the check to be deposited, or you can write "Pay to the Order of Jack Smith" if you want the check to be used by Jack Smith.

If you lose your paycheck, you will have to follow your company's procedure for canceling it and issuing a new one.

Myth I'm too young to pay taxes.

Truth Even teenagers have to pay taxes. Age doesn't matter when it comes to paying taxes. If you receive a paycheck from a company, that company will withhold taxes and Social Security. If you make over a certain amount, you will even have to file an income tax form.

Even money earned babysitting or mowing lawns is potentially taxable. This is considered self-employment income. If you earn more than $400.00 in self-employment income in a year, you are required to report it to the Internal Revenue Service (IRS).

Understanding Your Pay Stub

A pay stub is attached to the paycheck and provides a lot of information about the money you earned. It has no cash value, and you cannot exchange it for money at the bank. Most pay stubs have four sections.

- *Personal information about the employee.* This usually includes the check number and date, the starting and ending dates of the pay period, your name, and your employee number.
- *Information about earnings.* This usually includes the number of hours you worked, your hourly wage, and the amount you are being paid this pay period.
- *Information about deductions.* Employers withhold state and federal taxes, as well as **FICA**, which is Social Security. They may also withhold local taxes. The amount of these deductions is based on a percentage of how much you earn. You might have other deductions such as contributions to a health care plan or to a savings account.

■ *Information summarizing earnings and withholdings.* You usually get this information for the current pay period and the year-to-date (YTD), which is since January 1 of the current year. In this section, you can see your **gross income**, which is your pay before withholdings, and your **net income**, which is your pay after withholdings. Some people call net pay take-home pay, because it is the amount you actually take home.

It is important to look closely at your pay stub to make sure the information is correct, particularly the number of hours worked. If there are any errors, you will have to follow your company's procedure for correcting them.

	Current		M /02
...nings Information	4,389.30		
...mal Gross	0.00		
...uctions	0.00		
...itions	0.00	Year to Date	
...rtime			
EARNINGS TOTAL	4,389.30	5,277.30	
...-Taxable Gross	351.14	418.18	
...able Gross	3,971.12	4,859.12	

...atutory & Other Deductions	Current	Year to Date
...eral Withholding	311.17	311.17
...itional Federal Withholding	0.00	*****
...te Withholding	135.96	135.96
...itional State Withholding	0.00	*****
...DI	0.00	55.06
...icare	62.67	75.55
...icare Buyout	0.00	0.00
...te Disability Insurance	0.00	0.00
	351.14	351.14
	0.00	0.00

What can you learn by looking at your pay stub?

CAREER

COUNSEL

21st Century Learning

Anthony's school counselor suggested he take accelerated classes next year with the hopes of getting advanced placement credit for college. Though Anthony did well in his advanced math classes last year, he also had to study hard. Often when his friends would be out playing soccer, he would be huddled over a mountain of homework.

Taking accelerated classes next year might put him on the college track, but he is afraid of how much more work would be involved. If the classes are too difficult, he might spend all of his time studying and still do poorly. He knows that bad grades, even in tough classes, won't help him get into college. Anthony's parents want him to take the harder classes.

What should Anthony do? Should he take the advanced courses even if it means more work? Or should he take easier classes that he knows he can do well in and have a little more free time? Use your 21st Century Skills, such as decision making, goal setting, and being flexible, to pick a path for Anthony's education. Make up a list of pros and cons for each decision. Form small groups and debate Anthony's options, then come back together and discuss as a class.

Choosing a Method of Payment

You use money to pay for expenses. At the beginning of this chapter, you read that there are many types of money including cash, checks, credit cards, debit cards, and electronic funds. The type of money you use to make a payment depends on many things, including the type of purchase.

■ For a purchase you make in person, you might use cash, a debit card, or a credit card.

■ For a payment you send in the mail, you might use a check.

■ For a payment you make over the phone, you might use a debit card or credit card.

■ For a payment you make over the Internet, you might use a debit card, credit card, or electronic funds.

Other factors include the amount of the purchase and convenience. For example, if something costs a lot of money, you might choose to use a credit card because you can pay for it later. A debit card might be convenient because you do not have to keep going to the bank for more cash.

Each method has benefits and drawbacks. You can use your decision-making skills to consider each option before choosing a method of payment.

Payment Method	Benefits	Drawbacks
Cash	You know you can afford what you are buying.	If you lose it, there is no way to get it back.
Check	Generally safer than cash, especially when mailed.	Often requires identification. Some businesses don't take personal or out-of-town checks.
Debit card	Convenient. Withdraws directly from checking account, so no interest is charged.	Can overdraw checking account.
Credit card	Convenient. Allows you to make purchases even when you don't have enough money available.	Can end up costing a lot more in the long run due to interest charges.

When to Use Cash

Between debit cards, check cards, electronic funds, and credit cards, it almost seems as if no one uses cash anymore. But cash is a good option for most purchases. When you use cash, you know you have enough money to pay for the purchase. You don't have to worry about whether there is enough money in your bank account to cover a check or a debit, or if you will have enough money to pay a credit card bill in the future.

Cash is also universal. Some businesses take only certain credit cards or no cards at all. Some won't take a personal check. Just about everyone takes cash. Cash is useful if you need to buy a drink from a vending machine, pay for a parking meter, or pay a toll. You may also need it to tip for service.

The biggest drawback to using cash is that it can be lost or stolen. You have very little chance of recovering cash once someone else has it. You may also find it inconvenient to keep going to the bank or ATM to withdraw cash so you have it when you need it. And, of course, you cannot make purchases online with cash.

When to Write a Check

When you write a check, you are **authorizing**—giving permission to—your bank to transfer money from your account to the account of the **payee**—the person whose name you write on the check. In order to pay by check, you must have a checking account with a bank, and you must have enough money in the account to cover the amount of the check.

Paying by check can be convenient.

■ You do not have to carry cash.

■ You can send a check through the mail.

■ If a check is lost or stolen, your bank can stop payment, or cancel the check so that it cannot be exchanged for money.

Why is it important to always keep track of your bank balance?

If you use a checking account, it is important to keep the account **balanced**. That means you must keep track of how much money is in your account, as well as the amounts of all the payments you have made. If you make more payments than you have money, your account will be **overdrawn**. Most banks charge a large fee if you overdraw your account.

Checks have other disadvantages that you should be aware of.

■ Banks may charge a fee for every check you write.

■ Not every business accepts checks.

■ Some businesses require a valid photo I.D. with each check.

■ Some businesses will not accept a check from a bank in a different city or state.

■ Checks take time to clear—time for the check to be verified and the bank to make the transfer.

How Will You Be Paying For This?

Look over the following purchases. Which method of payment would you use for each?

- ✔ Downloading music from the Internet
- ✔ Buying a new sweater from a catalog
- ✔ Paying a phone bill by mail
- ✔ Buying a snack at a ball game
- ✔ Purchasing a drink from a vending machine
- ✔ Buying a new computer at a store

Credit and debit cards may look the same, but they don't work the same way. What are the main differences?

When to Use a Debit Card

A **debit card** is just like cash except it is more convenient. You must have a bank account in order to use a debit card, and you must have enough money in the account to cover your purchases. Most cards will be declined if there is not enough money in the account to cover the expense.

When you use a debit card, the money is automatically and immediately transferred out of your bank account, just as if you withdrew it as cash. Most debit cards require you to enter a **personal identification number** (PIN) with each use. By entering the PIN, you prove that you are the person authorized to use the card.

The biggest risk of a debit card is that if someone else gets hold of your debit card and knows your PIN, he or she can use it to access your money. Because they are just like cash, debit cards are accepted for payment almost everywhere you can buy something, including stores, restaurants, and online.

When to Use a Credit Card

A credit card lets you use **credit**—a loan—to buy now and pay later. Every time you use a credit card, you are borrowing money from the business that issued the card, such as the bank, store, or credit card company. The business pays for the purchase, and then you repay the business by paying your credit card bill.

Credit cards may be convenient, because you do not have to have enough money to pay at the time you make the purchase. You can also make a lot of purchases, and then pay them all at once with a single check or electronic fund transfer by paying your credit card bill. However, if you don't pay your credit card bill in full each month, you will be charged interest, usually between 20 and 30 percent on the balance. You can end up spending a lot more than the original purchase price.

Using an Installment Plan

Another payment option—especially for items that you can't afford to pay for upfront—is *installment buying*. With this method of payment, you buy something, such as a car or a piece of furniture, on credit, with a series of future payments to be made at specified intervals. Of course with such a payment plan, you don't actually own the thing you purchased until your last payment is made, and if you fail to make your payments, the seller can take that car or couch back. While most often used with automobiles and major appliances, many stores offer layaway programs that also allow you to pay for items over time.

Using Electronic Funds

You use **electronic fund transfers** (EFT) to transfer money from one bank account to another. To use an EFT, you must have electronic access to your bank account and enough money in your bank account to cover your purchases. There are three common methods of using EFT.

- *A debit card.* When you use your debit card, the money is transferred from your account to the seller.

- *Online banking.* If your bank account is set up for online banking, you can use the bank's online banking software to transfer money from your account to other accounts. You can make the transfer from your home computer or from a bank machine. You can transfer the money to almost any other account, so you can pay bills such as utilities, credit cards, and even taxes.

- *Online payment services.* Many online retailers such as eBay have their own online banking system that you can use to transfer funds electronically. You must set up an account and make sure you have money available to cover your purchases.

Tech Connect

Even now, many people are nervous about using the Internet to transfer funds, make purchases, or pay bills. However, advances in technology have made most online transactions quite safe. The key as a consumer is to know if the Web site you are using is secure.

A secure Web site uses **encryption**—codes—and authentication standards to protect online transaction information. That means your personal information including debit card numbers and PINs are safe when you shop online.

You can tell that you are viewing a secure Web site because the letters https display to the left of the Web site name in the Address bar of your browser. On an unsecured site, there is no "s." Also, a small lock icon displays in your Web browser's status bar. You can double-click the lock icon to display details about the site's security system.

Why do you think it is important to use a secure Web site when you are shopping or banking online?

Is shopping online just as safe as going to the store or the mall?

Dos and Don'ts of Credit Card Use

While credit cards can be convenient, they can also be dangerous. Think about how you will use a credit card once you get one.

- 👎 Paying only the minimum amount each month

- 👎 Charging much more than you can reasonably expect to pay off

- 👎 Paying your credit card bill late

- 👎 Applying for a new credit card when the first has reached its spending limit

- 👍 Choosing credit cards with the lowest interest rates

- 👍 Choosing credit cards with no annual or hidden fees

- 👍 Paying the balance off in full each month

- 👍 Only making purchases that you know you will be able to pay for in the future

Though you may not be old enough to have one yet, it won't be too long before you get your first credit card offer. Do you think you are old enough to use a credit card responsibly?

Alisha received a preapproved credit card in the mail. She started using it right away to buy clothes and jewelry and to take her friends out for lunch. She bought things she didn't need and things she would never use. She bought gifts for her family and friends. She felt rich. When the first bill arrived, Alisha owed $650.00!

At first she thought the bill was wrong, but when she added up everything she had bought, she realized it was correct. Alisha started to panic. She knew she didn't have that much money in her bank account. She did not know what to do.

■ What problems and choices are Alisha facing?

■ Why do you think she spent so much?

■ What do you recommend Alisha do now??

Web Extra

When most teens get their first paycheck, they are shocked at how little they actually get to take home after all of the deductions are taken out. But they might also be surprised to see how much other people have taken from their paychecks.

Use the Internet to learn more about federal income and Social Security taxes. Who pays the most? What does Social Security cover? Why do you think people who earn more pay a higher percent in taxes? Do you think this is fair? Write a paragraph explaining why or why not and share it with your class.

Answer It!

1. **What is money?**
2. **What currency do we use in the United States?**
3. **What is purchasing power?**
4. **List four factors to consider when you make a financial decision.**
5. **What is a budget?**

6. **List three types of income.**
7. **List three types of fixed expenses.**
8. **What is the difference between a deficit and a surplus?**
9. **List three things that are printed on a pay stub.**
10. **List three drawbacks to paying by check.**

Career-Ready Practices

Career-ready individuals take regular action to contribute to their financial well-being. They understand that personal financial security provides the peace of mind they need to pursue their own career success.

Divide into teams of four or five. Spend 10 to 15 minutes thinking of and writing down all the things on which you spend money in a typical week. Be sure to include things you need, things you want, and things you buy on impulse. Write down the amount you spend on each item. Then, for each item, think of an alternative that would either eliminate the expense or reduce it. There may be some items for which there is no alternative, like medications or bus fare. How much could you save? Share your findings with the class.

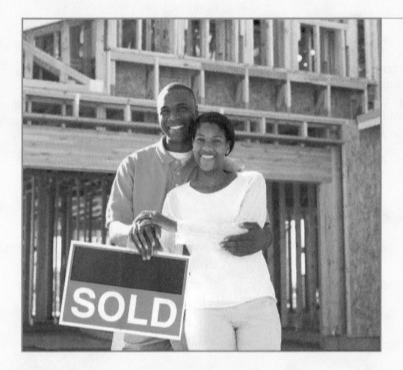

Write Now

Can you imagine how you will be spending money twenty years from now? Will you have an income? What type of lifestyle will you have? What types of expenses will you have? Will you have achieved any of the financial goals you have now? Will you have new goals? Will you have the same needs and wants that you have today? Will you have financial security? How about financial freedom?

Use the questions in the previous paragraph as a guide for writing a personal essay about your future self's personal finances. Share your essay with the class.

Career Portfolio

A career portfolio should showcase your successes. That includes any successes you've had running your own business. Think about all the ways you can earn extra income as a teenager, from babysitting to cleaning gutters to taking care of animals while their owners are away. This is the only kind of employment history many people your age have to draw from. Earning money through self-employment shows that you are motivated, organized, and responsible.

But how do you represent these in your portfolio? First, don't underestimate the kindness of satisfied customers. See if one of your regular customers or clients will write you a letter of recommendation. Or, you could create and print out your own comment cards and have people fill them out. Finally, if you do create a budget for your "business," you should include that as well.

What else could you include in your portfolio to show off your skills and successes if you don't have much work experience?

Business Plan Project

Use a spreadsheet program to create a list of all the expenses you think you will have for your business. Do not include amounts. Categorize the expenses according to whether they are on-going or if they are for the start-up phase only, and sort them based on these two categories. Then, for the on-going expenses, identify whether these are variable or fixed expenses. Include the spreadsheet in your **Business Plan Project**.

21 Personal Financial Planning

Skills in This Chapter . . .

- **Choosing a Bank and a Bank Account**
- **Managing Your Bank Account**
- **Saving and Investing**
- **Analyzing Credit and Debt**
- **Paying Taxes**
- **Keeping Your Personal and Financial Information Safe**
- **Analyzing Banking and Credit Regulations**

GETTING STARTED

When asked, most people will say that they wouldn't mind being rich but that mostly they just want to "live comfortably." What does it mean to live comfortably? For most people, it means knowing they will have enough money to pay their bills and afford most of the things they want in life. It means having financial security. People who are financially secure know how to earn money, save for the future, and avoid debt. They don't worry about money, because they have enough to live a lifestyle that makes them happy.

➤ On a sheet of paper, write down all of the things you would like to own and activities you would like to do when you become an adult. This could include a house, a car, nice clothes, electronics, vacations, and leisure activities. Feel free to dream a little, but try to be realistic (no solid gold mansions or trips to the moon). Next to each item on your list, estimate how much you think it would cost. Ask your teacher for help. When you have finished, add up your costs. Then compare your totals with those of your classmates. Who had the highest total? Who had the lowest? How do people's goals affect their financial planning needs? Discuss your findings as a class.

Choosing a Bank and a Bank Account

A **bank** is a financial institution, which is a fancy way of saying a business that stores and manages money for individuals and other businesses. The bank invests that money or loans it to people and other businesses so that the bank can earn even more money.

There are basically three reasons to put your money in a bank.

1. *To keep it safe.* When your cash is in a bank account, it cannot be lost or stolen.

2. *To earn interest.* For some account types, the bank pays you for using your money. That means you earn money just by having a bank account.

3. *To make financial transactions easier.* Having a bank account makes it easier to cash paychecks, pay bills, and manage your money.

There are many types of banks and bank accounts. Understanding the differences helps you choose the one that is right for you.

> **Myth** The bank will pay a check I wrote even if I don't have enough money in the account.
>
> **Truth** While every bank is different, most banks will send the check back to the payee without paying. Then, the bank charges you an *overdraft fee*—a fee for spending more than you have in your account. It may also charge you a fee for returning the check. The payee may *then* charge you a fee for the returned check and still require you to pay the original amount. Be sure you have the money in your account before writing a check, or you'll end up owing a lot more in the long run.

Currency Exchange

Recall that most countries have their own currency. While some countries will accept U.S. dollars, if you are traveling internationally it is a good idea to have some local currency.

Banks can help you with this. Many banks will exchange your U.S. dollars for other currencies, such as euros, pesos, rupees, and yen, based on current exchange rates. For less commonly asked-for currencies, such as Icelandic kronur or Malaysian ringgits, you may have to go to your bank's central branch. Using the Internet, locate a site that lists exchange rates. See how much the dollar is worth in another currency.

Types of Banks

Do you have a savings account or a debit card? If you do, it's probably at a retail bank. Most of the banks that offer basic banking services to individuals are called **retail banks**. They provide services such as checking and savings accounts, credit cards, education loans, car loans, and home loans—also called **mortgages**. Most retail banks also provide resources for online banking. Commercial banks are like retail banks, except they provide their services to businesses.

Credit unions also offer basic banking services. They are nonprofit banks that are owned by the customers, or members. **Nonprofit** means their goal is not to earn money for the business, but to earn money for the customers. Credit unions are formed by a group of people with something in common, such as employees of the same company or residents of the same town.

If you use the Internet to do all of your banking, you might have an account at an online bank. **Online banks** are retail banks that operate only on the Internet. They do not have buildings where you can go to talk to a banker or make a deposit. You do all of your banking electronically.

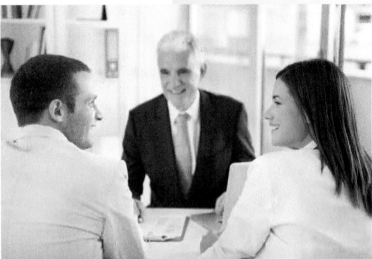

Investment banks help businesses and other organizations raise money by issuing stocks and bonds. They also provide consulting services when one business wants to buy another business.

A **central bank** is an organization responsible for managing the banking activity of a particular country. In the United States, the Federal Reserve is the central bank.

Are all banks the same? Why is it important to compare banks and their services?

Which Bank Is Right for You?

Most communities have several banks to choose from, not to mention all of the options available online. So, how do you decide which bank is best for you? If the bank has a **branch**—local office—nearby, you can go in and talk to the manager to learn more about the bank. You can also look online at a bank's Web site. Consider the following when choosing a bank.

- *Convenience.* You want a bank that is easy to get to and open when you need it. Does the bank have a branch nearby? Is it open in the evenings or on Saturdays? Does it provide free and secure ATM (Automated Teller Machine) service?

- *Services.* Different banks offer different services. Does the bank offer the type of account you need? Are there age limits for getting a debit card or ATM card? Does it offer online banking?

- *Interest rates.* Interest rates vary from bank to bank, and so does the way the bank credits the interest into your account. Does the bank offer the highest interest rate? How does the bank credit the interest? If monthly, the interest is added to your balance at the end of each month. If quarterly, interest is added to your balance at the end of every three months.

Finally, there are fees to consider. All banks charge fees—that's one way they make money. Before you choose a bank, you can compare the fees each bank charges for common services and transactions, including monthly service fees, check fees, and ATM transaction fees.

Some banks waive the monthly service fees if you maintain a minimum balance or sign up for direct deposit of your paycheck. Some allow you to use a certain number of transactions for free each month. Some banks also have low-fee or no-fee accounts for students.

NUMBERS GAME

How much should you save? Many financial experts recommend that you save at least 10% of your income.

To find the percentage of a number:

1. Change the percentage to a decimal by replacing the percent sign with a decimal point and moving the decimal point two spaces to the left.

2. Multiply the decimal by the number. For example, to find 20% of 150:

   20% = .20

   150 × .20 = 30

So imagine you receive $75.00 for your birthday—how much is 10%?

10% = .10

75.00 × .10 = $7.50

What if you wanted to save 15%?

Types of Bank Accounts

Banks keep track of the money you deposit and withdraw by using a bank account. A **bank account** is a record of the transactions between you and the bank. When you *deposit* money, the amount is *added* to your current bank account balance. This is known as a **credit**. When you *withdraw* money, the amount is *subtracted* from the balance. This is known as a **debit**.

The most common types of personal bank accounts are checking accounts and savings accounts.

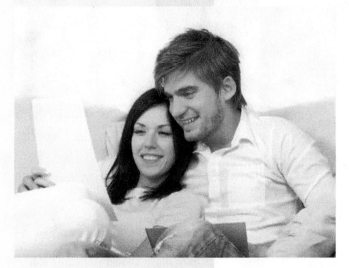

Most banks have several different kinds of accounts. How do you know which one is right for you?

- **Checking accounts** are set up so that you can access your money by writing checks. You can also sometimes use a debit card or automated teller machine (ATM) card. Most people use checking accounts so they can pay for things without carrying cash. For example, you can write a check to pay for groceries or use your debit card to buy movie tickets. You must have enough money in the account to cover all of the checks and debit transactions.

- **Savings accounts** are not linked to checks or debit cards, although you may be able to deposit or withdraw money using an ATM card. Savings accounts earn interest, which means the bank pays you a percentage of your **balance**—the amount of money in the account. That interest is an incentive for you to keep your money at that bank. People use savings accounts to save money for future use.

Of course there are many different kinds of savings and checking accounts, most of which will be discussed later in this chapter.

Career Trend

More and more people are having their paychecks automatically deposited into their bank accounts. People prefer direct deposit because it saves them the time of going to the bank. Businesses prefer it because they don't have to print checks or worry about them getting lost. Banks prefer it because they know that money will come into the account, at least for a short time. In fact, many banks offer incentives or higher interest rates if you agree to have your paycheck automatically deposited.

Opening a Savings Account

You open an account by going to a branch, filling out some forms, and making a deposit. Each bank has different rules, but usually you meet with a manager or assistant manager to show a picture I.D., such as a student I.D., a driver's license, or a passport. You may also need a birth certificate or Social Security card. Then you will do the following.

■ Fill out a signature card that the bank will keep on file. A signature card helps keep your account safe, because it identifies the person authorized to use the account.

■ Make the first deposit into the account when you open it. Some banks have a minimum deposit requirement, so it's a good idea to ask ahead of time how much money you will need.

■ Fill out forms for ordering personalized checks. If you are opening a checking account, you will need to pick out your checks. The cost of the checks is automatically subtracted from your account balance, though some banks offer checks for free.

■ Select personal identification numbers (PIN) for any debit or ATM cards, or for your online banking access, if available.

Using a Checking Account

A check is a piece of paper that tells the bank how much money to take from your account and put in someone else's—the payee's—account. A debit card—sometimes called a check card—authorizes an electronic transfer from your account to someone else's. It is important to keep enough money in the account to cover the amounts of every check or debit transaction you make.

When you open a checking account, the bank sends you personalized checks. Each check has printed information on it, including your personal information such as name and address in the upper-left corner, the check number in the upper-right corner, and your bank information such as the bank name and your account number across the bottom.

Why is it important that you understand all the rules and limitations of the type of account you choose?

What If I'm Not Old Enough?

Some banks have a minimum age requirement for opening certain accounts. For example, you might have to be 16 to open a checking account. What if you aren't old enough to open an account?

★ An adult can co-sign the account, which means he or she will sign the signature card, too.

★ You may be able to open a savings account instead of a checking account.

★ If your parents or guardians have an account at the bank, you may be able to open an account that is linked to theirs.

★ Consider a different bank with different age requirements.

If an adult co-signs on the account, the account will have your name and the adult's name on it—a joint account. You can both make transactions. What are benefits and drawbacks to having a joint account?

Each check also has blanks for you to fill in the following:

A Date

B Amount in words

C Payee

D Your signature

E Amount in numbers

F A memo line for noting what the check is for

Why would you bother writing anything in the memo line?

Write the Right Check!

It is important to fill out a check properly to avoid fraud and so that the bank can process it.

✔ Write neatly so the bank can read it.

✔ Use a pen, not a pencil, so the information cannot be erased and changed.

✔ Do not cross out mistakes.

✔ Remember to fill in all blanks, including the date.

✔ Make sure the numerical dollar amount matches the written dollar amount.

✔ Remember to sign the check in cursive—no printing!

If you make a mistake, tear up the check and write a new one. In your account register, enter the torn-up check as VOID, which means it is not available for use. What are some benefits of paying by check? What are some drawbacks?

Each time you write a check, you should record the transaction details in your **account register**, which is a book the bank provides along with your personalized checks. The register has spaces where you can enter the date, check number, payee, and amount. Then, you subtract the amount from your current balance, so you can see how much money is left in the account.

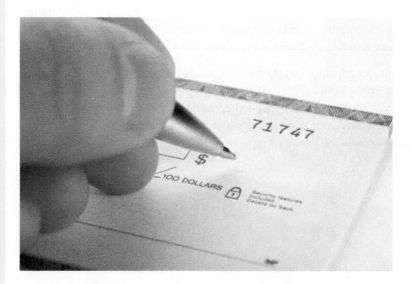

Sometimes people write checks and forget to record them in their registers. What happens then?

Can I Use a Debit Card?

If you have a debit card linked to your checking account, you can use it instead of writing a check. The card comes with your name and account number stamped on it. Some include your picture, too. There is a place on the back for your signature to help protect your identity.

To use the card, you run it through a machine at the store. You then punch in your PIN to authorize the transaction. The money is immediately transferred out of your account. Be sure to record debit transactions in your checking account register the same way you record checks.

Managing Your Bank Account

There are two important parts to managing your bank account:

■ Keeping records of every transaction you make

■ Making sure you and the bank enter each transaction correctly

Managing your bank accounts gives you control over your money. It allows you to make healthy financial decisions and to achieve your financial goals, because you know where your money is and how you are using it.

Recording Transactions

Even with ATMs, debit cards, and electronic transfers, banking still involves a lot of slips of paper. Bank records include canceled checks, bank statements, deposit receipts, ATM receipts, receipts for purchases you make using a check or debit card, and basically every other piece of paper that details a banking transaction.

For example, when you make a deposit into your bank account, you fill out a **deposit slip** with your name, account number, and the amount. When you make a withdrawal, you fill out a **withdrawal slip** with the same information. The teller uses the information to make sure the transaction is processed correctly.

How will keeping your accounts balanced help you reach your financial goals?

After any transaction—deposit, withdrawal, debit card or check purchase—you receive a receipt that shows the transaction details. Keep that receipt! You can use it to make sure the transaction is correct, and then save the receipt to compare to your bank statement. If you ever find an error on your bank statement, you can show the bank your receipt, and the bank can correct the information.

Also, be sure to record every transaction in your register. Do this as soon as possible. If you forget, it will not only make it harder to balance your accounts, it could also cost you more money in overdraft fees.

Ask your parents if you can look at their next bank statement. Are you surprised at how much they spend?

Balancing Your Account

Every month or so, the bank sends you a bank statement, which is a list of all the transactions for your bank account. The statement may come in the mail, the bank may send it via e-mail, or you may be able to access it online.

When you receive your statement, you can compare it to your account register and your transaction receipts to see if your information matches the bank's information. This is called *balancing your account*. If you keep complete and accurate records, you will be able to balance your account correctly with each statement.

The bank statement shows the following information:

■ Starting balance: the amount you had at the beginning of the month

■ Ending balance: the amount you have at the end of the month

■ Deposits and credits added to your balance

■ Withdrawals and fees subtracted from your balance

For checking accounts, the bank statement lists each transaction that has cleared, including the date, check number or debit location and amount, and sometimes the payee. Some banks also send a picture of every check that has been processed or allow you to view them online. Checking account statements usually come once a month.

For savings accounts, the statement also shows the interest that is credited to your account. Savings account statements may come once a month or four times a year (quarterly).

Career Tips

Want to be sure you have enough money in your account before making a purchase? Most banks have a number you can call to check your balance and even make transfers between accounts, or you may be able to look it up online. Sometimes, the bank charges a fee for these services.

Using an ATM

An Automated Teller Machine (ATM) lets you perform bank transactions without going to a branch office and waiting for a teller. You can use an ATM to:

- Deposit cash or checks
- Withdraw cash
- Transfer money from one account to another
- Check your account balance

To use an ATM, you need an ATM card that is linked to your bank account. The card has your name and account information stamped on it. When you apply for the ATM card at the bank, you choose a PIN. Every time you use the card, you must enter your PIN. Then you follow the on-screen instructions to choose a transaction type and your account. Most ATMs have instructions for hearing- and visually-impaired customers.

Remember: You must have enough money in your account to make a withdrawal at an ATM. Be sure to record the transaction in your account register and to adjust the balance by subtracting a withdrawal or adding a deposit. Some banks charge a fee each time you use an ATM, or if you use an ATM owned by a different bank, so subtract any fees from your account balance, too.

What should you consider before withdrawing money from an ATM?

My Account Doesn't Balance!

There are a number of reasons your account might not balance with your bank statement.

- 👎 You forgot to record a transaction you made.
- 👎 You forgot to record an automatic deposit or withdrawal.
- 👎 You forgot to record bank fees or credits.
- 👎 You recorded the incorrect amount.
- 👎 You made a math error adding a deposit or subtracting a withdrawal.
- 👎 The bank made a mistake.

- 👍 You carefully reviewed the bank statement and your records and found that the account does balance.

If the account still doesn't balance after you check it again, take your receipts and the bank statement to the bank and ask a manager or assistant manager to review it with you. If the bank is responsible for the error, they will correct it. What steps can you take to make sure your account will balance with your bank statement?

Money Madne$$

Greg started the month with $200.00 in his checking account. He wrote three checks this month, one for $25.00, one for $18.00 and the other for $15.00. He also withdrew $30.00 from an ATM (no fee was charged) and made a deposit of $120.00. When he got his statement, the bank listed his ending balance at $232.00. But he had calculated his ending balance at $262.00.

Can you explain the difference? Is the bank correct, or is Greg?

Saving and Investing

Saving money is one of the most important steps toward financial security. You put the money someplace safe—such as a bank or a credit union—so that it is available when you need it for an unexpected expense (such as medical bills), a planned expense (such as education), or for retirement. As a bonus, the bank will pay you just for leaving the money in your account. The longer it stays in your account, the more money you will have to spend later.

You might decide to invest some of your savings. Investing is riskier than saving, but it also provides an opportunity to earn more money or to increase your savings at a faster rate.

Saving and investing provide opportunities to increase your wealth, leading to financial security and freedom.

The Difference Between Saving and Investing

When you save, you put money aside on a regular basis. You might deposit it in a savings account, a checking account, or a certificate of deposit (CD). When you invest, you take a portion of your savings and purchase a product such as stocks, bonds, or mutual funds.

Investing is riskier than saving, because the deposit is usually not insured, and your **return on investment (ROI)**—the amount of money you earn compared to the amount of money you invest—is not guaranteed. It is possible that you will lose all of the money you invest. But you have the opportunity to earn more from an investment than from savings.

Most financial experts advise that you use a combination of saving and investing. Saving keeps your money safe and available, and investing gives you the chance to grow your wealth. The amount you save and the amount you invest depend on your financial goals, your financial resources, how old you are, and how much risk you are willing to take.

Children who learn to save at an early age are usually better savers as they get older. When did you first start saving money?

Career Tips

Ninety percent of the best-paying and fastest-growing jobs require some kind of postsecondary education, usually a two- or four-year degree. There are several ways to start saving for a college education. Most states offer college savings plans that are tax-friendly and may even offer rebates. Ask your parents to help you explore your options.

Using Savings Accounts

The safest, most reliable, and most convenient way to save is to deposit your money in a savings account at a retail bank or credit union. The money will earn a small amount of interest and be available when you need it. It is insured by the Federal Deposit Insurance Corporation (FDIC) or the National Credit Union Association (NCUA), so you won't lose the money.

There are three basic types of savings accounts.

■ *Passbook accounts* are the standard type of savings account. They earn a small amount of interest but are flexible, so you can withdraw your money at any time. A passbook account is a good way to get started saving.

■ *Time accounts* are savings accounts that require you to leave the money untouched for a set amount of time—or **term**. Usually, the longer the term, the higher the interest rate. If you withdraw the money before the end of the term, you may have to pay a penalty, or fee. **Certificates of deposit (CDs)** are an example of a time account. Many time accounts have a minimum deposit, often between $500 and $10,000 dollars.

■ *Money market accounts* are accounts that offer a higher interest rate than a passbook savings account. They usually have a minimum balance requirement and may limit the number of times per month that you can withdraw money.

Savings accounts, and any other investment for that matter, earn interest one of two ways. *Simple interest* is calculated based on the principal balance only. *Compounded interest* is calculated based on the principal plus any interest that has already been earned. Of the two, compounded interest is preferable as it results in greater savings over the long run.

Opening a Savings Account

To start saving, simply open a savings account at a retail bank or credit union. There are a few questions you want to ask about any savings account you are considering.

■ What is the interest rate?

■ Is the interest simple or compounded?

■ How often is interest calculated?

■ How often is the interest credited (added) to your account?

■ Are there service fees?

■ Can you withdraw your money at any time?

Why is it important to manage the resources you have available?

NUMBERS GAME

Have you ever heard of "The Rule of 72"? This theory is that to figure out the amount of time required to double an investment at a given compounded interest rate, you just divide the interest rate into 72. For example, if you want to know how long it will take to double your money at 6% interest, divide 6 into 72 and you get 12 years. You can also do the rule backwards to figure out what interest rate you need. So, if you know that you want to double your money in 12 years, you would divide 12 into 72 and then see that you need to invest your money at a 6% interest rate. The rule is very reliable with interest rates less than 20%.

1. How long would it take to double your money at an 8% interest rate?

2. If you want to double your money in 10 years, at what interest rate would you have to invest your money?

Try creating a spreadsheet to make projections using these formulas.

Investment Terms

If you plan to invest, it is important to speak the language of investors.

✔ **Bond:** A debt security issued by corporations, governments, or their agencies, in return for cash investors

✔ **Commodity:** An item such as gold, wheat, or coal that can be traded or sold

✔ **Portfolio:** All of the investments and accounts an investor owns

✔ **Return:** The money received annually from an investment, usually expressed as a percentage

✔ **Stock:** A share of ownership in a corporation

✔ **Risk:** The measurable likelihood of loss or less-than-expected returns

✔ **Security:** An asset that has financial value and that can be traded

✔ **Securities and Exchange Commission (SEC):** The government agency that regulates the securities industry

Does the idea of investing in stocks excite you? What stock would you invest in if you had the money?

Understanding Investments

Once you achieve your savings goals, you may decide to invest a portion of your savings to see if you can earn a higher return on investment. You may not be able to invest on your own until you are 18 years old, but you can ask a parent or other trusted adult to help you set up a joint investment.

Learning as much as possible about an investment before you commit money will go a long way toward minimizing your risk. Still, all investments involve risk, so it is a good idea to invest only as much as you are willing to lose. Here are two basic types of investments.

- **Equity investments**, in which you purchase **stock**—or ownership—in a company. Your ROI depends on the stock price. If the stock goes up—increases in value—you gain. If it goes down—decreases in value—you lose. Stock prices change by the minute, and you do not actually earn any money until you sell your stock.

- **Fixed income investments**, in which you lend money to a business or government agency in exchange for a **bond**. A bond provides fixed interest payments for a set period of time. The business or government agency uses your money for the term of the bond.

Bonds are generally safer than stocks. You are promised a specific rate of return, and most bonds are insured. However, stocks usually provide greater opportunity to earn money.

One way to minimize your risk when investing is to diversify—to purchase a variety of stocks and bonds. One of the easiest ways to diversify is to invest in a mutual fund. A **mutual fund** is a pool of money collected from many—maybe thousands—of investors, and then used to buy stocks, bonds, and other securities.

The success of a mutual fund is not dependent on a single company, the way a stock is. Some of the assets in the fund might decrease in value, but if overall the assets increase in value, then the fund increases in value. This diversity helps minimize your risk over time.

Planning for Retirement

Retirement is the stage of life after you stop working, when you can relax and have time to do things you enjoy. Of course, you still need money to pay for your needs and wants. That's why it is important to start saving for retirement as soon as possible.

While you can use regular savings and investment accounts to save for retirement, there are also some types of accounts designed specifically for retirement savings. Called **tax-deferred savings plans**, they have tax benefits that encourage people to save for the long term. Following are the two most common tax-deferred savings plans.

- An **individual retirement account (IRA)** is a personal savings plan that allows you to set aside money for retirement, usually up to $2,000.00 per year. You do not pay taxes on the money you deposit into the IRA. You can start withdrawing from your IRA when you are 59½ years old.

Do you think it's too early to start planning for retirement?

- A **401(k)** or **403(b)** plan is a savings plan offered by an employer to an employee. The employee contributes a percentage of his or her earnings to the 401(k)/403(b) account each pay period. Some employers then match the contribution. Such plans are considered to be *tax sheltered annuities* because employees are allowed to invest a portion of their paycheck *before* taxes are taken out. Keep in mind that not all companies offer retirement packages. If they do not, then it is up to the employee to start one.

In addition to the saving and investments you make independently, you also contribute to **Social Security**, a government program that pays monthly benefits to retired workers in the United States who paid their Social Security tax. It also pays benefits if you become disabled and cannot work, and to the spouse and children of workers who die before they retire. The benefits are based on the amount of Social Security tax you pay during your working life and the age when you retire.

Social Security provides a welcome income to many retirees, but it is usually not enough to cover living expenses. Experts estimate that if you have average earnings throughout your life, Social Security benefits add up to about 40% of the yearly income you earned while you were working. In addition, many people think the Social Security system is in trouble and may run out of money before all of the people who have been contributing are able to collect benefits. That's why many people save for their own retirement.

Career FACT

Most large companies used to offer *pensions*—a retirement plan wherein employers set aside money to be granted to employees upon retirement. The number of companies offering pensions has declined in recent decades, forcing more workers to contribute to their own retirement. There are still some careers that offer traditional pensions, namely those in public service. Police officers, firefighters, teachers, and judges generally receive pensions, provided they put in the required years of service.

Career Profile: Broker

**Finance
Career Cluster**

Job Summary

A broker, also called a securities and commodities sales agent, buys and sells stocks, bonds, and other products for clients who want to invest in the stock market. They explain the advantages and disadvantages of investments and keep their clients up to date with price quotes and economic changes. Some agents help clients with insurance, tax planning, and estate planning.

Being a broker is a stressful and demanding job. Brokers generally work long hours and are always under pressure to make important financial decisions. The job can also be very rewarding: It's not unusual for brokers to earn more than six figures per year. Most brokers have a bachelor's degree in business or finance.

Use the Internet, library, or your school's guidance resources to learn more about a career in financial planning. Write a job description, including the educational requirements, career pathway, and potential salary range.

What skills and interests do you think would be helpful for someone pursuing a career as a broker?

Analyzing Credit and Debt

Credit is money that you borrow and promise to pay back. **Debt** is the money that you borrowed and now owe. If you owe money, you are a **debtor**. If you loan money, you are a **creditor**.

When you use credit responsibly, it can be very convenient, because you can use it to buy things now and pay for them later. You might use a credit card to pay for a shirt, because you know your grandmother is going to give you money for your birthday next week. When you receive the money, you can pay the credit card bill. When you use credit irresponsibly, you might wind up with so much debt that you can never pay it back. What happens if you buy a shirt that costs more than your grandmother gives you? How will you pay the credit card bill?

Managing credit and debt responsibly shows that you are trustworthy, you understand the difference between needs and wants, and you can make healthy financial decisions.

Getting a Loan

A **loan** is a transaction in which the lender agrees to give the borrower money and expects to be repaid in full. You can get a loan from a bank, business, credit company, insurance company, relative, or friend.

Most loans have **terms** that are written in a contract that both the lender and the borrower sign. For example, you might agree to repay the loan by a certain date, and you might agree to pay a specific rate of interest. A **contract** protects both the lender and the borrower. It spells out all the conditions so everyone involved knows what to expect. Such conditions may include the need for a *cosigner* (someone who is responsible for the loan if you can't pay) or for *collateral* (something you own, such as a house or car, that the lender can take possession of if the loan is not repaid). Generally speaking, borrowing more money than you can repay is not good for your well-being. Your credit history will suffer, you will be unable to get new loans, and personal relationships with the lender will suffer.

At some point, you will want to buy something you can't afford. Where will you get the money?

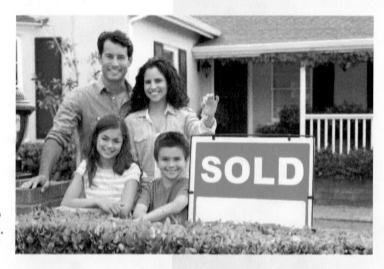

Can I Borrow 20 Bucks?

Borrowing from friends and family can help you achieve certain financial goals. You might be able to get a loan from a relative even if you don't qualify at the bank. But, it's still a loan, and you still have to pay it back. Taking advantage of a friend or relative by ignoring your responsibilities is likely to hurt your relationship.

👎 You skip payments.

👎 You use the money for frivolous wants.

👎 You borrow for something you can afford on your own.

👎 You forget to put the terms in writing.

👍 You make all payments on time and in full until the loan is repaid.

Borrowing from or loaning to a friend or relative can cause conflict in your relationship. How would you feel if you lent your friend money and she never paid you back?

Using a Credit Card

A credit card is useful and convenient. It lets you make a bunch of purchases and then pay for them all at the same time by writing a single check. A credit card can come in handy in an emergency, such as paying for repairs or towing if your car breaks down. If you use it responsibly, it helps you establish credit so you can get loans in the future.

Responsible credit card use means:

- Paying the entire balance by the due date each month
- Only using it to buy items that you can afford
- Using your credit card sometimes, but also using cash, checks, or your debit card
- Having only one or two credit cards in your name
- Saving all receipts and checking your statement carefully for errors each month

While it may be tempting to apply for more than one credit card, there are drawbacks to having too much plastic in your purse or wallet. If lenders believe you have too much credit, they may reject your loan application. You might not be able to borrow money for education or to buy a car.

Having too many cards can cause problems in the future. Why do you think some people have multiple credit cards?

Keep in mind that credit card companies are in business to make money. Each card comes with a set of terms and conditions that states the fees, penalties, and other charges that the company can impose. Common terms and conditions include:

- *Credit limit:* the maximum amount of purchases you can charge to the card
- *Annual percentage rate:* the interest you pay on your outstanding balance
- *Annual fee:* the yearly charge for using credit
- *Grace period:* the length of time from when you make a purchase to when you start accumulating interest
- *Late fee:* the fee charged when you make a payment past the due date
- *Over-limit fee:* the fee you pay when you charge an amount over your credit limit
- *Minimum payment:* a percentage of the outstanding balance that must be paid each month

The only way to avoid paying additional fees and charges is to pay your balance in full and on time every month. If you don't, the fees and charges are added to your balance, which continues to grow, even if you don't make any new purchases. If you only pay the minimum amount required, you will be paying that same bill for many years. In fact, you may never pay it off. This also becomes part of your credit history, and banks, landlords, and even employers will doubt your ability to make responsible decisions and repay loans.

Money Madne$$

Credit card companies charge an annual percentage rate on any outstanding balance. This rate varies tremendously, from as low as 5% to as high as 35%.

Imagine you made $150.00 in charges this month and you are only able to make the minimum payment of $20.00. Your credit card has an interest rate of 22%. How much will your finance charge be? Use a spreadsheet program to calculate what your financing costs will be.

How Do I Establish Credit?

At some point in your life, you will need a loan. You might need an education loan to go to college, an auto loan to buy a car, or a mortgage to buy a house. You might apply for a credit card to use to pay for purchases. You might apply for a small business loan to help start up a new business.

Before a bank or retailer will give you a loan or issue you a credit card, it checks your credit history to find out if you know how to manage money and make healthy financial decisions. Landlords check your credit history before they rent you an apartment. When it comes to small business loans, lenders scrutinize your credit history. No matter how good your business plan is or how brilliant your idea for a new product or service, a bank won't give you the money to get off the ground if you haven't managed your own personal finances well. After all, if you can't pay your own bills, how can they expect you to pay them back?

It takes time to establish credit, but it is worth the effort. There are positive steps for establishing credit.

- Maintaining bank account balances
- Earning a paycheck
- Paying bills on time
- Paying rent
- Using a credit card responsibly

What's a Credit Report?

A **credit report** is a summary of your credit history—usually for the past seven to ten years. If you have a good credit history, lenders will loan you money. If you have a poor credit history, they won't. For example, if you have a few loans and credit cards, and you pay all of your bills on time every month, banks, landlords, and other lenders will believe you are responsible. If you have many credit cards with high outstanding balances, and you regularly miss payments or pay late, the lenders will believe you are irresponsible.

Ways to Protect Your Credit

You can keep your credit safe by making sure your credit information does not get into the hands of an unauthorized person. To keep your credit safe:

✔ Keep a list of your account numbers.

✔ Keep a list of the contact information for your banks and lenders.

✔ Keep your credit, debit, and ATM cards in a safe place.

✔ Report lost or stolen cards immediately.

✔ Do not give your account number to anyone who calls, texts, or e-mails you.

✔ Do not give anyone your PIN.

✔ Shred documents that have your account number on them.

Why is it important to check your credit report every year?

A credit report lists the following.

■ All of the loans you have received, including all credit cards

■ Your outstanding balances—the money you owe

■ Whether you have paid your bills on time

■ The names of agencies or companies who have recently requested copies of your credit report

■ Your credit score, which is a three-digit number that ranks your likelihood of repaying your loans

The information is collected by a credit bureau, or consumer credit reporting company, and sold to banks and other lenders to help them determine whether they should lend you money.

There are three nationwide consumer credit reporting companies in the United States: Equifax, Experian, and TransUnion. By law, you can obtain one copy of your credit report for free, once a year, from each of the three credit bureaus. Looking over your credit report gives you the opportunity to see if there are any mistakes that might hurt your chances of getting a loan. You can also see if any unauthorized people have been trying to get credit in your name. If you find an error, notify the reporting agency immediately.

Managing Debt

Sometimes borrowing money is the easy part; paying it back is more difficult. As long as you make your payments in full and on time, you are managing your debt responsibly. The problems come when debt grows to the point where you do not have enough money to cover your payments as well as your other expenses.

Excessive debt may be caused by irresponsible use of credit cards and loans, but it can also be caused by unexpected expenses such as medical bills. The following tips can help you keep your debt in control.

■ Do not purchase more than you can afford.

■ Set financial goals and stick to them.

■ Pay all of your bills in full and on time every month.

■ Keep accurate records, so you always know how much you have and how much you owe.

■ Use a budget to track and analyze your expenses.

■ Save at least 10 percent of your income every pay period.

Myth All debt is bad.

Truth Some debt is inevitable. Very few people can afford to pay cash for a house, for example. A mortgage is a form of debt that allows you to work towards owning a home. Thus it is also a form of investment. The key is to manage your debt responsibly—not let it get out of hand.

If debt grows to the point that you cannot pay more than the monthly minimum, or maybe not even that, it will affect your well-being. It is not easy, but you can get out of debt.

- Figure out how much you owe.
- Stop using your credit cards.
- Analyze your budget and cut out all nonessential expenses.
- Allocate as much as possible to paying your bills.

If you have spent all of your money and cannot pay any of your bills, you may be faced with bankruptcy. **Bankruptcy** is a process in which you declare yourself legally unable to pay your outstanding debts. A judge approves your request, and most of your debts are cleared so you can start over. Bankruptcy negatively affects your credit history, making it very difficult to get credit again for a long time.

The World Bank

The World Bank is not really a bank at all. It is a part of the United Nations called a specialized agency. It includes two organizations: the International Bank for Reconstruction and Development and the International Development Association. Together, they support efforts to improve the lives of people in developing countries by providing low-interest loans, interest-free credit, and grants (monetary aid given to support a cause). The funds are used in a wide range of areas such as agriculture, water supply, science, and education.

Using resources in your library or on the Internet, research the World Bank and the areas that it supports. Select a project for which it provided a loan or credit and report on it to your class.

Too Much Debt?

In the United States, the number of credit cards in circulation ranks in the hundreds of millions. In fact, most Americans have between 3 and 12 credit cards in their pockets or purses. Unfortunately, the convenience of buying on credit comes with a cost.

★ As a nation, we owe over $850 billion dollars in credit card debt.

★ The average credit card balance per consumer is almost $3,800.

★ The average U.S. college graduate begins his or her career with more than $2,000 in credit card debt.

While most Americans do use credit cards responsibly, it's clear that many struggle to keep their plastic paid off. Do credit cards do more harm than good? Do you think it would be possible to live the lifestyle you want without them?

CAREER COUNSEL

21st Century Learning

Keyshan loves to fix things. He spends many Saturday afternoons working on upgrades to his home computer or helping his dad make repairs around the house. His favorite subjects in school are technology education, art, and computer science, though he is also pretty good at math. He is starting his junior year, which means he needs to think seriously about his future after high school. His grades might be good enough to get into one of the community colleges in town. He's also thinking about forgoing college and going directly to work after graduation, maybe as an apprentice.

Use your 21st Century Skills, such as goal setting, decision making, and critical thinking, to help Keyshan choose a career path that not only meets his interests, but also makes the most of his available resources. Make a list of five or ten options, then rank them from most to least desirable. Compare your rankings to other members of your class. Which option seems to be the best overall? What would you do if you were Keyshan?

Paying Taxes

A **tax** is money we pay the government. The government uses the money to pay for public resources. People complain about taxes all the time, but if we didn't pay them we wouldn't have things such as streets, sidewalks, parks, schools, and libraries. The government wouldn't be able to run programs to help citizens in need, pay for the military, or send astronauts into space.

There are three basic categories of taxes.

- *Income taxes* are based on wages and other earnings.

- *Consumption taxes* are based on things we buy, such as computers or gasoline.

- *Asset taxes* are based on things we already own, such as houses or cars.

You have to keep taxes in mind when making purchases, planning a budget, or setting financial goals. While a 5% sales tax on a candy bar won't have a big impact on your budget, that same sales tax on a $16,000 car would. There are all sorts of rules and measures in place to make sure that we pay our taxes when they are due.

One of the key issues prompting the Revolutionary War and the birth of our nation was unfair taxation. Do you think it's fair for a government to tax its people?

THE BOSTON TEA PARTY

Career FACT

Not everything you buy is taxed. For example, most food that you purchase in a grocery store is tax-free. Also, many states have "tax-free holidays"—usually weekends when you can make purchases without paying sales tax. Research the sales tax laws for various states online. Is there one state where it's cheaper to go shopping than the others?

Where Do Your Tax Dollars Go?

Governments use our tax dollars to pay for public resources. We pay different taxes at different rates according to who is collecting and using the money.

- Some taxes we pay to the federal—national—government. Federal taxes are the same for everyone, no matter where you live. We all pay income tax, Social Security tax, and federal fuel tax for gasoline.

- Some taxes we pay to the state government. State taxes are different depending on where you live. Each state sets its own rates, so one state might have a 5% sales tax, while another state might have an 8% sales tax.

- Some taxes we pay to the local government—the community where we live. Some communities have property taxes. Each community sets its own tax rates.

Often we don't even notice when we are paying taxes. Gas tax is already included in the price per gallon. Property taxes are usually a part of a homeowner's monthly mortgage payment. But it's always important to be aware of how taxes will affect your income and expenses.

Do you ever think about the sales tax when you buy something? Is everything you buy taxed?

Paying Income Tax

Income tax is a percentage of your income that you pay to the government. The federal government collects income tax, and most—but not all—state governments do, too. Income tax is automatically withheld from your paycheck by your employer.

The United States has a *progressive tax system*, which means the more you earn, the more you pay. Income is categorized into levels, called **tax brackets**. If your income falls into the lowest tax bracket, you pay 0%. If it falls in the next tax bracket, you pay 10%. Currently, the highest tax bracket pays 39.6%. The government changes the levels and percentages as necessary to keep up with economic changes, such as salary levels and the cost of living.

Your tax bracket is based on your **taxable income**, which is not the same as your annual salary. To calculate your taxable income, you add up all of your income and then subtract **tax deductions**, which are expenses that you are allowed to deduct from your income, such as contributions to charities and interest you pay on a mortgage. The remainder is your taxable income.

Once you know your tax bracket, you can calculate the amount of actual tax you owe. From that, you may be able to subtract tax credits, which are expenses you are allowed to subtract from your actual tax payment. Some typical tax credits include expenses for college and childcare.

Filing Income Tax Returns

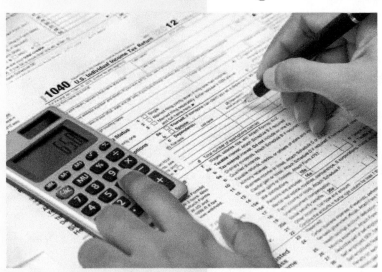

Each year by April 15, you must file income tax returns for the income you earned the previous year. **Income tax returns** are forms on which you calculate the amount of income tax you owe. You file federal tax returns to the **Internal Revenue Service (IRS)**, the agency responsible for collecting federal taxes, and you file state tax returns with your state's revenue department.

Once you calculate the amount you owe based on your tax bracket, you subtract the amount that your employer withheld throughout the year. If it is more than the amount you owe, the government sends you a refund check. If it is less than the amount you owe, you must send the government a check for the difference.

Do you think it would be better if everyone paid the same percent on income tax?

Career

FACT

According to recent data, the top 50% of U.S. taxpayers paid 98% of all income taxes collected, and the bottom half paid only 2%.

What If We Just Stopped Paying?

Some believe that without taxes we wouldn't have any government-funded programs. For example, what if people decided not to pay their local taxes? There would be no:

★ *Teachers and schools*

★ *Firefighters*

★ *Police officers*

★ *Trash collection and recycling*

★ *Street plowing and cleaning*

★ *Municipal parks*

Now think about what your community could be like if people were able to pay ten times the amount in local taxes that they do now.

Tech Connect

The days of taxpayers poring over reams of paper with W-2 forms flying and paper cuts galore are fading. More and more people are using software to file their taxes. Programs such as TurboTax® not only do the calculations for you, they also walk you through the process, helping you to find important deductions and exemptions that can save you money. In addition, tax returns computed and filed electronically usually have fewer errors, which is better for the taxpayer and the IRS alike.

In fact, the number of people filing their taxes online is up to 99 million and growing. To learn more about how to file your tax return online, go to irs.gov/Filing. Read about all of the options available to individual taxpayers. Then make a list of the pros and cons of filing your taxes using each method. If possible, prepare a sample EZ income tax form and 1040A income tax form both manually and electronically. Present your findings to the class.

Keeping Your Personal and Financial Information Safe

When was the last time you gave out personal information? Personal information includes your name, address, phone number, and e-mail address. It also includes your birth date, Social Security number (SSN)—the number assigned to you by the U.S. government to track your income and employment history—bank and credit card account numbers, and medical and insurance records. Protecting yourself from identity theft and fraud means protecting all of that information.

Identity theft occurs when someone steals your personal information and uses it to commit fraud. The thief might open new charge accounts, rent an apartment, make purchases, and take out loans. He might get a job using your Social Security number, or apply for a driver's license or passport. She might obtain medical care using your insurance information. The **Federal Trade Commission (FTC)**—the government agency responsible for protecting consumers—estimates that as many as 9 million Americans have their identities stolen each year.

Keeping your personal and financial information safe is an important part of financial responsibility.

Protect Your Records

Identity thieves will do almost anything to get their hands on your personal, financial, and medical records. They'll go through your trash, bribe clerks, and peek over your shoulder when you use your computer. It is important to keep track of these documents and make sure they are stored safely.

What types of documents should you secure?

- Personal records such as a birth certificate and Social Security card
- Medical records showing when you had immunizations
- School records showing what school you attend, report cards and standardized tests results, and your student identification.
- Financial records such as bank statements, credit and debit card numbers, and loan information
- Copies of tax returns, pay stubs, and insurance records
- Driver's license, marriage certificate, and passport

You can keep these items in a safe, or in a **safe deposit box**, which is a box in a fireproof vault that you can rent from your bank. The information will be safe from thieves, and you will know where to find it when you need it.

Do you have anything that you value highly, such as a diary or a journal or important papers? Where do you keep important items?

Who Is Responsible?

You cannot assume the banks, lenders, and regulatory agencies are always going to know what is going on with your accounts. You have to take responsibility as a consumer. What if you notice an unauthorized charge on your credit card statement?

★ Notify the credit card company by phone and in writing immediately.

★ Check your other statements to see if there are any other unauthorized charges.

★ Check your credit report to see if there are any signs of fraud.

★ Pay the undisputed charges in full and on time.

What would you do if you found an error on your credit report? Who would you contact if you felt a credit card company was treating you unfairly?

Protect Your Wallet

Think about the items you carry in your purse or wallet: cash, credit and debit cards, insurance card, driver's license or student I.D., cell phone, receipts, and keys. What could a thief do with all of that?

If you lose your wallet or purse, you should immediately take steps to protect your identity and your finances. If your wallet or purse is missing:

■ File a report with the police immediately and keep a copy.

■ Report the loss to the fraud department at your bank and other financial institutions.

■ Cancel your credit, debit, and ATM cards immediately.

■ Apply for new cards with new account numbers.

■ Call the fraud departments of the three major credit reporting agencies and ask each agency to put out a fraud alert on your accounts. A fraud alert is like a red flag on your accounts that shows your information may be in the hands of an unauthorized person.

■ Review your credit reports regularly and have them corrected when necessary.

■ Report a missing driver's license to your state's department of motor vehicles.

■ Change the locks on your home and car if your keys are missing.

■ Notify your cell phone service provider that your phone is missing.

Protect Yourself Online

It is certainly true that the Internet has made information more accessible. Unfortunately, it has also made your personal information easier to get as well. Experts believe that the wired world has led to the dramatic increase in identity theft over the last decade. **Phishing** is a scam designed to steal your personal and financial information over the Internet. Criminals use e-mail messages and fake Web sites to trick you into entering the information, which they can sell or use themselves.

What steps can you take to make sure your identity is safe, even online?

You can protect yourself by being wary.

■ Never reply to an e-mail message, text message, or pop-up browser window that asks for your personal information, even if the message looks as if it comes from a bank or credit card company you use.

■ Never call a phone number included in an e-mail message or text to contact your bank or credit card company. Use the phone number on the back of your account statements or credit card.

■ Keep your antivirus and antispyware software up to date, and use a firewall.

■ Keep your e-mail and online account passwords in a safe place and change them often. Don't use the same password for every account.

Analyzing Banking and Credit Regulations

The federal and state governments have passed many laws and regulations designed to protect you and your money. They have set up agencies such as the **FDIC—Federal Deposit Insurance Corporation**—to provide insurance for your deposits, and the **FTC—Federal Trade Commission**—to make sure businesses treat you fairly. They allow you to report problems, such as lenders that discriminate based on your race, and to ask questions, such as "What's my credit score?"

Regulating Banks

Banks must be chartered to operate in the United States. A **bank charter** is an agreement that controls how the bank operates. The agency that charters the bank is responsible for making sure the bank follows all rules and regulations. Each state has a regulatory agency responsible for regulating state-chartered banks. In addition, three federal agencies regulate banks:

- The Office of the Comptroller of the Currency (OCC) (occ.treas.gov)
- The Federal Reserve Board (federalreserve.gov)
- The Federal Deposit Insurance Corporation (FDIC) (fdic.gov)

All of these agencies have consumer protection departments. You can contact them with questions or problems at any time.

Protecting Credit

Consumer credit laws are designed to help consumers and creditors meet their legal responsibilities. Some federal acts regulating credit include:

- *The Fair Credit Reporting Act.* This act is enforced by the Federal Trade Commission (FTC). It promotes accuracy and ensures privacy of the information used in consumer reports such as your credit report.
- *The Equal Credit Opportunity Act.* This act protects you from discrimination by creditors for any reason other than your creditworthiness. Creditors cannot ask your race, sex, country of origin, religion, or age.
- *The Fair Credit Billing Act.* This act sets rules for when credit card bills are mailed and payments are credited, as well as procedures for settling billing errors.
- *Truth in Lending Act.* This law is designed to make sure you have all of the information you need to make a healthy decision about borrowing money. It lists the information that a creditor must disclose before lending you money. This is also called the *Consumer Credit Protection Act.*
- *The Credit Card Act of 2009.* This act restricts credit card issuers from raising interest rates without warning and charging excessive fees for late payments. It also set the minimum age for obtaining a credit card to 21.

Myth Deposits in all savings and investments account are insured by the federal government.

Truth Investment accounts are not insured by the government the way savings accounts are.

However, the **Securities and Exchange Commission (SEC)** is a government agency responsible for supervising and regulating companies to protect investors. The SEC monitors companies to make sure they provide investors with accurate and timely information. The SEC gives consumers rights to sue if the information is incomplete or inaccurate.

Case Study

Maggie has been putting money in a savings account for five years to help pay for college. She has $2,200.00. The savings account earns about 1.2% interest. She thinks she has enough saved now that she might be able to earn more interest if she puts the money in a different type of account, or invests it.

The bank manager recommends putting $1,500.00 in a CD for 12 months at 2.5% interest. Maggie is considering the CD, when her older brother offers to set up a stock trading account online for her. He recommends buying shares of the company where he works. The current stock price is $10.00 per share, so she has enough money to buy at least 200 shares, as well as pay the fees. He tells her the stock will go up; then she'll be able to sell and make a nice profit.

- What options does Maggie have?
- What are the pros and cons of each choice?
- What information does she need to make the best choice?
- What should Maggie do?

Web Extra

Many government Web sites provide consumers with information about finances and other money issues. Some, such as www.USA.gov, has a section specifically for teens.

Use the Internet to locate useful government Web sites, and make a directory of the sites. Include a brief description of the information available on the site. Post the directory on your school Web site, or make it available in your school library.

Answer It!

1. What are the three basic reasons for putting your money in a bank?
2. What is the main difference between a retail bank and a credit union?
3. Explain which is riskier, saving or investing.
4. What are the advantages of investing in a mutual fund?
5. What is the difference between credit and debt?

6. List three positive steps for establishing credit.
7. How often are you allowed to check your credit report for free?
8. By what date each year do you have to file your income tax return?
9. What government agency is responsible for protecting investors?
10. What is the purpose of consumer credit laws?

Career-Ready Practices

Divide into teams of four or five and play a version of the Stock Market Game. Each team will have the same amount of money to invest. Research different companies online and select those in which you want to invest. Consider mutual funds or other types of investments. Decide what you want to buy, and commit to your investments. Make sure you employ valid and reliable research strategies. Evaluate the sources from which you gather information about your investment choices. Delegate duties and tasks so that each member of your team is involved and makes a positive contribution.

Keep records of your purchases, including the purchase price, the number of shares, and any fees you have to pay. You may want to set up a spreadsheet to track your investments. Follow your portfolio for at least one week by checking the stock prices online. At the end of the week, sell everything. The team that has the greatest profit wins.

Discuss your experience as a class. How did you pick your investments? How did you assess your risk? Did you make smart choices? Could you have done anything?

Write Now

According to the Credit Card Act of 2009, you must be 21 to obtain a credit card. Do you think that's fair? Is there another age that makes more sense?

Write an opinion essay about the topic. State your thesis, and then support it with facts. The essay should be at least four paragraphs in length, including an introduction and conclusion. Read your essay to the class and discuss it.

Career Portfolio

A career portfolio is a treasure-trove of personal information. It often includes names, addresses, phone numbers, work history, transcripts, grade reports, and identification numbers. While you are encouraged to make a digital version of your portfolio, you also need to be aware of how you will make it available and to whom. For example, if you choose to post your portfolio online, is there a chance that someone could use the information in the files for fraudulent purposes? Are there ways you can limit access to your online portfolio or at least restrict the kinds of personal information you include with it?

A number of Web sites allow you to create an online portfolio or e-portfolio and store it on a secure server (try visualcv.com for starters—or check with your school to see if they have their own service). You can then restrict who can access the portfolio by sending them an e-mail or requiring a password. In addition, your school may have a secure place on their Web site for creating, storing, and posting your digital portfolio.

Explore your options for posting your portfolio online. Report your findings to the class.

Business Plan Project

Review the list of on-going expenses you created in Chapter 20. Map out the time to create one unit, if you are making anything or providing a service. Think about what you are selling and define your unit of sale. Picking one can help you keep track of your projections. Enter this in a new row in your spreadsheet. Identifying the unit of sale can help you keep track of your projections. Use a spreadsheet program to create an Economics of One Unit table, such as the one shown at right. Fill in the table. Set a price by doubling your variable expenses. Is this a price customers would pay? Is it competitive? Answer these questions in your **Business Plan Project**. Enter the table in your **Business Plan Project**. Refer to Appendix B to make sure you are on track.

Name of Business:	Unit of Sale:
Selling Price	
Cost of Goods Sold per unit	
Other Variable Expenses (commission)	
Total Variable Expenses	
Contribution Margin/unit	

Skills in This Chapter . . .

- **What Is Economics?**
- **Analyzing Supply and Demand**
- **Analyzing Economic Systems**
- **Taking Part in a Global Economy**

GETTING STARTED

Do you have *everything* you want? Do you have enough time to do all of the activities you'd like? Are there times when you wish you had an extra hour to study for an exam or an extra $10.00 for a movie? Economics is the study of choices. Economists—those who study and apply economic theory—understand that resources are limited, and that every day people, businesses, and governments have to make important decisions in order to make the best use of those resources. The laws and principles that govern those decisions and that predict their results form the basis of economics. Understanding the basic principles of economics can help you not only to choose your best career path, but also to understand why you make the choices you do in the first place.

➤ Make a list of all of the classes you are taking and the grades you are currently earning in each. Now imagine you can raise each grade by a full letter for only a dollar. For example, $2.00 could raise a grade of C to an A. Now imagine that you have only $3.00 to spend on your grades. How would you spend it? What grades would you change? Or would you save your money to spend on another report card? How did you make these decisions? What if in order to raise one grade, you had to lower another? Would you do it?

417

What Is Economics?

When most people think about economics, they think about money. But to an economist, money is just one of many tools that people, businesses, and governments use to make producing and distributing goods and services easier. Economists are more interested in how limited resources can be used to produce all the goods and services that people want and need.

All countries have to answer three major economic questions.

- What goods and services will be produced?
- How will those goods and services be produced?
- For whom will those goods and services be produced?

Economics is the study of how people produce, distribute, and use goods and services. An economic system is a country's way of using limited resources to provide those goods and services.

What? How? For whom? If you were going to start your own business, how would you answer these questions?

Analyzing Scarcity

Scarcity is one of the most important principles of economics. It means that there is never enough of everything to satisfy everyone completely. Money doesn't grow on trees, and there's never enough time in the day.

Every day, you are faced with the economic principle of scarcity. Have you ever stood in front of a vending machine with only a dollar to spend and debated between two equally desirable options? Because your resources were limited (were scarce), you were forced to make a choice.

Scarcity isn't limited to the amount of money you have to buy things. All resources are limited to some degree. Think about the time you have in the evenings during the week. You could spend that time in a number of ways. Some of them you probably *should* do.

- Do your homework
- Brush your teeth
- Straighten your room
- Take a shower

Others you simply *want* to do.

- Watch television
- Play video games
- Check e-mail
- Call a friend
- Play outside
- Ride your bike
- Go shopping
- Read for pleasure
- Spend time with your family

Your time is a limited resource. How do you choose to spend it from day to day?

Your time is a scarce resource. You have to decide how best to use that resource to maximize your return—that is, to make you happiest. You could argue that spending an hour in front of the television will make you happier than doing your homework, but you might not feel that way when you go to school the next day.

In the same way, economists are concerned with how people and societies use their resources to maximize—increase as much as possible—their happiness or satisfaction. They call this measure of happiness or satisfaction utility. Things that make you happy have high **utility**, and things that don't have low utility. The goal of both economists and people in general is to find the best way to allocate—distribute—limited resources in order to generate the most utility.

Every Choice Comes at a Cost

For economists, every choice you make comes at a cost. Without enough resources to satisfy every want, we have to make choices. **Opportunity cost** is the next best choice that you give up in order to do something else.

- Choosing to play soccer after school at the cost of giving up piano lessons
- Choosing to buy a new outfit at the cost of going out to dinner
- Choosing to volunteer in your community instead of hanging around with friends

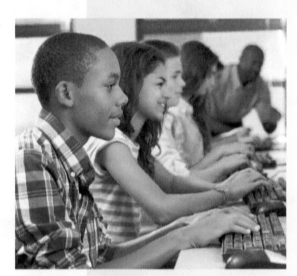

Now think about these choices on a larger scale. Each year, the government prepares a budget. The government's resources are limited, so government officials debate what they should spend tax dollars on. Often this becomes an either/or situation. Build more schools or hire more police officers? Increase funding for cancer research, the space program, or the arts? We could do *all* of these things, but *that* might require raising taxes. The trade-off for more government spending is less money in the pockets of consumers.

Imagine your school got a $50,000 improvement grant. How would you want the school to spend that money?

As you get older, the choices you make often have higher and higher opportunity costs.

- Do you buy a car or save for college?
- Do you rent an apartment or purchase a house?
- Do you go on vacation or save for retirement?

Even your career choices have opportunity costs. College students must choose a major or program of study. Choosing a major opens up many career opportunities, but it likely eliminates far more. Choosing to study business probably means you won't be a nurse or an engineer.

Career Profile: Forensic Science Technician

Law, Public Safety, Corrections and Security Career Cluster

Job Summary

Forensic science technicians investigate crimes by collecting and analyzing physical evidence—everything from a bullet to a fingerprint to a lock of hair. They use recording, measuring, and testing equipment to help police detectives and other law personnel catch criminals. They are also often asked to testify as expert witnesses during criminal trials. Forensic science technicians work primarily for state and local governments. A 2-year degree is usually the minimum requirement for these jobs, though 4-year degrees are becoming more and more common.

Use the Internet, library, or your school's guidance resources to learn more about a career as a forensic science technician. Write a job description, including the educational requirements, career pathway, and potential salary range.

What skills do you think you would need in order to be a forensic science technician?

Thinking About Resources

Remember that all of the things we want to buy and do—those goods and services—can't be produced without resources. Also remember that those resources are limited. Economics breaks resources down into three categories.

■ *Land.* This category includes all natural resources, including forests, minerals, and water.

■ *Labor.* This category represents the workers who make the goods and provide the services.

■ *Capital.* These are the goods that are used in production, such as factories, tools, and computers.

Economists are also concerned with how easily a resource can be replaced. A *renewable* resource is one that can be used again and again. Solar and wind power are renewable resources. A *nonrenewable* resource cannot be replaced. Coal and oil are examples of nonrenewable resources.

Economists, environmentalists, and other scientists are concerned about our dependence on nonrenewable resources. Not only do many nonrenewable resources contribute to pollution (such as the oil used to produce gasoline), but we are using them at faster and faster rates. Eventually, these resources will run out, and we will have to find or create new resources to replace them.

Career Trend

Today's businesses are concerned about sustainability. Sustainable economic development does not harm society or the environment and tries to preserve natural resources for future generations. More and more companies are recognizing that green business is good business.

Some resources are replaced each time they are used up. How many examples of renewable resources can you think of?

Resource Management

Sometimes individuals and businesses use resources inefficiently or rely too heavily on one kind of resource.

👎 Increased dependence on coal and oil as a source of power

👎 Deforestation (chopping down trees faster than they can be replanted)

👎 Overfishing (reducing fish populations faster than they can reproduce)

👍 Recycling (finding ways to reuse materials)

👍 Developing new fuel sources (such as creating ethanol from corn)

👍 Exploring alternative energy sources (wind, solar, and nuclear energy)

Can you think of other business practices that positively or negatively impact global resources?

Producers and Consumers

What do companies do to convince you to buy their products?

Another way to look at the economy is as a relationship between producers and consumers. **Producers** are the companies or individuals who make or provide goods and services. The people who purchase and use those goods and services are **consumers**.

Are you a producer? Maybe. If you babysit, mow lawns, or make items such as jewelry for sale, you are a producer. Are you a consumer? Definitely. When you buy a pair of jeans, download a song, go to a movie, or buy a snack, you are acting as a consumer.

Producers and consumers depend on each other for survival. You depend on the grocer to sell you food. And the grocer depends on you to buy it. In fact, companies spend millions of dollars in market research to try to figure out what people just like you want and need. They also spend millions trying to convince you that you want or need what they have.

A Smart Consumer

You have a responsibility as a consumer to be a smart shopper.

✔ *Shop around. Read the sales advertisements, check out your options online, and wait for the things you want to come down in price. Also research brands, prices, and options using consumer resources such as Consumer Reports and other product review magazines and Web sites.*

✔ *Consider used or second-hand items. Previously owned clothes, CDs, and video games can often be purchased at much lower prices.*

✔ *Pay more for better quality. A $50.00 pair of shoes that will last four years is a better investment than a $20.00 pair that will last only one year.*

Measuring the Economy

Individuals, businesses, and governments count on economists to tell them how strong the economy is and where it is headed. The condition of the economy is important to everybody. It affects how much things cost, how much people earn, and how many jobs are available.

Economists use a variety of mathematical tools and equations, often called **indicators**, to measure the health of the economy. For example, the total value of all goods and services produced in a country is called the **gross domestic product (GDP)**. Economists believe that by comparing GDP of the current year to years past, they can get a good sense of whether the economy is growing, and by how much.

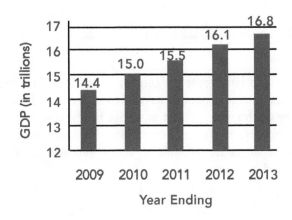

What might an economist learn about the economy from this chart?

Economists also use the **consumer price index (CPI)** to measure changes in the prices of goods and services. For example, the CPI shows whether milk, cars, or houses are more or less expensive from month to month. When the average price of goods goes up sharply, it's called **inflation**.

Economists also watch unemployment carefully. When the **unemployment rate** is high, more people are out of work. Fewer people earning a paycheck usually means fewer people spending, which can lead to a slower economy. When statistics show unemployment to be rising, investments falling, and GDP decreasing over a long period of time, it often indicates an economic downturn, or **recession**.

Career FACT

Prices of goods and services generally rise over time. In response most companies try to provide what's called a "cost of living" raise—an annual increase in wages to account for those rising costs.

Money Madne$$

Due to inflation affecting the cost of fuel and maintenance, the bus company announced it is raising its prices by 9% this year. If you paid $35.49 for a ticket to visit your cousins last summer, how much will the ticket cost this summer?

What can a government do to positively impact the quality of life of its citizens?

No World Standard

Economists are primarily concerned with people's standard of living—their quality of life based on what they can afford. Here in the United States, we enjoy one of the highest standards of living in the world. The United States enjoys relatively high earnings; decent access to education, health care, and other public services; and a relatively low poverty rate. However, not all countries enjoy the same quality of life. Many countries suffer from hunger and poverty, high unemployment, and high inflation.

Use the Internet to research the standard of living in a country of your choice. Be sure to look at important economic factors such as average income, unemployment, and poverty rates. Compare that country to the United States. Are we better or worse off? What can be done to improve the standard of living in any country?

Analyzing Supply and Demand

Businesses provide goods and services because consumers will pay money for them. Businesses typically want to get the most money possible for the goods and services they offer. Consumers typically want to pay the least amount of money possible for what they buy. These two opposing forces actually work together to create a price that everyone is satisfied with.

Supply is the quantity of goods and services a business is willing to sell at a specific price and a specific time. **Demand** is the quantity of goods and services consumers are willing to buy at a specific price and a specific time. As you can see, both price and timing are important when considering supply and demand.

Can you think of times when the supply of something is always greater than the demand or vice versa?

The Law of Supply and Demand

Imagine you are a potato farmer in Idaho. This year, the weather conditions were just right and you had a bumper crop—more potatoes than expected. So did every other potato farmer in the region. Now the country has twice as many potatoes as it usually does. Let's assume that the demand for potatoes is the same this year as it was last year. Now you and the other potato farmers have too many potatoes on your hands. What will you do to convince consumers to eat more potatoes? Most likely, you will lower the price.

Supply and demand have a direct impact on the price of goods and services.

■ When the supply is greater than the demand, the price goes down.

■ When the demand is greater than the supply, the price goes up.

Think about lawnmowers. In the spring, demand for lawnmowers is usually high, so the price is also high. As winter approaches, demand for lawnmowers drops sharply in regions of the country where it snows in winter and prices fall.

Meeting in the Middle

In a market economy, the price of a particular good or service is determined by supply and demand. Suppliers decide what quantity of a good or service they are willing to sell at a particular price. Consumers decide how much they are willing to pay for a good or service. Most of the time, the two meet in the middle.

▪ A **surplus** exists when the quantity supplied is greater than the demand.

▪ A **shortage** exists when the quantity supplied can't meet demand.

Maybe you remember when Nintendo first introduced its Wii™ gaming system. Production problems and a poor forecast of how popular it would be led to a supply problem. Demand was so great that some people were paying twice the suggested retail price to get their hands on one, and the company was forced to tell hundreds of would-be purchasers that they wouldn't be getting a Wii for Christmas. To avoid having a surplus or a shortage, businesses try to establish an **equilibrium**. They try to find the ideal quantity *and* price so that they can meet demand and maximize profits.

Visualizing Supply and Demand

Look at the figure below. This is a *supply curve*. It shows the quantity of a product or service a supplier is willing to sell across a range of prices. As you can see, the supplier is willing to provide more product as the price increases.

SUPPLY CURVE

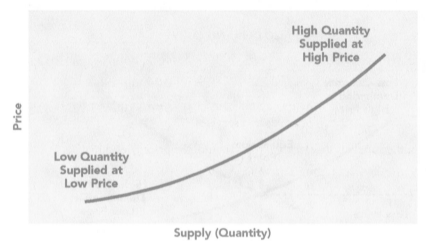

High Quantity Supplied at High Price

Low Quantity Supplied at Low Price

Price

Supply (Quantity)

NUMBERS GAME

Imagine you are making custom t-shirts to celebrate your school's homecoming. Use graph paper and the following supply and demand data to draw a supply and demand curve and find the equilibrium point. Along the horizontal (x-axis) list the quantities from 10 to 100. Along the vertical (y-axis) list the prices from $5 to $25. Plot the supply possibilities listed and draw a line connecting them. Then plot the five demand possibilities listed and draw a line connecting them. Use the example graphs in this chapter as a guide. Where do the two lines meet?

How many t-shirts should you produce? What price should you charge for each shirt? Why?

Supply				
Quantity	20	40	60	80	100
Price	$5	$10	$15	$20	$25

Demand			
Quantity	100	70	40	10
Price	$10	$15	$20	$25

Why are businesses willing to provide more goods at higher prices?

Now look at following figure. This is a *demand curve*. It shows the quantity that consumers are willing to buy across a range of prices. In contrast to the demand curve, here the consumer is willing to buy more as the price decreases.

DEMAND CURVE

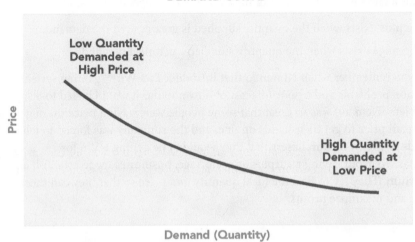

Why does the demand curve slope in the opposite direction as a supply curve?

Put the two together and you have a *supply and demand curve* (see below). This shows the relationship between price and quantity. The *equilibrium point* is where the supply curve and the demand curve meet. This is the point at which supply and demand are balanced. It also represents the quantity that a business should produce of a given item (the *equilibrium quantity*) and how much the business should charge for it (the *equilibrium price*).

SUPPLY AND DEMAND CURVE

Why would businesses or consumers want to reach the equilibrium point?

Entrepreneurial Thinking on Supply and Demand

As an entrepreneur, you have two ways to think about demand. You can try to sell a product in *high* demand, either because no such product is available or because competing businesses can't keep up with consumer wants and needs.

Or, you can try to meet demand *better*. Just because the demand for a good or service is being met already doesn't mean that customers are fully satisfied. Improved quality, better or faster service, lower prices—there are lots of ways to convince consumers to choose your business over others. You haven't increased demand for *the* product—you've just increased demand for *your* product.

Think of a product or service you buy regularly. What could you do to improve it? How could you convince consumers to buy your version over your competitor's version?

Analyzing Economic Systems

There are two basic types of economic systems: the command economy and the market economy.

In a **command economy**, the government owns or manages the nation's resources and businesses. The government controls what suppliers produce, how much is produced, and how it is produced. The government also regulates how goods and services are distributed throughout the country and at what prices.

In a **market economy**, suppliers produce whatever goods and services they wish and set prices based on what consumers are willing to pay.

In reality, no country has a pure command economy or a pure market economy. This leads to a third type of economic system, a *mixed economy*, one that blends elements of the command economy and the market economy. Most economies lean heavily one way or the other, however.

Career FACT

In a free market economy, businesses are owned by individuals, not the government. The cash and goods a business owns are often called its *capital*. That's why the market economy or free enterprise system is sometimes referred to as *capitalism*.

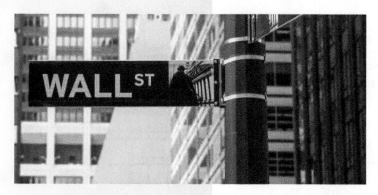

In a free market economy, people can invest their money however they want to. If you had one thousand dollars, how would you invest it?

In command economies, the government has strict control over social and economic affairs. China, Saudi Arabia, Syria, Iran, Cuba, and North Korea are said to have command economies. In these countries, government planners usually make economic decisions and long-term plans for the nation. The government controls most resources and businesses.

In a market economy, the government does not tell businesses what to produce or tell consumers what to buy. In this system, individuals have freedom of choice. The United States, Australia, Canada, and most Western European countries have market economies.

The Free Enterprise System

Another name for a market economy is **free enterprise system**. In a free enterprise system, individuals or businesses operate with little government interference. People are free to become entrepreneurs and to own and operate a business. Individuals can invest money however they please.

In general, free enterprise systems share the same five characteristics.

- *Private property.* Individuals are free to own as much property as they can afford. Property includes cars, houses, factories, and other goods.
- *Freedom of choice.* Workers choose the work they will do, businesses choose what they will sell, and consumers choose what they will buy.
- *Voluntary exchange.* Individuals are free to trade anything they want for something they value more.
- *Economic incentive.* Money, more specifically profit, provides the incentive for the economy to grow and produce more.
- *Competition.* Individuals and businesses are free to compete with each other for resources and consumer demand.

Under a free enterprise system, you are free to start or work for any business you'd like (as long as it's legal), and spend your paycheck any way you please (after taxes).

Of course, the government does have some *role* in all free market systems. The United States has one of the freest market economies in the world. Suppliers and consumers largely determine which goods and services are offered for sale and at what prices. However, the U.S. government still regulates businesses, enforces labor and product safety laws, and imposes taxes. For example, the Federal Trade Commission watches out for unfair trade practices among corporations, and the Consumer Product Safety Commission issues recalls on unsafe products. The government also makes policy decisions that can have a direct impact on interest rates, inflation, unemployment, and other economic factors.

Myth Capitalism promotes greed.

Truth Companies are interested in making a profit. Often this means making much more money than they *need*. This self-interest forces those companies to hire talented workers, produce goods cheaper and faster, reduce prices to encourage consumers to spend money, and constantly invest in research and development. However, when the quest for profits leads to unsafe or illegal business practices or endangers people's livelihood or the environment, then it goes too far. Luckily the government has systems in place to keep such motives in check.

The Role of Competition

In a free enterprise economy, *competition* is a driving force. Suppliers often offer similar products or services. WalMart, Target, and Sears all compete for your retail dollars. Movie studios carefully plan their releases to compete directly with another studio's title or to avoid competing with a potential blockbuster.

Consumers also compete against each other to be successful. The best-paying, most secure, or most high-status jobs aren't available to everyone. To get such a job, you will probably need to get the right education, work hard, and save money.

Competition has many benefits.

■ Competition between businesses can result in bigger and better selection, lower prices, and better service.

■ Competition between businesses encourages innovation—introducing new items or methods—and variety by forcing employees to work smarter and harder.

■ Competition between individuals can lead to higher earnings as businesses compete for talented workers.

To see competition in action, all you need to do is turn on the television and wait for a commercial. When is the last time you saw a commercial asking you to compare the product being advertised with the "leading brand"? Did you know what brand the commercial was referring to? While advertisers don't always say it, every advertisement is designed to compete for your hard-earned money.

Like any kind of competition, economic competition forces those behind the leader to work harder to catch up. What do you compete for?

If a business has no competition, then it controls all of the supply and demand for the product or service it sells. Such a business is called a **monopoly**. Monopolies can charge the highest possible price that consumers are willing to spend. The government attempts to make sure there is fair competition among businesses through anti-trust laws. Such laws are designed to prevent monopolies and other challenges to competition such as price fixing. This is especially important for entrepreneurs looking to start a new business as it gives them room to compete.

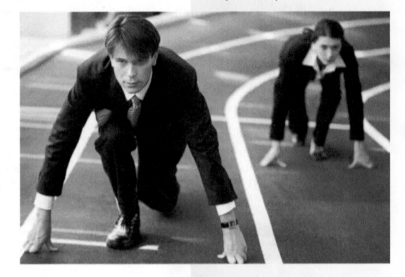

The Role of Profit

Businesses provide goods and services in an effort to satisfy consumers' demands. Profit is a business's reward for succeeding in this effort.

In very simple terms, a business makes a **profit** when the amount of money coming in from sales is greater than the business's expenses. Businesses can then save that profit, spend it, invest it, or donate it to worthy causes. If a business is unsuccessful, it will make no profit, and it is likely to fail.

Profit is a strong incentive in a market economy. Starting a business is a risky thing to do. The opportunity to earn a profit encourages entrepreneurs to accept those risks. New businesses lead to new jobs. That leads to more paychecks, which leads to more spending, which leads to greater profits, and so on.

Money Madne$$

Profit is the money left over after expenses have been paid. Shonda's Special Sunday Afternoon Lemonade sells for $1.00 a glass. The lemonade mix costs $3.20 per can and will make an estimated 8 glasses of lemonade. The cups she uses cost $4.00 for a package of 50. In addition, Shonda floats a slice of lemon in each glass. Lemons go for $1.20 a piece and yield 8 slices each. Assuming that she doesn't have to pay for water and that the lemonade stand and other equipment are free to use, how much profit does Shonda make on each glass of lemonade she sells?

Career Tips

As a consumer and a worker, you have a direct impact on how the economy operates. Understanding how the U.S. economic system works can help you to make important career decisions, such as whether or not to go to college, what fields will be growing in the future, and what jobs will be moved to other countries.

Taking Part in a Global Economy

The English poet John Donne once wrote, "No man is an island, entire of itself." The same can be said of nations—even if they really are islands—or at least their economies.

Globalization is the term commonly used for the growing integration of the world's economies. As economies become more dependent on each other, they are able to grow faster and learn more, making the most of other countries' economic strengths.

What does it mean to have a global economy?

Nations are becoming more open to each other by removing political, social, and economic barriers. As a result, U.S. companies frequently partner with foreign companies to gain access to the larger world market. Businesses market globally, investing in the economies of other countries all across the world.

Take McDonald's®, for example, a company whose golden arches are one of the enduring symbols of the American economy. The company operates 34,500 restaurants in 118 different countries worldwide. To create a global presence, they even adapt their menu to cater to different eating preferences around the world. At an Indian McDonald's, you can order lamb burgers with veggie nuggets. In Japan, you can get a teriyaki burger and a green-tea shake.

Planning for your career means learning how to take your place in the global economy. It means reevaluating your options to take advantage of some of the opportunities globalization makes possible. It also means understanding how this smaller world will lead to more competition from abroad. As a citizen of the world, you are not just competing with millions of workers for the best jobs and opportunities. You are competing with billions.

Is Globalization a Good Thing?

Not everyone agrees that globalization is a positive thing. In fact, many believe that the costs outweigh the potential benefits. Some of the benefits of globalization include the following.

■ *Increased trade.* Countries are expanding their trade, whether it's money, goods, services, information, or labor. Look at your clothes, shoes, wallet, watch, or digital music player. Where was it made? What company designed it? Where was it shipped from?

■ *Increased prosperity.* Developing countries especially benefit from globalization. According to the World Bank, over the last 20 years, more than 200 million people in the world have risen above the poverty level. Countries such as China and India have become world economic powers, nearly doubling their average income per person in recent years.

Living Within Your Means

It's estimated that 80% of the world lives on less than $10.00 a day. What if you had only $10.00 a day for all your needs?

★ What would you eat?

★ What would you wear?

★ How would you get around?

★ Where would you live?

★ What would you do to entertain yourself?

★ How would you pay for your education?

Could you survive on $10.00 a day? Would you be happy?

Countries such as India and China are becoming world economic super powers. Is this good or bad for the United States?

■ *Increased cultural exchange.* By increasing trade and opening borders, we not only provide for the free exchange of goods and services, but also of ideas, cultural practices, art, and beliefs. This can ultimately lead to a more accepting and peaceful world culture.

Globalization presents the following problems as well.

■ *Increased interdependence.* Problems with one country's economy can have a dramatic impact on the whole world. This was apparent with the housing market collapse in the United States in 2008. While initially a national problem, the effects of the recession that followed were felt throughout the world.

■ *Loss of jobs.* Globalization has led to an increase in **offshoring**—hiring people in other countries to do certain jobs. Thanks to new technology and a wired world, workers in India, China, and other countries are capable of providing more cheaply the same work that used to be done in the United States.

Career Tips

If you can, take advantage of any opportunities to travel abroad. International travel not only exposes you to different cultures, it also shows employers and college recruiters that you are open to new experiences. Class trips, foreign exchange programs, and other opportunities for traveling abroad can broaden your horizons as well as your career options.

International Trade

Globalization may be a relatively recent term, but the basic forces driving it are ancient. Whether it's Marco Polo's 24-year-long visit to China or Columbus's attempt to find a trade route to the Indies, countries have always looked to expand their economic influence by trading with other countries.

Most international trade consists of exports and imports.

■ **Exports** are goods or services that are sent from one country and sold to foreign consumers. Common U.S. exports include wheat, corn, pharmaceuticals, paper, steel, and the latest Hollywood movies.

■ **Imports** are goods and services that are brought into a country from foreign suppliers. Common U.S. imports include oil, coffee, bananas, automobiles, and electronics.

Even in a free global market there are limits. Most nations put restrictions on imports for two reasons.

■ They want to give their domestic businesses—those that produce their goods and services *within* the country—a competitive advantage over foreign ones selling the same product or service. If there is a comparative advantage, we are better off as a country if our citizens buy a car produced in the United States rather than one produced in, say, Italy. The money spent on the American-made car goes back into American businesses and goes to pay American workers' salaries.

■ They want to protect their consumers from foreign goods that might be unsafe or of poor quality. For example, foreign countries may not have the same safety or health inspections as those that are common in this country.

To help control trade, governments use trade barriers. A **trade barrier** is a governmental restriction on international trade. The most common trade barriers are tariffs and quotas on imports.

Why would one country want to limit the products it imports from another country?

■ A **tariff** is a fee, similar to a tax, that importers must pay on goods they import.

■ A **quota** is a limit on the quantity of a product that can be imported into a country.

Countries use tariffs and quotas to give their domestic businesses the best possible chance to meet demand within the country.

CAREER

COUNSEL

21st Century Learning

Marcia's uncle owns a fruit stand. Every week he must dispose of unsold fruit before it becomes rotten. Marcia and her friend Celia offer to buy the fruit before it spoils for a low price. They set up a fruit smoothie cart at an indoor flea market on weekends. Because they get a good price on the fruit, they can charge less than other smoothie stands and still earn a profit. They believe it is a win-win situation: Marcia's uncle benefits because he earns some money where before he earned none. Consumers benefit because they can buy inexpensive smoothies. Marcia and Celia benefit because they have a business that earns a profit.

Marcia's uncle sees that they are successful and decides to start selling fruit smoothies at his fruit stand. He tells the girls he cannot sell them the fruit anymore, because he is going to use it himself. The girls try to find another source of inexpensive fruit, but they cannot. Marcia and Celia don't know what to do. They don't want to close their business, but they don't know how they can continue to offer smoothies at a price customers will pay and earn a profit.

Use your 21st Century Skills such as decision making, problem solving, and critical thinking to help the girls determine what they should do next. Write an ending to the story and read it to your class, or work with a group of classmates to present it as a skit.

Technology and the Global Economy

In Chapter 11, you learned how advances in technology have changed the way businesses operate. Those same advances in technology provide much of the driving force behind globalization as well.

Advancements in shipping, travel, and telecommunications permit much more international trade than in the past. Goods can circle the world in a matter of days. Airlines have added more foreign destinations to their routes, allowing goods and businesspeople greater access to international trading. Satellite and broadband communications connect suppliers and consumers around the world.

The Internet, in particular, has made international trade easier, faster, and more convenient than ever before. Through the Internet, you can order a kimono directly from a dressmaker in Japan and have it delivered to your door 72 hours later.

Advances in telecommunications and computer technology have made it possible for people to work together from anywhere in the world. Have you ever worked on a project with someone you have never met in person?

Technology also makes it easier for companies to employ people from all over the world. The ability to telecommute allows workers from different countries to come together to complete a project. While this means more U.S. companies are outsourcing work to qualified foreigners, it also means other countries are turning to U.S. workers for their knowledge and expertise.

Myth The United States is the richest nation in the world.

Truth Studies of countries with the greatest stability and prosperity often rank several countries above the United States, including Singapore, Luxembourg, Norway, and Qatar. While these studies are limited and open to interpretation, they do prompt the question: What does it mean to be prosperous?

Think Globally, Act Locally

The phrase, "Think globally, act locally" can have different meanings depending on context. For those concerned with the environment, it means that everyone should consider how their daily actions impact the health of the Earth and the world as a whole. In business, it means that multinational corporations must be willing to build local roots and relationships and adapt to the cultures and customs of each country's people. Visit your library or use the Internet to research how business is conducted in a country that interests you. How does it differ from the way business is done in the United States?

Respecting Other Cultures

Culture includes a people's language, beliefs, attitudes, customs, manners, and habits. Obviously, a nation can include people of many different cultures; however, many people within a country often share general characteristics.

In addition, businesspeople in most societies follow particular social rules and customs called **etiquette**. For example, if you are at lunch as part of a business trip in China, cultural courtesy says that you don't discuss business.

Of course, as you learned in earlier chapters, being successful at work and in your career means building relationships and learning to communicate with people from a wide variety of backgrounds. That means avoiding stereotypes and being sensitive to others' needs. But it also means recognizing the specific talents and abilities of the people around you, no matter where they are from. Doing so will make others more open to seeing the abilities and talents you possess as well.

Do all cultures and nationalities have the same basic social customs?

Becoming a Citizen of the World

Over 2,500 years ago, the philosopher Socrates wrote, "I am not an Athenian or a Greek, but a citizen of the world." Socrates' known world was much smaller than our own, which only makes being a world citizen an even loftier goal now than before. How can you become a citizen of the world?

✔ Learn about other countries and cultures.

✔ Take an interest in local, national, and international news.

✔ Learn a second language, or even a third.

✔ Understand the far-reaching impact your actions can have on others and the environment.

✔ Speak out against racism, bias, and intolerance.

✔ Take an active part in your own community.

✔ Learn about the histories of other nations and civilizations.

✔ Take advantage of any opportunity to travel.

✔ Use the Internet to make friendships across national borders.

Case Study

Michael's parents have a small store where they print and sell custom clothing, such as T-shirts and baseball caps. Michael works at the store after school and on weekends. He runs the printing machine and sometimes develops new designs. His parents pay him a commission on sales of items he designs himself.

One day Michael sees a picture of a basketball player in a magazine. The player has a tattoo that looks like a Chinese character on his arm. Michael likes the look of it and incorporates it into a design for a T-shirt. He hangs samples in the store window, hoping to attract attention. Unfortunately, he does. It turns out the character is actually a word that Chinese people consider insulting and offensive. They write letters to local newspapers about it and organize a boycott of the store. Some young people rush to buy the shirts before Michael's parents insist he stops printing them, but overall, business suffers.

■ Do you think Michael did anything wrong? If so, what?

■ What were the consequences of Michael's actions?

■ What steps can Michael take to solve the problems he has created?

Web Extra

Economic statistics can be overwhelming and even mystifying to those without specialized training. The U.S. Bureau of Labor Statistics offers a quick and easy Web site for checking on the health of the U.S. Economy. Called Economy at a Glance (bls.gov/eag), it shows the most important economic data at the national and state level, as well as for major metropolitan areas.

Use the above Web site or one like it to research how well the economy is doing in your state or city. Be sure to research important economic factors such as unemployment rates and average earnings. Write a brief (one to two paragraphs) synopsis of your findings and share it with the class.

Answer It!

1. What are the three economic questions every country has to answer?

2. Give two examples of both renewable and nonrenewable resources.

3. What indicators do economists measure to see how well an economy is doing?

4. How is standard of living defined?

5. What happens to prices when demand is greater than supply?

6. What is the equilibrium price?

7. What are the differences between a command economy and a market economy?

8. Identify the five characteristics of a free market economy.

9. What are two benefits of competition in an economic system?

10. List one possible drawback of globalization.

Career-Ready Practices

With your teacher's permission, create a mini-economy in your classroom. Divide into teams of three or four. Decide as a team on one kind of snack you will purchase and then resell. Decide how you will price it, and market it. Your goal is to make a profit while delivering a quality product. Career-ready individuals realize that the decisions they make—no matter how minor they might seem—have an impact on others. For example, if you have a quality product that you price lower in order to beat the competition, you may run out and your customers will go elsewhere to shop. Create advertisements to post in the room. Begin marketing your snack at the start of the week. Then, on Friday, have every student bring in exactly $1.00 to spend in the "free market." Students will have five minutes to spend their dollar. Tell each student that they must buy at least one thing, but they are not required to spend the whole dollar.

When the market closes, have each team add up their total earnings and subtract their expenses. Did your team make a profit? Did you have a surplus? Were you able to meet demand? What did you learn about consumer preferences? What did you learn about marketing? How did you make your own decision as an individual consumer, and was it different from the decisions you made as a group? Discuss your experience as a class..

Write Now

How would your life be different if the United States switched to a command economic system? Could you accept limitations? Would you be willing to if the government promised to eliminate poverty? Write a four paragraph response paper answering the questions above. Be sure to include an introduction, a thesis, and a conclusion. Alternatively, compose a series of three diary entries wherein you imagine yourself as an adult in a command economic system. Share those entries with the class.

Career Portfolio

College recruiters and employers alike appreciate applicants who are able to live and work in a multicultural environment. It helps if you can showcase your ability to get along with people from diverse backgrounds. That includes being able to speak more than one language, having experience working in a multicultural environment, forming relationships with people in other countries, or traveling internationally.

Be sure to include any evidence of these skills and activities in your portfolio. Perhaps include an essay written in a second-language or excerpts from a travel journal kept during your visit to another country. Or, you could research a country you might like to live or work in one day and create a fact sheet about that country including why you would like to spend time there. Remember that one goal of your portfolio is to show how well-rounded you are. It doesn't hurt to be worldly as well.

Business Plan Project

For an entrepreneur, an income statement is similar to a personal budget. It shows the business the total sales minus all expenses, and, most importantly, the net profit. Use a spreadsheet program to create and fill in the income statement shown below. You will need to estimate the total number of units sold. Enter the spreadsheet in your **Business Plan Project** Refer to Appendix B to make sure you are on track.

Yearly Income Statement for: _____   Date: _____

	# of Units Sold	Unit Price	Total
Revenue			
Cost of Goods Sold			
Other Variable Costs			
Total Variable Cost			
Gross Profit			
Fixed Expenses			
Utilities			
Salaries			
Advertising			
Insurance			
Interest			
Rent			
Depreciation			
Total Fixed Expenses			
Pre-Tax Profit			
Taxes at 20%			
Net Profit			

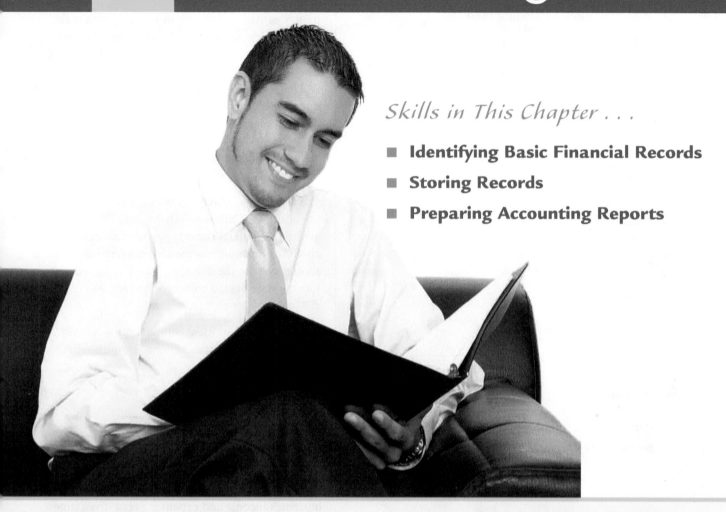

Skills in This Chapter . . .

- **Identifying Basic Financial Records**
- **Storing Records**
- **Preparing Accounting Reports**

GETTING STARTED

Business financial management may seem overwhelming. Why should you bother learning about financial statements and records? If you're not an accountant, why do you need to recognize accounting methods?

Studies show that one of the major reasons that businesses fail is that they lack financial management. In simple terms, financial management is keeping track of how much money is coming in, and how much money is going out. It involves monitoring and balancing bank accounts, keeping track of business records, such as bank statements and receipts, and maintaining clear and organized financial statements.

The success of the American economy may rest on future business innovation. Does that mean you must be a business entrepreneur to find a career or earn a living? Not necessarily. But an understanding of business finances and an understanding of how to manage them, will help you no matter what type of career you choose.

➤ Of the 16 career clusters, which one do you think offers the most opportunity for jobs in financial management?

Identifying Basic Financial Records

Joe's Furniture Mart
General Ledger
As of December 31, 2015

Date	Num	Debit	Credit	Balance
Medical Insurance				7,103.06
12/15/2015	5118	609.15		7,712.21
Total Medical Insurance		609.15	0.00	7,712.21
Total Insurance		609.15	0.00	7,712.21
Internet access				280.00
Total Internet access				280.00
Marketing & Promotional Expense				0.00
Total Marketing & Promotional Expense				0.00
Miscellaneous				576.77
12/30/2015	5119	100.90		677.67
12/30/2015	5119	24.74		702.41
Total Miscellaneous		125.64	0.00	702.41
Office Equipment				1,592.62
12/30/2015	5119	285.77		1,878.39
12/30/2015	5119	40.35		1,918.74
12/30/2015	5119		58.43	1,860.31
12/30/2015	5119		47.23	1,813.08
Total Office Equipment		326.12	105.66	1,813.08
Office Supplies				201.00
12/16/2015	EFT	28.32		229.32
12/30/2015	5119	81.27		310.59
Total Office Supplies		109.59	0.00	310.59
Payments to Subcontractors				1,700.00
12/16/201	1058	600.00		2,300.00
Total Payments to Subcontractors		600.00	0.00	2,300.00
Professional Fees				1,304.52
Accounting Fees				1,160.00
12/16/2015	1059	160.00		1,320.00
Total Accounting Fees		160.00	0.00	1,320.00
Telephone & Fax				1,334.94
12/30/2015	5119	108.03		1,442.97
Total Telephone & Fax		108.03	0.00	1,442.97
TOTAL		**26,049.07**	**26,049.07**	**0.00**

Simon's Sign Shop
Income Statement
For the Quarter ended September 30

Sales (4,300 units) (from sales budget)	$301,000
Cost of goods sold (4,300 units × $35.20 per sign)	
(from budgeted manufacturing costs per unit schedule)	(151,360)
Gross profit	149,640
Operating expenses (from operating expenses budget)	(22,414)
Operating income	127,226
Less: Provision for income tax (35% tax rate)	(44,529)
Net income	$ 82,697

Does the income statement from this business report a healthy or a failing business? How can you tell?

At the heart of every business is a balance between money earned and money owed. Imagine a scale, with one side representing business income, and the other side representing business debt. If a business is doing well, the side representing income will be heavier. A business doing poorly is the opposite: The side representing debt is heavier. A business that has both sides balanced—an even debt-to-income ratio—is said to "break even." That means it is neither making money nor losing money.

Of course, no one actually uses a scale to measure the health of a business. What is used, however, are basic **financial records**—written statements about the business's performance. Every business should prepare the following financial records: an income statement, a balance sheet, and a cash flow statement.

Looking at each of these components separately will help you understand the basics of financial records as a whole.

The Income Statement

One of the most important documents for any business is an income statement. An **income statement** is a financial document that summarizes a business's income and expenses over a given time period. It shows whether the business made a profit or took a loss. For this reason, it's also called a **profit-and-loss statement**. Income statements may be prepared once a month, four times a year, or once a year.

If a business's **revenue**—money taken in, possibly from sales—is greater than its expenses—money spent, or operating costs—the income statement will show a profit. If a business's sales are less than its expenses, the income statement will show a negative number, or loss.

A basic income statement has three parts.

■ *Revenue.* This is the money a company receives from selling its products, before taking into account how much money was spent on making and selling them.

■ *Expenses.* This is a list of everything a company pays to operate the business. It includes the cost of making, storing, and selling its products, as well as rent for the company and wages for employees.

■ *Net profit (or loss).* **Net Profit** is the amount of money a company actually makes, and **net loss** is the amount of money a company loses. Both are calculated by subtracting the expenses from the revenue. You can think of net profit as a company's entire income.

The health of a company is reflected by the numbers listed on an income statement. For this reason, it is extremely important to keep accurate records. A company that did not prepare an accurate income statement would have great difficulty keeping track of how much money it spends, how much it can spend, and how much it is making.

Money Madne$$

Laura's Lilies is a company that sells flowers. Its monthly revenue is $2,500.00 from roses, $1,225.00 from lilies, and $3,000.00 from dahlias. Its expenses include $3,500.00 for rent, $2,100.00 for wages to one employee, and the wholesale cost of flowers, which totals $5,000.00. At this rate, is Laura's Lilies taking in a net profit, or does it have a net loss? If it is a profit, how much is it? If it is a loss, how much more does the company need to make before breaking even? Create a table called "Laura's Lilies Income Statement" and use these numbers to show the calculations you used.

The Balance Sheet

Like income statements, balance sheets are essential financial records. A **balance sheet** shows a business's financial situation at a particular time, such as at the end of a quarter. A balance sheet shows the relationship between the business's **assets**, **liabilities**, and **owner's equity**.

■ Assets include cash on hand, checking or other money accounts, *accounts receivable* (money that is owed to the business), real estate that the business owns, office equipment, and even vehicles such as company cars or trucks.

■ Liabilities include all debts that the business must pay to creditors, suppliers, or banks. These are also called *accounts payable*.

■ Owner's equity (or shareholder's equity) is the amount of money invested in the business by its owners or shareholders.

In a financially healthy business, assets equal liabilities plus owner's equity; that is, the liabilities and owner's equity must *balance* with the assets, which is why this financial record is called a balance sheet.

Joe's Furniture Mart
Balance Sheet
As of January 20, 2015

	Jan 20, 15
ASSETS	
Current Assets	
Checking/Savings	
checking	9,586.26
Total Checking/Savings	9,586.26
Total Current Assets	9,586.26
TOTAL ASSETS	**9,586.26**
LIABILITIES & EQUITY	
Liabilities	
Current Liabilities	
Other Current Liabilities	
Payroll Liabilities	6,189.65
Total Other Current Liabilities	6,189.65
Total Current Liabilities	6,189.65
Total Liabilities	6,189.65
Equity	
Owner's draw	-109,450.42
Retained Earnings	109,204.30
Net Income	3,642.73
Total Equity	3,396.61
TOTAL LIABILITIES & EQUITY	**9,586.26**

Why do you think businesses need to keep careful records of their assets and liabilities?

IRS Tax Records

There are many forms of financial records, but some of the most important are related to taxes. The IRS requires that businesses have many tax-related documents and records on their books. Here is a list of some common tax records.

✔ *The Employer Identification Number lets the IRS easily track and process a business's taxes.*

✔ *Businesses must generate and maintain documents that show they have paid Federal taxes, Social Security taxes, and Medicaid (insurance) taxes.*

✔ *Companies must keep records about their employees, including their Social Security numbers, work authorization, and tax information.*

✔ *Sales taxes are almost always included in the price of goods you buy. Since this money eventually is given to the IRS and state tax agencies, businesses must keep records of how much sales tax it collects as a part of its sales.*

Ask a local business owner how much their business usually pays in taxes. Then think about where this tax money goes (for instance, to schools, roads, our military, etc.).

Career Trend

There is a trend in the banking and finance world toward greater emphasis on financial responsibility. In the U.S., the government is setting new regulations and watching financial institutions closely to make sure consumers' rights are protected.

Color Accounting

In America, would-be accountants start out by learning four basic principles:

■ *The cost principle*, which says that goods and services should be recorded at their original cost and not their current market value

■ *The accrual principle*, which accounts for the lag between when a business spends money and when it makes money

■ *The matching principle*, which reminds accountants to match a business's costs with its revenue

■ *The disclosure principle*, which reminds them that they must disclose both good and bad financial information

But our system for training accountants is not the only one in the world, nor is it necessarily the best. Just ask Australian-born and South African-raised accountant Peter Frampton, who invented an alternative system for teaching basic accounting, called "Color Accounting."

Instead of the four basic principles, Frampton's system uses nothing more than some crayons, paper, and plastic cups. By drawing two green rectangles on the paper and labeling one "Assets" and the other "Expenses," he demonstrates how a business uses funds. Then, by drawing three yellow rectangles, each labeled "Liabilities," "Profit/Equity," and "Income," respectively, he demonstrates where a business gets its funds. Finally, Frampton uses small plastic cups and strips of green and yellow paper to represent how the sums in each of the five rectangles rise and fall with a business's transactions. (You can learn more about Color Accounting at Frampton's Web site, coloraccounting.com.)

There are many options for you to learn more about accounting. You could start by taking accounting courses in school. Then, you could branch out and explore alternative ways of understanding accounting, like Peter Frampton's. Try to imagine yourself teaching accounting to someone. What system would you use?

The Cash Flow Statement

A **cash flow statement** shows how cash comes into and goes out of a business over a specific period of time. Money coming into a business is called *cash inflow*. Money going out is called *cash outflow*.

Cash inflows can include sales of a company's products or services, interest from investments, and money from loans made to the company. Cash outflows include wages and salaries, tax payments, loan repayments, and even the payment of dividends to shareholders.

In a formal cash flow statement, the cash inflows and outflows are organized into three categories.

■ *Operating cash flows.* These include cash flows that relate to the running of the business. This part of the cash flow statement would show inflows such as sales receipts from customers as well as outflows such as payments to suppliers and employees.

■ *Investing cash flows.* These include cash flows that relate to the business's assets. Cash inflows in this area would include dividends from investments. Cash outflows would include monies used to invest in new equipment.

■ *Financing cash flows.* These include cash flows that relate to loans and investments by shareholders. Cash inflows would include money coming into the business from new loans or shareholder investments. Cash outflows would include repayments on loans or payments of dividends to shareholders.

The cash flow statement can give you important information about the business's general health by showing you where money is coming from and going to. A healthy business should be generating most of its income through sales, so operating cash flows should exceed those from the other sources. If you review your cash flow statement and discover that most of your money is coming in from bank loans or shareholder investments rather than sales, your business may not be a long-term success.

THE CRAB SHACK
Cash Flow Statement
For period ending 31 Dec, 2015

CASH FLOWS FROM OPERATING ACTIVITIES

Cash receipts from customers	27,500	
Cash paid to suppliers and employees	(20,000)	
Cash generated from operations (sum)	7,500	
Interest paid	(2,000)	
Income taxes paid	(4,000)	
Net cash flows from operating activities		1,500

CASH FLOWS FROM INVESTING ACTIVITIES

Proceeds from the sale of equipment	7,500	
Dividends received	3,000	
Net cash flows from investing activities		10,500

CASH FLOWS FROM FINANCING ACTIVITIES

Dividends paid	(2,500)	
Net cash flows used in financing activities		(2,500)

Net increase in cash and cash equivalents	9,500
Cash and cash equivalents, beginning of year	1,000
Cash and cash equivalents, end of year	$10,500

What can you tell about the cash inflow of this company? Is it positive or negative?

Career FACT

Whether your company is large or small, the IRS can do what is called an **audit**, or official inspection of your accounts, if they suspect that you are not paying your taxes properly. If you are audited, you must turn over all of your financial statements. If you do not keep good records, you will be penalized.

The Importance of Financial Statements

Large or small, any business must keep careful track of all the financial statements it receives so that it can record every single **transaction**, or instance of buying or selling, in its accounting books. The reason for this level of accounting detail is that for a business to be successful, it must always know precisely how much money it currently has and how much it currently owes. The only way to accurately keep track of this is to know exactly how much money comes in as revenue and how much goes out as expenses. And if a business is seeking a loan, would-be investors typically look at the business's financial statements to determine if it is a good risk. For these reasons, financial statements are one of the most important parts of **accounting**—or the system of recording, summarizing, and reporting business and financial transactions.

If you decide to start your own business, you will be responsible for collecting, understanding, and saving financial statements. Although an entrepreneur is ultimately responsible for understanding and managing all financial records for his or her company, this doesn't mean he or she has to do it all alone. Business owners have many options for handling their accounting work. They can take accounting classes and do most of the work themselves, hire an accountant, or invest in computer software.

Even if you do not plan on starting your own business, you will encounter financial statements in your life at some point. For instance, if you have a bank account, then you have already been given a financial statement in the form of a bank deposit slip. Finally, the Internal Revenue Service (IRS), the government agency that collects federal taxes, also insists that you keep accurate records for its tax-collecting purposes.

Can you imagine saving every one of these paper receipts? Why do you think it is important to do so?

Storing Records

Keeping accurate records might be the most important part of business financial management. Considering how important it is to keep good records, and the large amount of records a business accumulates over time, a good filing system is critical. Yet this is only one of the concerns about maintaining financial records for a company. Other issues include security and access.

Since companies must keep all records of all financial transactions, these issues are concerns for even the smallest of businesses. This also means that as companies grow in size, the issues become more complicated and important.

Career Tips

You don't necessarily need to be great at math to be an accountant. On the contrary, the most important skill for a career in accounting is attention to detail!

Maintaining the Security of Financial Records

If a company is **publicly traded**—owned by members of the general public, called **shareholders,** who pay to own a certain percentage—financial records must be made public. But privately owned companies, particularly those with many competitors, might not want investors, competitors, and others to access sensitive financial data.

For instance, would you buy a product from a company if you thought the company was failing? Would you be more interested in opening a shoe store if you knew the only other shoe store in town was doing very well?

There are two ways a company must store its financial records. If the records are physical files and documents, they must be physically secured by being put in a locked location. Moreover, only trusted individuals should be allowed access to them, as information contained within them must not be released. If the records are on a computer, they must be **encrypted**, or digitally secured so that only authorized people can access them. Encryption uses complicated mathematical *algorithms* (programs or formulas designed to solve problems)

What do you think a company can do to ensure its financial records are secure?

A Position with Great Responsibility

Accountants are perhaps the most trusted people in any company. This is because they deal directly with all of the money that a company makes and spends. An accountant must never abuse the trust placed upon his or her position by making false documents or stealing money. This is called embezzlement, and it is a serious crime. Here are wrong and right ways to deal with situations if you are an accountant.

👎 You tell your friend who works in a competing business about the financial status of your company.

👎 You borrow money from your company's income for your own personal use.

👎 You fail to record some transactions.

👎 You falsify sales numbers so the business looks better.

👍 You make careful, detailed records of all the business income and expenses.

👍 You keep all of the income safely locked away.

👍 You report any problems with the financial records.

👍 You get your work done as soon as you can.

Brainstorm at least two other examples of good accounting and bad accounting. Then, share your thoughts with a partner.

to turn regular data into unreadable data that can be transformed back with a special password, called a "key." These days, financial records are usually both physical and computerized, so both methods of security are necessary.

Coding and Accessing Files

Even small companies have a large number of financial records. As these records accumulate, they become harder to find and access when needed. You can imagine how this issue becomes more challenging as a company grows.

To solve this problem, a wise accountant will use some type of system to keep track of where all the records are. This is called a **coding system**, or method of keeping track of files through unique names. A coding system has two components.

The first is the labels. For every file that goes into storage, a special label with a unique name goes on the file. This name can have any number of formats, as long as it is given to that specific file only. For instance, it can be a color, number, or name.

The second part of a coding system is an **index**, or a list of the names given to each file and a corresponding location for each. So, if a certain file is put in one filing cabinet, the index would record the name of the file as labeled and where it went. That way, an accountant can easily find exactly where that file is located.

Computerized systems make access to files much easier. In fact, the computer applies the coding system for you. The difficult part of computerized systems is inputting the financial records into the computer in the first place (unless they are already computerized). Most records are entered manually, but some are scanned.

Why do you think color-coding can be an effective way to keep track of financial documents?

Malcolm works in a neighborhood candy store on weekends. One day, the store owner asks him to move some cardboard boxes from a back room to the basement. Malcolm stacks the boxes in a corner of the basement behind the water heater.

Three weeks later the water heater bursts. The basement floods, soaking the cardboard boxes. When Malcolm arrives at work that week, the store owner yells at him. The boxes contained the store's financial records for the past two years. He does not know if he will be able to salvage them.

Was it Malcolm's fault the records were ruined? Is there anything Malcolm could do to help the store owner? Use 21st Century Skills such as decision making, problem solving, and critical thinking to think of an ending to the story. Write the ending, or present it as a skit to your class.

Tech Connect

It is no secret that the world's information is moving increasingly into cyberspace. For instance, many companies find it necessary to have all of their financial statements on their private **intranet**—or restricted company-only communications network—systems so that they can be easily accessed and read by employees.

Since large companies have so many financial records, the task of putting them all into a computer is daunting. To do so, "intelligent" scanners were invented to scan many pages of text in a short amount of time. Designers felt that the best way to do this was to create scanners that acted as a human would, by picking up a piece of paper, putting it in a scanner, and then taking it out afterward. The result was a computer with arms and fingers that can grasp and move pieces of paper; in other words, a robot that can scan.

Use the Internet to research one other way that high technology has affected the way businesses keep financial records. Then, type up your report and be prepared to share it with the class.

Preparing Accounting Reports

Now that we have discussed the purpose of keeping good financial records and what these records are, we will outline some of the ways these records can be used to prepare accounting reports. All accounting reports help businesses keep track of where their money is coming from and where it is going, but they can be quite varied. What they look like and how they are prepared depends on the needs of the business.

Accounting systems are categorized as either manual or computerized, but with today's technology, most businesses use some type of computerized system. Since both manual and computerized accounting systems produce the same financial documents—usually income statements, balance sheets, and cash flow statements—we will examine the reasons for and against using each type of system.

Remember: All accounting systems rely on some method of recording every business transaction, which includes all income received and all expenditures made. Therefore, careful records are essential no matter what method one uses.

Manual Accounting Systems

The most basic type of accounting system is a manual system, which means it is managed by hand. Depending on the size of the business, it may or may not be the easiest method. Generally (though not always), the smaller the company is, the more likely it is that a manual system will be the most efficient.

Using only a journal, an accountant can prepare all the necessary financial statements using the manual system. For example, the accountant would:

■ Prepare a clear list of all transactions for a given period, with each transaction on its own line and including the date of transaction.

■ For each transaction, record the amount of income or expense.

Then, at the end of a designated period, for instance once per month or year, the accountant can use all of the recorded information about every transaction to prepare other financial statements.

Some of the reasons why a company would want to use the manual accounting method are as follows.

■ It is straightforward and requires no advanced knowledge or expertise. As long as the accountant keeps track of every transaction, this method is a piece of cake!

■ It is very inexpensive. Compared to the computerized systems, this method is practically free. All that is required is a blank book or journal and a pencil.

If the business dealings of a company are relatively straightforward, and the company is small enough, the manual method is perfectly adequate to keep track of the company's finances. One major risk, however, is human error. When people are responsible for entering and manipulating the information, mistakes are possible.

Do you think this old-fashioned method of accounting is better than a computerized system? Why or why not?

Myth Computerized accounting systems do all the work of an accountant automatically.

Truth While computerized systems may make accounting easier in certain circumstances, there is still a great deal of human work required to keep track of financial records and interpret the results of financial statements.

Computerized Accounting Systems

Manual accounting systems may be inexpensive and straightforward, but they are not usually adequate for larger and more complex businesses. For instance, for a large multimillion-dollar business to use a manual accounting system, they would need hundreds of accountants working around the clock to enter all of the daily transactions into the system. In fact, any business that has numerous transactions and many different accounts may find it easier to use a computerized accounting system.

To use any type of computerized accounting system, an accountant must enter each financial statement into a database. Then, various reports can be generated depending on the level of sophistication of the software. For instance, some small businesses can use spreadsheet software to track their accounting data. This type of software can perform accounting calculations, but the formulas used must be set up manually. Other companies use more sophisticated software that already has these formulas, which makes less work for the accountant. Finally, large corporations must use much more sophisticated (and expensive) software solutions to handle more complicated financial information. The levels of sophistication in computerized accounting systems vary. But any computerized system is generally more expensive than a manual system. It also requires training and set-up time. These drawbacks are usually worthy tradeoffs when businesses consider the ease of use and accuracy of computerized systems.

6.47	16.52	14.21	30.73	33.69	$1,010.80
11.2	17.00	14.02	31.02	32.55	$976.43
15.1	17.65	14.09	31.74	33.15	$994.37
22.9	18.14	14.38	32.52	34.08	$1,022.43
13.6	17.49	14.39	31.88	33.58	$1,007.52
26.3	17.76	14.34	32.10	33.45	$1,003.55
10.3	16.40	15.13	31.52	33.09	$992.62
4.51	16.16	15.23	31.39	31.51	$945.38
7.05	16.08	15.27	31.35	29.91	$897.27
25.9	16.85	15.71	32.56	31.06	$931.67
23.8	17.44	15.65	33.09	32.04	$961.09
19.7	17.12	16.17	33.28	32.28	$968.37
15.8	16.78	16.94	33.72	32.34	$970.29
11.9	15.31	17.55	32.87	31.79	$953.70
2.86	15.06	17.95	33.01	30.95	$928.44

What are the benefits and drawbacks of using a computerized accounting system?

What If There Were No Computers?

How would a world without computers affect basic business financial management? What if all companies, small and large, had to use the manual accounting system?

★ *Companies might be limited in size by their ability to keep accurate accounting records.*

★ *There would need to be many more accountants in charge of recording the transactions and income/expenses of very large companies.*

★ *We would go through much more paper, because every transaction would need to be recorded in a journal or ledger.*

★ *There might be more errors in accounting, because large companies would need to rely on large numbers of people, which increases the likelihood of human error.*

Can you think of other consequences for accounting practices in a world without computers? Do you think that such a world would be very different from ours? Why or why not?

Career Profile: Accountant

Business Management & Administration Career Cluster

Job Summary

An accountant is a person in charge of keeping track of, preparing statements about, and analyzing the finances of a company. Accountants are the gatekeepers of the financial well-being of a company. They are the first to know when a company is doing well or poorly. In fact, they are the people in charge of tracking a company's health.

To be an accountant, you must have a college degree, such as a Bachelor's degree. Accountants can also receive specialized training, such as that required to become a Certified Public Accountant, or CPA. CPAs are generally higher paid and can take more varied financial roles in both the public and private sector. In addition to these educational and training requirements, any type of accountant must not mind doing math often, must be detail-oriented, and must be good at keeping detailed records. As a reward for all of these requirements, accountants can expect to be very well paid. This is because the job is quite specialized, and very important.

Use resources such as the Internet, your library, your parents, or a school counselor to find out more about a career in accounting. Prepare a half-page write-up with your findings, including whether you would ever want to be an accountant and why or why not.

Case Study

LeTwan has been given a small weekly allowance of $5.00 per week. However, the new leather jacket that he wants to buy costs $300.00. He has already asked his parents, and they suggested that either he wait until he has saved enough from his allowance to buy it, or that he uses his allowance to start an after-school business.

He figures that it will take him too long to save his allowance every week to buy the leather jacket he wants. Therefore, he plans on saving for a certain amount of weeks and then starting a business.

■ What kind of business could LeTwan reasonably start and run after school? Consider how much revenue it would generate and in what amount of time.

■ Suppose LeTwan partners up with his friend Lindsay. Lindsay does not receive an allowance, but has saved $50.00 from her birthdays. How could the two new business partners use their investment to grow their business?

■ How should LeTwan and Lindsay decide to split the work and profits for their business?

■ With their combined initial investment, the size and scope of their business, how long do you think it will take for LeTwan and Lindsay's business to generate the amount of money LeTwan needs for his leather jacket?

■ What types of financial records should they keep?

Web Extra

Use the Internet to learn about various types of computerized accounting systems. Create a list of at least three different programs and do research on each one. Identify which you think is best based on its ease of use, the amount of human input required, and the price.

Answer It!

1. What is at the heart of every business?

2. Why is a cash-flow statement necessary for a business?

3. What will an income statement show if a company's sales are greater than its expenses?

4. What will an income statement show if a company's sales are less than its expenses?

5. What is the difference between an income statement and a balance sheet?

6. What are the three cash flow categories shown on a cash flow statement?

7. Why must a company record every transaction?

8. Why is cash inflow an important figure for a business to track?

9. Why is security an issue for the storage of financial records?

10. What are the two ways a company must secure its financial records?

Career-Ready Practices

Form a group with three or four others. Pick a business from your community. For example, you might pick a local pizza or sandwich shop, a veterinarian's office, or a clothing store. Imagine that your team is responsible for managing the company's financial information. Work together to create financial records for the company. Set the records up using a spreadsheet program. Career-ready individuals are proficient with basic computer applications, such as spreadsheet, word processing, and presentation programs. They recognize the importance of using new and existing technology tools to accomplish basic workplace tasks and improve productivity. Using examples from the text, create an income statement, a balance sheet, and a cash flow statement. Present your business records to the class.

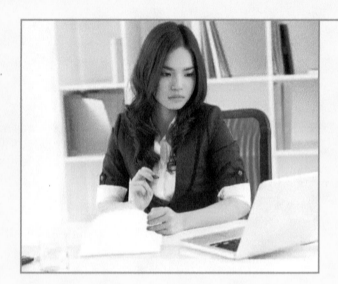

Write Now

You are in a position similar to LeTwan and Lindsay in the Case Study on page 450. You need to write an executive summary of your business plan for your new venture! Your initial investment was the combined savings of one month of weekly allowances totaling $5.00 each, and $50.00 in cash.

Recall that an executive summary is a one- or two-page written summary of highlights on how you plan on running a company, including the key selling points of the investment opportunity. Plan on devoting one paragraph to each of the following: what product or service your business will sell; how much you plan on spending on your products or services and where your investment will come from; how much you plan on making after one year and where the revenue will come from (for instance, what type of people will buy your goods or services?); and finally, where you see the company in five years.

After you have written this executive summary, think of a name for your company that somehow relates to the goods or services it will sell. Put it at the top of the page and submit it to your teacher.

Career Portfolio

Businesses rely on sharp people like you to keep them running. This is because there are many important roles "behind the scenes" in any business. For instance, account managers, accountants, and bookkeepers are all people who keep any company running.

In order to identify good candidates for these essential roles, companies look for people who possess certain skills. Whether or not you will eventually go into a business in one of these roles, you probably possess at least some of these desirable skills. For instance, being good at paying attention to details is an essential skill for people working behind the scenes in a business. Another important skill is being good at math.

Using what you have learned so far about financial management, make a list of all the skills you have that you think would be necessary for someone in a "behind the scenes" role at a business. Rate your level of accomplishment for each skill, using a "Beginner," "Intermediate," or "Expert" rating for each. Then, put this list in your Career Portfolio labeled "Business Management Skills."

Business Plan Project

Think about the different ways that an entrepreneur can manage financial records. In your **Business Plan Project**, make a chart listing the pros and cons of different ways your business could handle financial records. Then, write a paragraph explaining which method you would choose, and why.

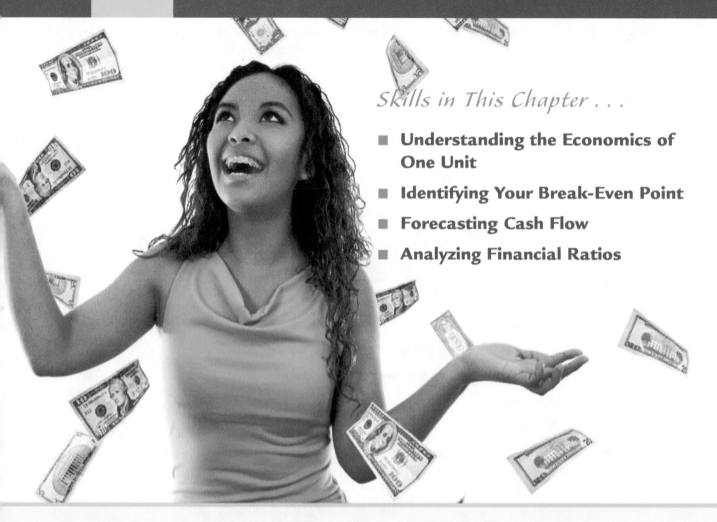

Skills in This Chapter . . .

- **Understanding the Economics of One Unit**
- **Identifying Your Break-Even Point**
- **Forecasting Cash Flow**
- **Analyzing Financial Ratios**

GETTING STARTED

Do you have to be an accountant to manage a company's finances? Even if you have an accountant, it is important to know how to track and analyze financial information to keep a business on track for success.

Although business finances may seem complex, certain key financial calculations require only basic math skills, such as addition, subtraction, multiplication, and division. If you can master these calculations, you will be better prepared to achieve your business goals.

➤ Fold a sheet of paper in half. On the left side, list specific elements you think demonstrate that a business is successful. On the right side, list what a business needs to achieve each element.

Understanding the Economics of One Unit

An entrepreneur needs to know that his or her business is profitable. One important way to examine profitability is to look at how much profit the business makes every time a customer buys a unit of sale. A **unit of sale** is one of whatever customers buy from the business. For example, a customer might buy one T-shirt from a retail store.

The **economics of one unit** is a calculation that determines the profit—or loss—that a business earns every time a customer buys a unit of sale.

- A T-shirt business might earn a $5.00 profit every time a customer buys a T-shirt.

- A hair salon might earn $3.00 every time a client buys a haircut.

Identifying Your Unit of Sale

Sometimes, it is easy to identify your unit of sale. If your business sells T-shirts, your unit of sale is one T-shirt. If your business sells haircuts, your unit of sale is one haircut.

Sometimes, it is harder to figure out your unit of sale. What if you sell decorated tooth picks? Your unit of sale might be a box of 50 toothpicks. What if you provide child care? Your unit of sale might be one hour of service.

Different business types have different units of sale.

- A retail business might sell one T-shirt at a time.

- A wholesaler might sell a box of 25 shirts.

- The manufacturer that produces the shirts might sell cartons containing five boxes each.

- A house cleaning service might charge $50.00 per apartment.

- Another house cleaning service might charge $20.00 per hour.

Career Tips

The easiest way to determine your unit of sale is to ask yourself this question: What is your customer actually buying from you? That is your unit of sale.

Calculating the Economics of One Unit

Every unit of sale has a selling price that the consumer pays, and an expense—or cost—that the entrepreneur spends. Depending on the business, expenses might include the cost of materials, production, labor, storage, and transportation. You calculate the economics of one unit by subtracting the expenses for the unit of sale from its selling price.

Selling Price – Expense = Profit (or Loss)

If the equation results in a positive number, you've made a profit. If it results in a negative number, you have a loss.

For example, if your T-shirt business spends $15.00 in expenses for every T-shirt, and you sell each T-shirt for $20.00, you earn $5.00 on every sale.

$20.00 – $15.00 = $5.00

If you spend $22.00 in expenses for every T-shirt, you would lose $2.00 on every sale:

$20.00 – $22.00 = –$2.00

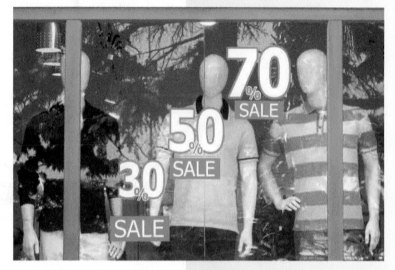

How might a business suffer if it has to offer deep discounts in order to sell products?

The Importance of the Economics of One Unit

Making a profit is the primary goal of every business. Business owners use their profits to pay themselves, to expand their businesses, and to start other businesses. Because the unit of sale is the basic building block of a business, analyzing the economics of one unit lets you accurately identify whether or not your business is—or will be—profitable.

For a business to be successful financially, the economics of one unit must result in a profit. A business that cannot make a profit from one unit of sale will never make a profit, no matter how many units it sells.

Money Madne$$

An entrepreneur buys plain backpacks for $11.00 each. She decorates them at home with painted artwork, embroidery, and decorative buttons. It costs her $3.00 for supplies and $6.00 for labor to complete each backpack. She sells them at a flea market for $25.00 each. What is her economics of one unit of sale? What if she spends $3.50 for supplies? Can you think of ways she might be able to increase her economics of one unit to earn a greater profit?

Identifying Your Break-Even Point

What if you looked at your income statement and saw that your expenses were exactly equal to your sales? That means there is neither a profit nor a loss. The net income at the bottom of the statement would be zero.

When the net income is zero, you are at the **break-even point**. It means that the business has sold exactly enough units to cover all expenses.

Identifying the break-even point is important, because it helps you determine what you have to do to make a profit and to avoid a loss. To identify the break-even point, you perform a **break-even analysis**, which lets you determine how many units of sale you must sell to cover all of your expenses. To perform the break-even analysis, you calculate your gross profit per unit, and then calculate your break-even unit.

Calculate Your Gross Profit per Unit

Using information from your income statement, you can calculate your **gross profit per unit**, which is the amount of profit you use to pay operating expenses. The formula for calculating your gross profit per unit is:

Selling Price per Unit – Cost of Goods Sold per Unit = Gross Profit per Unit

For example, if you sell one unit for $10.00, and your **cost of goods sold**—expenses you incur in order to sell the unit—is $6.00, then your gross profit per unit is $4.00.

$10.00 – $6.00 = $4.00

Once you know your gross profit per unit, you can use information from your income statement to determine your break-even unit.

Calculate Your Break-Even Unit

A **break-even unit** is the number of units of sale you must sell to arrive at the break-even point. That means that if you sell fewer than your break-even unit, you will lose money. If you sell more, you will earn a profit. If you sell exactly the number of your break-even unit, you will break even—no profit or loss.

The formula for calculating your break-even unit is:

Operating Expenses ÷ Gross Profit per Unit = Break-Even Unit

For example, if your operating expenses are $3,000.00 per month, and your gross profit per unit—the amount of profit you earn before expenses—is $4.00, your break-even unit is 750. You must sell 750 units in order to break even

$3,000 ÷ $4.00 = 750

The Importance of Breaking Even

It usually takes time for a new business to increase sales enough to make a profit. Until then, it has to have enough cash to cover its losses as the business grows. A break-even analysis and realistic sales forecasting can help a business estimate how long it will take to earn a profit.

Why might an entrepreneur celebrate when he or she reaches the break-even point?

Because sales and expenses can change frequently, it is important to reevaluate your break-even point every once in a while. Knowing your break-even point will help you make sure your business becomes and remains profitable.

Tech Connect

With so much important financial information stored on computers, it is essential for all businesses to set procedures for backing up data. Backing up means creating a copy of your electronic files and storing them someplace safe.

In the past, backups were made manually by copying the data to a disk drive attached to the company's computer system. Now, many businesses—and individuals—are using online backup services to store their backup data on the Internet.

Online backup services have the advantage of capacity—which means they can store a lot of data. Online data is also saved far from the original location, so it is not damaged if there is a fire or flood. Of course, there are risks with online storage, too. Most important is the risk of losing data, or of having it stolen.

Do you think online backup services are a good idea? Create a spreadsheet or table comparing the benefits and risks of an online backup service with a manual backup system.

Career Profile:
Agricultural Scientist

Job Summary

Agricultural scientists include plant scientists, such as agronomists and crop scientists; soil scientists; food scientists; and animal scientists, such as dairy scientists, poultry scientists, and animal breeders. They participate in research into advancements such as ways of improving crop yield, controlling pests and weeds, turning crops into energy sources, and conserving soil and water. In addition, they work to develop healthy food products for consumers.

What interests do you think might lead someone to a career as an agricultural scientist?

The type of education and training varies depending on the type of work the scientist performs. Most jobs in the farming and food processing industry require a bachelor's degree. Research positions require a master's or doctoral degree. To succeed in senior research positions or teaching, an agricultural scientist must have a Ph.D.

Most agricultural scientists work regular hours in offices and laboratories. Some may work in specialized environments, such as a food scientist who works in a test kitchen, or an animal scientist who works in a farm facility.

Agricultural scientists should be able to work independently or as part of a team and be able to communicate clearly and concisely, both verbally and in writing. Most also need an understanding of basic business principles, the ability to apply statistical techniques, and the ability to use computers to analyze data and to control biological and chemical processing.

Use the Internet, a library, or career center to research the responsibilities, education and training requirements, and salary range of an agricultural scientist. Select one specific type of agricultural scientist and develop a list of courses a student would have to take—starting in high school—in order to achieve success in the field.

Forecasting Cash Flow

Cash for a business is like gasoline for an automobile—without it, the business does not have the fuel necessary to operate. It doesn't matter if the business is large or small. If it doesn't have enough cash to pay its bills, the creditors can force the business to close.

To ensure that you have enough money to operate, you must track your cash flow. **Cash flow** is the money received minus the money spent over a set period of time. As you read in Chapter 23, you use a cash flow statement to monitor the inflow and outflow of cash as it occurs. You use a **cash budget** to **forecast**—predict based on past experience—inflow and outflow of cash in the future, for a set period of time, and to compare your prediction to the actual amounts.

Predicting the future is, of course, difficult. However, you can base your prediction on facts, such as how much you spent in the past and how much you expect to take in.

Setting Up a Cash Budget

A cash budget usually covers one month. It includes four columns.

■ Descriptions of the source of cash inflow and the recipient of cash outflow

■ Forecasted amount for each

■ Actual amount for each

■ Difference between the forecasted amount and the actual amount

Setting up a cash budget is a three-step process.

1. List and total any expected incoming cash payments over the next month. You should include only cash you really expect and can count on, such as payments from trusted customers.

2. List and total any expected outgoing cash payments for the next month. You should include expenses such as rent and salaries that you know you must pay.

3. Subtract the expected cash outflows from the expected cash inflows. The result provides an estimate of the surplus or shortage of cash for the next month.

Cash Budget for the Month of _____

	Forecast	Actual	Difference
Cash Inflows			
Cash Sales			
Credit Collections			
Bank Loans			
Other Income			
Total Cash Inflows			
Cash Outflows			
Estimated Variable Expenses			
Insurance			
Salaries			
Advertising			
Interest			
Utilities			
Rent/Mortgage			
Other Fixed Expenses			
Total Cash Outflows			
Cash Available			

What steps might you take if your cash budget estimate shows a shortage of cash for the next month?

Ways to Reduce Cash Outflows and Increase Cash Inflows

✔ Take advantage of trade credit offered by other businesses.

✔ Collect payments from customers as soon as possible.

✔ Offer discounts to customers who pay in cash.

✔ Insist that customers who have overdue bills pay in cash, not credit.

✔ Be insistent on collecting overdue payments.

✔ Shorten the payment time for customers using credit.

✔ Do not purchase excess inventory.

✔ Protect inventory from loss, damage, or theft.

✔ If necessary, reduce cash paid out in salaries and wages by eliminating positions and cutting back on hours.

Improving Cash Flow

If your estimate shows that you will not take in enough cash to cover your expenses, you may have to use money saved for emergencies, take out a loan, or seek new investments. You can also take steps to improve the flow of cash.

It is common for new businesses to spend more cash than they earn during their early months. That is why it is important that the initial start-up investment is great enough to cover anticipated expenses and emergencies (refer to Chapter 19).

In general, all businesses should continuously work to reduce cash outflows and increase cash inflows. You can manage your business in a way that helps make sure your cash flow intake is sufficient. For example, you can do the following.

■ Collect cash as soon as possible.

■ Pay bills close to the due date.

■ Check your cash balance every day.

■ Lease equipment instead of buying it.

■ Minimize the amount of inventory you keep in stock.

Tech Connect

Even the slightest change in cash flow can have a big impact on a small business that operates with a narrow profit margin. Entrepreneurs must keep up with industry and economic trends so they can foresee and predict how changes will affect their businesses. One way an entrepreneur can keep up is to read online blogs about entrepreneurial thinking.

A blog—short for Web log—usually features regular entries of text, photos, and links to other sites. It is maintained by one person who has expertise or interest in a topic. Most blogs also have comment sections where readers can post comments or ask questions and communicate with the blogger and other readers. Blogs on entrepreneurial thinking focus on the concerns of small businesses and can be a great resource for the latest information about how to run a company efficiently and navigate changing market conditions. Why do you think blogs might be useful to an entrepreneur?

Analyzing Financial Ratios

Entrepreneurs rely on financial records such as income statements and balance sheets to determine if their company is successful. One of the most effective ways to analyze the data from financial records is to use **financial ratios**. These are relationships between important financial information that are expressed as fractions or as percentages.

■ Some financial ratios are based on the information in an income statement. They help you monitor expenses, compare the performance of the company with competitors, and measure profitability.

■ Some financial ratios are based on the information on a balance sheet. They help you monitor debt, compare debt with equity, and make sure the business has enough cash to pay its debts.

Financial ratios are calculated by dividing one number by another. It is important for an entrepreneur to examine many financial ratios rather than relying on just one or two. Each ratio provides important information about a different aspect of the business.

Operating Ratios

The **operating ratio** is based on information from an income statement. It is the percentage of each dollar of revenue, or sales, needed to cover expenses. The formula for calculating the operating ratio is:

(Expenses ÷ Sales) × 100 = Operating Ratio (%)

For example, if an income statement shows sales of $20,000.00 and an insurance expense of $1,000.00, the operating ratio for insurance is 5%.

($1,000.00 ÷ $20,000.00) × 100 = 5%

An operating ratio is often used to compare one company with other businesses in the industry. For instance, if you are paying a higher operating ratio for insurance than other, similar businesses, you might consider looking for a different insurance company or negotiating a lower rate with your current company.

Myth When you deposit a check in your bank account, the cash becomes available immediately.

Truth Each bank sets its own rules about how quickly check deposits become available. Most have at least a one-day wait time, and some have up to five business days. Understanding your bank's policy will help you manage your cash flow.

Return on Sales

The *return on sales (ROS) ratio* is also based on information from an income statement. ROS shows how much of each dollar of sales a company keeps as profit. It may also be called **net margin**, **net profit ratio**, **net profit on sales ratio**, or **profit margin**.

The formula for calculating ROS is:

(Net Profit ÷ Sales) × 100 = ROS (%)

For example, if the income statement shows sales of $30,000.00 and a net profit of $6,000.00, the ROS percentage is 20%.

($6,000.00 ÷ $30,000.00) × 100 = 20%

A high ROS ratio is *usually* a good indicator of success for a business. However, the ROS percentage alone doesn't provide a complete picture. A business selling high-priced items, such as luxury automobiles, can be very profitable with an ROS in the 5% range, while a retailer selling less expensive items, such as hats or T-shirts, may need an ROS in the 25% range to be successful.

Same-Size Analysis

A **same-size analysis ratio** is a comparison of the total revenue or other financial data against that same data converted into percentages. It is called a same-size analysis because you are comparing the same data, just using a different format—percentage. To perform a same-size analysis, you divide a line item on the income statement by the sales, and then multiply the results by 100. This shows the line item as a percentage of sales:

(Line Item ÷ Sales) × 100 = % of Sales

For example, if your expenses are $3,500.00 and your sales are $10,000.00, you calculate your expenses as a percentage of sales like this:

($3,500.00 ÷ $10,000.00) × 100 = 35%

Same-size analysis makes it clear how each item affects the business's pre-tax profit. It also lets you easily compare income statements from different time periods. Even if the sales are different from month to month or quarter to quarter, you can see the patterns and trends in the percentages, rather than looking at the sales.

Debt Ratio

One ratio calculated using data from a balance sheet is a **debt ratio**. It is the ratio of a business's total debt—or liabilities—divided by its total assets. The formula for calculating debt ratio is:

(Total Debts ÷ Total Assets) × 100 = Debt Ratio (%)

For example, if you have $100,000.00 in total debts and $500,000.00 in total assets, your debt ratio is 20%.

($100,000.00 ÷ $500,000.00) × 100 = 20%

A high debt ratio indicates that a business has a high percentage of debt relative to assets. Banks and other investors often look at the debt ratio to determine whether a business is a good risk, or if it has already borrowed more than it might be able to pay back.

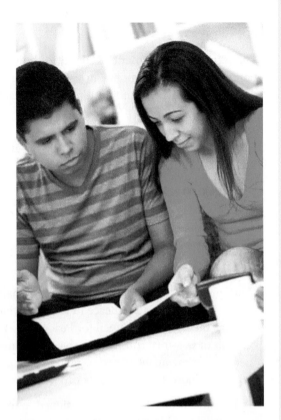

Why might a bank refuse to loan money to a business that has a high debt ratio?

Debt-to-Equity Ratio

The **debt-to-equity ratio** shows the relationship between total debts and the *owner's equity*, which is the value of the business calculated by subtracting the total debts from the total assets as listed on the balance sheet. The formula for calculating the debt-to-equity ratio is:

(Total Debts ÷ Owner's Equity) × 100 = Debt-to-Equity Ratio (%)

For example, if you have $100,000.00 in total debts and the owner's equity is $400,000.00, your debt-to-equity ratio is 25%.

($100,000.00 ÷ $400,000.00) × 100 = 25%

Managing Your Debt Ratio

A business might choose a high debt ratio by using creditors and suppliers instead of cash as a source of financing. What are some of the benefits and risks that might result?

- Banks won't provide loans, or provide loans with high interest rates.
- Suppliers insist on cash payments instead of credit.
- The business is unable to pay its debts
- The business is able to stay in business long enough to start generating profits.
- The owners are able to achieve a high return on their investment.

Can you think of the benefits and drawbacks of maintaining a low debt ratio?

Return on Investment Ratio

The **return on investment (ROI) ratio** shows how well a business is doing in relation to the amount of money invested. It is calculated by dividing the net profit by the initial investment, and multiplying the result by 100. The formula is:

(Net Profit ÷ Initial Investment) × 100 = Return on Investment (%)

For example, if your net profit is $1,500.00, and your initial investment was $10,000.00, your ROS is 15%.

($1,500.00 ÷ $10,000.00) × 100 = 15%

Entrepreneurial Thinking

Entrepreneurial thinking can create more than just new products and opportunities. It can also lead to peace in locations that need it most. Organizations such as the Business Council for Peace work to encourage small-business growth in war-torn countries such as Afghanistan and Rwanda. Local entrepreneurs can provide jobs, income, and a feeling of self-worth to the people of the region. A more stable economy can help lead to political stability.

Peaceworks is another venture designed to foster understanding through entrepreneurial thinking. It is a global business that has Arabs and Israelis working together to create a line of food products. United by profit, former foes become partners in business, gaining understanding and tolerance for one another.

Can you think of an area abroad or in the United States where small businesses might help create peace and cooperation between enemies?

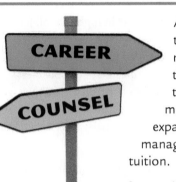

CAREER

COUNSEL

Andre has always loved action figures. By the time he was in high school, he had collected so many that he had no more room to store them. He started having one yard sale a month to sell some of his action figures. He used the money he made to buy more. In college, he expanded the business to include online sales. He managed to earn enough to pay a portion of his tuition.

After graduation, he decided he wanted to open a real store to sell action figures and other collectibles. He found a store to rent, stocked it with inventory, and hired two part-time employees. Almost immediately, he ran into a cash-flow problem. He was not selling enough items to earn enough money to pay all his expenses. He was at risk of losing his lease for not paying his rent. He was not sure he would have enough money to pay his employees. He began to regret his decision to open a store.

What are the problems and challenges facing Andre? What decisions does he have to make? Use 21st Century Skills such as problem solving, decision making, critical thinking, and effective communication to help Andre deal with his situation. Write an ending to the story and share it with your class.

21st Century Learning

Doing the Math

Managing and growing a business depends on your ability to perform, understand, and analyze many financial calculations. What if you stop taking math in high school?

★ *You will not be able to calculate your economics of one unit.*

★ *You will not be able to identify your business's break-even point.*

★ *You will not understand the information on your company's income statement and balance sheet.*

★ *You will not be prepared to manage your company's cash flow.*

Can you think of problems you might have starting and growing a business if you are unable to understand basic math calculations?

Case Study

For a team fundraiser their junior year in high school, Jenny and Kelsey made and sold chocolate-covered strawberries. The items were a big hit. The girls decided to take orders and sell the treats in boxes of ten for Valentine's Day. The business took off from there. By the time they started college, they were running a successful enterprise selling custom chocolate-covered fruit for parties, events, and individuals. They called their business *Sweet and Fresh*.

Jenny was a good manager. She monitored the orders, hired employees, and made sure the products met quality standards. Kelsey was good at math. She took control of the financial aspects of the business. She negotiated with suppliers, monitored their cash flow, and made sure everyone was paid on time. They asked their friend Patrice who was creative and liked selling things to join the business to handle marketing. Patrice helped them expand their business to the Internet using a Web site.

The girls plan to keep their business growing while they attend college. They believe that because they provide fresh, high-quality items and are willing to work closely with clients to create customized products, they will continue to succeed.

■ What factors do you think have contributed to the success of Sweet and Fresh?

■ What challenges might face the girls in the future?

■ Can you think of ways the girls might expand their business in the future?

Web Extra

Blogs on entrepreneurial thinking can be an excellent source of information and tips for someone trying to start a business. A good blogger updates the site often to address current issues. Some notable blogs include: smallbiztrends.com, youngentrepreneur.com/blog, and ducttapemarketing.com/blog.

Use the Internet to explore these and other small business blogs, and make a directory of the ones you think would be most useful.

Answer It!

1. Give an example of a unit of sale.
2. What is the formula for calculating the economics of one unit?
3. How do business owners use their profits?
4. How can you tell if your business is at the break-even point?
5. What information do you need to calculate your break-even unit?
6. What is the formula for calculating your gross profit per unit?
7. What is cash flow?
8. List at least five steps you can take to make sure your cash flow intake is sufficient.
9. In what format are financial ratios expressed?
10. Which financial ratio is used to compare one company with other businesses in the industry?

Career-Ready Practices ------

Form teams of three or four. As a team, select one of the 16 career clusters, and then think of a small business in that cluster area. Determine the data you would need to calculate the economics of one unit, the break-even point, and the break-even unit. Write the data on a piece of paper. Employ the skills you have acquired through math, business, and economics classes to complete the calculations. Career-ready individuals know when it is appropriate to apply academic and technical skills to real-world, on-the-job situations. Trade papers with another team. Use the information provided by the other team to calculate the economics of one unit, the break-even point, and the break-even unit for their business.

Write Now

Write an article for a financial newspaper or Web site giving advice to small business owners on how they can use financial information to track the progress and success of their business. Cover the importance of the economics of one unit, performing a break-even analysis, and setting up a cash flow budget. Include information on how to use financial ratios.

Career Portfolio

You can make an impression on an employer or investor by showing that you understand how to use financial calculations in business. Set up a worksheet or table listing and explaining important financial calculations. Include the formula for each calculation, how to use the calculation in a business situation, and an example of the calculation using real numbers. Add the document to your career portfolio.

Business Plan Project

Review the chart you entered on page 1 of your **Business Plan Project** back in Chapter 1. Have you completed all the elements of the business plan project? If not, go back and complete it. When it is complete, review your work. Use Appendix B as a reference. Make corrections and improvements and share it with a partner.

A Business Management Issues

Skills in This Chapter . . .

- **Managing Insurance**
- **Managing Contracts and Other Legal Issues**
- **Interpreting Government Regulations**
- **Managing Business Credit**
- **Managing Business Taxes**

Business management includes a wide range of responsibilities. This appendix examines some of the more advanced business issues that every business owner and manager should understand.

Managing Insurance

"Hope for the best, but prepare for the worst" is a **proverb**—saying—that explains why every business needs insurance. Recall that insurance is an investment that protects you financially against everyday risks. There is risk in all business ventures, just as there is risk in everyday life. The goal for businesses and individuals is to manage the risk so that there is a higher chance of success than there is of failure.

Just as individuals count on insurance to cover losses due to illness, fire, and other emergencies, businesses count on insurance to help minimize and protect them from business losses. The three most common business insurance needs are to cover:

■ Property damage

■ Liability

■ Workers' compensation

Types of Risk

There are two basic types of risk.

■ **Speculative risk** is risk that holds the possibility of either gain or loss. For example, when a restaurant adds a new dish to the menu, there is a risk that customers won't like it, and a chance that they will.

■ **Pure risk** is the chance of loss with no chance of gain. Kitchen fires are a pure risk in running a restaurant.

To manage risk, business owners take different steps. For example, the restaurant owner can minimize the risk of introducing a new dish by first carrying out market research or by having focus groups taste the food. He or she can minimize the risk of fire by serving only cold foods, enforcing safety rules, installing sprinklers, and keeping fire extinguishers handy.

Another option is to shift the risk to someone else—called **risk transfer**. For business owners and individuals, that means purchasing insurance so the insurance company takes on the risk.

Property Insurance

Property insurance protects a business's possessions in case of fire, theft, or damage from the weather. A basic policy could cover the building, its furnishings, and the equipment, supplies, cash, and inventory.

Individuals usually purchase *homeowner's* or *renter's insurance* to protect their personal property in case of fire, theft, or damage. In fact most banks will not issue a mortgage unless the home buyer shows proof that there is property insurance in place.

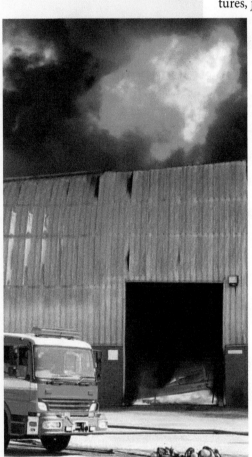

How can you protect yourself and your business from the cost of an unexpected emergency?

Property can be insured for its actual worth, called **cash value**. Or it can be insured for its **replacement cost**, which is the amount it would cost to replace the lost item. Business owners may also choose business interruption insurance, which covers losses if a business can't operate as the result of a covered event, such as a storm or fire.

Most basic property insurance is limited to protecting the business from predictable events. Policies do not cover loss resulting from a catastrophe or disaster such as a hurricane. Business owners may be able to purchase disaster coverage, but it is expensive.

Automobiles and other vehicles are property, but they require a separate type of insurance policy. There are specific insurance policies to cover cars, trucks, motorcycles, boats, and even airplanes. Most states require owners to purchase insurance before they can register the vehicle for use. Vehicle insurance usually includes coverage for collision damage, as well as for damage caused to someone else's property or person.

Liability Insurance

Liability insurance protects a business when the business's action, or lack of action, injures someone or another business. The injury may be physical, such as a defective hair dryer that burns a customer, or financial, such as a defective hairdryer that causes a salon to lose business.

Business owners can purchase a variety of liability insurance policies.

- *General liability insurance* covers expenses related to injuries that occur on the business's property.
- *Product liability insurance* protects a business from losses caused by a product it produced or developed.
- *Professional liability insurance* covers harm done by a business's actions, or failure to act.
- *Identity theft insurance* protects a business against damage done by the theft of sensitive information.
- *Employment practices liability insurance* covers claims of discrimination, sexual harassment, and other unfair treatment.

Individuals can purchase personal liability insurance. Sometimes, it is part of a homeowner's or automobile insurance policy, or it may be purchased separately. For example, personal liability insurance may protect a homeowner if someone slips on the front walk and sues for damages.

Why is it important for a business to have liability insurance?

Workers' Compensation

Workers' compensation insurance covers losses to employees resulting from job-related injury or illness. All businesses are required by law to have workers' compensation insurance. Worker's compensation—or workers' comp—is **no-fault insurance**, which means it pays regardless of who is responsible. It usually covers the employee's medical bills and reimburses him or her for lost wages.

Each state has its own regulations for workers' compensation, and within a state, different rules may be applied to different industries. Even if workers' compensation is not required for a specific situation, a business owner may choose to purchase it because it protects the company from lawsuits filed by employees injured at work.

Life Insurance

Some businesses purchase life insurance policies for vital employees, such as owners and high level executives. Life insurance pays a benefit if the insured person dies. Such insurance helps protect the company financially for the loss of a key manager, without whom the business might fail.

Life insurance is important for most people, particularly working parents. If the parent dies, the family might lose the income, but the insurance benefit will provide money to pay bills and support the children. Companies often subsidize the cost of life insurance for all employees.

Managing Contracts and Other Legal Issues

Every business must be aware of legal issues in order to protect its rights, as well as the rights of owners, investors, employees, customers, and suppliers. Legal issues range from ownership of **intellectual property**—defined as artistic and industrial creations of the mind—to what makes a contract valid.

Understanding the law can be complicated. Most businesses hire lawyers who are trained to interpret rules and regulations to manage legal issues. However, anyone involved in owning or managing a business will benefit from a basic understanding of important legal issues.

Reducing Business Risk

In addition to purchasing insurance, businesses can take steps to reduce risk by limiting the chances that an event will occur. A business can:

✔ Install fire safety protection devices such as sprinkler systems and fire extinguishers

✔ Install antitheft devices such as locks, lighting, and alarms

✔ Train employees in business ethics

✔ Secure computers and sensitive information

✔ Provide a safe workplace

✔ Encourage health and wellness among employees

Why is it important for a manager or entrepreneur to understand basic legal issues?

Types of Contracts

A **contract** is an agreement between competent parties in which each promises to take or avoid a specified action. Some common types of contracts include the following.

- **Sales contracts** and **service contracts** are agreements that include the service provided on items sold, the selling price and how it will be paid, and the date and location of the transaction. They also describe each party's rights and obligations. For example, a landscaper's service contract may state that his company will replace any plant that dies within 30 days, or that the customer will be charged a fee for canceling on less than 48 hours notice. Sales contracts typically give the buyer the right to inspect the goods and to refuse them if there is sufficient reason.

- A **lease** is a written contract in which a property owner gives temporary use of that property to another party. Terms of leases include the length of the contract, the amount of rent, and how often payment will be made. Limitations may be placed on the use of the property, and penalties may be imposed for damages or late payments. Leases are usually associated with real estate, such as for renting an apartment or office space, but can apply to any type of item, such as furniture, vehicles, and other machinery.

- A **confidentiality agreement**—also called a **nondisclosure agreement**—binds parties to secrecy. It usually concerns employees, investors, or others with whom a business owner needs to share sensitive information—information that he or she does not want made available to the general public. Confidentiality agreements describe the specific information that is considered confidential and how the parties may and may not use the information.

Collective Bargaining

Collective bargaining is negotiation between workers and their union representatives on one side and employers represented by management on the other. The result of the negotiation is a labor contract, usually called the **collective bargaining agreement**.

The contract defines such employment conditions as wages, benefits, scheduling, vacation time, paid holidays, health and safety, nondiscrimination clauses, length of contract, and seniority requirement.

Collective bargaining agreements usually include provisions for disciplinary and grievance procedures. *Disciplinary procedures* define why and how the employer may discipline an employee. *Grievance procedures* define why and how an employee can bring workplace concerns to management. The procedures typically involve notifying all parties of the situation and allowing a set amount of time to resolve the problem. If the problem is not resolved, it may be brought to a higher level, and finally to an arbitrator, who is someone trained to settle an issue between parties in dispute.

What Makes a Contract Legal?

For a contract to be valid—or legally enforceable—all the conditions mentioned in the contract must be met. The three basic conditions found in all contracts include:

- *Agreement between the parties.* The parties must agree on the **conditions**, or the events or circumstances that must occur for the contract to be legal.

- *Competence.* All parties must be **competent**, or capable of understanding the terms and consequences of the contract.

- *Mutual exchange.* There must be **consideration**, or a benefit that each party provides for the other.

Verbal—or spoken—contracts may be valid. However, it is usually safer for both parties to put the contract in writing. That way, there can be no misunderstanding of the terms. Some contracts, such as the sale of land, must be in writing in order to be valid.

Protection of Intellectual Property

Ownership of intellectual property is protected by law. That means that when someone plays music, reprints text, displays artwork, uses an invention, or recreates an architectural design, he or she must name the owner and provide payment. As a business owner, you cannot use someone else's intellectual property. To help make sure no one uses your intellectual property, you should make sure it is protected.

Artistic creations are protected by copyright. **Copyright** is the exclusive right to perform, display, copy, or distribute an artistic work. It covers all forms of expression, including words, music, images, or actual objects. It also includes information published on the Internet. Copyright applies automatically as soon as a work is created. To identify your work as having a copyright, you can use the traditional notice: COPYRIGHT © [YEAR] BY [COPYRIGHT HOLDER]. This informs others that they can reproduce the work only by permission and possibly with payment. You can also register the work with the Library of Congress's Copyright Office. Copyright generally applies for the lifetime of the creator plus 70 years.

A doctrine called **fair use** provides for the limited quotation of a copyrighted work without permission from or payment to the copyright holder. Also, some creative works or inventions are in the **public domain**, which means they are available for free use because their copyright or patent has expired.

Industrial inventions are protected by **patent**. A patent is the exclusive right to make, use, or sell a device or process. Many types of inventions can be patented, from an improved design for a ketchup bottle to a variety of tomato used to make the ketchup to a process for bottling the ketchup. To qualify for a patent, an invention must be different from anything that already exists, have some feature that is unexpected or out of the ordinary, and be useful. To obtain a patent, you apply to the U.S. Patent and Trademark Office (USPTO).

A **trademark** is a symbol that indicates that a brand or brand name is legally protected and cannot be used by other businesses. A trademarked brand or brand name is a type of intellectual property. You can register a trademark with the USPTO, but it is not necessary. Registering helps you make sure the mark is not owned by someone else and gives you some legal rights to limit the use of the trademark by others.

Trade secrets are information that a business or individual keeps confidential to gain an advantage over competitors. Each state has a version of the Uniform Trade Secrets Act, which protects trade secrets.

Seeking Remedy

Entering into a business contract usually gives the right to take action against the other party if they breach the agreement. Violating the rights provided by a copyright or patent is called **infringement**. Failing to carry out the conditions of a contract is referred to as **breach of contract**.

The law allows different types of remedies, depending on the violation. For infringement, the common remedy is injunctive relief, which is an order for the violator to stop the illegal activity, such as selling purses printed with a company's trademark without permission. In breach of contract, the violator must agree to carry out the agreed-upon terms. In any case, the violator may be forced to pay damages—a payment to reimburse the injured party for a loss.

Seeking remedy can be a lengthy and complicated process. It should be taken only with an attorney's advice.

Interpreting Government Regulations

Every level of government imposes regulations on business and industry. The goals of regulation are to protect employees and customers as well as to help ensure fair trade. All business owners must be aware of the regulations controlling their industry in order to make sure they comply with all laws.

What's That Symbol?

There are two symbols associated with U.S. trademarks and one associated with copyrights:

✔ ™ is used to indicate that a brand is protected in a general way, but does not have formal legal protection.

✔ ® is the registered trademark symbol. It can only be used if the owner has registered the brand or brand name with the U.S. Patent and Trademark Office.

✔ © is used to indicate that a creation is protected by copyright laws.

Federal Regulations

The federal government protects consumers with a series of product safety laws such as the Fair Packaging and Labeling Act, which requires all product packaging to identify the item, its manufacturer, and the quantity. The Food, Drug, and Cosmetic Act forbids any false or deceptive labeling. Many packaged foods require a list of ingredients and nutrition facts, and all health-related claims must meet the definition set by the Food and Drug Administration and the U.S. Department of Agriculture. Products that contain hazardous substances must be labeled with safety-related information, and manufacturers must describe the dangers associated with the product, its proper use and precautions, and first-aid or emergency treatment if it's misused or mishandled.

The Federal Deposit Insurance Corporation (FDIC) administers the Consumer Leasing Act, which is part of the federal Truth in Lending Act. Passed in 1976, it requires anyone issuing a lease to disclose specific financial information about the lease terms, such as the monthly payment, the total amount of payments, and the allowance for a trade-in. The information lets consumers make an educated decision about which lease to choose, or even whether it makes more sense to purchase the item rather than lease it.

The Federal Trade Commission enforces regulations designed to ensure that one business does not have an unfair advantage. It enforces detailed truth-in-advertising laws that require businesses to provide accurate and fair information. It uses antitrust laws to restrict practices such as price fixing—when companies agree to set the price of goods or services instead of allowing free trade; price discrimination—charging competing buyers different prices for the same product; and monopolies—when a single company is the only supplier of a certain product.

State and Local Regulations

States and local communities usually impose regulations on business and industry. For example, many local governments have zoning laws that control where a business may be located.

States and local governments may require a business owner to have a license in order to operate. A **license** is a legal document issued by a state or local government that allows a business to provide a regulated product or service. A hair salon usually needs a license, as does a builder or electrician. (Some industries require federal licenses, such as broadcasting, investment consulting, and meats preparation.) Licensing usually requires some type of certification, which may mean passing an exam or supplying documentation to prove education and ability.

Sometimes a business needs a **permit**, which is a legal document that allows a business to take a specific action. For example, a builder may need a permit to construct a new home, and a restaurant may need a permit to serve alcoholic beverages.

Environmental Regulations

Business owners must be aware of laws designed to reduce the harmful impact the business may have on the environment. Many of these regulations are set by the U.S. Environmental Protection Agency (EPA). These cover a wide range of business activities in almost every field. For example:

■ The Clear Air Act limits the types and amounts of chemicals that factories with smokestacks may release into the atmosphere. It also regulates farmers burning crop stubble in their fields, which might damage air quality, and whether a road-construction firm must avoid traffic delays that might increase pollutants emitted by cars in the area.

■ The Clean Water Act may require a business to get a permit to discharge wastewater, and then control the amount of water released and the chemical content of the water.

■ The Endangered Species Act regulates whether builders can develop land near a wildlife preserve.

Workplace Laws and Regulations

Employers are responsible for the health, safety, and well-being of employees. Some of the most notable regulations concerning employee rights are covered in Chapter 15, including the Civil Rights Act of 1964, the Americans with Disabilities Act (ADA), the Occupational Safety and Health Act, and the Family and Medical Leave Act (FMLA).

In addition, the Equal Employment Opportunity Commission (EEOC) enforces the Fair Labor Standards Act, which guarantees most hourly workers a minimum hourly wage, a maximum number of hours worked, and extra pay for working overtime. Some states have a minimum wage that is higher than the national level and add requirements for conditions such as lunch and rest breaks, pay periods, and severance pay. **Severance pay** is an amount of money given to employees when they are terminated for reasons other than performance.

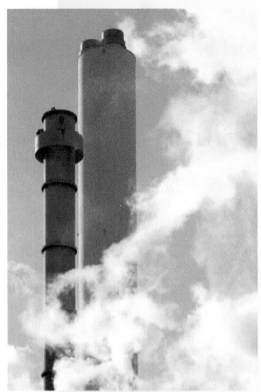

What do you think are the benefits and drawbacks of regulations that protect the environment?

Hiring Regulations

Employers must take care to abide by all laws and regulations during the hiring process. For example:

■ The Civil Rights Act forbids employers from making hiring decisions based on the assumption that married candidates are more responsible than unmarried ones.

■ Employers cannot pass over a qualified individual from a minority group for promotion.

■ Job ads that imply that older workers are not qualified for a position violate the Age Discrimination in Employment Act.

■ Employers cannot ask a disabled job candidate how he or she became disabled.

■ Employers cannot make a medical exam a condition of being hired, unless it is required of all employees.

Termination Policies

Before letting an employee go, an employer should confirm that the termination is legally justified and lawful. It is imperative that the grounds for dismissal are clearly stated in the company's policies and in the employee's handbook. If there is a contract between the employer and the employee, it should include specific information about grounds for termination.

All conversations between the employer and the employee regarding performance and termination should be documented in writing and kept in the employee's file. Termination cannot be based on personal feelings or bias of any kind, nor can it violate any federal or state employment laws. An employee may file a *wrongful termination* lawsuit against the employer if he or she believes the termination was unlawful.

Managing Business Credit

What problems might arise from mismanaging business credit?

Recall that credit is the granting of extended time to pay off a debt, which is money you owe to someone else. A business must also manage its credit and debt in order to succeed.

A business might use credit in order to buy supplies. In that case, it is responsible for paying back the credited funds, according to the specified terms. The business might also act as a creditor by extending credit to customers. In that case, the business expects to be repaid according to the specified terms. In both situations, it is important to know how to grant credit and collect payments to keep a business operating.

Types of Credit

Two types of credit are of particular interest to business owners.

■ **Trade credit** is when one business allows another business to take an extended time before paying for purchased goods or services. For example, a textile supplier might extend credit to a clothing manufacturer who buys bolts of cloth to use to create T-shirts. Trade credit can be useful for managing cash flow, because the buyer does not have to pay for the supplies immediately, but can wait until he or she sells the product and has more cash on hand.

■ **Consumer credit** is when a business gives consumers an extended payment time for purchased goods or services. For example, a furniture store may allow customers up to 12 months to pay for a purchase.

Terms of Trade Credit

Terms of trade credit usually define when payment is due and what penalties there will be for late payment. For example, a business might grant 30 days or 60 days for repayment if it is confident the buyer will pay. It might grant 10 days for repayment if it is worried that the buyer will not pay.

It is important for buyers to understand when a trade period begins. The starting date is often called the reference date. It may be the date the goods or services are purchased or are received by the buyer. It may be the last day of the month, or a specifically designated date.

Vendors who allow trade credit often provide a small discount to the buyer if full payment is made early and in cash. The discount may range from 1 to 3 percent of the total.

Granting Credit and Collecting Payments

A sale made on credit is based on trust that the person or business will pay the debt in the future. Deciding whether to grant credit involves some risk. Will the person or business repay the debt?

Many businesses follow specific procedures when deciding whether or not to grant credit to an applicant. The first step is to ask the applicant to supply personal and financial information, such as employment and income history. Next, the business can check the applicant's credit history.

Every person or business that has ever used credit has a credit history, which is a record of credit transactions. The credit history includes information about whether or not payment was made in accordance with the credit terms set by the creditor. (Refer to Chapter 21 for more information on credit histories.) A business can request a credit history report from a credit bureau. If the business grants the credit, it has certain obligations.

The federal Truth in Lending Act requires creditors to inform customers about the credit terms, including any finance charges. In addition, the creditor must send a routine bill to the customer when the debt is due. If the customer does not pay, the creditor may hire a business that specializes in collecting unpaid debt. Debt collection agencies charge a fee, which may be a percentage of the amount collected.

Managing Business Taxes

A tax is money we pay the government. The government uses the money to pay for public resources, such as trash collection, public schools, and medical care. Like individuals, businesses must pay taxes in order to support public services.

Taxes may seem like a burden to many companies, particularly to a small business. However, they are necessary, and a company—or individual—that does not pay taxes is committing a federal crime called **tax evasion**. Tax evasion is punishable by fine, seizure of property, or imprisonment.

Payroll Taxes

The government pays for workers' retirement and disability insurance using money collected from payroll taxes, which are also called FICA. FICA is an acronym for the Federal Insurance Contributions Act.

Both employers and employees contribute to the tax through deductions from wages and income. The employer is responsible for calculating and sending the payments to the Internal Revenue Service (IRS). FICA includes two deductions: one for Social Security and one for Medicare. The amount is calculated as a percentage of the employee's wages or salary. The employer's contribution equals the contribution of the employee. Most states also require employers to deduct state income taxes and send the amount to the state government.

How do individuals benefit when businesses pay taxes?

Federal Unemployment Tax

Payments to fund unemployment insurance are called FUTA, which stands for the Federal Unemployment Tax Act. The tax is used to pay workers who have lost a job. FUTA is paid solely by the employer—not by the employee. It is calculated as a percentage of employee wages.

FUTA is run jointly by the federal and state governments. In some states, employers may be required to make payments to the state as well as to the federal government. Payments are typically made quarterly, which means every three months.

Percentage Method Tables for Income Tax Withholding

(For Wages Paid in 2014)

TABLE 1—WEEKLY Payroll Period

(a) SINGLE person (including head of household)—

If the amount of wages (after subtracting withholding allowances) is: Not over $43 . . . . The amount of income tax to withhold is: $0

Over—	But not over—		of excess over—
$43	—$218 . .	$0.00 plus 10%	—$43
$218	—$753 . .	$17.50 plus 15%	—$218
$753	—$1,762 . .	$97.75 plus 25%	—$753
$1,762	—$3,627 . .	$350.00 plus 28%	—$1,762
$3,627	—$7,834 . .	$872.20 plus 33%	—$3,627
$7,834	—$7,865 . .	$2,260.51 plus 35%	—$7,834
$7,865	. . . .	$2,271.36 plus 39.6%	—$7,865

(b) MARRIED person—

If the amount of wages (after subtracting withholding allowances) is: Not over $163 . . . . The amount of income tax to withhold is: $0

Over—	But not over—		of excess over—
$163	—$512 . .	$0.00 plus 10%	—$163
$512	—$1,582 . .	$34.90 plus 15%	—$512
$1,582	—$3,025 . .	$195.40 plus 25%	—$1,582
$3,025	—$4,525 . .	$556.15 plus 28%	—$3,025
$4,525	—$7,953 . .	$976.15 plus 33%	—$4,525
$7,953	—$8,963 . .	$2,107.39 plus 35%	—$7,953
$8,963	. . . .	$2,460.89 plus 39.6%	—$8,963

TABLE 2—BIWEEKLY Payroll Period

(a) SINGLE person (including head of household)—

If the amount of wages (after subtracting withholding allowances) is: Not over $87 . . . . The amount of income tax to withhold is: $0

Over—	But not over—		of excess over—
$87	—$436 . .	$0.00 plus 10%	—$87
$436	—$1,506 . .	$34.90 plus 15%	—$436
$1,506	—$3,523 . .	$195.40 plus 25%	—$1,506
$3,523	—$7,254 . .	$699.65 plus 28%	—$3,523
$7,254	—$15,667 . .	$1,744.33 plus 33%	—$7,254
$15,667	—$15,731 . .	$4,520.62 plus 35%	—$15,667
$15,731	. . . .	$4,543.02 plus 39.6%	—$15,731

(b) MARRIED person—

If the amount of wages (after subtracting withholding allowances) is: Not over $325 . . . . The amount of income tax to withhold is: $0

Over—	But not over—		of excess over—
$325	—$1,023 . .	$0.00 plus 10%	—$325
$1,023	—$3,163 . .	$69.80 plus 15%	—$1,023
$3,163	—$6,050 . .	$390.80 plus 25%	—$3,163
$6,050	—$9,050 . .	$1,112.55 plus 28%	—$6,050
$9,050	—$15,906 . .	$1,952.55 plus 33%	—$9,050
$15,906	—$17,925 . .	$4,215.03 plus 35%	—$15,906
$17,925	. . . .	$4,921.68 plus 39.6%	—$17,925

The government publishes tables such as this one to help employers calculate payroll tax. How much would an employer withhold per pay period from a single employee who earns $1,500 a week and is paid weekly?

Consumption Taxes

Most goods and services that people buy are subject to consumption taxes. Business owners who sell goods and services that are taxed decide who pays the consumption tax. They may pay it themselves, or pass some or all of it on to the customer.

The most common consumption tax is a sales tax, which is a percentage of the sales price of a good or service. The percentage—or sales tax rate—is usually set by the state or local government. Some items have federal taxes, and some may be tax-free. For example, in most states, food is not taxed, but meals purchased in a restaurant are. It is a business owner's responsibility to collect and pay the required sales tax.

Another type of consumption tax is called an **excise tax**, which is a tax imposed on a specific product or activity. For example, a local government may charge an excise tax for registering a vehicle, or a state may have an excise tax on diesel fuel to pay for road maintenance. Some excise taxes are temporary and are intended to raise the funds required for a specific project. For example, a city may impose a hotel room tax to fund a convention center.

Business Income Tax

Calculating business income tax depends on the type of business ownership. For C corporations, a corporate income tax is assessed on the business's earnings. For sole proprietorships, partnerships, S corporations, and limited liability corporations (LLCs), the income earned as a business owner is taxed in the same way as income earned as an employee (refer to Chapter 21 for information on individual income tax). The main difference is that the business owner is responsible for estimating and sending in the payments at regular intervals throughout the year.

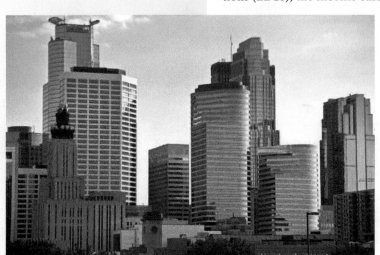

Most communities have a commercial tax rate that is different from the residential tax rate. Which one do you think is higher, and why?

Property Tax

A business that owns the land or building where the business operates must also pay an annual commercial property tax. As with personal property, the tax rate for commercial property is set by the local government. In addition, some states assess a tax on personal property used in business, such as furniture, vehicles, supplies used for daily operations, and inventory held for sale.

Tax-Saving Strategies

A business can take steps to minimize its tax burden. This is called tax avoidance, or using legal strategies to reduce your tax liability. The two most common methods of tax avoidance are deductions and tax credits.

■ *Deductions* are items or expenses that you subtract from your gross income on a tax return. Expenses that are considered ordinary and necessary for operating a business are usually tax-deductible. That includes utilities, rent, employee compensation, costs of goods sold, travel, vehicle use, taxes, and insurance.

■ *Tax credits* are subtracted from the tax owed. They are available for a wide range of business activities and change from year to year depending on the current tax law. For example, tax credits may be available for using green energy sources, donating goods to a charitable organization, or hiring workers who are reentering society after serving time in prison. A small business may take a credit for making the workplace accessible to disabled workers.

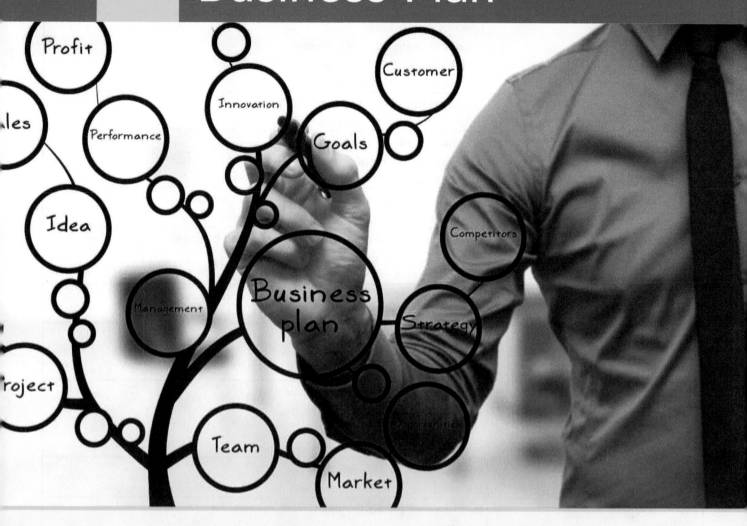

A business plan is like a map showing how you will get from your current situation to your successful business. You use it as a guide for yourself, and also to show potential *investors*— the people who will loan you money to start and run your business—that you have thought through the challenges to come and know how to make the business profitable. The following business plan can be used as a guide as you develop your own business plan.

Business Plan Chart

Your Business Idea	Describe your business idea. What is the name of your business? Explain how your idea will satisfy a customer need. Explain your business ownership.
Economics of One Unit	What type of business are you starting? Calculate the economics of one unit.
Return on Investment	What are your business goals? What are your personal goals? How much education will you need?
Opportunity Recognition	What resources and skills do you have to run this business? Perform a SWOT analysis.
Core Beliefs	Describe the core beliefs you will use to run this business. Choose a motto/slogan for your company. Create your philanthropic plan.
Supply and Demand	What factors will influence the demand for your product or service? What factors will influence the supply for your product or service?
Competitive Advantage	Describe your company's competitive advantage. Who are the primary competitors? How will your business help others?
Marketing and Market Research	Describe the Four Ps for your business. Fill out a marketing plan for your business. Describe your target market. Brainstorm five market research questions.
Operating Costs	List and describe your operating costs. List and describe your monthly variable costs.
Record Keeping	Describe your record-keeping system. List all bank accounts you will open for your business.
Projected Income Statement	Complete a monthly projected budged and a one-year income statement for your business. Use your projected one-year income statement to calculate: ■ Projected ROI for one year ■ Projected ROS for one year
Financial Strategy	Describe the legal structure you have chosen for your business. Make a list of the items you will need to start your business. What is your total start-up investment?

Basic Sample Student Business Plan

Your Business Idea

1. Describe your business idea.

   I would like to sell pens, pencils, erasers, notebooks, and other kinds of school supplies to my classmates at Wingate High School in Williamsburg, Brooklyn.

2. What is the name of your business?

   School Supply Solutions

3. Explain how your idea will satisfy a consumer need.

   Students are busy and on the go. Sometimes they don't have the things they need for class—such as pencils or notebooks. Maybe they left a book bag at home or a pen ran out of ink. School Supply Solutions will be there to help them when this happens.

4. Provide contact information for each owner.

   Lisa Johnson, President and Owner

5. If there is more than one owner, describe how the business ownership will be shared.

   I do not plan to share ownership.

Economics of One Unit

1. What type of business are you starting?

   School Supply Solutions will be a retail business.

2. Calculate the Economics of One Unit for your business.

   My business will sell different products, such as pens, notebooks, pocket calculators, and erasers. I plan to add new products if I see that there is a need for them. While some products will cost more than others, I am assuming that, on average, School Supply Solutions will earn $2.00 per sale. My business will use "keystoning" as a pricing strategy, so for every $1.00 I pay in COGS, my customers will pay twice that amount.

ECONOMICS OF ONE UNIT (EOU)

Retail Business: average unit of sale = $2.00

Selling Price per Unit:			$2.00
Cost of Goods Sold per Unit:		$1.00	
Sales Commission @10%:	$0.20		
Total Other Variable Costs per Unit:	$0.20	0.20	
Total Variable Costs per Unit:		$1.20	1.20
Gross Profit per Unit:			$0.80

Return on Investment

Business Goals:

1. What is your short-term business goal (less than one year)? What do you plan to invest to achieve this goal? What is your expected ROI?

   My short-term goals are to:

   ■ **Operate my business during my senior year of high school.**

   ■ **Generate $600 in sales within the first three months.**

   ■ **Use a portion of my net profit to pay for my senior prom and school activities.**

2. What is your long-term business goal (from one to five years)? What do you plan to invest to achieve this goal? What is your expected ROI?

   My longer-term goals are to:

   ■ **Operate my business when I am in college.**

   ■ **Use a portion of my net profit to buy a used car.**

   ■ **Generate $8,000 in sales by the end of my third year of operations.**

Personal Goals:

3. What are your long-term personal and career goals?

   Career Goals:

   ■ **Become an international business lawyer**

   ■ **Live and work overseas**

   ■ **Run my own law firm**

   Life Goals:

   ■ **Learn to speak another language fluently**

   ■ **Travel around the world**

   ■ **Use my skills to help others**

4. How much education will you need for your career?

- ■ **High School Diploma**
- ■ **College Degree (BA)**
- ■ **Law Degree (JD)**
- ■ **Master's Degree in Business Administration (MBA)**

5. Have you tried to get a part-time job related to your chosen career?

Last summer I worked part-time at a law firm in New York City.

Opportunity Recognition

1. What resources and skills do you (and the other owners of your business) have that will help make your business successful?

I am very outgoing and have been told that I am a good listener. I think that being successful in sales requires both of these skills. Even more importantly, I stick with things, even in the face of obstacles. I refuse to give up on a goal until I achieve it.

2. Perform a SWOT analysis of your business (see below).

Strengths (Entrepreneur's abilities and contacts)

**My customers will be my classmates, and these people are also my friends.
I understand their needs and preferences. My customers trust me.**

Weaknesses (The problems the entrepreneur faces, from lack of money or training to lack of time or experience.)

I will not have a fixed location for my business. This could make it difficult to connect with customers since they will not always be able to find me. To take care of this, I plan to use a cell phone for my business and include the number on all my promotional material.

Opportunities (Lucky breaks or creative advantages the entrepreneur can use to get ahead of the competition.)

At school, no one else is selling the kinds of products I plan to provide. Students can't succeed without school supplies.

Threats (Anything that might be bad for the business, from competitors to legal problems.)

Once other people see what a good idea I have, they could try to copy me, and then my business would have competition. If this happened, I would need to figure out how to stay ahead of competitors.

Core Beliefs

1. Describe three core beliefs you will use in running your company.

I believe in honesty, providing people with a quality product, and that businesses exist to solve other people's problems.

2. Choose a motto—or slogan—for your company.

"School Supply Solutions: We Supply You with the Tools for Success"

Supply and Demand

1. What factors will influence the demand for your product or service?

   Demand for my products will depend on how often students forget to bring their own supplies to school or run out of something, or discover that the supplies they have don't work properly.

2. What factors will influence the supply for your product or service?

   My supply will depend upon me. I need to make arrangements to purchase new inventory regularly. I also need to remember to bring my products to school. I plan to store my inventory in my locker.

Competitive Advantage

1. What is your competitive advantage?

Competitive Advantage	Yes/No	Description
Quality	No	
Price	Yes	My products sell for 10% less than those sold by my closest competitor —a stationery store three blocks from the school.
Location	Yes	My business offers students convenience. They can get the products they need for school without leaving the building.
Selection	Yes	I know what products my customers will want to buy because I need the same supplies that they do.
Service	No	
Speed	Yes	I can deliver the products right at school.
Reputation	Yes	People will buy from me because they know and trust me.

2. Who are your primary competitors? Where are they located?

   Sunshine Cards and Gifts: 536 Metropolitan Avenue, Brooklyn, NY 11211

   All in the Cards: 305 Broadway, Brooklyn, NY 11211

3. How will your business help others? List all organizations to which you plan to contribute. (Your contribution may be time, money, your product, or something else.)

   I will be helping my classmates to succeed in school. Without the basic supplies - notebook, pen, and pencils - students can't take notes. And if they can't take notes then they won't do well on tests and their grades will go down. I plan to donate 5% of my net profit to a local homeless shelter.

Operating Costs

1. List and describe your monthly fixed costs.

Utilities:	$10.00
Salaries:	$25.00
Advertising (printing flyers and posting them around school):	$10.00
Insurance:	$30.00
Interest:	$0.00
Rent:	$0.00
Depreciation:	<u>$10.00</u>
Total Monthly Fixed Costs:	$85.00

2. List and describe your monthly variable costs.

Monthly Variable Costs

Cost of Goods Sold per Unit	# of Units Sold for month of September	Total COGS
$1.00	200	$200.00

3. Re-calculate your economics of one unit, allocating as many variable costs as possible.

Other Variable Costs

Commission	Total Sales Revenue	Total Commission
10%	$400.00	$40.00

Total Monthly Variable Costs

Cost of Goods Sold per Unit	Commission	
$200.00 +	$40.00 =	$240.00

Marketing

1. Describe the Four P's for your business.

Product—Why will your product meet a consumer need?

Students need school supplies and they often forget to bring their own to school or they run out.

Place—Where do you intend to sell your product?

I will sell supplies from my locker before school and between classes. During lunch, I will sell in the cafeteria. This will be very convenient for my customers.

Price—What price do you plan to sell your product for, and why?

I plan to keystone, or double the price that I paid for the products. I need to make sure, though, that I get a good deal on the products I purchase. A lot of students don't have much spending money so I'll need to keep my prices low.

Promotion—How do you plan to advertise and promote your product?

Word of mouth will help me to promote School Supply Solutions. I will also put up flyers in the school hallways and in the cafeteria.

2. Fill out a marketing plan for your business.

Methods	Description	Target Market	Amount to Be Spent
Brochures	Brochures will describe my products and include an order form.	Students and teachers	$10.00
Business Cards	Cards will feature my name, e-mail, phone number, and slogan.	Students and teachers	$17.00
Flyers	Flyers will feature my business name, slogan, and contact information.	Students	$5.00
Promo Items	I will give out pencils, pens, and erasers with my business card the first week of each grading period.	Students	$0.50 per packet × 100 = $5.00
Special Events	Visibility at sports events, plays, assemblies, and other events at my school.	Students, teachers, and parents	No additional cost.
E-mail	My mailing list will allow me to notify customers about special events, sales, and promotions.	Students	No additional cost. My monthly Internet fee of $10.00 is already accounted for in my fixed costs.

3. Do you intend to publicize your philanthropy? Why or why not? If you do, explain how you will work your philanthropy into your marketing.

I plan to inform customers through my promotional materials that 5% of my profits will go to the local homeless shelter.

Market Research

1. Describe your target market.

   My target market consists of:

   - **850 teenagers ages 14 to 18 who attend the High School for Enterprise and Technology in Williamsburg, Brooklyn.**
   - **Teachers who work at my school.**
   - **Parents who attend special school events such as sports events and concerts.**

   Through my market research, I learned that on average, each student at my school spends $75 per year on supplies. This means that students at my school are investing a total of $63,750 into the school supplies market each and every year! My goal is to capture at least 5% market share or about $3,200.

2. Brainstorm five market research questions.

   A. **What are your favorite school supply products?**

   B. **What kinds of school supplies do you buy the most (and least) frequently?**

   C. **How much do you spend on school supplies each year?**

   D. **Where do you buy your school supplies now?**

   E. **Are there school supplies that you like/need that are difficult to find? What are they?**

Record Keeping

1. Describe your record-keeping system.

   - **I will keep electronic records for my business on my computer.**
   - **My accounting system will be "cash-only."**
   - **I plan to file my receipts in a filing cabinet so that I will have records of all my expenses.**
   - **Each day, I will fill in my electronic spreadsheet to track which products I have sold and in what quantities. This way, I can see how my business is progressing.**

2. List all bank accounts you will open for your business.

   I already have a savings account for my own personal use. I plan to open a second savings account at the same bank so that I can keep my business income separate from my personal savings.

Projected Income Statement

1. Complete a monthly projected budget and one-year income statement for your business.

MONTHLY INCOME STATEMENT

School Supply Solutions   Date: October, 2014

	# of Units	Unit Price		
Revenue:	200	$2.00		$400.00
Cost of Goods Sold		$1.00	$200.00	
Other Variable Costs				
Commission @10%:		0.20	40.00	
Total Variable Costs:			$240.00	240.00
Gross Profit:				$160.00
Fixed Operating Costs				
Utilities:		$10.00		
Salaries:		25.00		
Advertising:		10.00		
Insurance:		30.00		
Interest:		0.00		
Rent:		0.00		
Depreciation:		10.00		
Total Fixed Operating Costs:		$85.00		85.00
Pre-Tax Profit:				$75.00
Taxes (estimated 20%):				15.00
Net Profit:				$60.00

YEARLY INCOME STATEMENT
(My business will operate for ten months of the year.)

School Supply Solutions   Date: 2014

	# of Units	Unit Price		
Revenue:	2,000	$2.00		$4,000.00
Cost of Goods Sold		$1.00	$2,000.00	
Other Variable Costs				
Commission @10%:		0.20	400.00	
Total Variable Costs:			$2,400.00	2,400.00
Gross Profit:				$1,600.00

YEARLY INCOME STATEMENT (con't)

School Supply Solutions   Date: 2014

	# of Units	Unit Price	
Revenue:	2,000	$2.00	$4,000.00
Gross Profit:			$1,600.00
Fixed Operating Costs			
Utilities:	$10.00	$100.00	
Salaries:	25.00	250.00	
Advertising:	10.00	100.00	
Insurance:	30.00	300.00	
Interest:	0.00	0.00	
Rent:	0.00	0.00	
Depreciation:	10.00	100.00	
Total Fixed Operating Costs:	$85.00	$850.00	850.00
Pre-Tax Profit:			$750.00
Taxes (estimated 20%):			150.00
Net Profit:			$600.00

2. Use your projected one-year income statement to calculate:

Projected ROI for one year: (Net Profit ÷ Start-Up Investment × 100)

$600 ÷ $1,555 × 100 = 39%

Projected ROS for one year: (Net Profit ÷ Sales × 100)

$600 ÷ $4,000 × 100 = 15%

Financing Strategy

1. What legal structure have you chosen for your business? Why?

School Supply Solutions will operate as a sole proprietorship. I understand that incorporating has advantages because it protects the business owner from losing personal assets if the business is sued or goes bankrupt. However, my business (school supplies) is not likely to cause a customer harm so my liability risk is low. It is also expensive to incorporate and I cannot afford this cost right now.

2. Make a detailed list of the items you will need to start your business. What is your total start-up investment?

Item	Quantity	Cost per item	Total
Equipment:			
Used Computer	1	@ $500.00/each =	$500.00
Cell Phone	1	@ $80.00/each =	$80.00
Printer/Fax/Copier	1	@ $100.00/each =	$100.00
Beginning Inventory (First 1-2 months):			
Pocket Folders	25	@ .60/each =	$15.00
Pencils	50	@ .03/each =	$1.50
Gelly Roll® Pens	50	@ .75/each =	$37.50
Large Spiral Notebooks	25	@ 1.00/each =	$25.00
Small Spiral Notebooks	15	@ .50/each =	$7.50
Erasers	20	@ .05/each =	$1.00
Liquid Eraser	5	@ 1.50/each =	$7.50
Looseleaf Paper Packets	3	@ 1.00/each =	$3.00
Other Costs:			
Flyers	100	@ .05/each =	$5.00
Copyright and Trademark Costs	1	@ $500.00/each =	$500.00
Business Cards	200	@ .10/each =	$20.00
Cash reserve covering 3 months of fixed costs	3	@ $85.00/each =	$255.00
Total Start-Up Investment:			$1,558.00

3. List the sources of financing for your start-up investment. Identify whether each source is equity, debt, or a gift. Indicate the amount and type for each source.

   My start-up investment will come from my own personal savings.

4. What is your debt ratio? What is your debt-to-equity ratio?

   My debt ratio is 0. My debt to equity ratio is 0:100. In other words, I have 100% equity in my business and zero debt.

5. What is your payback period? In other words, how long will it take you to earn enough profit to cover start-up capital?

   Total Start-Up Investment = $1,555

   Monthly Net Profit = $60

   1,555 ÷ 60 = 26

   My payback period will be 26 months (a little over two years).

C Joining a Student Organization

Career and Technical Student Organizations (CTSOs) are groups of students who are enrolled in a career and technical education program that engages in career and technical activities as part of the curriculum. There are different CTSOs for different career and technical programs; students join the organization related to the CTE program in which they are enrolled.

CTSOs provide members with a range of individual and group programs and activities. They promote career education and training and provide opportunities for leadership, teamwork, competition, and citizenship. CTSOs offer a unique program of career and leadership development, motivation, and recognition for students in grades 6 through 12. Members benefit from:

- Belonging to a positive and supportive group of their peers
- Examining firsthand the relationship between academics and the world of work
- Identifying career opportunities
- Building confidence and knowledge through competition
- Exercising leadership and teamwork skills
- Practicing personal skills for success
- Developing employability skills
- Recognizing and developing interests and abilities that align with career goals

Common Career and Technical Student Organizations

There are CTSOs to support every career cluster and pathway. The national CTSOs supported by educators in most states include the following:

- Family, Career and Community Leaders of America (FCCLA) for students in Family and Consumer Sciences programs (fcclainc.org)
- Future Business Leaders of America-Phi Beta Lambda (FBLA-PBL) for students in business, government, and public service programs (fbla-pbl.org)
- Business Professionals of America (BPA) for students in business and marketing programs (bpa.org)
- DECA for students in marketing programs (deca.org)
- HOSA (Health Occupations Students of America) for students in health services programs (hosa.org)
- National FFA Organization for students in agriculture programs (ffa.org)
- National Young Farmer Educational Association (NYFAE) for students in agriculture programs (nyfae.org)
- SkillsUSA for students in technical, skills, and service programs (skillsusa.org)
- Technology Student Association (TSA) for students in technology, innovation, design and engineering programs (tsaweb.org)

For more information on CTSOs at the national level, contact:

U.S. Department of Education
Office of Vocational and Adult Education
Washington, DC 20202
(202) 205-5440
National Website Address: ed.gov/about/offices/list/OVAE/index.html

D Language Arts Review

Being able to use basic grammar and punctuation in your writing is essential. How will you get the job without being able to fill out the application, write the cover letter, and create a resume? Written communication is an indispensable skill.

Grammar

Subjects and Verbs

The basic unit of writing is the simple sentence. A simple sentence expresses a complete thought. Every simple sentence must contain two basic building blocks: a **subject** and a **verb**. The subject is the main topic of the sentence—who or what the sentence is about. The verb says what the subject does.

Example of a simple sentence:
Donna bakes cupcakes for the New York Cupcake Café.

Subject: *Who?* <u>Donna</u>

Verb: *What does Donna do?* She <u>bakes</u>.

All sentences are built from subjects and verbs, so understanding how to find them is an important first step in mastering other sentence skills.

Find the Subject

When you write a sentence, you write about someone or something: the subject. To find the subject of a simple sentence, ask who or what the sentence is about. Subjects can be people, places, things, or ideas.

■ Maddie eats cheese every day.
  Who? <u>Maddie</u> (person)

■ Expensive restaurants intimidate me.
  What? Expensive <u>restaurants</u> (place)

Find the Verb

When writing about someone or something (the subject), to complete the thought you must write what the subject does: the **verb**. A verb often conveys the idea of action. To find the verb, ask what the subject does.

Action Verbs

Verbs often show action. These verbs are called **action verbs**. They tell us what somebody or something *does*.

■ Maddie eats cheese every day.
  What does Maddie do? She <u>eats</u>.

■ Expensive restaurants intimidate me.
  What do expensive restaurants do? They <u>intimidate</u>.

NOTE
Since not all verbs express action, it is helpful to keep in mind that verbs are also words that change their forms to indicate the tense or time of a sentence.

For example:
Reading is my favorite activity.

What is the verb?

Change to past tense:
Reading was my favorite activity.

Which word has changed?
So what is the verb?

Linking Verbs

Some verbs, called **linking verbs**, do not show action. Instead, a linking verb connects a noun in front of the verb with a word or group of words that comes after it. In doing so, the linking verb tells something about the subject: what the subject is or was.

Some Common Linking Verbs

am	be	feel
is	become	seem
are		look
was		appear
were		

- Pizza <u>is</u> my favorite food. (connects *pizza* with *favorite food*)
- Your outfit <u>looks</u> good. (connects *outfit* with *good*)

Prepositional Phrases

A **prepositional phrase** is a group of words beginning with a part of speech called a preposition and ending with a noun. Writers often use prepositional phrases to show time or location, as in before the game, during the party, below the table, or inside the box.

Common Prepositions

about	behind	despite	in	onto	until
above	before	down	inside	over	up
across	beneath	during	into	through	upon
after	beside	except	of	to	with
around	between	for	off	toward	within
at	by	from	on	under	without

NOTE
Linking verbs sometimes relate to the five senses: sight, sound, taste, touch, and smell.

NOTE
Prepositional phrases often answer the question *when* or *where*.

For example:
When?
   before breakfast
Where?
   over the fence

The subject never appears within a prepositional phrase, so you should ignore prepositional phrases when looking for the subject of a sentence. In the examples below, the prepositional phrases are crossed out.

■ ~~Through the night~~, we heard a strange tapping sound.
Subject: *Who?* <u>We</u>
Verb: *What did we do?* We <u>heard</u>.

■ The music ~~at the party~~ was boring.
Subject: *What?* The <u>music</u>
Verb: *What about the music?* It <u>was</u>.

Helping Verbs and Verb Phrases

Both action and linking verbs often are accompanied by other special verbs called **helping verbs**. Helping verbs frequently show time. Listed below are some frequently used helping verbs.

Helping Verbs

can	may	shall	will
could	might	should	
have	must	used to	
is	need	was	

Main verbs accompanied by one or more helping verbs are called **verb phrases**. For example, following are some verb phrases formed by adding helping verbs to the main verb learn:

Helping Verbs and Verb Phrases

is learning	has learned	should have learned
was learning	will learn	should have been learned
	had been learning	had learned
	has been learned	should have been learning

Below are sentences that contain verb phrases:

■ Eliza will be moving to Washington next week.
      Subject: *Who?* <u>Eliza</u>
      Verb phrase: *What about her?* She <u>will be moving</u>.
■ We should have left hours ago.
      Subject: *Who?* <u>We</u>
      Verb phrase: *What about us?* We <u>should have left</u>.

NOTE
Helping verbs must always accompany (help) another verb.

NOTE
Words like *not, never, always,* and *just* are not considered part of the verb even though they may be in the middle of the verb.
   I will not *be going with you today.*
   Kate had never *flown on an airplane before*

Fragments

A word group that lacks a subject or a verb and that does not show a complete thought is called a **fragment**. Because fragments are incomplete thoughts punctuated as complete ones, they can confuse readers and must be avoided. One key to eliminating fragments from your writing is knowing the difference between two types of word-groups: **phrases** and **clauses**.

NOTE
Fragment literally means "a part broken off."

Phrases and Clauses

A group of words without a subject/verb unit is called a **phrase**. A group of words with a subject/verb unit is called a **clause**.

■ **Phrase (Fragment):**
My relatives in Chicago. (no verb)

Clause:
My relatives live in Chicago. (contains a subject, *relatives,* and a verb, *live*)

■ **Phrase (Fragment):**
Rounding the corner. (no subject)

Clause:
A red convertible was rounding the corner.
(contains a subject, *convertible,* and a complete verb phrase, *was rounding*)

Independent and Dependent Clauses

Though clauses contain both a subject and a verb, that does not mean that all clauses are complete sentences. There are two types of clauses: **independent clauses** and **dependent clauses**.

A clause that can stand alone as a complete sentence is called an **independent clause**.

A **dependent clause** cannot stand alone. Dependent clauses always start with a word called a **subordinator**. Words like *although* and *since* are subordinators. Because they are incomplete thoughts, dependent clauses must be attached to independent clauses.

NOTE
Use a comma after a dependent clause if it comes at the beginning of a sentence:
  After I started exercising, I had a lot more energy.
Do not use a comma if the dependent clause comes at the end of a sentence:
  I had a lot more energy after I started exercising.

Common Subordinators

after	if	until	wherever
although	in order that	what	whether
as	since	whatever	which
because	that	when	while
before	though	whenever	who
even though	unless	where	whose

For example:

- **Independent Clause:**
  Dwane likes professional basketball.

  Dependent Clause (Fragment):
  Although Dwane likes professional basketball.

  Correction:
  Although Dwane likes professional basketball, he enjoys watching football even more. (attached dependent clause)

- **Independent Clause:**
  Richard came home for summer vacation.

  Dependent Clause (Fragment):
  Since Richard came home for summer vacation.

  Correction:
  Since Richard came home for summer vacation, he has not done a single thing. (attached dependent clause)

Correcting Fragments

Sentence fragments are phrases or dependent clauses punctuated as if they were complete sentences. Fragment literally means a "part broken off." In keeping with this definition, a sentence fragment can usually be fixed by attaching the fragment to a sentence. Thus, the "broken part" is glued back to its original position.

For example:

- **Phrase (Fragment):**
  Stanley has no patience for people. Especially his sister-in-law Blanche.

  Correction:
  Stanley has no patience for people, especially his sister-in-law Blanche.

- **Dependent Clause (Fragment):**
  Because Donna took so long to get ready. We all missed the first act of the play.

  Correction:
  Because Donna took so long to get ready, we all missed the first act of the play.

Hints on Proofreading for Fragments

Focus on each sentence separately, reading slowly. Do not be tempted to skim over your work.

Try reading out loud when you are trying to decide whether a group of words is complete or incomplete. You can often "hear it" when something is incomplete.

Learn to identify phrases and dependent clauses in writing. If you see a word group that is unattached, you know it must be a fragment.

What Are Run-on Sentences?

While some writers make the mistake of not putting enough information in a sentence, resulting in sentence fragments, others try to cram too much into their sentences. **Run-on sentences** result when two complete sentences (independent clauses) are joined with either no punctuation or only a comma. This construction makes it unclear where one thought ends and the next one begins.

Like fragments, run-ons cause readers to become confused. People often write run-ons when they sense that two thoughts belong together *logically* but do not realize that the two thoughts are separate sentences *grammatically*, as in the following examples.

■ **Run-on:**

   Dave and Rhonda are crazy about figure skating they watch it on television constantly.

   Run-on:

   Dave and Rhonda are crazy about figure skating, they watch it on television constantly.

   Correction:

   Dave and Rhonda are crazy about figure skating. They watch it on television constantly.

Generally, good writers will often join sentences which are logically related to make a more complex point. However, complete sentences *cannot* be joined with just a comma or no punctuation at all.

Correcting Run-on Sentences

Following are three useful ways to correct run-ons:

■ Make two separate sentences of the run-on thoughts by inserting a **period and a capital letter**.

   Dave and Rhonda are crazy about figure skating. They watch it on television constantly.

■ Use a **comma plus a coordinating conjunction** (*and, but, for, or, nor, so, yet*) to connect the two complete thoughts. Coordinating conjunctions are joining words that, when used with a comma, show the logical connection between two closely related thoughts.

   Dave and Rhonda are crazy about figure skating, *so* they watch it on television constantly.

■ Use a **subordinator**. You can also show the relationship between two sentences by using a subordinator (words like *after, because,* and *although*) to change one of them into a dependent clause.

   Because Dave and Rhonda are crazy about figure skating, they watch it on television constantly.

NOTE

Technically, run-ons that have no punctuation to mark the break between complete thoughts are called *fused sentences*.

Run-ons that use only a comma to attempt to join complete thoughts are called *comma splices*.

NOTE

If you have trouble recognizing the seven coordinating conjunctions, remember them by the handy acronym "FANBOYS": For, And, Nor, But, Or, Yet, So.

Common Subordinators

after	even though	unless	whenever
although	if	until	where
as	in order that	what	wherever
because	since	whatever	whether
before	though	when	while

Words That Often Lead to Run-on Sentences

Frequently the second sentence in a run-on begins with one of the words in the following list. These words often refer to something in the first sentence or seem like joining words. Beware of run-ons whenever you use one of these words in your writing.

Words That Often Lead to Run-ons

I	we	there	now
you	they	this	then
he		that	next
she			
it			

Making Subjects and Verbs Agree

Being able to identify subjects and verbs is important. But you must also make sure that the subjects and verbs agree in number. This grammatical rule is called **subject-verb agreement**.

- A singular subject (one person or one thing) is used with a singular verb.
  For example:
  Her <u>habit annoys</u> me. (singular)
  The <u>plane was</u> late. (singular)

- A plural subject (more than one person or thing) is used with a plural verb.
  For example:
  Her <u>habits annoy</u> me. (plural)
  The <u>planes were</u> late. (plural)

Writers sometimes make mistakes in subject-verb agreement in sentences with more than one subject—a compound subject—or with verbs separated from subjects. It's also common for writers to confuse subject-verb agreement when using pronouns (I, you, he, she, it, we, you, and then), either/or, neither/nor connectors, or "there" sentences. Examples of these follow.

NOTE

The rules of subject-verb agreement apply mostly to *present tense* verbs since the form of a verb changes in the present tense singular.

Present	Past
I write	I wrote
you write	you wrote
he/she *writes*	he/she wrote
we write	we wrote
they write	they wrote

NOTE

The verb *to be* causes agreement problems in the past tense as well as the present because it has many different forms.

Present	Past
I *am*	I *was*
you *are*	you *were*
he/she *is*	he/she *was*
we *are*	we *were*
they *are*	they *were*

You must learn these forms to avoid any agreement problems in your writing.

Compound Subjects

Subjects joined by **and** are typically paired with a plural verb. These are called **compound subjects.** The only exception to this rule would be subjects considered singular because they are taken as a single unit, such as *Rock 'n' Roll*.

■ For example:

<u>John and Tina</u> <u>are</u> very close. (plural)

<u>Corned beef and cabbage</u> <u>is</u> my favorite meal. (singular)

<u>Hot cocoa and a good book</u> <u>make</u> Sandra happy. (plural)

<u>Hide-and-seek</u> <u>is played</u> by almost all children. (singular)

Verbs Separated from Subjects

When words, such as prepositional phrases, come between the subject and verb, the interrupting words do not change subject-verb agreement. The verb still must agree with the subject of the sentence.

■ For example:

The <u>coins</u> ~~on the table~~ <u>are</u> mine. (plural)

The <u>price</u> ~~of the dining room chairs~~ <u>is</u> ridiculous. (singular)

That <u>woman</u> ~~with plaid bell bottoms~~ <u>seems</u> strange. (singular)

Those <u>shirts,</u> ~~as well as that coat,~~ <u>need</u> a thorough cleaning. (plural)

Punctuation

Commas

Writers use commas to mark slight pauses or breaks in sentences. When used properly, commas clarify meaning in a sentence. When overused, however, commas can interrupt the smooth flow of sentences and cause confusion. Whenever you add a comma to a sentence, you should be conscious of the specific comma usage rule you are applying. All good writers should know the six primary comma rules covered in this topic.

NOTE
Inexperienced writers tend to overuse commas rather than omit them. If you cannot think of a specific reason to use a comma, *leave it out*.

1. Use a comma after an introductory word or word group that leads into the main sentence.

    ■ Strolling down the nature trail, Zac saw a brown bear.

    ■ When you have finished eating your broccoli, you may leave the table.

A dependent clause that comes at the beginning of a sentence always needs to be followed by a comma. The second example above illustrates this concept. However, if the dependent clause comes at the end of the sentence, no comma is necessary:

    ■ You may leave the table when you have finished eating your broccoli.

2. Use commas to enclose a word or word group that interrupts the flow of a sentence.

   ■ Jane, however, will not be coming tonight.

   ■ Richard, knowing that it was going to rain, bought a new umbrella.

If you are unsure whether Rule 2 applies to a sentence, try reading the sentence without the interrupting word or words. If the sentence still makes sense without the missing material, set off the interrupting expression with commas. Note how **nonessential information** is set off with commas in the following example:

   ■ Marty Lasorda, who sat next to me in high school, is now a trader on Wall Street.

The words *who sat next to me in high school* are added information and not needed to identify the subject of the sentence, *Marty Lasorda*. However, in the next sentence the added information is necessary:

   ■ The guy who sat next to me in high school is now a trader on Wall Street.

The words *who sat next to me in high school* are **essential** to the sentence. Without them, we would have no idea to which *guy* the writer is referring.

3. Use commas to separate items in a series.

   ■ Steve ordered a large coke, large fries, and a double cheeseburger.

   ■ Tanya did her laundry, cleaned the bedroom, washed the dishes, and painted the kitchen on Sunday.

Use a comma between descriptive words in a series if *and* sounds natural between them, as in the following:

   ■ We immediately left the crowded, noisy restaurant.
   (We immediately left the crowded *and* noisy restaurant.)

   ■ Pablo wore an expensive, well-tailored suit to the party.
   (Pablo wore an expensive *and* well-tailored suit to the party.)

Notice, however, how commas are not necessary in the following sentences:

   ■ Brenda bit into a juicy red apple.

   Awkward:

   Brenda bit into a juicy *and* red apple.

In the above example *and* does not sound natural between descriptive words, so no comma is used.

4. Use a comma before the conjunctions and, but, for, or, nor, yet, or so when they connect two independent clauses.

   ■ Dwane thought he had enough money for the movie, but he was fifty cents short.

   ■ The running back broke through the line for a thirty yard gain, and the home crowd began cheering wildly.

NOTE
Nonessential information: information that can be removed from a sentence without changing its meaning.

5. Use commas around direct addresses.

When addressing a person, set off the person's name or title with commas. If the direct address comes at the beginning or end of a sentence, only one comma is necessary.

- ■ Ernest, your pants are on backwards.
- ■ Ladies and gentlemen, you are cordially invited to a reception after the show.

6. Use a comma to set off a direct quotation.

A comma separates what is said from who said it.

- ■ "Never tell me the odds," said Han Solo.
- ■ "Seeing the movie version," continued Samantha, "is never as good as reading the book."

NOTE
Commas and end punctuation marks go on the *inside* of quotation marks.

Possessive Apostrophes: Singular Nouns

The possessive form of a noun shows ownership—or possession. There are several ways to show ownership without changing the noun itself, such as:

- ■ the sweater belonging to the *girl*

   OR

- ■ the sweater of the *girl*

However, a simpler, more efficient way to show ownership is to change the possessive noun using a punctuation mark called an **apostrophe** ('):

- ■ the *girl's* sweater

NOTE
When using an apostrophe to show possession, the owner is always followed by the thing possessed. To determine the owner simply ask, "*To whom does it belong?*" The answer to this question takes the 's or the '.

Rule 1: To make a singular noun possessive, add an apostrophe and an s ('s).

- ■ the test of the *student* = the *student's* test
- ■ the ending of the *movie* = the *movie's* ending

Be careful: Do not use 's when you are simply forming a plural.

- ■ Incorrect:
   Barbecue short rib's are the specialty here.
- ■ Correct:
   Barbecue short ribs are the specialty here.

Possessive Apostrophes: Plural Nouns

A plural noun names two or more persons, places, things, or ideas. Most commonly a noun is made plural by adding an *s*: one *girl* becomes several *girls*; one *book* becomes several *books*. Making a plural noun ending in s possessive is simple:

Rule 2: To make a plural noun ending in s possessive, place an apostrophe after the s (s').

- the tests of the *students* = the *students'* tests
- the endings of the *movies* = the *movies'* endings

Some nouns change their spellings to form the plural: *child* becomes *children*; *woman* becomes *women*, for example. To make this kind of plural noun possessive simply add an apostrophe and an *s* ('*s*).

- the children's toys
- the women's self defense class

Contractions

Sometimes writers combine two words to form a single shorter word. Such a construction is called a **contraction**. An apostrophe is added to show where letters have been omitted. For example:

- I + am = I'm (the apostrophe replaces the missing *a*)
- you + will = you'll (the apostrophe replaces the missing *w* and *i*)

Here are some other common contractions:

cannot = can't	is not = isn't	they have = they've
did not = didn't	it is = it's	was not = wasn't
do not = don't	let us = let's	we are = we're
he is = he's	she is = she's	we have = we've
I will = I'll	there is = there's	will not = won't

Be careful: The possessive form of the word *it* is *its*. Do **not** add an apostrophe to show possession in this case; *it's* always means *it is* or *it has*.

- Vlada's car blew out *its* right front tire. (possessive)
- The plant outgrew *its* pot. (possessive)
- *It's* been a pleasure to meet you. (contraction: *it has*)
- I think *it's* time to go home now. (contraction: *it is*)

NOTE

When a proper noun (a name) ends in s, you may choose to add either 's or ', depending on your preference in pronunciation.

For example:
Charles's room
OR
Charles' room

NOTE

Although contractions are very common in everyday speech, try to avoid them in formal writing.

NOTE

To test if "its" is correct in a sentence, substitute the word "its" with "his."

For example:
Give the dog its bone.
Give the dog his bone.

Other Punctuation Marks

Punctuation is necessary to help make sentence meanings clearer. Commas and apostrophes are the most commonly misused punctuation marks. However, they are not the only marks that give writers trouble. Listed below are the rules for other punctuation marks that are used in writing.

Period

Use a **period** (.) at the end of all sentences except for direct questions and exclamations.

Use a period at the end of any indirect question.

■ **Example:**
John asked Beth why there were no cookies left.

Use a period after most abbreviations.

■ **Example:**
Dr.
Ms.
Jr.

Question Mark

Use a **question mark** (?) at the end of a direct question. But, as illustrated above, do not use a question mark to end an indirect question.

■ **Examples:**
How cold is it outside?
When was the Civil War fought?
John asked Beth, "Why are there no cookies left?"
"Why are there no cookies left?" asked John.

Exclamation Point

An **exclamation point** (!) is used to at the end of a statement of strong feeling or after an interjection.

■ **Example:**
Look out for that truck!
Hey! Somebody stole my wallet!

NOTE
Before the advent of computers, two spaces were always inserted after a period. However, the current trend is to use only one space after a period.

NOTE
Do not use periods in acronyms (abbreviations made up of the first letter from a series of words).

Example:
NATO

NOTE
Never use exclamation points in formal writing. Save them for casual e-mail correspondence and written dialog.

Colon

Use a **colon** (:) to introduce a list. The words that come before the colon must be a complete sentence.

- **Incorrect:**

  Two things that I hate are: rainy days and Sundays.

- **Correct:**

  There are two things that I hate: rainy days and Sundays.

A colon is used to help explain the statement that precedes the colon. It is also used to set off an explanation or final word.

- **Examples:**

  There are only two things I like to do on Sundays: go to the movies and have pizza for dinner.

  We all had the same goal: success.

Use a colon after salutations in business correspondence, even if you address the person by their first name.

- **Examples:**

  Dear Ms. Smith:

  Dear Verna:

NOTE
Do not use semicolons to set off a list; use a colon.

Semicolon

A **semicolon** (;) is used to separate closely related independent clauses. Often the semicolon is used in place of the word *because*.

- **Example:**

  Sarah was excited about the party; she knew that Greg was going to be there.

Use a semicolon to separate items in a series when the items themselves contain commas.

- **Example:**

  There are four pizza toppings that I enjoy: pepperoni, sausage, and mushrooms; green peppers, onions, and olives; eggplant, garlic, and anchovies; and spinach, goat cheese, and sun-dried tomatoes.

NOTE
If you are not sure if you should hyphenate a compound word, try looking the word up in the dictionary. As a rule of thumb, words ending in *ly* are not hyphenated.

Incorrect: *freshly-cut flowers*
Correct: *fresh-cut flowers*

Hyphens

Hyphenating documents has become much easier on the computer since you can automatically hyphenate the document, move the word to the next line, or compress the word to keep it on one line. However, hyphens have other functions, as discussed below.

Use a **hyphen** (-) to combine two nouns when they are acting as a singular, descriptive word. To see if the two words should be hyphenated into one descriptive word, ask yourself "what kind" of noun is being described.

■ **Examples:**

a three-legged dog (What kind of dog? *three-legged*)

a four-day convention (What kind of convention? *four-day*)

Incorrect:

I went to a convention that lasted four-days.
(Four days does not answer the question "what kind.")

In writing, hyphenate the numbers twenty-one through ninety-nine and all fractions:

■ **Examples:**

thirty-three

one-half

Do not hyphenate three-word numbers.

■ **Example:**

four hundred five

Use a hyphen with the prefix *mid* when referring to time.

■ **Example:**

the mid-sixties

Do not hyphenate the prefix *mid* when referring to other things:

■ **Example:**

midlife crisis

Hyphenate the prefix *re* only for ease of reading.

■ **Examples:**

re-edited

re-evaluated

restated (no hyphen needed)

Dashes

Use a **dash** (—) to show a sudden break in thought or to set off parenthetical information. The dash is also called an **em dash** because it is about the width of a capital M.

Use an **em dash** (—) to interrupt a sentence or to add additional information. Em dashes can be used in place of commas to add additional drama to the sentence. Em dashes can also be used to set off contrasting remarks.

■ **Examples:**

The bank robbers—with guns in hand—fired the first shot.

We plan to revise the book in two—not three—months.

An **en dash** (–) is longer than a hyphen and shorter than an em dash. Its length is about the width of a capital N. Use an en dash to show continuation in time, dates, or other numbers. Think of using an en dash instead of the words *to* or *through*.

NOTE

In Microsoft Word you can create an em dash (—) by typing two hyphens (--) with no spaces between them or before or after them. Word will automatically create an em dash for you.

■ **Examples:**

9:00 AM–5:00 PM   1990–94

March–May   pages 220–284

Parentheses

Like dashes or commas, **parentheses ( )** are used to set off information that is extra or inessential to the meaning of the sentence.

NOTE
Do not overuse parentheses in your writing.

■ **Example:**

The chapter on medieval art (pages 172–184) is very interesting.

Quotation Marks

NOTE
Quotation marks always come in pairs.

Quotation Marks ("") are used to set off someone's exact words. A comma always separates what is said from who said it. Periods and commas go inside of quotation marks.

■ **Examples:**

"There are too many rules to punctuation," he stated.

The clerk told me, "There are no more bananas today."

Use **single quotes** (' ') to enclose titles of poems, stories, movie titles, or other quoted material within quoted material.

■ **Examples:**

"'Survivor' is my favorite TV show," the teenage girl proclaimed.

"If you call Johnny 'stinky toes' one more time," Mom told Suzy, "you're going to your room."

E | Math Review

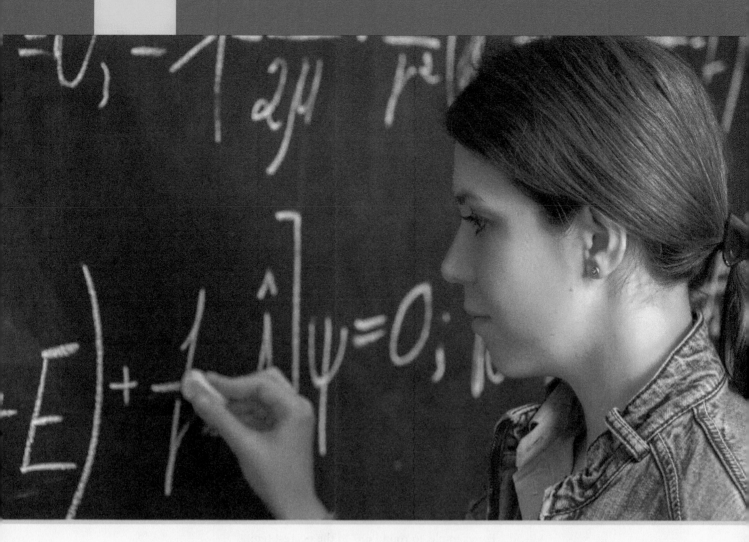

Knowing basic math concepts and knowing when to apply them are essential skills. You should know how to add, subtract, multiply, divide, calculate percentages, and manipulate fractions. This section will help you accurately apply basic math concepts and skills necessary to your success at school, work, and to manage your personal finances at home.

Numbers

Numbers are expressed in different forms:

■ Whole numbers, which are the counting numbers and zero. Whole numbers do not contain decimals or fractions. *Examples:* 1, 2, 3, 10, 15, 18, 0. Ignore zeros before whole numbers. For example, 025 is the same as 25.

■ Nonwhole numbers, which are numbers that have decimals, such as 6.25 or 9.85.

■ Mixed numbers, which are numbers that combine whole numbers and a fraction, such as $6^1/_4$ or $7^2/_3$.

■ Percentages, which are portions in relation to a whole, such as 65% or 22%.

Place Value

Numbers that have more than one digit are defined by their place value. Place value is the value of a digit based on where it is in a number. For example, the number 7777 is given the following values:

This number is described by saying "seven thousand, seven hundred seventy-seven." Numbers are written with a comma placed to the left of every third digit. The number 7777 is properly written 7,777.

Rounding Whole Numbers

1. Find the place to be rounded.
2. If the digit to the right is 5 or more, add 1 to the place to be rounded. If the digit to the right is 4 or less, leave the place to be rounded unchanged.
3. Change all digits to the right of the rounded place to zeroes.

For example, to round 687 to the nearest ten:

1. The place to be rounded is the number in the tens column.
2. The digit to the right of the tens column is greater than 5, so you add 1 to the digit in the place to be rounded, making it 9.
3. Change the 7 to a zero. The result is 690.

Working with Decimals and Percentages

Recall that a percentage is a portion of a whole. 100 percent = the whole or all of something. The symbol for percent is %. In the figure to the right, four turtles = 100% or all of the turtles. One turtle is ¼ of the total, or 25%. Two turtles = ½ of the total, or 50%. Three turtles = ¾ or 75%. Numbers to the left of a decimal are whole numbers. Numbers to the right of a decimal are less than one.

Four turtles = 100%.

One turtle or 25% of the turtles are sold.

To divide decimals by whole numbers:

$24.5 \div 4 = 4\overline{)24.5}$ Place the decimal point in the answer directly above the decimal point in the dividend.

Add 0s to carry answer.

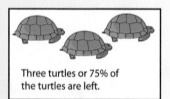

Three turtles or 75% of the turtles are left.

Numbers to the right of a decimal point indicate less than one whole. For example, 1.5 is the same as 1½.

If there were five turtles in the figure, what percentage would one turtle represent?

Examples:

Decimal		Percentage		Fraction(s)
0.10	=	10%	=	¹⁰/₁₀₀ or ¹/₁₀
0.25	=	25%	=	²⁵/₁₀₀ or ¼
6.25	=	625%	=	6 ²⁵/₁₀₀ or 6¼

To change a decimal number into a percentage: Move the decimal two places to the right.

Examples:

0.5 = 0.5 0. = 50%

30.0 = 30.0 0. = 3000%

0.04 = .0 4. = 4%

To change a percentage into a decimal number: Replace the percent sign with a decimal and move the decimal two spaces to the left.

To find the percentage of a number:

1. Change the percentage to a decimal.
2. Multiply that decimal by the number.

Examples:

15% of 63   change 15% to 0.15 then multiply 0.15 × 63 = 9.45

9.45 is 15% of 63

20% of 100   change 20% to 0.20 then multiply 0.20 × 100 = 20

20 is 20% of 100

Addition

Addition is the totaling of two or more numbers. Each number you are adding is called an *addend*. The result is called the *sum* or *total*. For example, 2 computers in the reception area + 3 computers in accounting = a total of 5 computers in the office.

To add:

1. Write the addends in columns, making sure each digit lines up correctly according to its place value. That means putting ones in the ones column, tens in the tens column, hundreds in the hundreds column, and so on.
2. Draw a line under the last addend in the column.
3. Add all the addends above the line and write the total or sum below the line.

Examples:

```
   2      34      <— addends
 + 3     + 4      <— addends
   5      38      <— totals
```

When adding more than one column of numbers, always start adding numbers in the right column—place value ones—first.

Adding by Carrying Numbers

When the numbers in a column add up to more than 10, you must *carry* all digits to the left of the place value ones column. To carry means to move the digits to the top of the next place value column. You then add the carried digits with all the numbers in that column.

For example, to add 81 + 384 + 10 + 9:

1. Write the numbers in columns, lining them up according to place value.
2. Add the numbers in the ones column. The total is 14.
3. Write the 4 in the ones column below the total line, and carry the 1 to the top of the tens column.
4. Add the numbers in the tens column, including the 1 you carried. The total is 18.
5. Write the 8 in the tens column below the total line, and carry the 1 to the top of the hundreds column.
6. Add the numbers in the hundreds column, including the 1 you carried. The total is 4.
7. Write the 4 in the hundreds column below the total line. The sum of the numbers is 484.

Example 1:

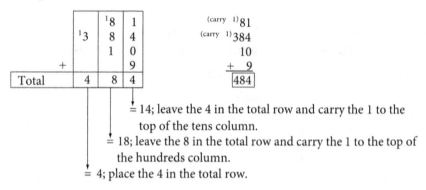

= 14; leave the 4 in the total row and carry the 1 to the
  top of the tens column.

= 18; leave the 8 in the total row and carry the 1 to the top of
  the hundreds column.

= 4; place the 4 in the total row.

Example 2:

= 14; leave the 4 in the total row and carry the 1 to the
  top of the tens column.

= 35; leave the 5 in the total row, carry the 3 to the top of
  the hundreds column.

= 12; leave the 2 in the total row, and carry the 1 to the top
  of the thousands column. 1 is the only number in the thousands
  columns, so you write the 1 in the total column.

Subtraction

Subtraction is the opposite of addition. Subtracting numbers means taking one
number—called the *subtrahend*—away from another number—called the *minuend*. The result is called the *difference*. Write a subtraction problem in columns,
just like you write an addition problem. Put the minuend on top, and the subtrahend below it. Make sure you line up the digits in the proper place value column.

Subtract the number in the ones column first, and write the difference below the
line. Then, subtract the number in the tens column, then the hundreds column,
and so on.

```
    84        <— minuend —>         136
  – 23        <— subtrahend —>     – 12
   [61]       <— difference —>     [124]
```

Check your answer by adding the difference to the subtrahend. If your answer is
correct, your total will equal the minuend

For example, you can check your subtraction for the first equation above by
adding 61 (the answer) to 23 (the number you subtracted). 61 + 23 = 84, which is
the number you started with at the top of the equation. The answer is correct.

Subtracting by Borrowing Numbers

When the number you are subtracting is greater than the number above it in the column, you can borrow a one from the column to the left. Borrowing makes the number at the top of the equation greater, so you can complete the subtraction.

When you borrow the one, you must do two things:

1. Cross out the number in the column to the left, and replace it with a number that is one less than the number that was there. For example, if there is a 3 in the column to the left, you cross out the 3 and replace it with a 2. If there is a 7, you cross out the 7 and replace it with a 6.
2. Write the borrowed 1 to the left of the number that is currently in the column you are subtracting. So, if there is a 5 in the column you are subtracting, you write the borrowed 1 to the left of the 5; the 5 becomes 15.

Examples:

$$^2\cancel{3}\,^15$$
$$-\ \underline{1\ 8}$$
$$\boxed{1\ 7}$$

8 is greater than 5, so you can borrow a one from the tens column.
Cross out the 3 in the tens column and replace it with a 2.
Write the borrowed 1 to the left of the 5, making it 15.
Subtract 8 from 15 and write the result (7) below the line in the ones column.
Subtract 1 from 2 and write the result (1) below the line in the tens column.

Adding and Subtracting Decimals

For decimals, the process of adding and subtracting numbers is similar to the process for adding and subtracting whole numbers. The only difference is how the numbers are aligned in the column. Numbers should be aligned by the decimal point as in the following examples:

$$\begin{array}{r} 12.136 \\ +\ \underline{10.246} \\ 22.382 \end{array}$$

$$\begin{array}{r} 23.453 \\ -\ \underline{10.37} \\ 13.083 \end{array}$$

Adding and Subtracting Fractions

A fraction is made up of two parts: a *numerator*, which is the number on top, and a *denominator*, or the number on the bottom. To add or subtract a fraction, the denominator must be the same. Consider the following examples:

Example 1:

$$\frac{1}{4} + \frac{3}{4} = \frac{1+3}{4} = \frac{4}{4} = \frac{1}{1} = 1$$

Example 2:

$$\frac{1}{5} + \frac{2}{5} + 12\frac{4}{5} = \frac{1}{5} + \frac{2}{5} + \frac{64}{5} = \frac{1+2+64}{5} = \frac{67}{5} = 13\frac{2}{5}$$

Example 3:

$$\frac{2}{3} - \frac{1}{3} = \frac{2-1}{3} = \frac{1}{3}$$

Note that Example 1 shows a simplified fraction, or a fraction that does not have any common factors (other than 1) for the numerator and denominator. Example 2 shows a mixed number, which is converted to a fraction to be added or subtracted.

In some cases, fractions will need to be converted so each fraction being added has a common denominator. Consider the following example:

$$\frac{1}{3} + \frac{1}{2} = ?$$

Step 1: Convert each fraction so they have a common denominator.

The denominators, 2 and 3, are factors of 6, so multiply both the nominator and the denominator of each fraction by the number that makes the denominator equal to 6.

$$\frac{1}{3} \times \frac{2}{2} = \frac{2}{6}$$

$$\frac{1}{2} \times \frac{3}{3} = \frac{3}{6}$$

Step 2: Add fractions.

$$\frac{2}{6} + \frac{3}{6} = \frac{5}{6}$$

For subtraction, follow the same process to make fractions that have the same denominator. Simplify fractions after adding and subtracting as needed.

$$\frac{3}{4} - \frac{1}{3} = ?$$

Step 1: Convert each fraction so they have a common denominator.

$$\frac{3}{4} \times \frac{3}{3} = \frac{9}{12}$$

$$\frac{1}{3} \times \frac{4}{4} = \frac{4}{12}$$

Step 2: Subtract fractions.

$$\frac{9}{12} - \frac{4}{12} = \frac{5}{12}$$

Add or subtract the following:

3.45 + 2.34 + 5.6

$$3\frac{3}{4} + \frac{2}{3} + \frac{4}{5}$$

3.4 − 1.28

$$2\frac{3}{4} - 1\frac{1}{3}$$

What will happen if you don't convert fractions to a common denominator before adding or subtracting them?

Multiplication

Multiplication, the process of finding the product of two factors, is a quick, easy way to add. For example, 9 + 9 + 9 = 27, but an easier process is 3 × 9 = 27.

To multiply numbers easily, memorize the multiplication table.

Multiplication Table

	1	2	3	4	5	6	7	8	9	10
1	1	2	3	4	5	6	7	8	9	10
2	2	4	6	8	10	12	14	16	18	20
3	3	6	9	12	15	18	21	24	27	30
4	4	8	12	16	20	24	28	32	36	40
5	5	10	15	20	25	30	35	40	45	50
6	6	12	18	24	30	36	42	48	54	60
7	7	14	21	28	35	42	49	56	63	70
8	8	16	24	32	40	48	56	64	72	80
9	9	18	27	36	45	54	63	72	81	90
10	10	20	30	40	50	60	70	80	90	100

Multiplying Fractions

To multiply fractions:

1. Multiply the first **numerator**—the number above the line in the fraction—by the second numerator. Write the answer as the numerator in the result.
2. Multiply the first **denominator**—the number below the line in the fraction— by the second denominator. Write the answer as the denominator in the result.

The numerators, or top numbers of the fractions, are multiplied; and the denominators, or bottom numbers of the fractions, are multiplied. For example:

$$\frac{3}{4} \times \frac{12}{15} = \frac{36}{60}$$

If possible, reduce the fraction, which means dividing both the numerator and the denominator by the largest number than goes into both. In the following example, 12 is the largest number that goes into both. 36 divided by 12 equals 3. 60 divided by 12 equals 5. You can reduce the fraction to $3/5$.

$$\frac{36}{60} \text{ to } \frac{3}{5}$$

401(k) plan	a savings plan offered by an employer to an employee
403(b) plan	a savings plan offered by an employer to an employee
abstinence	avoiding or refraining from certain behavior
accommodation	a change that makes it possible for a disabled employee to perform his or her job responsibilities in a safe and accessible work environment
accomplishments	things you have achieved at home, in school, or in the community
account register	a book the bank provides to customers to keep track of their transactions
addend	the numbers totaled in an addition equation
addiction	a need to continue using a substance even though it has negative consequences
addition	the totaling of two or more numbers
aggressive	forcing your opinions on others
algorithms	programs designed to solve mathematical problems
Americans with Disabilities Act (ADA)	a law that makes it illegal to discriminate based on age or physical disability
angel investors	a wealthy individual or group interested in investing money in a start-up in exchange for an equity share
app	a computer program designed for use on a mobile device
apprentice	someone who works with a professional to learn a skill or trade
apprenticeship	a paid training program in a given trade
arbitrator	a person who is trained to settle an issue between parties in dispute
assertive	stand up for yourself in a strong and positive way
assets	everything owned by a business that has monetary value
associate's degree	a degree that usually requires two years of study after high school to earn
attitude	the way you think, feel, or behave, particularly when you are with other people
audit	an official inspection of records and accounts
auditory learners	people who take in information best when they hear it
authorizing	giving permission or allowing
automation software	programs that enable computers to perform repetitive, time-consuming tasks
average	the sum of two or more quantities divided by the number of quantities
axis	the horizontal or vertical lines in a graph or chart
bachelor's degree	a degree that usually requires four years of study after high school to earn

balance sheet	a financial record that summarizes the assets and liabilities of a business
balance	the amount of money in an account
balanced	in banking, keeping track of money coming in and going out of an account
bank account	a record of the transactions between a bank and its client
bank charter	an agreement that controls how a bank operates
bank	a business that stores and manages money for individuals and other businesses
bankruptcy	a legal process in which you declare yourself legally unable to pay your outstanding debts
bar graph	a graph that displays comparisons among individual items
barter	negotiate the value of traded goods
base pay	hourly wage or annual salary that you earn
beneficiary	the person who collects insurance money if there is a claim
biometric time clock	a time-clock that uses a fingerprint or handprint to record when an employee comes and goes
bond	a debt security issued by corporations, governments, or their agencies, in return for cash from lenders and investors
bonus	a lump sum paid in addition to base pay
Boolean operators	words, terms, or symbols that set criteria for an Internet search
bootstrapping	doing something for yourself without help from anyone else
branch	local bank office
branding	a method of creating a strong, identifiable, and sometimes emotional attachment between your customers and your product
breach of contract	failure to carry out the conditions of a contract
break-even analysis	a process used to determine how many units of sale a business must sell to cover all of its expenses
break-even point	when expenses equal sales, and a business has a net income of zero
break-even unit	the number of units of sale a business must sell to arrive at its break-even point
budget	a plan for spending and saving money
business ethics	moral principles applied to business issues and actions
business management	the skillful use and coordination of a business's resources in an organized and efficient way to achieve business goals
business opportunity	a consumer need or want that can be met by a new business
business plan	a statement of your business goals, the reasons you think these goals can be met, and how you are going to achieve them
business	an organization that provides goods or services, usually to earn money
calorie	a unit of food energy

candidate	possible employee
career cluster	a category used to identify occupations in a similar area or industry
career fair	an event organized so that people searching for jobs may meet and collect information from a large number of employers in one place; also called a job fair
career plan	a map that shows you the way to achieve your career goals
career requirements	the responsibilities that you must perform in order to succeed in the career
career self-assessment	a process that helps you identify career-related interests, values, and abilities
career	a chosen field of work in which you try to advance over time by gaining responsibility and earning more money; another word for career is occupation
cash budget	a forecast of the inflow and outflow of cash in the future, for a set period of time
cash flow statements	a financial record that shows the inflow and outflow of cash when they occur
cash flow	money received minus money spent over a set period of time
cash reserves	money set aside for emergencies
cash value	the actual worth of something
central bank	an organization responsible for managing banking activity
certificates of deposit (CDs)	time account with minimum balance and set term
character	the personal qualities or traits that make you unique
chart	a picture that displays data; also called a graph
check	written order to a bank to transfer funds from one account to another
checking account	a bank account that allows you to withdraw funds using checks and/or a debit card
civic responsibility	service that you owe to a community of which you are a part
Civil Rights Act of 1964	a law which states that employers may not use race, skin color, religion, sex, or national origin as a reason to promote, not promote, hire, or fire an employee
cloud computing	a type of computing in which all files and programs are stored online and accessed through the Internet
co-curricular	activities such as athletic teams, clubs, and career student organizations, offered to students in addition to class subjects
code of ethics	a document that describes a business's moral values and sets guidelines for behavior
coding system	a method of keeping track of files using unique names
collaborative software	programs that allow more than one person to work on a document at a time
colleagues	co-workers
collective bargaining agreement	the labor contract that is the result of collective bargaining
collective bargaining	negotiation between workers and their union representatives on one side and employers represented by management on the other
command economy	economic system in which the government owns or manages the nation's resources and businesses

commission	a payment based on a percentage of sales
commodity	an item such as gold, wheat, or coal that can be traded, processed, and sold
communication barriers	differences that can be obstacles to effective communication
community resources	services that the government provides, such as public parks, public schools, libraries, and police and fire departments
community	a group of people who have a common goal
compensation	wages and benefits provided in exchange for work
competent	capable; in law, someone who is capable of understanding the terms and consequences of a contract
competition	businesses that offer the same or similar product, with which you are competing for the dollars your target market spends
competitive advantage	something that makes your business more appealing to your target market than the competitors' businesses
computer application	a software program that enables you to perform specific tasks using a computer
computer program	a software application that enables you to perform specific tasks using a computer
computer virus	a software program that spreads from computer to computer destroying data
conditions	events or circumstances that must occur for a contract to be legal
confidentiality agreement	a contract that binds parties to secrecy; also called a nondisclosure agreement
conflict	a disagreement between two or more people who have different ideas
consequences	results that happen in response to a decision or action
consideration	in law, a benefit that each party provides for the other
constructive criticism	helpful suggestions from others on how to improve
consumer credit	when a business gives consumers an extended payment time for purchased goods or services
consumer price index (CPI)	a measure of the changes in the prices of goods and services
consumers	people who purchase goods and services
contract	a legal document that defines the conditions of an agreement between two parties; an agreement between competent parties in which each promises to take or avoid a specified action
cooperative	a business owned, controlled, and operated for the mutual benefit of its members
coping skills	actions and thoughts that help you deal with or overcome problems and difficulties that you might not be able to solve
copyright	the exclusive right to perform, display, copy, or distribute an artistic work
corporate social responsibility	when a business acts in ways that balance profit and growth with the good of society
corporation	a type of business ownership arrangement in which the business is considered an entity under the law, and owners are called shareholders

cost of goods sold	expenses incurred in order to sell one unit
cost/benefit analysis	the process of adding up all the expected benefits of an opportunity and subtracting all the expected costs
cover letter	a short, one-page summary of who you are, why you are applying for the job, and why you are the best person for it, that you send to a potential employer with your resume
credit card	a card you use in place of cash to buy something and pay for it later
credit limit	the maximum amount you can charge to a credit card or borrow from a bank
credit report	a summary of your credit history
credit union	nonprofit banks that are owned by the customers or members
credit	money that you borrow and promise to pay back
creditor	someone who loans money
critical reading	thinking about what is written and why, while you read
critical thinking	the ability to be honest, rational, and open-minded
criticism	advice about how to make positive changes in your actions or behavior
culture	language, beliefs, attitudes, customs, manners, and habits that define a group of people or community
currency	the unit of money used in a country
current ratio	current assets divided by current liabilities
customer objections	reasons a customer may be wary or unwilling to buy a product or service
customer profile	a description of an ideal customer for a particular product or service
data analysis	a type of math used to collect, organize, and analyze data; another term for statistics
data	information
debit card	card you use in place of cash to make purchases or withdrawals
debt financing	borrowing money from a source such as a bank, credit union, relative, or friend
debt ratio	the ratio of a business's total debt—or liabilities—divided by its total assets
debt	the money that you borrowed and owe
debtor	someone who owes money
debt-to-equity ratio	a comparison of a business's total debts and the owner's equity
decimal point	the period used to separate whole numbers and numbers less than one in a written decimal
decimal	a fraction written using a decimal point to separate whole numbers and numbers less than one, representing multiples of ten
decision	the process of choosing one option over one or more alternative options
deductible	a set amount an insurance beneficiary must pay toward a claim before the insurance company pays any money

deduction	an amount that your employer withholds from your earnings to pay for things such as taxes or insurance
deference	courteous regard or respect
deficit	when more money is spent than earned
degree	a certificate awarded by an institution such as a college or university when you complete the requirements of an academic or vocational program
demand	the quantity of goods and services consumers are willing to buy at a specific price and specific time
demographics	facts about a population
denomination	the face value of money
denominator	the number below the fraction bar in a written fraction
deposit slip	a form you fill out when you deposit money in a bank account
devil's advocate	a label used to describe taking a position you do not necessarily agree with, but pretend you do for the sake of argument
dictate	speak so someone or something can write down your words
diet	the food you eat
difference	the measurement between two values; in math, you find the difference by subtracting one value from another
diploma	the document which certifies that you successfully completed your high school study
direct competitors	businesses that sell a product or service similar to yours
direct deposit	paycheck that is automatically deposited into an account
discrimination	unfair treatment of a person or group based on age, gender, race, or religion
diversity	an environment that includes variety, such as people of different ages, cultural backgrounds, and race
dividend	the total or whole in a division equation; also, the amount of a corporation's after-tax earnings that it pays to its shareholders
division	the process of separating a whole into parts; the opposite of multiplication
divisor	the number by which you divide a dividend in a division equation
docent	guide
dropout	someone who leaves school without receiving a diploma
dual-income family	a family in which both parents have paying jobs
dues	fees paid for membership
dysfunctional	not working correctly
e-commerce (electronic commerce)	buying and selling goods or services over the Internet
economic system	the way a country uses limited resources to provide goods and services

economics of one unit	a calculation that determines the profit—or loss—that a business earns every time a customer buys a unit of sale
economics	the study of the way people produce, distribute, and use goods and services and other resources to achieve their needs and wants
economy	activity related to the production and distribution of goods and services
elapsed time	the amount of time that has passed from one time to another
electives	classes you choose because you are interested in the subject
electronic fund transfer (EFT)	transfer of money from one bank account to another electronically
elevator pitch	a business plan presentation that is short enough to be delivered during an elevator ride
emotional well-being	well-being that depends on your ability to deal with problems and stress
employability	having and using your life skills and abilities to be hired and stay hired
employee handbook	a document that describes company policies and procedures
employee	a person who works in a business owned by someone else
emulate	copy in a respectful manner
encrypted	digitally coded for security purposes
encryption	code
endorse	approve or sign
entrepreneur	a person who organizes and runs his or her own business
entrepreneurship	the process of starting a new business
environmental well-being	well-being that depends on your comfort and satisfaction with the environment in which you live and work
Equal Employment Opportunity Commission (EEOC)	the federal agency responsible for investigating charges of discrimination against employers
equilibrium	the ideal quantity and price to meet consumer demand exactly
equity financing	selling shares of ownership in a business to sources such as relatives, friends, venture capitalists, or partners
equity investments	stock—or ownership—in a company
equity	ownership
estimate	guess, using past experience and knowledge as a guide
ethics	a set of beliefs about what is right and what is wrong
etiquette	a culture's social rules and customs
exchange rate	a calculation that determines how much foreign currency you can buy for one dollar
excise tax	a consumption tax imposed on a specific product or activity
exit interview	a meeting with your supervisor or human resources representative to discuss why you are leaving

expenses	all the ways you use money
exports	goods or services that are sent from one country and sold to foreign consumers
face value	the number printed or stamped on money
factors	numbers multiplied in a multiplication equation
fair use	a legal provision that allows for the limited quotation of a copyrighted work without permission from or payment to the copyright holder
Family and Medical Leave Act (FMLA)	a law that provides certain employees with up to 12 weeks of unpaid, job-protected leave per year
FDIC (Federal Deposit Insurance Corporation)	the government agency that provides insurance for bank deposits
Federal Reserve	institution responsible for creating and tracking all of the country's money
FICA	Social Security tax
financial aid	money provided by others to help you pay for education
financial decision	a decision about how to manage your money
financial goals	plans you have for using your money
financial needs	the things you must buy in order to survive
financial ratios	relationships between items of important financial information that are expressed as fractions or as percentages
financial record	written statements about a business's performance
financial wants	the things you need to maintain a certain standard of living
financing	raising money for a business
firewalls	software that restricts unauthorized access to a site
fixed expense	known expenses that stay the same every month
fixed income investments	money lent to a business or government agency in exchange for a bond
fixed income	income that does not change month to month
flexible (variable) expense	expenses that change from month to month
flexible (variable) income	income that changes month to month
flexible standards	standards that you can adapt to different situations
focus group	a discussion about a product or service held among a small number of potential customers
forecast	predict or estimate future occurrences based on past experience
formula	rule or method of doing something
fraction bar	the line between a numerator and denominator in a written fraction
fraction	a ratio, or comparison of two whole numbers, or one whole number divided by another whole number

franchise	an arrangement in which an established company sells the right for others to use the company's name and operating plan to sell products or services
franchisee	someone who buys a franchise
franchisor	a company that sells franchises
free enterprise system	a market economy in which individuals or businesses operate and invest with little government interference
frequency	the number of times an event occurs
FTC (Federal Trade Commission)	the federal agency responsible for the fair treatment of consumers
fungible	the ability to trade one item or quality for another
geometry	math that deals with the size, position, and shape of 2- and 3-dimensional objects
give notice	tell your employer you are leaving your job
globalization	the growing integration of the world's economies
goal	something you are trying to achieve
governance	making decisions about how government will act
grade point average	the average of all grades that you receive
grant	financial aid you do not have to repay
graph	a picture that displays data; also called a chart
graphical representation	way of conveying information without words
gross domestic product (GDP)	the total value of all goods and services produced in a country
gross income	pay before withholdings
gross profit per unit	the amount of profit used to pay operating expenses
harassment	unwanted, repeated behavior or communication that bothers, annoys, frightens, or stresses another person
help wanted ads	job listings for specific positions; also called classified ads
human resources	resources people provide that things cannot
hydraulic arm	a machine that creates power by pumping water through a confined space
imports	goods and services that are brought into a country from foreign suppliers
impulsive	inclined to act without thinking
income statement	a financial document that summarizes a business's income and expenses over a given time period; also called a profit and loss statement
income tax returns	forms you fill out and send in to the government stating how much income you earned and how much tax you must pay
income	all the money that you earn or receive
indecisive	unable to make a decision

index	a list of the names of all items in a set, such as the names given to each file in a filing system, and the corresponding location where each can be found
indicators	mathematical tools used to measure the health of the economy
indirect competitors	businesses that sell different products or services than yours, but fill the same need or want
individual retirement account (IRA)	a personal retirement savings plan
inflation	when the average price of goods goes up sharply
influence	something that affects the way you think and act
information technology (IT)	computer and telecommunication systems that transmit and store information
informational interview	the opportunity to sit down with someone who is employed to ask questions and learn about his or her career or industry
infringement	violating the rights provided by a copyright or patent
instrumental value	value based on an item's usefulness for acquiring something else
insurance agent	someone who sells insurance
insurance claim	a request for payment to cover a loss
insurance policy	a contract issued by the insurance company
insurance premium	the amount of money paid by an insurance policy holder
insurance	an investment that protects you financially against everyday risks
integral	necessary or essential
intellectual property	artistic and industrial creations of the mind
intellectual well-being	well-being that depends on your ability to think and learn new things
interests	subjects or activities that attract your attention and that you enjoy doing or learning about
Internal Revenue Service (IRS)	the federal government agency responsible for collecting federal taxes
internship	a temporary job, usually for students, that may or may not pay a salary, but provides other useful benefits, such as the opportunity to gain experience
intrapreneurship	acting like an entrepreneur while working as an employee
intrinsic value	value based on an item's own merits
inventory	goods you have available to sell
investment bank	banks that help businesses and other organizations raise money by issuing stocks and bonds
irradiation	a process that exposes fresh food to a source of radiation in order to kill bacteria and insects
job application	a standard form you fill out when you apply for a job
job interview	a meeting between a job seeker and a potential employer—the interviewer

job lead	information that might lead you to find a job
job outlook	a prediction of future opportunities for a particular occupation
job search resources	tools designed to help you find job leads
job security	knowing you will have a job for a long time
job shadowing	to follow someone around at work for a day, or part of a day
job	any activity that you do in exchange for money or other payment
job-share	a position in which two employees share the responsibilities for one job
just-in-time	a method of reducing costs while improving quality and efficiency by limiting the amount of inventory a manufacturer keeps in stock
labor market	any situation in which workers compete for jobs and employers compete for workers
layoff	a job loss caused when a company has no work for certain employees for a period of time
leader	someone who unites people to work toward common goals
learning style	a way of taking in information so that you remember it and can use it in a practical way
lease	a written contract in which a property owner gives temporary use of that property to another party
least common denominator (LCD)	the smallest number that two different denominators can divide into evenly
leisure	fun activities outside of work
liability insurance	type of corporate structure that protects a business when the business's action, or lack of action, injures someone or another business
liability	debt, or any outstanding bill or loan that must be repaid; also, the legal obligation of a business owner to use personal money and possessions to pay the debts of the business
license	a legal document issued by a state or local government that allows a business to provide a regulated product or service
lifestyle factors	things about your job that affect the way you live your life
lifestyle	the way you think and behave every day
limited liability	liability that protects owners from being legally responsible for paying business debt
line graph	a graph that uses lines to display data that shows trends over time
liquidity	the ability of an investment to be easily converted into cash with little or no loss of capital and a minimum of delay
loan	a transaction in which the lender agrees to give the borrower money and expects to be repaid in full
local time	current time in the time zone where a person is located
long-term goals	something you want to achieve in the more distant future
majority	a greater number or part

manager	someone who makes decisions, solves problems, and uses resources to achieve specific goals
man-hour	a measurement unit equal to the amount of work one employee performs in one hour
manufacturer	a type of business that uses materials to build goods that it can sell to others
manufacturing	using machines to design and build products
market economy	an economic system in which suppliers produce whatever goods and services they wish and set prices based on what consumers are willing to pay
market research	research used to learn as much as possible about potential customers
market share	the percentage of total sales captured by a product or a business in a particular market
market	a group of potential customers
marketing plan	a detailed guide that identifies your marketing goals and strategies
marriage	an institution that grants a couple a unique set of legal, social, and religious rights and responsibilities
mass market	attempt to sell a product to a wide range of customers
mean	a typical value calculated by adding all values and dividing the total by the number of values; another term for average
median	the middle value in a set
mentor	someone knowledgeable and experienced in your field who is willing to teach you, advise you, and help you reach your goals
milestones	a series of short-term goals achieved in the process of working toward a long-term goal
minority	a lesser number or part
mixed fraction	a mix of whole numbers and fractions, such as $1\frac{1}{4}$
mode	the number that occurs most often in a set
monetary compensation	compensation in the form of money
money	anything you exchange for goods or services
monopoly	a business that has no competition
moral values	personal values based on what one thinks is good compared to what one thinks is wrong
mortgage	a loan to purchase a home
motivator	something that encourages you to set goals and make decisions
motive	a reason for doing something
multiplication	a quick method of adding numbers by repeating an addition problem in one step
mutual fund	a pool of money collected from multiple investors and then used to buy stocks, bonds, and other securities
natural resources	things that exist in nature and are available for everyone
need	something you can't live without

negative attitude	behavior that shows someone is unhappy, has little confidence in himself or herself or in others, and believes that life is unfair
negotiate	discuss options that will lead to an agreement or compromise that will satisfy everyone
net income	pay after withholdings
net margin	the portion of each dollar of sales a company keeps as profit; also called return on investment ratio, net profit ratio, net profit on sales ratio, or profit margin
net profit on sales ratio	*see* net margin
net profit ratio	*see* net margin
networking	sharing information about yourself and your career goals with personal contacts
no-fault insurance	a policy that pays regardless of who is responsible for the loss
nonhuman resources	things, such as money and cars
nonprofit organizations	companies that are in business to serve the good of society, not to make a profit
nonrenewable resources	natural resources that are available in limited quantities and may one day be used up
nontraditional occupation	any job that a man or woman does that is usually done by someone of the other gender
numerator	the number above the fraction bar in a written fraction
nutrients	the parts of food that your body requires
nutrition	a science that studies the way the food you eat nourishes your body
objective	fairly, without emotion or prejudice; also, another word for goal
occupation	a job or career
Occupational Outlook Handbook (OOH)	a book published by the U.S. Bureau of Labor Statistics that describes more than 200 occupations, including responsibilities, working conditions, education requirements, salary ranges, and job outlook
Occupational Safety and Health Act	a law requiring all employers to provide a safe and healthful workplace
Occupational Safety and Health Administration (OSHA)	the federal agency responsible for inspecting companies and enforcing safety laws
offshoring	hiring people in other countries to do certain jobs
on-call	available at any time to cope with emergencies
online bank	retail bank that operates only on the Internet
operating ratio	a ratio that shows the percentage of each dollar of sales needed to cover expenses
opportunity cost	the value of what you are willing to give up to achieve something else
organizational structure	the system that assigns work, authority, and responsibility within a company
overdrawn	the condition when there are not enough funds in an account to cover expenses
owner's equity	the value of a business on a specific date if all assets were sold and all the liabilities were paid; also, an accounting term that means total assets minus total liabilities according to a company's balance sheet

partners	people who assume a percentage of the ownership of a business in exchange for equity financing
partnership	a business ownership arrangement in which at least two individuals share the management, profit, and liability
passive reading	reading without thinking critically about the written words; reading to take in information or be entertained
patent	the exclusive right to make, use, or sell a device or process
pathway	a group of jobs within a career cluster
pay stub	a printed record of information about your pay, including how much you have earned and how much your employer has deducted from your pay
payback	the amount of time, measured in months, that it takes a business to earn enough in profit to cover its start-up investment
paycheck	a written document that tells your employer's bank how much money to give to you
payee	the person a check is written to
peer pressure	when peers such as friends, classmates, or co-workers influence you to do something
peers	people your own age
pension	a regular payment given to a retired person by a former employer
percentage	a part of a whole
performance review	a report that rates how well you do your job
perks	compensation in addition to wages or salary
permit	a legal document that allows a business to take a specific action
personal academic plan	a document that you use to set goals for the things you want to accomplish while you are in school; some schools call it a personal education plan, a personal career plan, or even a personal life plan
personal identification number (PIN)	identification number used with a debit card
personal information card	an index card—or other piece of paper—on which you write or print the information you might need to fill out a job application accurately
personal qualities	the characteristics and traits that make you unique
personal well-being	well-being that depends on how satisfied and confident you are with yourself
phishing	a scam designed to steal your personal and financial information over the Internet
physical well-being	well-being that depends on your health
population	the number of people in a country or area
portfolio	a collection of information and documents; for investors, all the investment and accounts they own
positive attitude	behavior that shows someone is happy, has confidence in himself or herself or in others, and believes that life is good

postsecondary education	school after high school
prejudice	negative opinions that are not based on fact
press release	a written statement of information about a product or company, sent to media outlets for publication or distribution
probability	the chance that something will happen
problem	a difficulty or challenge that you must resolve before you can make progress
process	a series of steps that leads to a conclusion
producers	companies or individuals who make or provide goods and services
product	the result of a multiplication equation; also, goods manufactured and sold
productivity	the amount of work an employee accomplishes
professional development	training in your chosen career
professional organization	an association of people who are all employed in the same field or industry
professionalism	the ability to show respect to everyone around you while you perform your responsibilities as best you can
profit and loss statement	a financial document that summarizes a business's income and expenses over a given time period; also called an income statement
profit margin	*see* net margin
profit	earnings greater than a business's expenses, or the money left over after all the bills are paid
promotion	an advance in your career that includes a new job title and additional responsibilities; also, actions that raise awareness of a product
promotional mix	a combination of different methods of product promotion
property insurance	insurance that protects possessions in case of fire, theft, or damage from the weather
proportion	two ratios that equal each other
prospect	a potential customer
proverb	a saying
public domain	available for free use
publically traded	owned by shareholders
purchasing power	the number of goods or services that can be purchased with a unit of currency
pure risk	the chance of loss with no chance of gain
qualify	evaluate
quick ratio	a comparison of cash to debt
quota	a limit on the quantity of a product that can be imported into a country
quotient	the result of a division equation
raise	an increase in pay

range	the difference between the lowest and highest values in a set
ratio	a comparison between two values
recession	a slow economic period marked by high unemployment, falling investments, and decreased production
reciting	speaking out loud
recreation	fun activities outside of work
reference	someone who knows you well and is willing to speak to employers about your qualifications
relating	interacting with someone else
relationship	a connection or association between two or more people
Renaissance	a historical time period of artistic and intellectual revival in Europe
renewable resources	natural resources that can be recreated in unlimited quantities, such as air and sunlight
replacement cost	the amount it would cost to replace a lost or damaged item
resent	to blame someone else for your unhappiness
resources	things you can use to get something else
responsibility	something people expect you to do, or something you must accomplish
resume	a document that summarizes you, your skills, and your abilities and provides a snapshot image of your qualifications for potential employers
retail bank	a for-profit financial institution providing services such as checking and savings accounts, credit cards, education loans, car loans, and home loans
retailer	a type of business that buys goods, often from wholesalers, and sells them directly to consumers
retirement	when someone leaves a job or career after many years and does not return to a paid job
return on investment (ROI) ratio	a comparison of net profit to initial investment
return on investment	the amount of money you earn compared to the amount of money you invest
return on sales (ROS)	the portion of each dollar of sales a company keeps as profit; also called net margin, net profit ratio, net profit on sales ratio, or profit margin
return	the money received annually from an investment, usually expressed as a percentage
revenue	money earned from sales
risk transfer	to shift risk to someone else, such as an insurance company
risk	the chance of losing something; also, the measurable likelihood of loss or less-than-expected returns
risky behavior	activity that puts your health and wellness in danger
role	the way a person behaves in a specific situation
room and board	cost of meals and a place to live

rule	a written or unwritten statement about how something is supposed to be done
safe deposit box	a box in a fireproof vault that you can rent from your bank
salary	the money that you receive in exchange for work performed
sales force	salespeople, or sales representatives
sales lead	a person or company that has some characteristics of your target market and might become a potential customer
sales tax	a consumption tax calculated as a percentage of the sales price of a good or service
same-size analysis ratio	a comparison of the total revenue or other financial data against that same data converted into percentages
savings account	interest-bearing bank account
scale	to change the size of something
scarcity	the principle that there are never enough resources or goods to satisfy everyone
scholarship	a type of grant, usually based on specific criteria
secondary data	existing information collected by someone else
Securities and Exchange Commission (SEC)	the government agency that regulates the securities industry
security	an asset that has financial value and that can be traded
severance package	compensation a company pays an employee when the employee is dismissed
severance pay	an amount of money given to employees when they are terminated for reasons other than performance
share of stock	a unit of ownership in a corporation
shareholders	owners of a corporation; also called stockholders
shortage	when the quantity supplied can't meet demand
short-term goals	goals you can accomplish in the near future—maybe even today
skill	an ability or talent—something you do well
smartphone	a cell phone that has the ability to run computer programs
Social Security	a government program that pays monthly benefits to workers who pay the Social Security tax (FICA)
social well-being	well-being that depends on how you get along with other people
sole proprietorship	a business that is owned by a single individual
speculative risk	risk that holds the possibility of either gain or loss
spyware	a program that lets others access your computer and monitor your keystrokes and other actions
stage of life	how old you are
standard of living	a measure of how comfortable you are based on the things you own

standards	guidelines for whether or not something meets expectations
start-up investment	the one-time sum required to start a business and cover start-up expenses
statistics	a type of math used to collect, organize, and analyze data; also called data analysis
stock	a share of ownership in a corporation
stockholders	owners of a corporation; also called shareholders
strategies	careful plans and methods
strengths	positive qualities and skills
stress	the way your body reacts to a difficult or demanding situation
stressor	a cause of stress
subjective	affected by existing opinions, feelings, and beliefs
subordinates	employees supervised by a manager
subsidy	a cash payment toward a specific work-related need
substance abuse	using substances—such as food, drugs, or alcohol—that are bad for your health and wellness
subtle	unmentioned or implied
subtraction	taking one number away from another number; the opposite of addition
success	setting and achieving a goal
sum	the result of an addition equation
supply	the quantity of goods and services a business is willing to sell at a specific price and a specific time
surplus	when more money is earned than spent
SWOT analysis	a business method used to evaluate four areas: Strengths, Weaknesses, Opportunities, and Threats
tactile learners	people who learn best by touching things
target market	the group of customers most likely to buy a product or service
tariff	a fee that importers must pay on the goods they import
tax brackets	levels dictating how much tax is due based on income
tax deductions	expenses that you are allowed to deduct from your income when calculating taxes
tax evasion	the federal crime of failing to pay taxes
tax	money citizens pay the government
taxable income	income minus deductions
tax-deferred savings plans	retirement savings plans with tax benefits
team	a group of two or more people who work together to achieve a common goal
technological resources	resources provided by technology such as computers, automated teller machines (ATMs), or medical equipment

technology infrastructure	the computer systems, networking, and other devices that form the core or backbone of an organization's technological capabilities
technology	the use of resources such as scientific knowledge and methods to make lives easier or better
telecommuter	an employee who works from home
templates	sample documents
term	the set amount of time you have to earn the return on an investment or pay back a loan
time clock	a machine that automatically records the time an employee arrives and leaves
time sheet	a table used for entering the time in, time out, and total hours spent at work
time zones	geographic regions that use the same standard time
tolerant	willing to consider the opinions of others
total	the result of an addition equation; also, the whole of something
trade barrier	a governmental restriction on international trade
trade credit	when one business allows another business to take an extended time before paying for purchased goods or services
trade secret	information that a business or individual keeps confidential to gain an advantage over competitors
trade union	an organization of people who do similar work, that acts on behalf of members regarding employment issues such as compensation and working conditions
trademark	a symbol that indicates that a brand or brand name is legally protected and cannot be used by other businesses
trade-off	a compromise, or giving up one thing in order to get something
transaction	a financial exchange
transcript	a record of the courses you took in high school and the grades you earned
transferable skills	skills that can be used on almost any job; they are called transferable skills because you can transfer them from one situation or career to another
trend	a general move in a certain direction
tuition	cost of education
twitpitch	a business idea summarized in no more than 140 characters
U.S. Bureau of Labor Statistics (BLS)	a government agency responsible for tracking information about jobs and workers
unemployment rate	the percentage that measures the number of unemployed people looking for jobs
unique	one of a kind
unit of sale	one of whatever customers buy from a business
utility	a measure of happiness or satisfaction
value	a measure of the quality or importance of something

values	the thoughts, ideas, and actions that are important to you
venture capitalists	companies that invest in businesses
videoconference	a meeting conducted over distances using video cameras and an Internet connection so that people do not have to travel to the same location
virtual reality	a computer-generated simulation of the world
virtues	positive character traits, such as honesty, compassion, and loyalty
visual aids	pictures, graphs, charts, or anything without words that conveys a message or idea
visual learners	people who take in information best when they see it
volunteering	doing work without pay
volunteers	unpaid workers
W-4 (Employee's Withholding Allowance Certificate)	a form employees fill out to provide information the employer needs in order to calculate how much money to withhold from wages to pay taxes
wages	the money that you receive in exchange for work performed
want	something you desire
Web host	a business that stores Web site information on its server computers
well-being	the feeling and understanding that things are going right
wellness	an overall feeling of well-being
wholesaler	a business that buys goods in large quantities, typically from manufacturers, and resells them in smaller batches to retailers
Wi-Fi	a technology that enables connection to the Internet without wires or cords
withdrawal slip	a form you fill out when you withdraw money from a bank account
work ethics	beliefs and behaviors about what is right and wrong in a work environment
work history	a list of jobs you have held from the past through the present, showing your experience as an employee
work week	the number of hours a person works per week
work-related values	values that refer to how you like to work and the results that you produce
work-study program	the opportunity to work while you are in school so you can earn money to help pay your costs
x-axis	the horizontal line that shows categories in a chart or graph
y-axis	the vertical line that shows values in a chart or graph

Index

Photo Credits

Title page: olesiabilkei/Fotolia; Andres Rodriguez/Fotolia; michaeljung/Fotolia; Monkey Business/Fotolia

Part I: p 1 ryanking999/Fotolia

Chapter 1: p 3 Patrick Hermans /Fotolia; p 4 imagedb.com/Fotolia; p 5 wellphoto/Fotolia; Monkey Business/Fotolia; p 6 Monkey Business/Fotolia; p 7 Minerva Studio/Fotolia; Tsiumpa/Fotolia; p 8 Darren Baker/Fotolia; ra2 studio/Fotolia; p 9 Gabriel Blaj/Fotolia; p 10 Nick Freund/Fotolia; EastWest Imaging/Fotolia; p 12 Monkey Business/Fotolia; p 14 Jenner/Fotolia; p 15 Andres Rodriguez/Fotolia; p Rido/Fotolia; p 17 viappy/Fotolia; emde71/Fotolia; Monkey Business/Fotolia; Andres Rodriguez/Fotolia; vadymvdrobot/Fotolia; p 18 ryflip/Fotolia; p 19 Andres Rodriguez/Fotolia; Maya Kruchancova/Fotolia

Chapter 2: p 21 Darrin Henry/Fotolia; p 22 chunumunu/Fotolia; p 23 Africa Studio/Fotolia; p 24 ndoeljindoel/Fotolia; p 26 juiceteam2013/Fotolia; p 27 michaeljung/Fotolia; p 28 zoomyimages/Fotolia; micromonkey/Fotolia; p 29 Marco Govel/Fotolia; p 31 serranostock/Fotolia; p 32 Tsiumpa/Fotolia; ra2 studio/Fotolia; p 33 viappy/Fotolia; emde71/Fotolia; Monkey Business/Fotolia; Monkey Business/Fotolia; Andres Rodriguez/Fotolia; olesiabilkei/Fotolia; kerdazz/Fotolia; p 34 ryflip/Fotolia; p 35 Andres Rodriguez/Fotolia; Actionpics/Fotolia

Chapter 3: p 37 Ljupco Smokovski/Fotolia; p 38 vadymvdrobot/Fotolia; p 39 Ljupco Smokovski/Fotolia; p 40 Jelena Ivanovic/Fotolia; p 41 yanlev/Fotolia; pressmaster/Fotolia; p 42 Kurhan/Fotolia; p 43 ra2 studio/Fotolia; p 44 Klaus Eppele/Fotolia; Minerva Studio/Fotolia; p 45 Pixsooz/Fotolia; BlueOrange Studio/Fotolia; p 47 viappy/Fotolia; emde71/Fotolia; Monkey Business/Fotolia; Monkey Business/Fotolia; Andres Rodriguez/Fotolia; Andres Rodriguez/Fotolia; kerdazz/Fotolia; p 48 desaif/Fotolia; p 49 FotolEdhar/Fotolia; p 50 ryflip/Fotolia; p 51 Andres Rodriguez/Fotolia; Monkey Business/Fotolia

Chapter 4: p 53 Andres Rodriguez/Fotolia; p 54 Africa Studio/Fotolia; ra2 studio/Fotolia; p 55 José 16/Fotolia; p 56 ndoeljindoel/Fotolia; p 57 Dirima/Fotolia; p 58 FotolEdhar/Fotolia; kerdazz/Fotolia; p 59 Rido/Fotolia; desaif/Fotolia; p 60 michaeljung/Fotolia; p 61 auremar/Fotolia; p 62 wong yu liang/Fotolia; p 63 viappy/Fotolia; emde71/Fotolia; Monkey Business/Fotolia; Monkey Business/Fotolia; Andres Rodriguez/Fotolia; kerdazz/Fotolia; p 64 TessarTheTegu/Fotolia; p 65 Monkey Business/Fotolia; desaif/Fotolia; p 66 dmitrimaruta/Fotolia; p 67 aijohn784/Fotolia; p 68 ndoeljindoel/Fotolia; p 69 Ariwasabi/Fotolia; Tsiumpa/Fotolia; p 70 Semen Barkovskiy/Fotolia; p 71 CandyBox Images/Fotolia; p 72 paffy/Fotolia; p 73 FotolEdhar/Fotolia; kerdazz/Fotolia; desaif/Fotolia; p 74 ryflip/Fotolia; p 75 Andres Rodriguez/Fotolia; Web Buttons Inc/Fotolia

Chapter 5: p 77 Andres Rodriguez/Fotolia; p 78 Glenda Powers/Fotolia; kerdazz/Fotolia; p 79 Monkey Business/Fotolia; p 80 Alliance/Fotolia; p 81 Monkey Business/Fotolia; p 82 rnl/Fotolia; p 83 rnl/Fotolia; michaeljung/Fotolia; p 84 Tsiumpa/Fotolia; p 85 Monkey Business/Fotolia; p 86 viappy/Fotolia; emde71/Fotolia; Monkey Business/Fotolia; Monkey Business/Fotolia; Andres Rodriguez/Fotolia; auremar/Fotolia; p 87 WavebreakMediaMicro/Fotolia; p 88 ryflip/Fotolia; p 89 Andres Rodriguez/Fotolia; Monkey Business/Fotolia

Part II: p 91 DenisNata/Fotolia

Chapter 6: p 93 phoenix021/Fotolia; p 94 Kalim/Fotolia; p 95 Monkey Business/Fotolia; p 96 Gajus/Fotolia; desaif/Fotolia; p 97 Monkey Business/Fotolia; biglama/Fotolia; p 98 lucadp/Fotolia; chagin/Fotolia; p 100 viappy/Fotolia; emde71/Fotolia; Monkey Business/Fotolia; Monkey Business/Fotolia; Andres Rodriguez/Fotolia; nyul/Fotolia; Tsiumpa/Fotolia; p 101 Rido/Fotolia; p 102 michaeljung/Fotolia; p 103 Minerva Studio/Fotolia; p 104 Monkey Business/Fotolia; p 105 spaxiax/Fotolia; p 107 Syda Productions/Fotolia; ra2 studio/Fotolia; p 108 ryflip/Fotolia; p 109 Andres Rodriguez/Fotolia; Minerva Studio/Fotolia

Chapter 7: p 111 Hugo Félix/Fotolia; p 112 michaeljung/Fotolia; p 113 Monkey Business/Fotolia; Tsiumpa/Fotolia; p 114 Lisa F. Young/Fotolia; p 115 Arto/Fotolia; p 116 ra2 studio/Fotolia; p 117 cfarmer/Fotolia; p 118 hartphotography/Fotolia; p 119 Edie Layland/Fotolia; p 120 Felix Mizioznikov/Fotolia;

P 121 wong yu liang/Fotolia; desaif/Fotolia; p 122 SeanPavonePhoto/Fotolia; Sam Spiro/Fotolia; desaif/Fotolia; p 124 viappy/Fotolia; emde71/Fotolia; Monkey Business/Fotolia; Monkey Business/Fotolia; Andres Rodriguez/Fotolia; George Wada/Fotolia; p 125 chunumunu/Fotolia; p 126 mangostock/Fotolia; p 128 ryflip/Fotolia; p 129 Andres Rodriguez/Fotolia; Bronwyn Photo/Fotolia

Chapter 8: p 131 eurobanks/Fotolia; p 132 eurobanks/Fotolia; p 133 Tsiumpa/Fotolia; bst2012/Fotolia; p 134 kerdazz/Fotolia; p 135 michaeljung/Fotolia; p 136 fotosmile777/Fotolia; pressmaster/Fotolia; p 137 michaeljung/Fotolia; p 138 Andy Dean/Fotolia; p 139 xy/Fotolia; viappy/Fotolia; emde71/Fotolia; Monkey Business/Fotolia; Monkey Business/Fotolia; Andres Rodriguez/Fotolia; p 140 slasnyi/Fotolia; WavebreakmediaMicro/Fotolia; WavebreakmediaMicro/Fotolia; p 141 Monkey Business/Fotolia; p 142 Photographee.eu/Fotolia; p 143 Ljupco Smokovski/Fotolia; Ljupco Smokovski/Fotolia; p 144 desaif/Fotolia; Monkey Business/Fotolia; p 145 Glenda Powers/Fotolia; ra2 studio/Fotolia; p 146 DragonImages/Fotolia; p 147 michaeljung/Fotolia; p 148 ryflip/Fotolia; p 149 Andres Rodriguez/Fotolia; Andres Rodriguez/Fotolia

DATE DUE